Reading Literature and Writing Argument

Reading Literature and Writing Argument

SEVENTH EDITION

Missy James
Tallahassee Community College, Emeritus

Alan P. Merickel
Tallahassee Community College, Emeritus

Jenny McHenry
Tallahassee Community College

 Pearson

Executive Portfolio Manager: Aron Keesbury
Content Producer: Barbara Cappuccio
Content Developer: Len Neufeld
Portfolio Manager Assistant:
  Christa Cottone
Senior Product Marketing Manager:
  Michael Coons
Product Marketing Manger: Nicholas Bolt
Content Producer Manager: Ken Volcjak

Managing Editor: Cynthia Cox
Digital Studio Course Producer:
  Elizabeth Bravo
Full-Service Project Management: Integra
  Software Services Pvt. Ltd.
Printer/Binder: LSC Communications, Inc.
Cover Printer: Phoenix Color/Hagerstown
Senior Art Director: Cate Barr
Cover Design: Cadence Design Studio

Acknowledgments of third party content appear on the appropriate page within the text, which constitutes an extension of this copyright page.

Copyright © 2020, 2017, 2013 by Pearson Education, Inc. 221 River Street, Hoboken, NJ 07030. All Rights Reserved. Printed in the United States of America. This publication is protected by copyright, and permission should be obtained from the publisher prior to any prohibited reproduction, storage in a retrieval system, or transmission in any form or by any means, electronic, mechanical, photocopying, recording, or otherwise. For information regarding permissions, request forms and the appropriate contacts within the Pearson Education Global Rights & Permissions department, please visit www.pearsoned.com/permissions/.

This work is solely for the use of instructors and administrators for the purpose of teaching courses and assessing student learning. Unauthorized dissemination or publication of the work in whole or in part (including selling or otherwise providing to unauthorized users access to the work or to your user credentials) will destroy the integrity of the work and is strictly prohibited.

PEARSON, ALWAYS LEARNING, and Revel are exclusive trademarks in the U.S. and/or other countries owned by Pearson Education, Inc. or its affiliates.

Unless otherwise indicated herein, any third-party trademarks that may appear in this work are the property of their respective owners and any references to third-party trademarks, logos or other trade dress are for demonstrative or descriptive purposes only. Such references are not intended to imply any sponsorship, endorsement, authorization, or promotion of Pearson's products by the owners of such marks, or any relationship between the owner and Pearson Education, Inc. or its affiliates, authors, licensees or distributors.

Library of Congress Cataloging-in-Publication Data

Names: James, Missy, author. | Merickel, Alan, author.
Title: Reading literature & writing argument / James-Merickel.
Description: Seventh edition. | Hoboken, N.J. : Pearson, [2020]
Identifiers: LCCN 2018039924 | ISBN 9780135164754 (paperback : alk. paper) |
  ISBN 0135164753 (paperback : alk. paper)
Subjects: LCSH: English language—Rhetoric. | Persuasion (Rhetoric) |
  College readers. | Report writing.
Classification: LCC PE1408 .J36 2020 | DDC 808.06/6378—dc23
LC record available at https://lccn.loc.gov/2018039924

Instructor's Review Copy
ISBN-10:   0-13-528542-9
ISBN-13: 978-0-13-528542-8

Access Code Card
ISBN-10:   0-13-516475-3
ISBN-13: 978-0-13-516475-4

Pearson

Brief Contents

Contents

Part 2 Anthology 127

Preface

*R*eading Literature and Writing Argument springs directly from our more than three decades of classroom experiences as teachers of two college composition courses: "Writing about Literature" and "Writing Argument and Persuasion." We believe that all students should experience the combined essence of these two courses—an enrichment as readers and as writers through engagement with ideas in written texts. Through this engagement with literature and through their application of the principles of argument, students deepen and expand their thinking and practice the skills of analysis and evaluation. The complementary study of literature and argument empowers students to cultivate critical standards for judging ideas and forming opinions.

Reading Literature and Writing Argument also is based on the premise that writing is valued when it makes readers think. This premise implies that a person must have ideas—something to say—in order to put pen to paper or fingers to keyboard. However, the notion that writing must have valuable ideas can be daunting to the individual staring at a blank page or screen. Here is where literature—fiction, poetry, drama, nonfiction—can play a vital role. Students can examine the implied arguments in stories by Louise Erdrich, Sir Arthur Conan Doyle, and Lucia Berlin; in poems by Margaret Engle, D. H. Lawrence, and Gwendolyn Brooks; and in plays by Sharon E. Cooper, Susan Glaspell, and William Shakespeare. Encountering issues in imaginative literature, students are invited to explore diverse perspectives on topics that may be familiar or foreign, thereby generating fresh thinking and new ideas. Nonfiction pieces—such as Barry Meier's "Origins of an Epidemic: Purdue Pharma Knew Its Opioids Were Widely Abused"—typically present explicit arguments. Reading Meier's piece, students can examine the merits of his case against Purdue Pharma and develop an informed opinion on the issue. Other nonfiction works—from Francis Bacon's "Of Revenge" (1597) to Major Sullivan Ballou's letter to his wife (1861) to Lisa H. Lewis's "Why We Still Allow Bullying to Flourish in Kids' Sports" (2018)—give students the opportunity to experience and evaluate issues and arguments from across the centuries and to understand how those issues and arguments resonate in their own lives and times.

To borrow from Robert Frost's statement on poetry, *Reading Literature and Writing Argument* is designed to bring both "delight" and "wisdom" to the first-year college student's composition experience. We believe that students will enjoy reading the literature pieces, practicing creative and critical thinking skills, and exploring multiple perspectives on issues related to their own lives. Moreover, we believe that students will discover that they have a wealth of ideas as well as the creative and critical skills to compose written arguments that will compel their readers to think. The blank page or computer screen will present a welcome invitation to speak out and to be heard—to participate in shaping viewpoints on issues that matter in their own lives and in the lives of others.

What's New In This Edition

For Both the Rhetoric and the Anthology Chapters

- An extensively revised and updated array of reading selections, with more than 25 new selections, including both contemporary and classic works.
- Engaging new multimodal activities, designed to give students opportunities to practice composing in modalities that are integral to twenty-first century modes of communication.
- Extensively updated and revised end-of-chapter Chapter Activities sections.

For the Rhetoric Chapters

- Substantial revisions, including an almost entirely new Chapter 2, emphasizing both creative and critical reading.
- New examples of student writing, including one literary argument.
- New, thought-provoking midchapter Journal writing tasks and Look It Up activities directing students to online sources for research and writing tasks.
- New Take Note boxes, summarizing and organizing important information, providing tips, and posing challenging tasks.

For the Anthology Chapters

- A chapter-opening artwork for thematic prewriting and discussions, providing students practice with reading visual images creatively and critically.
- Updated critical thinking and writing topics following each reading selection, reflecting recent events and issues.

To Complement Both Parts of the Text

- An extensively revised, comprehensive glossary of the key terms called out in the text.
- New and updated biographical notes on the authors of reading selections.

Organization
Part 1: Rhetoric

The five Rhetoric chapters, indeed the entire text, are based on this premise: *Literature liberates thinking, and argument disciplines it.* Through their engagement with literature and application of the principles of argument, students will exercise creative thinking, practice the skills of analysis and evaluation, and develop their own critical lenses through which to view the diverse perspectives within the global community.

Chapter 1: Connecting Argument and Literature
This chapter introduces the concept of academic argument and the essential link between academic argument and critical thinking. The chapter also demonstrates how the study of argument and the study of literature provide separate yet complementary reading and writing experiences.

Chapter 2: Reading Creatively and Reading Critically
This chapter offers students tips for improving reading skills and demonstrates the application of those skills to reading imaginative literature. It also models how to read the four genres—fiction, poetry, drama, nonfiction—through the lenses of creative reading and of critical reading and how to synthesize the two reading experiences to foster independent thinking.

Chapter 3: Analyzing Argument
This chapter introduces the components of an argument—claims, evidence, assumptions, and concessions and refutations to counterarguments. It defines and illustrates ten common logical fallacies, rhetorical context, and Aristotle's basic argument model, including the rhetorical appeals of *pathos, logos,* and *ethos.* Lastly, the chapter discusses visual argument, reading an image as an argument.

Chapter 4: Writing an Argument Essay
This chapter takes students through the process of planning and developing an argument essay—finding a subject and clarifying a purpose and an audience; writing a claim statement; and designing an argument strategy. The chapter also introduces Rogerian argument strategy, thereby encouraging students to view an argument as an opportunity to exercise the creative skills of problem solving and compromise.

Chapter 5: Researching and Documenting an Argument Essay
This chapter guides students in developing proficiency in finding and documenting credible sources. It overviews documentation systems and the purposes of creating both a preliminary and an annotated bibliography; it discusses and illustrates incorporating sources within the text of their own writing; and it models the process of purposeful reading of secondary source articles—to detect biases and to compare the perspectives of different sources.

Part 2: Anthology

The three Anthology chapters contain reading selections centered on three enduring themes:

- **Chapter 6: Individual and Community Identity**
- **Chapter 7: Crime and Punishment**
- **Chapter 8: Power and Responsibility**

For these anthology chapters, we purposefully selected broad cultural themes. We believe that students appreciate the opportunity to explore their own thinking within these contexts. Rather than offering answers or solutions to issues, the reading selections spark questioning and prompt students to arrive at their own conclusions. The chapter themes invite students to draw connections, not only among the readings within a single chapter, but also across the three chapters. Students may identify an issue in a Chapter 6 reading, for example, that they can relate to a Chapter 8 reading.

The chapter-theme-based introduction to each Anthology chapter ends with Prewriting and Discussion tasks, including a task related to the chapter-opening artwork. In the body of the chapter, following each reading selection, Critical Thinking Topics encourage students to apply the concepts, terms, and tools covered in the five Rhetoric chapters to the reading selection. The Critical Thinking Topics are followed by one or more Writing Topics, writing tasks that prompt students to reflect on specific issues raised in the selection and to generate ideas for writing arguments.

Chapter Activities

Each chapter concludes with Chapter Activities designed to engage students in applying their learning and reading experiences to the chapter's topics, themes, and issues; in synthesizing their reading and writing experiences; and in developing their own arguments.

- In both the Rhetoric and Anthology chapters, the Chapter Activities conclude with Multimodal Activities that encourage students to apply their critical and creative reading and writing skills to visual, aural, digital, or other nonliterary modes and media.
- In the Rhetoric chapters, the Chapter Activities include Think About It questions, covering all the main topics explored in the chapter, and Read and Respond activities, allowing students to apply what they have learned in the chapter to poems, short prose pieces, and excerpts from longer works.
- In the Anthology chapters, the Chapter Activities include Topics for Writing Arguments, writing tasks focusing on the chapter theme in relation to one or more of the chapter's reading selections, and a final writing task asking students to look back at and reflect on their responses to the chapter-opening Prewriting and Discussion tasks; Taking a Global Perspective,

calling on students to develop a chapter-theme-related argument on an issue of worldwide concern; Collaborating on a Rogerian Argument, requiring students to work in small groups to develop a Rogerian compromise on a contentious issue related to the chapter theme; and Arguing Themes from Literature, asking students to develop narrowly focused arguments on theme-related issues brought out in the chapter's reading selections.

REVEL™

Revel is an interactive learning environment that deeply engages students and prepares them for class. Media and assessment integrated directly within the authors' narrative lets students read, explore interactive content, and practice in one continuous learning path. Thanks to the dynamic reading experience in Revel, students come to class prepared to discuss, apply, and learn from instructors and from each other.

Learn more about Revel
www.pearson.com/revel

Pearson English Assignments Library

Available with your adoption of any © 2019 or © 2020 Pearson English course in Revel is the English Assignments Library comprising 500 essay and Shared Media prompts:

- A series of 300 fully editable essay assignments invites students to write on compelling, wide-ranging writing topics. You can choose from an array of writing prompts in the following genres or methods of development: Argument/Persuasion; Comparison/Contrast; Critique/Review; Definition; Description; Exposition; Illustration; Narration; Process Analysis; Proposal; and Research Project. Assignments can be graded using a rubric based on the WPA Outcomes for First-Year Composition. You can also upload essay prompts and/or rubrics of your own.

- 200 Shared Media assignments ask students to interpret and/or produce various multimedia texts to foster multimodal literacy. Shared Media activities include analyzing or critiquing short professional videos on topics of contemporary interest; posting brief original videos or presentation slides; and sharing original images—such as posters, storyboards, concept maps, or graphs.

Supplements

Make more time for your students with instructor resources that offer effective learning assessments and classroom engagement. Pearson's partnership with educators does not end with the delivery of course materials; Pearson is there with you on the first day of class and beyond. A dedicated team of local Pearson representatives will work with you to not only choose course materials but also integrate them into your class and assess their effectiveness. Our goal is your goal—to improve instruction with each semester.

Pearson is pleased to offer the following resource to qualified adopters of *Reading Literature and Writing Argument*. This supplement is available to instantly download from Revel or on the Instructor Resource Center (IRC); please visit the IRC at **www.pearson.com/us** to register for access.

- **INSTRUCTOR'S RESOURCE MANUAL** Create a comprehensive road-map for teaching classroom, online, or hybrid courses. Designed for new and experienced instructors, the Instructor's Resource Manual includes learning objectives, lecture and discussion suggestions, activities for in or out of class, research activities, participation activities, and suggested readings, series, and films as well as a Revel features section. Available within Revel and on the IRC.

Acknowledgments

First, we thank our students, who, throughout our more than three decades of teaching college composition, have been our teachers; they are the primary reason we have written this text. We are especially grateful to students Cale Blount, Christian Garcia, Doralicia Giacoman-Soto, Josh Griep, Marlee Head, and John Miller for sharing their creative and critical writing. We thank the following college composition teachers for their reviews of the sixth edition: Melissa Edwards, Middlesex County College–Edison; Michael Harker, Georgia State University; Burgsbee Lee Hobbs, Saint Leo University; Gina Hochhalter, Clovis Community College; Arlandis Jones, Tarrant County College; Jordine Logan, Montclair State University; and Christine Pipitone, Raritan Valley Community College. Their comments and suggestions provided both encouragement and constructive guidance.

We offer a hearty thank you to Pearson Collegiate English Executive Producer and Publisher Aron Keesbury and Ohlinger Publishing Services Managing Editor Cynthia Cox for their steadfast support and good humor throughout the revision process. We are also grateful to Ohlinger Studios Senior Rights and Permissions Manager Joseph Croscup and his team for their persistence on our behalf, and to these other members of the Ohlinger team who made significant contributions to the development of this text: Senior Managing Editor Maggie Barbieri; Senior Managing Editor Beth Jacobson; and Project Manager, Development–English Kate Hoefler. Among the editors who have assisted us, we thank our boots-on-the-ground developmental editor Len Neufeld for his incisive and insightful edits and suggestions; he has been a key player on our team.

Lastly, we wish to thank our families for their encouragement and unwavering support. We are especially grateful to Jessica James-Tomasello Ireland, Jace James, Victoria Merickel, Cole Perkins, and Iain McHenry.

Missy James

Alan Merickel

Jenny McHenry

Part 1
Rhetoric

The five Rhetoric chapters, indeed the entire text, are based on this premise: *Literature liberates thinking, and argument disciplines it.* Through your engagement with literature and your application of the principles of argument, you will have the opportunity to exercise creative thinking and to practice the skills of analysis and evaluation. In this way, you will develop your own critical lenses through which to view the diverse perspectives flooding the global community. Moreover, you will develop the skills and confidence needed to make your voice heard and, thereby, to take part in conversations on issues that matter to our lives. Following is a brief overview of the Rhetoric chapters:

Chapter 1: Connecting Argument and Literature

This chapter introduces you to the concept of academic argument and to the essential link between academic argument and critical thinking. Also, the chapter demonstrates the purpose in combining the study of argument and literature—two disciplines that provide separate yet complementary reading and writing experiences.

Chapter 2: Reading Creatively and Reading Critically

This chapter offers you tips for improving your reading skills and demonstrates the application of those skills to reading imaginative literature. It also demonstrates how to read each of the four genres—fiction, poetry, drama, nonfiction—through the lenses of creative reading and of critical reading and how to synthesize the two reading experiences to arrive at your own independent thinking.

Chapter 3: Analyzing Argument

This chapter introduces you to the components of an argument—claims, evidence, assumptions, and concessions and refutations to counterarguments—the tools of argument analysis. It also defines and illustrates ten common logical fallacies, rhetorical context, and Aristotle's basic argument model, including the rhetorical appeals of *pathos, logos,* and *ethos*—a model that has molded successful argumentation for over two millennia. Lastly, the chapter discusses visual argument, reading an image as an argument.

Chapter 4: Writing an Argument Essay

This chapter takes you through the process of planning and developing an argument essay—finding a subject and clarifying a purpose and an audience; discovering and writing a claim statement; and designing an argument strategy. Furthermore, the chapter introduces Rogerian argument strategy, in which argument is viewed as an opportunity to exercise the complementary creative skills of problem solving and compromise when addressing a contentious issue.

Chapter 5: Researching and Documenting an Argument Essay

This chapter seeks to help you become more proficient in finding and documenting credible sources. It briefly overviews documentation systems and explains the purposes of creating both a preliminary and an annotated bibliography. In addition, it discusses and illustrates incorporating sources within the text of your own writing. Finally, the chapter models the process of purposeful reading of secondary source articles—to detect biases and to compare the perspectives of different sources.

Chapter 1
Connecting Argument and Literature

 ## Learning Objectives

In this chapter, you will learn to

- **1.1** Define academic argument.
- **1.2** Develop and practice the habit of critical thinking.
- **1.3** Read literature to expand thinking and to explore issues.

1.1 Academic Argument versus Confrontational Argument

Define academic argument.

"Everyone agrees in theory that we can't judge a new idea or point of view unless we enter into it and try it out, but the practice itself is rare."

—Peter Elbow

When people engage in a confrontational argument, they often close their minds. Their emotions displace their reason as their desire for victory overcomes any inclination to listen to their opposition's point of view (as illustrated in Figure 1.1).

As you read the dialogue below, you can see that neither participant really listens to the other. They hear each other, but neither of them makes a serious effort to enter into the other's perspective. As a result, the conversation rapidly disintegrates into a shouting match and ends with personal insults—nothing gained and, perhaps, a friendship eroded.

Figure 1.1

© Andriy Popov/Alamy Stock Photo

BLAKE: You need to come see the pit bull puppy I just adopted. She is one cuddly fur ball.

DREW: Are you out of your mind? Pit bulls are notorious for mauling children. You hear it in the news all the time.

BLAKE: The news, yeah, right. What you don't hear about is the adorable poodle biting a kid at the playground or the cocker spaniel biting its owner.

DREW: Those are exceptions, but not so for pit bulls. Pit bulls are bred to attack and kill. The breed should be banned.

BLAKE: You have no basis for saying that. It's simple-minded people like you who spread rumors and false alarms.

DREW: And it's selfish and irresponsible people like you who are making society worse.

Is this dialogue a discussion between two people trying to get at the truth? Of course not. At best, it is an unproductive and potentially destructive quarrel. Unfortunately, we can experience similarly unproductive, destructive confrontations every day on many media outlets. Let's see if we can rewrite the dialogue as a search for facts and mutual understanding.

BLAKE: You need to come see the pit bull puppy I just adopted. She is one cuddly fur ball.

DREW: Sure, I'd love to meet your puppy. What's her name?

BLAKE: I haven't decided yet.

DREW: I'm sure you know that you've adopted a breed with a reputation for transforming from a friendly companion pet into an attack dog that bites people out of the blue. I know not all pit bulls turn into attack dogs, but still...

BLAKE: Yeah, I know they have a bad rep, which they deserve to some extent, but mostly it's the owners who are the problem. I intend to be one of those owners who train and socialize their puppy from day one. Any breed of dog, if not trained properly, can turn into an attack machine.

DREW: You're right about that. Even so, pit bulls can be challenging because of their history of being bred to fight. But I understand that you're accepting your responsibility as a pit puppy's owner. I respect you for that, even though I, for one, would not be willing to take on the risk of owning a pit.

Now the dialogue is no longer a quarrel; rather, the participants are listening to each other and making a sincere effort to "try out" the other's point of view. While they do not come to the same conclusion about owning a pit bull, their discussion is constructive, respectful, and positive—minds were not necessarily changed, but they were opened. This second version of Blake and Drew's discussion exemplifies **academic argument**, where the goal is not to trample an opponent but to engage in a respectful exchange of viewpoints. Whether or not minds are changed, each side "wins" by attaining a deeper understanding of the issue.

Academic argument implies the willingness of participants to consider all sides of an issue and to listen to views that may differ from their own. Entering into an academic argument, we should work actively to cast aside our preconceived notions about the issue. In order to advance a conversation on a divisive or controversial issue, we need to demonstrate a broad understanding of the issue. For example, you may already have a strong view on health care reform, but if you were to engage in an academic argument on this issue, you would have a responsibility to understand and to acknowledge perspectives that differ from your own. In doing so, you would demonstrate to an audience that you are well informed; in addition, being well informed would prepare you to develop effective rebuttals to opposing viewpoints.

1.2 Academic Argument and Critical Thinking

Develop and practice the habit of critical thinking.

A willingness to take a broad, global perspective also promotes **critical thinking**, which involves analyzing all the elements of a situation and considering all the possible outcomes. Critical thinking skills are essential to developing academic arguments, which advance the discussion of issues with the goal of generating thought-provoking insights. Such insights prompt audience members to consider conflicting views and also challenge them to change or clarify their own stances on issues. Logic and reasoning prevail over impulsive reaction and raw emotion.

By choosing to attend college, you have chosen to be part of an academic community, one that thrives on conversation among its members—that is, on academic argument. As a member of this community, you have the responsibility to bring your best thinking to this conversation: to read about the issues and to consider diverse viewpoints, including those that may clash with your own views. Moreover, as a participant in the conversation, you have the responsibility to ask questions—ones that will compel you to examine your own ideas and thinking as well as those ideas you encounter in your reading, writing, and discussion.

Contemporary social issues continually wash across college campuses, touching the academic disciplines both directly and indirectly: freedom of speech, sexual harassment, immigration, social media, guns on campuses, the opioid epidemic, and so on. In the community at large, hotly contested debates emerge as people establish and hold fast to diverse positions around these issues; in the college setting, however, you have an opportunity to step back from the heat of these debates and establish some emotional distance. The college experience encourages you to probe the values and belief systems that underlie differing positions on issues and differing ideas, including your own positions and ideas. Looking inward and outward, you develop and practice the habit of critical thinking, which empowers you to make independent choices, deliberately and thoughtfully, and to participate in the debates that shape our society.

Former president Barack Obama showed that he understood the need for critical thinking when he said: "One of the dangers in the White House, based on my reading of history, is that you get wrapped up in groupthink and everybody agrees with everything and there's no discussion and there are no dissenting views."[1] Obama knows that thinking is strengthened, not weakened, through discussion and through addressing dissenting views. The academic community provides a place for you to participate in discussions with those who hold dissenting views and, thus, to develop and practice critical thinking.

Like the skills involved in repairing a motorcycle engine or playing a guitar, critical thinking skills are not innate; however, just as you can learn to repair an engine or to play a guitar through study and practice, so too can you learn to become a proficient critical thinker.

The first step in becoming a critical thinker is to adopt a willingness to question your own thinking. For example, consider the following scenario: Your college has a mandatory class attendance policy, which you adamantly oppose because, after all, you are the one who is paying to attend class. Given your strong feelings, you decide to write a letter to the editor for publication in your college newspaper. You know that among your audience, besides your parents, who have taught you to speak up for yourself, will be administrators, professors, and, of course, fellow students—quite

---

[1] Quoted in Peter Baker and Helene Cooper, "Appointments Begin a New Phase for Obama," *New York Times*, 2 Dec. 2008. Web. 10 June 2015.

a diverse group. As you prepare to write your letter, you might ask yourself these questions: Besides the fact that I pay for my classes, what other reasons do I have to support my position opposing the college's mandatory attendance policy? How might my readers—parents, administrators, professors, students—respond to each reason? Why do others, including most, if not all, administrators and professors and even some of my fellow students, believe that the policy is necessary? What might happen if the policy were dropped? Would I continue to attend class regularly and would most of my peers? What would be some of the consequences—on our attitudes, our learning, our grades—of allowing students to choose whether or not to attend class?

As you attempt to answer these questions, you may be surprised to discover that, while you have some strong personal opinions about the issue, you do not have a lot of solid information. After this critical examination of your own thinking, you might be ready to acknowledge that you need to seek out more information and a variety of viewpoints in order to develop an argument that will influence others—notably, administrators and professors.

1.2.1 Critical Inquiry

"It is not the answer that enlightens, but the question."

—Eugene Ionesco

How often have we sat silently instead of asking a question, perhaps out of fear of sounding ignorant in front of our peers or disrespectful to an authority figure? We need to keep in mind that asking questions is a human instinct and that college gives us the opportunity to exercise that instinct freely and openly. As we develop the habit of **critical inquiry**—by asking questions that advance our thinking about issues—we lay the groundwork for developing astute critical thinking skills. Take Note 1.1 illustrates how critical inquiry can be used to explore a controversial issue.

The following Journal task is intended to help you recognize biases that might interfere with your ability to think critically about certain issues.

Journal: Biases For and Biases Against

"The moment we want to believe something, we suddenly see all the arguments for it, and become blind to the arguments against it."—George Bernard Shaw

Reflect on this quotation and then consider your own biases, the things you "want to believe." Some may be completely harmless, but others may make it hard for you to think critically about certain issues—that is, to examine both sides of the issues fairly and objectively. Write out a list of these biases, step away from the list for an hour or so, and then review the entries. Put the entries in order, beginning with the biases that are most likely to influence your ability to be fair and objective and ending with the least likely. For the top two or three items, briefly describe the origin of each bias in your own life.

Take Note 1.1

The Use of Force by Law Enforcement Officers: How Critical Inquiry Can Help You Develop as a Critical Thinker

By applying critical inquiry to his initial thinking, this student opens his mind to the possibility of changing his stance on the issue.

Initial Thinking	Critical Inquiry
My mother is a police officer, as was her father before her. One day, a fellow officer in my mother's squad saw a driver run through a stop sign, so he pulled the guy over. As the officer walked up to the driver's window, the driver pulled a gun and shot him in the chest. This tragic incident makes me think that police officers in that situation should always have their weapon in their hand, ready for use; when an officer's life could be at stake—better safe than sorry.	This is a powerful example, but should I base my position on just one example, no matter how powerful? Do I have enough solid information to support my position? For example, do I know the relevant statistics about shootings of—or by—police officers during traffic stops? Would getting more information help me think more creatively about this incident?
Having grown up in a family of police officers, I know that almost all officers of the law are respectful and caring individuals who daily put their lives on the line to protect the public. That's why I get furious when an officer is crucified in the media for shooting an unarmed suspect. There's no way a reporter or newscaster or anyone else but another police officer could understand the split-second decisions that officers have to make under conditions of extreme fear and tremendous stress.	Do I recognize my own assumptions and how those assumptions might influence my reasoning? Do I think about whether those assumptions are valid? For instance, does my family background make me so biased that I automatically think the best of all police officers? How many officers do I actually know, out of the thousands upon thousands of officers in this country? Am I overlooking the harm suffered by unarmed suspects and their families because a police officer fired a weapon in the wrong situation?
I also resent those who claim that incidents of police brutality are not isolated but widespread. Almost always, if a suspect gets roughed up a bit, it's because he lost control and resisted arrest or even attacked an officer during questioning—and, of course, it's the guilty suspects who lose control and lash out at officers.	Am I seriously considering the factual data, or am I just making snap judgments? Have I examined all sides of the issue fairly and equally? Have I tried switching sides—that is, taking a different view of the issue? Can I imagine myself being accused of a nasty crime that I didn't commit and then being knocked around by an angry, hotheaded police officer who assumed I was guilty?
As a police officer, my mother has been in the line of fire for much of my life, all for the well-being and safety of others. She is my role model, and my respect for her is absolute. I know she speaks only the truth when she praises the honor, integrity, and self-sacrifice of her fellow officers. Accusations of widespread brutality and corruption among the police infuriate us both, and when I hear people making those types of accusations, I do not hold back from letting them know how I feel.	Am I letting my biases and my emotions push me to a particular conclusion? If my goal is to change people's minds—to persuade them that police officers generally have impeccable integrity—am I using a tone that will be effective with an audience that has a different perspective from mine?
"Violence by Police: Problem or Prevarication?" is one of the topics our professor gave us to write an essay on, and that's obviously a topic that I have strong opinions about. I showed a draft of my essay to my roommates, but they refuse to be serious about it—they just crack jokes. I also showed the draft to my mother, who says it's brilliant. I trust her judgment. Being a police officer puts her in a perfect position to critique my essay.	Have I shared my ideas with people who will assess them carefully and honestly? For example, should I show the draft to classmates who are outspoken and seem to enjoy challenging other people's ideas?

1.3 Reading Literature to Expand Thinking and to Explore Issues

Read literature to expand thinking and to explore issues.

The study of argument and the study of literature are complementary and mutually empowering; both contribute to creative envisioning and critical thinking. Even as we differ by holding fast to opposing viewpoints, we are alike in sharing the common ground of our humanity. This text tries to demonstrate that reading literature can lead us to this common ground. Through careful and close reading of literature, we become better prepared to articulate thoughtful positions and to argue those positions with heartfelt emotion and with clear and valid reasoning.

One way to develop and practice the habit of critical thinking is to explore ideas and experiences through different lenses. Imaginative literature provides readers with an array of such lenses. While reading literature, you are transported from the particulars of your own life to the lives of others, to their places and their times. You may emerge from the pages of the literary work with fresh perspectives, new lenses for examining both the personal issues that sometimes cloud your daily life and the social issues that often divide communities. Reading fiction, poetry, drama, and nonfiction not only entertains you but also prompts you to explore your own thinking, through the process of critical inquiry. This exploration can provide inspiration when you are trying to generate ideas for an argument essay. To illustrate, let's briefly examine a poem and excerpts from a short story. (But first, try the following Journal task.)

Journal: "Inner City" 1

Before reading the poem that follows, spend a few moments writing out your reflections when you hear the phrase "inner city": What images come to mind? What are the sources of these images?

Now read this poem by Mercedez Holtry:

Something out of Nothing (2015)

I hand them Popsicle sticks,
String
And glue,
I tell them, "Make something of it."

Their smallish brains occupied for about a good 30 minutes.
Generating methods for creation.

5

They hand me these funky crafted,
Spider web,
Thing-a-ma-bobs,

And answer the question before I can ask it.   10

"They're dream catchers Ms. Mercedez!"

I smile at their pride
How much joy they get knowing,
They created something,
Out of nothing.   15

You see these kids,
These inner city kids.
They do this often.
Create something out of nothing.
They're used to getting second hand shit   20
Then being told, be thankful for it.
Unlike kids in Paradise Hills, Taylor Ranch, Rio Rancho,
And the Heights,
We know nothing,
of brand new.   25

I wake up every morning to come work in an icebox.
The gym heater broken,
Leaves them bundled in big jackets.
Our basketballs, flat.
Games from Good Will fill the old recycled shelves,   30
Donated years ago.
The kids fight over a deck of cards
missing two jacks and a deuce.
Press the marker to the paper,
Attempting to get the last bit of color.   35

Search, for at least one sharpened color pencil,
In a bucket full of broken ones,
Because our pencil sharpener
Is Broken.
Our ball pump,   40
Broken.
Our chairs,
Broken.
Our books,
Broken.   45
Their spirits,
Are not yet broken.
My heart breaks for them sometimes.

I tell them,
"Finish your homework"   50
"So you can get a job"
"So you can go to college"
"So you don't end up a SCUMMY BUMMY HOBO!"
They giggle, at my attempt to be funny,
A 5th grader,   55
Amelia raises her hand for the first time and says,
"Ms. Mercedez, I've been homeless before.
It's like not really that fun."

Speechless and stupid,
I apologize.   60
Apologize for being ignorant to the fact,
that some of these kids
know struggle better than their ABC's.

Out of the 36 that attend,
five are raised by grandparents,   65
fifteen are raised by single mothers,
eighteen are here on welfare contracts,
two are foster kids,
and all of them know what it means
to make something of nothing.   70

It is what they will have to do
for the rest of their lives.

They are brilliant in this way.
They are grateful for seconds of snack,
angry when they fist fight,   75
embarrassed because they can't read very well,
frustrated when I make them finish homework,
and irritated when I tell them to try harder,
as if they aren't trying hard enough.
But when they finally breakthrough   80
to success...overjoyed.

"I did it Ms. Mercedez!
            I did it!
                    I did it!
                            I did it!"   85
I tell them,
        "I told you so."

See what happens when you're not a quitter?
When you don't give up.
Never give in to your environment.   90

If your environment tells you,
you can only be its product.

Don't give in to poverty,
to a system that gives you nothing.
Build something.   95
Keep making dream catchers out of Popsicle sticks.
Let dreams be the foundation for built realities.
keep building,
keep moving,
Keep rising,   100
and remember,

Your capability for making something
out of nothing
is going to take you far in life.

So make something of it.   105

Source: "Something out of Nothing." MY BLOOD IS BEAUTIFUL, by Mercedez Holtry, Swimming with Elephants Publications, LLC, 2015, pp. 25–28.

The speaker, who teaches "inner city kids," addresses the kids directly and implores them: "Never give in to your environment" and "Build something." You can feel her belief in "these kids" and her passion for motivating them to go "far in life" and to "make something of nothing." The "inner city" becomes a vibrant and living place. Does the following Journal task reveal any new perspectives of your own on the "inner city"?

Journal: "Inner City" 2

Read back over the reflections you wrote before reading Holtry's poem. Do you note any similarities or contrasts between yours and those implied by the poem's speaker? What fresh perspectives can you create by synthesizing (blending) the speaker's and your own perspectives on the "inner city"?

Writing reflective responses to poems or other types of literature can enrich and deepen your reading experience: Imagination and thinking are opened and stretched, as ideas and topics begin to take shape. For example, densely populated urban neighborhoods (like the "inner city" of Holtry's poem) face issues involving poverty, prejudice, funding for schools, crime, law enforcement, housing, and homelessness. By exploring one of these broad topics, you could identify a narrower issue on which to write an argument essay. Then, when reading sources for your essay, you would want to consider your initial reflections on each source, as well as the reflections inspired by your reading of Holtry's poem.

Now compare another artist's very different take to Holtry's perspective on the inner city (see the Look It Up feature "A Hip Hop Artist's Perspective on the Inner City").

Look It Up: A Hip Hop Artist's Perspective on the Inner City

Hip hop artist Nas presents another view of life in the inner city in his song "Life's a Bitch," from his album *Illmatic* (1994). Do an Internet search for the lyrics of this song. How does the perspective in the song differ from the perspective in Holtry's poem? How do the two perspectives complement each other in representing life in the inner city? Also, note that two decades separate the song (1994) and the poem (2015)—what has changed in the inner city, and what seems to have remained the same?

Watch the YouTube video of Mercedez Holtry's performance of "Something out of Nothing" at the 2015 Women of the World Poetry Slam Finals in Albuquerque, New Mexico. Then watch a video of Nas performing "Life's a Bitch." In what ways does your listening experience influence your previous responses to both the poem and the song? On the one hand, how does the tone of the two performances sharpen distinctions between the two perspectives, and, on the other hand, how does the tone imply a parallel message? What might that message be?

Now let's see how careful and creative explorations of a short story can similarly open up and sharpen your thinking. In "The Foundations of the Earth," a 1992 story by Randall Kenan (the full text is in Chapter 6), you witness the narrator Maggie's personal struggle in facing her rage over the tragic death of her 27-year-old grandson and in confronting the reality of his personal life as an adult: His longtime adult partner is not only male but of another race. You enter into Maggie's perspective and experience her difficult journey "to realign her thinking." Here are two excerpts from the early stages of that journey—not surprisingly, the journey begins with questions:

> *"Why? Why? Why did you kill him, you heartless old fiend.... Speak to me, damn it. Why? Why? Why?"*
>
> . . .
>
> "She saw herself looking, if not refreshed, calmed, and within her the rage had gone, replaced by a numb humility and a plethora of questions. Questions. Questions. Questions."

Traveling with Maggie on her inner journey of struggle and reconciliation, you bear witness to her anger, her resistance, her heartache, her questioning, and her seismic shifts in thinking. Responding to Maggie's story on a personal level, you may be prompted to explore moments in your own life when you confronted a disturbing and unexpected revelation that sent you on a journey.

Moreover, looking beyond the immediate context of Maggie's personal story, you can identify social issues that continue to deeply divide communities—race, religion, sexual orientation. Kenan addresses none of these issues explicitly, but certainly they are present. Reading literature allows you to confront contentious issues within the privacy and safety of your own mind, in your imagination and thinking. Then, moving from reading a work of literature to writing an argument essay—from the private to the public sphere of communication—you can identify specific social issues that you will find interesting to explore, to probe critically, and on which to articulate and support a position.

In delivering an academic argument, we speak knowledgably because we have explored our own viewpoint through critical inquiry and have listened openly to a diverse range of other viewpoints. As the classic rock music artist Jimi Hendrix said, *"Knowledge speaks, but wisdom listens."*

1.4 Chapter Activities

The series of activities on the following pages invite you to apply the concepts and ideas we have discussed and demonstrated throughout this chapter.

1.4.1 Think About It

Answer the following questions covering the topics discussed in this chapter.

1. Imagine the following scenario: The City Council is considering rezoning the property where the city's dog park is located to make it a commercial zone. The council hopes to attract a business, thus creating jobs and tax revenues. When you hear this news, you are outraged: You and your greyhound, Harper, are regular visitors to the dog park. The council is holding a public hearing next week, and you plan to attend and speak your mind. But Harper reminds you that you need to put your emotions on a short leash if you wish to make a serious dent in the thinking of your audience. Heeding Harper's sage counsel, you decide to develop a list of questions to help you examine the rezoning issue and take an objective look at your viewpoint. Write out at least six questions that will help you apply critical inquiry to your thinking about this issue.

2. Select an issue you feel strongly about, such as recreational marijuana legalization, border security, or paying college athletes:
   - Apply your critical thinking skills to the issue by writing out at least six questions and your response to each. (To help guide your thinking, look back at this feature in the "Critical Inquiry" section of this chapter: "The Use of Force by Law Enforcement Officers: How Critical Inquiry Can Help You Develop as a Critical Thinker.")
   - Read over your responses. Suppose you were planning to write an argument essay on the issue—what would be your first step?

3. Imagine that you are the parent of a son who is entering high school next year and who plans to try out for the high school football team:
   - Do you support or oppose your son's plan? Articulate two opposing positions on this issue, giving three reasons in support of each position.
   - What types of evidence did you use to articulate each position? For example, have you had personal experience as a spectator of or participant in high school football; have friends or family given you personal accounts of their experiences; have you seen media reports or fictionalized dramatizations (movies, miniseries) on the issue? List the sources of evidence that have influenced your thinking on this topic. (See Chapter 3 for a discussion of evidence as a component of argument.)

4. Imagine that you are the parent of a daughter who is entering high school next year and who plans to try out for the high school cheerleading squad:

   • Do you support or oppose your daughter's plan? Articulate two opposing positions on this issue, giving three reasons in support of each position.

   • What types and sources of evidence have influenced your thinking on the topic of high school cheerleading?

5. Write a paragraph reflecting on how practicing switching sides of an argument could be valuable to you.

6. Think about "switching sides" in an argument. Spend a few minutes reflecting on this quotation and then respond to the questions that follow:

   > *"The test of a first-rate intelligence is the ability to hold two opposed ideas in the mind at the same time, and still retain the ability to function."*
   > —F. Scott Fitzgerald

   • List at least three currently controversial issues that interest you. Write out your thinking on one of these issues: Do you already have a viewpoint? If so, what is it? Or are you undecided? If so, why? What observations, experiences, or other sources of evidence inform your thinking on the issue? (See the discussion of evidence in Chapter 3.)

   • Find two viewpoints that differ from your own on the issue you wrote about in the preceding question; then, for each of those two opposing viewpoints, write out three compelling reasons why the viewpoint is correct. How has this exercise in switching sides influenced your thinking? Has it prompted you to question or, perhaps, to strengthen your initial stance?

1.4.2 Read and Respond

1. Read the *New York Times* op-ed (meaning "opposite the editorial page") article below and respond to the writing task that follows.

"The Art of Thinking Well," by David Brooks (2017)

Richard Thaler has just won an extremely well deserved Nobel Prize in economics. Thaler took an obvious point, that people don't always behave rationally, and showed the ways we are systematically irrational.

Thanks to his work and others', we know a lot more about the biases and anomalies that distort our perception and thinking, like the endowment effect (once you own something you value it more than before you owned it), mental accounting (you think about a dollar in your pocket differently than you think about a dollar in the bank) and all the rest.

Before Thaler, economists figured it was good enough to proceed as if people are rational, utility-maximizing creatures. Now, thanks to the behavioral economics revolution he started, most understand that's not good enough.

But Thaler et al. were only scratching the surface of our irrationality. Most behavioral economists study individual thinking. They do much of their research in labs where subjects don't intimately know the people around them.

It's when we get to the social world that things really get gnarly. A lot of our thinking is for   5
bonding, not truth-seeking, so most of us are quite willing to think or say anything that will help
us be liked by our group. We're quite willing to disparage anyone when, as Marilynne Robinson once put it, "the reward is the pleasure of sharing an attitude one knows is socially approved." And when we don't really know a subject well enough, in T. S. Eliot's words, "we tend
always to substitute emotions for thoughts," and go with whatever idea makes us feel popular.

This is where Alan Jacobs's absolutely splendid forthcoming book "How to
Think" comes in. If Thaler's work is essential for understanding how the market can
go astray, Jacobs's emphasis on the relational nature of thinking is essential for
understanding why there is so much bad thinking in political life right now.

Jacobs makes good use of C. S. Lewis's concept of the Inner Ring. In every
setting — a school, a company or a society — there is an official hierarchy. But there
may also be a separate prestige hierarchy, where the cool kids are. They are the Inner Ring.

There are always going to be people who desperately want to get into the Inner Ring
and will cut all sorts of intellectual corners to be accepted. As Lewis put it, "The passion for
the Inner Ring is most skillful in making a man who is not yet a very bad man do very bad things."

People will, for example, identify and attack what Jacobs calls the Repugnant Cultural Other — the group that is opposed to the Inner Ring, which must be assaulted to
establish membership in it.

Other people will resent the Inner Ring, and they will cut all sorts of intellectual   10
corners in order to show their resentment. These people are quick to use combat
metaphors when they talk about thinking (he shot down my argument, your claims
are indefensible). These people will adopt shared vague slurs like "cuckservative" or
"whitesplaining" that signal to the others in the outsider groups that they are attacking
the ring, even though these slurs are usually impediments to thought.

Jacobs notices that when somebody uses "in other words" to summarize another's
argument, what follows is almost invariably a ridiculous caricature of that argument, in order to
win favor with the team. David Foster Wallace once called such people Snoots. Their motto is,
"We Are the Few, the Proud, the More or Less Constantly Appalled at Everyone Else."

Jacobs nicely shows how our thinking processes emerge from emotional life and
moral character. If your heart and soul are twisted, your response to the world will be,
too. He argues that by diagnosing our own ills, we can begin to combat them. And
certainly I can think of individual beacons of intellectual honesty today: George Packer,
Tyler Cowen, Scott Alexander, and Caitlin Flanagan, among many.

But I'd say that if social life can get us into trouble, social life can get us out. After all, think
of how you really persuade people. Do you do it by writing thoughtful essays that carefully
marshal facts? That works some of the time. But the real way to persuade people is to create
an attractive community that people want to join. If you do that, they'll bend their opinions to
yours. If you want people to be reasonable, create groups where it's cool to be reasonable.

Jacobs mentions that at the Yale Political Union members are admired if they can
point to a time when a debate totally changed their mind on something. That means
they take evidence seriously; that means they can enter into another's mind-set. It
means they treat debate as a learning exercise and not just as a means to victory.

How many public institutions celebrate these virtues? The U.S. Senate? Most TV   15
talk shows? Even the universities?

Back when they wrote the book of Proverbs it was said, "By long forbearing is a prince persuaded, and a soft tongue breaketh the bone." These days, a soft tongue doesn't get you very far, but someday it might again.

Source: David Brooks, Oct 10 2017, "The Art of Thinking Well." From *The New York Times*, 10/10/2017
© 2016 *The New York Times*. All rights reserved. Used by permission and protected by the Copyright Laws of the United States. The printing, copying, redistribution, or retransmission of this Content without express written permission is prohibited.

Writing Task

Find at least three sentences in "The Art of Thinking Well" that stand out for you. Write out each sentence and your reflections on it. Think about how each sentence relates to you directly and to the community at large. As you write, include examples to illustrate your thinking.

2. Read the poem below and answer the questions that follow.

"We Are the Renters," by Beth Ann Fennelly (2004)

You need no other name for us than that.
The good folk of Old Taylor Road
know who you mean. We are
the renters, hoarders of bloated boxes,
foam peanuts. When the Welcome Wagon   5
of local dogs visits our garbage,
we're not sure which houses to yell at. So
what if we leave the cans there a bit too long.
We have white walls, a beige futon, orange
U-Haul on retainer, checks with low numbers.   10
Scheming to get our security deposit back, nail holes
are spackled with toothpaste. Ooops, our modifiers
dangle. Our uncoiled hoses dangle, but the weeds
in our gutters do not, they grow tall,
they are Renters' Weeds, they are unafraid.   15
An old black one-speed leans against the carport.
So what. Maybe we were thinking about riding
past these houses with posters for Republican governors.
We have posters too: Garage Sale. "Can I hel—"
"No, just looking." We are just looked at, we renters.   20
Are we coming soon to your neighborhood?
We're the ones without green thumbs,
with too many references, the ones
whose invitation to the block party
must have gotten lost in the mail. If we're still here   25
come winter, tell the postman not to bother
searching our nameless mailbox for his Christmas check.

Source: "We Are the Renters," from TENDER HOOKS: POEMS, by Beth Ann Fennelly. Copyright © 2004 by Beth Ann Fennelly. Used by permission of W. W. Norton & Company, Inc.

Questions

1. What perspective on "renters" does Fennelly's poem suggest? Find quotes from the poem to support your response.

2. To what extent do you agree or disagree with the perspective on renters in Fennelly's poem? What experiences and observations underlie your opinion?

3. Fennelly's poem does not explicitly mention social and economic class divisions—the gap between the haves and the have nots—but it seems to suggest this topic. Rereading the poem with this topic in mind, can you say what the poem might be implying about class divisions in American society? What images in the poem lead you to this conclusion? Do you agree with this perspective on class divisions? Why or why not?

1.4.3 Multimodal Activity

From Verbal to Visual Representation

The poem "We Are the Renters" in the preceding activity presents vivid verbal images of renters. But an internet search for visual images of renters would yield hundreds of very different representations, such as the ones in Figure 1.2.

1. Compare and contrast the representations in Figure 1.2 to the verbal images in the poem "We Are the Renters."

2. Do an internet search to find visual images of renters that represent perspectives along a continuum between the perspective taken by the poem "We Are the Renters" and the perspective taken by the photos in Figure 1.2. Do you think visual images can convey differences in perspective as accurately as verbal images?

3. What are your thoughts about the persuasive power of verbal representations versus visual ones? To borrow a cliché, is a picture necessarily worth a thousand words?

Figure 1.2

Blend Images/Shutterstock   Monkey Business Images/Shutterstock

Chapter 2
Reading Creatively and Reading Critically

2.1 Active Reading

Read actively.

We read all the time. Think about what you read every day: Texts from friends? Facial expressions on Snapchat? Emails from professors? Celebrity news or sports writing? Opinion pieces in a newspaper? A novel? Poetry? Just as you are fluent at reading many different forms of communication, you most likely are also fluent at producing several different forms, automatically adopting the style appropriate for each. Take, for example, texting. You probably use a blend of fully spelled out words, punctuation, abbreviations, and emojis to talk with friends; not all generations are as comfortable with this style. It's a language some haven't learned. When the language is unfamiliar, communication breaks down.

Each form of literature—fiction, poetry, drama, nonfiction—has its own language and patterns; the more familiar you are with these conventions, the more successful and rewarding your reading will become. We hope to help you become more fluent in reading literature, both creatively and critically.

Synthesizing, or blending, creative and critical reading is a skill that serves all literate people, whatever their age or occupation. It is how we educate ourselves about politics and current events. It is how we learn about new trends and discoveries. And it is often how we engage with people from different cultures and generations. As practical as this skill is, reading serves another important function in our lives: It exposes us to art and to emotions, experiences, and perspectives that we might otherwise never encounter or acknowledge. Ursula Le Guin (1929–2018), a well-known science fiction writer, explains that

> One of the functions of art is to give people the words to know their own experience. There are always areas of vast silence in any culture, and part of an artist's job is to go into those areas and come back from the silence with something to say. It's one reason why we read poetry, because poets can give us the words we need. When we read good poetry, we often say, "Yeah, that's it. That's how I feel."[1]

Recognizing shared emotions connects all of us. We see the similarities in our experiences and learn from our differences. In order to accomplish this bridging—to see and appreciate our shared humanity—we must learn to become active readers. This chapter aims to promote **active reading**, the balancing of creative, or exploratory, responses with critical, or analytic, responses and the synthesizing of these responses to arrive at fresh insights and new conclusions.

2.2 Reading Carefully

Read carefully.

Before you can master reading creatively and critically, you must develop the patience for and confidence in reading carefully. Our daily reading habits often reinforce casual reading rather than careful reading—that is, thoughtful, purposeful reading. But as we will see, careful reading can yield rewarding results. You may wonder, how do you begin to improve your reading skills, to move beyond basic comprehension of a text to nuanced insight?

The answer is practice. Use the following Journal feature to better understand how you typically "practice" reading.

Journal: What Do You Read, and How Do You Read It?

Consider the reading you do most often: Social media? Advertisements? Class assignments? Web sites? Emails from professors? Novels?

Reflect on your current reading process and write about what you enjoy, using specific examples to highlight your strengths and your struggles.

---

[1]From an interview with Jonathan White (ed.), in *Talking on the Water: Conversations about Nature and Creativity.* San Antonio, Texas: Trinity University Press, 2016.

Now consider your goals as a reader. What would you like to accomplish? Are you an avid reader who wants to develop the skills for reading ever more challenging texts? Do you dislike reading and aim to read only what is necessary, as efficiently as possible? Do you aspire to do more reading but find yourself intimidated by complex literature? How do you see yourself meeting your goals? (See Take Note 2.1 for some tips.)

Take Note 2.1

Tips for Improving the Way You Read

- *Read the text more than once.*
  Do you sometimes read through a text one time, put it aside, and declare you did not understand it? That approach does a disservice to you and to the text. Reading for understanding requires both patience and effort—that is, it requires careful reading.

- *Read the text in small sections.*
  Sometimes trying to understand an entire piece can be overwhelming. All tasks seem easier when attacked in manageable chunks. Approach a poem line by line or stanza by stanza, a play by one speech or one scene at a time, or a short story or nonfiction piece by paragraphs or sections.

- *Read the text out loud.*
  Fascinating things happen when you slow down and take the time to read out loud. Concentration improves. Emphasis shifts. You notice words, phrases, tones, and rhythms that you might have missed when reading silently. This simple strategy can help you become more engaged in the piece and improve your understanding.

- *Take notes.*
  Like reading out loud, writing notes can increase your concentration and focus. Use whatever style you like for making notes—maybe you like to annotate digitally, or maybe you prefer writing notes on paper. Your approach doesn't matter. The key is to use the act of taking notes to help you pay close attention to what you are reading.

- *Look up unfamiliar terms and allusions.*
  Many readers do not make the effort to learn new vocabulary or understand allusions to history, mythology, religion, or other literature. You should refer to a dictionary or do some Internet research when you encounter an unfamiliar term or allusion.

- *Prepare for multiple interpretations.*
  Life experiences, age, gender, political preferences—all may contribute to how you understand a certain text. While you may understand a text differently than a classmate, both interpretations may have validity in the context of your individual backgrounds.

- ***Recognize ambiguity, tone, and subtext.***
  All writing is not straightforward in its presentation. Writers may use a variety of tones, such as satire and sarcasm, and may want readers to encounter ideas that are not directly written but are conveyed through undercurrents, in a subtext. Oftentimes, authors create ambiguity, leaving us wondering what happened. All these techniques add to the complexity of writing and require more effort from readers. We have to make judgments, decisions, and choices based on our understanding of different aspects of the piece and of our own perspective.

- ***Identify the theme.***
  A **theme** in a written work is a central or controlling idea in the work. A piece of literature may have more than one theme. When you read, it is up to you to articulate each theme clearly and specifically. One poem, for example, may be about love, but would "love" be an adequate statement of this theme? It might be too broad, because there are so many types of love—romantic, unrequited, familial, brotherly, obsessive, platonic, and so on—and the theme might be just one of these types or the interplay among multiple types of love.

2.3 Reading Creatively

Read creatively.

"There is creative reading as well as creative writing."
—Ralph Waldo Emerson

Reading creatively implies considering new ideas and new approaches and involves articulating your ideas and reflections on a text. Think about how you listen to music. You try out new artists, new styles, and new songs. When you hear a song that reflects your mood, how do you develop that connection? Do you immerse yourself in the song, listening to it more than once? Do you consider how it relates to something from your own life? Do you look up the lyrics to check your understanding? Do you find the video, check out the artist's other releases, or look up the singer's biography? The **creative reading** process is similar: You explore the text, considering its relevance to your own life or how it exposes you to a new viewpoint, and you try reading new works—you experience them, and you have fun with them.

Another way to think about creative reading is to compare it to creative writing. Imagine an assignment for a creative writing class. Perhaps you have to write a poem that emphasizes color imagery or a short story about a moment of fear. It does not matter too much what the specific requirements are. In every creative writing assignment, you, the writer, have some control. As a creative reader, you have control, too. It is not necessary to be an "expert" on the author or the piece. Your control consists of bringing your own life experiences and knowledge to your reading of the text. Problems with understanding become opportunities for growth. You might question the author's perspective or discover a willingness to accept change based on your exposure to new ideas.

Try applying the process of creative reading to the following poem by Dudley Randall.

Ballad of Birmingham (1968)

(On the bombing of a church in Birmingham, Alabama, 1963)

"Mother dear, may I go downtown
Instead of out to play,
And march the streets of Birmingham
In a Freedom March today?"

"No, baby, no, you may not go,   5
For the dogs are fierce and wild,
And clubs and hoses, guns and jails
Aren't good for a little child."

"But, mother, I won't be alone.
Other children will go with me,   10
And march the streets of Birmingham
To make our country free."

"No, baby, no, you may not go,
For I fear those guns will fire.
But you may go to church instead   15
And sing in the children's choir."

She has combed and brushed her night-dark hair,
And bathed rose petal sweet,
And drawn white gloves on her small brown hands,
And white shoes on her feet.   20

The mother smiled to know her child
Was in the sacred place,
But that smile was the last smile
To come upon her face.

For when she heard the explosion,   25
Her eyes grew wet and wild.
She raced through the streets of Birmingham
Calling for her child.

She clawed through bits of glass and brick,
Then lifted out a shoe.   30
"O, here's the shoe my baby wore,
But, baby, where are you?"

Source: Randall, Dudley. Reprinted by permission of the Dudley Randall Literary Estate. "Ballad of Birmingham" in "ROSES AND REVOLUTIONS: The Selected Writings of Dudley Randall."

After reading this poem, one of my students wrote that it is the saddest poem he ever read. This poem is tragic and heartbreaking. A creative reading of this poem might acknowledge that the emotion many of us feel after reading it comes from our shared values: protecting the innocent, recognizing the bond between mother and child, valuing the sanctity of a church. We might not know the history behind the poem or understand its symbolism, but our humanity knows the mother is in pain.

Beginning your reading with what you already understand and know is a valuable approach to developing complex reading skills. Reading creatively is not the only approach to developing those skills. Reading critically is a complementary process that enriches the creative approach.

2.4 Reading Critically

Read critically.

Critical reading implies analyzing the text—scrutinizing it and taking it apart to examine its components or elements. For example, to read a poem, short story, or play critically, you might examine theme, symbolism, tone and diction, characters and plot, and so on. To read a nonfiction piece, you might examine the author's purpose, intended audience, message, tone, biases, and so on. When you put on your critical lenses to read a text, you take time to identify the individual components and to engage in a dialogue with the text by asking questions and challenging ideas, by agreeing and disagreeing. Let's begin to delve into the process of reading critically by taking another look at "Ballad of Birmingham."

Look It Up: "Ballad of Birmingham"

Do an Internet search for information about the author, Dudley Randall, and the history of the Birmingham church bombing in 1963. Write down three facts about the author's professional life and three facts about the bombing.

Journal: "Ballad of Birmingham": Reading Critically

After researching the historical context of "Ballad of Birmingham," reread the poem to practice your critical reading skills. What do you see as a theme of the poem? What is the significance of the historical context? Analyze examples of symbolism in the poem, and describe the poem's tone. What might Dudley Randall's purpose have been in writing this poem? Who is the intended audience? How effective do you think Randall is in conveying his message to his audience?

Now read a student's critical analysis of "Ballad of Birmingham" and respond to the writing tasks that follow.

Doralicia Giacoman-Soto
Professor Jenny McHenry
ENC 1141
2 November 2017

"Ballad of Birmingham": A Mother's Grief Delivers a Message to Us All

Poetry, like other literature forms, can surpass time through its language, which can convey strong meaning and relevance to readers, no matter how much time has passed. Dudley Randall's 1968 poem "Ballad of Birmingham" is a fine example. Randall's poem centers on one of the most horrific demonstrations of the racial hate present during the era of the Civil Rights Movement, when the 16th Street Baptist Church in Birmingham was bombed. Within Randall's poem, an important idea stands out: innocence and the loss of innocence. The poet focuses on a narrative about a mother and her young daughter. The daughter wants to go to the Freedom March, but her mother, wary about the violence that may be caused by segregationists, wants her instead to attend church. The theme of innocence and its loss is exemplified throughout the poem through Randall's choice of diction, creating a stark contrast between the young girl's innocence and the violence that took her life. In this way, Dudley Randall delivers a powerful statement through "Ballad of Birmingham" about the inhumane and horrific nature of racial violence during the era of the Civil Rights Movement.

To illustrate the profound, race-based violence many African Americans experienced during the Civil Rights Movement, Randall presents it explicitly through his choice of diction and depiction of the young girl's innocence. The poet opens with the girl asking her mother if she may "go downtown" to "march the streets of Birmingham." These lines not only show the girl's awareness of social issues, but they also display her lack of awareness of the extent of the dangers she could face. Her mother responds by offering specific examples of these all too real dangers: "the dogs are fierce and wild" and the "clubs and hoses, guns and jails." Still, the girl persists, saying other "children will go with" her. Her persistence, despite her mother's accounting of the dangers, further emphasizes the girl's innocence. So, while the mother fears "those guns will fire," she compromises with her daughter by saying the girl instead can go to church, as she knows it to be a "sacred place," where her daughter will be safe. The mother's belief in the safety of the church symbolizes an innocence and purity much like her daughter's.

Randall further emphasizes the idea of innocence with images of the girl preparing for church by putting "white gloves on her small brown hands" and "white shoes." This focus on her special dressing up shows the young girl shares the same respect for the sacredness of the church as her mother. The white of her gloves and shoes symbolizes her purity and innocence and creates a symbolical contrast between the brown color of the girl's skin and the white color of her clothes during a racially charged time. But even a "sacred place" like the church couldn't keep the girl safe. As the girl is attending church—to "sing in the children's choir"—the 16th Street Baptist Church is bombed and destroyed. Hearing the explosion, the mother, "calling for her child," rushes out to the streets to find her. Arriving at the site of destruction, the mother "clawed through bits of glass and brick," only to find a single shoe. Most likely, the once white shoe is now blackened and marred, symbolizing the tragic loss of her daughter and the loss of her innocence. The bombing, an act of racial hatred, has destroyed a church and human life and blackened innocence. With the universal image of a smile on the mother's face, as she sends her child off to church, that "sacred place," Randall makes the mother's grief cry out to the reader, for "that smile was the last smile to come upon her face." Like the brick and mortar structure of the church, this mother has been destroyed, her daughter and her innocence forever lost—all because of racial hatred and violence.

Through his choice of diction and imagery and with simple and compelling grace, Dudley Randall delivers a profound message about racial hatred and violence in his 1968 poem "Ballad of Birmingham." With its narrative structure, the poem proceeds in an uncomplicated manner that makes the violence of the bombing even more shocking and horrific—a young child's life is snuffed out, and a mother, devastated, her heart broken forever. As readers, we all can relate to this mother who has lost her daughter in a tragic and senseless and violent act, one based on hatred over differences in skin color. Dudley Randall delivers a message for all readers, of all generations and of all backgrounds. Racial violence is all too real, in the past and in our present lives.

Source: Courtesy of Doralicia Giacoman-Soto

Describe your reaction to this student's point of view. Do you agree with her explanation of the poem? Use examples from her essay to show how she supports her critical reading of the poem.

The challenge (and the fun) of a critical approach to reading a work of literature often comes from the **ambiguity** in the piece, the way in which the piece invites diverse interpretations of its themes or characters. Sometimes, the term "ambiguity" has a negative connotation: a lack of clarity is not what we want in our politicians, instructors, coaches, or parents. In literature, however, the successful use of ambiguity does not make the work unclear; rather, it challenges us to interpret the piece in diverse ways, to debate and discuss its meaning. As a result, our reading experience is enriched, our thinking, expanded.

Read the following poem by Theodore Roethke. Most of you will probably agree that the poem is broadly about the relationship between a father and his son. But when you read the discussion following the poem, note how the ambiguity in this work opens up different possibilities of interpretation.

My Papa's Waltz (1942)

The whiskey on your breath
Could make a small boy dizzy;
But I hung on like death:
Such waltzing was not easy.

We romped until the pans   5
Slid from the kitchen shelf;
My mother's countenance
Could not unfrown itself.

The hand that held my wrist
Was battered on one knuckle;   10
At every step you missed
My right ear scraped a buckle.

You beat time on my head
With a palm caked hard by dirt,
Then waltzed me off to bed   15
Still clinging to your shirt.

Source: "My Papa's Waltz," copyright © 1942 by Hearst Magazines, Inc., copyright © 1966 and renewed 1994 by Beatrice Lushington; from COLLECTED POEMS by Theodore Roethke. Used by permission of Doubleday, an imprint of the Knopf Doubleday Publishing Group, a division of Penguin Random House LLC. All rights reserved.

When trying to make the broad subject more specific—to arrive at your own conclusion about the nature of the father–son relationship—you would examine the poem closely to discern what you think may be its theme. To do so, you would isolate specific images and debate the significance of the language. You might see this poem as an adult reflection on the rough play of a working-class father with his son. Other readers might find the language more violent and see evidence of abuse in the relationship. If you argue that the "waltz" is typical father–son roughhousing, you might point out that the young boy "clings to [the father's] shirt" and emphasize the use of playful language like "romped" and "waltzed." In contrast, those who see abuse in the relationship might argue that "whiskey," "death," "battered," "scraped," and "beat" indicate harmful violence. Both interpretations of the theme rely on textual evidence and on a meaningful assessment of the tone and the implications of the word choices. Maybe your interpretation of the ambiguities in the poem is influenced by your own relationship with a parent. If so, there also might be elements of creative reading in your impression of the poem's theme.

2.5 Synthesizing Creative and Critical Reading

Synthesize creative and critical reading.

If a literary work is read thoughtfully—both creatively and critically—it will usually be difficult to distinguish the creative elements from the critical ones in the reader's response to the work. And this is so for a reason—each mode of reading plays a role, but, finally, they function collectively. Synthesizing creative and critical reading yields the richest results for readers. This blending of reading experiences enhances curiosity and fosters intellectual growth.

Let's look at "The Red Wheelbarrow," by William Carlos Williams, to practice synthesizing creative and critical reading.

The Red Wheelbarrow (1923)

so much depends
upon

a red wheel
barrow

glazed with rain
water

beside the white
chickens.

Source: By William Carlos Williams, from THE COLLECTED POEMS: Volume I, 1909–1939, copyright ©1938 by New Directions Publishing Corp. Reprinted by permission of New Directions Publishing Corp.

The first step is to read the poem several times, including at least one time out loud. Your first response might be—why is this even called a poem? It doesn't rhyme, and a poem about a wheelbarrow? It's just words and ... ah, I see— three words, one word, three words, one word—it does have pattern and structure. And it is like a snapshot, a vivid picture. Now that you have given the poem a fair chance and allowed yourself to get engaged with it, you will be more likely to examine just what those sixteen words in a three–one pattern may have to say to you.

You might begin by considering what words stand out. "Glazed"? What do you think of when you read that word? Donuts? A glazed donut is a beautiful thing—sweet and shiny and lovely. Perhaps you think of glazed pottery, which is also shiny and beautiful. So, why is the wheelbarrow depicted as shiny?

Perhaps the wheelbarrow is shiny because of the rainwater, the cleansing rainwater. Most wheelbarrows are used for carting fertilizer or debris around a yard. A wheelbarrow is certainly a utilitarian item, dirty most of the time. In this poem, at this moment, it is clean and bright and red—why red?

You could consider the symbolism of colors. Red is powerful, passionate. It is a contrast to white, which typically symbolizes innocence or purity, perhaps simplicity. How does the color white connect to the chickens? Are they innocent? Pure? Simple?

Another item to consider is the first line's tiny word "so." The speaker doesn't tell us what depends on the red wheelbarrow, only that it is "so much." Why isn't he more specific; why is he ambiguous? Could it be that if he told us, we wouldn't use our imagination? Is it the farm? Is it the livelihood of the farmer and his family? Is it that so much depends on taking time to notice the beauty in ordinary everyday moments?

Finally, consider the theme of the poem. What could a poem of eight short lines and sixteen simple words tell us? Is it only about a wet red wheelbarrow standing beside some white chickens? It might be about how practical tools are sometimes more than just useful; they might be attractive and have an appeal of their own. This poem's theme could be the beauty of utilitarian objects and workaday scenes. You might find another theme, and that would be okay. Based on your own experience as the poem's reader, you can create your own interpretation of its theme. As a careful reader—one who has taken the time to read the poem creatively and critically—you would be able to support your interpretation of the theme with evidence from the poem.

Before continuing our discussion of creative and critical reading, let's spend a few moments on the question of whether the same kind of creative–critical approach can work with visual "texts." Could a photo like the one in Figure 2.1 arouse the same responses and take on the same significance as Williams's poem? Why or why not?

Another component of both creative and critical reading is the personal connection that powerful pieces can provide with social or political issues. When reading literature that presents a different perspective from your own, perhaps from another time or another culture, you might recognize parallels with contemporary issues and your own personal struggles. This discovery of shared

Figure 2.1 Is This Picture Worth Sixteen Words?

Heather Cameron

concerns can expand our thinking about issues, but only if we have some knowledge of the original context of the work, make the effort to engage in some personal reflection on the work and the issues it raises, and have an adequate awareness of current events.

For example, Arthur Miller's play *The Crucible* (1953), based on the Salem witch trials of 1692, illustrates how emotion, in this case, fear, can derail logical reasoning and clear thinking. In the play, as in historical Salem, Massachusetts, the townspeople jump to the conclusion that the women are witches, although the evidence for this conclusion, the testimony of young girls, is inadequate. At the close of Act 1, in the presence of two local men (Parris and Putnam), Reverend John Hale, known as an expert on witchcraft, interrogates Tituba (a woman slave in her forties) and two of the girls, Abigail and Betty (who has been lying in her bed, incapable of speech):

> HALE: Take courage, you must give us all their names. How can you bear to see this child suffering? Look at her, Tituba. *He is indicating Betty on the bed.* Look at her God-given innocence; her soul is so tender; we must protect her, Tituba; the Devil is out and preying on her like a beast upon the flesh of the pure lamb. God will bless you for your help.
>
> *Abigail rises, staring as though inspired, and cries out.*
>
> ABIGAIL: I want to open myself! *They turn to her, startled. She is enraptured, as though in a pearly light.* I want the light of God, I want the sweet love of Jesus! I danced for the Devil; I saw him; I wrote in his book; I go back to Jesus; I kiss His hand. I saw Sarah Good with the Devil! I saw Goody Osburn with the Devil! I saw Bridget Bishop with the Devil!
>
> *As she is speaking, Betty is rising from the bed, a fever in her eyes, and picks up the chant.*
>
> BETTY, *staring too:* I saw George Jacobs with the Devil! I saw Goody Howe with the Devil!
>
> PARRIS: She speaks! *He rushes to embrace Betty.* She speaks!
>
> HALE: Glory to God! It is broken, they are free!
>
> BETTY, *calling out hysterically and with great relief:* I saw Martha Bellows with the Devil!
>
> ABIGAIL: I saw Goody Sibber with the Devil! *It is rising to a great glee.*
>
> PUTNAM: The marshal, I'll call the marshal!
>
> *Parris is shouting a prayer of thanksgiving.*
>
> BETTY: I saw Alice Barrow with the Devil!
>
> *The curtain begins to fall.*
>
> HALE, *as Putnam goes out:* Let the marshal bring irons!

Source: Miller, Arthur. "Act I," from THE CRUCIBLE, by Arthur Miller, copyright 1952, 1953, 1954, renewed © 1980, 1981, 1982 by Arthur Miller. Used by permission of Viking Penguin, a division of Penguin Group (USA) Inc. Used by permission of The Wylie Agency LLC.

The dialogue and stage directions depict the strong emotions that surround this situation. The men, who very much *want* to believe the girls' accusations, readily leap to the conclusion that the accused women are guilty. In contrast, near the start of Act 2, Miller shows us two people (John and Elizabeth Proctor, husband and wife) for whom the testimony of young girls is inadequate evidence.

> ELIZABETH: … There be fourteen people in the jail now, she says. *Proctor simply looks at her, unable to grasp it.* And they'll be tried, and the courts have power to hang them too, she says.
>
> PROCTOR, *scoffing, but without conviction:* Ah, they'd never hang—
>
> ELIZABETH: The Deputy Governor promises hangin' if they'll not confess, John. The town's gone wild, I think. She speaks of Abigail, and I thought she were a saint, to hear her. Abigail brings the other girls into the court, and where she walks the crowd will part like the sea for Israel. And folks are brought before them, and if they scream and howl and fall to the floor—the person's clapped in the jail for bewitchin' them.
>
> PROCTOR, *wide-eyed:* Oh, it is a black mischief.
>
> ELIZABETH: I think you must go to Salem, John. *He turns to her.* I think so. You must tell them it is a fraud.

John Proctor does, indeed, go to Salem, but to no avail. The town has "gone wild," allowing emotion to overcome all reason. Based on inadequate evidence, fourteen people are unjustly hanged.

Perhaps we are inclined to tell ourselves that these events in Salem took place over three hundred years ago and, therefore, do not apply to our contemporary world. But of course, we only need to look at a newspaper to read about daily events in which reason and justice are overthrown by unreason and injustice. In fact, Miller was inspired to write *The Crucible* by a series of then-contemporary events dominated by emotion rather than reason—the so-called McCarthy hearings, in which the House Un-American Activities Committee, influenced by the fanatically anticommunist senator Joseph McCarthy, investigated persons accused of being communists. Appealing to fear—the "Red scare," the post–World War II fear of the spread of communism—this Congressional committee derailed and ruined the careers of many American journalists, actors, and others by smearing them as "card-carrying communists," mostly without any credible evidence. As in colonial Salem, reason was overcome by emotion. Indeed, the term "witch hunt," which has long been applied to the McCarthy hearings, has as much viability today as it did in the late 1600s. We must remain vigilant to avoid becoming victims of our own flawed reasoning, slaves to purely emotional appeals. Approaching our reading of literature such as *The Crucible* with both a creative and a critical eye helps us to practice this vigilance and to discover how a work of literature may relate to current issues and our own lives.

Now read through the following annotated fiction, drama, and nonfiction texts to see more examples of how creative and critical reading can be applied and synthesized. As you read, we would like you to keep the following in mind: There are no fixed rules for annotating a text. We encourage you to design an approach that works for you as a reader and that suits your style as a writer. Although there are no fixed rules, there is a principle we hope you will embrace: Be bold and expansive; take risks; and, above all, enjoy the process. As fiction writer Eudora Welty once declared about writing, "The joy is in the doing of it."

2.5.1 Creative and Critical Reading Annotations: Fiction

From "The Red Convertible," by Louise Erdrich (1984). (The full text is in Chapter 6.)

Lyman Lamartine

I was the first one to drive a convertible on my reservation. And of course it was red, a red Olds. I owned that car along with my brother Henry Junior. We owned it together until his boots filled with water on a windy night and he bought out my share. Now Henry owns the whole car, and his youngest brother Lyman (that's myself), Lyman walks everywhere he goes.

Source: Erdrich, Louise. "The Red Convertible" from the book LOVE MEDICINE, new and expanded Version by Louise Erdrich. Copyright © 1984, 1993 by Louise Erdrich. Reprinted by permission of Henry Holt and Company, LLC.

CREATIVE READING ANNOTATION: *Lyman and Henry Junior are brothers who live on a reservation, so a story about two Native American brothers. Awesome— a red Oldsmobile convertible. My dream car is a red Mustang convertible. Okay, boots filling with water on a windy night—what is that about, I wonder? Guess we'll find out later.*

CRITICAL READING ANNOTATION: *This paragraph tells me that Lyman and his brother are Native Americans who live on a reservation. From what I know about reservations, the living is hardscrabble—high rates of poverty and alcoholism—so owning a red Oldsmobile convertible would be a big deal. Hence, the story's title. This red Olds is going to play a key role in this story: "... until his boots filled with water ..."—something to watch out for as I continue reading.*

How did I earn enough money to buy my share in the first place? My own talent was I could always make money. I had a touch for it, unusual in a Chippewa. From the first I was different that way, and everyone recognized it. I was the only kid they let in the American Legion Hall to shine shoes, for example, and one Christmas I sold spiritual bouquets for the mission door to door. The nuns let me keep a percentage. Once I started, it seemed the more money I made the easier the money came. Everyone encouraged it. When I was fifteen I got a job washing dishes at the Joliet Cafe, and that was where my first big break happened.

CREATIVE READING ANNOTATION: Lyman is one of those guys who can make a buck out of nothing. And he and his brother are Chippewa? It sounds as though Lyman is an all-around good luck guy—things happen for him, but then he works for it. He sees an opportunity and goes for it. And he can charm nuns—not bad. I want some of his juice.

CRITICAL READING ANNOTATION: Lyman seems like a guy who will make it; he will escape the impoverished life of the reservation. He is a people guy, too; he charms nuns into letting him "keep a percentage." But looking back at that opening paragraph—maybe not—he says he "walks everywhere he goes."

The first time we saw it! I'll tell you when we first saw it. We had gotten a ride to Winnipeg, and both of us had money. Don't ask me why, because we never mentioned a car or anything, we just had all our money. Mine was cash, a big bankroll from the Joliet's insurance. Henry had two checks—a week's extra pay for being laid off, and his regular check from the Jewel Bearing Plant.

CREATIVE READING ANNOTATION: Henry doesn't seem to have Lyman's slick ways with money. And he's down on his luck—he's been laid off from his job at a factory. Drudgery.

CRITICAL READING ANNOTATION: Here we get a bit of information about Henry. He may be the oldest brother, but he seems to be, in contrast to the younger Lyman, a guy who never gets a break—or maybe he just doesn't have Lyman's imagination. He just puts one foot in front of the next.

We were walking down Portage anyway, seeing the sights, when we saw it. There it was, parked, large as life. Really as if it was alive. I thought of the word repose, because the car wasn't simply stopped, parked, or whatever. That car reposed, calm and gleaming, a for sale sign in its left front window. Then, before we had thought it over at all, the car belonged to us and our pockets were empty. We had just enough money for gas back home.

CREATIVE READING ANNOTATION: I can see this scene. This big shiny red Olds convertible, sitting there saying, come to me. And the brothers have money burning in their pockets. One day, that'll be me and my red Mustang convertible!

CRITICAL READING ANNOTATION: "The Red Convertible"—Here comes the title. For these brothers, the car is not just a machine to move you from a to b; it is a living creature—and a beauty. It is magical, and it is power. It is letting the moment move you, not playing it safe all the time but splurging—spending those bucks.

We went places in that car, me and Henry. We took off driving all one whole summer. We started off toward the Little Knife River and Mandaree in Fort Berthold and then we found ourselves down in Wakpala somehow, and then suddenly we were over in Montana on the Rocky Boy, and yet the summer was not even half over. Some people hang on to details when they travel, but we didn't let them bother us and just lived our everyday lives here to there.

CREATIVE READING ANNOTATION: *They are living the good life—going where they want, when they want—road-tripping. What happened to these kinds of summer days? My buddies and I all work part-time jobs and do classes year-round.*

CRITICAL READING ANNOTATION: *Two brothers on a summer road trip—the car is their ticket to freedom and independence. They have escaped the reservation. Ah, I get it—reservations are where Native Americans were, and have been, in a sense, trapped; they were forced to move there and enclosed. Before white settlers took over, Native Americans could go where they wanted—no boundaries.*

> I do remember this place with willows. I remember I laid under those trees and it was comfortable. So comfortable. The branches bent down all around me like a tent or a stable. And quiet, it was quiet, even though there was a powwow close enough so I could see it going on. The air was not too still, not too windy either. When the dust rises up and hangs in the air around dancers like that, I feel good. Henry was asleep with his arms thrown wide. Later on, he woke up and we started driving again. We were somewhere in Montana, or maybe on the Blood Reserve—it could have been anywhere. Anyway it was where we met the girl.

CREATIVE READING ANNOTATION: *This scene is peaceful—the two brothers taking some shut-eye out in nature. I am not sure what a powwow is; apparently, it involves dancers—some kind of Native American ceremony, maybe. Yes, enter the girl—now the real action begins!*

CRITICAL READING ANNOTATION: *I may be reading too much into this, but then that is what these annotations are about. Here the brothers are getting in touch with their Native American selves. The quiet. Nature. The powwow with dancers—googled it and found out it is a Native American ritual, a way that contemporary Native Americans stay connected to their heritage.*

Follow-up analysis:

CREATIVE READING ANNOTATIONS: *The annotations show that the reader is reading the text for pleasure. It is as though he is getting to know these two brothers, two young men who are different from him—Native Americans—yet similar: They love a sweet-looking, sleek car and the freedom of the road. Not concerning himself with understanding every aspect of the story, he gives himself license to enjoy imagining the scenes as they unfold.*

CREATIVE READING ANNOTATIONS: *The annotations show that the reader is reading the text from an objective rather than a subjective stance. He is not putting himself personally into the narrative; rather he is taking time to examine the possible significance of details. He draws an insightful contrast between the brothers, even as he points out their deep and natural bond, one that is manifested through their spontaneous joint purchase of the car and summer road trip. Moreover, he takes the time to look up some information about powwows, which helps to deepen his understanding of the significance of that specific detail.*

Synthesis of the creative and critical reading annotations:

Even though I am not Native American, I can relate to the brothers' longing to be free to travel where they want, when they want—the freedom of the road. And a car (or truck) is a symbol of that freedom—for teenagers and young adults of all backgrounds and ethnicities. Independence. The story, however, hints at darker moments ahead—Henry, down on his luck, and the opening image of "his boots filled with water on a windy night." Contrast the peacefulness of the scene under the willows with the disquieting image of boots filling with water on a windy night. There is trouble ahead for these Native American brothers.

I suspect that the story raises some serious issues about the status of Native Americans in their American "homeland"—ironically, today, the reservation. They are trying to hold onto their heritage, but the currents of society are pushing them apart from it. I looked up the bio info on the author; Erdrich is of mixed heritage, mother Chippewa (like Lyman and Henry) and father German-American—interesting combo, for sure. As I continue reading, I will be on the lookout for argument topics centered on Native Americans. Thinking about this story has gotten me interested in doing research on these true "original" Americans.

2.5.2 Creative and Critical Reading Annotations: Drama

An Ideal Husband, by Oscar Wilde (1895) (the full text is in Chapter 8), is a comedic play that satirizes the political and social lives of upper-class London society, illustrating the hypocrisy of their superficial displays of morality. The setting of this excerpt, from the opening scene, is a fashionable and formal party for members of high society, where even close friends call each other by their titles, and charming conversation is the main source of entertainment, even when the charm hides insults.

[... Lord Goring *saunters over to* Mabel Chiltern.]

MABEL CHILTERN:	You are very late!
LORD GORING:	Have you missed me?
MABEL CHILTERN:	Awfully!
LORD GORING:	Then I am sorry I did not stay away longer. I like being missed.
MABEL CHILTERN:	How very selfish of you!
LORD GORING:	I am very selfish.
MABEL CHILTERN:	You are always telling me of your bad qualities, Lord Goring.
LORD GORING:	I have only told you half of them as yet, Miss Mabel!
MABEL CHILTERN:	Are the others very bad?
LORD GORING:	Quite dreadful! When I think of them at night I go to sleep at once.

MABEL CHILTERN:	Well, I delight in your bad qualities. I wouldn't have you part with one of them.
LORD GORING:	How very nice of you! But then you are always nice.

CREATIVE READING ANNOTATION: These characters are very flirty here. They seem to follow the good girl/bad boy stereotype, like in Grease, Dirty Dancing, *or* 10 Things I Hate About You. *They appear to know each other quite well.*

CRITICAL READING ANNOTATION: The use of the word "saunters" in the opening of this passage gives the readers an important clue to Lord Goring's personality: He is nonchalant and relaxed, or desires to appear that way. He and Mabel Chiltern both appreciate this persona. In Victorian society, they often valued public morality over personal pleasure. Both Lord Goring and Miss Mabel prefer the opposite, and audiences are expected to like these two characters. Wilde implies that honest, though flawed, personalities are preferred.

LORD GORING:	By the way, I want to ask you a question, Miss Mabel. Who brought Mrs. Cheveley here? That woman in heliotrope, who has just gone out of the room with your brother?
MABEL CHILTERN:	Oh, I think Lady Markby brought her. Why do you ask?
LORD GORING:	I haven't seen her for years; that is all.
MABEL CHILTERN:	What an absurd reason!
LORD GORING:	All reasons are absurd.
MABEL CHILTERN:	What sort of a woman is she?
LORD GORING:	Oh! a genius in the daytime and a beauty at night!
MABEL CHILTERN:	I dislike her already.
LORD GORING:	That shows your admirable good taste.

CREATIVE READING ANNOTATION: Who is this other woman? Is there a love triangle in play now? What is heliotrope?!! Lord Goring compliments Mrs. Cheveley when he calls her a genius and a beauty, but he seems to agree with Mabel's dislike for (or jealousy of) Mrs. Cheveley.

CRITICAL READING ANNOTATION: Mrs. Cheveley invites comments and gossip; people notice her. Wilde must want her to seem extravagant to have the color of her dress described as "heliotrope" instead of pale purple, something more universally recognized. Lord Goring reveals more of his character when he equates reason with absurdity and shows disdain for "genius." Perhaps, too, his apparent compliment of being a "beauty at night" is more insulting, since one cannot see as well when it is dark.

VICOMTE DE NANJAC:	[*Approaching.*] Ah, the English young lady is the dragon of good taste, is she not? Quite the dragon of good taste.
LORD GORING:	So the newspapers are always telling us.
VICOMTE DE NANJAC:	I read all your English newspapers. I find them so amusing.

LORD GORING:	Then, my dear Nanjac, you must certainly read between the lines.
VICOMTE DE NANJAC:	I should like to, but my professor objects.
VICOMTE DE NANJAC:	[*To* Mabel Chiltern.] May I have the pleasure of escorting you to the music-room, Mademoiselle?
MABEL CHILTERN:	[*Looking very disappointed.*] Delighted, Vicomte, quite delighted! [*Turning to* Lord Goring.] Aren't you coming to the music-room?
LORD GORING:	Not if there is any music going on, Miss Mabel.
MABEL CHILTERN:	[*Severely.*] The music is in German. You would not understand it.

[*Goes out with the* Vicomte de Nanjac.]

CREATIVE READING ANNOTATION: *What is a dragon of good taste? I think he may have used the wrong word. He might be foreign because his name seems more French than English. Mabel does not want to leave Lord Goring, but she covers her disappointment with a small insult. She seems to be popular.*

CRITICAL READING ANNOTATION: *Vicomte de Nanjac brings some examples of low comedy to this scene with his malapropisms and contrasts well with Lord Goring's subversive remarks. Mabel Chiltern, too, demonstrates her polite subversion when she declares she is "delighted" to accompany the Vicomte, though she is "disappointed." The characters in this scene are also able to insult English newspapers and German music and, perhaps, English and French education.*

[Lord Caversham *comes up to his son.*]

LORD CAVERSHAM:	Well, sir! What are you doing here? Wasting your life as usual! You should be in bed, sir. You keep too late hours! I heard of you the other night at Lady Rufford's dancing till four o'clock in the morning!
LORD GORING:	Only a quarter to four, father.
LORD CAVERSHAM:	Can't make out how you stand London Society. The thing has gone to the dogs, a lot of damned nobodies talking about nothing.
LORD GORING:	I love talking about nothing, father. It is the only thing I know anything about.
LORD CAVERSHAM:	You seem to me to be living entirely for pleasure.
LORD GORING:	What else is there to live for, father? Nothing ages like happiness.
LORD CAVERSHAM:	You are heartless, sir, very heartless!
LORD GORING:	I hope not, father.

CREATIVE READING ANNOTATION: *How come Lord Caversham and Lord Goring have different names if they are father and son? Lord Caversham treats Lord Goring like many parents treat their sons, nagging and lecturing. Lord Goring is very amusing—What a great line: "I love talking about nothing, father. It is the only thing I know anything about." Is he teasing his father or is he being more honest than most?*

CRITICAL READING ANNOTATION: Lord Goring expresses his life's philosophy in a *very understated fashion: He lives for pleasure. Of course, his father would be dismayed at this confession, but, again, Lord Goring prefers honesty, even when disguised as wit.*

LORD GORING:	Good evening, Lady Basildon!
LADY BASILDON:	[*Arching two pretty eyebrows.*] Are you here? I had no idea you ever came to political parties!
LORD GORING:	I adore political parties. They are the only place left to us where people don't talk politics.
LADY BASILDON:	I delight in talking politics. I talk them all day long. But I can't bear listening to them. I don't know how the unfortunate men in the House stand these long debates.
LORD GORING:	By never listening.
LADY BASILDON:	Really?
LORD GORING:	[*In his most serious manner.*] Of course. You see, it is a very dangerous thing to listen. If one listens one may be convinced; and a man who allows himself to be convinced by an argument is a thoroughly unreasonable person.

CREATIVE READING ANNOTATION: Lord Goring makes more cynical and sly comments here—again, is he being honest and hiding it with his wit? Probably many modern politicians also never listen.

CRITICAL READING ANNOTATION: Lord Goring conveys apparent boredom with politics, reflecting again his preference for pleasure. Lord Goring states that listening is dangerous and changing one's mind is unreasonable—as is often the case with satire, the author implies the opposite.

Follow-up analysis:

CREATIVE READING ANNOTATIONS: The reader notes the conventional plot devices found even in today's romantic comedies: The good girl falls for the bad boy, possibly with hopes of reforming him; she identifies potential obstacles to the relationship with the entrance of romantic rivals; and she begins to recognize the use of humor in the conversations.

CRITICAL READING ANNOTATIONS: Here the reader focuses on the satire and social criticism in this section. The emphasis is on the historical and political connections, with some observations about the humor the playwright uses to convey his contempt for social institutions.

Synthesis of the creative and critical reading annotations:

Oscar Wilde creates, in An Ideal Husband, *a comedy that reflects our current romantic and political issues, yet feels rooted in its own period. He presents characters that are both appealing and manipulative, as well as ones that recognize the lazy intellect and selfishness of politicians. His use of humor makes audiences enjoy the presentation of his "lesson."*

Political hypocrisy and social judgment are issues that resonate with contemporary readers. After reading the complete play, it might be interesting to compare the moralists of today with the moralists of Victorian England; both societies project veneers of perfection while concealing underlying vices. The romantic and familial relationships are common to today's society, and an analysis of common tropes in An Ideal Husband *and a modern movie could be engaging. This play also reveals corruption in affairs of state, and issues in modern political corruption might be a potential topic for an argument essay.*

2.5.3 Creative and Critical Reading Annotations: Nonfiction

From "Bots at Work: Men Will Lose the Most Jobs to Robots. That's OK," by Laurie Penny. (The full text is in Chapter 6.)

> Robots are coming for our jobs—but not all of our jobs. They're coming, in ever increasing numbers, for a certain kind of work. For farm and factory labor. For construction. For haulage. In other words, blue-collar jobs traditionally done by men.

Source: Penny, Laurie. *Wired* (10/2017). Reprinted by permission of The David Higham Agency.

CREATIVE READING ANNOTATION: This writer seems to like to play around with sentence rhythm and style. It's as though she is thinking out loud as she writes—she makes writing seem like fun, not a bore or a chore.

CRITICAL READING ANNOTATION: After reading the title, I know where this writer's coming from. She doesn't seem to be a fan of men, most especially, blue-collar workers. I suppose she's assuming that blue-collar men (and women) don't read Wired *magazine, only white-collar men (and women).*

> This is why automation is so much more than an economic problem. It is a cultural problem, an identity problem, and—critically—a gender problem. Millions of men around the world are staring into the lacquered teeth of obsolescence, terrified of losing not only their security but also their source of meaning and dignity in a world that tells them that if they're not rich, they'd better be doing something quintessentially manly for money. Otherwise they're about as much use as a wooden coach-and-four on the freeway.

CREATIVE READING ANNOTATION: Gender problem—It seems these days most everything is called out as a gender problem. What's the problem—I'm not sure. Maybe it's that we're calling gender a "problem." The images are vivid, if not sharply pointed: "lacquered teeth of obsolescence" and "wooden coach-and-four on the freeway." It's funny to think of a coach on the freeway in an article about robots.

CRITICAL READING ANNOTATION: In this paragraph, the writer reveals her total disdain for the so-called blue-collar workers—"staring into the lacquered teeth of obsolescence, terrified" and then comparing them to "a wooden coach-and-four." Such a disrespectful and demeaning tone is a turn-off for many readers, this one included. And she claims to know that "millions of men around the world" are in this category.

There's hope for mankind, but it'll be a hard sell. The way we respond to automation will depend very much on what we decide it means to be a man, or a woman, in the awkward adolescence of the 21st century.

CREATIVE READING ANNOTATION: Good question—what does it mean to be a man or a woman? The default response is that to be a man is to be tough and assertive; to be a woman, soft and compliant. But that was back in the day. Today we are not so tied to those outdated models of manhood and womanhood.

CRITICAL READING ANNOTATION: This short paragraph provides a bit of breathing space after the biting tone and not so subtle attacks on men in the previous one—it seems more neutral and offers a glimmer of optimism.

Some political rhetoric blames outsourcing and immigration for the decline in "men's work," but automation is a greater threat to these kinds of jobs—and technological progress cannot be stopped at any border. A recent Oxford study predicted that 70 percent of US construction jobs will disappear in the coming decades; 97 percent of those jobs are held by men, and so are 95 percent of the 3.5 million transport and trucking jobs that robots are presently eyeing. That's scary, and it's one reason so many men are expressing their anger and anxiety at home, in the streets, and at the polls.

CREATIVE READING ANNOTATION: What is "men's work"—being a CEO or a lawyer or a doctor or a chef or a sports journalist or a store manager or a salesperson? And women's work is no different these days, really, when you think about it. And aren't women angry too? These days, plenty of women are expressing their anger over sexual harassment.

CRITICAL READING ANNOTATION: Why is "men's work" in quotation marks? Is it the writer's way of assuming that blue-collar jobs = men's work? If so, I do not buy that assumption: Men's work means a lot more—most CEOs are men; men are lawyers, doctors, teachers, etc. And the Oxford study data sound impressive—show me the numbers—but I would like to know more details about this "recent Oxford study." Recent as in within the last six months, three years, or decade? And who was involved in the study, and who at Oxford conducted it?

While all of this is going on, though, there's a counter-phenomenon playing out. As society panics about bricklaying worker droids and self-driving 18-wheelers, jobs traditionally performed by women—in the so-called pink-collar industries, as well as unpaid labor—are still relatively safe, and some are even on the rise. These include childcare. And service. And nursing, which the US Bureau of Labor Statistics predicts will need a million-plus more workers in the next decade.

CREATIVE READING ANNOTATION: *Rather than scary, I think it's hilarious to think of worker droids zipping around fixing potholes in the streets or laying new shingle for a roof—although I am not so sure how I would feel about a driverless 18-wheeler barreling up to my bumper on the interstate. Here is the writer with another colorful image, "pink-collar industries"—it makes me think of this dainty person in an industrial setting. I hadn't thought of childcare and nursing in that context.*

CRITICAL READING ANNOTATION: *I didn't realize that we all ("society") are in a panic about worker droids and self-driving 18-wheelers. In fact, I am not, and I would bet that neither are most of my peers. And now we hear about the "so-called pink-collar industries"—childcare, service, nursing. In contrast, the "blue-collar jobs," noted earlier, were not "so-called." This subtle difference seems significant; it suggests that blue-collar = men, but pink-collar should not be assigned exclusively to women. Citing the US Bureau of Labor Statistics does win some points for her—it is an authoritative source—but I would like to know the date of this information.*

Follow-up analysis:

CREATIVE READING ANNOTATIONS: *The annotations show that the reader is reading the text primarily for enjoyment and discovery. She engages with the language and style of the writing and gives herself the freedom to isolate phrases and passages and to engage with each as its own entity. Her approach to this initial reading experience is open-ended and exploratory.*

CRITICAL READING ANNOTATIONS: *Here the reader is reading the text with her critical sensors on high alert. Whether or not her personal stance tends to favor the writer's stance, she is playing the role of the skeptical reader and paying close attention to the nuances of language and phrasing, not for their creative and aesthetic qualities but for their subjective and biased qualities. She also questions assumptions and wonders whether reported information is accurate and complete.*

Synthesis of the creative and critical reading annotations:

Writer Laurie Penny presents an engaging and a provocative short argument. Even if some—or perhaps many—readers are offended by her biting and outright haughty tone (regarding "blue-collar" workers/men), they most likely will keep reading. She has a feisty style. As a student of writing and, specifically, argument, I admire Penny's creative flare, her lively and vivid language; however, I also see how critical it is to monitor your tone. As we have been taught in class, the purpose of writing an argument is, above all, to change your audience's thinking on a controversial issue. Although Penny's writing is likely to keep her readers reading to the end, I don't think her argument will change many readers' thinking.

The topic, "bots at work," is a fresh one and appeals to me. If robots are coming into the workplace, their presence is certainly going to impact me, in some way. And I just thought of a potential issue for our next argument essay: Should self-driving 18-wheelers become the primary mode for the transcontinental transportation of goods and products? Or another topic could center on employment policy regarding paternity leave, in order to encourage and support men in the pink-collar industry of childcare: Should paternity leave be the same as maternity leave?

2.6 Chapter Activities

The series of activities below on the following pages invite you to apply the concepts and ideas we have discussed and demonstrated throughout this chapter.

2.6.1 Think About It

Answer the following questions covering the topics discussed in this chapter.

1. You may approach your college education with concrete goals of getting a job and earning money, aspirations that often qualify as success in our society. The genres we are reading in this text (poetry, fiction, drama, nonfiction) may or may not be genres you will read in your eventual career. Consider and articulate how reading these genres and practicing the skills of reading creatively and reading critically may be beneficial in both your academic and your professional future.

2. Find a new musical artist or a song that appeals to you. Describe your initial connection to the music; consider the style, lyrics, or video version. Do some Internet research on the musician(s), and review the printed lyrics. Annotate the lyrics using both creative and critical reading skills.

3. Review assignments from other courses. In what ways do the assignments rely on reading for you to complete them? Think of one recent assignment and describe how applying creative and critical reading skills could help you to complete the assignment more proficiently.

2.6.2 Read and Respond

Read the poem below and respond to the writing tasks that follow.

"Porphyria's Lover," by Robert Browning (1836)

The rain set early in to-night,
    The sullen wind was soon awake,
It tore the elm-tops down for spite,
    And did its worst to vex the lake:
    I listened with heart fit to break.   5

When glided in Porphyria; straight
    She shut the cold out and the storm,
And kneeled and made the cheerless grate
    Blaze up, and all the cottage warm;
    Which done, she rose, and from her form   10

Withdrew the dripping cloak and shawl,
 And laid her soiled gloves by, untied
Her hat and let the damp hair fall,
 And, last, she sat down by my side
 And called me. When no voice replied,   15

She put my arm about her waist,
 And made her smooth white shoulder bare,
And all her yellow hair displaced,
 And, stooping, made my cheek lie there,
 And spread, o'er all, her yellow hair,   20

Murmuring how she loved me—she
 Too weak, for all her heart's endeavour,
To set its struggling passion free
 From pride, and vainer ties dissever,
 And give herself to me for ever.   25

But passion sometimes would prevail,
 Nor could to-night's gay feast restrain
A sudden thought of one so pale
 For love of her, and all in vain:
 So, she was come through wind and rain.   30

Be sure I looked up at her eyes
 Happy and proud; at last I knew
Porphyria worshipped me; surprise
 Made my heart swell, and still it grew
 While I debated what to do.   35

That moment she was mine, mine, fair,
 Perfectly pure and good: I found
A thing to do, and all her hair
 In one long yellow string I wound
 Three times her little throat around,   40

And strangled her. No pain felt she;
 I am quite sure she felt no pain.
As a shut bud that holds a bee,
 I warily oped her lids: again
 Laughed the blue eyes without a stain.   45

And I untightened next the tress
 About her neck; her cheek once more
Blushed bright beneath my burning kiss:
 I propped her head up as before,
 Only, this time my shoulder bore   50

Her head, which droops upon it still:
    The smiling rosy little head,
So glad it has its utmost will,
    That all it scorned at once is fled,
    And I, its love, am gained instead!   55

Porphyria's love: she guessed not how
    Her darling one wish would be heard.
And thus we sit together now,
    And all night long we have not stirred,
    And yet God has not said a word!   60

Writing Tasks

1. Taking a creative approach to reading Robert Browning's poem, compare the tone and message of this strange, almost bizarre, narrative to your idea of a traditional love story. How are they similar and how are they different?

2. Reading more critically, choose three of the following images from Browning's poem and explain the symbolic meaning: rain/wind, warm cottage, smooth white shoulder, yellow hair, burning kiss, smiling rosy little head.

3. The final line of "Porphyria's Lover" is "And yet God has not said a word!" Reading the poem with a blend of creative and critical perspectives, explain what the speaker means by this final line.

4. The name Porphyria is based on a Greek word that means "purple"; it is also the name of a disease that affects the nervous system. What might be the significance of Browning's choice of this name for his character?

5. Porphyria, by the end of the poem, has become an *objet d'art* (an object of art), almost like a sculpture. Consider at least three of the following works, each of which has a female character who becomes an object of art or, in reverse, a piece of art brought to life: the myth of Pygmalion or the play *Pygmalion*, by George Bernard Shaw; the poem "The Lady of Shalott," by Alfred, Lord Tennyson; the poem "Aspecta Medusa," by Dante Gabriel Rossetti; the tale "Snow White" or "Sleeping Beauty," collected by the Brothers Grimm; the poem "My Last Duchess," by Robert Browning; the 2007 film *Lars and the Real Girl*; and the 1987 film *Mannequin* (or consider other such works of your own choosing). What is the effect of comparing a woman to an art object or even transforming one into the other? What are the positive and negative connotations of such comparisons and transformations? Include quotations from your three chosen works to support your responses.

2.6.3 Multimodal Activities

1. **"Reading" a Song: The Unsolved Mystery of Billy Joe**
   For the writing task below, apply your skills as both a creative and a critical reader to a video performance and the lyrics of Bobbie Gentry's 1967 song, "Ode to Billy Joe" (performance and lyrics are available, for example, at this URL: https://www.google.com/search?q=ode+to+billy+joe&oq=ode+to+billy+joe&aqs=chrome.0.0l6.2493j0j9&sourceid=chrome&ie=UTF-8). Ever since the song's release, controversy has swirled around the mystery of Billy Joe: why he jumped off the Tallahatchie Bridge, what was thrown off the bridge, and what his relationship is to the song's narrator (Gentry has never offered definitive answers to any of these questions).

Writing Task

- Write out your creative and critical responses to the song and to the mystery of Billy Joe.
- Synthesize your responses to offer your own take on the song's mystery. Use excerpts from the lyrics to support your perspective.

2. **From Reading Words in a Book, to Words and Pictures on a Screen, to Symbols on a Smartphone**
   Reflect on the images in Figure 2.2, and then respond to the following writing tasks.
   - How does each image reflect an important aspect of reading?
   - How do the images illustrate the changing nature of reading?
   - Using the images as inspiration, choose three of these reading modalities and briefly describe the pros and cons of each: traditional books, newspapers, ebooks, digital essays, audio recordings. Which modalities do you prefer and under which circumstances? How do these preferences reflect your reading style?

Figure 2.2

© INTERFOTO/Alamy © Iain Masterton/Alamy Stock Photo   © Concepts/Alamy Stock Photo
Stock Photo

Chapter 3
Analyzing Argument

 Learning Objectives

In this chapter, you will learn to

3.1 Recognize the components of an argument.

3.2 Identify logical fallacies.

3.3 Understand rhetorical context and Aristotle's argument model.

3.1 Components of an Argument

Recognize the components of an argument.

In the sections that follow, we will describe some of the different types of claims, evidence, and assumptions used in constructing arguments, and we will look at how these components of argument appear in literature, either explicitly or implicitly. We also will examine how arguers can respond to counterarguments by making concessions and articulating refutations.

3.1.1 Claims

An academic argument requires a claim. The **claim** is the assertion made in an argument—it is the main point, the thesis, of the argument. We can also think of the claim as the conclusion the writer has drawn. A claim reveals a writer's purpose in addressing an audience. A solid argument is created when the writer takes the time to identify his or her claim and then develops a plan for conveying that claim to the audience.

Depending upon the subject matter, you may decide to make an **explicit claim**; that is, you might feel that directly stating your purpose in a focused thesis statement early in your argument essay is the best way to convey your claim. Other times, however, you may choose to make an **implicit claim**, beginning your essay with an interesting scenario or subtle clues that invite the reader to think deeply. An implicit claim can work by steering the reader on a thought-provoking journey toward understanding the claim.

Argument theorists identify several types of claims, including claims of fact, claims of policy, and claims of value. Suppose, for example, that you have decided to write an essay about rain forests. The topic may interest you, but what exactly do you wish to convey about rain forests? Let's look at how you could use these three types of claims to plan your argument (see Take Note 3.1).

3.1.2 Claims in Literature

Do you recall reading *The Scarlet Letter,* by Nathaniel Hawthorne, sometime during your four years in high school? Do you remember the novel well enough to state Hawthorne's main claim? Something about deception perhaps? Maybe something about values? You're not likely to find a single sentence in Hawthorne's novel equivalent to a thesis in an academic essay. However, in a classroom discussion, through the interplay of varying interpretations, readers can articulate a central claim for this novel.

Imaginative literature is often ambiguous or difficult to interpret, making it harder to identify a claim. Look, for example, at this short poem by Kenneth Rexroth:

Cold Before Dawn (1979)

Cold before dawn,
Off in the misty night,
Under the gibbous moon,
The peacocks cry to each other,
As if in pain.

Source: Rexroth, Kenneth. "Cold Before Dawn" By Kenneth Rexroth, from FLOWER WREATH HILL, copyright © 1979 by Kenneth Rexroth. Reprinted by permission of New Directions Publishing Corp.

Take Note 3.1

Claims of Fact, Policy, and Value

When you make a claim about rain forests, what type of claim are you making?

Claim	Type of Claim
You make the point that the world loses ten acres of rain forest every minute.	You are making a **claim of fact**, which may be useful as evidence in an argument calling for new environmental laws to protect the rain forest.
You call for new laws to protect the rain forest.	You are making a **claim of policy** because you are asking for a specific action to take place.
You state that rain forests are an invaluable and irreplaceable natural resource.	You have asserted a **claim of value**, a personal judgment about the value of rain forests.

Do you see a claim in this poem? You might sense the contrasts in this poem—
the contrast between the cold of night and the warmth of morning; the darkness of the mist and the light from the almost full moon; the beauty of peacocks
and the discord of their cries. The poem is eloquent and musical, but its abstract
qualities make it difficult to argue that it contains a claim.

Look at the following poem by the eighteenth-century British poet William
Blake:

London (1794)

I wander thro' each charter'd street,
Near where the charter'd Thames does flow,
And mark in every face I meet
Marks of weakness, marks of woe.

In every cry of every Man,   5
In every Infant's cry of fear,
In every voice, in every ban,
The mind-forg'd manacles I hear.

How the Chimney-sweeper's cry
Every black'ning Church appalls;   10
And the hapless Soldier's sigh
Runs in blood down Palace walls.

But most thro' midnight streets I hear
How the youthful Harlot's curse
Blasts the new born Infant's tear,   15
And blights with plagues the Marriage hearse.

What do you see as the claim in this poem? Is the claim about the young children
used as chimney sweeps and doomed to early deaths? Is it about venereal disease?
Yes, the poem says something about both of these subjects; indeed, a number of
subclaims usually can be identified in any example of writing. In this poem, however, Blake makes the implicit claim that the religious, military, and legal institutions of England in the late 1700s are responsible for the human suffering endured
by so many people then. No single line makes such a claim, but when you reread
the poem, you will see that this indictment is certainly the poem's central focus,
the conclusion the writer wishes the reader to draw (see the further discussion of
this point in the section "Evidence in Literature").

3.1.3 Evidence

No matter whether a writer opts to make a claim explicit or implicit, what must
be present in the argument is evidence. **Evidence** is the information used to support a claim. In building a body of evidence, the arguer draws on sources—both
primary sources and *secondary sources* (see Take Note 3.2).

Take Note 3.2

Primary and Secondary Sources of Evidence

Primary sources—firsthand accounts and examples, observations, interviews.

- An interview with a politician could be a primary source of evidence about the politician's opinions or attitudes.
- A video of an accident or testimony by an accident victim could be a primary source of evidence about what really happened.

Secondary sources—analyses and opinion pieces, reports based on primary sources, statistics.

- A compilation of information reported in various publications could be a secondary source of evidence about a politician.
- Testimony by police investigators could be a secondary source of evidence about an accident.

With relevant and substantive evidence to support a claim, an arguer earns credibility with an audience, and regardless of their stance on the issue, the individuals in the audience will seriously consider the arguer's viewpoint.

There are various types of evidence, but for our purposes, let's concentrate on three: personal experience, reports, and authority. To illustrate, in an essay, a student claims physician-assisted suicide should be legalized and offers as evidence his experience of watching his grandmother suffer a prolonged and painful death from cancer. The student employs descriptive details and a sincere tone to create a strong, emotional response in his readers. This use of **personal experience** provides compelling evidence for the validity of his argument, particularly among readers who have had similar experiences.

But what about readers who have not had any personal experience with cancer and have never experienced the death of a family member or loved one? For these readers, the emotional pull of the writer's personal experience may not be sufficient, and further evidence likely will be required to persuade them. In this case, the writer might want to provide statistics on the number of patients on life support in this country, as well as on the costs of prolonged treatment, both to families and to health care providers. A writer taking this approach is using **reports**, objective facts gathered from outside sources, to support his argument.

The student writer might take one further step toward validating his argument for legalizing physician-assisted suicide by citing an **authority**. In this case, a quote from a health care professional would be a strategic choice. In fact, every field has authorities, people who are widely recognized as experts. Citing a Centers for Disease Control scientist as an authority on the current influenza outbreak, Mark Zuckerberg as an authority on social media, or Supreme Court justice Sonia Sotomayor as an authority on women's careers in the judiciary, a writer could be certain readers would recognize these individuals as authorities. They have credibility in their respective fields.

In this way, academic argument is more than the mere expression of an opinion; the writer's opinion must be reinforced by primary and secondary sources that lend credibility to the author's claims in the eyes of the audience. Depending upon the assignment, your instructor may allow you to use personal experiences to support your claims. At the same time, many college-level writing classes require students to incorporate outside research materials from books or articles, either online or in print, to support their claims.

3.1.4 Evidence in Literature

Applying the concept of evidence to imaginative literature complicates and enriches our reading experience. To begin with, we must address the **dramatic context** of the work, including the actions, words, and thoughts of the characters. Examining the characters' claims and arguments, their positions, framed within the dramatic context, we look beyond ourselves and gain a clearer perception of our own positions. For example, readers of Harper Lee's novel *To Kill a Mockingbird* not only see the transformation of attitudes within the characters as they confront the issue of racial discrimination but may also come away from that reading experience examining their own attitudes about prejudice. In other words, analyzing the evidence in the dramatic context of a particular work can lead us to understand the positions of the characters within the work and to explore our own beliefs and values.

Moving beyond the dramatic context, we also can examine the **social context**—the conditions and events within society at the time a work was written—as evidence of the writer's claim. Often, however, we will need to gather additional information in order to understand that evidence.

Look back at the poem "London." If William Blake wants the reader to believe the social institutions of eighteenth-century England were to blame for much of the suffering endured by its citizens, he must offer us some evidence. At that time, poor families often sold one of their children to the chimney sweeps, who used them to slide down London's many tight chimneys. As they brushed the soot from those chimneys, the children's lungs filled with black dust, and they regularly died while still in their early teens. The fact that such an abuse of children was legal in London is clear evidence in support of Blake's claim. By acquainting ourselves with this historical background, we enrich our understanding of Blake's implied argument.

3.1.5 Assumptions

Assumptions are general principles, generalizations, or commonly accepted beliefs that underlie an argument. Typically, assumptions are based on values that an arguer believes the audience shares. Assumptions may be stated explicitly in an argument, but they frequently are unstated—that is, implied. Identifying unstated assumptions requires readers to exercise their critical reading skills

Take Note 3.3

Implied Assumptions

Identify the hidden assumptions.

* *Professor Schultz is a classy person because she teaches English.*

  What is the hidden assumption that the writer thinks readers will accept? It is that English professors are classy people. Of course, the authors of this textbook would accept that assumption, but undoubtedly it would not be universally accepted by readers.

* *Professor Schultz will be able to proofread the document because she is an experienced college English teacher.*

  In this case, the hidden assumption—that experienced college English teachers are competent proofreaders—is likely to be accepted by a general audience.

especially carefully. You can think of an implied assumption as the invisible ice chunk that lies beneath the visible tip of an iceberg—invisible but crucial to be aware of, as the sinking of the *Titanic* exemplifies. To illustrate the importance of recognizing a writer's unstated assumptions, let's begin with the two examples in Take Note 3.3.

Assumptions—whether stated or unstated—are an essential element in argument, the link between the claim and the evidence. As the second example above demonstrates, the claim that Professor Schultz will be able to proofread a document is supported by the evidence that the professor is an experienced college English teacher. The challenge for both the arguer and the reader is to identify and understand the assumptions and to determine their validity.

Let's move on to a more complex example illustrating the importance of understanding assumptions in argument, both as a writer and as a reader. In arguing for strict environmental regulation of rain forests, a writer may offer statistical data and scientific facts as evidence that rain forests are being destroyed. The unstated assumption—rain forests are valuable resources—may be readily accepted by most American readers, but a Brazilian landowner reading this argument may consider his property more valuable as a clear-cut and plowed field than as part of a rain forest. Depending on whom the writer envisions as her audience, she may need to back her assumption with evidence showing that rain forests are valuable.

Within our own boundaries, from the Pacific Northwest to the Florida Everglades, similar disputes rage over how to use our wilderness areas; writers engaging in these disputes also face issues concerning assumptions, evidence, and claims. First, what assumptions underlie the way we define *wilderness*? And how is our definition of wilderness affected by the economic or cultural factors in our lives? Individuals vary widely both in their definition of wilderness and in their ways of life, and acknowledging these individual variations is crucial to any discussion of wilderness issues. Our personal definition informs the value we assign to wilderness areas; this value assignment (the assumption) then shapes our viewpoint about specific land use issues.

Similarly, consider the issue of whether physician-assisted suicide should be legalized. Our position on this issue is influenced by the relative value we assign to the sanctity of human life versus the dignity of human life. An arguer opposed to the legalization of physician-assisted suicide probably assumes that the sanctity of human life is a higher value than the dignity of human life; whereas, an arguer in favor of legalization probably assumes the opposite.

3.1.6 Assumptions in Literature

Again, look back at Blake's poem "London." Now that we have identified a claim (the social institutions of eighteenth-century England were to blame for much of the suffering of its citizens) and pointed out evidence (the practice of selling children to chimney sweeps) in Blake's poem, we can consider the assumptions—the general principles or commonly accepted beliefs—that underlie Blake's argument. What assumption can you identify binding the evidence to the claim? Interestingly, the assumption, a **value assumption**, is so automatically accepted by contemporary readers that we might have trouble noticing it: The use of child labor is an affront to the principles of compassionate people everywhere. In eighteenth-century England, however, children, especially children of poor families, were viewed as property; therefore, the selling and buying of children was not widely condemned. Fortunately, enlightened thinkers, such as Blake, stood apart and questioned social institutions that supported the exploitation and abuse of children.

But the child labor issue is still complicated for contemporary readers. What about those expensive athletic shoes or the smartphone we may have recently purchased? Where were they manufactured? And by whom? In recent decades, the employment practices of several well-known U.S. manufacturers of name-brand shoes have come under critical scrutiny, and more currently, employment practices in Apple iPhone factories in China have come under attack. Many U.S. manufacturers have opened factories in foreign countries, where operating costs are far lower: Land is cheaper, and environmental and labor laws are often either nonexistent or far less stringent than in the United States. In some cases, boys and girls younger than sixteen work long hours under brutal conditions for meager wages. Is this practice not abusive and exploitative, an affront to our principles of compassion? Even though we are not directly responsible for hiring the twelve-year-old girl who works in the factory where our designer jeans were manufactured, do we share some portion of responsibility? Reading Blake's poem as an argument and examining its assumption about child labor from this perspective, we bridge the centuries that seem to separate twenty-first century readers from eighteenth century readers.

3.1.7 Counterarguments: Concessions and Refutations

How open-minded are you, especially about your own ideas? Complete the following Journal task to assess yourself on this point.

Journal: Are You Able to Question Your Own Ideas?

"It is the mark of an educated mind to be able to entertain a thought without accepting it."—Aristotle.

Spend a few minutes writing out your reflections on this quotation. Can you think of a recent example when you entertained a thought without accepting it?

A successful arguer keeps in mind that the target audience is not just people who already share the arguer's views but also, and more importantly, those who have opposing views or who are undecided. It is these groups of readers with whom a writer must work to connect. Consequently, in designing an argument strategy, a writer should determine which opposing views, or **counterarguments**, are significant and therefore merit attention. A writer can address counterarguments in two ways: through **concessions** (statements that acknowledge the validity of one or more points in a counterargument) and through **refutations** (arguments against one or more points in a counterargument). When trying to convince a broad audience, writers commonly make some concessions and also present refutations.

Consider, for example, the issue of climate change. An arguer in favor of the view that human activity is a major contributor to global warming might make a *concession* by acknowledging that accurate climate records don't go back very far in time. Therefore, the *counterargument*—climate change is not caused mainly by human activity but is, in fact, a naturally recurring phenomenon—might have some validity. The writer could then answer this concession with a detailed *refutation* by citing compelling factual evidence in support of the opinion that human activity is the primary cause of climate change.

By addressing opposing arguments thoroughly and fairly, an arguer strengthens her position with a large and diverse audience, one that is likely to include persons who are undecided, who are skeptical, who are adamantly opposed, or who readily accept the arguer's claim. In this way, the arguer reinforces a bond of respect and trust between writer and audience, which is fundamental to successful communication.

3.2 Logical Fallacies

Identify logical fallacies.

Not only should arguers look for areas of weakness in their opposition's logic, they should take inventory of their own logic. To identify and address any logical fallacies, successful writers examine the way they state and support their own beliefs and ideas.

Most of us would not knowingly choose to be flawed or biased thinkers. One way we can develop our skills as critical thinkers is to practice examining the logic in reasoning. An error or flaw in reasoning is called a **logical fallacy**. While dozens of logical fallacies have been identified, we have chosen to feature ten of the more common ones (see Take Note 3.4).

As you read through the list and definitions, you will see that understanding fallacies encourages you to practice clear thinking. Familiarizing yourself

Take Note 3.4

Common Logical Fallacies

Fallacy	Definition	Example
Ad hominem (from the Latin for "against the person")	Using personal attack instead of addressing the issue.	*Mrs. X has had an extramarital affair, so her opinion on the tax cuts isn't worth considering.*
Begging the question	Assuming exactly what the argument is attempting to prove.	*Capital punishment deters crimes because it prevents other people from committing crimes.*
Either–or reasoning	Oversimplifying by implying that there are only two ways of looking at an issue.	*If you don't vote for this school bond, we may as well shut down our public schools.*
Equivocation	Intentionally using a word that has more than one interpretation, in order to confuse an issue.	*In order to maximize my refund from the IRS, I am simply adjusting some figures on my tax return.*
False analogy	Making a false or illogical comparison ("comparing apples to oranges").	*Like Rome, America is destined for destruction.*
Hasty generalization	Jumping to a broad conclusion based on too little evidence (for example, stereotyping).	*English professors are nonathletic bookworms.*
Post hoc ergo propter hoc (from the Latin for "after this, therefore because of this"; also called the "false cause fallacy")	Incorrectly attributing a cause-and-effect relationship between events just because one comes after the other.	*Brock became a vegetarian, so he lost his muscle tone.*
Red herring	Distracting readers and leading them astray by bringing up a different issue as bait to capture the readers' interest.	*I really deserve a "B" in this class; I need the grade to keep my scholarship.*
Slippery slope	Falsely suggesting that a single event will trigger a series of increasingly undesirable effects.	*If the drinking age is lowered to eighteen, teenagers will drink to excess, and we will end up with a nation of alcoholics.*
Two wrongs make a right	Justifying wrongdoing by pointing to another's wrongdoing.	*Maybe I did fudge a bit when I reported my income to the IRS, but so do many of the nation's richest people.*

with common fallacies and practicing detecting them in arguments is not just an academic exercise. Rather, it sharpens your critical thinking skills and empowers you as an independent thinker.

Now test your analytical skills. In Exercise 3.1, can you match each logical fallacy with the example sentence that illustrates it?

Exercise 3.1: Identifying Logical Fallacies

Read these example sentences. Then, in the table below, write the number of the sentence that illustrates each logical fallacy.

1. Fossil fuel emissions are a huge problem, but people love driving, and a new car is a beautiful thing.

2. I stayed up late partying, and I scored an A on the exam the next morning — why study?

3. I've already indicated my unwillingness to discuss my finances, because I don't want to divert voters from the real issues.

4. If we criminalize gun possession, only criminals will have guns, and we'll all be at risk of our lives at every moment.

5. If you don't go to every class, you might as well withdraw from school.

6. She stood me up last week, so it's only fair that I didn't show up for our date yesterday.

7. Teenagers are interested in two things — having fun and rebelling against authority.

8. The support of the Spanish crown enabled Columbus's first voyage to the Americas, just as the first successful manned mission to Mars depends on the political commitment.

9. Why should we believe what that cheater says about the reason he cheated?

10. Richard is an excellent student because he makes superior grades.

Fallacy	Example
Ad hominem	
Begging the question	
Either–or reasoning	
Equivocation	
False analogy	
Hasty generalization	
Post hoc ergo propter hoc	
Red herring	
Slippery slope	
Two wrongs make a right	

3.3 Rhetorical Context and Aristotle's Argument Model

Understand rhetorical context and Aristotle's argument model.

As you develop an organizational strategy for your argument, you want to be cognizant of the **rhetorical context**, the conversation, both written and oral, surrounding the issue. To be persuasive, an arguer needs to be aware of the diverse viewpoints on the issue and the passionate feelings infusing those viewpoints.

The ancient Greek philosopher Aristotle offered a model of argument that you might find helpful as you begin to plan an essay or a speech. Aristotle's model includes three **rhetorical appeals**—fundamentals of persuasion used by most writers and speakers:

- *pathos* (emotion): An arguer should use sincere emotion and shared values to connect with the audience.
- *logos* (logic): An arguer should apply clear and sensible reasoning to draw in the audience.
- *ethos* (credibility): An arguer should make believable claims to earn the trust of the audience.

As shown in Figure 3.1, Aristotle's model can be represented as a "rhetorical triangle" in which the appeals of *pathos, logos,* and *ethos* are the three distinct vertices,

Figure 3.1

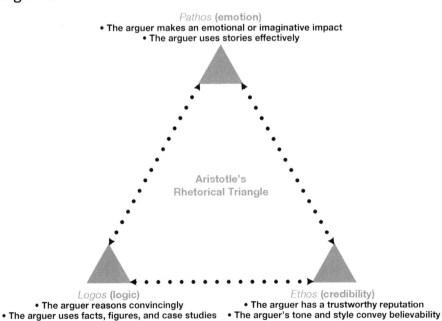

Pathos (emotion)
- The arguer makes an emotional or imaginative impact
- The arguer uses stories effectively

Aristotle's Rhetorical Triangle

Logos (logic)
- The arguer reasons convincingly
- The arguer uses facts, figures, and case studies

Ethos (credibility)
- The arguer has a trustworthy reputation
- The arguer's tone and style convey believability

yet each appeal feeds into the other two, to complete the triangle. Likewise, arguers strategically use the appeals to enhance the persuasiveness of their arguments.

Perhaps you have seen a television commercial asking you to support humane organizations that foster animals that have been subjected to horrible living conditions. Animal lovers are moved by tales of animal abuse told solely in words, but the commercial includes pictures of the faces of neglected animals, thus employing the power of *pathos*—the emotional impact of the pictures motivates many to make contributions who might not otherwise do so.

Whether or not you realize it, you demand a certain amount of *logos* from the world around you. Have you ever watched guests on an interview show and found yourself frustrated not only because their beliefs differed from your own, but also because you could not understand their arguments? If so, your need for logic was not satisfied.

Suppose one of your friends has repeatedly lectured you about the ills of smoking. One day, at a party, you see your friend in the backyard smoking. Likely you will also see his *ethos* as damaged. Credibility is paramount for an arguer to be taken seriously. Arguers who give their audience reason to think they are less than honest damage their chances of persuading their audience.

Drawing on these three rhetorical appeals, an arguer addresses the audience's basic human characteristics: emotion and empathy (*pathos*), logic and reasoning (*logos*), credibility and trust (*ethos*). Any lawyer who expects to win over a jury understands the necessity for using these appeals.

Barack Obama's second inaugural address stands as a model of argument and persuasion (the full text of the address appears in Chapter 8), in part because of Obama's use of rhetorical appeals (see Take Note 3.5).

Take Note 3.5

Rhetorical Appeals in Barack Obama's Second Inaugural Address (2013)

Pathos

Obama evokes his audience's empathy and appeals to common values—"Through blood drawn by lash and blood drawn by sword, we learned that no union founded on the principles of liberty and equality could survive half-slave and half-free."

Logos

Obama reasons deliberately and analytically about the nature of time and action—"We have always understood that when times change, so must we; that fidelity to our founding principles requires new responses to new challenges...."

Ethos

Obama builds trust with his audience as fellow Americans—"We recall that what binds this nation together is not the colors of our skin or the tenets of our faith or the origins of our names. What makes us exceptional—what makes us American—is our allegiance to an idea articulated in a declaration...."

We commonly associate Aristotle's rhetorical appeals with nonfiction prose. However, in the next sections we will see that by examining the use of appeals in poetry and fiction, we can deepen our understanding of the ways poets connect with their readers.

3.3.1 *Pathos*

"Federico's Ghost," by Martín Espada, strikingly illustrates the use of *pathos*. The poem tells the story of a boy's defiant gesture of protest against the abusive treatment of workers by those in positions of power:

Federico's Ghost (1990)

The story is
that whole families of fruitpickers
still crept between the furrows
of the field at dusk,
when for reasons of whiskey or whatever   5
the cropduster plane sprayed anyway,
floating a pesticide drizzle
over the pickers
who thrashed like dark birds
in a glistening white net,   10
except for Federico,
a skinny boy who stood apart
in his own green row,
and, knowing the pilot
would not understand in Spanish   15
that he was the son of a whore,
instead jerked his arm
and thrust an obscene finger.

The pilot understood
He circled the plane and sprayed again,   20
watching a fine gauze of poison
drift over the brown bodies
that cowered and scurried on the ground,
and aiming for Federico,
leaving the skin beneath his shirt   25
wet and blistered,
but still pumping his finger at the sky.

After Federico died,
rumors at the labor camp,
told of tomatoes picked and smashed at night,   30
growers muttering of vandal children

or communists in camp,
first threatening to call Immigration,
then promising every Sunday off
if only the smashing of tomatoes would stop.   35

Still tomatoes were picked and squashed
in the dark,
and the old women in camp
said it was Federico,
laboring after sundown   40
to cool the burns on his arms,
flinging tomatoes
at the cropduster
that hummed like a mosquito
lost in his ear,   45
and kept his soul awake.

Source: From REBELLION IS THE CIRCLE OF LOVER'S HANDS/Rebelión es el giro de manos del amante. Copyright © by Martín Espada. Translation Copyright © by Camilo Perez-Bustillo and Martín Espada. First printed in 1990 by Curbstone Press. Used by permission of the author.

Using sensory language and specific details, Espada pulls us inside—behind the words—to where we cannot avoid seeing the human faces of the tomato pickers, who are not unlike ourselves: "whole families," "a skinny boy," "old women." By acknowledging our common humanity, we must acknowledge the injustice and the oppression in the lives of the field laborers.

Poetic structure also heightens appeal to *pathos*. Because we are accustomed to reading margin-to-margin prose, the line breaks in the poem slow down our reading. We cannot rush or skip over words, as we may do in reading an essay. Espada isolates images in short lines, which surprise and shock us as readers:

over the pickers
who thrashed like dark birds
in a glistening white net

. . .

leaving the skin beneath his shirt
wet and blistered

Source: Espada, Martín. "Federico's Ghost" and "Bully" by Martín Espada from REBELLION IS THE CIRCLE OF A LOVER'S HANDS (Curbstone Press) © 1990 Martín Espada. Used by permission of the author.

With these images alive in our imaginations, we are compelled to confront the reality of "man's inhumanity to man" and to examine our own attitudes toward day laborers, migrant workers, and illegal aliens. Appealing to our emotions and moral values, Espada's poem makes a powerful statement about prejudice and power and about human dignity and heroism. "Federico's Ghost" may, indeed, keep our own "soul awake."

3.3.2 *Logos*

Shakespeare's sonnets can exemplify the *logos* point of Aristotle's triangle. Compare Espada's free-verse (open-form) poetry to the fixed form of the Shakespearean sonnet (fourteen lines—three quatrains and a couplet). The sonnet's structure reinforces the poem's argumentative emphasis. Whereas the free-form line breaks in Espada's poem counter logical structure and dramatize emotion, the ordered structure and regular rhythm of a Shakespearean sonnet underscore its pattern of reasoning and logic, as illustrated in Shakespeare's Sonnet 18:

Sonnet 18 (1609)

Shall I compare thee to a summer's day?
Thou art more lovely and more temperate:
Rough winds do shake the darling buds of May,
And summer's lease hath all too short a date:
Sometime too hot the eye of heaven shines,   5
And often is his gold complexion dimmed;
And every fair from fair sometimes declines
By chance or nature's changing course untrimmed;
But thy eternal summer shall not fade
Nor lose possession of that fair thou ow'st,   10
Nor shall death brag thou wander'st in his shade,
Whon in otornal linoc to timo thou grow'st:
    So long as men can breathe or eyes can see,
    So long lives this, and this gives life to thee.

In the sonnet, the poet's claim is explicitly stated in the final quatrain: For as long as there are people to read it, this poem shall live and so, too, shall the poet's beloved. In the preceding twelve lines, the poet provides evidence for his claim. Beginning with "a summer's day," he lists comparisons, each of which he finds deficient: "Sometime too hot the eye of heaven shines,/And often is his gold complexion dimmed." As readers, we are invited to think and reason with the poet as he makes his case for his beloved's immortality.

3.3.3 *Ethos*

Questioning the speaker's reliability leads us to the final point of Aristotle's rhetorical triangle: *ethos*—the attitude the speaker or writer conveys through specific word choices. Near the opening of Obama's second inaugural address, he provides a clear example of a highly effective appeal to *ethos*. In speaking personally and directly to all Americans ("what makes us American"), he clearly intends to offer his audience a verbal handshake as a gesture of respect and cordiality. However, other speakers or writers are not always as transparent in their purposes. As critical thinkers, we cannot always readily agree on whether a speaker or writer has credibility. For example, the following short fiction piece, "Girl," by Jamaica Kincaid, evokes an uncertain perspective on the narrator's *ethos:*

Girl (1983)

Wash the white clothes on Monday and put them on the stone heap; wash the color clothes on Tuesday and put them on the clothesline to dry; don't walk barehead in the hot sun; cook pumpkin fritters in very hot sweet oil; soak your little clothes right after you take them off; when buying cotton to make yourself a nice blouse, be sure that it doesn't have gum on it, because that way it won't hold up well after a wash; soak salt fish overnight before you cook it; is it true that you sing benna in Sunday school?; always eat your food in such a way that it won't turn someone else's stomach; on Sundays try to walk like a lady and not like the slut you are so bent on becoming; don't sing benna in Sunday school; you mustn't speak to wharf-rat boys, not even to give directions; don't eat fruits on the street—flies will follow you; *but I don't sing benna on Sundays at all and never in Sunday school;* this is how to sew on a button; this is how to make a buttonhole for the button you have just sewed on; this is how to hem a dress when you see the hem coming down and so to prevent yourself from looking like the slut I know you are so bent on becoming; this is how you iron your father's khaki shirt so that it doesn't have a crease; this is how you iron your father's khaki pants so that they don't have a crease; this is how you grow okra—far from the house, because okra tree harbors red ants; when you are growing dasheen, make sure it gets plenty of water or else it makes your throat itch when you are eating it; this is how you sweep a corner; this is how you sweep a whole house; this is how you sweep a yard; this is how you smile to someone you don't like too much; this is how you smile to someone you don't like at all; this is how you smile to someone you like completely; this is how you set a table for tea; this is how you set a table for dinner; this is how you set a table for dinner with an important guest; this is how you set a table for lunch; this is how you set a table for breakfast; this is how to behave in the presence of men who don't know you very well, and this way they won't recognize immediately the slut I have warned you against becoming; be sure to wash every day, even if it is with your own spit; don't squat down to play marbles—you are not a boy, you know; don't pick people's flowers—you might catch something; don't throw stones at blackbirds, because it might not be a blackbird at all; this is how to make a bread pudding; this is how to make doukona; this is how to make pepper pot; this is how to make a good medicine for a cold; this is how to make a good medicine to throw away a child before it even becomes a child; this is how to catch a fish; this is how to throw back a fish you don't like, and that way something bad won't fall on you; this is how to bully a man; this is how a man bullies you; this is how to love a man, and if this doesn't work there are other ways, and if they don't work don't feel too bad about giving up; this is how to spit up in the air if you feel like it, and this is how to move quickly so that it doesn't fall on you; this is how to make ends meet; always squeeze bread to make sure it's fresh; *but what if the baker won't let me feel the bread?;* you mean to say that after all you are really going to be the kind of woman who the baker won't let near the bread?

Source: Reprinted by permission of Farrar, Straus and Giroux: "Girl" AT THE BOTTOM OF THE RIVER by Jamaica Kincaid. Copyright © 1983 by Jamaica Kincaid.

The narrator in Kincaid's piece would seem to be a mother lecturing her daughter, the "girl." The mother's advice and admonitions are salt-of-the-earth, basic survival skills for a girl or woman: from how to cook, how to clean, and how to spit or smile, to how to take care of a man, or to administer her own birth control. Clearly, the mother is intent on her daughter's listening; the daughter manages only two brief rebuttals: *"but I don't sing benna on Sundays at all and never in Sunday school"* and *"but what if the baker won't let me feel the bread?"* Furthermore, the mother's tone is authoritative and domineering; her lecture is spiked with imperative clauses: Do this, do that, don't do that, never do this, etc. Yet it also is a catalogue of practical information: "this is how ... ; this is how...." The mother is passing on to her daughter all of her own hard-earned knowledge. As readers, what is our attitude toward this mother? Is she a "good" mother? Do we respect her? Trust her? Why or why not? Finally, would we describe the tone as simple yet elegant, a message of "tough love," or would we say it is crude and haranguing, a belittling message of misguided love? Kincaid's short fiction piece can provoke an energetic discussion among readers and prompt us to explore our underlying assumptions about the role of a parent or other authority figure.

3.3.4 Visual Argument

So far in this chapter we have used written examples to illustrate the principles of argument. These principles also apply to visual images, such as political cartoons, advertisements, and images that function as **propaganda** (usually, information spread by a government to promote a political cause).

Advertisers want their audience to buy a particular product, so their ads (including the visual images in the ads) often contain hidden assumptions and make use of rhetorical appeals to convince the audience that their product is needed. When analyzing visuals, we must consider what assumptions are present. For example, most of us believe that facial wrinkles are unattractive; knowing this, advertisers create commercials for antiaging products that prey on this belief by including it as an unstated assumption in the commercials. Visuals, like written arguments, often rely on appeals to *ethos, logos*, and *pathos* to persuade consumers to purchase products. As an appeal to *pathos*, a car commercial might include images of adorable animals or small children; an appeal to *logos* might include a car buyer looking pleased in response to high gas mileage or a low price; and an appeal to *ethos* might include dramatic videos of the car passing a crash test.

At the time this book was being written, the term "fake news" had become a political football, most especially on Twitter feeds (maybe it still is?). On one side, some politicians and government officials claim vociferously that

Figure 3.2

Library of Congress Prints and Photographs Division, [LC-DIG-ppmsca-27675]

mainstream media intentionally engage in a campaign of misleading the public with a barrage of "fake news" (intentionally fabricated or biased news reports); on the other side, journalists and others in the media proclaim it is their duty to serve as independent agents, to report news stories factually and objectively, and to investigate public and political affairs in an unbiased manner. You may or may not be aware that this controversy has a longstanding history, dating back to the earliest days of newspaper publication. Look, for example, at a political cartoon from 1910 (Figure 3.2) and then complete the following Journal task and Look It Up task.

Journal: Visual Argument and "Fake News"

Spend a few minutes writing about what the cartoon's creator may be arguing, based on the details of the cartoon. Also, reflect on why the "fake news" controversy has such a long history and why that controversy will continue.

Look It Up: The History of "Fake News"

To see other visual representations of "fake news" and to read more about its history, follow this link: http://publicdomainreview.org/collections/yellow-journalism-the-fake-news-of-the-19th-century/. Examine the illustration "The 'New Journalism' Beats Him" on that web page. How could this illustration be interpreted as applying to news reporting in the United States today?

3.4 Chapter Activities

The series of activities on the following pages invite you to apply the concepts and ideas we have discussed and demonstrated throughout this chapter.

3.4.1 Think About It

Answer the following questions covering the topics discussed in this chapter.

1. Imagine you were assigned an argument essay examining the effects of social media on the mental health of college students. Create three claims on the topic: a claim of fact, a claim of policy, and a claim of value.
2. Consider the evidence needed to support each of the claims you created for question 1. Review the three types of sources discussed in this chapter (personal experience, reports, authority), and, in the context of the essay topic in question 1, describe what specific evidence you might gather from each source, where you might find an example of each source, and how each source might appeal to *logos*, *ethos*, and *pathos*.
3. What assumptions might the following audiences hold regarding social media: other college students, parents of college students, and instructors of college students?
4. Suppose the administration of the high school that your child attends recently implemented a policy banning students' use of cellphones and laptops in the classroom. Proponents of this policy contend that these devices:

   - distract teachers from focusing on their role as teachers by making them monitor student use of the devices;
   - encourage students—who are not yet critically savvy in distinguishing reliable information sources from unreliable ones—to accept unreliable online sources as authoritative; and
   - interfere with students' focus on classroom tasks.

   Create a counterargument that includes at least one concession and two refutations.
5. Read the following examples of flawed reasoning. Which of the ten logical fallacies discussed in this chapter does each example illustrate?

   - We can trust Breakthrough News because it is a reliable source of information.
   - One afternoon, I fed some bread crumbs to several squirrels on campus. The next day, I saw the same squirrels hanging about and expecting more bread crumbs. The city's homeless people are the same: well trained to expect handouts.
   - Jones's book doesn't deserve a Pulitzer Prize; she has been married four times.
   - After the total solar eclipse in 2017, there were an unusual number of extreme weather events.

3.4.2 Read and Respond

1. Read the poem below and answer the questions that follow.

"Those Winter Sundays," by Robert Hayden (1966)

Sundays too my father got up early
and put his clothes on in the blueblack cold,
then with cracked hands that ached
from labor in the weekday weather made
banked fires blaze. No one ever thanked him.   5

I'd wake and hear the cold splintering, breaking.
When the rooms were warm, he'd call,
and slowly I would rise and dress,
fearing the chronic angers of that house,

Speaking indifferently to him,   10
who had driven out the cold
and polished my good shoes as well.
What did I know, what did I know
of love's austere and lonely offices?

Source: "Those Winter Sundays". Copyright © 1966 by Robert Hayden, from COLLECTED POEMS OF ROB-
ERT HAYDEN by Robert Hayden, edited by Frederick Glaysher. Used by permission of Liveright Publishing
Corporation.

Questions

- What is the poet's claim? (State it in one sentence.)
- What evidence in the poem supports that claim? Can you also find evidence within your own personal experience that would support the claim?
- Is the claim valid only within the dramatic context of the poem, or is the claim valid universally? What in the poem and in your own experience leads you to this conclusion?
- What assumption underlies the claim? Do you think it is likely that a broad range of readers would share that assumption? Explain why or why not.

2. Read the essay below and answer the questions that follow.

"Truer to the Game," by Randy Horick (2000)

Out in our driveway, where my 12-year-old daughter dreams of becoming the next Chamique Holdsclaw, we have been working together on a few of the finer points of competitive basketball. Like how to use your elbow semi-legally to establish position (an old Don Meyer bit of wisdom). Or how to inbound the ball to yourself by thunking it off the buttocks of an unsuspecting opponent. Or the deep personal satisfaction, to say nothing of the psychological advantage, gained from setting a teeth-rattling screen.

Horick offers examples of plays to demonstrate his sports knowledge and build his credibility.

As part of this regimen, I have tried to use games on TV as teaching tools. I point out, for example, a good blockout on a rebound, a properly executed pick and roll, or the way to run a two-on-one fast break (or, more often, the way *not* to run a break).

Being a quick study, my daughter has observed one of the game's truths just from viewing two telecasts: the women's Final Four games on Friday and the corresponding men's contests on Saturday evening. "Dad," she observed, "the guys can't shoot."

This is either basketball's deep, dark secret or a cause for excitement, depending on your point of view. The truth is that the women take better shots than their male counterparts. As their respective NCAA tournaments made it ever clearer this March, when it comes to putting the pill in the hoop, girls' basketball rocks. Boys' basketball, well, doesn't.

But not only that: The women play a superior brand of basketball. These are not   5
the tilted rantings of some addle-brained pot-stirrer, as accustomed as you may profess to be to seeing such things on these pages. You can find a whole pantheon of old NBA stars—including no less of a luminary than Bill Russell his own bad shot-blocking self—who proclaim that women's basketball is much truer to the game they played than the men's version today.

Horick presents explicit claim statements.

Claims of superiority, of course, all depend upon your definitions. If you measure quality by physical measures—speed, play above the rim, dazzling one-on-one moves—it's still a man's world. (Don't imagine, however, that the women in the Final Four aren't superbly conditioned athletes.)

If you're looking for solid fundamentals and all-around team play, well, um, fellas, y'all got next. Ironically, the relative physical inferiority of today's women players provides the basis for a superior game.

The ability of men to complete acrobatic, soaring drives and dunks increasingly has led them to become infatuated with "taking it to the tin"—regardless of which defenders are in the way or which teammates may be open elsewhere. It's as if the guys have all graduated from some funky basketball camp that teaches that style points count for even more than real ones.

If you had $250 for every time during the men's NCAAs that a player passed up a jump shot, faked with the ball, then put his head down and headed toward the hole, they'd make you an honorary member of the bar association. The predictable results of such reckless driving, all too often, are offensive fouls, ugly collisions, and loads of bricks. For every dunk, we are forced to witness several thunks. For every electrifying play, there are several short-circuits. The literal rise of countless would-be Jordans has corresponded with a steady fall in field goal and free throw percentages in the men's game.

Horick draws on first-hand observation to emphasize the negative characteristics of male basketball players.

Contrast that with the women's game, where the play is decidedly below the rim 10
and dunks are rarer than incorruptible state legislators.

Because the girls aren't yet throwing it down, they're forced to concentrate on the aspects of the game that many of the boys seem to regard as beneath them. Like practicing free throws. Running patterned offenses. Looking for back-door cutters. Making routine shots. Executing the fundamentals.

To support his argument and offer balance, Horick draws on first-hand observation to emphasize the positive characteristics of female basketball players.

For all of these reasons, if you want to teach someone to play the game, women's basketball today is far more instructive. In part, that's because their game runs at a slightly slower speed, allowing you more clearly to see plays develop. Much more, however, it has to do with better shot selection, better ball movement, and more faithful adherence to the concept of team play.

Horick offers specific aspects of female basketball he finds superior to the male game.

Off the court, of course, women's college basketball looks even better in comparison. At the Division I Level, men's hoops today less and less exemplifies the old ideals of amateur competition and more and more resembles a corporate leviathan.

In the way that drug cartels have corrupted the institutions in countries like Colombia and Mexico, those who control the money and labor supply have leeched into men's basketball. AAU coaches serve as talent brokers who wield inordinate influence. Shoe companies sponsor posh summer camps for top high school players and sign college coaches to cushy contracts, hoping to win future endorsements from those who become stars.

Meanwhile, the pressures to win are so enormous upon coaches, and the financial 15
allure of an NBA career so powerful to players, that almost any action can be rationalized in the name of winning. Top high school players with marginal grades may be shipped off to basketball trade schools that pass themselves off as institutions of academic learning.

Collegiate coaches recruit the nation's elite players knowing all too well that they will be gone within a year or two, and that their only real interest in the college experience lies in gaining experience that will prepare them for the pros.

Things are so whomperdejawed that the NCAA, which blithely presided over the creation of this mess, is now declaring that the entire culture of men's basketball is diseased and needs a radical cure. (Good luck, guys.)

*Horick adds support to his argument by examining reasons why **men's** basketball is not as loyal to the game as **women's** basketball.*

Against this backdrop, the women's game looks like a fount of purity. Star players don't bug out early for the professional league; they stay and earn their degrees.

Coaches don't have to hire bodyguards to protect their athletes from contact by predatory agents. The recruiting process does not begin in the eighth or ninth grades. There are no televised McDonald's all-American games or dunk contests that teach the best players that they belong to some sort of celebrity elite.

Those days may be coming. As the popularity of women's basketball continues to   20
increase (Sunday's championship between Tennessee and Connecticut was the most
watched women's game ever), so too will the pressures.

The retirement last week of Louisiana Tech coach Leon Barmore is a reminder
of where the game is going. Tech and Old Dominion are perhaps the last of the "little"
schools that remain powers in women's basketball today. It's easy to forget that, barely
two decades ago, the game was dominated by colleges you never heard of: Delta State,
Immaculata, Stephen F. Austin, Wayland Baptist.

Women's basketball belongs to the big schools now. With the WNBA suc-
cessfully established, it is conceivable that collegians might turn pro early if salaries
become attractive enough. Coaches might cut corners and grease palms to lure the
best high schoolers to their programs. A whole industry might rise up and enshroud
the game, as it has with men's basketball.

> *In recognizing that **women's** basketball has the potential to face the same issues as the*
> ***men's** game, Horick is acknowledging the complexity of the issue.*

Until then, though, I'll keep offering up as role models the kind of unspoiled, we-first
players who were evident in the women's tournament.

Meanwhile, we won't forget at our house that the men's pro league still offers
enormous entertainment value. Just last Sunday, during the Knicks-Lakers game, my
daughter came rushing in breathlessly. "Dad, dad, come check it out. Kobe Bryant and
Chris Childs are having a fight!"

Source: Horick, Randy. "Truer to the Game" appeared within Nashville Scene, April 10, 2000. Used by permission.

Questions

- Horick claims, "The women play a superior brand of basketball,...
  women's basketball is much truer to the game...than the men's version today," and every word in Horick's essay leads readers to accept
  this claim. What type of claim is it—fact, policy, or value? Explain your
  answer.
- What evidence does Horick use to support his claim?
- What assumptions are contained in the essay? Do you accept these assumptions? Why or why not?
- Suppose you were asked to create a counterargument to Horick's claim.
  Write at least one concession and two refutations that could be part of
  your counterargument.
- Do you think Horick makes a convincing argument that female players
  are "truer to the game" of basketball? Why or why not?

3. Read this *New York Times* letter to the editor and respond to the writing task
   that follows.

To the Editor

Daniel LaChance crafts a very reasonable economic argument against the death penalty.
And that's the problem.

Proponents of the death penalty are guided by retributive zeal rather than fiscal practicality. Even the stingiest of taxpaying death penalty supporters don't flinch at the titanic costs associated with their beloved institution.

Their bloodlust masked as justice is rooted in the primitive motivation for vengeance, which—at least with respect to this issue—reduces their ability to employ reason.

Thomas E. Templeton

Delmar, N.Y., Sept. 9, 2014

Source: Templeton, Thomas E., Delmar, NY. New York Times (9/9/2014). Used with permission.

Writing Task

Regardless of your personal stance on this controversial issue, write out one concession and two refutations that could be part of a counterargument to the letter writer's argument opposing the death penalty.

4. Read the excerpt below and respond to the writing task that follows.

From *Mein Kampf* (*My Struggle*), by Adolf Hitler (1925)

Thus men without exception wander about in the garden of Nature; they imagine that they know practically everything and yet with few exceptions pass blindly by one of the most patent principles of Nature's rule: the inner segregation of the species of all living beings on this earth.

Even the most superficial observation shows that Nature's restricted form of propagation and increase is an almost rigid basic law of all the innumerable forms of expression of her vital urge. Every animal mates only with a member of the same species. The titmouse seeks the titmouse, the finch the finch, the stork the stork, the field mouse the field mouse, the dormouse the dormouse, the wolf the she-wolf, etc. ...

The consequence of this racial purity, universally valid in Nature, is not only the sharp outward delineation of the various races, but their uniform character in themselves. The fox is always a fox, the goose a goose, the tiger a tiger, etc.

Source: Hitler, Adolph. "Mein Kampf." Translated by Ralph Manheim, 1943.

Writing task

Practice applying your critical thinking skills to this notorious work. Explain how Hitler's reasoning is flawed due to his use of the logical fallacies discussed in this chapter.

5. Read the poem below and answer the questions that follow.

"Dulce et Decorum Est," by Wilfred Owen (1917)

Bent double, like old beggars under sacks,
Knock-kneed, coughing like hags, we cursed through sludge,
Till on the haunting flares we turned our backs
And towards our distant rest began to trudge.
Men marched asleep. Many had lost their boots
But limped on, blood-shod. All went lame; all blind;
Drunk with fatigue; deaf even to the hoots
Of tired, outstripped Five-Nines that dropped behind.

5

Gas! GAS! Quick boys!—An ecstasy of fumbling,
Fitting the clumsy helmets just in time;   10
But someone still was yelling out and stumbling
And flound'ring like a man in fire or lime—
Dim, through the misty panes and thick green light,
As under a green sea, I saw him drowning.

In all my dreams, before my helpless sight,   15
He plunges at me, guttering, choking, drowning.

If in some smothering dreams you too could pace
Behind the wagon that we flung him in,
And watch the white eyes writhing in his face,
His hanging face, like a devil's sick of sin;   20
If you could hear, at every jolt, the blood
Come gargling from the froth-corrupted lungs,
Obscene as cancer, bitter as the cud
Of vile, incurable sores on innocent tongues,—
My friend, you would not tell with such high zest   25
To children ardent for some desperate glory,
The old Lie: *Dulce et decorum est*
Pro patria mori.

Background

Wilfred Owen was a young poet and English teacher who enlisted in the British
Army in 1915, during World War One. He served as a second lieutenant and died
in combat in 1918, about a week before the armistice (November 11, 1918). The
title of his poem, *"Dulce et Decorum Est,"* and the poem's final two lines are a
quotation from the Roman poet Horace (65–8 BCE) that translates as "it is sweet
and honorable to die for one's country."

Questions

- What is the poet's claim? (State it in one sentence.)
- How does the poet use Aristotle's three rhetorical appeals (*logos, ethos,*
  and *pathos*) to persuade or connect to his audience?
- Which type of evidence does Owen use to support his claim? How effective is this choice of evidence?

6. Read this excerpt from "The Dying Art of Disagreement," by Bret
Stephens (the full text is in Chapter 8), and respond to the writing tasks
that follow:

> According to a new survey . . . , a plurality of college students today—fully 44
> percent—do not believe the First Amendment to the U.S. Constitution protects
> so-called "hate speech," when of course it absolutely does. More shockingly,
> a narrow majority of students—51 percent—think it is "acceptable" for a student

group to shout down a speaker with whom they disagree. An astonishing 20 percent also agree that it's acceptable to use violence to prevent a speaker from speaking.

Stephens also asserts, "Free speech must ultimately be free, whether or not it's fair."

Writing Tasks

Do you agree or disagree with the students cited in the paragraph? Explain your reasoning on each point. Do you agree with Stephens's assertion under the paragraph? Why or why not? Use examples to support your stance on each of these issues.

3.4.3 Multimodal Activities

1. **Visual Argument**

   Look at the post–World War One British army recruitment poster in Figure 3.3 and respond to the questions and writing tasks that follow.

   - Describe the claim made by the poster in Figure 3.3.

   - What are the implied assumptions about the connection between sports and the military? Do you accept these assumptions? Why or why not?

   - How does the poster appeal to *logos, ethos*, and *pathos*?

   - Reread *"Dulce et Decorum Est"* and explain how the poem could be interpreted as refuting the argument of this poster.

Figure 3.3

Simmons, Graham, G P Ltd, British Army.
Courtesy of The Imperial War Museum

2. Meaning and the Spoken Word

Critical reading of *"Dulce et Decorum Est"* requires study and concentration, but as with most poetry, reading it out loud deepens one's understanding and appreciation of the poem. Listening to dramatic readings can provide insight into the tone and mood of the poem, as can visual imagery accompanying the reading. Consider the readings of *"Dulce et Decorum Est"* available at these Web addresses, and then respond to the questions that follow:

https://www.youtube.com/watch?v=qB4cdRgIcB8 (read by Christopher Eccleston)

https://www.youtube.com/watch?v=N0skWPCUFg0 (read by Kenneth Branagh)

https://www.youtube.com/watch?v=M5zT01lm3lw (read by Ben Whishaw)

https://www.youtube.com/watch?v=SgQhH67oPgY (animation)

Questions

- Discuss the ways in which the tone, imagery, and music of each reading affect how the claim is presented and how the appeals to *ethos, logos,* and *pathos* work.

- Which presentation most effectively conveys what you see as the main strength of the poem? Explain your answer.

Chapter 4
Writing an Argument Essay

 Learning Objectives

In this chapter, you will learn to

4.1 Focus an argument essay assignment by clarifying a subject, a purpose, and an audience.

4.2 Articulate a claim and develop a plan for writing an argument essay.

4.3 Create and revise a draft.

4.4 Use the Rogerian argument strategy for controversial topics.

4.1 Focusing an Argument Essay Assignment

Focus an argument essay assignment by clarifying a subject, a purpose, and an audience.

The educated person is, above all, one who is "open to new knowledge and able to advance it."

—William J. Bouwsma

When your instructor assigns an argument essay, what emotions initially hit you? Dread? Anxiety? Enthusiasm? Optimism? Such definite, even extreme, feelings are to be expected, most likely triggered by recent experiences with writing essays. And if these experiences have tended to be negative, you might find it difficult to let go of them and adopt a positive frame of mind—to see this new essay assignment as an opportunity for growth and an opportunity to influence the thinking of others.

In an academic community, you are called upon to advance knowledge and to shape your own and other people's thinking about ideas and issues. Approaching an argument essay assignment with this responsibility in mind can be empowering and liberating. The assignment calls upon you to participate in thoughtful conversation about your topic—to express your informed opinion in an academic argument.

The writing process for academic argument is neither simple nor fast; it requires patience and persistence—a steadfast commitment to hard work: to planning, reading, thinking, writing; to rereading, rethinking, rewriting. Because writing an argument is an investment of intellect, you are likely to produce your best work when you give yourself plenty of time to plan, read, write, and revise ahead of your deadline. In the following sections, we suggest guidelines and strategies to help you develop an academic argument that will satisfy, if not surpass, your goals as a writer and as a participant in an academic community.

4.1.1 Clarifying a Subject, a Purpose, and an Audience

After taking stock of your feelings about a new writing assignment, your next step should be to read the assignment carefully and to make sure you understand the instructor's expectations. As you saw in Chapter 2, reading carefully means reading through the assignment more than once, noting anything you are unsure about, so you can ask the instructor for clarification, if necessary. Most likely, both classmates and the instructor will appreciate your taking this initiative.

Once you understand the assignment and the instructor's expectations, you will need to find a topic to write about, one that interests you and works within the parameters of the assignment. Some instructors may assign a topic, while others may give you the freedom to create your own. Prewriting can help you connect to an assigned topic as well as discover and explore ideas for topics. There is no single, right way to get started; the key is to begin writing and to trust that ideas will come—listing, freewriting in phrases or sentences, creating webs of words, or using a technique of your own design. Consider this stage of the writing process to be writing off-leash: you are free to explore where your thoughts may take you. Once you are satisfied that you have a topic, you will focus on clarifying a subject, a purpose, and an audience—three considerations that are integral to creating a successful academic argument.

The **subject** of an argument is, by definition, an *issue*, a debatable topic. You can test a subject to make sure that it is, in fact, a debatable topic by framing it as an **issue question**, a question on which reasonable people might disagree. For example, "gun control" is a subject; to show that is a debatable topic, we can frame it as an issue question, such as, "Should semiautomatic weapons and assault rifles be banned?"

Let's further explore the idea of subjects as debatable topics. No one will argue that many people recognize December 25 as Christmas Day or that the police have the authority to make arrests. Both statements are accepted facts, not really open to debate. However, a worthwhile conversation—an academic argument—on the topic of Christmas or the police can be advanced by considering controversies surrounding the topic. With regard to Christmas, for example, some people claim that the diversity of religious and cultural celebrations around the time of Christmas means that a socially conscious society should abandon the greeting "merry Christmas" and replace it with the more inclusive "happy holidays." And with regard to the police, many people contend that all too often the power to make arrests is exercised arbitrarily and is accompanied by excessive force, especially against minorities. Ideas for topics often come to us as broad concepts, like Christmas or the police, but a successful arguer is able to narrow the range of discussion by delving into specific areas of disagreement within a topic. Framing a topic as an issue question can help you focus on the cutting edge of controversy. With a specific issue articulated, you have identified a subject for an argument essay.

The **purpose** of an argument is found in a writer's motivation for initiating a conversation on a subject. Granted, most of you would not choose to write research papers if they were not assigned by your instructors. But to offer your best writing performance, you must move past this feeling of obligation and search for what you can add to the dialogue on a subject, thereby advancing knowledge. For example, in writing an essay about holidays and political correctness, is your purpose to persuade the audience to do more to acknowledge religious and cultural differences, or is your purpose to persuade the audience that political correctness has gone too far when an expression of goodwill is defined as offensive? Likewise, in writing an essay about police officers' abuse of power, if your purpose is to persuade your audience that police often abuse their power, merely describing a recent case of alleged police misconduct is not enough to accomplish that purpose in an academic argument; you would also want to immerse your audience in specific points about the case and to show that the case is not an isolated incident but part of a pattern of many such cases. Establishing a clear purpose empowers you as an argument writer: you have specific goals for addressing an audience.

Knowing your **audience** is another essential component in creating a successful academic argument. When you are completing a college assignment, consider your audience to be the global academic community. You are addressing an educated body of your peers. Educated members of your community bring a baseline of knowledge to their reading. Therefore, part of knowing your audience is realizing that readers expect you to contribute to the ongoing conversation on a controversial subject and not simply to report summary information. Another critical aspect of knowing your audience is recognizing that they bring to their reading a diverse range of backgrounds and viewpoints. Switching sides, as discussed in Chapter 1 (see the section on critical inquiry), can help make you aware of your audience's range of viewpoints. You will want to take time to imagine your audience as individuals who may hold opposing views from yours and to consider how you might address them in a way that invites them into the conversation rather than shuts them out. This point was made by journalist Sydney J. Harris (1917–1986) when he said, *"The most important thing in an argument, next to being right, is to leave an escape hatch for your opponent, so that he can gracefully swing over to your side without too much apparent loss of face."* By acknowledging that an opposing viewpoint has at least some validity, even as you endeavor to undermine it, you do just as Harris advises: You create "an escape hatch." (For a more detailed discussion of this topic, see the section on counterarguments in Chapter 3.)

4.2 Articulating a Claim and Developing a Plan for Writing an Argument Essay

Articulate a claim and develop a plan for writing an argument essay.

At the beginning of the chapter, we acknowledged that the writing process for an argument essay requires a commitment to hard work. With a clear sense of a subject, a purpose, and an audience, you take control of this work—it has value for you that extends beyond the completion of the assignment with an acceptable grade. Now is the time to create a plan of action for achieving your goal and enhancing your success as an arguer. We suggest that your plan include these fundamental steps:

- Explore multiple perspectives on your subject through reading, writing, and conversation, in order to expand, deepen, and complicate your thinking; as you explore, be willing to let go of preconceived ideas.

- Analyze and evaluate those perspectives to construct your own argument, one centered on a clear claim that you can support with credible and specific evidence.

- Map out an outline and argument strategy based on your specific goals for your audience.

- Draft your argument essay and seek feedback to "field-test" it with a live audience; this will help you view your writing as writing for "real" readers and gain a more objective perspective.

- Rethink your argument, based on the feedback you have gotten and on your enhanced perspective.

- Revise, edit, and proofread to produce an argument essay that will compel your audience (a global academic community) to engage thoughtfully with your position and, finally, prompt them to change their initial thinking.

In the next sections, we discuss the specifics of writing a claim and designing an argument, but first we recommend that you look back at the section in Chapter 1 on critical inquiry and take the time to consider how you would evaluate your thinking on your subject.

4.2.1 Articulating a Claim Statement

You have thought about your issue, discussed it with friends and classmates, and read about it in periodicals, books, and electronic sources. You have a collection of notes, photocopies of sources, and perhaps an annotated bibliography (see the section on annotated bibliography in Chapter 5). The heart of an argument is its claim. Now is the time for you to make that heart come alive. To do so, you will engage in higher-order critical thinking by synthesizing your ideas and source information to arrive at one essential and arguable point.

Once you have reread the issue question, which has been the focus of your research efforts, you are prepared to write an informed opinion in response to that question—that is, a claim for which you can create a compelling case. Although this claim should be a single statement, succinct yet specific, be prepared to spend some time—and many words—to arrive at it by a process of writing, scratching out, writing, and rewriting. This process can be time-consuming and frustrating; it requires patience, persistence, and, above all, confidence in your ability to find your way. Allow your first efforts in wording a claim to be rough, even awkward and simplistic. Once you see on paper (or on your screen) a fairly clear version of the point you want to argue, you can revise the wording to make the claim more concise and compelling.

As you revise, determine which type of claim—fact, policy, or value—best suits your purpose (see the Chapter 3 discussion of these three types of claims). Consider, for example, the differences among these three types of claims in response to this issue question: "Should the city place a moratorium on the construction of fast-food restaurants in lower-income neighborhoods?"

- *Claim of fact.* Residents of lower-income neighborhoods are targeted by the fast-food industry, and as a result, they are particularly prone to health problems associated with high-fat and processed foods.

- *Claim of policy.* The city should not implement a moratorium on fast-food restaurant construction in lower-income neighborhoods.

- *Claim of value.* A proposal to ban fast-food restaurant construction in lower-income neighborhoods unfairly stereotypes and discriminates against the residents of those neighborhoods.

If a moratorium on the construction of fast-food restaurants in lower-income neighborhoods were the subject of your argument essay, most likely your claim would be the claim of policy, with the claims of fact and value serving as main supporting points or subclaims.

Exercise 4.1: Identifying Types of Claims

In the table below, circle the correct type of claim next to each claim statement.

Claim Statement	Type of Claim
High school students should be encouraged to take a gap year.	claim of fact claim of policy claim of value
Requiring professional athletes to stand for the national anthem restricts their individual freedom.	claim of fact claim of policy claim of value
Soda beverages are a primary cause of obesity.	claim of fact claim of policy claim of value
Performance-enhancing drugs have tainted the integrity of the Olympic Games.	claim of fact claim of policy claim of value
Public schools should no longer be gun-free zones.	claim of fact claim of policy claim of value
Fossil burning fuels are a leading factor in increased greenhouse gases.	claim of fact claim of policy claim of value

Now check your skill in distinguishing among the three types of claims—fact, policy, and value. In Exercise 4.1, identify the type of claim illustrated by each claim statement.

4.2.2 Creating an Informal Outline

Many of you probably have an automatic, less than positive response to the words "essay assignment," a response that probably becomes even less positive when you hear the instruction to "outline the essay." Some of you may be outline resisters who prefer to draft your way into finding structure for your essay; others of you may be outline advocates and would not think of writing a draft without an outline in hand. To help resolve this conflict, we suggest that you consider yet another approach: begin by writing a fast first draft (often called a "zero draft" or an "exploratory draft") and then outline. While one approach is not necessarily more efficient than another, outlining—at whatever stage and in whatever form you may choose—can streamline the process of drafting your essay. Take Note 4.1 shows a bare-bones organizational framework for an informal outline, to serve as a guide.

4.2.3 Designing an Argument Strategy

An outline provides you with a blueprint for writing a first draft of an argument essay. Jotting down responses to the strategy questions in Take Note 4.2 can further prepare you for the drafting process.

After creating an outline and jotting down strategy notes, you should have a steady dialogue running through your mind; most definitely, you will have

Take Note 4.1

Framework for an Informal Outline

As you fill out this framework with some of the specifics of your argument, the outline will become a starting point for planning an essay that will achieve your goals as a writer of argument.

Introduction
* Lead-in "hook" sentences
* Concise overview of the issue, including its rhetorical context (see the discussion in Chapter 3)
* Explicit claim of fact, policy, or value

Opposition
* Concise summary of key points of counterarguments
* Concessions to counterarguments, to acknowledge the validity of aspects of opposing viewpoints
* Refutations of counterarguments, to address and weaken aspects of opposing viewpoints

Supporting Arguments
* Specific proof of claim
* Evidence grouped under three or so key points (subclaims)
* Strongest point presented last

Conclusion
* Restatement of claim, without repeating it verbatim
* Resolution, compromise, or call to action

generated plenty of words on the subject. Reviewing your pages of notes, you may choose to first revise and expand your outline and then write a draft—or you may be ready to crank out that first draft.

4.3 Creating and Revising a Draft

Create and revise a draft.

Armed with your prep work—outline and strategy notes—you are ready to write a first draft. Here are two important tips about how to proceed:

* Think of yourself as an expert on the issue; most certainly, you are more informed than many other laypersons.
* Put your sources aside—*out of sight*—and write a fast first draft by using only your outline and other planning notes and the knowledge you have gained through intensive study of the issue.

Take Note 4.2

Strategy Questions for Organizing Your Argument Essay

1. How can you "hook" your readers from the start—for instance, with an opening example, anecdote, scenario, startling statistic, or provocative question?
2. How much background information and rhetorical context should you include to acquaint readers with the issue?
3. Will you present your claim early in your essay (at the end of your introduction is the conventional placement) or delay it until your conclusion?
4. What are your main supporting points (subclaims)?
5. Do you have sufficient evidence for each of these points? Have you located authoritative (expert) sources that add credibility to your argument?
6. How will you address opposing viewpoints? Have you identified the key points in the counterarguments? Are you prepared to make some concessions and to build strong refutations?
7. Have you considered aspects of tone (for example, serious, comical, inquisitive, humble, thoughtful, or assertive) that would suit the issue and would lead your audience to respect and trust you?
8. How will you conclude in a meaningful way? Will you call upon readers to take action? Will you explain why the issue is important? Will you offer a compromise that benefits all sides?

By writing a fast first draft—*on your own*—you can avoid the common pitfall of overrelying on source material and, consequently, losing ownership of your writing. Moreover, without switching back and forth between a draft and sources, you may find your writing is more fluid and coherent. Once you have written this first draft, you can return to your sources and notes and identify relevant information to flesh out the draft and give your argument a more authoritative basis.

4.3.1 Revising a Draft

The golden rule of revising is to give yourself some breathing room between drafts: take a break and allow your vision to clear. Once you are ready to tackle the work of revising, begin by reviewing the big picture—the substance and structure of the draft as an argument. Save the details of editing, such as sentence by sentence review, for a later round.

With the caveat that there is not one right method for revising an argument essay, consider the guidelines in Table 4.1, which are based on the essential components of argument (see the discussion in Chapter 3) and on the rhetorical appeals in Aristotle's argument model (also discussed in Chapter 3).

Based on your review notes, you can determine how to proceed most efficiently with the task of writing a second draft. You may choose to work with

Table 4.1 Reviewing Components of Argument and Rhetorical Appeals When Revising an Argument Essay

Components of Argument	
Claim	Since the claim is the heart of an argument, it should be the first component you review. What if, in the process of drafting, you ended up with a sharp and concise claim statement in your conclusion—but not the same statement you began with in your introduction? This is not a problem, but a perk. With this retooled claim in clear view, you can reshape your introduction and proceed confidently and efficiently with the work of revising the full draft.
Evidence	If you wrote out your first draft without relying on your sources, now is the time to build them in—to fortify key supporting points with solid evidence. As you read your draft, underline, highlight, or annotate to indicate where you should build in source information (if you are using Microsoft Word, the commenting tool will make it easy to write annotations). Review your sources and notes and identify compelling information to incorporate into the revision (see Chapter 5 for a discussion of incorporating sources).
Assumptions	Comb through your draft and underline, highlight, or annotate assumptions. Ask yourself if your audience—keeping in mind the diverse range of backgrounds and viewpoints—is likely to accept those assumptions. If not, think about how you can provide backing or whether you should consider removing any unsupported assumptions.
Rhetorical Appeals	
Pathos	How can you connect to your audience's emotions, imagination, and values? Annotate your draft to indicate which evidence is likely to appeal to *pathos*. Where should you locate that evidence? Should you weave it in throughout the essay? Should you open and close your essay with appeals to *pathos*? In making these decisions, consider the temperature of the issue on the table: Is it a hotly contested issue, about which many readers may have strong feelings? If so, you may want to show restraint early on—to build your appeal to *ethos* and to avoid the appearance of bias. Consider placing your strongest appeals to *pathos* later in the essay, after you have earned readers' respect and trust.
Logos	How do you demonstrate logic, reasoning, and analytical thinking? Annotate your draft to mark which evidence appeals to *logos*. Where should you place that evidence? Follow this general rule—but also remember that you can feel free to break it—place appeals to *logos* early in the essay to help create an objective stance. In this way, you build your appeal to *ethos* with a broad range of readers.
Ethos	How do you build trust and establish credibility with an audience? Using an appropriate tone is one way; using authoritative sources, another; and addressing opposing viewpoints fairly but assertively, another. Also, writing predominately from a third-person point of view helps establish an objective stance and an authoritative tone. Most academic writing avoids using "you" to address the reader and is sparing in its use of "I" and "we." As you read your draft, annotate it to mark places where you need to consider these aspects.

your original document file or to create a new draft file. Whichever approach you choose, save all drafts as separate files—a seemingly minor housekeeping matter, but one that may help you avoid problems.

Now read the following student essay and our annotations to see how one student applied the revision principles in Table 4.1 to produce his revised draft (the student's annotated bibliography is presented in Chapter 5); then respond to the writing tasks that follow. Note that this essay is making a claim of policy.

John Miller
Professor Missy James
ENC 1102
4 December 2014

Domestic Oil Drilling: Providing Little, Wasting a Lot

As human civilization has progressed and spread across the world, nature has paid a price for humans' appetite for space and resources. There are few remaining areas of true wilderness in the world today, and these are threatened by oil and gas companies that seek to ravage them for resources. The United States is currently one of the largest energy consumers in the world. According to data from 2011, the Energy Information Administration estimates that the United States is responsible for approximately 20% of the world's total annual energy consumption (U.S. Energy). To satisfy the large demand and take advantage of economic opportunity, many oil companies are eager to expand their drilling into delicate and protected lands throughout the United States. The United States government must enforce strict regulations of drilling and prevent drilling in new areas to protect the environment and to preserve the remaining wilderness.

> The writer opens with a provocative statement to "hook" readers. He provides rhetorical context for the issue, reinforced with factual data from an authoritative source (appeals to *logos* and *ethos*). He concludes the introduction with a specific claim of policy.

The United States has many areas with untapped oil and gas stores that environmentalists are fighting to protect while oil companies aggressively try to gain access to them. Currently, the debate is centered on oil and gas drilling in the Arctic; areas such as the Arctic National Wildlife Refuge (ANWR) and the Alaskan Arctic outer continental shelf hold billions of barrels of oil and are home to some of the world's most delicate ecosystems. For over thirty years, the U.S. government has prevented large scale oil and gas drilling in arctic lands and waters by denying companies access and passing environmental protection laws ("Arctic National Wildlife"). In addressing this issue as a presidential candidate in 2008, then Senator Barack Obama stated, "I strongly reject drilling in the Arctic National Wildlife Refuge because it would irreversibly damage a protected national wildlife refuge without creating sufficient oil supplies to meaningfully affect the global market price or have a discernible impact on US energy security" (ProCon.org). However, oil companies and politicians, who support drilling, continue to raise the issue, claiming that the environmental impacts are minimal and the economic benefits outweigh potential risks. According to Ken Salazar, the U.S. Interior Secretary, Alaska's resources hold great promise of economic opportunity, and cautious exploration can "help us expand our understanding of the area and its resources, and support our goal of continuing to increase safe and responsible domestic oil and gas production" (Freedman). Although some oil companies take safety precautions to protect the environment, there have been many cases where companies have failed to demonstrate proper care, and, consequently, the environment has suffered. Allowing companies to drill when they cannot ensure the safety of the environment is an invitation for a major catastrophe.

> The writer elaborate s on the rhetorical context of the issue and balances the overview with authoritative quotes—one opposing and one supporting drilling (appeal to *ethos*). He concludes by reinforcing his opposing position.

The detrimental effects of the oil industry are apparent in the western United States. Since 1980, oil and natural gas companies have drilled nearly 270,000 wells in pristine western lands. This infrastructure has changed the western landscape, possibly caused irreversible environmental damage, and endangered the western water supply (Horwitt). Dusty Horwitt, an analyst for the Environmental Working Group, has expressed that drilling in the West has resulted in oil operations "injecting toxic chemicals, consuming millions of gallons of water, clawing out pits for their hazardous waste and slashing the ground for sprawling road networks." Government agencies, including the Environmental Protection Agency (EPA), have found that oil and gas drilling produces air pollution and toxic waste and may lead to contaminated wastewater. The United States Bureau of Land Management documented toxic benzene, a chemical related to oil drilling, in groundwater in a small county in Wyoming, where over 4,000 wells had been drilled (Horwitt). Even without large scale oil well drilling, oil companies make mistakes and threaten the environment. In 2012, while Royal Dutch Shell was conducting exploratory drilling, a drilling rig, which did not meet EPA emission standards, presented a threat to the ecosystem because it was emitting dangerous levels of nitrous oxide and ammonia (Freedman). While some may argue that these mistakes are uncommon, when they occur, they pose a serious threat to ecosystems and only show the tip of the iceberg of potential damage from oil companies' drilling.

> The writer begins to lay out evidence in support of his position in opposition to allowing drilling in wilderness areas. Evidence is bolstered with source information (appeals to *ethos* and *logos*).

In 2010, British Petroleum's Deepwater Horizon rig exploded off the coast of Louisiana, spilling approximately 170 million gallons of oil into the Gulf of Mexico. According to the National Wildlife Federation, over 8,000 birds, seas turtles, and marine mammals were injured or killed within the first six months of the spill. In addition to the contamination of oil, nearly two million gallons of chemicals were used to clean up the spill. Although presently there is no visible oil in the water, it remains on the ocean floor and on beaches along with the chemical dispersants used to clean it up. To this day, the damage is still being assessed, but the long-term damage may not be understood for years to come ("How Does BP?"). Many of the world's precious lands and waters have been destroyed or damaged due to oil drilling. These accidents and mistakes by oil and gas companies demonstrate that they are unable to conduct drilling operations without harming ecosystems. Therefore, it is crucial that the federal government pass laws to prevent additional oil drilling and to protect the environment from the threat of destruction from current drilling operations.

> The writer elaborates on a recent and catastrophic example of an oil spill, one that his audience can readily recall. He concludes the paragraph by reiterating his claim (appeals to *logos* and *pathos*).

Despite the risk of environmental damage, companies are eager to drill. Currently, a select number of companies are permitted to conduct exploratory drilling in the Arctic and to construct a small number of oil wells. Proponents of opening the Arctic to oil and natural gas drilling argue that it is an excellent economic opportunity for the United States. If the government allows drilling in protected lands and waters, it could generate hundreds of thousands of jobs and billions of dollars in federal revenue. Oil companies also claim that if they are allowed to drill in an area such as the Arctic National Wildlife Refuge, it would be a significant step for the United States towards energy independence (Webb). While it may be true that drilling would create jobs, provide federal revenue, and help establish energy independence, these benefits are overestimated and do not justify irreversibly disturbing the ecosystems. If companies were allowed to drill in areas such as ANWR, the amount of oil extracted would only be a drop in the bucket for America's immense appetite. According to the Energy Information Administration, ANWR could produce about 0.8 million barrels per day, but this would still require the United States to import 10.6 million barrels a day to satisfy demand. The total amount of oil that could be drilled in the area would only meet the nation's energy needs for approximately nine months ("Arctic National Wildlife"). Clearly, drilling in ANWR would have a limited effect on the United States' goal of energy independence. Moreover, in terms of economic benefit, ANWR would provide federal revenue but not enough to have a significant impact on the economy or to provide long-term revenue. Like other oil-rich areas, ANWR has a finite amount of oil. Drilling would only be a short-term solution for satisfying America's energy needs and for solving post-Recession economic problems.

> The writer transitions to present drilling proponents' position (appeal to *ethos*). He then offers a brief concession and begins to lay out his counterargument, citing factual data as he attempts to deconstruct drilling proponents' position (appeals to *ethos* and *logos*).

Allowing companies to exploit lands and waters for oil and natural gas exploration poses risks that would permanently damage precious ecosystems, while providing only short-term economic benefits. The United States federal government must, therefore, take actions to defend and protect our lands and waters from companies, whose practices consistently demonstrate that they are unable to operate without harming the environment. In a testimony before the Senate Energy and Natural Resources Committee, Debbie Miller, an author and environmental activist, made this statement regarding drilling in the Arctic National Wildlife Refuge: "The oil industry argues that the 19 million-acre refuge can stand to lose the 1.5 million-acre coastal plain.... the industry's argument is like saying that I shot the man but the bullet only made a small hole through his heart" ("Top Arctic"). While this statement specifically addresses ANWR, the fundamental message is important for the protection of all nature. It is critical that the United States regulates oil drilling to preserve its few remaining wilderness areas and to protect the environment from permanent damage. Human-caused environmental disasters demonstrate our ability to destroy nature and also solidify our obligation to protect the environment so that it may flourish and be admired and enjoyed by generations to come.

> The writer transitions to a conclusion with a summation statement that echoes his claim and is laced with appeal to *pathos*. He restates his claim with the signal transition word "therefore" and continues to draw on appeals to *pathos* through his word choices and by quoting a provocative statement by an environmental activist.

Over sixty years ago, writer and conservationist Aldo Leopold underscored the incalculable value of wilderness areas in this passage:

> We all strive for safety, prosperity, comfort, long life, and dullness.... A measure of success in this is all well enough, and perhaps is a requisite to objective thinking, but too much safety seems to yield only danger in the long run. Perhaps this is behind Thoreau's dictum: In wildness is the salvation of the world. Perhaps this is the hidden meaning in the howl of the wolf, long known among mountains, but seldom perceived among men. (133)

As we move forward in the twenty-first century, we need to look beyond our thirst for oil and not silence "the howl of the wolf."

> The writer adds a short closure paragraph and draws on the figurative language of the quoted passage to conclude his argument (appeal to *pathos*).

Works Cited

"Arctic National Wildlife Refuge Drilling." *Opposing Viewpoints Online Collection*, Gale, 2014. *Opposing Viewpoints in Context*, http://db28.linccweb.org/login?url=http://link .galegroup.com/apps/doc/PC3010999229/OVIC?u=lincclin_tcc&xid=25ca1755.

Freedman, Ethan. "Groups Vow to Fight Arctic Drilling." *Global Information Network*, 31 Jul. 2012. *SIRS Issues Researcher*, https://sks-sirs-com.db28.linccweb.org.

Horwitt, Dusty. "Oil and Gas Drilling Operations Have Degraded the Environment of the Western United States." *Oil*, edited by Debra A. Miller, Greenhaven Press, 2010. Current Controversies, *Opposing Viewpoints in Context*, http://db28. linccweb.org/login?url=http://link.galegroup.com/apps/doc/EJ3010734214/O VIC?u=lincclin_tcc&xid=2db11d2c.

"How Does the BP Oil Spill Impact Wildlife and Habitat?" *National Wildlife Federation*. National Wildlife Federation, http://www.energybc.ca/cache/oilspill/www.nwf .org/Oil-Spill/Effects-on-Wildlife.html.

Leopold, Aldo. "Thinking Like a Mountain." *A Sand County Almanac,* Library of America, 2013, pp. 129–133.

ProCon.org. "Should Drilling for Oil in the Arctic National Wildlife Refuge (ANWR) Be Allowed?" *ProCon.org*, 2 June 2009, https://2008election.procon.org/view.resource .php?resourceID=001669.

"Top Arctic Wilderness Quotes." *Northern Alaska Environmental Center*, 2009, www.northern.org/what-we-value/wilderness/arctic-refuge-quotes.

U.S. Energy Information Administration. U.S. Energy Information Administration, https://www.eia.gov.

Webb, K.J. "Oil Industry Regulation Hurts the American Economy." *Oil Spills*, edited by Tamara Thompson, Greenhaven Press, 2014. Current Controversies, *Opposing Viewpoints in Context*, http://db28.linccweb.org/login?url=http://link.galegroup.com/apps/doc/ EJ3010893221/OVIC?u=lincclin_tcc&xid=2327da3e.

source: Used with permission from John Miller.

Now that you have read "Domestic Oil Drilling: Providing Little, Wasting a Lot," complete the following writing tasks:

1. Describe the writer's tone. Does the tone change as the essay progresses? Do you think his tone is likely to appeal to *ethos* within his audience, a global academic community? Why or why not?

2. Find at least two assumptions in the writer's argument. Are these assumptions likely to be shared by his audience? Why or why not?

3. The writer holds to the third-person point of view until his closing sentence, where he shifts to first-person plural with "our" and "we." Why do you think he made this shift? In doing so, what assumption is he making about his audience? In your view, is this assumption valid?

4. What was your opinion on drilling in wilderness areas before reading the student's argument essay? To what degree did he change your initial thinking?

4.4   Rogerian Argument Strategy: Creative Problem Solving

Use the Rogerian argument strategy for controversial topics.

Academic argument is designed to respect the diversity of viewpoints within an audience; even so, it can incite heated emotional responses and exacerbate disagreements. However, avoiding discussion of divisive issues does nothing to bring about progress or resolve conflicts. Thus, the question is how you can approach a highly charged issue with the goal of advancing the dialogue constructively. **Rogerian argument strategy** is one viable approach.

American psychotherapist and communication theorist Carl R. Rogers (1902–1987) is renowned for his promotion of empathetic listening and consensus-building dialogue. According to Rogers, constructive dialogue is more likely to occur if participating parties demonstrate understanding of opposing arguments and, moreover, approach an issue as an opportunity to solve a mutual problem.

Look It Up: Carl Rogers

Spend some time online reading about Carl Rogers's life and work (access material on three or more different websites). Jot down at least five points that stand out for you. Write out your ideas on at least two of those points. As you reflect, consider whether Rogers's theories are relevant to you, individually, and to society, collectively.

Any dialogue that addresses a controversial issue through Rogerian argument strategy has a nonconfrontational structure and a consensus-building tone. The idea behind this strategy is that traditional Western argument structure, which begins with an assertive stance, often fosters resistance on the part of the "target" audience—those who hold an opposing position. Using Rogerian argument strategy, the writer seeks out "common ground" among readers by adopting an outwardly neutral and objective stance toward the issue. In place of the traditional argument structure—claim, support, counterargument, and reaffirmation of claim—Rogerian argument substitutes this structure: question, alternatives, consideration of alternatives, and advocacy of a middle-ground, or compromise, position (the argument's claim).

As a writer of Rogerian argument, your purpose is to build bridges of communication among opposing sides, thereby bringing the sides together in support of a middle-ground position or compromise, as illustrated in Figure 4.1. To develop a reasonable compromise, you will apply the higher-order critical thinking skills of synthesis and creative problem solving.

Figure 4.1 Rogerian Argument: Common Ground and Compromise

levranii/123RF

Journal: The Pros and Cons of Compromising

Some might say that compromising is a sign of weakness—and certainly it can be in some contexts. Proponents of that viewpoint might argue that compromise is the opposite of conviction. But those with a different point of view might say that compromising is a sign of flexibility and understanding. They might assert that compromise is the opposite of intolerance. Write about the range of interpretations of compromising. Include examples or scenarios (real or imagined) to illustrate the range of perspectives.

4.4.1 Rogerian Argument Organizational Plan

Take Note 4.3 presents a basic framework for organizing a Rogerian argument essay. Adapt the guidelines to suit your subject and your individual writing style. Two principles, however, hold for all Rogerian arguments:

- Maintain a stance of neutrality and fair-mindedness;
- Conclude by advocating a compromise, a middle-ground position.

Now read the following student essay and our annotations to see how one student used the framework in Take Note 4.3 to craft a Rogerian argument essay; then respond to the writing tasks that follow.

Take Note 4.3

Framework for a Rogerian Argument Essay

Introduction

- Lead-in sentences ("hook" strategies: a scenario or an example, a related current event in the news, a startling statistic, a provocative question or statement).
- Synopsis of the discussion surrounding the issue (rhetorical context).
- Issue stated as an issue question to set a tone of inquiry and investigation.

  Note that this is a statement of the issue, rather than a claim statement.

Body

- Two or three paragraphs covering key points that support one prominent position on the issue.
- Two or three paragraphs covering key points that support alternative positions. (Using transitional "signal sentences"—*On the other hand, critics argue . . .* or *Despite these compelling arguments for . . . , many people strongly oppose . . .* —helps prepare readers for the writer's switch from examining one position to examining an opposing position.)
- An alternative pattern would be to focus each body paragraph on a topic related to the issue and to present the supporting and opposing positions on that topic within the paragraph.

Conclusion

- Paragraph that presents a balanced and concise summation of the most compelling points for each opposing side of the argument.
- One or more paragraphs that present the writer's middle-ground, or compromise, position; in advocating for this position, the writer would draw on elements from the diverse positions examined earlier.

  This middle-ground position constitutes the writer's claim—the key is not only to state it but to persuade the audience that it is viable and beneficial.

Christian Garcia
Professor Missy James
ENC 1102
10 April 2007

A Bull's Life

Where does one draw the line in determining acts of animal cruelty? Is it punishing a domestic animal for not following a person's command? Is it training an animal to perform stunts to please the crowd in a circus? Or is animal cruelty the slow and painful killing of an animal simply to entertain the public?

> The writer leads in with a series of questions designed to engage his readers in the subject.

Approximately 1,100 bulls are killed by Matadors during bullfights in Southern France, which is a fraction of the number killed in Spain every year (Mulholland). Bullfighting has been around for centuries, and in Spain and most Latin American countries, it is considered a tradition. Bullfighting originated in Spain, where the best Matadors still come from today. Is bullfighting a cruel process of torture for the animal? Is it a respectful tradition, a way of living that should never cease or be forgotten?

> The writer provides a brief overview of the subject (rhetorical context) and concludes this introduction section by focusing the issue as a two-sided question. Note that he does not reveal his stance.

Despite its value as a tradition, bullfighting clearly is not valued by all persons. However, if one thinks of a bullfight as a cruelty to the bull, then one also should think about the bull's first four to five years. Before a bull is sent to a bullfight, he is basically treated like a champion, sometimes even better than an average person. Raised on a well-tended farm, he receives top quality food and care. The bull runs freely in an open field, unlike captured exotic animals such as panthers, which are trapped in a cage whether they are located in a zoo or a circus. In the poem "The Panther," Rainer Maria Rilke states, "His vision, from the constantly passing bars,/ has grown so weary that it cannot hold/anything else. It seems to him there are/a thousand bars; and behind the bars, no world" (lines 1–4). In a zoo, some may acknowledge the cruelty to the panther, as it is locked in its cage, for the simple purpose of entertaining the public. As the poem implies, the panther might as well be dead.

> The writer raises points in support of bullfighting as a sport and incorporates an excerpt from a poem to contrast a fighter bull's life with that of a caged zoo animal.

Certainly, many persons may view bullfighting as cruelty to the bull because of the way this event is often publicized to feature the gore and blood. They, therefore, associate bullfights exclusively with the violence of the kill without understanding the art of bullfighting. In fact, it is hard to imagine a bullfight without the kill (Nash); it is like playing basketball without a basket. Meanwhile, animals die each day for the purpose of developing or testing new cosmetics or medicines for our personal benefit. This type of animal cruelty is not publicized; it is unlikely to see a company advertising its product by stating that thanks to testing on an animal we are healthier (or more beautiful) today. Millions of Americans readily swallow down a Nyquil when a cold is coming on, but few, if any, stop to wonder how many animals may have been sacrificed before this cold medicine hit the market.

> The writer acknowledges the position of those opposed to bullfighting. He then prepares for a shift to the supporting position by pointing out the hypocrisy of condemning bullfighting as cruelty while ignoring the cruelty of animal testing.

If understood correctly, bullfighting is an art, similar to ballet. The moments of danger are beautiful, rather than simply thrilling, because the Matador controls them (Hannan, "Moments"). However, one may never understand this type of art until one experiences it by being in the stadium watching the bullfight. Words cannot describe the feeling and rush from watching how the Matador dodges and cheats death, time after time. No matter what anyone says, it takes a lot of guts for a man to stand alone in the middle of the stadium waiting for a 1,100-pound bull to charge. Also, there is an allotted time for a bullfight; the Matador has approximately 16 minutes to perform a series of passes with his cape and deliver the deathblow (Schwartz). After the event is completed, the bull is taken out of the stadium, butchered, and sold as meat. The bull is not wasted because it is following its "natural" course, the course that any other bull would go through of being sold as meat.

> The writer continues to elaborate on the supporting position.

Nevertheless, opponents argue that bullfights are cruel to the bull because he goes through a slow and painful death. In a bullfighting event, there are three Matadors; each will kill two bulls (Hannan, "Bulls"). Before the Matador faces the bull, the bull is weakened, and in most cases, one can find blood in the bull's mouth and on his back due to darts. The bull is weakened by men called banderillos, whose sole purpose is to approach the bull and pierce him with two, bright-colored darts on his back. The bull essentially has no chance of survival, once he meets the Matador at the end of the match. Furthermore, a Matador is supposed to kill a bull with one blow of the sword. Unfortunately, this is not always the case; there are incidents where the Matador missed or stabbed the wrong section of the bull. This serves to prolong his slow and painful death—all to entertain the public.

> With the transition signal sentence "Nevertheless, opponents argue...," the writer shifts to the opposing position.

Even though the bull chosen for this event has been given the best care throughout his life, it does not justify the way he is killed. The bull does not have an option as to how to live or lose his life. In the short story "May's Lion" by Ursula Le Guin, a mountain lion wanders into May's yard and lies down under a fig tree: "It just laid there looking around. It wasn't well" (230). Not knowing what to do, May called the sheriff, who sent out two carloads of county police. "'I guess there was nothing else they knew how to do, so they shot it,'" May said (149). Likewise, matadors think that the only option for the bull is for it to die after the bullfight. Many people therefore claim that bullfighting is a barbaric and unethical tradition that should be abolished. The only purpose bullfighting serves is to show the Matador's manliness to the world and to feed people's appetite for blood and gore.

> Continuing to develop the opposing position, the writer includes a passage from a short story and draws a parallel between the fictional event and bullfighting.

Although it is difficult for one to watch a bull being stabbed six times and eventually a sword penetrating his heart to end his life, it is equally hard to imagine a bullfight without the kill. Perhaps over time, this change could be effected, but it would take generations to bring about an end to this tradition. Meanwhile, many people depend on bullfights to make a living and consider it an honorable livelihood, one that is a strong family tradition and community bond. Given the contrasting perspectives, bullfighting as animal cruelty and bullfighting as an honorable tradition, an alternative to abolishing bullfights would be to reduce the numbers of bulls that are killed.

> The writer transitions to his conclusion with a sentence that articulates points on both sides of the issue. In the paragraph's closing sentence, the writer prepares readers for the middle-ground, or compromise, position, which he lays out in his final paragraph.

Specifically, the number of events should be limited to 500 bullfights per year. Also, as with many other sports, there should be a fine for the Matador if he does not kill the bull on his first attempt. This will ensure that the Matador understands there is a lot at stake for his having the privilege to take the bull's life. The number of banderillos should be decreased to only four banderillos per bull, which would increase the bull's chance of survival. These terms will require the Matador to be strong and have the sufficient endurance to fight against a bull. If the bull is not killed by the Matador in his first opportunity, the match will end; the bull will be euthanized if he is badly hurt or be treated and earn his freedom if he has minor injuries. If the bull injures the Matador and the bull is in a decent condition, then that bull has earned his freedom, and he shall be allowed to live out his life on the farm where he was raised. Understanding these new regulations will help the Matador understand the value of the life of the bull and the privilege it is to take a bull's life. Furthermore, these regulations will increase the chances a bull has to win his freedom and minimize the animal cruelty in bullfighting.

> The writer offers a specific plan of action as a compromise, briefly clarifying each of its points. Moreover, in an attempt to persuade both parties to accept the compromise, the writer articulates the benefits for supporters and for opponents of bullfighting.

Works Cited

Hannan, Daniel. "The Bulls Have It." *The Spectator Ltd*, 17 May 2003, p. 81. *InfoTrac OneFile*, www.linccweb.org.

———. "Moments of Truth." *The Spectator Ltd*, 19 July 2003: 44. *InfoTrac OneFile*, www .linccweb.org.

Le Guin, Ursula K. "May's Lion." *The Unreal and the Real*, Saga Press, 2017, pp. 145–155.

Mulholland, Rory. "Most French Disapprove, but Bullfighting Battles on in South." *Agence France*, 3 Aug. 2004. *NewsBank Online*, www.linccweb.org.

Nash, Elizabeth. "A Bloody Fight to the Death." *The Independent*, 13 Dec. 2004. *NewsBank Online*, www.linccweb.org.

Rilke, Rainer Maria. "The Panther." *The Selected Poetry of Rainer Maria Rilke*, translated by Stephen Mitchell, Random House, 1982, p. 25.

Schwartz, Jeremy. "Super Bowl of Bullfighting." *American Statesman*, 6 Feb. 2005. *NewsBank Online*, www.linccweb.org.

Source: Garcia, Christian. "A Bull's Life"

Now that you have read "A Bull's Life," complete the following writing tasks:

1. Is the writer effective in promoting a fair exploration of bullfighting?

2. Before reading the essay, did you have an opinion about bullfighting? If so, briefly explain your viewpoint. Did the writer change your initial thinking on bullfighting? Explain your response by pointing to specific parts of the essay.

3. Do you think the writer's compromise is effective in allowing each side of the controversy to walk away with a "win"? Why or why not?

4. What were your thoughts when you first read the title, "A Bull's Life"? Now that you have read the essay, do you think the title is well suited to the Rogerian argument that follows? Why or why not?

Rogerian argument strategy offers one approach to fostering constructive dialogue on a controversial issue. However, compromise is not always possible; indeed, oftentimes, opposing positions must go head to head in order to bring about the best thinking on an issue, and, as a result, one position prevails. Entrepreneur and author Margaret Heffernan avows, "For good ideas and true innovation, you need human interaction, conflict, argument, debate." An academic community provides the setting for you to engage in the experiences Heffernan champions. Practicing and honing your skills as a writer of argument prepares you to be a valuable participant in the global marketplace of ideas.

4.5   Chapter Activities

The series of activities on the following pages invite you to apply the concepts and ideas we have discussed and demonstrated throughout this chapter.

4.5.1   Think About It

Answer the following questions covering the topics discussed in this chapter.

1. Practice writing claims based on this issue question: Should public school teachers be armed with guns? Write three types of claims: a claim of fact, a claim of policy, and a claim of value. In crafting the claim statements, maintain a third-person point of view by avoiding the use of "I" or "we" (first person). By doing so, you will keep the readers' focus on the issue, rather than on you, the writer. Be prepared to share your three claim statements with classmates for discussion and debate.

2. Which of the following assumptions are not likely to be shared by a global academic community? Revise each such assumption—or add backing—to render it more likely to be accepted by most readers. (For example, the assumption "Smoking e-cigarettes causes teens to become tobacco smokers" is unlikely to be widely accepted, whereas the revised assumption "Smoking e-cigarettes may encourage teens to become tobacco smokers" is much more likely to be shared by your audience.)

   - Children should feel safe in their schools.
   - To keep their students safe, caring teachers want to have access to a gun.
   - Glued to smartphones and tablets, children no longer engage in hands-on exploration of their own backyards.
   - For many people, print media are taking a backseat to online media.

3. Imagine you were writing an argument essay on this issue question: Should public school teachers be armed? Write a paragraph reflecting on the advantages and disadvantages of approaching the issue by asserting and then supporting a clear position, either for or against arming teachers. Write a second paragraph reflecting on the advantages and disadvantages of using Rogerian argument strategy to address the issue. Read back over the two paragraphs and determine which approach you would choose for writing an argument essay. In a few sentences, explain why you would make this choice.

4.5.2 Read and Respond

Read this student essay and respond to the writing tasks that follow.

Cale Blount
Professor Greg Loyd
ENC 1102
18 November 2015

The Last Words of Power

Language is powerful. From the first grunt shared between our cave-dwelling ancestors to the thoughts disseminated among the youth in our schools, this has always been true. Language brought its own magic to the world, giving man something no other creature before or since had: the power to conjure in the mind of another exactly what that person was thinking. Until the end of the Middle Ages, language was so powerful that to know the name of another person was to have a hold over their very soul. Ceremonies and wars could be stopped with a word or two, and all of Europe followed the words of the Pope. Storytellers of old would enthrall communities by the fireside at night, weaving whole tales into the minds of those listening, like a gentle breeze across their face, to bring joy to a mundane life.

Today, language has lost its luster. Where once a sentence or two could rile a nation, today that same passage would not even gain the attention of the random passerby. The traditions of old have become forgotten as the world modernized and cultures have come together. Individual words, even whole stories, have lost their power to move people. Only one group of words can still elicit the same strength as those of old. The actual words change for every language, yet all fall into the same group. They are the words of pure emotion: swear words.

Many an academic would laugh at the proposition that swear words hold any power. It has long been the tradition of teachers and the academic community as a whole to shun such words as vulgar terms that debase language. The oft-told expression "Swearing is just the sign of an ignorant mind" is fairly common among teachers and intellectuals when talking to children or less educated peers. Many refrain from using them in certain formal settings for fear of seeming ignorant or rude. This mindset seems to be a warped mirror of the truth. Those who hear swear words tend to look at the reactions, the emotional state of those using the words and rationalize the outbursts as weakness. However, when has emotion been weakness? Have countless leaders and heroes not been idolized for such things? This argument is just an excuse to not look at the truth. When some people are at an emotional peak, they swear. Why they swear is not always easily discerned, but this argument refuses to answer that.

In truth, cussing is an extension of pain because these groups of words are the closest any language has to pure emotion in written form. The definition of such words rarely matters as much as the feeling they give off, the cathartic release of pent up stimulus and an end to aggression (Joelving). We swear to do one of two things: either in the throes of pain or emotion, for our own benefit, or when lobbing them like loaded bombs to another person to rile them up or cause them harm. There is no wonder why curse words are viewed with such disdain; they are nothing but the manifestation of all the emotion put behind them (Burton). They are a forced unmasking of truly negative emotions, the very base nature of our race.

Perhaps that is the truth behind the argument of curse words being only part of an ignorant mind. These words ally themselves with the very basic part of our brains: the part of our mind that we suppress in good society, the one that speaks to our true nature, the nature of what is left of our more bestial ancestors (Jay & Janschewitz). We fear this part of ourselves, what we cannot control. Society has always tried to reign in this beast, and yet this area of the lexicon of any language is part of that. Such words used in hushed tones between giggling children, or in the throes of passion, when the humors override our intellect, and we can only think of one thing to say to help ease our frazzled nerves.

But those who wish to erase such utterances fail to grasp their true importance. Science has finally begun to delve into the why of swearing. They have found that using curse words has a real, physical benefit, especially with pain. When in pain, a person who cusses acti- vates the human "Fight or Flight" response, which in turn releases adrenaline throughout the body (Burton). A study at the University of England found that subjects told to place their hands in ice water for as long as they could were able to keep the limbs in the water for twice as long when allowed to swear (Burton). When someone stubs his or her toe or gets a paper cut in real life, one of the first reactions, if he or she does not force self-censorship, is to curse. It is a natural reaction to such stimulus. The benefits extend far beyond just pain though. Swearing can increase circulation, elevate endorphin levels, and even bring about a sense of calm in a person (Burton). From the health benefits alone, swearing can be seen as a good thing.

Cursing is not limited to just being beneficial physically; there is a real social aspect that is only now being realized. Most English speakers learn to curse at around the age of 2 (Jay & Janschewitz). They also learn the implications society has given them. Swearing is a socializa- tion tool for many young adults and children, as it shows a sense of comfort around members within a group to curse (Burton). It can also symbolize trust and honesty toward other people. These taboo words that society shuns are being spoken within this group. They must be close, we think, to not be offended by them. A person using a curse word is rarely joking or idly throwing it out there. We as a society view these words as serious, so to use them is to either harm a person, give oneself relief, or show comfort around one another.

There exists in many societies the idea of decency. In fact, many civilized nations have what are called anti-decency laws in place to prevent the corruption of youth. The corruption of youth has long been a rallying cry for censorship, the idea that a word or action is the cause of strife among the generational gap. Today we have censorship of curse words rampant in the media, as it is thought that the impressionable youth will easily absorb such material and use it as a gateway down a dark path. The truth is words alone rarely have an impact anymore (Jay & Janschewitz). It is the underlying emotions that children pick up on. But beyond that, most children enter school knowing from 30-40 vulgarities, and their lexicon of "filth" only grows as they do. Children begin learning to swear by about age 2, far before most have the opportunity to view any programs or movies that would utilize curse words. Thus, it seems that swearing is more than part of the environment (Jay & Janschewitz). It is innate, hidden deep within the brain in areas that are still primal (Joelving).

Society has always had a stigma when it came to the taboo lexicon. Whether for the idea of the ignorant, to the idea of corruption in some way, there has been a never-ending battle to rid the language of these monstrosities. Yet, despite their attempts, the language finds new words to use, new ways of expressing this innate nature. It has been so prevalent that science is now forced to look into the matter and is finding surprising results. Swearing is a part of humanity, and it goes beyond any kind of intellectual debate. There are words of power left, which with an utterance cast a spell on whomever they are directed to. They are lost until we need them, and no matter what we do, they will always be there. Perhaps one day humanity will learn to celebrate its baser nature, instead of condemning it. Until that day comes, however, we are left with these mighty pillars of the id, constant reminders of who we truly are.

Works Cited

Burton, Neel. "Hell Yes: The 7 Best Reasons for Swearing." *Psychology Today*, 19 May 2012, https://www.psychologytoday.com/us/blog/hide-and-seek/201205/hell-yes-the-7-best-reasons-swearing.

Jay, Timothy, and Kristin Janschewitz. "The Science of Swearing." *Association for Psychological Science*, May-June 2012, https://www.psychologicalscience.org/observer/the-science-of-swearing.

Joelving, Frederick. "Why the #$%! Do We Swear? For Pain Relief." *Scientific American,* 12 July 2009, https://www.scientificamerican.com/article/why-do-we-swear.

Source: Blount, Cale. The Last Words of Power student essay.

Writing Tasks

1. This argument essay illustrates the use of an implicit claim. Can you determine what that claim is? Write a sentence that articulates a claim (remember, an implicit claim is not stated outright, which is why you will need to craft your own sentence). What type of claim is it (fact, policy, or value)?

2. Why do you think the writer may have chosen to present an implicit claim instead of an explicit claim? What audience considerations may have contributed to this decision?

3. The writer's subject is the use of swear words, yet his essay quotes no such words. Why do you think he chose not to include explicit examples?

4. In what ways does the writer appeal to *ethos*? How effective are his appeals?

5. Find at least two examples each of appeals to *logos* and to *pathos*. How effective is each one of these appeals?

6. To what degree did the writer change your thinking on the use of swear words?

4.5.3 Multimodal Activities

1. Audiences and Modes of Communication

Argument skills have applications beyond writing an academic essay. You may encounter both personal and professional situations when you need to apply these skills to make a persuasive case. Imagine the following scenario: You are on your way to class, and your car breaks down, again. Now, you will have to miss class; however, due to an illness earlier in the semester, you already have had the maximum number of absences your professor allows. You also worry about how you will get to work and to school going forward, since you can't afford to buy a new car or to continue paying the repair costs for this one. How will you handle the consequences of this event? Communication is key. You might need to

- ask a friend for rides,
- request a loan from a family member, and
- plead with the professor to excuse your absence.

Considering these different audiences and your goals with each, what tone will you adopt, what claims will you make, and what evidence will you offer in each situation? Draft an appropriate text message, letter, note, email, or voice mail for each recipient, using whichever of those modes of communication you think will work best with that audience.

2. Creative Disagreement

View the video of Margaret Heffernan's TED Global 2012 "Dare to disagree": https://www.ted.com/talks/margaret_heffernan_dare_to_disagree/ up-next#t-755906.

- Write your reflections on Heffernan's presentation. What stood out for you? How does Heffernan's message apply to you, now and in the future?

- Consider this issue question: Should immigrants and their children who came to this country illegally be required to leave? Practice applying Heffernan's message to the issue: Write out your initial response to the issue; then "dare to disagree"—that is, write out an internal debate on the issue.

- Heffernan asserts, "It's a fantastic model of collaboration—thinking partners who aren't echo chambers." Returning to the issue question about immigrants, write out any new ideas and perspectives that have emerged for you. Can you propose a creative solution?

Chapter 5
Researching and Documenting an Argument Essay

Learning Objectives

In this chapter, you will learn to

5.1 Research to discover a range of perspectives on your topic.

5.2 Locate credible sources.

5.3 Incorporate sources.

5.4 Document sources.

5.5 Use an annotated student essay as a model.

5.1 Researching to Discover

Research to discover a range of perspectives on your topic.

"Research is formalized curiosity; it is poking and prying with a purpose."
—Zora Neale Hurston

You may not have thought about it this way, but you already are an experienced researcher. Most likely, you search for information on your smartphone or a computer multiple times a day. And when you do, you have a purpose—to explore a topic of interest. Oftentimes, this search prompts you to delve deeper or to branch off in a wholly new direction. With your curiosity aroused, you are "poking and prying with a purpose." Now you can apply this experience to your goals as a writer of an argument essay.

As the previous chapters have emphasized, one of your primary goals as a writer of an argument essay is to establish credibility with your audience—in this case, the global academic community. These readers expect you to lead them on a journey of discovery in examining a complex topic; they expect you to demonstrate a sophisticated understanding of the controversies surrounding the topic and to bring clarity and insight to the conversation. High expectations they are, but they can be addressed by means of your thorough research of the topic.

When you set out to research a topic for an argument essay, it can be tempting to focus your efforts on proving a particular position on the issue and, either subconsciously or consciously, to overlook compelling evidence supporting other positions. However, if you consider this research to be a journey of discovery for you as the writer, as well as for your audience, then you can see that your purpose should be to seek out a broad range of perspectives in order to become well informed about the competing positions. Thus, before beginning the journey, reflect on your willingness to address the issue with an open mind—to examine different positions with balance and fair-mindedness. Suppose, for example, that your topic is whether semiautomatic and assault-style weapons should be banned. You may well already have a clear opinion, either for or against such a ban, but will you be able to separate yourself from that viewpoint when conducting research on the issue? And if the evidence you locate through your research supports an alternative position, will you be willing to modify your position or even adopt a different position? If your answer is no, perhaps you should consider choosing a different issue. Of course, your research may lead you to an even stronger commitment to your initial position; if so, you will be better prepared to construct convincing counterarguments as a result of your thorough examination of the opposing positions. Above all, you will have demonstrated an open mind and, thereby, have earned credibility with your audience.

Look It Up: Change Your Position on Felony Disenfranchisement?

In many U.S. states, convicted felons lose their right to vote (this is known as "felony disenfranchisement"). What is your position on this issue? Do some online research to see whether there are compelling reasons for changing your position. Write a paragraph or two explaining why your position has or has not changed.

American historian and Pulitzer Prize–winning author Daniel J. Boorstin (1914–2004) declared, "The greatest obstacle to discovery is not ignorance—it is the illusion of knowledge." Research will allow you to dispel the "illusion of knowledge." Moreover, research will empower you, as an argument essay writer, to dispel illusions of knowledge that your audience may have about your topic and thus to advance understanding and move the conversation in a constructive direction.

5.2 Locating Credible Sources

Locate credible sources.

As you strive for credibility as a writer, you will also search for credibility in your source material. You certainly could write an essay that expresses your opinions and insights on an issue by using personal experience or observations to support your claims. However, in an academic community, your audience expects you to move beyond personal experience and to make use of evidence from authoritative sources. You may wonder how you can determine if a source is authoritative—credible and worth using—especially when we hear so much about "fake news," "alternative facts," flawed studies, and bias in the media.

For published sources, the first criteria to consider are the credentials of each author and each publication. An author should be an expert in his or her field, usually determined by professional experience and by education (for example, by having earned an advanced degree such as a PhD). The publication should be widely respected, published by a professional, academic, or government organization, such as the Centers for Disease Control and Prevention or the Institution of Civil Engineers. Articles in the publication should also be peer reviewed, evaluated by other experts before publication. You will want to note the date of the source; the most recent sources provide current research and data and, therefore, are usually considered more credible. Even so, older sources can be useful for providing historical context, and in some areas, as in the case of literary criticism, the date of a source's publication is often irrelevant. While most of your source material may be in text format (either digital or print), you may also want to evaluate other modalities, such as podcasts and videos. Many experts now share their opinions in varied formats, to appeal to a broader audience.

Beginning your research process with your campus library, an academic library, allows you to locate "pre-sifted" information—that is, source material that has already been deemed credible. An academic library houses thousands of peer-reviewed scholarly journals, in print and online in academic library databases, including articles written by professionals in a specific discipline both for students and for other professionals. Thus, to find articles from the *Journal of the American Medical Association* (*JAMA*), from *Women's Studies,* or from *Film Journal International,* you would use an academic library database, such as *Academic Search Complete.*

Even when using scholarly, professional, peer-reviewed sources, it is essential that you maintain a critical eye when evaluating research materials. Well-respected authors might still have a bias or an agenda, and it is up to you to recognize the purpose of each source. You might find you disagree with an expert's position on your chosen issue. This difference of opinion does not mean that you cannot use the source; it only requires you to refute or qualify the author's position with an explanation of your own position or by citing an expert who supports your position. In selecting sources, keep in mind that you should include a broad range of perspectives.

As you examine materials from your research, you will need to record useful facts and ideas. Whether you take your notes on index cards or in electronic format, one concept is particularly important to keep in mind: Make a clear distinction between your words and the words of the authors of the sources. Always place quotation marks around any words or phrases that are an author's and clearly note when you have paraphrased someone else's ideas (see the section "Paraphrase and Summary" later in this chapter). Otherwise, when you write your essay, you will be unable to distinguish your words or ideas from those of your sources' authors.

5.2.1 Reading Sources Creatively and Critically

Imagine that you have read Louise Erdrich's short story "The Red Convertible" (the full text is in Chapter 6), which centers on two Native American brothers in the 1970s. The older brother, Henry, is a recent Vietnam veteran, and the story has prompted you to think about veterans and posttraumatic stress disorder (PTSD). Certainly, PTSD among veterans has been a focus of discussion for many years now, and you wonder, are things significantly better for veterans with PTSD today than they were in Henry's time? You also wonder whether Henry's being Native American affected the degree to which he suffered. Suppose that your next essay writing assignment requires you to create a source-based argument on a topic of your choice. Now is an opportunity to seek out answers to your questions about that topic—to start, as Zora Neale Hurston said, "poking and prying with a purpose."

For the topic of veterans, Native Americans, and PTSD, we accessed the following three sources online by using the search terms "veterans and PTSD treatment" and "Native American veterans and PTSD" (the sources are not listed in MLA format). An excerpt from each source is followed by commentary to illustrate reading sources creatively and critically—that is, reading sources in ways that will help you create a conversation—between you as reader and your sources and among the sources themselves. (The commentary also illustrates notes you might write for an annotated bibliography, as discussed later in this chapter.)

- "PTSD Help with Cognitive Processing Therapy—Taking the Blinders Off: Veteran Christopher Tyler's Experience with CPT," by George Decker, Public Affairs, National Center for PTSD, Veterans Health Administration, June 14, 2016.

  Chris Tyler joined the Army in 1996, right after he graduated from high school. During his nine years of service he was deployed to Kosovo for six months and to Iraq for 17 months.

  In Iraq he was part of the 168th Military Police Battalion. He did guard-tower duty. He transported fuel and ammunition. He worked the front gate of his base. But the most dangerous part of his job was prisoner transport.

Tyler's vehicle frequently came under attack. One incident in particular would haunt him for years to come.

. . .

Finally, eight years after leaving the military, Tyler sought help from the VA. He was diagnosed with PTSD and decided to enter a residential treatment program where he began Cognitive Processing Therapy (CPT). In CPT, patients are taught how the way they think can negatively affect the way they live, and how to recognize the thoughts that are making life difficult. Tyler would spend the course of his therapy learning how to reframe those thoughts. . . .

. . .

The tools Tyler learned in CPT gave him a new perspective on how ingrained and rigid his thoughts had become. He became more flexible in his thinking. From this new vantage point, Tyler could see his traumatic event in a more realistic light. The dark clouds started to lift, and relief, at one time unimaginable, was in sight.

His life began to change for the better.

When Tyler began treatment, he worried that therapy would push him over the edge—that he'd come out worse than when he went in. Instead, Cognitive Processing Therapy helped him break the cycle of his negative thinking, and reframe his perspective on the past. . . and the present.

COMMENTARY: *This article showcases cognitive processing therapy (CPT) as an effective treatment for veterans with posttraumatic stress disorder (PTSD). Because the article is published on the VHA's National Center for PTSD site, I infer that at the time of its publication, 2016, CPT was the go-to treatment at VA centers. However, as compelling and poignant as Tyler's personal story is, I wonder if his success is representative of the many other veterans who have participated in this therapy or if this is a somewhat isolated case. I also would like to know if CPT continues to be the first line of treatment for veterans or if, in the last several years, new treatments and alternative therapies have emerged and what those might be. Importantly, related to "The Red Convertible," I wonder what treatment options are available to Native American veterans with PTSD and how effective they are.*

- "Psychological Trauma for American Indians Who Served in Vietnam: The Matsunaga Vietnam Veterans Project," National Center for PTSD, U.S. Department of Veterans Affairs, last updated January 25, 2017.

  The Matsunaga Project involved two parallel studies. The American Indian Vietnam Veterans Project surveyed a sample of Vietnam in-country Veterans residing on or near two large tribal reservations, one in the Southwest and the other in the Northern Plains. These populations had sufficient numbers of Vietnam military Veterans to draw scientifically and culturally sound conclusions about the war and readjustment experiences.

  . . .

. . . Military training was a shocking new experience with good and bad aspects. For the good, many found the discipline, skills, and team spirit an invaluable preparation both for war and later adulthood.

On the other hand, many felt torn between traditional spiritual and community values and the military emphasis on aggression and killing. Many faced racial prejudice and discrimination, often for the first time up close, and felt disillusioned when they or other Indians encountered racial hostility or disrespect.

. . .

About one in three American Indian Vietnam Veterans who served in-country suffered from full or partial PTSD at the time of the study, a quarter century or more after the war. More than two in three American Indian Vietnam Veterans suffered from full or partial PTSD sometime since Vietnam. PTSD prevalence for American Indians is very high, more than twice as high as for White or Japanese American Vietnam Veterans.

COMMENTARY: *This report shines a bright, and even disturbing, spotlight on Native American Vietnam veterans and their experiences with PTSD. It suggests that cultural attributes have made them particularly susceptible to PTSD. And, strikingly, it also suggests that racial prejudice is a significant factor. Reflecting on Henry's depiction in Erdrich's story, I can see how he substantiates the study's conclusion regarding cultural attributes. My curiosity is again roused: What PTSD treatment options are out there for Native Americans? Thinking about the success of CPT in Tyler's case, I wonder if there are similar stories featuring Native Americans. I am glad to see the VA publicizing the Matsunaga Project—a federal agency paying positive attention to Native Americans.*

- "Featured Project: *Healing the Warrior's Heart*," by Federal/State Staff. October 22, 2014. National Endowment for the Humanities.

Healing the Warrior's Heart examines the emotional trauma of war, known as Post Traumatic Stress Disorder (PTSD), through the prism of Native American tradition and ceremony. Native Americans have long understood that helping warriors heal emotionally and spiritually is key to maintaining a healthy society. Within many tribal communities, tradition bearers continue to use ceremonies, prayers, and sacred objects to help returning warriors reintegrate into society, reconnect with the natural world, and cope with the guilt, shame, and fears they bring home with them.

. . .

For centuries, tribal cultures have used healing songs and ceremonies to cleanse their warriors of the emotional scars of war. Despite the loss of language and culture among many tribes, these traditions remain vital on several reservations in the West, and they hold lessons for the nation as it struggles to bring comfort to the latest generation of warriors suffering from PTSD. Despite great efforts by medical and military professionals to treat PTSD, many veterans continue to suffer from it, and there is a small but growing community of psychologists, counselors, and clergy who are looking toward Native American traditions to bring healing to suffering soldiers.

Researching and filming *Healing the Warrior's Heart* has generated an ongoing dialogue with the Navajo, Ute, Zuni, Crow and Blackfeet nations, and has led to relationships with veterans and spiritual leaders within those communities. The filmmakers learned that at Zuni Pueblo, for example, a medicine group associated with the War Gods conducts purification ceremonies for returning veterans at the reservation's border before they are escorted to a welcoming feast on tribal land. . . .

Since 2004, the VA Center in Salt Lake City has held a weekly sweat lodge ceremony. Most attendees are not Native Americans. Speaking of his experience in a sweat lodge ceremony, one veteran said that it had "lightened the load a lot."

COMMENTARY: As the report on the Matsunaga Project suggests, cultural attributes do make a difference for Native American veterans, not only in their elevated rate of exposure to PTSD, but also and importantly, regarding effective treatments. This NEH review of the documentary film **Healing the Warrior's Heart** *verifies that concrete steps have been taken to address the needs of Native Americans. And it opens up a fresh angle: the use of Native American tradition and ceremony in treating veterans for PTSD—not only Native Americans, but also, interestingly, veterans who are not Native Americans. According to this piece, Native Americans already have taken matters into their own hands, as exemplified by the medicine group at Zuni Pueblo. Also, based on the predominance of non–Native Americans attending the weekly sweat lodge ceremony at the Salt Lake City VA Center, I infer that conventional treatments, such as CPT, which worked well for Tyler, are not as effective for many other veterans, regardless of their background or ethnicity. Eager to view the documentary, I checked online and found out that it is readily available. To preview it, I watched a trailer—stunning, beautiful, and compelling! This film will provide a powerful primary source for my argument essay. I may even embed some clips. Meanwhile, I want to focus my next research efforts on the use of sweat lodges and other alternative therapies at VA centers around the country. Since 2004, when the weekly sweat lodge ceremony was initiated at the Salt Lake center, have other VA centers followed suit? Have concrete steps been taken to address not only the specific needs of Native American veterans, but also the diverse needs of all veterans? I can see an argument essay taking shape—from Erdrich's fictional character Henry to present-day veterans and PTSD treatments: what alternative therapies should be advocated?*

Journal: Locating Credible Sources for Nonacademic Issues

Reflect on the guidelines for locating credible sources and on the critical and creative reading strategies you will use to analyze sources. Now, write about at least two situations outside the classroom where you would need to apply these research skills by finding sources and assessing their credibility.

5.3 Incorporating Sources

Incorporate sources.

The first step in drafting your research essay is to develop a claim and then an organizational plan that includes information from your research notes (for a review, see the Chapter 4 section "Articulating a Claim and Developing a Plan for Writing an Argument Essay"). While you should have an awareness of sources as you draft, you may find it useful to begin without incorporating quotations or research material. When you write without using your sources, your own thoughts and voice are primary. Sometimes, it is tempting for students to rely too heavily on experts' opinions instead of emphasizing their own ideas. Drafting without source material can help you avoid this issue.

Once your draft is complete and you are satisfied with your argument, you can begin the process of introducing source material in your essay. Review your notes and research plan; decide where to place the material and whether to quote that material directly or to paraphrase or summarize it as you integrate it into your essay.

You must also follow a documentation system to give credit to your sources and to allow interested readers to access those sources (see the section "Documenting Sources" later in this chapter).

5.3.1 Direct Quotations

A **direct quotation** is an exact, word-for-word restatement of a writer's or a speaker's words. You should weave the quotation smoothly into the text of your own writing. A common way of illustrating how to integrate quotations is the "research sandwich" (see Figure 5.1): Before inserting quoted material, introduce the source (bottom slice of bread); then connect the introduction to the quoted material (the filling of the sandwich); and close with a sentence or more of your own analysis and commentary (top slice of bread).

In the following example (from a student essay in Chapter 4), notice how the writer lets readers know who is being quoted (an author and environmental

Figure 5.1 The Research Sandwich.

Your own analysis and commentary (top slice of bread)

Quoted material (delicious filling)

Introduction to the source (bottom slice of bread)

glevalex/123RF

activist—bottom slice), embeds the quotation, along with its in-text parentheti-cal citation (sandwich filling, indicated here with boldface), and follows the quote with his own commentary (top slice):

> In a testimony before the Senate Energy and Natural Resources Committee, Debbie Miller, an author and environmental activist, made this statement regarding drilling in the Arctic National Wildlife Refuge: **"The oil industry argues that the 19 million-acre refuge can stand to lose the 1.5 million-acre coastal plain. . . . the industry's argument is like saying that I shot the man but the bullet only made a small hole through his heart" ("Top Arctic").** While this statement specifically ad-dresses ANWR, the fundamental message is important for the protection of all nature. It is critical that the United States regulates oil drilling to preserve its few remaining wilderness areas and to protect the environ-ment from permanent damage.

Also, in the text quoted above, note the writer's use of *ellipsis points*—three periods with a space before and after each period (. . .). In this case, the ellipsis indicates that he has omitted words spanning two different sentences within the passage quoted. (Keep in mind that when omitting words from quoted material, you must not alter the context or meaning of the original material.)

Longer direct quotations—more than four typed lines—are introduced with your own sentence, are indented one-half inch from the left margin, and are double-spaced. Because the indented format signals a direct quotation, the quotation marks are omitted; also, the parenthetical citation follows, rather than precedes, the quoted passage's closing period. In the following example (from the same student essay in Chapter 4), notice not only the format but also the writer's lead-in and follow-up sentences, which provide a smooth integration of the source material into the writer's text (again note his use of ellipsis points—in this case, to indicate his omission of words between two different sentences—and note, too, that the concluding parenthetical citation consists of just the page num-ber, as the author's name, Aldo Leopold, is given in the introductory sentence):

> Over sixty years ago, writer and conservationist Aldo Leopold under-scored the incalculable value of wilderness areas in this passage:
>
> > We all strive for safety, prosperity, comfort, long life, and dullness. . . . A measure of success in this is all well enough, and perhaps is a requisite to objective thinking, but too much safety seems to yield only danger in the long run. Perhaps this is behind Thoreau's dictum: In wildness is the salvation of the world. Perhaps this is the hidden meaning in the howl of the wolf, long known among mountains, but seldom per-ceived among men. (133)
>
> As we move forward in the twenty-first century, we need to look beyond our thirst for oil and not silence "the howl of the wolf."

In addition to denoting the omission of words between quoted sentences, ellipsis points can also indicate the omission of words within a single sentence, as illustrated in the following text from a student essay that appears in full in the activities at the end of this chapter:

> Lisa Sanders of the *New York Times Magazine* goes so far as to call him "oblivious to the rhythm and courtesies of normal social intercourse. . . coldblooded."

Another tool writers often find useful when quoting material is brackets, to clarify the quotation or provide context for readers, as in the following text from the same student essay:

> At the beginning of the story, John is woken from a dead sleep to find "Sherlock Holmes standing, fully dressed, by the side of [his] bed" (Doyle 397).

In this case, the wording in the Sherlock Holmes story being quoted is "by the side of my bed," but that could be confusing to the reader of the student essay if "my" were misread as referring to the writer of the essay. The bracketed "[his]," in contrast, clearly refers to John (the narrator of the Sherlock Holmes story), and the brackets indicate that "his" is substituting for a different word in the quoted text.

In the following example, also from the same essay, the writer uses brackets to add a word in order to facilitate smooth incorporation of a quotation into the text of her own sentence (and she includes two sets of ellipsis points to indicate omitted words):

> But consider how he describes the scene in "The Adventure of the Speckled Band" where the two of them wait all night for the murderer to reveal his tricks: "[a]. . . dreadful vigil. . . . I could not hear a sound, not even the drawing of a breath" (Doyle 419).

One question that often arises regarding direct quotation is, how much quoting is too much? As with most writing strategy questions, there is no fixed rule. Even so, a useful guideline is to consider limiting yourself to two or three quotations per paragraph, depending on the length of the quotes and of the paragraph. Of course, you can adjust this guideline to suit your purpose and goals with your audience. If you follow the "research sandwich" method of incorporating quotations, you most likely will not fall into the trap of depending too much on sources' exact wording. Above all, keep in mind that you, as the writer, are the authority and that your sources are your support.

5.3.2 Paraphrase and Summary

Quoting directly is not the only way of incorporating sources; you can also choose either to paraphrase or to summarize passages from your sources. Of the two methods, **paraphrasing** is probably the more challenging way to use source material. To paraphrase a passage, it is not sufficient for you simply to change or rearrange a few words here and there; the paraphrase should be in your own original phrasing. Thus, to paraphrase a passage effectively, you should read and reread the original passage until you know what it is saying, and using your own words, you can express the ideas accurately in a passage of approximately the same length as the original. One way to ensure that the wording is your own is to rewrite the passage *without looking at it*. Although paraphrased material is not enclosed in quotation marks (since the wording is, in fact, your own), you still must document its source with an in-text parenthetical citation because the ideas, concepts, and information are not your own but your source's (see the section on in-text parenthetical citations later in this chapter):

> According to the Energy Information Administration, ANWR could produce about 0.8 million barrels per day but this would still require the United States to import 10.6 million barrels a day to satisfy demand. The total amount of oil that could be drilled in the area would only meet the nation's energy needs for approximately nine months ("Arctic National Wildlife").

Summarizing is similar to paraphrasing in that you are rewriting a passage from a source in your own words. The important distinction, however, between paraphrasing and summarizing is that a summary is concise, much shorter than the original passage, whereas a paraphrase is approximately the same length as the original. As with paraphrasing, when you summarize, you must document your use of the source with an in-text parenthetical citation:

> Proponents of opening the Arctic to oil and natural gas drilling argue that it is an excellent economic opportunity for the United States. If the government allows drilling in protected lands and waters, it could generate hundreds of thousands of jobs and billions of dollars in federal revenue. Oil companies also claim that if they are allowed to drill in an area such as the Arctic National Wildlife Refuge, it would be a significant step for the United States towards energy independence (Webb).

5.3.3 Signal Phrases and a Review

You may introduce a paraphrase, summary, or quotation with a **signal phrase**, which should include the author's name and a verb, usually in present tense. Table 5.1 lists some verbs commonly used in signal phrases.

Table 5.1 Verbs Commonly Used in Signal Phrases

acknowledge	charge	discuss	refute
advise	claim	emphasize	remark
advocate	concede	express	report
affirm	conclude	interpret	respond
agree	confirm	list	state
allow	contend	object	suggest
answer	criticize	observe	think
assert	declare	offer	write
avow	deny	oppose	
believe	disagree	recommend	

Direct quotations, paraphrases, and summaries provide explicit evidence of your research efforts; however, maintain your responsibility as the author of your essay. Be selective in quoting or paraphrasing research material and frame your use of research with lead-in sentences to provide context and with follow-up sentences to provide commentary. All of these uses of sources (direct quotations, paraphrases, and summaries) must be documented with in-text parenthetical citations that refer to the sources on the Works Cited page. Take Note 5.1 reviews the important principles and guidelines discussed above for incorporating sources into your argument essay.

Take Note 5.1

Direct Quotation, Paraphrase, and Summary: A Review

DIRECT QUOTATION

DEFINITION: Exact, word-for-word restatement of a writer's or a speaker's words.
When quoting sources directly, be sure to:

- Weave the quotation smoothly into the text of your own writing, and include an in-text parenthetical citation.
- Use ellipsis points and brackets to indicate omissions and modifications in the quoted material.
- Avoid overusing quotations—remember, you are the writer, and your sources are your support.

EXAMPLE:

In addressing this issue as a presidential candidate in 2008, then Senator Barack Obama stated, "I strongly reject drilling in the Arctic National Wildlife Refuge because it would irreversibly damage a protected national wildlife refuge without. . . meaningfully affect[ing] the global market price or hav[ing] a discernible impact on US energy security" (ProCon.org). However, oil companies and politicians, who support drilling, continue to raise the issue, claiming that the environmental impacts are minimal and the economic benefits outweigh potential risks.

Note how the quotation and the surrounding pieces of text make a "research sandwich," and note the writer's use of a signal phrase with the verb "stated" to introduce the quotation. Also note the writer's use of ellipsis points and brackets (to understand exactly how ellipsis points and brackets are being used here, compare this passage to the corresponding passage in the student essay by John Miller, in Chapter 4).

PARAPHRASE

DEFINITION: Rewriting a passage of source material in your own words.
When paraphrasing, be sure to:

- Read and reread the passage until you understand what it is saying.
- Rewrite the passage using your own original phrasing—do not simply change or rearrange a few words in the source material—and include an in-text parenthetical citation.
- End up with a passage of approximately the same length as the source passage.

EXAMPLE:

The following excerpt from a student essay (which appears in full later in this chapter) includes a direct quotation:

> However, owners of exotic animals disagree: "Ninety-nine percent of the people with exotic animals look after them properly. Of course, you only hear about that one percent that don't," claims Mark Killman, owner of the Killman Zoo which keeps exotic pets (Nikolovsky).

Here is one way the direct quotation could have been rewritten as a paraphrase instead:

> However, owners of exotic animals disagree. Mark Killman, owner of the Killman Zoo which keeps exotic pets, claims that the vast majority of exotic animals are well cared for by their owners, but that news reports focus on the few cases of improper care (Nikolovsky).

Note the writer's use of a signal phrase with the verb "disagree" to introduce the paraphrase.

SUMMARY

DEFINITION: Concisely recasting the information in a passage of source material in your own words. When summarizing, be sure to:

* Read and reread the passage until you understand what it is saying.
* Condense the passage using your own original phrasing, and include an in-text parenthetical citation.
* End up with a passage that is much shorter than the source passage.

EXAMPLE:

Suppose that a student's essay included a direct quotation from Abraham Lincoln's second inaugural address (the full address appears in Chapter 8):

> In his second inaugural address (delivered March 4, 1865), Lincoln drew sharp distinctions between the opposing parties at the time before the outbreak of the Civil War:
>
>> On the occasion corresponding to this four years ago all thoughts were anxiously directed to an impending civil war. All dreaded it, all sought to avert it. While the inaugural address was being delivered from this place, devoted altogether to *saving* the Union without war, insurgent agents were in the city seeking to *destroy* it without war—seeking to dissolve the Union and divide effects by negotiation. Both parties deprecated war, but one of them would *make* war rather than let the nation survive, and the other would *accept* war rather than let it perish, and the war came.

Here is one way the student could have summarized the quotation:

> In his second inaugural address (delivered March 4, 1865), Lincoln drew sharp distinctions between the opposing parties at the time before the outbreak of the Civil War. While noting that both parties said they did not want war, Lincoln pointed out that one party was trying to destroy the Union and would make war to do that, whereas the other party was trying to save the Union and would accept war for that purpose.

Note that the summary is about half the length of the original quotation. Also note the writer's use of the signal phrase "drew a sharp distinction" to introduce the summary.

5.4   Documenting Sources

Document sources.

Another step in establishing credibility as a writer is to document research accurately. One important purpose of documentation is to give credit to the originators of any material that is not your own, thereby recognizing the ownership of intellectual property and avoiding **plagiarism**—a writer's failure to give credit for words or concepts from another source. Documentation serves another important purpose: It enables your readers to locate the information you used and to evaluate it for themselves. In effect, you are sharing the information you have found, a consideration that becomes increasingly important as you become an increasingly active participant in an academic community.

In order to fulfill these two purposes, you must enable your readers to find the complete bibliographic information for each of your sources. To this end, within your essay, you provide the key name or title in a parenthetical citation, immediately after your use of information from a source (see the section "In-Text Parenthetical Citations" later in this chapter). Now the reader can turn to the last part of your essay—the Works Cited page—and locate the full bibliographic entry for each of your sources (see the section "The Works Cited Page" later in this chapter).

5.4.1   Common Knowledge

Some information from sources—information known as **common knowledge** —may not require documentation. For instance, if you read that the U.S. military suffered hundreds of thousands of casualties during World War II, you can include that information without documentation in your essay because it is common knowledge. However, if you read that 75,000 Americans were wounded or killed at the Battle of the Bulge, during December 1944 and January 1945—information that is not common knowledge—you would need to document a source for that information (e.g., United States Army Center of Military History: https://history.army.mil/html/reference/bulge/index.html). What is or is not common knowledge may not always be clear. When in doubt, cite the source, and if time allows, check with your campus writing center specialists or your instructor.

5.4.2   Documentation Systems

Whether your essay is in anthropology or chemistry, economics or English, geology or art history, you will need to learn how to use outside sources accurately and correctly. All academic disciplines require a systematic approach to research and documentation, but different disciplines often use different documentation systems. The humanities typically use a system created by the Modern Language Association (MLA), while the social sciences often use a

---

Look It Up: Documentation and the Avoidance of Plagiarism

Read the explanations of how to avoid plagiarism on two websites, both of which are authoritative sources:

- The MLA site "Plagiarism and Academic Dishonesty" (https://style.mla.org/plagiarism-and-academic-dishonesty/).
- The Purdue OWL site "Avoiding Plagiarism" (https://owl.english.purdue.edu/owl/resource/589/1/).

Which website do you think offers the most useful information and is the site that you might recommend to a friend? Briefly explain why.

---

system devised by the American Psychological Association (APA). Other academic documentation systems include those found in Kate L. Turabian's *Manual for Writers of Research Papers, Theses, and Dissertations* (usually just referred to as *Turabian*) and in the *Chicago Manual of Style*. However, since essays written for this English course will fall under the category of the humanities, the following explanation will center on the MLA documentation system.

5.4.3 Compiling and Annotating a Preliminary Bibliography

The list of sources that you end up actually citing in your essay will appear on the essay's Works Cited page (as discussed later in this chapter). However, in your initial research, as you begin to locate *potential* sources, you will want to maintain a list of those sources; this list is called a **preliminary bibliography**. To facilitate creating a preliminary bibliography for each essay you write, you should get into two important habits regarding each potential source: first, record all the available bibliographic information for the source; second, annotate your entry for the source.

RECORDING BIBLIOGRAPHIC INFORMATION   The bibliographic information for a source includes the author, title, publisher, date of publication, page or paragraph numbers, name of online database, URL, and so on. You will need this information when you compose the Works Cited page for your essay. Nothing is more frustrating than getting close to finishing an essay only to discover that you must try to locate the source of a quotation you found three weeks earlier when you began the project. In fact, when using online sources, you will find it useful to save the web pages as files or to print out the web pages, to ensure that you will have the information you need for citing sources on your Works Cited page.

Articles accessed from academic databases, such as those to which your college library subscribes, often include source citations. When you open the link to an article in an academic database, look to see if the article's citation is included, and if it is, make sure you record the information from the citation in the format required for your assignment (for example, MLA or APA). Clearly, whether or not you access a source via an academic database, you will save time by recording bibliographic information in the required format.

CREATING AN ANNOTATED BIBLIOGRAPHY   Annotating your preliminary bibliography means writing notes about each potential source. These notes, usually written as complete sentences, may primarily be a summation of key points, but for the purpose of writing an argument essay, sentences of critical commentary—that is, evaluations of the information in the sources—are particularly useful. Creating this **annotated bibliography** serves at least two valuable purposes:

1. The process of reviewing and assessing each source may make you aware of gaps, a lack of information on particular aspects of the issue. You also may note overlaps or disjunctions in the perspectives taken by sources and in the information that sources provide, enabling you to identify significant perspectives and information.

2. You can take the opportunity to synthesize information from multiple sources, thus moving toward developing a claim for your argument. Thinking critically about source information can jump-start the process of writing a claim.

Write your annotation of each source in paragraph form, as a summary and/or an evaluation, depending on the requirements of your assignment. The length of the annotations will also depend on those requirements, as well as on the complexity of the source you are annotating. But regardless of whether you are summarizing or evaluating, these annotations should be written *in your own words*.

In the following excerpts from an annotated preliminary bibliography, note how the student has written sentences of both summation and critical evaluation, thus focusing his review of sources on the process of creating an argument essay (the full essay is in Chapter 4).

John Miller
Professor Missy James
ENC 1102
25 November 2014

United States Oil and Natural Gas Drilling:
Annotated Bibliography

"Arctic National Wildlife Refuge Drilling." *Opposing Viewpoints Online Collection*, Gale, 2014. *Opposing Viewpoints in Context*, http://db28.linccweb.org/login?url=http://link. galegroup.com/apps/doc/PC3010999229/OVIC?u=lincclin_tcc&xid=25ca1755.

This article provides an overview of the issue of drilling in the Arctic National Wildlife Refuge (ANWR). In 1960, 8.9 million acres in northeastern Alaska were set aside as a wildlife refuge and labeled "wilderness" to protect them from development. Since then, ANWR has expanded, but certain areas have not received the same legal designation and protection, making them vulnerable to development and causing the long political debate over oil exploration and extraction in the area. Most Republican politicians, who support drilling for oil in ANWR, feel that it will yield great economic benefit for the country and increase our energy independence. Most Democrats advocate for continued protection of the area, and they argue that the irreversible environmental damage is not worth the small economic benefit that oil drilling would provide. Both sides stand firm in their opinions and neither party has achieved its goals in this debate. Republicans have failed to open the area for drilling, while Democrats have failed to establish complete protection. This article provides an excellent history and analysis of oil drilling in ANWR. Although the article attempts to be impartial, it reveals a slight bias in favor of protecting ANWR, in that it goes into much greater detail about the Democrats' argument. Nevertheless, this article provides relevant information regarding both sides of the issue and presents statistics about oil production that can help substantiate an argument about the issue.

Freedman, Ethan. "Groups Vow to Fight Arctic Drilling." *Global Information Network*, 31 Jul. 2012. *SIRS Issues Researcher*, https://sks-sirs-com.db28.linccweb.org.

In his article, Ethan Freedman discusses the plans of many oil companies to drill in the Arctic and their opposition's efforts to prevent this. Companies such as Royal Dutch Shell are pushing for more freedom in drilling in the Arctic. However, environmentalists argue that drilling by these industries endangers the precious and delicate ecosystem. Many companies do not meet necessary safety measures mandated by the Environmental Protection Agency. Opponents of Arctic drilling argue that if companies cannot ensure the safety of the environment, allowing them to drill risks a major catastrophe for the environment. Despite a strong organized opposition, Shell received permission to drill in the Arctic. While some companies feel that the potential environmental and financial risks are outweighed by the possible reward from drilling in the Arctic, many companies, such as BP, have abandoned their efforts. Freedman provides an unbiased synopsis of the struggle between environmentalists and oil companies over Arctic drilling. In addition to providing information to help readers understand each side of the issue, the article provides helpful statistics upon which to build a logical argument.

Horwitt, Dusty. "Oil and Gas Drilling Operations Have Degraded the Environment of the Western United States." *Oil*, edited by Debra A. Miller, Greenhaven Press, 2010. Current Controversies, *Opposing Viewpoints in Context*, http://db28.linccweb.org/login?url=http:// link.galegroup.com/apps/doc/EJ3010734214/OVIC?u=lincclin_tcc&xid=2db11d2c.

Arguing against oil and gas drilling in his article, Dusty Horwitt describes the lack of federal environmental protection and the detrimental effects of the oil industry on the environment (specifically in the western United States). Since 1980, oil and natural gas companies have drilled over 250,000 wells in the West. However, the federal government has failed to protect the lands that are negatively impacted by this industry. Multiple government agencies have confirmed that oil and natural gas drilling generates hazardous and toxic waste. As oil and natural gas drilling continues, it threatens the western environment, particularly, the water supply. Contaminated water has been found in several states, such as Colorado and New Mexico. Many of the negative and dangerous effects caused by drilling for these resources are irreversible. Horwitt provides excellent detail and practical examples of the dangers of oil and natural gas drilling. However, his strong bias makes the author seem less trustworthy and may alienate some readers.

Webb, K. J. "Oil Industry Regulation Hurts the American Economy." *Oil Spills*, edited by Tamara Thompson, Greenhaven Press, 2014. Current Controversies, *Opposing Viewpoints in Context*, http://db28.linccweb.org/login?url=http://link .galegroup.com/apps/doc/EJ3010893221/OVIC?u=lincclin_tcc&xid=2327da3e.

> In this article, K. J. Webb claims that regulating the oil industry in the United States hurts the economy. Webb argues that, considering the country's dependence on oil and natural gas and the potentially huge financial benefit, we are hurting the economy by strictly regulating and preventing industries from drilling for these resources in the United States. There are many untapped areas that hold billions of barrels of oil, such as the Arctic National Wildlife Refuge and Alaskan Arctic outer continental shelf. If companies were allowed to explore these areas, it would create hundreds of thousands of jobs, generate billions of dollars in federal revenue, and be a major step towards energy independence. However, government agencies such as the Environmental Protection Agency threaten energy industries' ability to explore areas and mine resources. Webb's argument helps readers understand his position and why many support expanding domestic oil production. Despite his bias, Webb provides useful facts and information to help the reader develop a position on the issue.

Source: Used with permisssion from John Miller.

5.4.4 In-Text Parenthetical Citations

In-text parenthetical citations are references within an essay that link specific information to its source on the Works Cited page, where the reader will find the full bibliographic information for the source. In MLA style, in-text parenthetical citations usually include the author's last name—or if an author's name is not given with a source, the source's title—and a page number, all enclosed in parentheses. (If there are two authors, the in-text citation should include both last names joined by "and"; if there are three or more authors, the citation should include just the first author's last name followed by "et al.") Again, remember this key principle: You must use in-text parenthetical citations for direct quotations, paraphrases, or summaries of another person's words and for facts, figures, and concepts that originated in someone else's work. The current edition of the *MLA Handbook for Writers of Research Papers* and the Purdue University Online Writing Lab (Purdue OWL) are excellent sources of guidelines for constructing in-text citations (as well as for other aspects of documenting sources). For updates, examples, and further explanations, go to the MLA website (mla.org).

PRINT SOURCES   If you were citing information from an article by Danielle S. Furlich entitled "Field Studies," appearing on page 54 of the spring 2009 issue of the magazine *Nature Conservancy*, the parenthetical citation would look like this: (Furlich 54). It would be placed at the end of the sentence containing the information you are citing and before the ending punctuation. In cases where your source does not identify an author, use key words of the title, enclosed in quotation marks, to identify the source, as in this example: ("Postmodern Culture" 398).

ELECTRONIC SOURCES   Like citations for print sources, in-text parenthetical citations for electronic sources should identify the source either by the author's last name, if the source has an author, or by the first key words in the title, for example: (Bishop) or ("Newsroom Integrity"). However, unlike citations for print sources, which require page numbers, citations for electronic sources include the page number only if the source is formatted in "page display format" (PDF): PDF example—(Johnson 5); non-PDF example—("Fighting with Microbes"). As you type in your in-text parenthetical citations, keep this guideline in mind: The author's last name or the key words from the source's title in your in-text parenthetical citation should match the first word(s) of the source citation on your Works Cited page (excluding articles—*A, An, The*). The in-text citation functions as a "shorthand" guide that allows readers to locate the source on your Works Cited page, where they can see its entire bibliographical entry.

5.4.5 The Works Cited Page

The final element of your essay is the Works Cited page, a list of the sources cited in the in-text parenthetical citations in your essay. On the Works Cited page, citations are arranged alphabetically by the author's last name or by the first word in the source's title (excluding *A, An,* and *The*). They should also be double-spaced with no extra space between entries or after the title, "Works Cited," which should be centered on the page. The entire essay, including the Works Cited page, should be in the same font (for example, Times New Roman 12 point). Each entry on the Works Cited page should use reverse indentation, also called "hanging indent." The current (8th) edition of the *MLA Handbook* indicates that the core elements of each entry should follow a specific order, with specific punctuation separating elements, as follows:

> author. title of source. title of container (such as a journal), other contributors, version, number, publisher, publication date, location.

However, not every element in this list will appear in every entry. The elements to include will vary according to the type of source—book, article, website, interview, or electronic source. Here are some sample source citations typically found on the Works Cited page of first-year college essays (the online MLA Style

Center provides additional guidance on citing specific types of sources, including guidance on the use of italics in citations):

Book by one author

Herzog, Hal. *Some We Love, Some We Hate, Some We Eat: Why It's So Hard to Think Straight About Animals*, Harper, 2010.

Story, poem, or essay from a collection in a book

Poe, Edgar Allen. "The Cask of Amontillado." *Reading Literature and Writing Argument*, edited by Missy James et al., 6th ed., Pearson, 2017, pp. 243–248.

Article from a print magazine

Tidwell, Mike. "The Low-Carbon Diet." *Audubon,* Feb. 2009, pp. 46+.

Personal interview

Pekins, John. Interview. By Jenny McHenry. 23 March 2018.

Film on DVD

Gone Girl. Directed by David Fincher, performance by Rosamund Pike, Ben Affleck, Neil Patrick Harris, and Tyler Perry. Twentieth Century Fox, 2014.

Article in an online journal

McQueen, Tena F., and Robert A. Fleck, Jr. "Changing Patterns of Internet Usage and Challenges at Colleges and Universities." *First Monday,* vol. 9, no.12, 2004, http://firstmonday.org/ojs/index.php/fm/article/view/1197/1117.

Article in an online database

Hughes, John. "Owen's *'Dulce et Decorum Est.'*" *Explicator,* vol. 64, no. 3, Spring 2006, pp.160–162. *Poetry Criticism*, edited by Michelle Lee, vol. 102, 2010. *Literature Resource Center*, www.linccweb.org.

Article with no author specified from an electronic database

"Being Stalked by Intelligent Design." *American Scientist,* Nov./Dec. 2005. *OmniFile Full Text Mega*, www.linccweb.org.

Article with more than two authors from an electronic database

Beard, Lawrence A., et al. "Online Versus On-Campus Instruction: Student Attitudes & Perceptions." *TechTrends: Linking Research & Practice to Improve Learning,* Nov./Dec. 2004, pp. 29–31. *Academic Search Premier*, www.linccweb.org.

Literary work from an online source

Yeats, W. B. "To a Wealthy Man." *Responsibilities and Other Poems*, Macmillan, 1916. *Bartleby.com*, http://www.bartleby.com/147/4.html.

Online magazine article

Keegan, Rebecca. "Sexual Harassment Allegations Plunge the Academy into Its Own Game of Thrones." *Vanity Fair*, Condé Nast, 22 March 2018, https://www.vanityfair.com/hollywood/2018/03/academy-president-allegations.

Website

"Battle of the Bulge." *United States Army Center of Military History*, United States Army, 27 Sept. 2017, https://history.army.mil/html/reference/bulge/index.html.

"Psychological Trauma for American Indians Who Served in Vietnam." *National Center for PTSD*, U.S. Department of Veterans Affairs, 25 January 2017, https://www.ptsd.va.gov/professional/treatment/cultural/psych-trauma-native-american.asp.

5.5 Using an Annotated Student Essay as a Model

Use an annotated student essay as a model.

The following student essay presents a research-based argument centered on a claim of policy.

Josh Griep
Professor Missy James
ENC 1102
14 April 2012

Wild Captives: The Exotic Animal Trade

An estimated five thousand tigers live freely in the wild today; the number of tigers living in captivity is approximately the same (Brook). The latter figure, however, is only the tip of the animal-trading iceberg. Each year, approximately thirty thousand animals are taken from the wild to be sold to private owners (Elton). It has been estimated that fifty to ninety percent of these animals die before ever reaching the United States to be sold.

> The writer opens his essay with factual data, substantiated by citations, which readers can verify on the Works Cited page.

Clearly, the traders of these animals care only about profits; the animals' welfare is the least of their concerns. Jorge Risemberg, who heads up the Ecological Police's Animal Division in Peru, says, "On the global level, after drug trafficking and the contraband arms trade, the contraband trade of animals is the most profitable" (Elton). The animals that are strong enough to survive are sold for as little as fifty dollars in the United States. These animals were not put on this earth to be conversation pieces or to simply look exotic in someone's backyard in Ohio. These wild animals belong in their natural habitats where they can roam their native habitat freely. The United States Government must step in and outlaw the shipping of exotic animals into this country.

> Elaborating on the issue's rhetorical context, the writer incorporates authoritative testimony. By introducing Risemberg and, notably, his credentials, the writer validates the source's perspective on the gravity of the issue.

Twelve states currently have bans against large exotic animals, and seven have partial bans. There is no federal law, however, that restricts anyone from selling or owning nonendangered, exotic animals ("HSUS"). U.S. Representative George Miller has been the prime supporter of HR 5226, a bill which would halt private ownership of many exotic animals: "Wild animals, especially such large and uniquely powerful animals as lions and tigers, should be kept in captivity by professional zoological facilities" (Woolf, "Lions"). Opponents of the bill argue that some people have the resources to care for these animals as well as or even better than zoos. This may be true, but this justification also begs the central question: the humane treatment of the wild animals. If zoos are unable to provide sufficient habitat, they should not be allowed to house the animals. Furthermore, how would the animals' living conditions be evaluated and qualified as suitable or not? Who would continue to monitor these facilities to make sure living conditions remain sufficient? Partial bans, while suggesting a compromise solution, would only serve the selfish needs of the human owners, not the basic needs of the captive animals. Therefore, a complete federal ban must be established to protect these wild creatures and to preserve the natural balance of species of the native lands from which they have been stolen.

> The writer provides further context for the issue as it relates to laws at the state and federal levels; to lend credibility to this information, he documents it with a citation. He follows with a quotation, again, by introducing the individual (Miller) and his credentials: note the "research sandwich"—source introduction; quotation; follow-up commentary. The in-text citation for the direct quotation includes not only the source's author but also the first key word of the article title. Reviewing the Works Cited list, readers see that the writer uses two Woolf articles as sources and, thus, must distinguish between the two in his in-text citations.

Not only is a total ban necessary to maintain the well-being of the animals and their native habitats, but it also is a prime factor in the safety of humans. The director of governmental affairs for the Humane Society states, "Each wild animal kept as a pet in a community is a time bomb waiting to go off. They're genetically programmed to kill" (Brook). Most people are not qualified to own wild animals. The United States Department of Agriculture "believes that only qualified, trained professionals should keep these animals, even if they are only to be pets" (Woolf, "Movie Stars"). However, owners of exotic animals disagree: "Ninety-nine percent of the people with exotic animals look after them properly. Of course, you only hear about that one percent that don't," claims Mark Killman, owner of the Killman Zoo which keeps exotic pets (Nikolovsky). One percent seems extremely low, so perhaps Killman has a point. However, that minute percentile includes the following: a Toronto man who was killed by one of his twenty Burmese pythons (Nikolovsky); the wild boar (Nikolovsky) and three lions found roaming around small towns that had to be executed (Brook); the leopard found in a freezing garage; and the two thousand exotic animals found in an animal breeder's home—all must be factored in to Killman's so-called "one percent" (Elton). Apparently, Killman and other opponents of the ban need a math lesson. Ten thousand fewer exotic animals survive being imported each year, and two thousand are found in single homes. That adds up to one-fifth or twenty percent of the animals imported that, Killman claims, are "properly taken care of."

> As the writer delves into the opposing viewpoints surrounding the issue, he laces the paragraph with quotes, introduced to provide context and cited to provide credibility. Midway in the paragraph, the writer catalogs examples of escaped exotic animals; in doing so, he cites several different sources to validate the information.

The problem extends far beyond the animals having to be put down when they are beyond rehabilitation. These animals are killing machines, and unpredictably they will return to their basic predatory instincts. For example, a three-year-old boy in Texas was killed by a "pet" tiger; another three-year-old had part of his arm ripped off; and a woman was bitten on the head by a 750-pound Siberian-Bengal tiger mix ("HSUS"). Cases such as these convincingly demonstrate that these wild creatures are not only dangerous to their owners, but to other people as well.

> To highlight graphic examples of exotic animals on the loose, the writer begins a new paragraph. Citing the source for the examples, the writer allows readers to draw their own conclusions about the source's potential bias.

Paris Griep, who has been a wildlife biologist for thirty years, believes that no one should be allowed to own these animals: "Well-regulated and monitored zoos are the only facilities with highly trained personnel who can truly care for these animals properly. They cannot be stuck in an 8´ by 8´ cage and expect to live any kind of a life." Not only does this importation of wild animals harm the individual animals, but it also endangers the ecosystem from which they are captured. "Whenever those animals are taken out of the wild, it depletes the natural diversity from the place where they are taken from," Griep points out. These animals already have a difficult time trying to maintain their species populations without humans' further interfering through the exotics trade.

> Closing out his argument and toning down the pitch of the previous paragraph, the writer provides reasoned and authoritative testimony by an expert, which he accessed by way of a personal interview, noted on the Works Cited page.

Wild animals are called wild for a reason; they should be allowed to live freely in their native habitats. Furthermore, wild animals are by their natures unpredictable and cannot safely interact with people. A complete federal ban on the selling and housing of exotic animals is the only rational and humane policy. Such a ban would not remove these animals from the public eye; in fact, that is quite the contrary. If a complete ban is established by law, the populations of these animals can be returned to the flourishing populations they once were. These animals can still be loved and viewed in the safety of well-regulated zoos and licensed wildlife preserves. If owners of exotic pets truly care for their animals, as they insist, they will realize that keeping the animals in a cage or in an environment that they are not accustomed to is unreasonable, unsafe, and inhumane.

Written almost a century ago, the poem, "The Panther" by Rainer Maria Rilke, offers powerful support for a complete ban on the wild animal trade:

His vision, from the constantly passing bars,
has grown so weary that it cannot hold
anything else. It seems to him there are
a thousand bars; and behind the bars, no world. (lines 1–4)

Let's not take away these animals' vision. We must make sure that they can roam freely in a world without bars.

> In a closing appeal to *pathos*, the writer introduces and embeds an excerpt from a poem (the full citation for the poem is on the Works Cited page).

Works Cited

Brook, Tom Vanden. "Exotic pets growing more accessible in USA." *USA TODAY*, sec. NEWS, 6 Dec. 2002, p. 16A. *NewsBank*, www.linccweb.org.

Elton, Catherine. "Peru's Eco-Police Make Barely a Dent in Trade of Exotic Pets." *Christian Science Monitor*, 5 May 2007. *Academic Search Premier*, www.linccweb.org.

Griep, Paris. Interview. By Josh Griep, 20 March 2008.

"HSUS Applauds Rep. George Miller for Introducing Legislation." *HSUS.org*, The Humane Society of the United States, July 2002, http://www.humanesociety.org/news/press_releases.

Nikolovsky, Boris. "Critics Growl over Keeping of Exotic Pets: Zoo Animals Live in Basements and Backyards." *Zoocheck Canada Inc.*, Aug. 2004, www.zoocheck.com.

Rilke, Rainer Maria. "The Panther." *The Selected Poetry of Rainer Maria Rilke*, translated by Stephen Mitchell, Random House, 1982, p. 25.

Woolf, Norma Bennett. "Lions and Tigers and Bears, Oh No!" *Naiaonline.org*, National Animal Interest Alliance, 9 Jan. 2012, http://www.naiaonline.org/articles/article/lions-and-tigers-and-bears-oh-no#sthash.cyOV3zaI.dpbs.

———. "Movie Stars Want Federal Restrictions on Private Ownership of Exotic Animals." *Naiaonline.org*, National Animal Interest Alliance, Feb. 2005, http://www.naiaonline.org/articles/article/movie-stars-want-federal-restrictions-on-private-ownership-of-exotic-animal#sthash.XoxfORjz.dpbs.

Sources are in alphabetical order to facilitate readers' quick access to full bibliographic information as they read the essay. The in-text citations throughout the essay link directly to the sources listed on the Works Cited page, by an author's last name (Elton) or, if no author is available, by a shortened title ("HSUS"). In the last source listed, the three dashes (———) indicate that the source is by the same author as the previous source (in this case, Woolf).

Source: "Griep, Josh. "Wild Captives: The Exotic Animal Trade." Student Paper. 20 Mar. 2003.

5.6 Chapter Activities

The series of activities on the following pages invite you to apply the concepts and ideas we have discussed and demonstrated throughout this chapter.

5.6.1 Think About It

Answer the following questions covering the topics discussed in this chapter.

1. Read the following quotation from the U.S. Department of Veteran Affairs's PTSD website report, "Psychological Trauma for American Indians Who Served in Vietnam." Then read the paraphrase that follows the quotation.

   [quotation]
   "Military training was a shocking new experience with good and bad aspects. For the good, many found the discipline, skills, and team spirit an invaluable preparation both for war and later adulthood."

   [paraphrase]
   Training for the military was shocking, with good and bad sides. On the good side, trainees learned skills, discipline, and team spirit that would prepare them for war and adulthood ("Psychological Trauma").

Does the paraphrase accurately convey the information in the quotation? Has the writer effectively rewritten the sentence in his or her own words? Is the paraphrase overall acceptable, or should it be revised? If you think the paraphrase is acceptable, explain why it works. If you think it should be revised, show how, and briefly explain the reasons for your revisions.

2. Select one of the following issue questions:
   - Should e-cigarettes be banned for teenagers?
   - Should students be allowed to skip senior year of high school and go directly to college?
   - Are some youth sports too intense?
   - Should college administrators have the final say on who can be invited to speak on campus?

   Imagine that you will be developing an argument essay on your chosen issue. Looking ahead to the research process, create a strategy:
   - Write out at least three questions for focusing your research.
   - List the types of sources you think may be most useful in helping you answer your questions.
   - List a few criteria for deciding whether personal testimony is authoritative and credible—that is, when you select personal quotations to use in your essay, what credentials and background will you want the individuals being quoted to have?

3. Since the advent of the World Wide Web at the end of the twentieth century, the accessibility of information has continually increased. Reflect on the benefits and difficulties of having so much information available. In a well-developed paragraph, discuss the pros and cons of researching online.

5.6.2 Read and Respond

1. Read this excerpt from Jennifer Bussey's "Critical Essay on 'The Red Convertible.'" Then respond to the writing tasks that follow.

   In "The Red Convertible," Erdrich uses symbolism in a variety of ways. The most important symbol is the title car, the significance of which changes as the story unfolds. Erdrich's use of symbolism in this way gives her story depth and complexity and enables her to communicate ideas and character developments without lengthy explanations. As a result, the red convertible embodies, at various points in the story, everything the story is meant to express. Fraternal bonds, freedom, innocence, control, and wisdom—all of these themes are carried by one red convertible.

   Perhaps the convertible's greatest contribution to the story is as a symbol of the relationship between Lyman and Henry. Initially, it represents their close companionship. They bought it together on a whim, which demonstrates their willingness to share a major responsibility and to do so on impulse. After buying it, they took a summer-long road trip together. The decision to take the trip was mutual, and their unplanned approach to the trip also was mutual. That they enjoyed the extended trip shows that they were close and genuinely enjoyed each other's company.

Source: From Short Stories for Students. © 2002 Gale, a part of Cengage, Inc. Reproduced by permission. www.cengage.com/permissions

Writing Tasks

Imagine you are writing an essay in which you want to use some of the above material from Bussey's article. Using the guidelines from the chapter for effective incorporation of source material, write three short passages for this imaginary essay:

- A passage with a direct quotation from Bussey's article.
- A passage in which you paraphrase material from Bussey's article.
- A passage in which you summarize material from Bussey's article.

2. Read the following student essay (an example of a literary argument essay). Then respond to the writing tasks that follow.

Writing Tasks

1. Find three instances of direct quotation in the student's essay. Describe how the student integrates each quotation and how effectively she uses the concept of the "research sandwich" to introduce and analyze each quotation.
2. Find direct quotations that the writer does not fully embed or sandwich. Is this problematic for you as the reader? Why or why not?

Marlee Head
Professor Jenny McHenry
ENC 1141
31 October 2017

A Study in Sherlock

Sir Arthur Conan Doyle opens his story "The Adventure of the Speckled Band" by acknowledging his protagonist's exceptionality, citing Sherlock Holmes' decision to work "rather for the love of his art than for the acquirement of wealth" and his "[refusal] to associate himself with any investigation which did not tend towards the unusual, even the fantastic" (Doyle 397). From this line alone the audience is left with the vision of a lofty, principled man with a penchant for adventure. Although this is certainly accurate, it does little justice to Sherlock's vast and multilayered personality. Through the course of just one story, Sherlock reveals himself to be enigmatic at the least, and Doyle no doubt explores and develops the character in his other stories. It is immensely difficult, then, to attempt to recreate this character in a manner that stays true to the author's intentions. But that is exactly what Mark Gatiss and Steven Moffat do in their 2010-2017 television series *Sherlock*. They place the cast, originally developed in the nineteenth century, in a modern setting. Although this idea could have easily brought shame to the Holmes franchise, Gatiss and Moffat combine their artistic liberties with details drawn directly from the original text to create a show so captivating it leaves audiences begging for more. By examining these two renditions, it is possible to examine Sherlock's personality traits more clearly, as well as prove he is largely reflective of his only friend, Dr. John Watson.

As mentioned, Doyle alludes to Sherlock's eccentricities early on. But as the story continues, it becomes clearer and clearer how extraordinary he really is. For example, after solving the murder in the "Speckled Band" case and catching the criminal red-handed, he comments to John Watson that he "had come to these conclusions before [he] had ever entered [the murderer's] room" (Doyle 422). Without seeing the crime scene, Sherlock used his previous knowledge and enormous mental capacity to craft a version of what may have occurred. Nor does it exactly surprise him when he is right. One critic sums up the whole story in the context of Sherlock's expertise: "'The Speckled Band' [is] a story in which Holmes extricates himself from the ties which bind him to his specular double by using the other's own weapons against him" (Levine). As this researcher so aptly points out, the story would be pointless if it were not for Sherlock's reasoning skills.

And this is by no means the only aspect of Sherlock's personality that comes off as a bit strong; he is revealed to be incredibly irritating at times. At the beginning of the story, John is woken from a dead sleep to find "Sherlock Holmes standing, fully dressed, by the side of [his] bed" (Doyle 397). There is almost nothing as horrifying as waking to see someone staring at you, yet Sherlock treats it as a matter of course. If it gets him what he wants, then the discomfort it may cause his friend is not an obstacle. Later on in the story, his rudeness and disregard for others are further illustrated in these lines of dialogue between John and Sherlock, respectively: "'You speak of danger. You have evidently seen more in these rooms than was visible to me.' 'No, but I fancy that I may have deduced a little more. I imagine that you saw all that I did'" (Doyle 416). This tendency to condescend or even terrify those close to him becomes a trademark of Sherlock's throughout the narrative. Lisa Sanders of the *New York Times Magazine* goes so far as to call him "oblivious to the rhythm and courtesies of normal social intercourse. . . coldblooded."

But these are all easily observable facts about Sherlock. The more interesting information is revealed by examining his interactions with that which is dear to him, his friend and partner, Dr. John Watson. Although he can be tough on John at times, there can be no doubt that they have a special relationship. Sanders points out that he has "no other friends" and calls John "extremely tolerant." But is John merely tolerant, or does he genuinely care about Sherlock? The evidence can be found directly in the text, because nearly all of the Sherlock Holmes stories are told from John's perspective. Take, for example, the moments immediately following the scene mentioned earlier, where Sherlock wakes John up by staring at him. Although John expresses "surprise. . . and resentment" at being roused in such an unorthodox fashion, he goes on to explain his gratitude to his colleague. "I had no keener pleasure," he exclaims, "than following Holmes in his professional investigations, and in admiring the rapid deductions, as swift as intuitions" (Doyle 397-398). This could be interpreted as doglike loyalty, the affections of a man blind from the stars in his eyes. But consider how he describes the scene in "The Adventure of the Speckled Band" where the two of them wait all night for the murderer to reveal his tricks: "[a]. . . dreadful vigil. . . I could not hear a sound, not even the drawing of a breath" (Doyle 419). No sane man would put himself in the line of such danger and fear if he didn't unconditionally trust and admire the person he was with. The only light in all this darkness is the person himself: ". . . yet I knew that my companion sat open-eyed, within a few feet of me" (Doyle 419). No, John Watson is not a puppy dog sycophant—he is a true and loyal friend.

Sherlock is brilliant but brusque. John's affections are not lost on him, but he does not always do a good job of reciprocating them. But what happened to these literary nuances when they were translated into a television series? The short answer would be that they were exaggerated. If the print Sherlock is smart, rude, and loyal, the TV Sherlock is ten times that. For example, in an episode called "A Scandal in Belgravia," a client gives Sherlock a string of what she believes to be code and asks him to unscramble it. After just five seconds, he delivers this rapid-fire speech:

> It's not code, these are seat allocations on a passenger jet. Look! There's no letter I because it can be mistaken for a 1. No letters past K, the width of the plane is the limit. The numbers always appear randomly and not in sequence, but the letters have little runs of sequence all over the place—families and couples sitting together. Only a jumbo is wide enough to need a letter K, or rows past fifty-five, which is why there's always an upstairs. There's a row thirteen, which eliminates the more superstitious airlines. Then there's the style of the flight number, 007, that eliminates a few more. And assuming the British point of origin, which would be logical, considering the original source of the information, and assuming from the increased pressure on you lately that the crisis is imminent, the only flight that matches all the criteria and departs within the week is the six-thirty to Baltimore tomorrow evening from Heathrow airport. ("Scandal in Belgravia")

And it is not just his intellect that has been enhanced. Sherlock now acknowledges his off-putting personality first-hand. In an earlier episode, he nonchalantly remarks to one of his rivals, "I've been reliably informed that I don't have [a heart]" ("The Great Game"). This saucy, razor-sharp attitude makes him both an engaging protagonist and a fascinating companion to the original.

But as always, it is John Watson that is the greatest measure of Sherlock's personality. In the series, John's character is exponentially developed. He was previously described as "a patient and sensitive observer [whose] detecting capabilities are no match for the lightning-swift deductive reasoning of Holmes" ("Watson, Dr."). He is now established as a stand-alone character, more of Sherlock's equal than his sidekick. Although he no longer has the advantage of narrating the story, in some ways this gives the viewers more insight into his nature. He can no longer hide behind the mask of interpreter; he has to share the spotlight. Because of this, the TV John no longer employs the same fawning, awe-inspired phrases when referring to Sherlock. He freely expresses his annoyance with his friend and colleague. In one episode, it is necessary for Sherlock to bear facial bruises in order to maintain a disguise. He begs John to punch him, and when John refuses, he goads and berates him until he finally gets his wish. Except John is not content with one, cursory punch. He proceeds to beat Sherlock up, apparently to exact a little revenge for all the times he has annoyed him. But just a few moments later, their client points out an emotionally charged fact: "'Somebody loves you,'" she remarks to Sherlock. "'If I had to punch that face, I'd avoid your nose and teeth, too'" ("Scandal in Belgravia"). No matter how much Sherlock drives John mad, both parties are aware they have a deep and irrevocable bond.

Because of this bond, John nearly always knows when Sherlock is in danger or in trouble. He helps him on cases and in the home, often against Sherlock's will. But mostly, he serves to humanize his wild companion, softening some of Sherlock's unforgivable behaviors for the audience. As viewers, we are able to understand and even sympathize better with some of the mad genius's decisions because we see them through the lens of John Watson. If someone as funny, kind, talented, and moral as John can find a reason to stay loyal to Sherlock, there must be something really worthwhile behind his indelicate appearance.

Regardless of which version of Sherlock is examined, he is not a perfect man. He can be crude, even cruel, and his brain moves too quickly for anyone else to keep up. John sometimes glorifies him, sometimes humanizes him, but always out of genuine devotion. Doyle's stories and the show complement each other nicely and easily lend themselves to character analysis. But in the end, the same conclusion is always reached: "'Sherlock Holmes is a great man, and someday, if we're very, very lucky, he might even be a good one'" ("A Study in Pink").

Works Cited

Doyle, Sir Arthur Conan. "The Adventure of the Speckled Band." *Sherlock Holmes: The Complete Novels and Stories: Vol. 1*, Bantam Classics, 1986, pp. 396–422.

"The Great Game." *Sherlock*, created by Mark Gatiss and Steven Moffat, performance by Benedict Cumberbatch and Martin Freeman, Season 2, Episode 3, BBC 2012. *Netflix*, www. netflix.com.

Levine, Michael G. "The Vanishing Point: Sherlock Holmes and the Ends of Perspective." *Criticism*, vol. 39, no. 2, 1997, p. 249. *Literature Resource Center*, www.linccweb.org.

Sanders, Lisa. "Hidden Clues." *The New York Times Magazine*, 2009, p. 22. *Literature Resource Center*, www.linccweb.org.

"A Scandal in Belgravia." *Sherlock*, created by Mark Gatiss and Steven Moffat, performance by Benedict Cumberbatch and Martin Freeman, Season 2, Episode 1, BBC, 2012. *Netflix*, www.netflix.com.

"A Study in Pink." *Sherlock*, created by Mark Gatiss and Steven Moffat, performance by Benedict Cumberbatch and Martin Freeman, Season 1, Episode 1, BBC, 2010. *Netflix*, www.netflix.com.

"Watson, Dr." *Merriam Webster's Encyclopedia of Literature*, 1995. *Literature Resource Center*, www.linccweb.org.

Source: Used with permission from Marlee Head.

5.6.3 Multimodal Activities

1. Imagine you were assigned to write a research-based argument essay on the Watergate scandal from the early 1970s, and you have yet to determine a focus or a claim. Perhaps you will argue that the effects of this corrupt behavior at the highest level of government influence our government today; perhaps you will argue that then President Richard Nixon did not need to resign or that his vice president and successor, Gerald Ford, should not have pardoned him. Or maybe you will choose some other topic related to this scandal. Decide on and describe your topic, and then conduct some preliminary research on it. Locate three sources of different modalities (such as news articles, government websites, podcasts, documentaries, and academic essays). Evaluate the credibility of each source and explain your conclusions.

2. Imagine that you have been assigned a research-based argument essay on the topic of sports teams' use of Native American names and mascots. If you have an opinion on this issue, you should attempt to put it aside and seek out sources—not simply to satisfy the requirements of the assignment but also to become well informed about different perspectives on the issue.

   - Locate and read two online sources that you deem to be informative and credible.
   - To show that you have read the sources creatively and critically, write sentences of commentary on the material in the sources. As modeled in this chapter, create a conversation between the two sources. Ask questions and explore points of interest.
   - If you were going to write this argument essay, what claim would you make? Briefly explain why.

Part 2
Anthology

The following three Anthology chapters present literature—selections of fiction, poetry, drama, and nonfiction—centered on three enduring themes: Individual and Community Identity, Crime and Punishment, and Power and Responsibility. Rather than offering answers or solutions to issues, the literature selections spark questioning and reflection and invite you the reader to arrive at your own conclusions. Following each reading selection, questions presented as Critical Thinking Topics encourage you to apply the concepts, terms, and tools covered in the five Rhetoric chapters in Part 1. These critical thinking questions are followed by one or more writing tasks (Writing Topics), prompting you to reflect on issues raised in the selection and to generate ideas for creating your own arguments. Each Anthology chapter concludes with Chapter Activities designed to engage you in applying your reading experiences to the chapter's themes and issues; to synthesize your reading experiences, reflections, and ideas; and to develop your own arguments.

Chapter 6: Individual and Community Identity

The readings in this chapter bring out themes and issues rooted in the concepts of individual and community identity—for example, ethnic and gender diversity, family bonds, cultural heritage, and community ties. The selections will lead you to explore a range of ways in which these concepts of identity sometimes can blend harmoniously and, at other times, can clash.

Chapter 7: Crime and Punishment

The readings in this chapter delve into the dramatic themes and issues related to crime and punishment. Some selections, for example, immerse you in questioning an individual's motives for committing or contemplating committing a criminal act; others prompt you to explore the concept of justice, especially as it relates to meting out punishment for a crime committed.

Chapter 8: Power and Responsibility

The readings in this chapter center on themes and issues surrounding the concepts of power and responsibility, the dynamics sparked by the interplay of these concepts—dynamics that are sometimes positive and constructive, at other times negative and destructive. In the readings, individuals confront the challenges involved in attempting to balance the desire for power with a sense of responsibility, and you as reader will arrive at your own conclusions about their success or failure.

Chapter 6
Individual and Community Identity

Americans have long prided themselves on their individuality and, most importantly, on each individual's freedom to choose how to live, think, and believe. Even so, dating back to the American Revolution, the slogan, "united we stand," has been a rallying cry, especially in times of crisis. We cherish our individual identity, but we also value the bonds of community. Rather than being at odds, it seems that individuality and identification with a community work hand in hand.

However, this partnership of individual and community identity is not without its challenges, challenges that grow increasingly complex as society becomes increasingly diverse. For example, it is commonly accepted that America was founded by immigrants, first by Native Americans migrating across the Bering Strait from Asia and then, in subsequent waves, by immigrant settlers from around the globe. Most immigrants sought out the new country for a fresh start; however, many others were forcibly transported from their homelands, including millions of Africans brought into slavery. The result of this history is that the American people represent a mix of ethnicities seen in few other countries. Diversity would seem to be a concept that binds all of us together—diverse in ethnicities and ways of life.

Meanwhile, technology has melted geographical and other boundaries, giving individuals ready access to a multitude of communities, and hence, to a broad range of experiences, information, ideas, and perspectives. Thus, the theme of individual and community identity would seem to be ever metamorphosing; this dynamic is reflected both in popular culture and in the literature selections in this chapter.

In popular culture, two recent films highlight ethnic diversity and the constant shifts of individual and community identity. The 2018 Marvel Studios film *Black Panther* (among the biggest box office hits of all time) not only features primarily black actors but also delves into themes revolving around the challenges faced by the individual members of a mythical community—an ancient, technologically advanced, and isolated African civilization. The 2017 film *The Shape of Water* (winner of four Academy Awards) depicts the confrontation of communities of power (government, science, industry) with individuals from two other communities—a community of diverse ordinary people (diverse in ethnicity, gender, and sexual identity) and an other-than-human community (a semihuman, semidivine water dweller). In accepting the 2018 Oscar for best director for the film, Mexican-born Guillermo del Toro said, "I am an immigrant," and went on to note the power of art "to erase the lines in the sand" between people of different ethnicities. "We should continue doing that when the world tells us to make them deeper," he said.[1] Like del Toro, many people embrace the idea of erasing lines between people, but others, striving to maintain the values and traditions of their ethnic identity, seek to engrave deep lines of distinction.

This chapter's reading selections explore these same topics of ethnic and individual diversity, as well as other identity issues. In the 2014 nonfiction piece "The Trouble with Too Much T," Katrina Karkazis and Rebecca Jordan-Young relate the story of South African female middle-distance runner Caster Semenya, who was required to undergo "sex testing" after fellow athletes questioned her sex. When doctors were brought in to determine whether she was really a woman, she simply asserted, "I know who I am." Other selections explore the idea that, across centuries, individual family members have found support and refuge, but also denial and peril, within the family community. In Kate Chopin's 1898 short story "The Storm," a woman, frightened by lightning, allows herself to fall into a sexual encounter with a married man who is not her husband; despite this apparent disregard for social convention and propriety and the implied peril for both marriages, the story comes to a surprising end. From quite a different perspective, Gary Snyder's 1970 poem "Not Leaving the House" expresses the feelings and perceptions of a father who seems to have been reborn upon the birth of his child.

Bringing your own experiences and ideas to the reading selections in this chapter, you will encounter a range of emotional and intellectual reactions to the depictions of individual and community identity. Some pieces will reinforce your assumptions and opinions, while others will provoke self-questioning. Such is the essence of literature—to spark imagination and to stir up thinking.

6.1 Prewriting and Discussion: Individual and Community Identity

1. Read the image in Figure 6.1 creatively and critically. What ideas does it suggest about individual and community identity?
2. What does it mean to be an *individual* in our contemporary society? What qualities signal one's individuality? Think of one of your close friends—how might he or she describe you as an individual?

---

[1] "'The Shape of Water' Wins Best Picture as Oscars Project Diversity," Brooks Barnes and Cara Buckley, Mar. 4, 2018, *New York Times*. www.nytimes.com/2018/03/04/movies/oscars-academy-awards.html. Retrieved 15 Mar. 2018.

Figure 6.1 *Night Fair*, by Richard Barnett.

'Night Fair' © Richard Barnett

3. What does the word "community" mean to you? What factors contribute to the formation or dissolution of communities? What pressures do communities exert on individuals and with what positive and negative effects? Most people identify with several different communities. For two or three of *your* communities, reflect on how each has influenced your *identity as an individual*.

6.2 Fiction

The eight short stories in this section, spanning the years 1898 through 2002, explore issues related to the theme of individual and community identity.

6.3 Kate Chopin, The Storm
(written 1898; first published 1969)

I

The leaves were so still that even Bibi thought it was going to rain. Bobinôt, who was accustomed to converse on terms of perfect equality with his little son, called the child's attention to certain sombre clouds that were rolling with sinister intention from the west, accompanied by a sullen, threatening roar. They were at Friedheimer's store and decided to remain there till the storm had passed. They sat within the door on two empty kegs. Bibi was four years old and looked very wise.

"Mama'll be' fraid, yes," he suggested with blinking eyes.

"She'll shut the house. Maybe she got Sylvie helpin' her this evening," Bobinôt responded reassuringly.

"No; she ent got Sylvie. Sylvie was helpin' her yistiday," piped Bibi.

Bobinôt arose and going across to the counter purchased a can of shrimps, of   5
which Calixta was very fond. Then he returned to his perch on the keg and sat stolidly holding the can of shrimps while the storm burst. It shook the wooden store and seemed to be ripping great furrows in the distant field. Bibi laid his little hand on his father's knee and was not afraid.

II

Calixta, at home, felt no uneasiness for their safety. She sat at a side window sewing furiously on a sewing machine. She was greatly occupied and did not notice the approaching storm. But she felt very warm and often stopped to mop her face on which the perspiration gathered in beads. She unfastened her white sacque at the throat. It began to grow dark, and suddenly realizing the situation she got up hurriedly and went about closing windows and doors.

Out on the small front gallery she had hung Bobinôt's Sunday clothes to air and she hastened out to gather them before the rain fell. As she stepped outside, Alcée Laballière rode in at the gate. She had not seen him very often since her marriage, and never alone. She stood there with Bobinôt's coat in her hands, and the big rain drops began to fall. Alcée rode his horse under the shelter of a side projection where the chickens had huddled and there were plows and a harrow piled up in the corner.

"May I come and wait on your gallery till the storm is over, Calixta?" he asked.

"Come 'long in, M'sieur Alcée."

His voice and her own startled her as if from a trance, and she seized Bobinôt's   10
vest. Alcée, mounting to the porch, grabbed the trousers and snatched Bibi's braided jacket that was about to be carried away by a sudden gust of wind. He expressed an intention to remain outside, but it was soon apparent that he might as well have been out in the open: the water beat in upon the boards in driving sheets, and he went inside, closing the door after him. It was even necessary to put something beneath the door to keep the water out.

"My! what a rain! It's good two years sence it rain' like that," exclaimed Calixta as she rolled up a piece of bagging and Alcée helped her to thrust it beneath the crack.

She was a little fuller of figure than five years before when she married; but she had lost nothing of her vivacity. Her blue eyes still retained their melting quality; and her yellow hair, dishevelled by the wind and rain, kinked more stubbornly than ever about her ears and temples.

The rain beat upon the low, shingled roof with a force and clatter that threatened to break an entrance and deluge them there. They were in the dining room—the sitting room—the general utility room. Adjoining was her bed room, with Bibi's couch along side her own. The door stood open, and the room with its white, monumental bed, its closed shutters, looked dim and mysterious.

Alcée flung himself into a rocker and Calixta nervously began to gather up from the floor the lengths of a cotton sheet which she had been sewing.

"If this keeps up, *Dieu sait* if the levees goin' to stan' it!" she exclaimed.   15

"What have you got to do with the levees?"

"I got enough to do! An' there's Bobinôt with Bibi out in that storm—if he only didn' left Friedheimer's!"

"Let us hope, Calixta, that Bobinôt's got sense enough to come in out of a cyclone."

She went and stood at the window with a greatly disturbed look on her face. She wiped the frame that was clouded with moisture. It was stiflingly hot. Alcée got up and joined her at the window, looking over her shoulder. The rain was coming down in sheets obscuring the view of far-off cabins and enveloping the distant wood in a gray mist. The playing of the lighting was incessant. A bolt struck a tall chinaberry tree at the edge of the field. It filled all visible space with a blinding glare and the crash seemed to invade the very boards they stood upon.

Calixta put her hands to her eyes, and with a cry, staggered backward. Alcée's arm encircled her, and for an instant he drew her close and spasmodically to him.

Bonté!" she cried, releasing herself from his encircling arm and retreating from the window, "the house'll go next! If I only knew w'ere Bibi was!" She would not compose herself; she would not be seated. Alcée clasped her shoulders and looked into her face. The contact of her warm, palpitating body when he had unthinkingly drawn her into his arms, had aroused all the old-time infatuation and desire for her flesh.

"Calixta," he said, "don't be frightened. Nothing can happen. The house is too low to be struck, with so many tall trees standing about. There! aren't you going to be quiet? say, aren't you?" He pushed her hair back from her face that was warm and steaming. Her lips were as red and moist as pomegranate seed. Her white neck and a glimpse of her full, firm bosom disturbed him powerfully. As she glanced up at him the fear in her liquid blue eyes had given place to a drowsy gleam that unconsciously betrayed a sensuous desire. He looked down into her eyes and there was nothing for him to do but to gather her lips in a kiss. It reminded him of Assumption.

"Do you remember—in Assumption, Calixta?" he asked in a low voice broken by passion. Oh! she remembered; for in Assumption he had kissed her and kissed and kissed her; until his senses would well nigh fail, and to save her he would resort to a desperate flight. If she was not an immaculate dove in those days, she was still inviolate; a passionate creature whose very defenselessness had made her defense, against which his honor forbade him to prevail. Now—well, now—her lips seemed in a manner free to be tasted, as well as her round, white throat and her whiter breasts.

They did not heed the crashing torrents, and the roar of the elements made her laugh as she lay in his arms. She was a revelation in that dim, mysterious chamber; as white as the couch she lay upon. Her firm, elastic flesh that was knowing for the first time its birthright, was like a creamy lily that the sun invites to contribute its breath and perfume to the undying life of the world.

The generous abundance of her passion, without guile or trickery, was like a white flame which penetrated and found response in depths of his own sensuous nature that had never yet been reached.

When he touched her breasts they gave themselves up in quivering ecstasy, inviting his lips. Her mouth was a fountain of delight. And when he possessed her, they seemed to swoon together at the very borderland of life's mystery.

He stayed cushioned upon her, breathless, dazed, enervated, with his heart beating like a hammer upon her. With one hand she clasped his head, her lips lightly touching his forehead. The other hand stroked with a soothing rhythm his muscular shoulders.

The growl of the thunder was distant and passing away. The rain beat softly upon the shingles, inviting them to drowsiness and sleep. But they dared not yield.

The rain was over; and the sun was turning the glistening green world into a palace of gems. Calixta, on the gallery, watched Alcée ride away. He turned and smiled at her with a beaming face; and she lifted her pretty chin in the air and laughed aloud.

III

Bobinôt and Bibi, trudging home, stopped without at the cistern to make them-   30
selves presentable.

"My! Bibi, w'at will yo' mama say! You ought to be ashame'. You oughtn' put on those good pants. Look at' em! An' that mud on yo' collar! How you got that mud on yo' collar, Bibi? I never saw such a boy!" Bibi was the picture of pathetic resignation. Bobinôt was the embodiment of serious solicitude as he strove to remove from his own person and his son's the signs of their tramp over heavy roads and through wet fields. He scraped the mud off Bibi's bare legs and feet with a stick and carefully removed all traces from his heavy brogans. Then, prepared for the worst—the meeting with an over-scrupulous housewife, they entered cautiously at the back door.

Calixta was preparing supper. She had set the table and was dripping coffee at the hearth. She sprang up as they came in.

"Oh! Bobinôt! You back! My! but I was uneasy. W'ere you been during the rain? An' Bibi? he ain't wet? he ain't hurt?" She had clasped Bibi and was kissing him effusively. Bobinôt's explanations and apologies which he had been composing all along the way, died on his lips as Calixta felt him to see if he were dry, and seemed to express nothing but satisfaction at their safe return.

"I brought you some shrimps, Calixta," offered Bobinôt, hauling the can from his ample side pocket and laying it on the table.

"Shrimps! Oh, Bobinôt! you too good to' anything!" and she gave him a smacking kiss   35
on the cheek that resounded. "*J'vous réponds,* we'll have a feas' to night! umph-umph!"

Bobinôt and Bibi began to relax and enjoy themselves, and when the three seated themselves at table they laughed much and so loud that anyone might have heard them as far away as Laballière's.

IV

Alcée Laballière wrote to his wife, Clarisse, that night. It was a loving letter, full of tender solicitude. He told her not to hurry back, but if she and the babies liked it at Biloxi, to stay a month longer. He was getting on nicely; and though he missed them, he was willing to bear the separation a while longer—realizing that their health and pleasure were the first things to be considered.

V

As for Clarisse, she was charmed upon receiving her husband's letter. She and the babies were doing well. The society was agreeable; many of her old friends and acquaintances were at the bay. And the first free breath since her marriage seemed to restore the pleasant liberty of her maiden days. Devoted as she was to her husband, their intimate conjugal life was something which she was more than willing to forego for a while.

So the storm passed and everyone was happy.

Source: Chopin, Kate. "The Storm." Reprinted by permission of Louisiana State University Press. All rights reserved.

Critical Thinking Topics

1. How does Bobinôt's role as a husband shape his self-identity? How does Calixta's role as a wife inform hers?

2. What claim about marriage does "The Storm" imply? Point to specific evidence in the story that supports this claim. Are you convinced? Why or why not?

Writing Topics

1. The closing line asserts, "So the storm passed and everyone was happy." Is this a "happy ending"? Do you think Calixta is happy about allowing herself to have a passionate sexual encounter with Alcée? Why or why not? What assumptions about happiness would underlie a literal interpretation of the narrator's assertion? Do you accept or reject those assumptions? Why?

2. Imagine that you have been asked to write a continuation of the story, flashing forward two years. Do you think Calixta will have put her sexual encounter with Alcée into the past and out of her thoughts? How would you describe the state of Calixta's and Bobinôt's marriage and family life? Explain your responses.

6.4 O. Henry, The Gift of the Magi (1905)

One dollar and eighty-seven cents. That was all. And sixty cents of it was in pennies. Pennies saved one and two at a time by bulldozing the grocer and the vegetable man and the butcher until one's cheeks burned with the silent imputation of parsimony that such close dealing implied. Three times Della counted it. One dollar and eighty-seven cents. And the next day would be Christmas.

There was clearly nothing to do but flop down on the shabby little couch and howl. So Della did it. Which instigates the moral reflection that life is made up of sobs, sniffles, and smiles, with sniffles predominating.

While the mistress of the home is gradually subsiding from the first stage to the second, take a look at the home. A furnished flat at $8 per week. It did not exactly beggar description, but it certainly had that word on the lookout for the mendicancy squad.

In the vestibule below was a letter-box into which no letter would go, and an electric button from which no mortal finger could coax a ring. Also appertaining thereunto was a card bearing the name "Mr. James Dillingham Young."

The "Dillingham" had been flung to the breeze during a former period of prosperity when its possessor was being paid $30 per week. Now, when the income was shrunk to $20, the letters of "Dillingham" looked blurred, as though they were thinking seriously of contracting to a modest and unassuming D. But whenever Mr. James Dillingham Young came home and reached his flat above he was called "Jim" and greatly hugged by Mrs. James Dillingham Young, already introduced to you as Della. Which is all very good.

Della finished her cry and attended to her cheeks with the powder rag. She stood by the window and looked out dully at a gray cat walking a gray fence in a gray backyard. Tomorrow would be Christmas Day, and she had only $1.87 with which to buy Jim a present. She had been saving every penny she could for months, with this

5

result. Twenty dollars a week doesn't go far. Expenses had been greater than she had calculated. They always are. Only $1.87 to buy a present for Jim. Her Jim. Many a happy hour she had spent planning for something nice for him. Something fine and rare and sterling—something just a little bit near to being worthy of the honor of being owned by Jim.

There was a pier-glass between the windows of the room. Perhaps you have seen a pier-glass in an $8 flat. A very thin and very agile person may, by observing his reflection in a rapid sequence of longitudinal strips, obtain a fairly accurate conception of his looks. Della, being slender, had mastered the art.

Suddenly she whirled from the window and stood before the glass. Her eyes were shining brilliantly, but her face had lost its color within twenty seconds. Rapidly she pulled down her hair and let it fall to its full length.

Now, there were two possessions of the James Dillingham Youngs in which they both took a mighty pride. One was Jim's gold watch that had been his father's and his grandfather's. The other was Della's hair. Had the Queen of Sheba lived in the flat across the airshaft, Della would have let her hair hang out the window some day to dry just to depreciate Her Majesty's jewels and gifts. Had King Solomon been the janitor, with all his treasures piled up in the basement, Jim would have pulled out his watch every time he passed, just to see him pluck at his beard from envy.

So now Della's beautiful hair fell about her rippling and shining like a cascade of   10
brown waters. It reached below her knee and made itself almost a garment for her. And then she did it up again nervously and quickly. Once she faltered for a minute and stood still while a tear or two splashed on the worn red carpet.

On went her old brown jacket; on went her old brown hat. With a whirl of skirts and with the brilliant sparkle still in her eyes, she fluttered out the door and down the stairs to the street.

Where she stopped the sign read: "Mme. Sofronie. Hair Goods of All Kinds." One flight up Della ran, and collected herself, panting. Madame, large, too white, chilly, hardly looked the "Sofronie."

"Will you buy my hair?" asked Della.

"I buy hair," said Madame. "Take yer hat off and let's have a sight at the looks of it."

Down rippled the brown cascade.   15

"Twenty dollars," said Madame, lifting the mass with a practised hand.

"Give it to me quick," said Della.

Oh, and the next two hours tripped by on rosy wings. Forget the hashed metaphor. She was ransacking the stores for Jim's present.

She found it at last. It surely had been made for Jim and no one else. There was no other like it in any of the stores, and she had turned all of them inside out. It was a platinum fob chain simple and chaste in design, properly proclaiming its value by substance alone and not by meretricious ornamentation—as all good things should do. It was even worthy of The Watch. As soon as she saw it she knew that it must be Jim's. It was like him. Quietness and value—the description applied to both. Twenty-one dollars they took from her for it, and she hurried home with the 87 cents. With that chain on his watch Jim might be properly anxious about the time in any company. Grand as the watch was, he sometimes looked at it on the sly on account of the old leather strap that he used in place of a chain.

When Della reached home her intoxication gave way a little to prudence and rea- 20
son. She got out her curling irons and lighted the gas and went to work repairing the
ravages made by generosity added to love. Which is always a tremendous task, dear
friends—a mammoth task.

Within forty minutes her head was covered with tiny, close-lying curls that made
her look wonderfully like a truant schoolboy. She looked at her reflection in the mirror
long, carefully, and critically.

"If Jim doesn't kill me," she said to herself, "before he takes a second look at me,
he'll say I look like a Coney Island chorus girl. But what could I do—oh! what could I do
with a dollar and eighty-seven cents?"

At 7 o'clock the coffee was made and the frying-pan was on the back of the stove
hot and ready to Cook the chops.

Jim was never late. Della doubled the fob chain in her hand and sat on the corner
of the table near the door that he always entered. Then she heard his step on the stair
away down on the first flight, and she turned white for just a moment. She had a habit
of saying little silent prayers about the simplest everyday things, and now she whispered: "Please God, make him think I am still pretty."

The door opened and Jim stepped in and closed it. He looked thin and very 25
serious. Poor fellow, he was only twenty-two—and to be burdened with a family! He
needed a new overcoat and he was without gloves.

Jim stopped inside the door, as immovable as a setter at the scent of quail. His
eyes were fixed upon Della, and there was an expression in them that she could not
read, and it terrified her. It was not anger, nor surprise, nor disapproval, nor horror, nor
any of the sentiments that she had been prepared for. He simply stared at her fixedly
with that peculiar expression on his face.

Della wriggled off the table and went for him.

"Jim, darling," she cried, "don't look at me that way. I had my hair cut off and sold it
because I couldn't have lived through Christmas without giving you a present. It'll grow
out again—you won't mind, will you? I just had to do it. My hair grows awfully fast. Say
'Merry Christmas!' Jim, and let's be happy. You don't know what a nice—what a beautiful, nice gift I've got for you."

"You've cut off your hair?" asked Jim, laboriously, as if he had not arrived at that
patent fact yet even after the hardest mental labor.

"Cut it off and sold it," said Della. "Don't you like me just as well, anyhow? I'm me 30
without my hair, ain't I?"

Jim looked about the room curiously.

"You say your hair is gone?" he said, with an air almost of idiocy.

"You needn't look for it," said Della. "It's sold, I tell you—sold and gone, too. It's
Christmas Eve, boy. Be good to me, for it went for you. Maybe the hairs of my head
were numbered," she went on with a sudden serious sweetness, "but nobody could
ever count my love for you. Shall I put the chops on, Jim?"

Out of his trance Jim seemed quickly to wake. He enfolded his Della. For ten seconds let us regard with discreet scrutiny some inconsequential object in the other direction. Eight dollars a week or a million a year—what is the difference? A mathematician
or a wit would give you the wrong answer. The magi brought valuable gifts, but that was
not among them. This dark assertion will be illuminated later on.

Jim drew a package from his overcoat pocket and threw it upon the table. 35

"Don't make any mistake, Dell," he said, "about me. I don't think there's anything in the way of a haircut or a shave or a shampoo that could make me like my girl any less. But if you'll unwrap that package you may see why you had me going a while at first."

White fingers and nimble tore at the string and paper. And then an ecstatic scream of joy; and then, alas! a quick feminine change to hysterical tears and wails, necessitating the immediate employment of all the comforting powers of the lord of the flat.

For there lay The Combs—the set of combs, side and back, that Della had worshipped for long in a Broadway window. Beautiful combs, pure tortoise shell, with jewelled rims—just the shade to wear in the beautiful vanished hair. They were expensive combs, she knew, and her heart had simply craved and yearned over them without the least hope of possession. And now, they were hers, but the tresses that should have adorned the coveted adornments were gone.

But she hugged them to her bosom, and at length she was able to look up with dim eyes and a smile and say: "My hair grows so fast, Jim!"

And then Della leaped up like a little singed cat and cried, "Oh, oh!"   40

Jim had not yet seen his beautiful present. She held it out to him eagerly upon her open palm. The dull precious metal seemed to flash with a reflection of her bright and ardent spirit.

"Isn't it a dandy, Jim? I hunted all over town to find it. You'll have to look at the time a hundred times a day now. Give me your watch. I want to see how it looks on it."

Instead of obeying, Jim tumbled down on the couch and put his hands under the back of his head and smiled.

"Dell," said he, "let's put our Christmas presents away and keep' em a while. They're too nice to use just at present. I sold the watch to get the money to buy your combs. And now suppose you put the chops on."

The magi, as you know, were wise men—wonderfully wise men—who brought   45
gifts to the Babe in the manger. They invented the art of giving Christmas presents. Being wise, their gifts were no doubt wise ones, possibly bearing the privilege of exchange in case of duplication. And here I have lamely related to you the uneventful chronicle of two foolish children in a flat who most unwisely sacrificed for each other the greatest treasures of their house. But in a last word to the wise of these days let it be said that of all who give gifts these two were the wisest. Of all who give and receive gifts, such as they are wisest. Everywhere they are wisest. They are the magi.

Critical Thinking Topics

1. In the final paragraph, the narrator tells us of Della and Jim "that of all who give gifts these two were the wisest." How do you interpret this? Based on your reading, what type of claim is being argued (fact, policy, or value)? Give reasons for your choice.

2. Though Jim and Della no longer have the items that would make their gifts to each other complete, what do you think each has learned of the other as a result of this experience?

3. In closing the story, the narrator explains the significance of the gifts, but does so a bit indirectly. Try to state O. Henry's claim more clearly.

Writing Topic

Americans are often criticized for being too materialistic. They camp out to be the first in line for the latest iPhone. They begin shopping on Black Friday at 12:01 a.m. In 2017, the average credit card debt for balance-carrying households was over sixteen thousand dollars. And yet consumer spending drives the American economy. According to the Federal Reserve, consumer spending accounts for 70% of the gross domestic product. The basic purpose of the economy is to provide goods and services that people need. But "need" is rather ambiguous. Does your neighbor "need" that new $75,000 Tesla? The workers in the Tesla factory certainly hope your neighbor buys one. The question of whether Americans are too materialistic does not have a simple yes-or-no answer. Using evidence from outside sources as well as personal experience, support, refute, or qualify the claim that Americans are too materialistic.

6.5 Katherine Mansfield, The Garden Party (1922)

And after all the weather was ideal. They could not have had a more perfect day for a garden-party if they had ordered it. Windless, warm, the sky without a cloud. Only the blue was veiled with a haze of light gold, as it is sometimes in early summer. The gardener had been up since dawn, mowing the lawns and sweeping them, until the grass and the dark flat rosettes where the daisy plants had been seemed to shine. As for the roses, you could not help feeling they understood that roses are the only flowers that impress people at garden-parties; the only flowers that everybody is certain of knowing. Hundreds, yes, literally hundreds, had come out in a single night; the green bushes bowed down as though they had been visited by archangels.

Breakfast was not yet over before the men came to put up the marquee.

"Where do you want the marquee put, mother?"

"My dear child, it's no use asking me. I'm determined to leave everything to you children this year. Forget I am your mother. Treat me as an honoured guest."

But Meg could not possibly go and supervise the men. She had washed her hair   5 before breakfast, and she sat drinking her coffee in a green turban, with a dark wet curl stamped on each cheek. Jose, the butterfly, always came down in a silk petticoat and a kimono jacket.

"You'll have to go, Laura; you're the artistic one."

Away Laura flew, still holding her piece of bread-and-butter. It's so delicious to have an excuse for eating out of doors, and besides, she loved having to arrange things; she always felt she could do it so much better than anybody else.

Four men in their shirt-sleeves stood grouped together on the garden path. They carried staves covered with rolls of canvas, and they had big tool-bags slung on their backs. They looked impressive. Laura wished now that she had not got the bread-and-butter, but there was nowhere to put it, and she couldn't possibly throw it away. She blushed and tried to look severe and even a little bit short-sighted as she came up to them.

"Good morning," she said, copying her mother's voice. But that sounded so fearfully affected that she was ashamed, and stammered like a little girl, "Oh—er—have you come—is it about the marquee?"

"That's right, miss," said the tallest of the men, a lanky, freckled fellow, and he shifted   10
his tool-bag, knocked back his straw hat and smiled down at her. "That's about it."

His smile was so easy, so friendly that Laura recovered. What nice eyes he had, small, but such a dark blue! And now she looked at the others, they were smiling too. "Cheer up, we won't bite," their smile seemed to say. How very nice workmen were! And what a beautiful morning! She mustn't mention the morning; she must be business-like. The marquee.

"Well, what about the lily-lawn? Would that do?"

And she pointed to the lily-lawn with the hand that didn't hold the bread-and-butter. They turned, they stared in the direction. A little fat chap thrust out his under-lip, and the tall fellow frowned.

"I don't fancy it," said he. "Not conspicuous enough. You see, with a thing like a marquee," and he turned to Laura in his easy way, "you want to put it somewhere where it'll give you a bang slap in the eye, if you follow me."

Laura's upbringing made her wonder for a moment whether it was quite respectful   15
of a workman to talk to her of bangs slap in the eye. But she did quite follow him.

"A corner of the tennis-court," she suggested. "But the band's going to be in one corner."

"H'm, going to have a band, are you?" said another of the workmen. He was pale. He had a haggard look as his dark eyes scanned the tennis-court. What was he thinking?

"Only a very small band," said Laura gently. Perhaps he wouldn't mind so much if the band was quite small. But the tall fellow interrupted.

"Look here, miss, that's the place. Against those trees. Over there. That'll do fine."

Against the karakas. Then the karaka-trees would be hidden. And they were so   20
lovely, with their broad, gleaming leaves, and their clusters of yellow fruit. They were like trees you imagined growing on a desert island, proud, solitary, lifting their leaves and fruits to the sun in a kind of silent splendour. Must they be hidden by a marquee?

They must. Already the men had shouldered their staves and were making for the place. Only the tall fellow was left. He bent down, pinched a sprig of lavender, put his thumb and forefinger to his nose and snuffed up the smell. When Laura saw that gesture she forgot all about the karakas in her wonder at him caring for things like that— caring for the smell of lavender. How many men that she knew would have done such a thing? Oh, how extraordinarily nice workmen were, she thought. Why couldn't she have workmen for her friends rather than the silly boys she danced with and who came to Sunday night supper? She would get on much better with men like these.

It's all the fault, she decided, as the tall fellow drew something on the back of an envelope, something that was to be looped up or left to hang, of these absurd class distinctions. Well, for her part, she didn't feel them. Not a bit, not an atom... And now there came the chock-chock of wooden hammers. Some one whistled, some one sang out, "Are you right there, matey?" "Matey!" The friendliness of it, the—the—Just to prove how happy she was, just to show the tall fellow how at home she felt, and how she despised stupid conventions, Laura took a big bite of her bread-and-butter as she stared at the little drawing. She felt just like a work-girl.

"Laura, Laura, where are you? Telephone, Laura!" a voice cried from the house.

"Coming!" Away she skimmed, over the lawn, up the path, up the steps, across the veranda, and into the porch. In the hall her father and Laurie were brushing their hats ready to go to the office.

"I say, Laura," said Laurie very fast, "you might just give a squiz at my coat before   25
this afternoon. See if it wants pressing."

"I will," said she. Suddenly she couldn't stop herself. She ran at Laurie and gave him a small, quick squeeze. "Oh, I do love parties, don't you?" gasped Laura.

"Ra-ther," said Laurie's warm, boyish voice, and he squeezed his sister too, and gave her a gentle push. "Dash off to the telephone, old girl."

The telephone. "Yes, yes; oh yes. Kitty? Good morning, dear. Come to lunch? Do, dear. Delighted of course. It will only be a very scratch meal—just the sandwich crusts and broken meringue-shells and what's left over. Yes, isn't it a perfect morning? Your white? Oh, I certainly should. One moment—hold the line. Mother's calling." And Laura sat back. "What, mother? Can't hear."

Mrs. Sheridan's voice floated down the stairs. "Tell her to wear that sweet hat she had on last Sunday."

"Mother says you're to wear that sweet hat you had on last Sunday. Good. One   30
o'clock. Bye-bye."

Laura put back the receiver, flung her arms over her head, took a deep breath, stretched and let them fall. "Huh," she sighed, and the moment after the sigh she sat up quickly. She was still, listening. All the doors in the house seemed to be open. The house was alive with soft, quick steps and running voices. The green baize door that led to the kitchen regions swung open and shut with a muffled thud. And now there came a long, chuckling absurd sound. It was the heavy piano being moved on its stiff castors. But the air! If you stopped to notice, was the air always like this? Little faint winds were playing chase, in at the tops of the windows, out at the doors. And there were two tiny spots of sun, one on the inkpot, one on a silver photograph frame, playing too. Darling little spots. Especially the one on the inkpot lid. It was quite warm. A warm little silver star. She could have kissed it.

The front door bell pealed, and there sounded the rustle of Sadie's print skirt on the stairs. A man's voice murmured; Sadie answered, careless, "I'm sure I don't know. Wait. I'll ask Mrs Sheridan."

"What is it, Sadie?" Laura came into the hall.

"It's the florist, Miss Laura."

It was, indeed. There, just inside the door, stood a wide, shallow tray full of pots   35
of pink lilies. No other kind. Nothing but lilies—canna lilies, big pink flowers, wide open, radiant, almost frighteningly alive on bright crimson stems.

"O-oh, Sadie!" said Laura, and the sound was like a little moan. She crouched down as if to warm herself at that blaze of lilies; she felt they were in her fingers, on her lips, growing in her breast.

"It's some mistake," she said faintly. "Nobody ever ordered so many. Sadie, go and find mother."

But at that moment Mrs. Sheridan joined them.

"It's quite right," she said calmly. "Yes, I ordered them. Aren't they lovely?" She pressed Laura's arm. "I was passing the shop yesterday, and I saw them in the window. And I suddenly thought for once in my life I shall have enough canna lilies. The garden-party will be a good excuse."

"But I thought you said you didn't mean to interfere," said Laura. Sadie had gone.   40
The florist's man was still outside at his van. She put her arm round her mother's neck
and gently, very gently, she bit her mother's ear.

"My darling child, you wouldn't like a logical mother, would you? Don't do that.
Here's the man."

He carried more lilies still, another whole tray.

"Bank them up, just inside the door, on both sides of the porch, please," said Mrs.
Sheridan. "Don't you agree, Laura?"

"Oh, I do, mother."

In the drawing-room Meg, Jose and good little Hans had at last succeeded in   45
moving the piano.

"Now, if we put this chesterfield against the wall and move everything out of the
room except the chairs, don't you think?"

"Quite."

"Hans, move these tables into the smoking-room, and bring a sweeper to take
these marks off the carpet and—one moment, Hans—" Jose loved giving orders to the
servants, and they loved obeying her. She always made them feel they were taking part
in some drama. "Tell mother and Miss Laura to come here at once."

"Very good, Miss Jose."

She turned to Meg. "I want to hear what the piano sounds like, just in case I'm   50
asked to sing this afternoon. Let's try over 'This life is Weary.'"

Pom! Ta-ta-ta Tee-ta! The piano burst out so passionately that Jose's face changed.
She clasped her hands. She looked mournfully and enigmatically at her mother and
Laura as they came in.

"This Life is Wee-ary,
A Tear—a Sigh.
A Love that Chan-ges,
This Life is Wee-ary,
A Tear—a Sigh.
A Love that Chan-ges,
And then...Good-bye!"

But at the word "Good-bye," and although the piano sounded more desperate
than ever, her face broke into a brilliant, dreadfully unsympathetic smile.

"Aren't I in good voice, mummy?" she beamed.

"This Life is Wee-ary,
Hope comes to Die.
A Dream—a Wa-kening."

But now Sadie interrupted them. "What is it, Sadie?"

"If you please, m'm, Cook says have you got the flags for the sandwiches?"   55

"The flags for the sandwiches, Sadie?" echoed Mrs. Sheridan dreamily. And the
children knew by her face that she hadn't got them. "Let me see." And she said to
Sadie firmly, "Tell Cook I'll let her have them in ten minutes."

Sadie went.

"Now, Laura," said her mother quickly, "come with me into the smoking-room. I've
got the names somewhere on the back of an envelope. You'll have to write them out for

me. Meg, go upstairs this minute and take that wet thing off your head. Jose, run and finish dressing this instant. Do you hear me, children, or shall I have to tell your father when he comes home to-night? And—and, Jose, pacify Cook if you do go into the kitchen, will you? I'm terrified of her this morning."

The envelope was found at last behind the dining-room clock, though how it had got there Mrs. Sheridan could not imagine.

"One of you children must have stolen it out of my bag, because I remember   60
vividly—cream cheese and lemon-curd. Have you done that?"

"Yes."

"Egg and—" Mrs. Sheridan held the envelope away from her. "It looks like mince. It can't be mince, can it?"

"Olive, pet," said Laura, looking over her shoulder.

"Yes, of course, olive. What a horrible combination it sounds. Egg and olive."

They were finished at last, and Laura took them off to the kitchen. She found Jose   65
there pacifying the Cook, who did not look at all terrifying.

"I have never seen such exquisite sandwiches," said Jose's rapturous voice. "How many kinds did you say there were, Cook? Fifteen?"

"Fifteen, Miss Jose."

"Well, Cook, I congratulate you."

Cook swept up crusts with the long sandwich knife, and smiled broadly.

"Godber's has come," announced Sadie, issuing out of the pantry. She had seen   70
the man pass the window.

That meant the cream puffs had come. Godber's were famous for their cream puffs. Nobody ever thought of making them at home.

"Bring them in and put them on the table, my girl," ordered Cook.

Sadie brought them in and went back to the door. Of course Laura and Jose were far too grown-up to really care about such things. All the same, they couldn't help agreeing that the puffs looked very attractive. Very. Cook began arranging them, shaking off the extra icing sugar.

"Don't they carry one back to all one's parties?" said Laura.

"I suppose they do," said practical Jose, who never liked to be carried back. "They   75
look beautifully light and feathery, I must say."

"Have one each, my dears," said Cook in her comfortable voice. "Yer ma won't know."

Oh, impossible. Fancy cream puffs so soon after breakfast. The very idea made one shudder. All the same, two minutes later Jose and Laura were licking their fingers with that absorbed inward look that only comes from whipped cream.

"Let's go into the garden, out by the back way," suggested Laura. "I want to see how the men are getting on with the marquee. They're such awfully nice men."

But the back door was blocked by Cook, Sadie, Godber's man and Hans.
Something had happened.   80

"Tuk-tuk-tuk," clucked Cook like an agitated hen. Sadie had her hand clapped to her cheek as though she had toothache. Hans's face was screwed up in the effort to understand. Only Godber's man seemed to be enjoying himself; it was his story.

"What's the matter? What's happened?"

"There's been a horrible accident," said Cook. "A man killed."

"A man killed! Where? How? When?"

But Godber's man wasn't going to have his story snatched from under his very nose.   85

"Know those little cottages just below here, miss?" Know them? Of course, she knew them. "Well, there's a young chap living there, name of Scott, a carter. His horse shied at a traction-engine, corner of Hawke Street this morning, and he was thrown out on the back of his head. Killed."

"Dead!" Laura stared at Godber's man.

"Dead when they picked him up," said Godber's man with relish. "They were taking the body home as I come up here." And he said to the Cook, "He's left a wife and five little ones."

"Jose, come here." Laura caught hold of her sister's sleeve and dragged her through the kitchen to the other side of the green baize door. There she paused and leaned against it. "Jose!" she said, horrified, "however are we going to stop everything?"

"Stop everything, Laura!" cried Jose in astonishment. "What do you mean?"   90

"Stop the garden-party, of course." Why did Jose pretend?

But Jose was still more amazed. "Stop the garden-party? My dear Laura, don't be so absurd. Of course we can't do anything of the kind. Nobody expects us to. Don't be so extravagant."

"But we can't possibly have a garden-party with a man dead just outside the front gate."

That really was extravagant, for the little cottages were in a lane to themselves at the very bottom of a steep rise that led up to the house. A broad road ran between. True, they were far too near. They were the greatest possible eyesore, and they had no right to be in that neighbourhood at all. They were little mean dwellings painted a choc-olate brown. In the garden patches there was nothing but cabbage stalks, sick hens and tomato cans. The very smoke coming out of their chimneys was poverty-stricken. Little rags and shreds of smoke, so unlike the great silvery plumes that uncurled from the Sheridans' chimneys. Washerwomen lived in the lane and sweeps and a cobbler, and a man whose house-front was studded all over with minute bird-cages. Children swarmed. When the Sheridans were little they were forbidden to set foot there because of the revolting language and of what they might catch. But since they were grown up, Laura and Laurie on their prowls sometimes walked through. It was disgusting and sordid. They came out with a shudder. But still one must go everywhere; one must see everything. So through they went.

"And just think of what the band would sound like to that poor woman," said Laura.   95

"Oh, Laura!" Jose began to be seriously annoyed. "If you're going to stop a band playing every time some one has an accident, you'll lead a very strenuous life. I'm every bit as sorry about it as you. I feel just as sympathetic." Her eyes hardened. She looked at her sister just as she used to when they were little and fighting together. "You won't bring a drunken workman back to life by being sentimental," she said softly.

"Drunk! Who said he was drunk?" Laura turned furiously on Jose. She said, just as they had used to say on those occasions, "I'm going straight up to tell mother."

"Do, dear," cooed Jose.

"Mother, can I come into your room?" Laura turned the big glass door-knob.

"Of course, child. Why, what's the matter? What's given you such a colour?" And   100
Mrs. Sheridan turned round from her dressing-table. She was trying on a new hat.

"Mother, a man's been killed," began Laura.

"Not in the garden?" interrupted her mother.

"No, no!"

"Oh, what a fright you gave me!" Mrs. Sheridan sighed with relief, and took off the big hat and held it on her knees.

"But listen, mother," said Laura. Breathless, half-choking, she told the dread- 105 ful story. "Of course, we can't have our party, can we?" she pleaded. "The band and everybody arriving. They'd hear us, mother; they're nearly neighbours!"

To Laura's astonishment her mother behaved just like Jose; it was harder to bear because she seemed amused. She refused to take Laura seriously.

"But, my dear child, use your common sense. It's only by accident we've heard of it. If some one had died there normally—and I can't understand how they keep alive in those poky little holes—we should still be having our party, shouldn't we?"

Laura had to say "yes" to that, but she felt it was all wrong. She sat down on her mother's sofa and pinched the cushion frill.

"Mother, isn't it terribly heartless of us?" she asked.

"Darling!" Mrs. Sheridan got up and came over to her, carrying the hat. Before 110 Laura could stop her she had popped it on. "My child!" said her mother, "the hat is yours. It's made for you. It's much too young for me. I have never seen you look such a picture. Look at yourself!" And she held up her hand-mirror.

"But, mother," Laura began again. She couldn't look at herself; she turned aside.

This time Mrs. Sheridan lost patience just as Jose had done.

"You are being very absurd, Laura," she said coldly. "People like that don't expect sacrifices from us. And it's not very sympathetic to spoil everybody's enjoyment as you're doing now."

"I don't understand," said Laura, and she walked quickly out of the room into her own bedroom. There, quite by chance, the first thing she saw was this charming girl in the mirror, in her black hat trimmed with gold daisies, and a long black velvet ribbon. Never had she imagined she could look like that. Is mother right? she thought. And now she hoped her mother was right. Am I being extravagant? Perhaps it was extravagant. Just for a moment she had another glimpse of that poor woman and those little children, and the body being carried into the house. But it all seemed blurred, unreal, like a picture in the newspaper. I'll remember it again after the party's over, she decided. And somehow that seemed quite the best plan...

Lunch was over by half-past one. By half-past two they were all ready for the fray. 115 The green-coated band had arrived and was established in a corner of the tennis-court.

"My dear!" trilled Kitty Maitland, "aren't they too like frogs for words? You ought to have arranged them round the pond with the conductor in the middle on a leaf."

Laurie arrived and hailed them on his way to dress. At the sight of him Laura remembered the accident again. She wanted to tell him. If Laurie agreed with the others, then it was bound to be all right. And she followed him into the hall.

"Laurie!"

"Hallo!" He was half-way upstairs, but when he turned round and saw Laura he suddenly puffed out his cheeks and goggled his eyes at her. "My word, Laura! You do look stunning," said Laurie. "What an absolutely topping hat!"

Laura said faintly "Is it?" and smiled up at Laurie, and didn't tell him after all. 120

Soon after that people began coming in streams. The band struck up; the hired waiters ran from the house to the marquee. Wherever you looked there were couples strolling, bending to the flowers, greeting, moving on over the lawn. They were like bright birds that had alighted in the Sheridans' garden for this one afternoon, on their way to—where? Ah, what happiness it is to be with people who all are happy, to press hands, press cheeks, smile into eyes.

"Darling Laura, how well you look!"

"What a becoming hat, child!"

"Laura, you look quite Spanish. I've never seen you look so striking."

And Laura, glowing, answered softly, "Have you had tea? Won't you have an ice? 125 The passion-fruit ices really are rather special." She ran to her father and begged him. "Daddy darling, can't the band have something to drink?"

And the perfect afternoon slowly ripened, slowly faded, slowly its petals closed.

"Never a more delightful garden-party. . ." "The greatest success. . ." "Quite the most. . ."

Laura helped her mother with the good-byes. They stood side by side in the porch till it was all over.

"All over, all over, thank heaven," said Mrs. Sheridan. "Round up the others, Laura. Let's go and have some fresh coffee. I'm exhausted. Yes, it's been very successful. But oh, these parties, these parties! Why will you children insist on giving parties!" And they all of them sat down in the deserted marquee.

"Have a sandwich, daddy dear. I wrote the flag." 130

"Thanks." Mr. Sheridan took a bite and the sandwich was gone. He took another. "I suppose you didn't hear of a beastly accident that happened to-day?" he said.

"My dear," said Mrs. Sheridan, holding up her hand, "we did. It nearly ruined the party. Laura insisted we should put it off."

"Oh, mother!" Laura didn't want to be teased about it.

"It was a horrible affair all the same," said Mr. Sheridan. "The chap was married too. Lived just below in the lane, and leaves a wife and half a dozen kiddies, so they say."

An awkward little silence fell. Mrs. Sheridan fidgeted with her cup. Really, it was 135 very tactless of father. . .

Suddenly she looked up. There on the table were all those sandwiches, cakes, puffs, all uneaten, all going to be wasted. She had one of her brilliant ideas.

"I know," she said. "Let's make up a basket. Let's send that poor creature some of this perfectly good food. At any rate, it will be the greatest treat for the children. Don't you agree? And she's sure to have neighbours calling in and so on. What a point to have it all ready prepared. Laura!" She jumped up. "Get me the big basket out of the stairs cupboard."

"But, mother, do you really think it's a good idea?" said Laura.

Again, how curious, she seemed to be different from them all. To take scraps from their party. Would the poor woman really like that?

"Of course! What's the matter with you to-day? An hour or two ago you were 140 insisting on us being sympathetic, and now—"

Oh well! Laura ran for the basket. It was filled, it was heaped by her mother.

"Take it yourself, darling," said she. "Run down just as you are. No, wait, take the arum lilies too. People of that class are so impressed by arum lilies."

"The stems will ruin her lace frock," said practical Jose.

So they would. Just in time. "Only the basket, then. And, Laura!"—her mother followed her out of the marquee—"don't on any account—"

"What mother?" 145

No, better not put such ideas into the child's head! "Nothing! Run along."

It was just growing dusky as Laura shut their garden gates. A big dog ran by like a shadow. The road gleamed white, and down below in the hollow the little cottages were in deep shade. How quiet it seemed after the afternoon. Here she was going down the hill to somewhere where a man lay dead, and she couldn't realize it. Why couldn't she? She stopped a minute. And it seemed to her that kisses, voices, tinkling spoons, laughter, the smell of crushed grass were somehow inside her. She had no room for anything else. How strange! She looked up at the pale sky, and all she thought was, "Yes, it was the most successful party."

Now the broad road was crossed. The lane began, smoky and dark. Women in shawls and men's tweed caps hurried by. Men hung over the palings; the children played in the doorways. A low hum came from the mean little cottages. In some of them there was a flicker of light, and a shadow, crab-like, moved across the window. Laura bent her head and hurried on. She wished now she had put on a coat. How her frock shone! And the big hat with the velvet streamer—if only it was another hat! Were the people looking at her? They must be. It was a mistake to have come; she knew all along it was a mistake. Should she go back even now?

No, too late. This was the house. It must be. A dark knot of people stood outside. Beside the gate an old, old woman with a crutch sat in a chair, watching. She had her feet on a newspaper. The voices stopped as Laura drew near. The group parted. It was as though she was expected, as though they had known she was coming here.

Laura was terribly nervous. Tossing the velvet ribbon over her shoulder, she said 150 to a woman standing by, "Is this Mrs. Scott's house?" and the woman, smiling queerly, said, "It is, my lass."

Oh, to be away from this! She actually said, "Help me, God," as she walked up the tiny path and knocked. To be away from those staring eyes, or to be covered up in anything, one of those women's shawls even. I'll just leave the basket and go, she decided. I shan't even wait for it to be emptied.

Then the door opened. A little woman in black showed in the gloom.

Laura said, "Are you Mrs. Scott?" But to her horror the woman answered, "Walk in please, miss," and she was shut in the passage.

"No," said Laura, "I don't want to come in. I only want to leave this basket. Mother sent—"

The little woman in the gloomy passage seemed not to have heard her. "Step this 155 way, please, miss," she said in an oily voice, and Laura followed her.

She found herself in a wretched little low kitchen, lighted by a smoky lamp. There was a woman sitting before the fire.

"Em," said the little creature who had let her in. "Em! It's a young lady." She turned to Laura. She said meaningly, "I'm 'er sister, miss. You'll excuse 'er, won't you?"

"Oh, but of course!" said Laura. "Please, please don't disturb her. I—I only want to leave—"

But at that moment the woman at the fire turned round. Her face, puffed up, red, with swollen eyes and swollen lips, looked terrible. She seemed as though she couldn't understand why Laura was there. What did it mean? Why was this stranger standing in the kitchen with a basket? What was it all about? And the poor face puckered up again.

"All right, my dear," said the other. "I'll thenk the young lady."   160

And again she began, "You'll excuse her, miss, I'm sure," and her face, swollen too, tried an oily smile.

Laura only wanted to get out, to get away. She was back in the passage. The door opened. She walked straight through into the bedroom, where the dead man was lying.

"You'd like a look at 'im, wouldn't you?" said Em's sister, and she brushed past Laura over to the bed. "Don't be afraid, my lass,"—and now her voice sounded fond and sly, and fondly she drew down the sheet—"'e looks a picture. There's nothing to show. Come along, my dear."

Laura came.

There lay a young man, fast asleep—sleeping so soundly, so deeply, that he was far,   165
far away from them both. Oh, so remote, so peaceful. He was dreaming. Never wake him
up again. His head was sunk in the pillow, his eyes were closed; they were blind under the
closed eyelids. He was given up to his dream. What did garden-parties and baskets and
lace frocks matter to him? He was far from all those things. He was wonderful, beautiful.
While they were laughing and while the band was playing, this marvel had come to the lane.
Happy…happy…All is well, said that sleeping face. This is just as it should be. I am content.

But all the same you had to cry, and she couldn't go out of the room without saying something to him. Laura gave a loud childish sob.

"Forgive my hat," she said.

And this time she didn't wait for Em's sister. She found her way out of the door,
down the path, past all those dark people. At the corner of the lane she met Laurie.

He stepped out of the shadow. "Is that you, Laura?"

"Yes."   170

"Mother was getting anxious. Was it all right?"

"Yes, quite. Oh, Laurie!" She took his arm, she pressed up against him.

"I say, you're not crying, are you?" asked her brother.

Laura shook her head. She was.

Laurie put his arm round her shoulder. "Don't cry," he said in his warm, loving   175
voice. "Was it awful?"

"No," sobbed Laura. "It was simply marvellous. But Laurie—" She stopped, she
looked at her brother. "Isn't life," she stammered, "isn't life—" But what life was she
couldn't explain. No matter. He quite understood.

"Isn't it, darling?" said Laurie.

Source: Mansfield, Katherine. "The Garden Party." The Garden Party and Other Stories. New York: Knopf, 1922.

Critical Thinking Topics

1. When Laura suggests to her mother that the garden party be canceled due to
   the tragedy involving their neighbor, Mrs. Sheridan responds icily, "People
   like that don't expect sacrifices from us. And it's not very sympathetic to
   spoil everybody's enjoyment as you're doing now" (par. 113). Would you
   agree with Mrs. Sheridan that her working-class neighbors would not expect
   any show of sympathy, compassion, or respect from their wealthy, upper-
   class neighbors? Imagine yourself in Mrs. Sheridan's position: Suppose you
   have a neighbor whom you do not know personally and who belongs to a
   much lower socioeconomic group than your own. If that neighbor died in
   an accident close to your home on the day you have an extravagant party
   planned, would you postpone the party? Explain your reasoning.

2. Why do you think Mrs. Sheridan sent Laura over to the neighbors' house with the food basket? Describe the scene when Laura visits her neighbors. What lesson do you feel Laura took away from the experience? Is it the lesson her mother intended?

3. Laura's life has essentially been lived within the boundaries of her house and the idyllic garden, and her identity is founded on her family's identity. Does Laura's view of herself change with her exposure to the community of her working-class neighbors? If your answer is yes, explain how her view of herself changes. If no, why do you think it does not change?

Writing Topic

In "The Garden Party," the Sheridan family is clearly divided socially from the poor families who live in the cottages down the hill from their estate. Though we would like to believe we have evolved into a society in which we treat each other equally, regardless of socioeconomic status, in reality divisions based on such status are still quite prevalent. Do you think these divisions will lessen over time, or will there always be divisions based on wealth? Why do you think people seem to care so much about being perceived as wealthy (or at least not being perceived as poor)? How do these socioeconomic perceptions limit relationships? (In responding, you also might want to consider how Beth H. Piatote's short story "Beading Lesson," also in this chapter, relates to this question.)

6.6 Shirley Jackson, The Lottery (1948)

The morning of June 27th was clear and sunny, with the fresh warmth of a full-summer day; the flowers were blossoming profusely and the grass was richly green. The people of the village began to gather in the square, between the post office and the bank, around ten o'clock; in some towns there were so many people that the lottery took two days and had to be started on June 26th, but in this village, where there were only about three hundred people, the whole lottery took less than two hours, so it could begin at ten o'clock in the morning and still be through in time to allow the villagers to get home for noon dinner.

The children assembled first, of course. School was recently over for the summer, and the feeling of liberty sat uneasily on most of them; they tended to gather together quietly for a while before they broke into boisterous play, and their talk was still of the classroom and the teacher, of books and reprimands. Bobby Martin had already stuffed his pockets full of stones, and the other boys soon followed his example, selecting the smoothest and roundest stones; Bobby and Harry Jones "Dellacroy"—eventually made a great pile of stones in one corner of the square and guarded it against the raids of the other boys. The girls stood aside, talking among themselves, looking over their shoulders at the boys, and the very small children rolled in the dust or clung to the hands of their older brothers or sisters.

Soon the men began to gather, surveying their own children, speaking of planting and rain, tractors and taxes. They stood together, away from the pile of stones in the corner, and their jokes were quiet and they smiled rather than laughed. The women, wearing faded house dresses and sweaters, came shortly after their menfolk. They greeted one another and exchanged bits of gossip as they went to join their husbands. Soon the women, standing by their husbands, began to call to their children, and the children came reluctantly, having to be called four or five times. Bobby Martin ducked under his mother's grasping hand and ran, laughing, back to the pile of stones. His father spoke up sharply, and Bobby came quickly and took his place between his father and his oldest brother.

The lottery was conducted—as were the square dances, the teen-age club, the Halloween program—by Mr. Summers, who had time and energy to devote to civic activities. He was a round-faced, jovial man and he ran the coal business, and people were sorry for him, because he had no children and his wife was a scold. When he arrived in the square, carrying the black wooden box, there was a murmur of conversation among the villagers, and he waved and called, "Little late today, folks." The postmaster, Mr. Graves, followed him, carrying a three-legged stool, and the stool was put in the center of the square and Mr. Summers set the black box down on it. The villagers kept their distance, leaving a space between themselves and the stool, and when Mr. Summers said, "Some of you fellows want to give me a hand?" there was a hesitation before two men, Mr. Martin and his oldest son, Baxter, came forward to hold the box steady on the stool while Mr. Summers stirred up the papers inside it.

The original paraphernalia for the lottery had been lost long ago, and the black box   5
now resting on the stool had been put into use even before Old Man Warner, the oldest man in town, was born. Mr. Summers spoke frequently to the villagers about making a new box, but no one liked to upset even as much tradition as was represented by the black box. There was a story that the present box had been made with some pieces of the box that had preceded it, the one that had been constructed when the first people settled down to make a village here. Every year, after the lottery, Mr. Summers began talking again about a new box, but every year the subject was allowed to fade off without anything's being done. The black box grew shabbier each year; by now it was no longer completely black but splintered badly along one side to show the original wood color, and in some places faded or stained.

Mr. Martin and his oldest son, Baxter, held the black box securely on the stool until Mr. Summers had stirred the papers thoroughly with his hand. Because so much of the ritual had been forgotten or discarded, Mr. Summers had been successful in having slips of paper substituted for the chips of wood that had been used for generations. Chips of wood, Mr. Summers had argued, had been all very well when the village was tiny, but now that the population was more than three hundred and likely to keep on growing, it was necessary to use something that would fit more easily into the black box. The night before the lottery, Mr. Summers and Mr. Graves made up the slips of paper and put them in the box, and it was then taken to the safe of Mr. Summers's coal company and locked up until Mr. Summers was ready to take it to the square next morning. The rest of the year, the box was put away, sometimes one place, sometimes another; it had spent one year in Mr. Graves's barn and another year underfoot in the post office, and sometimes it was set on a shelf in the Martin grocery and left there.

There was a great deal of fussing to be done before Mr. Summers declared the lottery open. There were the lists to make up—of heads of families, heads of households in each family, members of each household in each family. There was the proper swearing-in of Mr. Summers by the postmaster, as the official of the lottery; at one time, some people remembered, there had been a recital of some sort, performed by the official of the lottery, a perfunctory, tuneless chant that had been rattled off duly each year; some people believed that the official of the lottery used to stand just so when he said or sang it, others believed that he was supposed to walk among the people, but years and years ago this part of the ritual had been allowed to lapse. There had been, also, a ritual salute, which the official of the lottery had had to use in addressing each person who came up to draw from the box, but this also had changed with time, until now it was felt necessary only for the official to speak to each person approaching. Mr. Summers was very good at all this; in his clean white shirt and blue jeans, with one hand resting carelessly on the black box, he seemed very proper and important as he talked interminably to Mr. Graves and the Martins.

Just as Mr. Summers finally left off talking and turned to the assembled villagers, Mrs. Hutchinson came hurriedly along the path to the square, her sweater thrown over her shoulders, and slid into place in the back of the crowd. "Clean forgot what day it was," she said to Mrs. Delacroix, who stood next to her, and they both laughed softly. "Thought my old man was out back stacking wood," Mrs. Hutchinson went on, "and then I looked out the window and the kids was gone, and then I remembered it was the twenty-seventh and came a-running." She dried her hands on her apron, and Mrs. Delacroix said, "You're in time, though. They're still talking away up there."

Mrs. Hutchinson craned her neck to see through the crowd and found her husband and children standing near the front. She tapped Mrs. Delacroix on the arm as a farewell and began to make her way through the crowd. The people separated good-humoredly to let her through; two or three people said, in voices just loud enough to be heard across the crowd, "Here comes your Missus, Hutchinson," and "Bill, she made it after all." Mrs. Hutchinson reached her husband, and Mr. Summers, who had been waiting, said cheerfully, "Thought we were going to have to get on without you, Tessie." Mrs. Hutchinson said, grinning, "Wouldn't have me leave m'dishes in the sink, now, would you, Joe?," and soft laughter ran through the crowd as the people stirred back into position after Mrs. Hutchinson's arrival.

"Well, now," Mr. Summers said soberly, "guess we better get started, get this over with, so's we can go back to work. Anybody ain't here?"   10

"Dunbar," several people said. "Dunbar, Dunbar."

Mr. Summers consulted his list. "Clyde Dunbar," he said. "That's right. He's broke his leg, hasn't he? Who's drawing for him?"

"Me, I guess," a woman said, and Mr. Summers turned to look at her. "Wife draws for her husband," Mr. Summers said. "Don't you have a grown boy to do it for you, Janey?" Although Mr. Summers and everyone else in the village knew the answer perfectly well, it was the business of the official of the lottery to ask such questions formally. Mr. Summers waited with an expression of polite interest while Mrs. Dunbar answered.

"Horace's not but sixteen yet," Mrs. Dunbar said regretfully. "Guess I gotta fill in for the old man this year."

"Right," Mr. Summers said. He made a note on the list he was holding. Then he   15
asked, "Watson boy drawing this year?"

A tall boy in the crowd raised his hand. "Here," he said. "I'm drawing for m'mother and me." He blinked his eyes nervously and ducked his head as several voices in the crowd said things like "Good fellow, Jack," and "Glad to see your mother's got a man to do it."

"Well," Mr. Summers said, "guess that's everyone. Old Man Warner make it?"

"Here," a voice said, and Mr. Summers nodded.

A sudden hush fell on the crowd as Mr. Summers cleared his throat and looked at the list. "All ready?" he called. "Now, I'll read the names—heads of families first—and the men come up and take a paper out of the box. Keep the paper folded in your hand without looking at it until everyone has had a turn. Everything clear?"

The people had done it so many times that they only half listened to the directions;   20 most of them were quiet, wetting their lips, not looking around. Then Mr. Summers raised one hand high and said, "Adams." A man disengaged himself from the crowd and came forward. "Hi, Steve," Mr. Summers said, and Mr. Adams said. "Hi, Joe." They grinned at one another humorlessly and nervously. Then Mr. Adams reached into the black box and took out a folded paper. He held it firmly by one corner as he turned and went hastily back to his place in the crowd, where he stood a little apart from his family, not looking down at his hand.

"Allen," Mr. Summers said. "Anderson. . . . Bentham."

"Seems like there's no time at all between lotteries any more," Mrs. Delacroix said to Mrs. Graves in the back row. "Seems like we got through with the last one only last week."

"Time sure goes fast," Mrs. Graves said.

"Clark. . . . Delacroix."

"There goes my old man," Mrs. Delacroix said. She held her breath while her hus-   25 band went forward.

"Dunbar," Mr. Summers said, and Mrs. Dunbar went steadily to the box while one of the women said, "Go on, Janey," and another said, "There she goes."

"We're next," Mrs. Graves said. She watched while Mr. Graves came around from the side of the box, greeted Mr. Summers gravely, and selected a slip of paper from the box. By now, all through the crowd there were men holding the small folded papers in the large hands, turning them over and over nervously. Mrs. Dunbar and her two sons stood together, Mrs. Dunbar holding the slip of paper.

"Harburt. . . .Hutchinson."

"Get up there, Bill," Mrs. Hutchinson said, and the people near her laughed.

"Jones."   30

"They do say," Mr. Adams said to Old Man Warner, who stood next to him, "that over in the north village they're talking of giving up the lottery."

Old Man Warner snorted. "Pack of crazy fools," he said. "Listening to the young folks, nothing's good enough for *them*. Next thing you know, they'll be wanting to go back to living in caves, nobody work any more, live *that* way for a while. Used to be a saying about 'Lottery in June, corn be heavy soon.' First thing you know, we'd all be eating stewed chickweed and acorns. There's *always* been a lottery," he added petulantly. "Bad enough to see young Joe Summers up there joking with everybody."

"Some places have already quit lotteries," Mrs. Adams said.

"Nothing but trouble in *that*," Old Man Warner said stoutly. "Pack of young fools."

"Martin." And Bobby Martin watched his father go forward. "Overdyke. . . .Percy."   35

"I wish they'd hurry," Mrs. Dunbar said to her older son. "I wish they'd hurry."

"They're almost through," her son said.

"You get ready to run tell Dad," Mrs. Dunbar said.

Mr. Summers called his own name and then stepped forward precisely and selected a slip from the box. Then he called, "Warner."

"Seventy-seventh year I been in the lottery," Old Man Warner said as he went   40
through the crowd. "Seventy-seventh time."

"Watson." The tall boy came awkwardly through the crowd. Someone said, "Don't be nervous, Jack," and Mr. Summers said, "Take your time, son."

"Zanini."

After that, there was a long pause, a breathless pause, until Mr. Summers, holding his slip of paper in the air, said, "All right, fellows." For a minute, no one moved, and then all the slips of paper were opened. Suddenly, all the women began to speak at once, saying, "Who is it?," "Who's got it?," "Is it the Dunbars?," "Is it the Watsons?" Then the voices began to say, "It's Hutchinson. It's Bill," "Bill Hutchinson's got it."

"Go tell your father," Mrs. Dunbar said to her older son.

People began to look around to see the Hutchinsons. Bill Hutchinson was stand-   45
ing quiet, staring down at the paper in his hand. Suddenly, Tessie Hutchinson shouted to Mr. Summers, "You didn't give him time enough to take any paper he wanted. I saw you. It wasn't fair!"

"Be a good sport, Tessie," Mrs. Delacroix called, and Mrs. Graves said, "All of us took the same chance."

"Shut up, Tessie," Bill Hutchinson said.

"Well, everyone," Mr. Summers said, "that was done pretty fast, and now we've got to be hurrying a little more to get done in time." He consulted his next list. "Bill," he said, "you draw for the Hutchinson family. You got any other households in the Hutchinsons?"

"There's Don and Eva," Mrs. Hutchinson yelled. "Make *them* take their chance!"

"Daughters draw with their husbands' families, Tessie," Mr. Summers said gently.   50
"You know that as well as anyone else."

"It wasn't *fair*," Tessie said.

"I guess not, Joe," Bill Hutchinson said regretfully. "My daughter draws with her husband's family, that's only fair. And I've got no other family except the kids."

"Then, as far as drawing for families is concerned, it's you," Mr. Summers said in explanation, "and as far as drawing for households is concerned, that's you, too. Right?"

"Right," Bill Hutchinson said.

"How many kids, Bill?" Mr. Summers asked formally.   55

"Three," Bill Hutchinson said. "There's Bill, Jr., and Nancy, and little Dave. And Tessie and me."

"All right, then," Mr. Summers said. "Harry, you got their tickets back?"

Mr. Graves nodded and held up the slips of paper. "Put them in the box, then," Mr. Summers directed. "Take Bill's and put it in."

"I think we ought to start over," Mrs. Hutchinson said, as quietly as she could. "I tell you it wasn't *fair*. You didn't give him time enough to choose. *Every*body saw that."

Mr. Graves had selected the five slips and put them in the box, and he dropped 60 all the papers but those onto the ground, where the breeze caught them and lifted them off.

"Listen, everybody," Mrs. Hutchinson was saying to the people around her.

"Ready, Bill?" Mr. Summers asked, and Bill Hutchinson, with one quick glance around at his wife and children, nodded.

"Remember," Mr. Summers said, "take the slips and keep them folded until each person has taken one. Harry, you help little Dave." Mr. Graves took the hand of the little boy, who came willingly with him up to the box. "Take a paper out of the box, Davy," Mr. Summers said. Davy put his hand into the box and laughed. "Take just *one* paper," Mr. Summers said. "Harry, you hold it for him." Mr. Graves took the child's hand and removed the folded paper from the tight fist and held it while little Dave stood next to him and looked up at him wonderingly.

"Nancy next," Mr. Summers said. Nancy was twelve, and her school friends breathed heavily as she went forward, switching her skirt, and took a slip daintily from the box. "Bill, Jr.," Mr. Summers said, and Billy, his face red and his feet overlarge, nearly knocked the box over as he got a paper out. "Tessie," Mr. Summers said. She hesitated for a minute, looking around defiantly, and then set her lips and went up to the box. She snatched a paper out and held it behind her.

"Bill," Mr. Summers said, and Bill Hutchinson reached into the box and felt around, 65 bringing his hand out at last with the slip of paper in it.

The crowd was quiet. A girl whispered, "I hope it's not Nancy," and the sound of the whisper reached the edges of the crowd.

"It's not the way it used to be," Old Man Warner said clearly. "People ain't the way they used to be."

"All right," Mr. Summers said. "Open the papers. Harry, you open little Dave's."

Mr. Graves opened the slip of paper and there was a general sigh through the crowd as he held it up and everyone could see that it was blank. Nancy and Bill, Jr., opened theirs at the same time, and both beamed and laughed, turning around to the crowd and holding their slips of paper above their heads.

"Tessie," Mr. Summers said. There was a pause, and then Mr. Summers looked at 70 Bill Hutchinson, and Bill unfolded his paper and showed it. It was blank.

"It's Tessie," Mr. Summers said, and his voice was hushed. "Show us her paper, Bill."

Bill Hutchinson went over to his wife and forced the slip of paper out of her hand. It had a black spot on it, the black spot Mr. Summers had made the night before with the heavy pencil in the coal-company office. Bill Hutchinson held it up, and there was a stir in the crowd.

"All right, folks," Mr. Summers said. "Let's finish quickly."

Although the villagers had forgotten the ritual and lost the original black box, they still remembered to use stones. The pile of stones the boys had made earlier was ready; there were stones on the ground with the blowing scraps of paper that had come out of the box. Mrs. Delacroix selected a stone so large she had to pick it up with both hands and turned to Mrs. Dunbar. "Come on," she said. "Hurry up."

Mrs. Dunbar had small stones in both hands, and she said, gasping for breath, "I 75 can't run at all. You'll have to go ahead and I'll catch up with you."

The children had stones already, and someone gave little Davy Hutchinson a few pebbles.

Tessie Hutchinson was in the center of a cleared space by now, and she held her hands out desperately as the villagers moved in on her. "It isn't fair," she said. A stone hit her on the side of the head.

Old Man Warner was saying, "Come on, come on, everyone." Steve Adams was in the front of the crowd of villagers, with Mrs. Graves beside him.

"It isn't fair, it isn't right," Mrs. Hutchinson screamed, and then they were upon her.

Source: Reprinted by permission of Farrar, Straus and Giroux: "The Lottery" from THE LOTTERY by Shirley Jackson. Copyright © 1948, 1949 by Shirley Jackson. Copyright renewed 1976, 1977 by Laurence Hyman, Barry Hyman, Mrs. Sarah Webster and Mrs. Joanne Schnurer.

Critical Thinking Topics

1. When Tessie finds out the Hutchinson family will have to draw in the final round of the lottery, she complains that this is unfair because, she says, her husband was not given enough time to draw whichever slip of paper he wanted. Then she suggests that her daughter and son-in-law should be counted among the Hutchinson clan. Were you surprised by this? Why does Tessie want to have her daughter and son-in-law included among the Hutchinsons? What truths about her character does her behavior reveal?

2. Do you think that all the villagers are firm believers in the lottery? If they are not, why do they participate in something they might otherwise deplore—killing a neighbor? How does this story reflect the themes of peer pressure and hypocrisy?

Writing Topics

1. When Old Man Warner complains that the younger members of some villages are considering doing away with lotteries, he refers to them as "a pack of young fools." How do you think this compares to the modern-day generation gap? In what ways do people today clash generationally and over what issues?

2. Think of a community—not your own—that observes a particular custom, festival, or celebration. Research the history of the observance: How did it start? Why does it continue? In what ways does it reflect the identity of the community and the beliefs of its people? In what ways is the observance similar to or different from observances you have experienced in your own community?

6.7 Louise Erdrich, The Red Convertible (1984)

Lyman Lamartine

I was the first one to drive a convertible on my reservation. And of course it was red, a red Olds. I owned that car along with my brother Henry Junior. We owned it together until his boots filled with water on a windy night and he bought out my share. Now Henry owns the whole car, and his youngest brother Lyman (that's myself), Lyman walks everywhere he goes.

How did I earn enough money to buy my share in the first place? My own talent was I could always make money. I had a touch for it, unusual in a Chippewa. From the first I was different that way, and everyone recognized it. I was the only kid they let in the American Legion Hall to shine shoes, for example, and one Christmas I sold spiritual bouquets for the mission door to door. The nuns let me keep a percentage. Once

I started, it seemed the more money I made the easier the money came. Everyone encouraged it. When I was fifteen I got a job washing dishes at the Joliet Cafe, and that was where my first big break happened.

It wasn't long before I was promoted to busing tables, and then the short-order cook quit and I was hired to take her place. No sooner than you know it I was managing the Joliet. The rest is history. I went on managing. I soon became part owner, and of course there was no stopping me then. It wasn't long before the whole thing was mine.

After I'd owned the Joliet for one year, it blew over in the worst tornado ever seen around here. The whole operation was smashed to bits. A total loss. The fryalator was up in a tree, the grill torn in half like it was paper. I was only sixteen. I had it all in my mother's name, and I lost it quick, but before I lost it I had every one of my relatives, and their relatives, to dinner, and I also bought that red Olds I mentioned, along with Henry.

The first time we saw it! I'll tell you when we first saw it. We had gotten a ride to   5
Winnipeg, and both of us had money. Don't ask me why, because we never mentioned a car or anything, we just had all our money. Mine was cash, a big bankroll from the Joliet's insurance. Henry had two checks—a week's extra pay for being laid off, and his regular check from the Jewel Bearing Plant.

We were walking down Portage anyway, seeing the sights, when we saw it. There it was, parked, large as life. Really as *if* it was alive. I thought of the word *repose,* because the car wasn't simply stopped, parked, or whatever. That car reposed, calm and gleaming, a for sale sign in its left front window. Then, before we had thought it over at all, the car belonged to us and our pockets were empty. We had just enough money for gas back home.

We went places in that car, me and Henry. We took off driving all one whole summer. We started off toward the Little Knife River and Mandaree in Fort Berthold and then we found ourselves down in Wakpala somehow, and then suddenly we were over in Montana on the Rocky Boy, and yet the summer was not even half over. Some people hang on to details when they travel, but we didn't let them bother us and just lived our everyday lives here to there.

I do remember this place with willows. I remember I laid under those trees and it was comfortable. So comfortable. The branches bent down all around me like a tent or a stable. And quiet, it was quiet, even though there was a powwow close enough so I could see it going on. The air was not too still, not too windy either. When the dust rises up and hangs in the air around dancers like that, I feel good. Henry was asleep with his arms thrown wide. Later on, he woke up and we started driving again. We were somewhere in Montana, or maybe on the Blood Reserve—it could have been anywhere. Anyway it was where we met the girl.

All her hair was in buns around her ears, that's the first thing I noticed about her. She was posed alongside the road with her arm out, so we stopped. That girl was short, so short her lumber shirt looked comical on her, like a nightgown. She had jeans on and fancy moccasins and she carried a little suitcase.

"Hop on in," says Henry. So she climbs in between us.   10

"We'll take you home," I says. "Where do you live?"

"Chicken," she says.

"Where the hell's that?" I ask her.

"Alaska."

"Okay," says Henry, and we drive.   15

We got up there and never wanted to leave. The sun doesn't truly set there in summer, and the night is more a soft dusk. You might doze off, sometimes, but before you know it you're up again, like an animal in nature. You never feel like you have to sleep hard or put away the world. And things would grow up there. One day just dirt or moss, the next day flowers and long grass. The girl's name was Susy. Her family really took to us. They fed us and put us up. We had our own tent to live in by their house, and the kids would be in and out of there all day and night. They couldn't get over me and Henry being brothers, we looked so different. We told them we knew we had the same mother, anyway.

One night Susy came in to visit us. We sat around in the tent talking of this and that. The season was changing. It was getting darker by that time, and the cold was even getting just a little mean. I told her it was time for us to go. She stood up on a chair.

"You never seen my hair," Susy said.

That was true. She was standing on a chair, but still, when she unclipped her buns the hair reached all the way to the ground. Our eyes opened. You couldn't tell how much hair she had when it was rolled up so neatly. Then my brother Henry did something funny. He went up to the chair and said, "Jump on my shoulders." So she did that, and her hair reached down past his waist, and he started twirling, this way and that, so her hair was flung out from side to side.

"I always wondered what it was like to have long pretty hair," Henry says. Well, we   20
laughed. It was a funny sight, the way he did it. The next morning we got up and took leave of those people.

On to greener pastures, as they say. It was down through Spokane and across Idaho then Montana and very soon we were racing the weather right along under the Canadian border through Columbus, Des Lacs, and then were in Bottineau County and soon home. We'd made most of the trip, that summer, without putting up the car hood at all. We got home just in time.

I don't wonder that the army was so glad to get my brother that they turned him into a Marine. He was built like a brick outhouse anyway. We liked to tease him that they really wanted him for his Indian nose. He had a nose big and sharp as a hatchet, like the nose on Red Tomahawk, the Indian who killed Sitting Bull, whose profile is on signs all along the North Dakota highways. Henry went off to training camp, came home once during Christmas, then the next thing you know we got an overseas letter from him. It was 1970, and he said he was stationed up in the northern hill country. Whereabouts I did not know. He wasn't such a hot letter writer, and only got off two before the enemy caught him. I could never keep it straight, which direction those good Vietnam soldiers were from.

I wrote him back several times, even though I didn't know if those letters would get through. I kept him informed all about the car. Most of the time I had it up on blocks in the yard or half taken apart, because that long trip did a hard job on it under the hood.

I always had good luck with numbers, and never worried about the draft myself. I never even had to think about what my number was. But Henry was never lucky in the same way as me. It was at least three years before Henry came home. By then I guess the whole war was solved in the government's mind, but for him it would keep on going. In those years I'd put his car into almost perfect shape. I always thought of it as his car while he was gone, even though when he left he said, "Now it's yours," and threw me his key.

"Thanks for the extra key," I'd said. "I'll put it in your drawer just in case I need it."   25
He laughed.

When he came home, though, Henry was very different, and I'll say this: the change was no good. You could hardly expect him to change for the better, I know. But he was quiet, so quiet, and never comfortable sitting still anywhere but always up and moving around. I thought back to times we'd sat still for whole afternoons, never moving a muscle, just shifting our weight along the ground, talking to whoever sat with us, watching things. He'd always had a joke, then, too, and now you couldn't get him to laugh, or when he did it was more the sound of a man choking, a sound that stopped up the throats of other people around him. They got to leaving him alone most of the time, and I didn't blame them. It was a fact: Henry was jumpy and mean.

I'd bought a color TV set for my mom and the rest of us while Henry was away. Money still came very easy. I was sorry I'd ever bought it though, because of Henry. I was also sorry I'd bought color, because with black-and-white the pictures seem older and farther away. But what are you going to do? He sat in front of it, watching it, and that was the only time he was completely still. But it was the kind of stillness that you see in a rabbit when it freezes and before it will bolt. He was not easy. He sat in his chair gripping the armrests with all his might, as if the chair itself was moving at a high speed and if he let go at all he would rocket forward and maybe crash right through the set.

Once I was in the room watching TV with Henry and I heard his teeth click at something. I looked over, and he'd bitten through his lip. Blood was going down his chin. I tell you right then I wanted to smash that tube to pieces. I went over to it but Henry must have known what I was up to. He rushed from his chair and shoved me out of the way, against the wall. I told myself he didn't know what he was doing.

My mom came in, turned the set off real quiet, and told us she had made something for supper. So we went and sat down. There was still blood going down Henry's chin, but he didn't notice it and no one said anything, even though every time he took a bite of his bread his blood fell onto it until he was eating his own blood mixed in with the food.

While Henry was not around we talked about what was going to happen to him. 30 There were no Indian doctors on the reservation, and my mom couldn't come around to trusting the old man, Moses Pillager, because he courted her long ago and was jealous of her husbands. He might take revenge through her son. We were afraid that if we brought Henry to a regular hospital they would keep him.

"They don't fix them in those places," Mom said; "they just give them drugs."

"We wouldn't get him there in the first place," I agreed, "so let's just forget about it." Then I thought about the car.

Henry had not even looked at the car since he'd gotten home, though like I said, it was in tip-top condition and ready to drive. I thought the car might bring the old Henry back somehow. So I bided my time and waited for my chance to interest him in the vehicle.

One night Henry was off somewhere. I took myself a hammer. I went out to that car 35 and I did a number on its underside. Whacked it up. Bent the tail pipe double. Ripped the muffler loose. By the time I was done with the car it looked worse than any typical Indian car that has been driven all its life on reservation roads, which they always say are like government promises—full of holes. It just about hurt me, I'll tell you that! I threw dirt in the carburetor and I ripped all the electric tape off the seats. I make it look just as beat up as I could. Then I sat back and waited for Henry to find it.

Still, it took him over a month. That was all right, because it was just getting warm enough, not melting, but warm enough to work outside.

"Lyman," he says, walking in one day, "that red car looks like shit."

"Well, it's old," I says. "You got to expect that."

"No way!" says Henry. "That car's a classic! But you went and ran the piss right out of it, Lyman, and you know it don't deserve that. I kept that car in A-one shape. You don't remember. You're too young. But when I left, that car was running like a watch. Now I don't even know if I can get it to start again, let alone get it anywhere near its old condition."

"Well you try," I said, like I was getting mad, "but I say it's a piece of junk."   40

Then I walked out before he could realize I knew he'd strung together more than six words at once.

After that I thought he'd freeze himself to death working on that car. He was out there all day, and at night he rigged up a little lamp, ran a cord out the window, and had himself some light to see by while he worked. He was better than he had been before, but that's still not saying much. It was easier for him to do the things the rest of us did. He ate more slowly and didn't jump up and down during the meal to get this or that or look out the window. I put my hand in the back of the TV set, I admit, and fiddled around with it good, so that it was almost impossible now to get a clear picture. He didn't look at it very often anyway. He was always out with that car or going off to get parts for it. By the time it was really melting outside, he had it fixed.

I had been feeling down in the dumps about Henry around this time. We had always been together before. Henry and Lyman. But he was such a loner now that I didn't know how to take it. So I jumped at the chance one day when Henry seemed friendly. It's not that he smiled or anything. He just said, "Let's take that old shitbox for a spin." Just the way he said it made me think he could be coming around.

We went out to the car. It was spring. The sun was shining very bright. My only sister, Bonita, who was just eleven years old, came out and made us stand together for a picture. Henry leaned his elbow on the red car's windshield, and he took his other arm and put it over my shoulder, very carefully, as though it was heavy for him to lift and he didn't want to bring the weight down all at once.

"Smile," Bonita said, and he did.   45

That picture. I never look at it anymore. A few months ago, I don't know why, I got his picture out and tacked it on the wall. I felt good about Henry at the time, close to him. I felt good having his picture on the wall, until one night when I was looking at television. I was a little drunk and stoned. I looked up at the wall and Henry was staring at me. I don't know what it was, but his smile had changed, or maybe it was gone. All I know is I couldn't stay in the same room with that picture. I was shaking. I got up, closed the door, and went into the kitchen. A little later my friend Ray came over and we both went back into that room. We put the picture in a brown bag, folded the bag over and over tightly, then put it way back in a closet.

I still see that picture now, as if it tugs at me, whenever I pass that closet door. The picture is very clear in my mind. It was so sunny that day Henry had to squint against the glare. Or maybe the camera Bonita held flashed like a mirror, blinding him, before she snapped the picture. My face is right out in the sun, big and round. But he might have drawn back, because the shadows on his face are deep as holes. There are two shadows curved like little hooks around the ends of his smile, as if to frame it and try to keep it there—that one, first smile that looked like it might have hurt his face. He has his field jacket on and the worn-in clothes he'd come back in and kept wearing ever since. After Bonita took the picture, she went into the house and we got into the car. There was a full cooler in the trunk. We started off, east, toward Pembina and the Red River because Henry said he wanted to see the high water.

The trip over there was beautiful. When everything starts changing, drying up, clearing off, you feel like your whole life is starting. Henry felt it, too. The top was down and the car hummed like a top. He'd really put it back in shape, even the tape on the seats was very carefully put down and glued back in layers. It's not that he smiled again or even joked, but his face looked to me as if it was clear, more peaceful. It looked as though he wasn't thinking of anything in particular except the bare fields and wind-breaks and houses we were passing.

The river was high and full of winter trash when we got there. The sun was still out, but it was colder by the river. There were still little clumps of dirty snow here and there on the banks. The water hadn't gone over the banks yet, but it would, you could tell. It was just at its limit, hard swollen, glossy like an old gray scar. We made ourselves a fire, and we sat down and watched the current go. As I watched it I felt something squeez-ing inside me and tightening and trying to let go all at the same time. I knew I was not just feeling it myself; I knew I was feeling what Henry was going through at that moment. Except that I couldn't stand it, the closing and opening. I jumped to my feet. I took Henry by the shoulders and I started shaking him. "Wake up," I says, "wake up, wake up, wake up!" I didn't know what had come over me. I sat down beside him again.

His face was totally white and hard. Then it broke, like stones break all of a sudden   50
when water boils up inside them.

"I know it," he says. "I know it. I can't help it. It's no use."

We start talking. He said he knew what I'd done with the car. It was obvious it had been whacked out of shape and not just neglected. He said he wanted to give the car to me for good now, it was no use. He said he'd fixed it just to give it back and I should take it.

"No way," I says. "I don't want it."

"That's okay," he says, "you take it."

"I don't want it, though," I says back to him, and then to emphasize, just to empha-   55
size, you understand, I touch his shoulder. He slaps my hand off.

"Take that car," he says.

"No," I say. "Make me," I say, and then he grabs my jacket and rips the arm loose. That jacket is a class act, suede with tags and zippers. I push Henry backwards, off the log. He jumps up and bowls me over. We go down in a clinch and come up swinging hard, for all we're worth, with our fists. He socks my jaw so hard I feel like it swings loose. Then I'm at his rib cage and land a good one under his chin so his head snaps back. He's dazzled. He looks at me and I look at him and then his eyes are full of tears and blood and at first I think he's crying. But no, he's laughing. "Ha, ha!" he says. "Ha! Ha! Take good care of it."

"Okay," I says. "Okay, no problem. Ha! Ha!"

I can't help it, and I start laughing, too. My face feels fat and strange, and after a while I get a beer from the cooler in the trunk, and when I hand it to Henry he takes his shirt and wipes my germs off. "Hoof-and-mouth disease," he says. For some reason this cracks me up, and so we're really laughing for a while, and then we drink all the rest of the beers one by one and throw them in the river and see how far, how fast, the cur-rent takes them before they fill up and sink.

"You want to go on back?" I ask after a while. "Maybe we could snag a couple nice   60
Kashpaw girls."

He says nothing. But I can tell his mood is turning again.

"They're all crazy, the girls up here, every damn one of them."

"You're crazy too," I say, to jolly him up. "Crazy Lamartine boys!"

He looks as though he will take this wrong at first. His face twists, then clears, and
he jumps up on his feet. "That's right!" he says. "Crazier'n hell. Crazy Indians!"

I think it's the old Henry again. He throws off his jacket and starts springing his legs   65
up from the knees like a fancy dancer. He's down doing something between a grass
dance and a bunny hop, no kind of dance I ever saw before, but neither has anyone
else on all this green growing earth. He's wild. He wants to pitch whoopee! He's up and
at me and all over. All this time I'm laughing so hard, so hard my belly is getting tied up
in a knot.

"Got to cool me off!" he shouts all of a sudden. Then he runs over to the river and
jumps in.

There's boards and other things in the current. It's so high. No sound comes from
the river after the splash he makes, so I run right over. I look around. It's getting dark. I
see he's halfway across the water already, and I know he didn't swim there but the current took him. It's far. I hear his voice, though, very clearly across it.

"My boots are filling," he says.

He says this in a normal voice, like he just noticed and he doesn't know what to
think of it. Then he's gone. A branch comes by. Another branch. And I go in.

By the time I get out of the river, off the snag I pulled myself onto, the sun is down.   70
I walk back to the car, turn on the high beams, and drive it up the bank. I put it in first
gear and then I take my foot off the clutch. I get out, close the door, and watch it plough
softly into the water. The headlights reach in as they go down, searching, still lighted
even after the water swirls over the back end. I wait. The wires short out. It is all finally
dark. And then there is only the water, the sound of it going and running and going and
running and running.

Source: Erdrich, Louise. "The Red Convertible" from the book LOVE MEDICINE, new and expanded Version by Louise
Erdrich. Copyright © 1984, 1993 by Louise Erdrich. Reprinted by permission of Henry Holt and Company, LLC.

Critical Thinking Topics

1. How would you characterize the brothers' relationship? Do certain aspects
   of their relationship seem related to their Native American heritage, while
   others seem cross-cultural? Explain your response by identifying specific
   images and phrases that support your conclusions.

2. The word "pariah" refers to someone who is despised or rejected, an outcast. When Vietnam veterans returned to American society, some said they
   felt like pariahs. In what way does Henry demonstrate this attitude?

3. At the Red River, Henry and Lyman fight over their car, then laugh and
   joke—"pitch whoopee." When Lyman says, "Crazy Lamartine boys!" Henry
   responds, "Crazier'n hell. Crazy Indians!" Is Henry crazy? Does his final act
   suggest that he is in control or out of control? Use evidence from the story to
   discuss how you arrived at your claim judging whether or not Henry is crazy.

Writing Topics

1. Write a three-part response to the story's closing paragraph:
   • a creative reading response
   • a critical reading response
   • a synthesis of the two responses
2. Do you know a veteran of World War II, the Korean War, the Vietnam War, the wars in the Persian Gulf, or the wars in Iraq or Afghanistan? If so, interview him or her to learn about his or her wartime and postwar experiences; if not, do some research to find a veteran's first-person account of such experiences. Also, contact your local veterans' affairs office to find out about benefits for veterans who have sustained disabilities. Do you think wounded and/or disabled wounded veterans receive adequate treatment and fair compensation?

6.8 Rick Bass, Antlers (1990)

Halloween brings us all closer, in the valley. The Halloween party at the saloon is when we all, for the first time since last winter, realize why we are all up here—all three dozen of us—living in this cold, blue valley. Sometimes there are a few tourists through the valley in the high green grasses of summer, and the valley is opened up a little. People slip in and out of it; it's almost a regular place. But in October the snows come, and it closes down. It becomes our valley again, and the tourists and less hardy-of-heart people leave.

Everyone who's up here is here because of the silence. It is eternity up here. Some are on the run, and others are looking for something; some are incapable of living in a city, among people, while others simply love the wildness of new untouched country. But our lives are all close enough, our feelings, that when winter comes in October there's a feeling like a sigh, a sigh after the great full meal of summer, and at the Halloween party everyone shows up, and we don't bother with costumes because we all know one another so well, if not through direct contact then through word of mouth—what Dick said Becky said about Don, and so forth—knowing more in this manner, sometimes. And instead of costumes, all we do is strap horns on our heads—moose antlers, or deer antlers, or even the high throwback of elk antlers—and we have a big potluck supper and get drunk as hell, even those of us who do not drink, that one night a year, and we dance all night long, putting nickels in the jukebox (Elvis, the Doors, Marty Robbins) and clomping around in the bar as if it were a dance floor, tables and stools set outside in the falling snow to make room, and the men and women bang their antlers against each other in mock battle. Then around two or three in the morning we all drive home, or ski home, or snowshoe home, or ride back on horses—however we got to the party is how we'll return.

It usually snows big on Halloween—a foot, a foot and a half. Sometimes whoever drove down to the saloon will give the skiers a ride home by fastening a long rope to the back bumper, and we skiers will hold on to that rope, still wearing our antlers, too drunk or tired to take them off, and we'll ride home that way, being pulled up the hill by the truck, gliding silently over the road's hard ice across the new snow, our heads tucked against the wind, against the falling snow...

Like children being let off at a bus stop, we'll let go of the rope when the truck passes our dark cabins. It would be nice to leave a lantern burning in the window, for coming home, but you don't ever go to sleep or leave with a lantern lit like that—it can burn your cabin down in the night and leave you in the middle of winter with nothing. We come home to dark houses, all of us. The antlers feel natural after having been up there for so long. Sometimes we bump them against the door going in and knock them off. We wear them only once a year: only once a year do we become the hunted.

We believe in this small place, this valley. Many of us have come here from other   5
places and have been running all our lives from other things, and I think that everyone who is up here has decided not to run anymore.

There is a woman up here, Suzie, who has moved through the valley with a regularity, a rhythm, that is all her own and has nothing to do with our—the men's—pleadings or desires. Over the years, Suzie has been with all the men in this valley. All, that is, except Randy. She won't have anything to do with Randy. He still wishes very much for his chance, but because he is a bowhunter—he uses a strong compound bow and wicked, heart-gleaming aluminum arrows with a whole spindle of razor blades at one end for the killing point—she will have nothing to do with him.

Sometimes I wanted to defend Randy, even though I strongly disagreed with bowhunting. Bowhunting, it seemed to me, was wrong—but Randy was just Randy, no better or worse than any of the rest of us who had dated Suzie. Bowhunting was just something he did, something he couldn't help; I didn't see why she had to take it so personally.

Wolves eviscerate their prey; it's a hard life. Dead's dead, isn't it? And isn't pain the same everywhere?

I would say that Suzie's boyfriends lasted, on the average, three months. Nobody ever left her. Even the most sworn bachelors among us enjoyed her company—she worked at the bar every evening—and it was always Suzie who left the men, who left us, though I thought it was odd and wonderful that she never left the valley.

Suzie has sandy-red hair, high cold cheeks, and fury-blue eyes; she is short, no   10
taller than anyone's shoulders. But because most of us had known her for so long—and this is what the other men had told me after she'd left them—it was fun, and even stirring, but it wasn't really that *great*. There wasn't a lot of heat in it for most of them—not the dizzying, lost feeling kind you get sometimes when you meet someone for the first time, or even glimpse them in passing, never to meet. . . . That kind of heat was missing, said most of the men, and it was just comfortable, they said—*comfortable*.

When it was my turn to date Suzie, I'm proud to say that we stayed together for five months—longer than she's ever stayed with anyone—long enough for people to talk, and to kid her about it.

Our dates were simple enough; we'd go for long drives to the tops of snowy mountains and watch the valley. We'd drive into town, too, seventy miles away down a one-lane, rutted, cliff-hanging road, just for dinner and a movie. I could see how there was not heat and wild romance in it for some of the other men, but for me it was warm, and *right*, while it lasted.

When she left, I did not think I would ever eat again, drink again. It felt like my heart had been torn from my chest, like my lungs were on fire; every breath burned. I couldn't understand why she had to leave; I didn't know why she had to do that to me. I'd known it was coming, someday, but still it hurt. But I got over it; I lived. She's lovely. She's a nice girl. For a long time, I wished she would date Randy.

Besides being a bowhunter, Randy was a carpenter. He did odd jobs for people in the valley, usually fixing up old cabins rather than ever building any new ones. He kept his own schedule, and stopped working entirely in the fall so that he could hunt to his heart's content. He would roam the valley for days, exploring all of the wildest places, going all over the valley. He had hunted everywhere, had seen everything in the valley. We all hunted in the fall—grouse, deer, elk, though we left the moose and bear alone because they were rarer and we liked seeing them—but none of us were clever or stealthy enough to bowhunt. You had to get so close to the animal, with a bow.

Suzie didn't like any form of hunting. "That's what cattle are for," she'd say. "Cattle are like city people. Cattle expect, even deserve, what they've got coming. But wild animals are different. Wild animals enjoy life. They live in the woods on purpose. It's cruel to go in after them and kill them. It's cruel."   15

We'd all hoo-rah her and order more beers, and she wouldn't get angry, then— she'd understand that it was just what everyone did up here, the men and the women alike, that we loved the animals, loved seeing them, but that for one or two months out of the year we loved to hunt them. She couldn't understand it, but she knew that was how it was.

Randy was so good at what he did that we were jealous, and we admired him for it, tipped our hats to his talent. He could crawl right up to within thirty yards of wild animals when they were feeding, or he could sit so still that they would walk right past him. And he was good with his bow—he was deadly. The animal he shot would run a short way with the arrow stuck through it. An arrow wouldn't kill the way a bullet did, and the animal always ran at least a little way before dying—bleeding to death, or dying from trauma—and no one liked for that to happen, but the blood trail was easy to follow, especially in the snow. There was nothing that could be done about it; that was just the way bowhunting was. The men looked at it as being much fairer than hunting with a rifle, because you had to get so close to the animal to get a good shot—thirty-five, forty yards was the farthest away you could be—but Suzie didn't see it that way.

She would serve Randy his drinks and would chat with him, would be polite, but her face was a mask, her smiles were stiff.

What Randy did to try to gain Suzie's favor was to build her things. Davey, the bartender—the man she was dating that summer—didn't really mind. It wasn't as if there were any threat of Randy stealing her away, and besides, he liked the objects Randy built her; and, too, I think it might have seemed to add just the smallest bit of that white heat to Davey and Suzie's relationship—though I can't say that for sure.

Randy built her a porch swing out of bright larch wood and stained it with tung   20 oil. It was as pretty as a new truck; he brought it up to her at the bar one night, having spent a week sanding it and getting it just right. We all gathered around, admiring it, running our hands over its smoothness. Suzie smiled a little—a polite smile, which was, in a way, worse than if she had looked angry—and said nothing, not even "thank you," and she and Davey took it home in the back of Davey's truck. This was in June.

Randy built her other things, too—small things, things she could fit on her dresser: a little mahogany box for her earrings, of which she had several pairs, and a walking stick with a deer's antler for the grip. She said she did not want the walking stick, but would take the earring box.

Some nights I would lie awake in my cabin and think about how Suzie was with Davey, and then I would feel sorry for Davey, because she would be leaving him eventually. I'd lie there on my side and look out my bedroom window at the northern lights flashing above the snowy mountains, and their strange light would be reflected on the river that ran past my cabin, so that the light seemed to be coming from beneath the water as well. On nights like those I'd feel like my heart was never going to heal—in fact, I was certain that it never would. I didn't love Suzie anymore—didn't think I did, anyway—but I wanted to love someone, and to be loved. Life, on those nights, seemed shorter than anything in the world, and so important, so precious, that it terrified me.

Perhaps Suzie was right about the bowhunting, and about all hunters.

In the evenings, back when we'd been together, Suzie and I would sit out on the back porch after she got in from work—still plenty of daylight left, the sun not setting until very late—and we'd watch large herds of deer, their antlers covered with summer velvet, wade out into the cool shadows of the river to bathe, like ladies. The sun would finally set, and those deer bodies would take on the dark shapes of the shadows, still out in the shallows of the rapids, splashing and bathing. Later, well into the night, Suzie and I would sit in the same chair, wrapped up in a single blanket, and nap. Shooting stars would shriek and howl over the mountains as if taunting us.

This past July, Randy, who lives along a field up on the side of the mountains at   25
the north end of the valley up against the brief foothills, began practicing: standing out in the field at various marked distances—ten, twenty, thirty, forty yards—and shooting arrow after arrow into the bull's-eye target that was stapled to bales of hay. It was unusual to drive past in July and not see him out there in the field, practicing—even in the middle of the day, shirtless, perspiring, his cheeks flushed. He lived by himself, and there was probably nothing else to do. The bowhunting season began in late August, months before the regular gun season.

Too many people up here, I think, just get comfortable and lazy and lose their real passions—for whatever it is they used to get excited about. I've been up here only a few years, so maybe I have no right to say that, but it's what I feel.

It made Suzie furious to see Randy out practicing like that. She circulated a petition in the valley, requesting that bowhunting be banned.

But we—the other men, the other hunters—would have been doing the same thing, hunting the giant elk with bows for the thrill of it, luring them in with calls and rattles, right in to us, hidden in the bushes, the bulls wanting to fight, squealing madly and rushing in, tearing at trees and brush with their great dark antlers. If we could have gotten them in that close before killing them, we would have, and it would be a thing we would remember longer than any other thing. . . .

We just weren't good enough. We couldn't sign Suzie's petition. Not even Davey could sign it.

"It's wrong," she'd say.   30

"It's personal choice," Davey would say. "If you use the meat, and apologize to the spirit right before you do it and right after—if you give thanks—it's okay. It's a man's choice, honey," he'd say—and if there was one thing Suzie hated, it was that man-woman stuff.

"He's trying to prove something," she said.

"He's just doing something he cares about, dear," Davey said.

"He's trying to prove his manhood—to me, to all of us," she said. "He's dangerous."

"No," said Davey, "that's not it. He likes it and hates it both. It fascinates him is all."   35

"It's sick," Suzie said. "He's dangerous."

I could see that Suzie would not be with Davey much longer. She moved from man to man almost with the seasons. There was a wildness, a flightiness, about her—some sort of combination of strength and terror—that made her desirable. To me, anyway, though I can only guess for the others.

I'd been out bowhunting with Randy once to see how it was done. I saw him shoot an elk, a huge bull, and I saw the arrow go in behind the bull's shoulder where the heart and lungs were hidden—and I saw, too, the way the bull looked around in wild-eyed surprise, and then went galloping off through the timber, seemingly uninjured, running hard. For a long time Randy and I sat there, listening to the clackclack of the aluminum arrow banging against trees as the elk ran away with it.

"We sit and wait," Randy said. "We just wait." He was confident and did not seem at all shaky, though I was. It was a record bull, a beautiful bull. We sat there and waited. I did not believe we would ever see that bull again. I studied Randy's cool face, tiger-striped and frightening with the camouflage painted on it, and he seemed so cold, so icy.

After a couple of hours we got up and began to follow the blood trail. There wasn't   40 much of it at all, at first—just a drop or two, drops in the dry leaves, already turning brown and cracking, drops that I would never have seen—but after about a quarter of a mile, farther down the hill, we began to see more of it, until it looked as if entire buckets of blood had been lost. We found two places where the bull had lain down beneath a tree to die, but had then gotten up and moved on again. We found him by the creek, a half mile away, down in the shadows, but with his huge antlers rising into a patch of sun and gleaming. He looked like a monster from another world; even after his death, he looked noble. The creek made a beautiful trickling sound. It was very quiet. But as we got closer, as large as he was, the bull looked like someone's pet. He looked friendly. The green-and-black arrow sticking out of him looked as if it had hurt his feelings more than anything; it did not look as if such a small arrow could kill such a large and strong animal.

We sat down beside the elk and admired him, studied him. Randy, who because of the scent did not smoke during the hunting season—not until he had his elk—pulled out a pack of cigarettes, shook one out, and lit it.

"I'm not sure why I do it," he admitted, reading my mind. "I feel kind of bad about it each time I see one like this, but I keep doing it." He shrugged. I listened to the sound of the creek. "I know it's cruel, but I can't help it. I have to do it," he said.

"What do you think it must feel like?" Suzie had asked me at the bar. "What do you think it must feel like to run around with an arrow in your heart, knowing you're going to die for it?" She was furious and righteous, red-faced, and I told her I didn't know. I paid for my drink and left, confused because she was right. The animal had to be feeling pain—serious, continuous pain. It was just the way it was.

In July, Suzie left Davey, as I'd predicted. It was gentle and kind—amicable—and we all had a party down at the saloon to celebrate. We roasted a whole deer that Holger Jennings had hit with his truck the night before while coming back from town with supplies, and we stayed out in front of the saloon and ate steaming fresh meat on paper plates with barbecue sauce and crisp apples from Idaho, and watched the lazy little river that followed the road that ran through town. We didn't dance or play loud music or anything—it was too mellow. There were children and dogs. This was back when

Don Terlinde was still alive, and he played his accordion: a sad, sweet sound. We drank beer and told stories.

All this time, I'd been uncertain about whether it was right or wrong to hunt if you   45 used the meat and said those prayers. And I'm still not entirely convinced, one way or the other. But I do have a better picture of what it's like now to be the elk or deer. And I understand Suzie a little better, too: I no longer think of her as cruel for hurting Randy's proud heart, for singling out, among all the other men in the valley, only Randy to shun, to avoid.

She wasn't cruel. She was just frightened. Fright—sometimes plain fright, even more than terror—is every bit as bad as pain, and maybe worse.

What I am getting at is that Suzie went home with me that night after the party; she had made her rounds through the men of the valley, had sampled them all (except for Randy and a few of the more ancient ones), and now she was choosing to come back to me.

"I've got to go somewhere," she said. "I hate being alone. I can't stand to be alone." She slipped her hand in mine as we were walking home. Randy was still sitting on the picnic table with Davey when we left, eating slices of venison. The sun still hadn't quite set. Ducks flew down the river.

"I guess that's as close to 'I love you' as I'll get," I said.

"I'm serious," she said, twisting my hand. "You don't understand. It's horrible. I   50 can't stand it. It's not like other people's loneliness. It's worse."

"Why?" I asked.

"No reason," Suzie said. "I'm just scared, is all. Jumpy. Spooky. Some people are that way. I can't help it."

"It's okay," I said.

We walked down the road like that, holding hands, walking slowly in the dusk. It was about three miles down the gravel road to my cabin. Suzie knew the way. We heard owls as we walked along the river and saw lots of deer. Once, for no reason, I turned and looked back, but I saw nothing, saw no one.

If Randy can have such white-hot passion for a thing—bowhunting—he can,   55 I understand full well, have just as much heat in his hate. It spooks me the way he doesn't bring Suzie presents anymore in the old, hopeful way. The flat looks he gives me could mean anything: they rattle me.

It's like I can't see him.

Sometimes I'm afraid to go into the woods.

But I do anyway. I go hunting in the fall and cut wood in the fall and winter, fish in the spring, and go for walks in the summer, walks and drives up to the tops of the high snowy mountains—and there are times when I feel someone or something is just behind me, following at a distance, and I'll turn around, frightened and angry both, and I won't see anything, but still, later on into the walk, I'll feel it again.

But I feel other things, too: I feel my happiness with Suzie. I feel the sun on my face and on my shoulders. I like the way we sit on the porch again, the way we used to, with drinks in hand, and watch the end of day, watch the deer come slipping down into the river.

I'm frightened, but it feels delicious.   60

This year at the Halloween party, it dumped on us; it began snowing the day before and continued on through the night and all through Halloween day and then Halloween night, snowing harder than ever. The roof over the saloon groaned that night under the load of new snow, but we had the party anyway and kept dancing, all of us leaping around and waltzing, drinking, proposing toasts, and armwrestling, then leaping up again and dancing some more, with all the antlers from all the animals in the valley strapped to our heads—everyone. It looked pagan. We all whooped and danced. Davey and Suzie danced in each other's arms, swirled and pirouetted; she was so light and so free, and I watched them and grinned. Randy sat on the porch and drank beers and watched, too, and smiled. It was a polite smile.

All of the rest of us drank and stomped around. We shook our heads at each other and pretended we were deer, pretended we were elk.

We ran out of beer around three in the morning, and we all started gathering up our skis, rounding up rides, people with trucks who could take us home. The rumble of trucks being warmed up began, and the beams of headlights crisscrossed the road in all directions, showing us just how hard it really was snowing. The flakes were as large as the biggest goose feathers. Because Randy and I lived up the same road, Davey drove us home, and Suzie took hold of the tow rope and skied with us.

Davey drove slowly because it was hard to see the road in such a storm.

Suzie had had a lot to drink—we all had—and she held on to the rope with both   65 hands, her deer antlers slightly askew, and she began to ask Randy some questions about his hunting—not razzing him, as I thought she would, but simply questioning him—things she'd been wondering for a long time, I supposed, but had been too angry to ask. We watched the brake lights in front of us, watched the snow spiraling into our faces and concentrated on holding on to the rope. As usual, we all seemed to have forgotten the antlers that were on our heads.

"What's it like?" Suzie kept wanting to know. "I mean, what's it *really* like?"

We were sliding through the night, holding on to the rope, being pulled through the night. The snow was striking our faces, caking our eyebrows, and it was so cold that it was hard to speak.

"You're a real asshole, you know?" Suzie said, when Randy wouldn't answer. "You're too cold-blooded for me," she said. "You scare me, mister."

Randy just stared straight ahead, his face hard and flat and blank, and he held on to the rope.

I'd had way too much to drink. We all had. We slid over some rough spots in   70 the road.

"Suzie, honey," I started to say—I have no idea what I was going to say after that—something to defend Randy, I think—but then I stopped, because Randy turned and looked at me, for just a second, with fury, terrible fury, which I could *feel* as well as see, even in my drunkenness. But then the mask, the polite mask, came back down over him, and we continued down the road in silence, the antlers on our heads bobbing and weaving, a fine target for anyone who might not have understood that we weren't wild animals.

Source: Reprinted by permission of the author.

Critical Thinking Topics

1. The narrator speaks for himself as an individual, and he also speaks for the inhabitants of the valley: "We believe in this small place, this valley" (par. 5). Describe the identity he creates for the community. What elements, external

and internal, create a bond among the individuals? Use details from the story to elaborate.

2. Randy declines to defend or explain his choice to bowhunt. Based on what you know about Randy, why do you think he bowhunts?

3. Why is Suzie frightened? What does the narrator mean when he says, "I'm frightened, but it feels delicious" (par. 60)?

4. Explain the significance of the short story's title. Consider the narrator's depiction of the annual Halloween party costume: "The antlers feel natural after having been up there for so long....We wear them only once a year: only once a year do we become the hunted" (par. 4). Also, beginning with paragraph 61, reread the story's closing scene; discuss the significance of that scene, focusing in particular on the images in the last sentence.

Writing Topic

As this short story illustrates, the practice of hunting can stir up passionate emotions. Some people argue that, regardless of the means or ends, it is unethical to kill a wild animal. Others, however, contend that hunting can be practiced in ethically and responsible ways, and, they note, hunters often are staunch supporters of efforts to preserve natural habitats. Identify and evaluate the different viewpoints about the ethics of hunting represented in the short story. Also, consider personal experience or observations and other examples of hunting. Based on your analysis of this story, as well as your own experience, observation, or ideas from other sources, develop and support an argument on the issue of whether hunting is ethical, including at least one concession and one refutation.

6.9 Randall Kenan, The Foundations of the Earth (1992)

I

Of course they didn't pay it any mind at first: just a tractor—one of the most natural things in the world to see in a field—kicking dust up into the afternoon sky and slowly toddling off the road into a soybean field. And fields surrounded Mrs. Maggie Mac-Gowan Williams's house, giving the impression that her lawn stretched on and on until it dropped off into the woods far by the way. Sometimes she was certain she could actually see the earth's curve—not merely the bend of the small hill on which her house sat but the great slope of the sphere, the way scientists explained it in books, a monstrous globe floating in a cold nothingness. She would sometimes sit by herself on the patio late of an evening, in the same chair she was sitting in now, sip from her Coca-Cola, and think about how big the earth must be to seem flat to the eye.

She wished she were alone now. It was Sunday.

"Now I wonder what that man is doing with a tractor out there today?"

They sat on Maggie's patio, reclined in that after-Sunday-dinner way—Maggie; the Right Reverend Hezekiah Barden, round and pompous as ever; Henrietta Fuchee, the prim and priggish music teacher and president of the First Baptist Church Auxiliary Council; Emma Lewis, Maggie's sometimes housekeeper; and Gabriel, Mrs. Maggie

Williams's young, white, special guest—all looking out lazily into the early summer, watching the sun begin its slow downward arc, feeling the baked ham and the candied sweet potatoes and the fried chicken with the collard greens and green beans and beets settle in their bellies, talking shallow and pleasant talk, and sipping their Coca-Colas and bitter lemonade.

"Don't they realize it's Sunday?" Reverend Barden leaned back in his chair and   5
tugged at his suspenders thoughtfully, eyeing the tractor as it turned into another row. He reached for a sweating glass of lemonade, his red bow tie afire in the penultimate beams of the day.

"I...I don't understand. What's wrong?" Maggie could see her other guests watching Gabriel intently, trying to discern why on earth he was present at Maggie Mac-Gowan Williams's table.

"What you mean, what's wrong?" The Reverend Barden leaned forward and narrowed his eyes at the young man. "What's wrong is: it's Sunday."

"So? I don't..." Gabriel himself now looked embarrassed, glancing to Maggie, who wanted to save him but could not.

"'So?' 'So?'" Leaning toward Gabriel and narrowing his eyes, Barden asked: "You're not from a churchgoing family, are you?"

"Well, no. Today was my first time in...Oh, probably ten years."   10

"Uh-huh." Barden corrected his posture, as if to say he pitied Gabriel's being an infidel but had the patience to instruct him. "Now you see, the Lord has declared Sunday as His day. It's holy. 'Six days shalt thou labor and do all thy work: but the seventh day is the sabbath of the Lord thy God: in it thou shalt not do any work, thou, nor thy son, nor thy daughter, thy manservant, nor thy maidservant, nor thy cattle, nor thy stranger that is within thy gates: for in six days the Lord made heaven and earth, the sea, and all that in them is, and rested the seventh day: wherefore, the Lord blessed the sabbath day, and hallowed it.' Exodus. Chapter twenty, verses nine and ten."

"Amen." Henrietta closed her eyes and rocked.

"Hez." Maggie inclined her head a bit to entreat the good Reverend to desist. He gave her an understanding smile, which made her cringe slightly, fearing her gesture might have been mistaken for a sign of intimacy.

"But, Miss Henrietta—" Emma Lewis tapped the tabletop, like a judge in court, changing the subject. "Like I was saying, I believe that Rick on *The Winds of Hope* is going to marry that gal before she gets too big with child, don't you?" Though Emma kept house for Maggie Williams, to Maggie she seemed more like a sister who came three days a week, more to visit than to clean.

"Now go on away from here, Emma." Henrietta did not look up from her empty   15
cake plate, her glasses hanging on top of her sagging breasts from a silver chain. "Talking about that worldly foolishness on TV. You know I don't pay that mess any attention." She did not want the Reverend to know that she secretly watched afternoon soap operas, just like Emma and all the other women in the congregation. Usually she gossiped to beat the band about this rich heifer and that handsome hunk whenever she found a fellow TV-gazer. Buck-toothed hypocrite, Maggie thought. She knew the truth: Henrietta, herself a widow now on ten years, was sweet on the widower minister, who in turn, alas, had his eye on Maggie.

"Now, Miss Henrietta, we was talking about it t'other day. Don't you think he's apt to marry her soon?" Emma's tone was insistent.

"I *don't know,* Emma." Visibly agitated, Henrietta donned her glasses and looked into the fields. "I wonder who that is anyhow?"

Annoyed by Henrietta's rebuff, Emma stood and began to collect the few remaining dishes. Her purple-and-yellow floral print dress hugged her ample hips. "It's that ole Morton Henry that Miss Maggie leases that piece of land to." She walked toward the door, into the house. "He ain't no God-fearing man."

"Well, that's plain to see." The Reverend glanced over to Maggie. She shrugged.

They are ignoring Gabriel, Maggie thought. She had invited them to dinner after   20
church services thinking it would be pleasant for Gabriel to meet other people in Tims Creek. But generally they chose not to see him, and when they did it was with illconcealed scorn or petty curiosity or annoyance. At first the conversation seemed civil enough. But the ice was never truly broken, questions still buzzed around the talk like horseflies, Maggie could tell. "Where you from?" Henrietta had asked. "What's your line of work?" Barden had asked. While Gabriel sat there with a look on his face somewhere between peace and pain. But Maggie refused to believe she had made a mistake. At this stage of her life she depended on no one for anything, and she was certainly not dependent on the approval of these self-important fools.

She had been steeled by anxiety when she picked Gabriel up at the airport that Friday night. But as she caught sight of him stepping from the jet and greeted him, asking about the weather in Boston; and after she had ushered him to her car and watched him slide in, seeming quite at home; though it still felt awkward, she thought: I'm doing the right thing.

II

"Well, thank you for inviting me, Mrs. Williams. But I don't understand...Is something wrong?"

"*Wrong*? No, nothing's wrong, Gabriel. I just thought it'd be good to see you. Sit and talk to you. We didn't have much time at the funeral."

"Gee...I—"

"You don't want to make an old woman sad, now do you?"   25

"Well, Mrs. Williams, if you put it like that, how can I refuse?"

"Weekend after next then?"

There was a pause in which she heard muted voices in the wire.

"Okay."

After she hung up the phone and sat down in her favorite chair in the den, she   30
heaved a momentous sigh. Well, she had done it. At last. The weight of uncertainty would be lifted. She could confront him face to face. She wanted to know about her grandboy, and Gabriel was the only one who could tell her what she wanted to know. It was that simple. Surely, he realized what this invitation meant. She leaned back looking out the big picture window onto the tops of the brilliantly blooming crepe myrtle trees in the yard, listening to the grandfather clock mark the time.

III

Her grandson's funeral had been six months ago, but it seemed much longer. Perhaps the fact that Edward had been gone away from home so long without seeing her, combined with the weeks and days and hours and minutes she had spent trying not to think about him and all the craziness that had surrounded his death, somehow lengthened the time.

At first she chose to ignore it, the strange and bitter sadness that seemed to have overtaken her every waking moment. She went about her daily life as she had done for thirty-odd years, overseeing her stores, her land, her money; buying groceries, paying bills, shopping, shopping; going to church and talking to her few good living friends and the few silly fools she was obliged to suffer. But all day, dusk to dawn, and especially at night, she had what the field-workers called "a monkey on your back," when the sun beats down so hot it makes you delirious; but her monkey chilled and angered her, born not of the sun but of a profound loneliness, an oppressive emptiness, a stabbing guilt. Sometimes she even wished she were a drinking woman.

The depression had come with the death of Edward, though its roots reached farther back, to the time he seemed to have vanished. There had been so many years of asking other members of the family: Have you heard from him? Have you seen him? So many years of only a Christmas card or birthday card a few days early, or a cryptic, taciturn phone call on Sunday mornings, and then no calls at all. At some point she realized she had no idea where he was or how to get in touch with him. Mysteriously, he would drop a line to his half-sister, Clarissa, or drop a card without a return address. He was gone. Inevitably, she had to ask: Had she done something evil to the boy to drive him away? Had she tried too hard to make sure he became nothing like his father and grandfather? I was as good a mother as a woman can claim to be, she thought: from the cradle on he had all the material things he needed, and he certainly didn't want for attention, for care; and I trained him proper, he was a well-mannered and upright young fellow when he left here for college. Oh, I was proud of that boy, winning a scholarship to Boston University. Tall, handsome like his granddad. He'd make somebody a good...

So she continued picking out culprits: school, the cold North, strange people, strange ideas. But now in her crystalline hindsight she could lay no blame on anyone but Edward. And the more she remembered battles with the mumps and the measles and long division and taunts from his schoolmates, the more she became aware of her true anger. He owes me respect, damn it. The least he can do is keep in touch. Is that so much to ask?

But before she could make up her mind to find him and confront him with her fury, before she could cuss him out good and call him an ungrateful, no-account bastard just like his father, a truck would have the heartless audacity to skid into her grandchild's car one rainy night in Springfield and end his life at twenty-seven, taking that opportunity away from her forever. When they told her of his death she cursed her weakness. Begging God for another chance. But instead He gave her something she had never imagined. 35

Clarissa was the one to finally tell her. "Grandma," she had said, "Edward's been living with another man all these years."

"So?"

"No, Grandma. Like man and wife."

Maggie had never before been so paralyzed by news. One question answered, only to be replaced by a multitude. Gabriel had come with the body, like an interpreter for the dead. They had been living together in Boston, where Edward worked in a book-store. He came, head bowed, rheumy-eyed, exhausted. He gave her no explanation; nor had she asked him for any, for he displayed the truth in his vacant and humble glare and had nothing to offer but the penurious tribute of his trembling hands. Which was more than she wanted.

In her world she had been expected to be tearless, patient, comforting to other   40
members of the family; folk were meant to sit back and say, "Lord, ain't she taking it
well. I don't think I could be so calm if my grandboy had've died so young." Magisterially
she had done her duty; she had taken it all in stride. But her world began to hopelessly
unravel that summer night at the wake in the Raymond Brown Funeral Home, among
the many somber-bright flower arrangements, the fluorescent lights, and the gleaming
bronze casket, when Gabriel tried to tell her how sorry he was . . . How dare he? This
pathetic, stumbling, poor trashy white boy, to throw his sinful lust for her grandbaby in
her face, as if to bury a grandchild weren't bad enough. Now this abomination had to
be flaunted. — Sorry, indeed! The nerve! Who the hell did he think he was to parade their
shame about?

Her anger was burning so intensely that she knew if she didn't get out she would
tear his heart from his chest, his eyes from their sockets, his testicles from their sac.
With great haste she took her leave, brushing off the funeral director and her brother's
wives and husband's brothers — they all probably thinking her overcome with grief
rather than anger — and had Clarissa drive her home. When she got to the house she
filled a tub with water as hot as she could stand it and a handful of bath oil beads, and
slipped in, praying her hatred would mingle with the mist and evaporate, leaving her
at least sane.

Next, sleep. Healing sleep, soothing sleep, sleep to make the world go away,
sleep like death. Her mama had told her that sleep was the best medicine God ever
made. When things get too rough — go to bed. Her family had been known as the
family that retreated to bed. Ruined crop? No money? Get some shut-eye. Maybe
it'll be better in the morning. Can't be worse. Maggie didn't give a damn where
Gabriel was to sleep that night; someone else would deal with it. She didn't care
about all the people who would come to the house after the wake to the Sitting Up,
talking, eating, drinking, watching over the still body till sunrise; they could take
care of themselves. The people came; but Maggie slept. From deeps under deeps
of slumber she sensed her granddaughter stick her head in the door and whisper,
asking Maggie if she wanted something to eat. Maggie didn't stir. She slept. And in
her sleep she dreamed.

She dreamed she was Job sitting on his dung heap, dressed in sackcloth and
ashes, her body covered with boils, scratching with a stick, sending away Eliphaz and
Bildad and Zophar and Elihu, who came to counsel her, and above her the sky boiled
and churned and the air roared, and she matched it, railing against God, against her
life — *Why? Why? Why did you kill him, you heartless old fiend? Why make me live
to see him die? What earthly purpose could you have in such a wicked deed? You
are God, but you are not good. Speak to me, damn it. Why? Why? Why?* Hurricanes
whipped and thunder ripped through a sky streaked by lightning, and she was lifted
up, spinning, spinning, and Edward floated before her in the rushing air and quickly
turned around into the comforting arms of Gabriel, winged, who clutched her grandboy to his bosom and soared away, out of the storm. Maggie screamed and the
winds grew stronger, and a voice, gentle and sweet, not thunderous as she expected,
spoke to her from the whirlwind: *Who is this that darkeneth counsel by words without knowledge? Gird up now thy loins like a man; for I will demand of thee, and
answer thou me. Where wast thou when I laid the foundations of the earth? Declare
if thou hast understanding* . . . The voice spoke of the myriad creations of the universe,

the stupendous glory of the Earth and its inhabitants. But Maggie was not deterred in the face of the maelstrom, saying: *Answer me, damn you: Why?*, and the winds began to taper off and finally halted, and Maggie was alone, standing on water. A fish, what appeared to be a mackerel, stuck its head through the surface and said: *Kind woman, be not aggrieved and put your anger away. Your arrogance has clouded your good mind. Who asked you to love? Who asked you to hate?* The fish dipped down with a plip and gradually Maggie too began to slip down into the water, down, down, down, sinking, below depths of reason and love, down into the dark unknown of her own mind, down, down, down.

Maggie MacGowan Williams woke the next morning to the harsh chatter of a blue-jay chasing a mockingbird just outside her window, a racket that caused her to open her eyes quickly to blinding sunlight. Squinting, she looked about the room, seeing the chest of drawers that had once belonged to her mother and her mother's mother before that, the chairs, the photographs on the wall, the television, the rug thickly soft, the closet door slightly ajar, the bureau, the mirror atop the bureau, and herself in the mirror, all of it bright in the crisp morning light. She saw herself looking, if not refreshed, calmed and within her the rage had gone, replaced by a numb humility and a plethora of questions. Questions. Questions. Questions.

Inwardly she had felt beatific that day of the funeral, ashamed at her anger of the day before. She greeted folk gently, softly, with a smile, her tones honey-flavored but solemn, and she reassumed the mantle of one-who-comforts-more-than-needing-comfort. 45

The immediate family had gathered at Maggie's house—Edward's father, Tom, Jr.; Tom, Jr.'s wife, Lucille; the grandbaby, Paul (Edward's brother); Clarissa. Raymond Brown's long black limousine took them from the front door of Maggie's house to the church, where the yard was crammed with people in their greys and navy blues, dark browns, and deep, deep burgundies. In her new humility she mused: When, oh when will we learn that death is not so somber, not something to mourn so much as celebrate? We should wear fire reds, sun oranges, hello greens, ocean-deep blues, and dazzling, welcome-home whites. She herself wore a bright dress of saffron and a blue scarf. She thought Edward would have liked it.

The family lined up and Gabriel approached her. As he stood before her—raven-haired, pink-skinned, abject, eyes bloodshot—she experienced a bevy of conflicting emotions: disgust, grief, anger, tenderness, fear, weariness, pity. Nevertheless she *had* to be civil, *had* to make a leap of faith and of understanding. Somehow she felt it had been asked of her. And though there were still so many questions, so much to sort out, for now she would mime patience, pretend to be accepting, feign peace. Time would unravel the rest.

She reached out, taking both his hands into her own, and said, the way she would to an old friend: "How have you been?"

IV

"But now, Miss Maggie..."

She sometimes imagined the good Reverend Barden as a toad-frog or an impotent 50 bull. His rantings and ravings bored her, and his clumsy advances repelled her; and when he tried to impress her with his holiness and his goodness, well...

"...that man should know better than to be plowing on a Sunday. Sunday! Why, the Lord said..."

"Reverend, I know what the Lord said. And I'm sure Morton Henry knows what the Lord said. But I am not the Lord, Reverend, and if Morton Henry wants to plow the west field on Sunday afternoon, well, it's his soul, not mine."

"But, Maggie. Miss Maggie. It's—"

"Well,"—Henrietta Fuchee sat perched to interject her five cents into the debate—"but, Maggie. It's your land! Now, Reverend, doesn't it say somewhere in Exodus that a man, or a woman in this case, a woman is responsible for the deeds or misdeeds of someone in his or her employ, especially on her property?"

"But he's not an emplo—"   55

"Well,"—Barden scratched his head—"I think I know what you're talking about, Henrietta. It may be in Deuteronomy . . . or Leviticus . . . part of the Mosaic Law, which. . ."

Maggie cast a quick glance at Gabriel. He seemed to be interested in and entertained by this contest of moral superiority. There was certainly something about his face . . . but she could not stare. He looked so *normal*. . .

"Well, I don't think you should stand for it, Maggie."

"Henrietta? What do you. . .? Look, if you want him to stop, *you go* tell him what the Lord said. I—"

The Right Reverend Hezekiah Barden stood, hiking his pants up to his belly. "Well, *I*   60
will. A man's soul is a valuable thing. And I can't risk your own soul being tainted by the actions of one of your sharecroppers."

"My soul? Sharecropper—he's not a sharecropper. He leases that land. I— wait!. . . Hezekiah!. . . This doesn't. . ."

But Barden had stepped off the patio onto the lawn and was headed toward the field, marching forth like old Nathan on his way to confront King David.

"Wait, Reverend." Henrietta hopped up, slinging her black pocketbook over her left shoulder. "Well, Maggie?" She peered at Maggie defiantly, as if to ask: *Where do you stand?*

"Now, Henrietta, I—"

Henrietta pivoted, her moral righteousness jagged and sharp as a shard of glass.   65
"Somebody has to stand up for right!" She tromped off after Barden.

Giggling, Emma picked up the empty glasses. "I don't think ole Morton Henry gone be too happy to be preached at this afternoon."

Maggie looked from Emma to Gabriel in bewilderment, at once annoyed and amused. All three began to laugh out loud. As Emma got to the door she turned to Maggie. "Hon, you better go see that they don't get into no fist-fight, don't you think? You know that Reverend don't know when to be quiet." She looked to Gabriel and nodded knowingly. "You better go with her, son," and was gone into the house; her molasses-thick laughter sweetening the air.

Reluctantly Maggie stood, looking at the two figures—Henrietta had caught up with Barden—a tiny cloud of dust rising from their feet. "Come on, Gabe. Looks like we have to go referee."

Gabriel walked beside her, a broad smile on his face. Maggie thought of her grandson being attracted to this tall white man. She tried to see them together and couldn't. At that moment she understood that she was being called on to realign her thinking about men and women, and men and men, and even women and women. Together . . . the way Adam and Eve were meant to be together.

V

Initially she found it difficult to ask the questions she wanted to ask. Almost impossible. 70

They got along well on Saturday. She took him out to dinner; they went shopping. All the while she tried with all her might to convince herself that she felt comfortable with this white man, with this homosexual, with this man who had slept with her grandboy. Yet he managed to impress her with his easygoing manner and openness and humor.

"Mrs. W." He had given her a nickname, of all things. No one had given her a nickname since . . . "Mrs. W., you sure you don't want to try on some swimsuits?"

She laughed at his kind-hearted jokes, seeing, oddly enough, something about him very like Edward; but then that thought would make her sad and confused.

Finally that night over coffee at the kitchen table she began to ask what they had both gingerly avoided.

Why didn't he just tell me?" 75

"He was afraid, Mrs. W. It's just that simple."

"Of what?"

"That you might disown him. That you might stop . . . well, you know, loving him, I guess."

"Does your family know?"

"Yes." 80

"How do they take it?"

"My mom's fine. She's great. Really. She and Edward got along swell. My dad. Well, he'll be okay for a while, but every now and again we'll have these talks, you know, about cures and stuff and sometimes it just gets heated. I guess it'll just take a little more time with him."

"But don't you want to be normal?"

"Mrs. W., I am. Normal."

"I see." 85

They went to bed at one-thirty that morning. As Maggie buttoned up her nightgown, Gabriel's answers whizzed about her brain; but they brought along more damnable questions and Maggie went to bed feeling betrayal and disbelief and revulsion and anger.

In church that next morning with Gabriel, she began to doubt the wisdom of having asked him to come. As he sat beside her in the pew, as the Reverend Barden sermonized on Jezebel and Ahab, as the congregation unsuccessfully tried to disguise their curiosity—("What is that white boy doing here with Maggie Williams? Who is he? Where he come from?")—she wanted Gabriel to go ahead and tell her what to think: *We're perverts* or *You're wrong-headed, your church has poisoned your mind against your own grandson; if he had come out to you, you would have rejected him. Wouldn't you?* Would she have?

Barden's sermon droned on and on that morning; the choir sang; after the service people politely and gently shook Gabriel and Maggie's hands and then stood off to the side, whispering, clearly perplexed.

On the drive back home, as if out of the blue, she asked him: "Is it hard?"

"Ma'am?" 90

"Being who you are? What you are?"

He looked over at her, and she could not meet his gaze with the same intensity that had gone into her question. "Being gay?"

"Yes."

"Well, I have no choice."

"So I understand. But is it hard?"   95

"Edward and I used to get into arguments about that, Mrs. W." His tone altered a bit. He spoke more softly, gently, the way a widow speaks of her dead husband. Or, indeed, the way a widower speaks of his dead husband. "He used to say it was harder being black in this country than gay. Gays can always pass for straight; but blacks can't always pass for white. And most can never pass."

"And what do you think now?"

"Mrs. W., I think *life* is hard, you know?"

"Yes. I know."

VI

Death had first introduced itself to Maggie when she was a child. Her grandfather 100 and grandmother both died before she was five; her father died when she was nine; her mother when she was twenty-five; over the years all her brothers except one. Her husband ten years ago. Her first memories of death: watching the women wash a cold body: the look of brown skin darkening, hardening: the corpse laid out on a cooling board, wrapped in a winding-cloth, before interment: fear of ghosts, bodyless souls: troubled sleep. So much had changed in seventy years; now there were embalming, funeral homes, morticians, insurance policies, bronze caskets, a bureaucratic wall between deceased and bereaved. Among the many things she regretted about Edward's death was not being able to touch his body. It made his death less real. But so much about the world seemed unreal to her these dark, dismal, and gloomy days. Now the flat earth was said to be round and bumblebees were not supposed to fly.

What was supposed to be and what truly was. Maggie learned these things from magazines and television and books; she loved to read. From her first week in that small schoolhouse with Miss Clara Oxendine, she had wanted to be a teacher. School: the scratchy chalkboard, the dusty-smelling textbooks, labyrinthine grammar and spelling and arithmetic, geography, reading out loud, giving confidence to the boy who would never learn to read well, correcting addition and subtraction problems, the taste and the scent of the schoolroom, the heat of the potbellied stove in January. She liked that small world; for her it was large. Yet how could she pay for enough education to become a teacher? Her mother would smile, encouragingly, when young Maggie would ask her, not looking up from her sewing, and merely say: "We'll find a way."

However, when she was fourteen she met a man named Thomas Williams, he sixteen going on thirty-nine. Infatuation replaced her dreams and murmured to her in languages she had never heard before, whispered to her another tale: *You will be a merchant's wife*.

Thomas Williams would come a-courting on Sunday evenings for two years, come driving his father's red Ford truck, stepping out with his biscuit-shined shoes, his one good Sunday suit, his hat cocked at an impertinent angle, and a smile that would make cold butter drip. But his true power lay in his tongue. He would spin yarns and tell tales that would make the oldest storyteller slap his knee and declare: "Hot damn! Can't that boy lie!" He could talk a possum out of a tree. He spoke to Maggie about his dream of opening his own store, a dry-goods store, and then maybe two or three or four. An audacious dream for a seventeen-year-old black boy, son of a farmer in 1936—and he promised, oh, how he promised, to keep Maggie by his side through it all.

Thinking back, on the other side of time and dreams, where fantasies and wishing had been realized, where she sat rich and alone, Maggie wondered what Thomas Williams could possibly have seen in that plain brown girl. Himself the son of a farmer with his own land, ten sons and two daughters, all married and doing well. There she was, poorer than a skinned rabbit, and not that pretty. Was he looking for a woman who would not flinch at hard work?

Somehow, borrowing from his father, from his brothers, working two, three   105
jobs at the shipyards, in the fields, with Maggie taking in sewing and laundry, cleaning houses, saving, saving, saving, they opened their store; and were married. Days, weeks, years of days, weeks of days, weeks of inventory and cleaning and waiting on people and watching over the dry-goods store, which became a hardware store in the sixties while the one store became two. They were prosperous; they were respected; they owned property. At seventy she now wanted for nothing. Long gone was the dream of a schoolhouse and little children who skinned their knees and the teaching of the ABCs. Some days she imagined she had two lives and she preferred the original dream to the flesh-and-blood reality.

Now, at least, she no longer had to fight bitterly with her pompous, self-satisfied, driven, blaspheming husband, who worked seven days a week, sixteen hours a day, money-grubbing and mean though—outwardly—flamboyantly generous; a man who lost interest in her bed after her first and only son, Thomas Jr., arrived broken in heart, spirit, and brain upon delivery; a son whose only true achievement in life was to illegitimately produce Edward by some equally brainless waif of a girl, now long vanished; a son who practically thrust the few-week-old infant into Maggie's arms, then flew off to a life of waste, sloth, petty crime, and finally a menial job in one of her stores and an ignoble marriage to a woman who could not conceal her greedy wish for Maggie to die.

Her life now was life that no longer had bite or spit or fire. She no longer worked. She no longer had to worry about Thomas's philandering and what pretty young thing he was messing with now. She no longer had the little boy whom Providence seemed to have sent her to maintain her sanity, to moor her to the Earth, and to give her vast energies focus.

In a world not real, is there truly guilt in willing reality to cohere through the life of another? Is that such a great sin? Maggie had turned to the boy—young, brown, handsome—to hold on to the world itself. She now saw that clearly. How did it happen? The mental slipping and sliding that allowed her to meld and mess and confuse her life with his, his rights with her wants, his life with her wish? He would not be like his father or his grandfather; he would rise up, go to school, be strong, be honest, upright. He would be; she would be . . . a feat of legerdemain; a sorcery of vicariousness in which his victory was her victory. He was her champion. Her hope.

Now he was gone. And now she had to come to terms with this news of his being "gay," as the world called what she had been taught was an unholy abomination. Slowly it all came together in her mind's eye: Edward.

He should have known better. I should have known better. I must learn better.   110

VII

They stood there at the end of the row, all of them waiting for the tractor to arrive and for the Reverend Hezekiah Barden to save the soul of Morton Henry.

Morton saw them standing there from his mount atop the green John Deere as it bounced across the broken soil. Maggie could make out the expression on his face: confusion. Three blacks and a white man out in the fields to see him. Did his house burn down? His wife die? The President declare war on Russia?

A big, red-haired, red-faced man, his face had so many freckles he appeared splotched. He had a big chew of tobacco in his left jaw and he spat out the brown juice as he came up the edge of the row and put the clutch in neutral.

"How you all today? Miss Maggie?"

"Hey, Morton."   115

Barden started right up, thumbs in his suspenders, and reared back on his heels. "Now I spect you're a God-fearing man?"

"Beg pardon?"

"I even spect you go to church from time to time?"

"Church? Miss Maggie, I—"

The Reverend held up his hand. "And I warrant you that your preacher—where *do* 120 you go to church, son?"

"I go to—wait a minute. What's going on here? Miss Maggie—"

Henrietta piped up. "It's Sunday! You ain't supposed to be working and plowing fields on a Sunday!"

Morton Henry looked over to Maggie, who stood there in the bright sun, then to Gabriel, as if to beg him to speak, make some sense of this curious event. He scratched his head. "You mean to tell me you all come out here to tell me I ain't suppose to plow this here field?"

"Not on Sunday you ain't. It's the Lord's Day."

"The Lord's Day?" Morton Henry was visibly amused. He tongued at the wad of 125 tobacco in his jaw. "The Lord's Day." He chuckled out loud.

"Now it ain't no laughing matter, young man." The Reverend's voice took on a dark tone.

Morton seemed to be trying to figure out who Gabriel was. He spat. "Well, I tell you, Reverend. If the Lord wants to come plow these fields I'd be happy to let him."

"You..." Henrietta stomped her foot, causing dust to rise. "You can't talk about the Lord like that. You're using His name in vain."

"I'll talk about Him any way I please to." Morton Henry's face became redder by the minute. "I got two jobs, five head of children, and a sick wife, and the Lord don't seem too worried about that. I spect I ain't gone worry to much about plowing this here field on His day none neither."

"Young man, you can't—"   130

Morton Henry looked to Maggie. "Now, Miss Maggie, this is your land, and if you don't want me to plow it, I'll give you back your lease and you can pay me my money and find somebody else to tend this here field!"

Everybody looked at Maggie. How does this look, she couldn't help thinking, a black woman defending a white man against a black minister? Why the *hell* am I here having to do this? she fumed. Childish, hypocritical idiots and fools. Time is just slipping, slipping away and all they have to do is fuss and bother about other folk's business while their own houses are burning down. God save their souls. She wanted to yell this, to cuss them out and stomp away and leave them to their ignorance. But in the end, what good would it do?

She took a deep breath. "Morton Henry. You do what you got to do. Just like the rest of us."

Morton Henry bowed his head to Maggie, "Ma'am," turned to the others with a gloating grin, "Scuse me," put his gear in first, and turned down the next row.

"Well—"

Barden began to speak but Maggie just turned, not listening, not wanting to hear, thinking: When, Lord, oh when will we learn? Will we ever? *Respect,* she thought. Oh how complicated.

They followed Maggie, heading back to the house, Gabriel beside her, tall and silent, the afternoon sunrays romping in his black hair. How curious the world had become that she would be asking a white man to exonerate her in the eyes of her own grandson; how strange that at seventy, when she had all the laws and rules down pat, she would have to begin again to learn. But all this stuff and bother would have to come later, for now she felt so, so tired, what with the weekend's activities weighing on her three-score-and-ten-year-old bones and joints; and she wished it were sunset, and she alone on her patio, contemplating the roundness and flatness of the earth, and slipping softly and safely into sleep.

Source: "The Foundations of the Earth" from LET THE DEAD BURY THEIR DEAD AND OTHER STORIES by Randall Kenan. Copyright © 1992 by Randall Kenan. Reprinted by permission of Houghton Mifflin Harcourt Publishing Company. All rights reserved.

Critical Thinking Topics

1. If Reverend Barden and Henrietta can be said to represent the values of their community, Tims Creek, then Edward, Gabriel, and Morton Henry represent an implicit challenge to those values.
   - List the values that the reverend and Henrietta represent.
   - List the values that Edward, Gabriel, and Morton represent.
   - Write out at least two passages from the story that indicate Maggie is caught between these two forces.

2. While walking beside Gabriel, Maggie "understood that she was being called upon to realign her thinking…" (par. 69). Explain how Maggie reached this understanding.

3. Do some research on the name Gabriel and then examine Gabriel's role in the story. Using details from the story and keeping in mind the symbolism of Gabriel's name, explain how Gabriel influences Maggie's shift in thinking.

4. In closing, Maggie reflects, "and she wished it were sunset, and she alone on the patio, contemplating the roundness and flatness of the earth, and slipping softly and safely into sleep." What is the significance of the image of "the roundness and flatness of the earth," and how does it connect to the story's title?

Writing Topic

The events that unfold in this story lead Maggie to a new perspective. At the end of the story, when Reverend Barden begins to speak, she thinks, "When, Lord, oh when will we learn? Will we ever? *Respect,* she thought. Oh how complicated" (par. 136). What claim is the author implying in this passage? Using evidence from the story, as well as from your own observations and experiences, develop an argument to defend, refute, or qualify that claim.

6.10 Beth H. Piatote, Beading Lesson
(2002)

The first thing you do is, lay down all your hanks, like this, so the colors go from light to dark, like a rainbow. I'll start you out with something real easy, like I do with those kids over at the school, over at Cay-Uma-Wa.

How about—you want to make some earrings for your mama? Yeah, I think she would like that.

Hey niece, you remind me of those kids. That's good! That's good to be thinking of your mama.

You go ahead and pick some colors you think she would like. Maybe three or four is all, and you need to pick some of these bugle beads.

Yeah, that's good, except you got too many dark colors.   5

You like dark colors. Every time I see you you're wearin' something dark. Not me. I like to wear red and yellow, so people know I'm around and don't try talkin' about me behind my back, aay?

The thing is, you got to use some light colors, because you're makin' these for your mama, right, and she has dark hair, and you want 'em to stand out, and if they're all dark colors you can't see the pattern.

I got some thread for you, and this beeswax. You cut the thread about this long, a little longer than your arm, but you don't want it too long or it will tangle up or get real weak. You run it through the beeswax, like this, until it's just about straight. It makes it strong and that way it don't tangle so much.

You keep all this in your box now. I got this for you to take home with you, back to college, so you can keep doin' your beadwork.

How do you like it over there at the university? You know your cousin Rae is just   10 about gettin' her degree. She just has her practicum, then she'll be done. I think her boyfriend don't like her being in school though, and that's slowing her down. It's probably a good thing you don't have a boyfriend right now. They can really make a lot of trouble for you, and slow you down on things you got to do.

Now you gotta watch this part. This is how you make the knot. You make a circle like this, then you wrap the thread around the needle three times, see? You see how my hands are? If you forget later you just remember how my hands are, just like this, and remember you have to make a circle, OK? Then you pull the needle through all the way to the end—good—and clip off the little tail.

I'll show you these real easy earrings, the same thing I always start those men at the jail with. You know I go over there and give them beading lessons. You should see how artistic some of them are. They work real hard, and some of them are good at beadwork.

I guess they got a lot of time to do it, but it's hard, it's hard to do real good beadwork. You got to go slow and pay attention.

I know this one man, William, he would be an artist if he wasn't in jail. I'll show you,   15 he gave me a drawing he did of an eagle. It could be a photograph, except you can tell it's just pencil. But it's good, you would like it. There's a couple other Indian prisoners— I guess we're supposed to call them inmates, but I always call them prisoners—and sometimes I make designs for them for their beadwork from what they draw. The thing is, they don't get very many colors to work with.

They like the beadwork, though. They always got something to give their girlfriends when they come visit, or their mothers and aunties.

You have to hide the knot in the bead, see, like this, and that's why you got to be careful not to make the knot too big.

Maybe next time you come they will be having a powwow at the prison and you can meet my students over there, and they can show you their beadwork. I think they always have a powwow around November, around Veteran's Day. Your cousin Carlisle and his family come over from Montana last time, and the only thing is, you got to go real early because it takes a long time to get all your things through security. They have to check all your regalia and last time they almost wouldn't let Carlisle take his staff in because they said it was too dangerous or something.

What's that? Oh, that's all right. Just make it the same way on the other one and everyone will think you did it that way on purpose.

Your mama is really going to like these earrings. I think sometimes she wishes she learnt to bead, but she didn't want to when she was little. She was the youngest so I think she was a little spoiled, but don't tell her I said that. She didn't have to do things she didn't want to, she didn't even have to go to boarding school. I think she would have liked it. It wasn't bad for me at that school. Those nuns were good to me; they doted on me. I was their pet. I think your mama missed out on something, not going to St. Andrews, because that's when you get real close with other Indians.   20

I like that blue. I think I'm goin' to make you a wing dress that color.

I think you'll look real good when you're ready to dance. Once you get going on your beadwork I'll get you started on your moccasins, and you know your cousin Woody is making you a belt and I know this lady who can make you a cornhusk bag. You're goin' to look just like your mama did when she was young, except I think she was younger than you the last time she put on beadwork.

I used to wonder if you would look like your dad, but now that you're grown you sure took after her. I look at you and I think my sister, she must have some strong blood.

Hey, you're doin' real good there, niece. I think you got "the gift"—good eyesight! You know, you always got to be workin' on something, because people are always needing things for weddin's and memorials and going out the first time, got to get their outfits together. Most everything I make I give away, but people pay me to make special things. And they are always askin' for my work at the gift shop. My beadwork has got me through some hard times, some years of livin' skinny.

You got to watch out for some people, though. Most people aren't like this; most people are real big-hearted. But some people, when they buy your beadwork, they think it should last forever. Somebody's car breaks down, he knows he got to take it to the shop, pay someone to get it goin' again. But not with beadwork—not with something an Indian made. No, they bring it back ten years later and they want you to fix it for free! They think because an Indian makes it, it's got to last forever. Just think if the Indians did that with all the things the government made for us. Hey, you got to fix it for free!   25

You done with that already? Let me show you how you finish. You pull the thread through this line, see, then clip it, then the bead covers it up. That's nice.

That's good. I'm proud of you, niece. You got a good heart. Just like your mama and dad.

I think your mama is really goin' to like these earrings, and maybe she'll come and ask you to teach her how you do it. You think she'll ever want to learn beadwork? Maybe she'll come and ask me, aay?

What do you think of that? You think your mama would ever want to learn something from her big sister? I got a lot of students. There's a lady who just called me the other day, she works at the health clinic, and she's a lot older than you and she wants to learn how. I said sure I'll teach her. It's never too late. I teach anyone who wants to learn; that's our way to keep it goin'. I just keep thinkin' if I stay around long enough, everyone's goin' to come back and want to learn beadwork, even your mama.

Source: Piatote, Beth H. Reckonings: Contemporary Fiction by Native American Women; Oxford University Press. Copyright © 2008, CCC Republication.

Critical Thinking Topics

1. Think of and list at least five words that characterize the narrator. Using those words, write a paragraph that depicts her central qualities and her personality.
2. The aunt is teaching her niece beadwork, but what other lessons is she imparting—for example, in paragraph 25?

Writing Topic

One can infer that the short story's narrator, a Native American and a woman, is marginalized by mainstream society. She is presumed to be a working-class laborer, one who should expect to earn nothing more than the minimum wage, if that. How does she consciously defy this identity and thereby maintain her sense of self and her dignity? What else does this unspoken rebellion accomplish? What role does the practice of cultural traditions serve in preserving identity and building self-worth among individuals within an ethnic, cultural, familial, or other type of community? Explain your answer by using examples from personal experience, observation, reading, or popular culture.

6.11 Poetry

The fifteen poems in this section, spanning the years from 1862 through 2014, explore topics and issues related to the theme of individual and community identity.

6.12 Emily Dickinson, Much Madness is divinest Sense (1862)

Much Madness is divinest Sense—
To a discerning Eye—
Much Sense—the starkest Madness—
'Tis the Majority
In this, as All, prevail—   5
Assent—and you are sane—
Demur—you're straightway dangerous—
And handled with a Chain—

Critical Thinking Topics

1. What value assumptions about "Madness" does Dickinson's poem refute? To what extent do you agree or disagree with the poet? Cite evidence from your own observations and experiences to support your viewpoint. Consider how some people break the limits placed upon them by others who consider them different. Think of a work of popular culture that dramatizes the topic, such as the 2017 film *The Shape of Water*. Explain how the work has affected the way you think about people who are considered different.

2. Our democratic society values the principle of majority rule. As the antithesis of monarchy and other forms of dictatorial rule, it is meant to guarantee a government that is "of the people, for the people, by the people." Dickinson's poem, however, implies that "the Majority" is anything but liberating (lines 7–8). Do you agree or disagree with the poet's perspective on the majority? Explain your response.

Writing Topic

Read "Crazy Courage," by Alma Luz Villanueva (later in this chapter). Does Michael's "crazy courage" support Dickinson's viewpoint on madness? Build on your response to question 1 above and create your own argument about the value of individuality and what limits, if any, should be placed upon it. Cite evidence from the poems, as well as your own experiences and observations.

6.13 Thomas Hardy, The Ruined Maid (written 1866; first published 1903)

"O 'Melia, my dear, this does everything crown!
Who could have supposed I should meet you in Town?
And whence such fair garments, such prosperi-ty?" —
"O didn't you know I'd been ruined?" said she.

—"You left us in tatters, without shoes or socks, 5
Tired of digging potatoes, and spudding up docks;
And now you've gay bracelets and bright feathers three!" —
"Yes: that's how we dress when we're ruined," said she.

—"At home in the barton you said 'thee' and 'thou,'
And 'thik oon,' and 'theäs oon,' and 't'other'; but now 10
Your talking quite fits 'ee for high compa-ny!" —
"Some polish is gained with one's ruin," said she.

—"Your hands were like paws then, your face blue and bleak
But now I'm bewitched by your delicate cheek,
And your little gloves fit as on any la-dy!" — 15
"We never do work when we're ruined," said she.

—"You used to call home-life a hag-ridden dream,
And you'd sigh, and you'd sock; but at present you seem
To know not of megrims or melancho-ly!" —
"True. One's pretty lively when ruined," said she. 20

—"I wish I had feathers, a fine sweeping gown,
And a delicate face, and could strut about Town!"—
"My dear—a raw country girl, such as you be,
Cannot quite expect that. You ain't ruined," said she.

Critical Thinking Topics

1. By leaving her home life on the farm, what has 'Melia left behind? What has she gained by her new life in Town?

2. Look up the adjective "ruined" to see how it was used with regard to young women in nineteenth-century England. Is it possible to be "ruined" in this sense in contemporary American society? In responding to this question, think about the role of social media.

3. Her former acquaintance, who still lives in the country, seems to think that 'Melia has found prosperity and happiness in Town. Does 'Melia's prosperity offer happiness? Could the hard life on a nineteenth-century English farm offer happiness? Explain your response.

Writing Topic

'Melia is caught between two choices: the hard farm life and the life of a "ruined" woman. Today, women like 'Melia (growing up in "hard" circumstances) might have other choices, but when seeking independence and a better life, do contemporary women in this situation also find themselves caught, pulled in different directions when faced with paying rent, buying food, and perhaps caring for children? Answer this question using evidence from your own observations and experiences and from outside sources.

6.14 Edwin Arlington Robinson, Richard Cory
(1897)

Whenever Richard Cory went down town,
We people on the pavement looked at him:
He was a gentleman from sole to crown,
Clean favored, and imperially slim.
And he was always quietly arrayed,   5
And he was always human when he talked;
But still he fluttered pulses when he said;
"Good-morning," and he glittered when he walked.
And he was rich—yes, richer than a king—
And admirably schooled in every grace: 10
In fine, we thought that he was everything
To make us wish that we were in his place.
So on we worked, and waited for the light,
And went without the meat, and cursed the bread;
And Richard Cory, one calm summer night,   15
Went home, and put a bullet through his head.

Critical Thinking Topics

1. What does the speaker mean by "he was always human when he talked"?
2. What assumptions do the townspeople make about Richard Cory? On what evidence are those assumptions based? Do these assumptions seem to persist in contemporary communities? Explain your response.

Writing Topic

By implication, the poem urges the reader to accept a generalization—that money does not make people happy. Do your own observations and experiences lead you to accept or reject this implication? In answering this question, you might want to consider the converse: Money does not necessarily make people unhappy. Might it be that Robinson's generalization only applies to specific cases such as Richard Cory? Discuss this question using examples from your own observations and/or from other literary works.

6.15 Claude McKay, Outcast (1920)

For the dim regions whence my fathers came
My spirit, bondaged by the body, longs.
Words felt, but never heard, my lips would frame;
My soul would sing forgotten jungle songs.
I would go back to darkness and to peace,   5
But the great western world holds me in fee,
And I may never hope for full release
While to its alien gods I bend my knee.
Something in me is lost, forever lost,
Some vital thing has gone out of my heart,   10
And I must walk the way of life a ghost
Among the sons of earth, a thing apart.
For I was born, far from my native clime,
Under the white man's menace, out of time.

Critical Thinking Topics

1. Use Aristotle's rhetorical triangle (see Chapter 3) to analyze and evaluate this poem as an argument:
   - How does the speaker appeal to *ethos*?
   - How does the speaker appeal to *logos*?
   - How does the speaker appeal to *pathos*?
2. Which rhetorical appeal is most persuasive, and why?

Writing Topic

What images does the term "outcast" evoke for you? In contemporary society, what attributes contribute to being labeled an outcast? Do you think that people who accept that label for themselves reveal a weakness or an unwillingness to be confident in their own originality? Do you feel that people who label others as outcasts reveal a harshness in judging others? Have you ever felt like an outcast? Explain.

6.16 Adrienne Rich, Aunt Jennifer's Tigers (1951)

Aunt Jennifer's tigers prance across a screen,
Bright topaz denizens of a world of green.
They do not fear the men beneath the tree;
They pace in sleek chivalric certainty.
Aunt Jennifer's fingers fluttering through her wool   5
Find even the ivory needle hard to pull.
The massive weight of Uncle's wedding band
Sits heavily upon Aunt Jennifer's hand.
When Aunt is dead, her terrified hands will lie
Still ringed with ordeals she was mastered by.   10
The tigers in the panel that she made
Will go on prancing, proud and unafraid.

Source: "Aunt Jennifer's Tigers." copyright © 2016 by the Adrienne Rich Literary Trust. © 1951 by Adrienne Rich, from COLLECTED POEMS: 1950–2012 by Adrienne Rich. Used by permission of W.W. Norton & Company, Inc. and Frances Goldin Literary Agency.

Critical Thinking Topics

1. What implied claims are made by this poem regarding Aunt Jennifer's marriage and her own identity? Identify images from the poem that support your answer.

2. Aunt Jennifer creates art through needlework. Describe the tigers that she embroiders and explain the symbolism of these images. What role does art play in shaping Aunt Jennifer's identity?

3. How does the speaker view Aunt Jennifer, and how might Aunt Jennifer's life and art challenge the speaker's assumptions about gender roles and identity?

Writing Topic

Have you observed a friend or family member's identity seeming to change after getting married, or, if not, have you noticed such a change in a character from a movie, television show, or book? How did the individual's identity change for the better and/or worse after marrying? Does marrying imply that the members of the couple are expected to change or even sacrifice their own identities? Elaborate on your response with examples.

6.17 Gary Snyder, Not Leaving the House (1970)

When Kai is born
I quit going out

Hang around the kitchen—make cornbread
Let nobody in.
Mail is flat.   5
    Masa lies on her side, Kai sighs,
    Non washes and sweeps
We sit and watch
    Masa nurse, and drink green tea.

Navajo turquoise beads over the bed   10
A peacock tail feather at the head
A badger pelt from Nagano-ken
For a mattress; under the sheet;
A pot of yogurt setting
Under the blankets, at his feet.   15

Masa, Kai,
And Non, our friend
In the green garden light reflected in
Not leaving the house.
From dawn til late at night   20
    making a new world of ourselves
    around this life.

Source: By Gary Snyder, from REGARDING WAVE, copyright ©1970 by Gary Snyder. Reprinted by permission of New Directions Publishing Corp.

Critical Thinking Topics

1. What view of a father does this poem present? Point to specific lines and images that develop this view.

2. Contrast Snyder's view of fatherhood with the view presented by Michael Cleary in the poem "Boss's Son," later in this chapter.

Writing Topic

Is there a universal view of fatherhood in the United States, or does that view change from one community to another? Using this poem and other literature selections, as well as your own personal experience and observations, write and support a claim of value about a father's role in a family.

6.18 Judy Grahn, Ella, In a Square Apron, Along Highway 80 (1971)

She's a copperheaded waitress,
tired and sharp-worded, she hides
her bad brown tooth behind a wicked
smile, and flicks her ass
out of habit, to fend off the pass   5
that passes for affection.
She keeps her mind the way men

keep a knife—keen to strip the game
down to her size. She has a thin spine,
swallows her eggs cold, and tells lies.   10
She slaps a wet rag at the truck drivers
if they should complain. She understands
the necessity for pain, turns away
the smaller tips, out of pride, and
keeps a flask under the counter. Once,   15
she shot a lover who misused her child.
Before she got out of jail, the courts had pounced
and given the child away. Like some isolated lake,
her flat blue eyes take care of their own stark
bottoms. Her hands are nervous, curled, ready to scrape.   20
The common woman is as common
as a rattlesnake.

Source: Grahn, Judy. "Ella, in a Square Apron, along Highway 80" from THE WALK OF THE COMMON WOMAN: The Collected Poetry of Judy Grahn. Copyright (c) 1971 by Judy Grahn. Reprinted by permission of the author.

Critical Thinking Topics

1. If you are not familiar with basic facts about copperheads and rattlesnakes—for example, both are venomous predators—take a moment to find out about them online. Also, look up the definition of "venomous," as it relates not only to snakes but also to humans. Compare and contrast the snake imagery in the poem's opening and closing lines. How do these images shape your understanding of and attitude toward Ella?

2. What claim of value does the poem imply about Ella as a "common woman"? Point to specific images and explain how they support your conclusion. To what degree do you find this claim of value valid or invalid?

3. On which rhetorical appeal (*ethos*, *logos*, or *pathos*) is this poem's argument based? Is this an effective persuasive strategy? Why or why not?

Writing Topics

1. How does Grahn's waitress attempt to maintain her individuality within her environment? Are her efforts successful? What pressure does your environment exert on your sense of individuality? Describe a specific example to elaborate on your response.

2. The poem implies that Ella is a waitress at a highway diner. Based on your reading of the poem, how would you describe the atmosphere of the diner "along Highway 80"? A quick online search suggests that, in the almost half century since this poem was published, the highway diner was first on the path to becoming an endangered species but, in the last ten years or so, has become an in-vogue destination for many people. What do you think accounts for the rebirth and renewed popularity of highway diners?

6.19 Peter Meinke, Advice to My Son (1981)

—FOR TIM

The trick is, to live your days
as if each one may be your last
(for they go fast, and young men lose their lives
in strange and unimaginable ways)
but at the same time, plan long range   5
(for they go slow: if you survive
the shattered windshield and the bursting shell
you will arrive
at our approximation here below
of heaven or hell).   10
To be specific, between the peony and the rose
plant squash and spinach, turnips and tomatoes;
beauty is nectar
and nectar, in a desert, saves—
but the stomach craves stronger sustenance   15
than the honied vine.
Therefore, marry a pretty girl
after seeing her mother;
speak truth to one man,
work with another;   20
and always serve bread with your wine.
But, son,
always serve wine.

Source: Meinke, Peter, "Advice to My Son" from TRYING TO SURPRISE GOD, by Peter Meinke, (c) 1981.
Reprinted by permission of the University of Pittsburgh Press.

Critical Thinking Topics

1. In this poem, the speaker implies there is a "trick" to successful living and states that he will be "specific." Describe both the specific advice and the symbolic advice the speaker gives. Evaluate how you as an individual and how members of your community might follow this advice to achieve balance.

2. In lines 17 and 18, the speaker asserts, "Therefore, marry a pretty girl," with the qualifying phrase "after seeing her mother." What value assumptions underlie that statement? Are they valid? Why or why not?

Writing Topic

The speaker is giving advice to his son ("—FOR TIM"). Working with several other students (preferably in mixed-gender groups), create a female version of Meinke's poem—"Advice to My Daughter." Be prepared to present your poem to the rest of the class.

6.20 Cathy Song, Lost Sister (1983)

1

In China,
even the peasants
named their first daughters
Jade—
the stone that in the far fields   5
could moisten the dry season,
could make men move mountains
for the healing green of the inner hills
glistening like slices of winter melon.
And the daughters were grateful: 10
They never left home.
To move freely was a luxury
stolen from them at birth.
Instead, they gathered patience;
learning to walk in shoes   15
the size of teacups,
without breaking—
the arc of their movements
as dormant as the rooted willow,
as redundant as the farmyard hens.   20
But they traveled far
in surviving,
learning to stretch the family rice,
to quiet the demons,
the noisy stomachs.   25

2

There is a sister
across the ocean,
who relinquished her name,
diluting jade green
with the blue of the Pacific.   30
Rising with a tide of locusts,
she swarmed with others
to inundate another shore.
In America,
there are many roads   35
and women can stride along with men.
But in another wilderness,
the possibilities,

the loneliness,
can strangulate like jungle vines.   40
The meager provisions and sentiments
of once belonging—
fermented roots, Mah-Jong tiles and firecrackers—set but
a flimsy household
in a forest of nightless cities.   45
A giant snake rattles above,
spewing black clouds into your kitchen.
Dough-faced landlords
slip in and out of your keyholes,
making claims you don't understand,   50
tapping into your communication systems
of laundry lines and restaurant chains.
You find you need China:
your one fragile identification,
a jade link   55
handcuffed to your wrist.
You remember your mother
who walked for centuries,
footless—
and like her,   60
you have left no footprints,
but only because
there is an ocean in between,
the unremitting space of your rebellion.

Source: Song, Cathy. "Lost Sister" from PICTURE BRIDE. Copyright (c) 1983 by Cathy Song. Reprinted by permission of Yale University Press.

Critical Thinking Topics

1. How do the poem's first twenty-five lines depict life for daughters—for women—in China? Include specific lines to support your description. Compare this description to that of the sister's life as an immigrant in America (lines 26 and following); point to specific lines to elaborate. What is the implied claim in the poem? Use your comparison to support your answer. Do you agree with this claim? Why or why not?

2. Examine images related to feet and movement—for example, lines 15–20, and 57–61. How do these images support the claim you identified?

Writing Topic

What value assumptions about rebellion against one's cultural values and heritage does the speaker implicitly challenge (focus, in particular, on the poem's title and closing lines, 60–64)? Do you agree or disagree with those assumptions? Support your viewpoint with examples from your own experience and from current events.

6.21 Mary Oliver, Wild Geese
(1986)

You do not have to be good.
You do not have to walk on your knees
for a hundred miles through the desert, repenting.
You only have to let the soft animal of your body love what it loves.
Tell me about despair, yours, and I will tell you mine.   5
Meanwhile the world goes on.
Meanwhile the sun and the clear pebbles of the rain
are moving across the landscapes,
over the prairies and the deep trees,
the mountains and the rivers.   10
Meanwhile the wild geese, high in the clean blue air,
are heading home again.
Whoever you are, no matter how lonely,
the world offers itself to your imagination,
calls to you like the wild geese, harsh and exciting—   15
over and over announcing your place
in the family of things.

Source: Excerpts from DREAM WORK, copyright © 1986 by Mary Oliver. Used by permission of Grove/
Atlantic, Inc. Any third party use of this material, outside of this publication, is prohibited.

Critical Thinking Topics

1. What assumptions about being "good" does the speaker challenge in the poem's first four lines?
2. How does the phrase "family of things" create a distinct perspective on the idea of community? What implied claim does the speaker make about an individual's place within his or her community?
3. On which rhetorical appeal—*pathos, logos,* or *ethos*—does the speaker rely? Cite examples and discuss their effect on you as a reader.
4. How might the calls of the wild geese be both "harsh and exciting" (line 15)?

Writing Topic

What role does imagination play in your daily life? What settings provide a space for you to engage your imagination? How has the increasing presence of technology and media affected your imagination? Create your own claim about the value of imagination, and support your argument with evidence from Oliver's poem and from your own experiences and observations.

6.22 Margaret Walker, Lineage
(1989)

My grandmothers were strong.
They followed plows and bent to toil.

They moved through fields sowing seed.
They touched earth and grain grew.
They were full of sturdiness and singing.   5
My grandmothers were strong.
My grandmothers are full of memories.
Smelling of soap and onions and wet clay
With veins rolling roughly over quick hands
They have many clean words to say.   10
My grandmothers were strong.
Why am I not as they?

Source: Alexander, Margaret Walker. "Lineage" from THIS IS MY CENTURY: New and Collected Poems. The University of Georgia Press.

Critical Thinking Topics

1. What qualities does the speaker imply she has lost that her grandmothers possessed?
2. How does this poem define "strong"? Which words and phrases in the poem create this definition?
3. What value assumptions does the speaker make about the rewards of physical toil? Do you accept those assumptions? Why or why not?

Writing Topic

Many of us admire someone in our family from a generation preceding our own. Can you identify one of your own relatives whom you particularly admire? If not, can you identify an historical figure whom you admire? Tell the story of your chosen relative or historical figure, and explain why you admire her or him. In what ways would you be proud to be like that person? Compare your own personal qualities to those of your chosen relative or historical figure. In what ways are you the same, and in what ways are you different? For what qualities do you hope to be remembered by generations to come?

6.23 Alma Luz Villanueva, Crazy Courage (1998)

To Michael B.

Why do I think of Michael...
He came to my fiction class
as a man (dressed in men's
clothes); then he came
to my poetry class   5
as a woman (dressed in women's
clothes; but he was still
a man under the clothes).
Was I moved in the face of
such courage (man/woman   10

woman/man)...
Was I moved by the gentleness
of his masculinity; the strength
of his femininity...
His presence at the class poetry   15
reading, dressed in a miniskirt,
high boots, bright purple tights,
a scooped-neck blouse, carrying
a single, living, red rose, in a
vase, to the podium (the visitors,   20
not from the class, shocked—
the young, seen-it-all MTV crowd—
into silence as he's introduced,
"Michael...") And what it was, I think,
was his perfect dignity, the offering   25
of his living, red rose to the perceptive,
to the blind, to the amused, to the impressed,
to those who would kill him, and
to those who would love him.
And of course I remember the surprise   30
of his foamy breasts as we hugged
goodbye, his face blossomed
open, set apart, the pain of it,
the joy of it (the crazy courage
to be whole, as a rose is   35
whole, as a child is
whole before they're
punished for including
everything in their
innocence).   40

Source: "Crazy Courage," from DEISRE, pp, 72-73 by Alma Luz Villanueva. Bilingual Press/Editorial Bilingue, 1998, Arizona State University, Tempe, AZ. Reprinted by permission

---

Critical Thinking Topics

1. In judging Michael, what is the speaker's implied claim of value about courage? Point to specific images that provide evidence for this claim. Does the speaker present a convincing argument? Why or why not?
2. Reread lines 18–20 and 35–36? How does the image of the rose contribute to the poem's message?

Writing Topic

Americans often say they celebrate expressions of individuality, yet people who violate cultural norms or behave unconventionally sometimes face discrimination. What value assumptions underlie our attitudes about nonconformist or unconventional behavior? How do these assumptions affect our judgments about and our behavior toward nonconformist or unconventional people? Use at least two specific examples to elaborate.

6.24 Michael Cleary, Boss's Son (2005)

The first weeks were the worst.
They were all full-timers
half a generation older at least,
and me headed for college, pegged for sure
among beer drinking, beer trucking men.   5
And they let me know it,
their muscle cars and pick-ups more real
than jock glory and SAT's.

Whatever I'd done, they stuck
a big fat "but" on its skinny ass: 10
I was football captain, *but* I was quarterback—
just another name for bossing guys around.
I was strong enough, *but* I liked books.
I had a pretty girl, *but* I was pussywhipped.
My pride unraveled like a baseball's snarled insides.   15
So I did twice my share, blisters
torn til calluses covered my hands like shells.

Gradually, they taught me their secrets:
let your legs do the lifting and save your back.
Load last things first so pints, quarts, cans, kegs   20
come undone top to bottom, back to front,
first stop to last and handle everything just once.
Snugging the load, making it stay that way all day
so corners and dumbshit drivers don't tumble it away
in explosions of foam soaking up half a day's pay.   25

After work we hung around and drank for free.
I salvaged bottles from the cooler's breakage bin,
hosing off scum and bits of glass.
I guzzled, smoked, swore with the best of them.
Playing the boy at night, I played the man   30
next morning, showed up early
and tried not to puke on company time.

Paydays we went to sour-smelling hangouts
of touchy pride and easy violence. Once
I saw a logger bite off a chunk   35
of a guy's cheek like an apple, then promise
to wait til he got back from the emergency room.
We waited, too, and they went at it again
for what seemed a good half hour.
Blood splattered all over the alley.   40

Those summers I changed
into that life easy as T-shirts and steel-toed boots,
doing the grunt work and putting down salesmen

like my father with their soft hands and ties,
gloried in sweat and sore muscles and hangovers   45
like nobody's goddamn boss's son.
After four years I was out of college
and out of there forever. Three months later,
the artery that burst inside my father's head
dropped him to the warehouse floor and he was gone.   50

What did he wonder about me living so hard,
trying to prove myself to everyone but him?
It was one more thing between us
I couldn't explain and he wouldn't understand.
I wanted the world to love me, I suppose,   55
on its own rough terms,
but I wanted him to love me, too,
for whatever man I was or was trying to be,
for the first time not in the name of the father
but some pilgrim who could be any man's son.   60

Source: "Boss's Son," from Halfway Decent Sinners, by Michael Cleary © 2006 WordTech Communications LLC, Cincinnati, Ohio, USA.

Critical Thinking Topics

1. What are the connotations of the word "pride" in line 15 and then again in line 34?

2. How does pride help this young adult establish his independence and identity?

3. Reread the poem's closing four lines ("but I wanted him to love me, too...."), and exercising your creative and critical thinking, offer your interpretation of those lines. In framing your response, consider the phrase "in the name of the father," juxtaposed with the image of "some pilgrim."

Writing Topic

Read Scott Russell Sanders's essay "The Men We Carry in Our Minds," later in this chapter. Both Sanders's essay and Cleary's poem address issues of class differences. While we like to think of the United States as a "classless" egalitarian society, Sanders's essay and Cleary's poem suggest otherwise. In what ways do they challenge the notion of egalitarianism? Do you agree or disagree with the writers? Use evidence to support your opinion.

6.25 Meri Culp, Cayenne Warning
(2010)

Even the pepper's skin will burn to the touch, Mom, my son says
as he fingers the slim fire, the just-picked red ripeness.

Be careful, he reminds, all kindness, newfound protection,
as I watch him harvest the peppers, red-handed, soon-to-be a man.

I want to tell him of life's red hot sting,   5
of his grandmother's dying request

for me to paint her fingernails chili pepper red,
to unearth from her drawer a favorite lipstick,

Revlon's Marooned, the color of black/red gardens,
the deep bite of goodbye, an open wound.   10

I want to say, *I know of burning, my son,*
how one night, I fell hard into a sunset,

slammed into a slow-blaze burn
of every shade of red,

learned how crimson turns scarlet,   15
then fades, like nightfall, old chiffon, dusty and pink.

But instead, I heed his advice,
let him sound the warning alarm,

as if I had lived my life in a gentle garden,
in a place I notice is now: my son, me, our red cayennes.   20

Source: Culp, Meri. "Cayenne Warning," Apalachee Review #60 (2010). Used by permission.

Critical Thinking Topics

1. The speaker of the poem focuses on the color red. What does red symbolize in the poem? What does it mean to the son? To the mother? Use quotations from the poem for support.

2. What does the speaker mean by "a gentle garden"? Describe the significance of this metaphor.

Writing Topic

The young son in the poem is "soon-to-be a man." How does his young outlook affect his vision of his own identity? Of his mother's identity? Reflect on your childhood and describe a moment when you felt mature or protective. Looking back as an adult, do you understand this moment differently? Why or why not?

6.26 Margarita Engle, Counting (2014)

Harry Franck, from the United States of America – Census Enumerator

I came to Panama planning to dig
the Eighth Wonder of the World,
but I was told that white men
should never be seen working
with shovels, so I took a police job,   5
and now I've been transferred
to the census.

I roam the jungle, counting laborers
who live in shanties and those who live
on the run, fugitives who are too angry   10

to keep working for silver in a system
where they know that others
earn gold.

When islanders see me coming,
they're afraid of trouble, even though   15
I can't arrest them anymore—now
all I need is a record of their names, ages,
homelands, and colors.

The rules of this census confound me.
I'm expected to count white Jamaicans   20
as dark and every shade of Spaniard
as semi-white, so that Americans
can pretend
there's only one color
in each country.   25

How am I supposed to enumerate
this kid with the Cuban accent?
His skin is medium, but his eyes
are green.

And what about that Puerto Rican   30
scientist, who speaks like a New York
professor,
or the girl who says she doesn't know
where she was born or who her parents
are—she could be part native, or part French,   35
Jamaican, Chinese...

She could even be part American,
from people who passed through here
way back
in gold rush days.   40

Counting feels just as impossible
as turning solid mountains
into a ditch.

Source: "Counting" from SILVER PEOPLE: Voices from the Panama Canal by Margarita Engle. Copyright © 2014 by Margarita Engle. Reprinted by permission of Houghton Mifflin Harcourt Publishing Company. All rights reserved.

Critical Thinking Topics

1. Following the title, Engle introduces readers to the poem's speaker, American and census enumerator Harry Franck. Describe the speaker's tone as he travels about to conduct the census. Select details from the poem to elaborate on your description.

2. The first two lines reveal the poem's setting and also the speaker's purpose for being there. What does the image of digging the Eighth Wonder of the World suggest?

3. Discuss the implications of the closing three lines.
4. What is one claim implied by the poem? Point to details that lead you to this conclusion. What is your perspective on the poem's argument?

Writing Topic

Every ten years, the U.S. Census Bureau conducts its counting of residents in the United States, thereby collecting data that have significant implications, including for voting representation and funding. At the time of this writing, the next census will be conducted in 2020, and controversy is swirling around the Trump administration's addition of a question about citizenship status (a citizenship question has not been included since the 1950 census). By the time this book is published, that census will have occurred—with or without the citizenship question. Do some online research on the 2020 census and the citizenship question. What is your stance on including such a question? Explain why you would advocate either for or against its inclusion in the following census, in 2030.

6.27 Drama

The two plays in this section, one dating from 1601-02 and the other from 2017, explore topics and issues related to the theme of individual and community identity.

6.28 William Shakespeare, Twelfth Night; Or, What You Will (1601-02)

Dramatis Personae

ORSINO, Duke of Illyria
SEBASTIAN, brother to Viola
ANTONIO, a sea captain, friend to Sebastian
A SEA CAPTAIN, friend to Viola
VALENTINE, gentleman attending on the Duke
CURIO, gentleman attending on the Duke
SIR TOBY BELCH, uncle to Olivia
SIR ANDREW AGUECHEEK, friend to Sir Toby
MALVOLIO, steward to Olivia
FABIAN, servant to Olivia
FESTE, a clown, servant to Olivia
OLIVIA, a rich countess
VIOLA, an aristocratic woman, disguises herself as Cesario
MARIA, Olivia's waiting woman
Lords, Priests, Sailors, Officers, Musicians, and other Attendants

SCENE: A city in Illyria, and the sea-coast near it

6.28.1 ACT I. SCENE I. An apartment in the DUKE'S palace.

	[Enter DUKE, CURIO, and other LORDS; MUSICIANS attending.]	
DUKE.	If music be the food of love, play on;	
	Give me excess of it, that, surfeiting,	
	The appetite may sicken and so die.	
	That strain again! It had a dying fall;	
	O, it came o'er my ear like the sweet sound	5
	That breathes upon a bank of violets,	
	Stealing and giving odour! Enough; no more;	
	'Tis not so sweet now as it was before.	
	O spirit of love, how quick and fresh art thou!	
	That, notwithstanding thy capacity	10
	Receiveth as the sea, nought enters there,	
	Of what validity and pitch soe'er,	
	But falls into abatement and low price,	
	Even in a minute! so full of shapes is fancy	
	That it alone is high fantastical.	15
CURIO.	Will you go hunt, my lord?	
DUKE.	What, Curio?	
CURIO.	The hart.	
DUKE.	Why, so I do, the noblest that I have.	
	O, when mine eyes did see Olivia first,	20
	Methought she purg'd the air of pestilence!	
	That instant was I turn'd into a hart;	
	And my desires, like fell and cruel hounds,	
	E'er since pursue me.	
	[Enter VALENTINE.]	
	How now! what news from her?	25
VALENTINE.	So please my lord, I might not be admitted,	
	But from her handmaid do return this answer:	
	The element itself, till seven years' heat,	
	Shall not behold her face at ample view;	
	But, like a cloistress, she will veiled walk	30
	And water once a day her chamber round	
	With eye-offending brine; all this to season	
	A brother's dead love, which she would keep fresh	
	And lasting in her sad remembrance.	
DUKE.	O, she that hath a heart of that fine frame	35
	To pay this debt of love but to a brother,	
	How will she love when the rich golden shaft	

Hath kill'd the flock of all affections else
That live in her; when liver, brain, and heart,
These sovereign thrones, are all supplied, and fill'd— 40
Her sweet perfections—with one self king!
Away before me to sweet beds of flow'rs;
Love-thoughts lie rich when canopied with bow'rs.
[Exeunt.]

6.28.2 ACT I. SCENE II. The sea-coast.

[Enter VIOLA, a CAPTAIN, and SAILORS.]

VIOLA. What country, friends, is this?

CAPTAIN. This is Illyria, lady.

VIOLA. And what should I do in Illyria?
My brother he is in Elysium.
Perchance he is not drown'd. What think you, sailors? 5

CAPTAIN. It is perchance that you yourself were sav'd.

VIOLA. O my poor brother! and so perchance may he be.

CAPTAIN. True, madam: and, to comfort you with chance,
Assure yourself, after our ship did split,
When you, and those poor number sav'd with you, 10
Hung on our driving boat, I saw your brother,
Most provident in peril, bind himself,
Courage and hope both teaching him the practice,
To a strong mast that liv'd upon the sea;
Where, like Arion on the dolphin's back, 15
I saw him hold acquaintance with the waves
So long as I could see.

VIOLA. For saying so, there's gold:
Mine own escape unfoldeth to my hope,
Whereto thy speech serves for authority, 20
The like of him. Know'st thou this country?

CAPTAIN. Ay, madam, well; for I was bred and born
Not three hours' travel from this very place.

VIOLA. Who governs here?

CAPTAIN. A noble duke, in nature as in name. 25

VIOLA. What is his name?

CAPTAIN. Orsino.

VIOLA. Orsino! I have heard my father name him;
He was a bachelor then.

CAPTAIN.	And so is now, or was so very late;	30
	For but a month ago I went from hence,	
	And then 'twas fresh in murmur—as, you know,	
	What great ones do the less will prattle of—	
	That he did seek the love of fair Olivia.	
VIOLA.	What's she?	35
CAPTAIN.	A virtuous maid, the daughter of a count	
	That died some twelvemonth since, then leaving her	
	In the protection of his son, her brother,	
	Who shortly also died; for whose dear love,	
	They say, she hath abjur'd the company	40
	And sight of men.	
VIOLA.	O that I serv'd that lady,	
	And might not be delivered to the world,	
	Till I had made mine own occasion mellow,	
	What my estate is!	45
CAPTAIN.	That were hard to compass,	
	Because she will admit no kind of suit,	
	No, not the duke's.	
VIOLA.	There is a fair behaviour in thee, captain;	
	And though that nature with a beauteous wall	50
	Doth oft close in pollution, yet of thee	
	I will believe thou hast a mind that suits	
	With this thy fair and outward character.	
	I prithee, and I'll pay thee bounteously,	
	Conceal me what I am, and be my aid	55
	For such disguise as haply shall become	
	The form of my intent. I'll serve this duke:	
	Thou shalt present me as an eunuch to him;	
	It may be worth thy pains, for I can sing	
	And speak to him in many sorts of music	60
	That will allow me very worth his service.	
	What else may hap, to time I will commit;	
	Only shape thou silence to my wit.	
CAPTAIN.	Be you his eunuch, and your mute I'll be;	
	When my tongue blabs, then let mine eyes not see.	65
VIOLA.	I thank thee; lead me on.	
	[Exeunt.]	

6.28.3 ACT I. SCENE III. OLIVIA'S house.

[Enter SIR TOBY BELCH and MARIA.]

SIR TOBY.	What a plague means my niece, to take the death of her brother thus? I am sure care's an enemy to life.
MARIA.	By my troth, Sir Toby, you must come in earlier o' nights; your cousin, my lady, takes great exceptions to your ill hours.
SIR TOBY.	Why, let her except before excepted. 5
MARIA.	Ay, but you must confine yourself within the modest limits of order.
SIR TOBY.	Confine! I'll confine myself no finer than I am. These clothes are good enough to drink in, and so be these boots too; and they be not, let them hang themselves in their own straps.
MARIA.	That quaffing and drinking will undo you. I heard my lady talk of it 10 yesterday, and of a foolish knight that you brought in one night here to be her wooer.
SIR TOBY.	Who, Sir Andrew Aguecheek?
MARIA.	Ay, he.
SIR TOBY.	He's as tall a man as any's in Illyria. 15
MARIA.	What's that to th' purpose?
SIR TOBY.	Why, he has three thousand ducats a year.
MARIA.	Ay, but he'll have but a year in all these ducats; he's a very fool and a prodigal.
SIR TOBY.	Fio, that you'll say so! he plays o' th' viol-de-gamboys, and speaks 20 three or four languages word for word without book, and hath all the good gifts of nature.
MARIA.	He hath indeed, almost natural; for, besides that he's a fool, he's a great quarreller; and but that he hath the gift of a coward to allay the gust he hath in quarrelling, 'tis thought among the prudent he would 25 quickly have the gift of a grave.
SIR TOBY.	By this hand, they are scoundrels and subtractors that say so of him. Who are they?
MARIA.	They that add, moreover, he's drunk nightly in your company.
SIR TOBY.	With drinking healths to my niece. I'll drink to her as long as there 30 is a passage in my throat and drink in Illyria: he's a coward and a coystrill that will not drink to my niece till his brains turn o' th' toe like a parish-top. What, wench! Castiliano vulgo! for here comes Sir Andrew Agueface.
	[Enter SIR ANDREW AGUECHEEK.]
SIR ANDREW.	Sir Toby Belch; how now, Sir Toby Belch! 35
SIR TOBY.	Sweet Sir Andrew!
SIR ANDREW.	Bless you, fair shrew.
MARIA.	And you too, sir.
SIR TOBY.	Accost, Sir Andrew, accost.

SIR ANDREW.	What's that?	40
SIR TOBY.	My niece's chambermaid.	
SIR ANDREW.	Good Mistress Accost, I desire better acquaintance.	
MARIA.	My name is Mary, sir.	
SIR ANDREW.	Good Mistress Mary Accost—	
SIR TOBY.	You mistake, knight; "accost" is front her, board her, woo her, assail her.	45
SIR ANDREW.	By my troth, I would not undertake her in this company. Is that the meaning of "accost"?	
MARIA.	Fare you well, gentlemen.	
SIR TOBY.	An thou let part so, Sir Andrew, would thou mightst never draw sword again.	50
SIR ANDREW.	And you part so, mistress, I would I might never draw sword again. Fair lady, do you think you have fools in hand?	
MARIA.	Sir, I have not you by th' hand.	
SIR ANDREW.	Marry, but you shall have; and here's my hand.	
MARIA.	Now, sir, "thought is free." I pray you, bring your hand to th' buttery-bar and let it drink.	55
SIR ANDREW.	Wherefore, sweet-heart? what's your metaphor?	
MARIA.	It's dry, sir.	
SIR ANDREW.	Why, I think so; I am not such an ass but I can keep my hand dry. But what's your jest?	60
MARIA.	A dry jest, sir.	
SIR ANDREW.	Are you full of them?	
MARIA.	Ay, sir, I have them at my fingers' ends; marry, now I let go your hand, I am barren. [Exit.]	
SIR TOBY.	O knight, thou lack'st a cup of canary; when did I see thee so put down?	65
SIR ANDREW.	Never in your life, I think; unless you see canary put me down. Methinks sometimes I have no more wit than a Christian or an ordinary man has; but I am a great eater of beef, and I believe that does harm to my wit.	70
SIR TOBY.	No question.	
SIR ANDREW.	And I thought that, I'd forswear it. I'll ride home to-morrow,	
SIR TOBY.	Pourquoi, my dear knight?	
SIR ANDREW.	What is "pourquoi"? do or not do? I would I had bestow'd that time in the tongues that I have in fencing, dancing, and bear-baiting! O, had I but follow'd the arts!	75
SIR TOBY.	Then hadst thou had an excellent head of hair.	
SIR ANDREW.	Why, would that have mended my hair?	
SIR TOBY.	Past question; for thou seest it will not curl by nature.	
SIR ANDREW.	But it becomes me well enough, does't not?	80

SIR TOBY. Excellent; it hangs like flax on a distaff; and I hope to see a housewife take thee between her legs and spin it off.

SIR ANDREW. Faith, I'll home to-morrow, Sir Toby. Your niece will not be seen; or, if she be, it's four to one she'll none of me: the count himself here hard by woos her.

SIR TOBY. She'll none o' th' count. She'll not match above her degree, neither in estate, years, nor wit; I have heard her swear't. Tut, there's life in't, man.

SIR ANDREW. I'll stay a month longer. I am a fellow o' th' strangest mind i' th' world; I delight in masques and revels sometimes altogether.

SIR TOBY. Art thou good at these kickshawses, knight?

SIR ANDREW. As any man in Illyria, whatsoever he be, under the degree of my betters; and yet I will not compare with an old man.

SIR TOBY. What is thy excellence in a galliard, knight?

SIR ANDREW. Faith, I can cut a caper.

SIR TOBY. And I can cut the mutton to't.

SIR ANDREW. And I think I have the back-trick simply as strong as any man in Illyria.

SIR TOBY. Wherefore are these things hid? Wherefore have these gifts a curtain before 'em? Are they like to take dust, like Mistress Mall's picture? Why dost thou not go to church in a galliard, and come home in a coranto? My very walk should be a jig. What dost thou mean? Is it a world to hide virtues in? I did think, by the excellent constitution of thy leg, it was form'd under the star of a galliard.

SIR ANDREW. Ay, 'tis strong, and it does indifferent well in flame-colour'd stock. Shall we set about some revels?

SIR TOBY. What shall we do else? Were we not born under Taurus?

SIR ANDREW. Taurus! That's sides and heart.

SIR TOBY. No, sir; it is legs and thighs. Let me see the caper. Ha! higher! ha, ha, excellent!

[Exeunt.]

6.28.4 ACT I. SCENE IV. The DUKE'S palace.

[Enter VALENTINE, and VIOLA in man's attire.]

VALENTINE. If the duke continue these favours towards you, Cesario, you are like to be much advanc'd. He hath known you but three days, and already you are no stranger.

VIOLA. You either fear his humour or my negligence, that you call in question the continuance of his love. Is he inconstant, sir, in his favours?

VALENTINE. No, believe me.

VIOLA.	I thank you. Here comes the Count.
	[Enter DUKE, CURIO, and ATTENDANTS.]
DUKE.	Who saw Cesario, ho?
VIOLA.	On your attendance, my lord; here.
DUKE.	Stand you awhile aloof. Cesario,

Thou know'st no less but all; I have unclasp'd
To thee the book even of my secret soul.
Therefore, good youth, address thy gait unto her;
Be not denied access, stand at her doors,
And tell them, there thy fixed foot shall grow
Till thou have audience.

VIOLA. Sure, my noble lord,
If she be so abandon'd to her sorrow
As it is spoke, she never will admit me.

DUKE. Be clamorous and leap all civil bounds
Rather than make unprofited return.

VIOLA. Say I do speak with her, my lord, what then?

DUKE. O, then unfold the passion of my love,
Surprise her with discourse of my dear faith!
It shall become thee well to act my woes;
She will attend it better in thy youth
Than in a nuncio's of more grave aspect.

VIOLA. I think not so, my lord.

DUKE. Dear lad, believe it;
For they shall yet belie thy happy years,
That say thou art a man: Diana's lip
Is not more smooth and rubious; thy small pipe
Is as the maiden's organ, shrill and sound,
And all is semblative a woman's part.
I know thy constellation is right apt
For this affair. Some four or five attend him;
All, if you will; for I myself am best
When least in company. Prosper well in this,
And thou shalt live as freely as thy lord,
To call his fortunes thine.

VIOLA. I'll do my best
To woo your lady—[Aside] yet, a barful strife!
Whoe'er I woo, myself would be his wife.
[Exeunt.]

Line numbers: 10, 15, 20, 25, 30, 35, 40

6.28.5 ACT I. SCENE V. OLIVIA'S house.

	[Enter MARIA and CLOWN.]
MARIA.	Nay, either tell me where thou hast been, or I will not open my lips so wide as a bristle may enter in way of thy excuse. My lady will hang thee for thy absence.
CLOWN.	Let her hang me. He that is well hang'd in this world needs to fear no colours. 5
MARIA.	Make that good.
CLOWN.	He shall see none to fear.
MARIA.	A good lenten answer. I can tell thee where that saying was born, of "I fear no colours."
CLOWN.	Where, good Mistress Mary? 10
MARIA.	In the wars; and that may you be bold to say in your foolery.
CLOWN.	Well, God give them wisdom that have it; and those that are fools, let them use their talents.
MARIA.	Yet you will be hang'd for being so long absent; or to be turn'd away, is not that as good as a hanging to you? 15
CLOWN.	Many a good hanging prevents a bad marriage; and, for turning away, let summer bear it out.
MARIA.	You are resolute, then?
CLOWN.	Not so, neither; but I am resolv'd on two points.
MARIA.	That, if one break, the other will hold; or, if both break, your gaskins 20 fall.
CLOWN.	Apt, in good faith; very apt. Well, go thy way; if Sir Toby would leave drinking, thou wert as witty a piece of Eve's flesh as any in Illyria.
MARIA.	Peace, you rogue, no more o' that. Here comes my lady; make your excuse wisely, you were best. 25
	[Exit.]
CLOWN.	Wit, and 't be thy will, put me into good fooling! Those wits that think they have thee do very oft prove fools; and I, that am sure I lack thee, may pass for a wise man: for what says Quinapalus? "Better a witty fool than a foolish wit."
	[Enter LADY OLIVIA with MALVOLIO.]
	God bless thee, lady! 30
OLIVIA.	Take the fool away.
CLOWN.	Do you not hear, fellows? Take away the lady.
OLIVIA.	Go to, you're a dry fool; I'll no more of you: besides, you grow dishonest.
CLOWN.	Two faults, madonna, that drink and good counsel will amend; for, give the dry fool drink, then is the fool not dry: bid the dishon- 35 est man mend himself; if he mend, he is no longer dishonest; if he cannot, let the botcher mend him. Any thing that's mended is but patch'd; virtue that transgresses is but patch'd with sin; and sin that

amends is but patch'd with virtue. If that this simple syllogism will
serve, so; if it will not, what remedy? As there is no true cuckold but   40
calamity, so beauty's a flower. The lady bade take away the fool;
therefore, I say again, take her away.

OLIVIA. Sir, I bade them take away you.

CLOWN. Misprision in the highest degree! Lady, cucullus non facit
monachum; that's as much to say as I wear not motley in my brain.   45
Good madonna, give me leave to prove you a fool.

OLIVIA. Can you do it?

CLOWN. Dexteriously, good madonna.

OLIVIA. Make your proof.

CLOWN. I must catechize you for it, madonna; good my mouse of virtue,   50
answer me.

OLIVIA. Well, sir, for want of other idleness, I'll bide your proof.

CLOWN. Good madonna, why mourn'st thou?

OLIVIA. Good fool, for my brother's death.

CLOWN. I think his soul is in hell, madonna.   55

OLIVIA. I know his soul is in heaven, fool.

CLOWN. The more fool, madonna, to mourn for your brother's soul being in
heaven. Take away the fool, gentlemen.

OLIVIA. What think you of this fool, Malvolio? doth he not mend?

MALVOLIO. Yes, and shall do till the pangs of death shake him. Infirmity, that   60
decays the wise, doth ever make the better fool.

CLOWN. God send you, sir, a speedy infirmity, for the better increasing your
folly! Sir Toby will be sworn that I am no fox; but he will not pass his
word for twopence that you are no fool.

OLIVIA. How say you to that, Malvolio?   65

MALVOLIO. I marvel your ladyship takes delight in such a barren rascal; I saw
him put down the other day with an ordinary fool that has no more
brain than a stone. Look you now, he's out of his guard already; unless you laugh and minister occasion to him, he is gagg'd. I protest,
I take these wise men, that crow so at these set kind of fools, no   70
better than the fools' zanies.

OLIVIA. O, you are sick of self-love, Malvolio, and taste with a distemper'd
appetite. To be generous, guiltless, and of free disposition, is to
take those things for bird-bolts that you deem cannon bullets.
There is no slander in an allow'd fool, though he do nothing but   75
rail; nor no railing in a known discreet man, though he do nothing
but reprove.

CLOWN. Now Mercury endue thee with leasing, for thou speak'st well of
fools!

[Re-enter MARIA.]

MARIA. Madam, there is at the gate a young gentleman much desires to   80
speak with you.

OLIVIA. From the Count Orsino, is it?

MARIA.	I know not, madam; 'tis a fair young man, and well attended.	
OLIVIA.	Who of my people hold him in delay?	
MARIA.	Sir Toby, madam, your kinsman.	85
OLIVIA.	Fetch him off, I pray you; he speaks nothing but madman: fie on him! [Exit MARIA.] Go you, Malvolio: if it be a suit from the count, I am sick, or not at home; what you will, to dismiss it. [Exit MAL-VOLIO.] Now you see, sir, how your fooling grows old, and people dislike it.	90
CLOWN.	Thou hast spoke for us, madonna, as if thy eldest son should be a fool; whose skull Jove cram with brains! for—here he comes— [Enter SIR TOBY.] one of thy kin has a most weak pia mater.	
OLIVIA.	By mine honour, half drunk. What is he at the gate, cousin?	
SIR TOBY.	A gentleman.	95
OLIVIA.	A gentleman! what gentleman?	
SIR TOBY.	'Tis a gentleman here—a plague o' these pickle-herring! How now, sot!	
CLOWN.	Good Sir Toby!	
OLIVIA.	Cousin, cousin, how have you come so early by this lethargy?	
SIR TOBY.	Lechery! I defy lechery. There's one at the gate.	100
OLIVIA.	Ay, marry, what is he?	
SIR TOBY.	Let him be the devil, and he will, I care not; give me faith, say I. Well, it's all one. [Exit.]	
OLIVIA.	What's a drunken man like, fool?	
CLOWN.	Like a drown'd man, a fool, and a madman: one draught above heat makes him a fool; the second mads him; and a third drowns him.	105
OLIVIA.	Go thou and seek the crowner, and let him sit o' my coz; for he's in the third degree of drink, he's drown'd: go look after him.	
CLOWN.	He is but mad yet, madonna; and the fool shall look to the madman. [Exit.] [Re-enter MALVOLIO.]	110
MALVOLIO.	Madam, yond young fellow swears he will speak with you. I told him you were sick; he takes on him to understand so much, and therefore comes to speak with you. I told him you were asleep; he seems to have a foreknowledge of that too, and therefore comes to speak with you. What is to be said to him, lady? he's fortified against any denial.	115
OLIVIA.	Tell him he shall not speak with me.	
MALVOLIO.	Has been told so; and he says, he'll stand at your door like a sheriff's post, and be the supporter to a bench, but he'll speak with you.	
OLIVIA.	What kind o' man is he?	
MALVOLIO.	Why, of mankind.	120

OLIVIA.	What manner of man?
MALVOLIO.	Of very ill manner; he'll speak with you, will you or no.
OLIVIA.	Of what personage and years is he?
MALVOLIO.	Not yet old enough for a man, nor young enough for a boy; as a squash is before 'tis a peascod, or a codling when 'tis almost an apple: 'tis with him in standing water, between boy and man. He is very well-favour'd, and he speaks very shrewishly; one would think his mother's milk were scarce out of him.
OLIVIA.	Let him approach. Call in my gentlewoman.
MALVOLIO.	Gentlewoman, my lady calls.
	[Exit.]
	[Re-enter MARIA.]
OLIVIA.	Give me my veil; come, throw it o'er my face;
	We'll once more hear Orsino's embassy.
	[Enter VIOLA, and ATTENDANTS.]
VIOLA.	The honourable lady of the house, which is she?
OLIVIA.	Speak to me; I shall answer for her. Your will?
VIOLA.	Most radiant, exquisite, and unmatchable beauty—I pray you, tell me if this be the lady of the house, for I never saw her: I would be loath to cast away my speech; for, besides that it is excellently well penn'd, I have taken great pains to con it. Good beauties, let me sustain no scorn; I am very comptible, even to the least sinister usage.
OLIVIA.	Whence came you, sir?
VIOLA.	I can say little more than I have studied, and that question's out of my part. Good gentle one, give me modest assurance if you be the lady of the house, that I may proceed in my speech.
OLIVIA.	Are you a comedian?
VIOLA.	No, my profound heart; and yet, by the very fangs of malice I swear, I am not that I play. Are you the lady of the house?
OLIVIA.	If I do not usurp myself, I am.
VIOLA.	Most certain, if you are she, you do usurp yourself; for what is yours to bestow is not yours to reserve. But this is from my commission. I will on with my speech in your praise, and then show you the heart of my message.
OLIVIA.	Come to what is important in't; I forgive you the praise.
VIOLA.	Alas, I took great pains to study it, and 'tis poetical.
OLIVIA.	It is the more like to be feign'd; I pray you, keep it in. I heard you were saucy at my gates, and allow'd your approach rather to wonder at you than to hear you. If you be not mad, be gone; if you have reason, be brief; 'tis not that time of moon with me to make one in so skipping a dialogue.
MARIA.	Will you hoist sail, sir? here lies your way.

125

130

135

140

145

150

155

160

VIOLA.	No, good swabber; I am to hull here a little longer. Some mollification for your giant, sweet lady. Tell me your mind; I am a messenger.
OLIVIA.	Sure, you have some hideous matter to deliver, when the courtesy of it is so fearful. Speak your office.
VIOLA.	It alone concerns your ear. I bring no overture of war, no taxation of homage: I hold the olive in my hand; my words are as full of peace as matter.	165
OLIVIA.	Yet you began rudely. What are you? what would you?
VIOLA.	The rudeness that hath appear'd in me have I learn'd from my entertainment. What I am, and what I would, are as secret as maidenhead; to your ears, divinity; to any other's, profanation.	170
OLIVIA.	Give us the place alone; we will hear this divinity.
	[Exeunt MARIA and ATTENDANTS.] Now, sir, what is your text?
VIOLA.	Most sweet lady—
OLIVIA.	A comfortable doctrine, and much may be said of it. Where lies your text?	175
VIOLA.	In Orsino's bosom.
OLIVIA.	In his bosom! In what chapter of his bosom?
VIOLA.	To answer by the method, in the first of his heart.
OLIVIA.	O, I have read it; it is heresy. Have you no more to say?
VIOLA.	Good madam, let me see your face.	180
OLIVIA.	Have you any commission from your lord to negotiate with my face? You are now out of your text; but we will draw the curtain, and show you the picture. Look you, sir, such a one I was this present; is't not well done? [Unveiling.]
VIOLA.	Excellently done, if God did all.	185
OLIVIA.	'Tis in grain, sir; 'twill endure wind and weather.
VIOLA.	'Tis beauty truly blent whose red and white
	Nature's own sweet and cunning hand laid on.
	Lady, you are the cruell'st she alive,
	If you will lead these graces to the grave,	190
	And leave the world no copy.
OLIVIA.	O, sir, I will not be so hard-hearted; I will give out divers schedules of my beauty. It shall be inventoried, and every particle and utensil labell'd to my will: as, item, two lips, indifferent red; item, two grey eyes, with lids to them; item, one neck, one chin, and so forth.	195
	Were you sent hither to praise me?
VIOLA.	I see you what you are, you are too proud;
	But, if you were the devil, you are fair.
	My lord and master loves you; O, such love
	Could be but recompens'd, though you were crown'd	200
	The nonpareil of beauty!
OLIVIA.	How does he love me?

VIOLA.	With adorations, fertile tears,
	With groans that thunder love, with sighs of fire.
OLIVIA.	Your lord does know my mind; I cannot love him: 205
	Yet I suppose him virtuous, know him noble,
	Of great estate, of fresh and stainless youth;
	In voices well divulg'd, free, learn'd, and valiant;
	And, in dimension and the shape of nature,
	A gracious person: but yet I cannot love him; 210
	He might have took his answer long ago.
VIOLA.	If I did love you in my master's flame,
	With such a suffering, such a deadly life,
	In your denial I would find no sense;
	I would not understand it. 215
OLIVIA.	Why, what would you?
VIOLA.	Make me a willow cabin at your gate,
	And call upon my soul within the house;
	Write loyal cantons of contemned love,
	And sing them loud even in the dead of night; 220
	Halloo your name to the reverberate hills,
	And make the babbling gossip of the air
	Cry out, "Olivia!" O, you should not rest
	Between the elements of air and earth,
	But you should pity me! 225
OLIVIA.	You might do much. What is your parentage?
VIOLA.	Above my fortunes, yet my state is well;
	I am a gentleman.
OLIVIA.	Get you to your lord;
	I cannot love him: let him send no more; 230
	Unless, perchance, you come to me again,
	To tell me how he takes it. Fare you well;
	I thank you for your pains. Spend this for me.
VIOLA.	I am no fee'd post, lady; keep your purse:
	My master, not myself, lacks recompense. 235
	Love make his heart of flint that you shall love;
	And let your fervour, like my master's, be
	Plac'd in contempt! Farewell, fair cruelty.
	[Exit.]
OLIVIA.	"What is your parentage?"
	"Above my fortunes, yet my state is well; 240
	I am a gentleman." I'll be sworn thou art;
	Thy tongue, thy face, thy limbs, actions, and spirit,

Do give thee five-fold blazon. Not too fast! Soft, soft!

Unless the master were the man. How now!

Even so quickly may one catch the plague?   245

Methinks I feel this youth's perfections

With an invisible and subtle stealth

To creep in at mine eyes. Well, let it be.

What ho, Malvolio!

[Re-enter MALVOLIO.]

MALVOLIO.   Here, madam, at your service.   250

OLIVIA.   Run after that same peevish messenger,

The county's man: he left this ring behind him,

Would I or not; tell him I'll none of it.

Desire him not to flatter with his lord,

Nor hold him up with hopes; I am not for him.   255

If that the youth will come this way to-morrow,

I'll give him reasons for't. Hie thee, Malvolio.

MALVOLIO.   Madam, I will.

[Exit.]

OLIVIA.   I do I know not what; and fear to find

Mine eye too great a flatterer for my mind.   260

Fate, show thy force: ourselves we do not owe;

What is decreed must be, and be this so!

[Exit.]

6.28.6 ACT II. SCENE I. The sea-coast.

[Enter ANTONIO and SEBASTIAN.]

ANTONIO.   Will you stay no longer; nor will you not that I go with you?

SEBASTIAN.   By your patience, no. My stars shine darkly over me: the malig-
nancy of my fate might perhaps distemper yours; therefore I shall
crave of you your leave that I may bear my evils alone: it were a bad
recompense for your love, to lay any of them on you.   5

ANTONIO.   Let me know of you whither you are bound.

SEBASTIAN.   No, sooth, sir; my determinate voyage is mere extravagancy. But I
perceive in you so excellent a touch of modesty that you will not ex-
tort from me what I am willing to keep in; therefore it charges me in
manners the rather to express myself. You must know of me then,   10
Antonio, my name is Sebastian, which I called Roderigo. My father
was that Sebastian of Messaline whom I know you have heard of.
He left behind him myself and a sister, both born in an hour. If the
heavens had been pleas'd, would we had so ended! but you, sir,
alter'd that; for some hour before you took me from the breach of   15
the sea was my sister drown'd.

ANTONIO. Alas the day!

SEBASTIAN. A lady, sir, though it was said she much resembl'd me, was yet of many accounted beautiful; but, though I could not, with such esti- mable wonder, over-far believe that, yet thus far I will boldly publish 20 her: she bore mind that envy could not but call fair. She is drown'd already, sir, with salt water, though I seem to drown her remem- brance again with more.

ANTONIO. Pardon me, sir, your bad entertainment.

SEBASTIAN. O good Antonio, forgive me your trouble! 25

ANTONIO. If you will not murder me for my love, let me be your servant.

SEBASTIAN. If you will not undo what you have done, that is, kill him whom you have recover'd, desire it not. Fare ye well at once; my bosom is full of kindness, and I am yet so near the manners of my mother that upon the least occasion more mine eyes will tell tales of me. I am 30 bound to the Count Orsino's court; farewell.
[Exit.]

ANTONIO. The gentleness of all the gods go with thee!
I have many enemies in Orsino's court,
Else would I very shortly see thee there.
But, come what may, I do adore thee so 35
That danger shall seem sport, and I will go.
[Exit.]

6.28.7 ACT II. SCENE II. A street.

[Enter VIOLA, MALVOLIO following.]

MALVOLIO. Were you not ev'n now with the Countess Olivia?

VIOLA. Even now, sir; on a moderate pace I have since arriv'd but hither.

MALVOLIO. She returns this ring to you, sir; you might have sav'd me my pains, to have taken it away yourself. She adds, moreover, that you should put your lord into a desperate assurance she will none of him; and 5 one thing more, that you be never so hardy to come again in his affairs, unless it be to report your lord's taking of this. Receive it so.

VIOLA. She took the ring of me; I'll none of it.

MALVOLIO. Come, sir, you peevishly threw it to her; and her will is it should be so return'd. If it be worth stooping for, there it lies in your eye; if not, 10 be it his that finds it.
[Exit.]

VIOLA. I left no ring with her; what means this lady?
Fortune forbid my outside have not charm'd her!
She made good view of me; indeed, so much
That, methought, her eyes had lost her tongue, 15
For she did speak in starts distractedly.

She loves me, sure: the cunning of her passion
Invites me in this churlish messenger.
None of my lord's ring! why, he sent her none.
I am the man. If it be so, as 'tis,   20
Poor lady, she were better love a dream.
Disguise, I see thou art a wickedness,
Wherein the pregnant enemy does much.
How easy is it for the proper-false
In women's waxen hearts to set their forms!   25
Alas, our frailty is the cause, not we!
For such as we are made of, such we be.
How will this fadge? my master loves her dearly;
And I, poor monster, fond as much on him,
And she, mistaken, seems to dote on me.   30
What will become of this? As I am man,
My state is desperate for my master's love;
As I am woman—now, alas the day!—
What thriftless sighs shall poor Olivia breathe!
O time, thou must untangle this, not I;   35
It is too hard a knot for me to untie!
[Exit.]

6.28.8 ACT II. SCENE III. OLIVIA'S house.

[Enter SIR TOBY and SIR ANDREW.]

SIR TOBY.   Approach, Sir Andrew: not to be a-bed after midnight is to be up
                betimes; and *diluculo surgere*, thou know'st—

SIR ANDREW.   Nay, by my troth, I know not; but I know, to be up late is to be up late.

SIR TOBY.   A false conclusion; I hate it as an unfill'd can. To be up after mid-
                night, and to go to bed then, is early; so that to go to bed after   5
                midnight is to go to bed betimes. Does not our life consist of the
                four elements?

SIR ANDREW.   Faith, so they say; but I think it rather consists of eating and drinking.

SIR TOBY.   Thou'rt a scholar; let us therefore eat and drink. Marian, I say! a
                stoup of wine!   10

[Enter CLOWN.]

SIR ANDREW.   Here comes the fool, i' faith.

CLOWN.   How now, my hearts! did you never see the picture of "We Three"?

SIR TOBY.   Welcome, ass. Now let's have a catch.

SIR ANDREW.   By my troth, the fool has an excellent breast. I had rather than forty shil-
                lings I had such a leg, and so sweet a breath to sing, as the fool has. In   15

sooth, thou wast in very gracious fooling last night, when thou spokest of Pigrogromitus, of the Vapians passing the equinoctial of Queubus; 'twas very good, i' faith. I sent thee sixpence for thy leman; hadst it?

CLOWN. I did impeticos thy gratillity; for Malvolio's nose is no whipstock; my lady has a white hand, and the Myrmidons are no bottle-ale houses. 20

SIR ANDREW. Excellent! why, this is the best fooling, when all is done. Now, a song.

SIR TOBY. Come on; there is sixpence for you: let's have a song.

SIR ANDREW. There's a testril of me too. If one knight give a—

CLOWN. Would you have a love-song, or a song of good life?

SIR TOBY. A love-song, a love-song. 25

SIR ANDREW. Ay, ay; I care not for good life.

CLOWN. [Sings]

> O mistress mine, where are you roaming?
> O, stay and hear; your true love's coming,
> That can sing both high and low:
> Trip no further, pretty sweeting; 30
> Journeys end in lovers meeting,
> Every wise man's son doth know.

SIR ANDREW. Excellent good, i' faith.

SIR TOBY. Good, good.

CLOWN. [Sings]

> What is love? 'Tis not hereafter; 35
> Present mirth hath present laughter;
> What's to come is still unsure.
> In delay there lies no plenty,
> Then come kiss me, sweet and twenty,
> Youth's a stuff will not endure. 40

SIR ANDREW. A mellifluous voice, as I am true knight.

SIR TOBY. A contagious breath.

SIR ANDREW. Very sweet and contagious, i' faith.

SIR TOBY. To hear by the nose, it is dulcet in contagion. But shall we make the welkin dance indeed? shall we rouse the night-owl in a catch that 45 will draw three souls out of one weaver? shall we do that?

SIR ANDREW. And you love me, let's do't; I am dog at a catch.

CLOWN. By'r lady, sir, and some dogs will catch well.

SIR ANDREW. Most certain. Let our catch be, "Thou knave."

CLOWN. "Hold thy peace, thou knave," knight? I shall be constrain'd in't to 50 call thee knave, knight.

SIR ANDREW. 'Tis not the first time I have constrain'd one to call me knave. Begin, fool: it begins, "Hold thy peace."

CLOWN.	I shall never begin, if I hold my peace.	
SIR ANDREW.	Good, i' faith! Come, begin.	55
	[Catch sung.]	
	[Enter MARIA.]	
MARIA.	What a caterwauling do you keep here! If my lady have not call'd up her steward Malvolio, and bid him turn you out of doors, never trust me.	
SIR TOBY.	My lady's a Cataian, we are politicians, Malvolio's a Peg-a-Ramsey, and "Three merry men be we."	
	Am not I consanguineous? am I not of her blood? Tilly-vally;	60
	lady! [Sings] "There dwelt a man in Babylon, lady, lady!"	
CLOWN.	Beshrew me, the knight's in admirable fooling.	
SIR ANDREW.	Ay, he does well enough if he be dispos'd, and so do I too; he does it with a better grace, but I do it more natural.	
SIR TOBY.	[Sings]	
	"O, the twelfth day of December"—	65
MARIA.	For the love o' God, peace!	
	[Enter MALVOLIO.]	
MALVOLIO.	My masters, are you mad? or what are you? Have you no wit, manners, nor honesty, but to gabble like tinkers at this time of night? Do ye make an alehouse of my lady's house, that ye squeak out your coziers' catches without any mitigation or remorse of voice? Is there no respect of place, persons, nor time, in you?	70
SIR TOBY.	We did keep time, sir, in our catches. Sneck up!	
MALVOLIO.	Sir Toby, I must be round with you. My lady bade me tell you that, though she harbours you as her kinsman, she's nothing allied to your disorders. If you can separate yourself and your misdemeanours, you are welcome to the house; if not, and it would please you to take leave of her, she is very willing to bid you farewell.	75
SIR TOBY.	"Farewell, dear heart, since I must needs be gone."	
MARIA.	Nay, good Sir Toby.	
CLOWN.	"His eyes do show his days are almost done."	80
MALVOLIO.	Is't even so?	
SIR TOBY.	"But I will never die."	
CLOWN.	Sir Toby, there you lie.	
MALVOLIO.	This is much credit to you.	
SIR TOBY.	"Shall I bid him go?"	85
CLOWN.	"What and if you do?"	
SIR TOBY.	"Shall I bid him go, and spare not?"	
CLOWN.	"O, no, no, no, no, you dare not."	
SIR TOBY.	Out o' tune, sir? ye lie. Art any more than a steward? Dost thou think, because thou art virtuous, there shall be no more cakes and ale?	90

CLOWN.   Yes, by Saint Anne, and ginger shall be hot i' th' mouth too.

SIR TOBY.   Th'rt i' th' right. Go, sir, rub your chain with crumbs. A stoup of
wine, Maria!

MALVOLIO.   Mistress Mary, if you priz'd my lady's favour at any thing more   95
than contempt, you would not give means for this uncivil rule.
She shall know of it, by this hand.
[Exit.]

MARIA.   Go shake your ears.

SIR ANDREW.   'Twere as good a deed as to drink when a man's a-hungry, to challenge him the field, and then to break promise with him and make a   100
fool of him.

SIR TOBY.   Do't, knight: I'll write thee a challenge; or I'll deliver thy indignation to
him by word of mouth.

MARIA.   Sweet Sir Toby, be patient for to-night; since the youth of the
count's was to-day with my lady, she is much out of quiet. For   105
Monsieur Malvolio, let me alone with him; if I do not gull him into a
nayword, and make him a common recreation, do not think I have
wit enough to lie straight in my bed: I know I can do it.

SIR TOBY.   Possess us, possess us; tell us something of him.

MARIA.   Marry, sir, sometimes he is a kind of puritan.   110

SIR ANDREW.   O, if I thought that, I'd beat him like a dog!

SIR TOBY.   What, for being a puritan? thy exquisite reason, dear knight?

SIR ANDREW.   I have no exquisite reason for't, but I have reason good enough.

MARIA.   The devil a puritan that he is, or any thing constantly, but a time-
pleaser; an affection'd ass, that cons state without book, and utters 115
it by great swarths; the best persuaded of himself, so cramm'd, as
he thinks, with excellencies, that it is his grounds of faith that all that
look on him love him; and on that vice in him will my revenge find
notable cause to work.

SIR TOBY.   What wilt thou do?   120

MARIA.   I will drop in his way some obscure epistles of love; wherein, by
the colour of his beard, the shape of his leg, the manner of his gait,
the expressure of his eye, forehead, and complexion, he shall find
himself most feelingly personated. I can write very like my lady, your
niece; on a forgotten matter we can hardly make distinction of our   125
hands.

SIR TOBY.   Excellent! I smell a device.

SIR ANDREW.   I have't in my nose too.

SIR TOBY.   He shall think, by the letters that thou wilt drop, that they come from
my niece, and that she's in love with him.   130

MARIA.   My purpose is, indeed, a horse of that colour.

SIR ANDREW.   And your horse now would make him an ass.

MARIA.   Ass, I doubt not.

SIR ANDREW.	O, 'twill be admirable!
MARIA.	Sport royal, I warrant you; I know my physic will work with him. I 135 will plant you two, and let the fool make a third, where he shall find the letter; observe his construction of it. For this night, to bed, and dream on the event. Farewell. [Exit.]
SIR TOBY.	Good night, Penthesilea.
SIR ANDREW.	Before me, she's a good wench. 140
SIR TOBY.	She's a beagle, true-bred, and one that adores me. What o' that?
SIR ANDREW.	I was ador'd once too.
SIR TOBY.	Let's to bed, knight. Thou hadst need send for more money.
SIR ANDREW.	If I cannot recover your niece, I am a foul way out.
SIR TOBY.	Send for money, knight; if thou hast her not i' th' end, call me cut. 145
SIR ANDREW.	If I do not, never trust me; take it how you will.
SIR TOBY.	Come, come, I'll go burn some sack; 'tis too late to go to bed now. Come, knight; come, knight. [Exeunt.]

6.28.9 ACT II. SCENE IV. The DUKE'S palace.

	[Enter DUKE, VIOLA, CURIO, and others.]
DUKE.	Give me some music. Now, good morrow, friends.
	Now, good Cesario, but that piece of song,
	That old and antique song we heard last night;
	Methought it did relieve my passion much,
	More than light airs and recollected terms 5
	Of these most brisk and giddy-paced times.
	Come, but one verse.
CURIO.	He is not here, so please your lordship, that should sing it.
DUKE.	Who was it?
CURIO.	Feste, the jester, my lord; a fool that the lady Olivia's father took 10 much delight in. He is about the house.
DUKE.	Go seek him out, and play the tune the while.
	[Exit CURIO. Music plays]
	Come hither, boy. If ever thou shalt love,
	In the sweet pangs of it remember me;
	For such as I am all true lovers are, 15
	Unstaid and skittish in all motions else,
	Save in the constant image of the creature
	That is belov'd. How dost thou like this tune?
VIOLA.	It gives a very echo to the seat
	Where Love is thron'd. 20
DUKE.	Thou dost speak masterly:

My life upon't, young though thou art, thine eye
Hath stay'd upon some favour that it loves;
Hath it not, boy?

VIOLA.   A little, by your favour.   25
DUKE.   What kind of woman is't?
VIOLA.   Of your complexion.
DUKE.   She is not worth thee, then. What years, i' faith?
VIOLA.   About your years, my lord.
DUKE.   Too old, by heaven! let still the woman take   30

An elder than herself; so wears she to him,
So sways she level in her husband's heart:
For, boy, however we do praise ourselves,
Our fancies are more giddy and unfirm,
More longing, wavering, sooner lost and worn,   35
Than women's are.

VIOLA.   I think it well, my lord.
DUKE.   Then let thy love be younger than thyself,

Or thy affection cannot hold the bent;
For women are as roses, whose fair flower,   40
Being once display'd, doth fall that very hour.

VIOLA.   And so they are: alas, that they are so;

To die, even when they to perfection grow!
[Re-enter CURIO and CLOWN.]

DUKE.   O, fellow, come, the song we had last night.

Mark it, Cesario, it is old and plain;   45
The spinsters and the knitters in the sun,
And the free maids that weave their thread with bones,
Do use to chant it: it is silly sooth,
And dallies with the innocence of love,
Like the old age.   50

CLOWN.   Are you ready, sir?
DUKE.   Ay; prithee, sing.

[Music]
[Sings]

CLOWN.   Come away, come away, death,

And in sad cypress let me be laid;
Fly away, fly away, breath;   55
I am slain by a fair cruel maid.
My shroud of white, stuck all with yew,
O, prepare it!
My part of death, no one so true

	Did share it.	60
	Not a flower, not a flower sweet,	
	On my black coffin let there be strown;	
	Not a friend, not a friend greet	
	My poor corpse, where my bones shall be thrown.	
	A thousand thousand sighs to save,	65
	Lay me, O, where	
	Sad true lover never find my grave,	
	To weep there!	
DUKE.	There's for thy pains.	
CLOWN.	No pains, sir; I take pleasure in singing, sir.	70
DUKE.	I'll pay thy pleasure, then.	
CLOWN.	Truly, sir, and pleasure will be paid one time or another.	
DUKE.	Give me now leave to leave thee.	
CLOWN.	Now the melancholy god protect thee; and the tailor make thy doublet of changeable taffeta, for thy mind is a very opal. I would have men of such constancy put to sea, that their business might be every thing, and their intent every where; for that's it that always makes a good voyage of nothing. Farewell. [Exit.]	75
DUKE.	Let all the rest give place.	
	[CURIO and ATTENDANTS retire.]	
	Once more, Cesario,	80
	Get thee to yond same sovereign cruelty.	
	Tell her my love, more noble than the world,	
	Prizes not quantity of dirty lands;	
	The parts that fortune hath bestow'd upon her,	
	Tell her, I hold as giddily as fortune;	85
	But 'tis that miracle and queen of gems	
	That Nature pranks her in attracts my soul.	
VIOLA.	But if she cannot love you, sir?	
DUKE.	I cannot be so answer'd.	
VIOLA.	Sooth, but you must.	90
	Say that some lady, as perhaps there is,	
	Hath for your love as great a pang of heart	
	As you have for Olivia: you cannot love her;	
	You tell her so; must she not, then, be answer'd?	
DUKE.	There is no woman's sides	95
	Can bide the beating of so strong a passion	
	As love doth give my heart; no woman's heart	
	So big to hold so much; they lack retention.	
	Alas, their love may be call'd appetite—	

	No motion of the liver, but the palate—	100
	That suffer surfeit, cloyment, and revolt;	
	But mine is all as hungry as the sea,	
	And can digest as much. Make no compare	
	Between that love a woman can bear me	
	And that I owe Olivia.	105
VIOLA.	Ay, but I know—	
DUKE.	What dost thou know?	
VIOLA.	Too well what love women to men may owe;	
	In faith, they are as true of heart as we.	
	My father had a daughter lov'd a man,	110
	As it might be, perhaps, were I a woman,	
	I should your lordship.	
DUKE.	And what's her history?	
VIOLA.	A blank, my lord. She never told her love,	
	But let concealment, like a worm i' th' bud,	115
	Feed on her damask cheek; she pin'd in thought,	
	And with a green and yellow melancholy,	
	She sat, like patience on a monument,	
	Smiling at grief. Was not this love indeed?	
	We men may say more, swear more; but indeed	120
	Our shows are more than will; for still we prove	
	Much in our vows, but little in our love.	
DUKE.	But died thy sister of her love, my boy?	
VIOLA.	I am all the daughters of my father's house,	
	And all the brothers too; and yet I know not.	125
	Sir, shall I to this lady?	
DUKE.	Ay, that's the theme.	
	To her in haste; give her this jewel; say,	
	My love can give no place, bide no denay.	
	[Exeunt.]	

6.28.10 ACT II. SCENE V. OLIVIA'S garden.

	[Enter SIR TOBY, SIR ANDREW, and FABIAN.]	
SIR TOBY.	Come thy ways, Signior Fabian.	
FABIAN.	Nay, I'll come: if I lose a scruple of this sport, let me be boil'd to death with melancholy.	
SIR TOBY.	Wouldst thou not be glad to have the niggardly rascally sheep-biter come by some notable shame?	5

FABIAN.	I would exult, man; you know he brought me out o' favour with my lady about a bear-baiting here.	
SIR TOBY.	To anger him, we'll have the bear again; and we will fool him black and blue: shall we not, Sir Andrew?	
SIR ANDREW.	And we do not, it is pity of our lives.	10
	[Enter MARIA.]	
SIR TOBY.	Here comes the little villain.	
	How now, my metal of India!	
MARIA.	Get ye all three into the box-tree; Malvolio's coming down this walk. He has been yonder i' the sun practising behaviour to his own shadow this half hour. Observe him, for the love of mockery; for I know this letter will make a contemplative idiot of him. Close, in the name of jesting! Lie thou there [throws down a letter], for here comes the trout that must be caught with tickling. [Exit.]	15
	[Enter MALVOLIO.]	
MALVOLIO.	'Tis but fortune; all is fortune. Maria once told me she did affect me; and I have heard herself come thus near, that, should she fancy, it should be one of my complexion. Besides, she uses me with a more exalted respect than any one else that follows her. What should I think on't?	20
SIR TOBY.	Here's an overweening rogue!	
FABIAN.	O, peace! Contemplation makes a rare turkey-cock of him; how he jets under his advanc'd plumes!	25
SIR ANDREW.	'Slight, I could so beat the rogue!	
SIR TOBY.	Peace, I say.	
MALVOLIO.	To be Count Malvolio!	
SIR TOBY.	Ah, rogue!	30
SIR ANDREW.	Pistol him, pistol him.	
SIR TOBY.	Peace, peace!	
MALVOLIO.	There is example for't: the lady of the Strachy married the yeoman of the wardrobe.	
SIR ANDREW.	Fie on him, Jezebel!	35
FABIAN.	O, peace! now he's deeply in; look how imagination blows him.	
MALVOLIO.	Having been three months married to her, sitting in my state—	
SIR TOBY.	O, for a stone-bow, to hit him in the eye!	
MALVOLIO.	Calling my officers about me, in my branch'd velvet gown; having come from a day-bed, where I have left Olivia sleeping—	40
SIR TOBY.	Fire and brimstone!	
FABIAN.	O, peace, peace!	
MALVOLIO.	And then to have the humour of state; and, after a demure travel of regard, telling them I know my place, as I would they should do theirs, to ask for my kinsman Toby—	45
SIR TOBY.	Bolts and shackles!	

FABIAN.	O, peace, peace, peace! now, now.
MALVOLIO.	Seven of my people, with an obedient start, make out for him: I frown the while; and perchance wind up my watch, or play with my—some rich jewel. Toby approaches; curtsies there to me— 50
SIR TOBY.	Shall this fellow live?
FABIAN.	Though our silence be drawn from us with cars, yet peace.
MALVOLIO.	I extend my hand to him thus, quenching my familiar smile with an austere regard of control—
SIR TOBY.	And does not Toby take you a blow o' the lips, then? 55
MALVOLIO.	Saying, "Cousin Toby, my fortunes having cast me on your niece, give me this prerogative of speech"—
SIR TOBY.	What, what?
MALVOLIO.	"You must amend your drunkenness."—
SIR TOBY.	Out, scab! 60
FABIAN.	Nay, patience, or we break the sinews of our plot.
MALVOLIO.	"Besides, you waste the treasure of your time with a foolish knight"—
SIR ANDREW.	That's me, I warrant you.
MALVOLIO.	"One Sir Andrew."
SIR ANDREW.	I knew 'twas I; for many do call me fool. 65
MALVOLIO.	What employment have we here?
	[Taking up the letter.]
FABIAN.	Now is the woodcock near the gin.
SIR TOBY.	O, peace! and the spirit of humours intimate reading aloud to him!
MALVOLIO.	By my life, this is my lady's hand: these be her very C's, her U's, and her T's; and thus makes she her great P's. It is, in 70 contempt of question, her hand.
SIR ANDREW.	Her C's, her U's, and her T's; why that?
MALVOLIO.	[Reads] "To the unknown beloved, this, and my good wishes"—her very phrases! By your leave, wax. Soft! and the impressure her Lucrece, with which she uses to seal; 'tis my lady. To whom should this be? 75
FABIAN.	This wins him, liver and all.
MALVOLIO.	[Reads]

> "Jove knows I love;
> But who?
> Lips, do not move;
> No man must know." 80

"No man must know." What follows? the numbers alter'd!
"No man must know." If this should be thee, Malvolio?

SIR TOBY.	Marry, hang thee, brock!
MALVOLIO.	[Reads]

"I may command where I adore;

    But silence, like a Lucrece knife,   85

With bloodless stroke my heart doth gore:

    M, O, A, I, doth sway my life."

FABIAN.	A fustian riddle!
SIR TOBY.	Excellent wench, say I.
MALVOLIO.	"M, O, A, I, doth sway my life." Nay, but first, let me see, let me see, 90 let me see.
FABIAN.	What dish o' poison has she dress'd him!
SIR TOBY.	And with what wing the staniel checks at it!
MALVOLIO.	"I may command where I adore." Why, she may command me; I serve her; she is my lady. Why, this is evident to any formal capac- 95 ity; there is no obstruction in this: and the end—what should that alphabetical position portend? if I could make that resemble some- thing in me!—Softly! M, O, A, I—
SIR TOBY.	O, ay, make up that; he is now at a cold scent.
FABIAN.	Sowter will cry upon't for all this, though it be as rank as a fox. 100
MALVOLIO.	M—Malvolio; M—why, that begins my name.
FABIAN.	Did not I say he would work it out? the cur is excellent at faults.
MALVOLIO.	M—but then there is no consonancy in the sequel; that suffers under probation: A should follow, but O does.
FABIAN.	And O shall end, I hope. 105
SIR TOBY.	Ay, or I'll cudgel him, and make him cry O!
MALVOLIO.	And then I comes behind.
FABIAN.	Ay, an you had any eye behind you, you might see more detraction at your heels than fortunes before you.
MALVOLIO.	M, O, A, I; this simulation is not as the former; and yet, to crush this 110 a little, it would bow to me, for every one of these letters are in my name. Soft! here follows prose.—[Reads] "If this fall into thy hand, revolve. In my stars I am above thee; but be not afraid of great- ness: some are born great, some achieve greatness, and some have greatness thrust upon 'em. Thy Fates open their hands; let thy 115 blood and spirit embrace them; and, to inure thyself to what thou art like to be, cast thy humble slough and appear fresh. Be opposite with a kinsman, surly with servants; let thy tongue tang arguments of state; put thyself into the trick of singularity: she thus advises thee that sighs for thee. Remember who commended thy yellow stock- 120 ings, and wish'd to see thee ever cross-garter'd. I say, remember. Go to, thou art made, if thou desir'st to be so; if not, let me see thee a steward still, the fellow of servants, and not worthy to touch Fortune's fingers. Farewell. She that would alter services with thee, THE FORTUNATE-UNHAPPY. 125

Daylight and champain discovers not more; this is open. I will be
proud, I will read politic authors, I will baffle Sir Toby, I will wash off
gross acquaintance, I will be point-device the very man. I do not
now fool myself, to let imagination jade me; for every reason excites
to this, that my lady loves me. She did commend my yellow stock-   130
ings of late, she did praise my leg being cross-garter'd; and in this
she manifests herself to my love, and with a kind of injunction drives
me to these habits of her liking. I thank my stars, I am happy. I will
be strange, stout, in yellow stockings, and cross-garter'd, even with
the swiftness of putting on. Jove and my stars be praised!" Here is   135
yet a postscript.
[Reads] Thou canst not choose but know who I am. If thou entertain'st
my love, let it appear in thy smiling; thy smiles become thee well;
therefore in my presence still smile, dear my sweet, I prithee.
Jove, I thank thee. I will smile; I will do everything that thou   140
wilt have me.
[Exit.]

FABIAN.   I will not give my part of this sport for a pension of thousands to be
                   paid from the Sophy.

SIR TOBY.   I could marry this wench for this device.

SIR ANDREW.   So could I too.   145

SIR TOBY.   And ask no other dowry with her but such another jest.

SIR ANDREW.   Nor I neither.

FABIAN.   Here comes my noble gull-catcher.
                   [Re-enter MARIA.]

SIR TOBY.   Wilt thou set thy foot o' my neck?

SIR ANDREW.   Or o' mine either?   150

SIR TOBY.   Shall I play my freedom at tray-trip, and become thy bond-slave?

SIR ANDREW.   I' faith, or I either?

SIR TOBY.   Why, thou hast put him in such a dream, that when the image of it
                   leaves him he must run mad.

MARIA.   Nay, but say true; does it work upon him?   155

SIR TOBY.   Like aqua-vitae with a midwife.

MARIA.   If you will then see the fruits of the sport, mark his first approach
                   before my lady. He will come to her in yellow stockings, and 'tis a
                   colour she abhors; and cross-garter'd, a fashion she detests; and
                   he will smile upon her, which will now be so unsuitable to her dispo- 160
                   sition, being addicted to a melancholy as she is, that it cannot but
                   turn him into a notable contempt. If you will see it, follow me.

SIR TOBY.   To the gates of Tartar, thou most excellent devil of wit!

SIR ANDREW.   I'll make one too.
                   [Exeunt.]

6.28.11 ACT III. SCENE I. OLIVIA'S garden.

[Enter VIOLA, and CLOWN with a tabor.]

VIOLA.	Save thee, friend, and thy music! dost thou live by thy tabor?
CLOWN.	No, sir, I live by the church.
VIOLA.	Art thou a churchman?
CLOWN.	No such matter, sir: I do live by the church; for I do live at my house, and my house doth stand by the church. 5
VIOLA.	So thou mayst say, the king lies by a beggar, if a beggar dwell near him; or the church stands by thy tabor, if thy tabor stand by the church.
CLOWN.	You have said, sir. To see this age! A sentence is but a cheveril glove to a good wit; how quickly the wrong side may be turn'd outward! 10
VIOLA.	Nay, that's certain; they that dally nicely with words may quickly make them wanton.
CLOWN.	I would, therefore, my sister had had no name, sir.
VIOLA.	Why, man?
CLOWN.	Why, sir, her name's a word; and to dally with that word might make 15 my sister wanton. But, indeed, words are very rascals since bonds disgrac'd them.
VIOLA.	Thy reason, man?
CLOWN.	Troth, sir, I can yield you none without words; and words are grown so false, I am loth to prove reason with them. 20
VIOLA.	I warrant thou art a merry fellow, and car'st for nothing.
CLOWN.	Not so, sir; I do care for something; but in my conscience, sir, I do not care for you: if that be to care for nothing, sir, I would it would make you invisible.
VIOLA.	Art not thou the Lady Olivia's fool? 25
CLOWN.	No, indeed, sir; the Lady Olivia has no folly: she will keep no fool, sir, till she be married; and fools are as like husbands as pilchards are to herrings, the husband's the bigger. I am, indeed, not her fool, but her corrupter of words.
VIOLA.	I saw thee late at the Count Orsino's. 30
CLOWN.	Foolery, sir, does walk about the orb like the sun, it shines every-where. I would be sorry, sir, but the fool should be as oft with your master as with my mistress. I think I saw your wisdom there.
VIOLA.	Nay, and thou pass upon me, I'll no more with thee. Hold, there's expenses for thee. 35
CLOWN.	Now Jove, in his next commodity of hair, send thee a beard!
VIOLA.	By my troth, I'll tell thee, I am almost sick for one; [Aside] though I would not have it grow on my chin. Is thy lady within?
CLOWN.	Would not a pair of these have bred, sir?

VIOLA.	Yes, being kept together and put to use.	40
CLOWN.	I would play Lord Pandarus of Phrygia, sir, to bring a Cressida to this Troilus.	
VIOLA.	I understand you, sir; 'tis well begg'd.	
CLOWN.	The matter, I hope, is not great, sir, begging but a beggar. Cressida was a beggar. My lady is within, sir. I will construe to them whence you come; who you are and what you would are out of my welkin— I might say "element," but the word is over-worn.	45
	[Exit.]	
VIOLA.	This fellow is wise enough to play the fool;	
	And to do that well craves a kind of wit:	
	He must observe their mood on whom he jests,	50
	The quality of persons, and the time;	
	And, like the haggard, check at every feather	
	That comes before his eye. This is a practice	
	As full of labour as a wise man's art:	
	For folly that he wisely shows is fit;	55
	But wise men, folly-fall'n, quite taint their wit.	
	[Enter SIR TOBY and SIR ANDREW.]	
SIR TOBY.	Save you, gentleman!	
VIOLA.	And you, sir.	
SIR ANDREW.	Dieu vous garde, monsieur.	
VIOLA.	Et vous aussi; votre serviteur.	60
SIR ANDREW.	I hope, sir, you are; and I am yours.	
SIR TOBY.	Will you encounter the house? my niece is desirous you should enter, if your trade be to her.	
VIOLA.	I am bound to your niece, sir; I mean, she is the list of my voyage.	
SIR TOBY.	Taste your legs, sir; put them to motion.	65
VIOLA.	My legs do better understand me, sir, than I understand what you mean by bidding me taste my legs.	
SIR TOBY.	I mean, to go, sir, to enter.	
VIOLA.	I will answer you with gait and entrance. But we are prevented.	
	[Enter OLIVIA and MARIA.]	
	Most excellent accomplish'd lady, the heavens rain odours on you!	70
SIR ANDREW.	That youth's a rare courtier. "Rain odours"; well.	
VIOLA.	My matter hath no voice, lady, but to your own most pregnant and vouchsafed ear.	
SIR ANDREW.	"Odours," "pregnant," and "vouchsafed": I'll get 'em all three all ready.	75
OLIVIA.	Let the garden door be shut, and leave me to my hearing.	
	[Exeunt SIR TOBY, SIR ANDREW, and MARIA.]	
	Give me your hand, sir.	

VIOLA.	My duty, madam, and most humble service.	
OLIVIA.	What is your name?	
VIOLA.	Cesario is your servant's name, fair princess.	80
OLIVIA.	My servant, sir! 'Twas never merry world	
	Since lowly feigning was call'd compliment;	
	You're servant to the Count Orsino, youth.	
VIOLA.	And he is yours, and his must needs be yours;	
	Your servant's servant is your servant, madam.	85
OLIVIA.	For him, I think not on him; for his thoughts,	
	Would they were blanks, rather than fill'd with me!	
VIOLA.	Madam, I come to whet your gentle thoughts	
	On his behalf.	
OLIVIA.	O, by your leave, I pray you,	90
	I bade you never speak again of him;	
	But, would you undertake another suit,	
	I had rather hear you to solicit that	
	Than music from the spheres.	
VIOLA.	Dear lady—	95
OLIVIA.	Give me leave, beseech you. I did send,	
	After the last enchantment you did here,	
	A ring in chase of you; so did I abuse	
	Myself, my servant, and, I fear me, you.	
	Under your hard construction must I sit,	100
	To force that on you, in a shameful cunning,	
	Which you knew none of yours; what might you think?	
	Have you not set mine honour at the stake,	
	And baited it with all th' unmuzzled thoughts	
	That tyrannous heart can think? To one of your receiving	105
	Enough is shown. A cypress, not a bosom,	
	Hides my heart. So, let me hear you speak.	
VIOLA.	I pity you.	
OLIVIA.	That's a degree to love.	
VIOLA.	No, not a grize; for 'tis a vulgar proof,	110
	That very oft we pity enemies.	
OLIVIA.	Why, then methinks 'tis time to smile again.	
	O world, how apt the poor are to be proud!	
	If one should be a prey, how much the better	
	To fall before the lion than the wolf! [Clock strikes]	115
	The clock upbraids me with the waste of time.	
	Be not afraid, good youth, I will not have you;	
	And yet, when wit and youth is come to harvest,	
	Your wife is like to reap a proper man.	
	There lies your way, due west.	120

VIOLA.	Then westward-ho! Grace and good disposition
	Attend your ladyship!
	You'll nothing, madam, to my lord by me?
OLIVIA.	Stay:
	I prithee, tell me what thou think'st of me. 125
VIOLA.	That you do think you are not what you are.
OLIVIA.	If I think so, I think the same of you.
VIOLA.	Then think you right; I am not what I am.
OLIVIA.	I would you were as I would have you be!
VIOLA.	Would it be better, madam, than I am? 130
	I wish it might, for now I am your fool.
OLIVIA.	O, what a deal of scorn looks beautiful
	In the contempt and anger of his lip!
	A murd'rous guilt shows not itself more soon
	Than love that would seem hid; love's night is noon. 135
	Cesario, by the roses of the spring,
	By maidhood, honour, truth, and every thing,
	I love thee so, that, maugre all thy pride,
	Nor wit nor reason can my passion hide.
	Do not extort thy reasons from this clause, 140
	For that I woo, thou therefore hast no cause;
	But rather reason thus with reason fetter,
	Love sought is good, but given unsought is better.
VIOLA.	By innocence I swear, and by my youth,
	I have one heart, one bosom, and one truth, 145
	And that no woman has; nor never none
	Shall mistress be of it, save I alone.
	And so adieu, good madam; never more
	Will I my master's tears to you deplore.
OLIVIA.	Yet come again; for thou perhaps mayst move 150
	That heart, which now abhors, to like his love.
	[Exeunt.]

6.28.12 ACT III. SCENE II. OLIVIA'S house.

	[Enter SIR TOBY, SIR ANDREW and FABIAN.]
SIR ANDREW.	No, faith, I'll not stay a jot longer.
SIR TOBY.	Thy reason, dear venom, give thy reason.
FABIAN.	You must needs yield your reason, Sir Andrew.
SIR ANDREW.	Marry, I saw your niece do more favours to the count's serving-man
	than ever she bestow'd upon me; I saw't i' th' orchard. 5

SIR TOBY.	Did she see thee the while, old boy? tell me that.
SIR ANDREW.	As plain as I see you now.
FABIAN.	This was a great argument of love in her toward you.
SIR ANDREW.	'Slight, will you make an ass o' me?
FABIAN.	I will prove it legitimate, sir, upon the oaths of judgment and reason. 10
SIR TOBY.	And they have been grand-jurymen since before Noah was a sailor.
FABIAN.	She did show favour to the youth in your sight only to exasperate you, to awake your dormouse valour, to put fire in your heart, and brimstone in your liver. You should then have accosted her; and with some excellent jests, fire-new from the mint, you should have 15 bang'd the youth into dumbness. This was look'd for at your hand, and this was balk'd: the double gilt of this opportunity you let time wash off, and you are now sail'd into the north of my lady's opinion; where you will hang like an icicle on Dutchman's beard, unless you do redeem it by some laudable attempt either of valour or policy. 20
SIR ANDREW.	And't be any way, it must be with valour; for policy I hate: I had as lief be a Brownist as a politician.
SIR TOBY.	Why, then, build me thy fortunes upon the basis of valour. Challenge me the count's youth to fight with him; hurt him in eleven places: my niece shall take note of it; and assure thyself, there is no love-broker 25 in the world can more prevail in man's commendation with woman than report of valour.
FABIAN.	There is no way but this, Sir Andrew.
SIR ANDREW.	Will either of you bear me a challenge to him?
SIR TOBY.	Go, write it in a martial hand; be curst and brief; it is no matter 30 how witty, so it be eloquent and full of invention; taunt him with the license of ink; if thou thou'st him some thrice, it shall not be amiss; and as many lies as will lie in thy sheet of paper, although the sheet were big enough for the bed of Ware in England, set 'em down: go, about it. Let there be gall enough in thy ink; though thou write with a 35 goose-pen, no matter: about it.
SIR ANDREW.	Where shall I find you?
SIR TOBY.	We'll call thee at the cubiculo. Go.
	[Exit SIR ANDREW.]
FABIAN.	This is a dear manakin to you, Sir Toby.
SIR TOBY.	I have been dear to him, lad, some two thousand strong, or so. 40
FABIAN.	We shall have a rare letter from him; but you'll not deliver't?
SIR TOBY.	Never trust me, then; and by all means stir on the youth to an answer. I think oxen and wain-ropes cannot hale them together. For Andrew, if he were open'd, and you find so much blood in his liver as will clog the foot of a flea, I'll eat the rest of th' anatomy. 45
FABIAN.	And his opposite, the youth, bears in his visage no great presage of cruelty.

SIR TOBY.   Look where the youngest wren of nine comes.

[Enter MARIA.]

MARIA.   If you desire the spleen, and will laugh yourselves into stitches, follow me. Yond gull Malvolio is turn'd heathen, a very renegado; for   50
there is no Christian, that means to be sav'd by believing rightly, can
ever believe such impossible passages of grossness. He's in yellow
stockings.

SIR TOBY.   And cross-garter'd?

MARIA.   Most villainously; like a pedant that keeps a school i' th' church. I   55
have dogg'd him, like his murderer. He does obey every point of the
letter that I dropp'd to betray him; he does smile his face into more
lines than is in the new map, with the augmentation of the Indies:
you have not seen such a thing as 'tis. I can hardly forbear hurling
things at him. I know my lady will strike him; if she do, he'll smile,   60
and take't for a great favour.

SIR TOBY.   Come, bring us, bring us where he is.

[Exeunt.]

6.28.13 ACT III. SCENE III. A street.

[Enter SEBASTIAN and ANTONIO.]

SEBASTIAN.   I would not by my will have troubled you;

But, since you make your pleasure of your pains,

I will no further chide you.

ANTONIO.   I could not stay behind you: my desire,

More sharp than filed steel, did spur me forth;   5

And not all love to see you, though so much

As might have drawn one to a longer voyage,

But jealousy what might befall your travel,

Being skilless in these parts; which to a stranger,

Unguided and unfriended, often prove   10

Rough and unhospitable. My willing love,

The rather by these arguments of fear,

Set forth in your pursuit.

SEBASTIAN.   My kind Antonio,

I can no other answer make but thanks,   15

And thanks, and ever thanks; too oft good turns

Are shuffl'd off with such uncurrent pay:

But, were my worth as is my conscience firm,

You should find better dealing. What's to do?

Shall we go see the reliques of this town?   20

ANTONIO.	To-morrow, sir; best first go see your lodging.	
SEBASTIAN.	I am not weary, and 'tis long to night;	
	I pray you, let us satisfy our eyes	
	With the memorials and the things of fame	
	That do renown this city.	25
ANTONIO.	Would you'd pardon me;	
	I do not without danger walk these streets.	
	Once, in a sea-fight, 'gainst the count his galleys	
	I did some service; of such note indeed,	
	That, were I ta'en here, it would scarce be answer'd.	30
SEBASTIAN.	Belike you slew great number of his people.	
ANTONIO.	Th' offence is not of such a bloody nature;	
	Albeit the quality of the time and quarrel	
	Might well have given us bloody argument.	
	It might have since been answer'd in repaying	35
	What we took from them; which, for traffic's sake,	
	Most of our city did: only myself stood out;	
	For which, if I be lapsed in this place,	
	I shall pay dear.	
SEBASTIAN.	Do not then walk too open.	40
ANTONIO.	It doth not fit me. Hold, sir, here's my purse.	
	In the south suburbs, at the Elephant,	
	Is best to lodge. I will bespeak our diet,	
	Whiles you beguile the time and feed your knowledge	
	With viewing of the town; there shall you have me.	45
SEBASTIAN.	Why I your purse?	
ANTONIO.	Haply your eye shall light upon some toy	
	You have desire to purchase; and your store,	
	I think, is not for idle markets, sir.	
SEBASTIAN.	I'll be your purse-bearer, and leave you	50
	For an hour.	
ANTONIO.	To th' Elephant.	
SEBASTIAN.	I do remember.	
	[Exeunt.]	

6.28.14 ACT III. SCENE IV. OLIVIA'S garden.

	[Enter OLIVIA and MARIA.]
OLIVIA.	I have sent after him; he says he'll come.
	How shall I feast him? what bestow of him?
	For youth is bought more oft than begg'd or borrow'd.

	I speak too loud.	
	Where's Malvolio? He is sad and civil,	5
	And suits well for a servant with my fortunes.	
	Where is Malvolio?	
MARIA.	He's coming, madam, but in very strange manner.	
	He is, sure, possess'd, madam.	
OLIVIA.	Why, what's the matter? does he rave?	10
MARIA.	No, madam, he does nothing but smile. Your ladyship were best to have some guard about you, if he come; for, sure, the man is tainted in's wits.	
OLIVIA.	Go call him hither.	
	[Exit MARIA.]	
	I am as mad as he,	
	If sad and merry madness equal be.	15
	[Re-enter MARIA, with MALVOLIO.]	
	How now Malvolio!	
MALVOLIO.	Sweet lady, ho, ho.	
OLIVIA.	Smil'st thou?	
	I sent for thee upon a sad occasion.	
MALVOLIO.	Sad, lady! I could be sad; this does make some obstruction in the blood, this cross-gartering; but what of that? if it please the eye of one, it is with me as the very true sonnet is, "Please one, and please all."	20
OLIVIA.	Why, how dost thou, man? what is the matter with thee?	
MALVOLIO.	Not black in my mind, though yellow in my legs. It did come to his hands, and commands shall be executed; I think we do know the sweet Roman hand.	25
OLIVIA.	Wilt thou go to bed, Malvolio?	
MALVOLIO.	To bed! ay, sweet-heart, and I'll come to thee.	
OLIVIA.	God comfort thee! Why dost thou smile so and kiss thy hand so oft?	30
MARIA.	How do you, Malvolio?	
MALVOLIO.	At your request! yes; nightingales answer daws.	
MARIA.	Why appear you with this ridiculous boldness before my lady?	
MALVOLIO.	"Be not afraid of greatness"; 'twas well writ.	
OLIVIA.	What mean'st thou by that, Malvolio?	35
MALVOLIO.	"Some are born great"—	
OLIVIA.	Ha!	
MALVOLIO.	"Some achieve greatness"—	
OLIVIA.	What say'st thou?	
MALVOLIO.	"And some have greatness thrust upon them."	40
OLIVIA.	Heaven restore thee!	
MALVOLIO.	"Remember who commended thy yellow stockings"—	
OLIVIA.	Thy yellow stockings!	

MALVOLIO.	"And wish'd to see thee cross-garter'd."	
OLIVIA.	Cross-garter'd!	45
MALVOLIO.	"Go to, thou art made, if thou desir'st to be so;"—	
OLIVIA.	Am I made?	
MALVOLIO.	"If not, let me see thee a servant still."	
OLIVIA.	Why, this is very midsummer madness.	

[Enter SERVANT.]

SERVANT.	Madam, the young gentleman of the Count Orsino's is return'd: I could hardly entreat him back: he attends your ladyship's pleasure.	50
OLIVIA.	I'll come to him. [Exit SERVANT] Good Maria, let this fellow be look'd to. Where's my cousin Toby? Let some of my people have a special care of him; I would not have him miscarry for the half of my dowry.	55

[Exeunt OLIVIA and MARIA.]

MALVOLIO.	O, ho! do you come near me now? no worse man than Sir Toby to look to me! This concurs directly with the letter: she sends him on purpose, that I may appear stubborn to him; for she incites me to that in the letter. "Cast thy humble slough," says she; "be opposite with kinsman, surly with servants; let thy tongue tang with arguments of state; put thyself into the trick of singularity"; and, consequently, sets down the manner how; as, a sad face, a reverend carriage, a slow tongue, in the habit of some sir of note, and so forth. I have lim'd her; but it is Jove's doing, and Jove make me thankful! And when she went away now, "Let this fellow be look'd to"; fellow! not Malvolio, nor after my degree, but fellow. Why, every thing adheres together, that no dram of a scruple, no scruple of a scruple, no obstacle, no incredulous or unsafe circumstance—what can be said? Nothing that can be can come between me and the full prospect of my hopes. Well, Jove, not I, is the doer of this, and he is to be thank'd.	60 65 70

[Re-enter MARIA, with SIR TOBY and FABIAN.]

SIR TOBY.	Which way is he, in the name of sanctity? If all the devils of hell be drawn in little, and Legion himself possessed him, yet I'll speak to him.	
FABIAN.	Here he is, here he is. How is't with you, sir? how is't with you, man?	75
MALVOLIO.	Go off; I discard you: let me enjoy my private; go off.	
MARIA.	Lo, how hollow the fiend speaks within him! did not I tell you? Sir Toby, my lady prays you to have a care of him.	
MALVOLIO.	Ah, ha! does she so?	
SIR TOBY.	Go to, go to; peace, peace; we must deal gently with him: let me alone. How do you, Malvolio? how is't with you? What, man! defy the devil; consider, he's an enemy to mankind.	80
MALVOLIO.	Do you know what you say?	
MARIA.	La you, and you speak ill of the devil, how he takes it at heart!	

	Pray God, he be not bewitch'd! My lady would not lose him for more than I'll say.	85
MALVOLIO.	How now, mistress!	
MARIA.	O Lord!	
SIR TOBY.	Prithee, hold thy peace; this is not the way: do you not see you move him? let me alone with him.	90
FABIAN.	No way but gentleness; gently, gently: the fiend is rough, and will not be roughly us'd.	
SIR TOBY.	Why, how now, my bawcock! how dost thou, chuck?	
MALVOLIO.	Sir!	
SIR TOBY.	Ay, Biddy, come with me. What, man! 'tis not for gravity to play at cherry-pit with Satan. Hang him, foul collier!	95
MARIA.	Get him to say his prayers; good Sir Toby, get him to pray.	
MALVOLIO.	My prayers, minx!	
MARIA.	No, I warrant you, he will not hear of godliness.	
MALVOLIO.	Go, hang yourselves all! you are idle shallow things. I am not of your element; you shall know more hereafter.	100
	[Exit.]	
SIR TOBY.	Is't possible?	
FABIAN.	If this were play'd upon a stage now, I could condemn it as an improbable fiction.	
SIR TOBY.	His very genius hath taken the infection of the device, man.	105
MARIA.	Nay, pursue him now, lest the device take air and taint.	
FABIAN.	Why, we shall make him mad indeed.	
MARIA.	The house will be the quieter.	
SIR TOBY.	Come, we'll have him in a dark room and bound. My niece is already in the belief that he's mad: we may carry it thus, for our pleasure and his penance, till our very pastime, tired out of breath, prompt us to have mercy on him; at which time we will bring the device to the bar, and crown thee for a finder of madmen. But see, but see.	110
	[Enter SIR ANDREW.]	
FABIAN.	More matter for a May morning.	
SIR ANDREW.	Here's the challenge, read it; I warrant there's vinegar and pepper in't.	115
FABIAN.	Is't so saucy?	
SIR ANDREW.	Ay, is't, I warrant him; do but read.	
SIR TOBY.	Give me. [Reads] "Youth, whatsoever thou art, thou art but a scurvy fellow."	120
FABIAN.	Good and valiant.	
SIR TOBY.	[Reads] "Wonder not, nor admire not in thy mind, why I do call thee so, for I will show thee no reason for't."	
FABIAN.	A good note; that keeps you from the blow of the law.	

SIR TOBY.	[Reads] Thou com'st to the lady Olivia, and in my sight she uses	125
	thee kindly: but thou liest in thy throat; that is not the matter	
	I challenge thee for.	
FABIAN.	Very brief, and to exceeding good sense—less.	
SIR TOBY.	[Reads] "I will waylay thee going home; where if it be thy chance to	
	kill me" —	130
FABIAN.	Good.	
SIR TOBY.	[Reads.] "Thou kill'st me like a rogue and a villain."	
FABIAN.	Still you keep o' th' windy side of the law; good.	
SIR TOBY.	[Reads] "Fare thee well; and God have mercy upon one of our souls!	
	He may have mercy upon mine; but my hope is better, and so look	135
	to thyself. Thy friend, as thou usest him, and thy sworn enemy,	
	ANDREW AGUECHEEK."	
	If this letter move him not, his legs cannot; I'll give't him.	
MARIA.	You may have very fit occasion for't; he is now in some commerce	
	with my lady, and will by and by depart.	140
SIR TOBY.	Go, Sir Andrew; scout me for him at the corner of the orchard, like	
	a bum-baily. So soon as ever thou see'st him, draw; and as thou	
	drawest, swear horrible; for it comes to pass oft, that a terrible oath,	
	with a swaggering accent sharply twang'd off, gives manhood more	
	approbation than ever proof itself would have earn'd him. Away!	145
SIR ANDREW.	Nay, let me alone for swearing.	
	[Exit.]	
SIR TOBY.	Now will not I deliver his letter; for the behaviour of the young	
	gentleman gives him out to be of good capacity and breeding;	
	his employment between his lord and my niece confirms no less:	
	therefore this letter, being so excellently ignorant, will breed no	150
	terror in the youth; he will find it comes from a clodpole. But, sir, I	
	will deliver his challenge by word of mouth; set upon Aguecheek	
	a notable report of valour; and drive the gentleman, as I know his	
	youth will aptly receive it, into a most hideous opinion of his rage,	
	skill, fury, and impetuosity. This will so fright them both, that they	155
	will kill one another by the look, like cockatrices.	
	[Re-enter OLIVIA with VIOLA.]	
FABIAN.	Here he comes with your niece; give them way till he take leave,	
	and presently after him.	
SIR TOBY.	I will meditate the while upon some horrid message for a challenge.	
	[Exeunt SIR TOBY, FABIAN, and MARIA.]	
OLIVIA.	I have said too much unto a heart of stone,	160
	And laid mine honour too unchary out.	
	There's something in me that reproves my fault;	
	But such a headstrong potent fault it is,	
	That it but mocks reproof.	

VIOLA.   With the same haviour that your passion bears,   165
              Goes on my master's grief.
OLIVIA.   Here, wear this jewel for me, 'tis my picture:
              Refuse it not; it hath no tongue to vex you:
              And I beseech you come again to-morrow.
              What shall you ask of me that I'll deny,   170
              That honour sav'd may upon asking give?
VIOLA.   Nothing but this—your true love for my master.
OLIVIA.   How with mine honour may I give him that
              Which I have given to you?
VIOLA.   I will acquit you.   175
OLIVIA.   Well, come again to-morrow; fare thee well.
              A fiend like thee might bear my soul to hell.
              [Exit.]
              [Re-enter SIR TOBY and FABIAN.]
SIR TOBY.   Gentleman, God save thee!
VIOLA.   And you, sir.
SIR TOBY.   That defence thou hast, betake thee to't. Of what nature the wrongs   180
              are thou hast done him, I know not; but thy intercepter, full of
              despite, bloody as the hunter, attends thee at the orchard-end. Dis-
              mount thy tuck, be yare in thy preparation; for thy assailant is quick,
              skilful, and deadly.
VIOLA.   You mistake, sir; I am sure no man hath any quarrel to me: my   185
              remembrance is very free and clear from any image of offence done
              to any man.
SIR TOBY.   You'll find it otherwise, I assure you. Therefore, if you hold your life
              at any price, betake you to your guard; for your opposite hath in him
              what youth, strength, skill, and wrath can furnish man withal.   190
VIOLA.   I pray you, sir, what is he?
SIR TOBY.   He is knight, dubb'd with unhatch'd rapier and on carpet consid-
              eration; but he is a devil in private brawl: souls and bodies hath he
              divorc'd three; and his incensement at this moment is so implacable
              that satisfaction can be none but by pangs of death and sepulchre.   195
              Hob, nob, is his word; give't or take't.
VIOLA.   I will return again into the house and desire some conduct of the
              lady. I am no fighter. I have heard of some kind of men that put
              quarrels purposely on others, to taste their valour; belike this is a
              man of that quirk.   200
SIR TOBY.   Sir, no; his indignation derives itself out of a very competent injury.
              Therefore get you on and give him his desire. Back you shall not to
              the house, unless you undertake that with me which with as much
              safety you might answer him. Therefore on, or strip your sword stark
              naked; for meddle you must, that's certain, or forswear to wear iron   205
              about you.

VIOLA.	This is as uncivil as strange. I beseech you, do me this courte-ous office, as to know of the knight what my offence to him is; it is something of my negligence, nothing of my purpose.	
SIR TOBY.	I will do so. Signior Fabian, stay you by this gentleman till my return.	210
	[Exit.]	
VIOLA.	Pray you, sir, do you know of this matter?	
FABIAN.	I know the knight is incens'd against you, even to a mortal arbitre-ment; but nothing of the circumstance more.	
VIOLA.	I beseech you, what manner of man is he?	
FABIAN.	Nothing of that wonderful promise, to read him by his form, as you are like to find him in the proof of his valour. He is, indeed, sir, the most skilful, bloody, and fatal opposite that you could possibly have found in any part of Illyria. Will you walk towards him? I will make your peace with him, if I can.	215
VIOLA.	I shall be much bound to you for't. I am one that had rather go with sir priest than sir knight; I care not who knows so much of my mettle.	220
	[Exeunt.]	
	[Re-enter SIR TOBY, with SIR ANDREW.]	
SIR TOBY.	Why, man, he's a very devil; I have not seen such a firago. I had a pass with him, rapier, scabbard, and all, and he gives me the stuck in with such a mortal motion that it is inevitable; and, on the answer, he pays you as surely as your feet hit the ground they step on. They say he has been fencer to the Sophy.	225
SIR ANDREW.	Pox on't, I'll not meddle with him.	
SIR TOBY.	Ay, but he will not now be pacified; Fabian can scarce hold him yonder.	230
SIR ANDREW.	Plague on't; and I thought he had been valiant and so cunning in fence, I'd have seen him damn'd ere I'd have challeng'd him. Let him let the matter slip, and I'll give him my horse, gray Capilet.	
SIR TOBY.	I'll make the motion. Stand here, make a good show on't; this shall end without the perdition of souls. [Aside] Marry, I'll ride your horse as well as I ride you.	235
	[Re-enter FABIAN and VIOLA.]	
	[To FABIAN] I have his horse to take up the quarrel; I have persuad-ed him the youth's a devil.	
FABIAN.	He is as horribly conceited of him; and pants and looks pale, as if a bear were at his heels.	240
SIR TOBY.	[To VIOLA] There's no remedy, sir: he will fight with you for's oath sake. Marry, he hath better bethought him of his quarrel, and he finds that now scarce to be worth talking of: therefore draw, for the supportance of his vow; he protests he will not hurt you.	
VIOLA.	[Aside] Pray God defend me! A little thing would make me tell them how much I lack of a man.	245

FABIAN.   Give ground, if you see him furious.

SIR TOBY.   Come, Sir Andrew, there's no remedy; the gentleman will, for his
honour's sake, have one bout with you; he cannot by the duello
avoid it; but he has promis'd me, as he is a gentleman and a soldier, 250
he will not hurt you. Come on; to't.

SIR ANDREW.   Pray God, he keep his oath!

VIOLA.   I do assure you 'tis against my will. [They draw.]

[Enter ANTONIO.]

ANTONIO.   Put up your sword. If this young gentleman

Have done offence, I take the fault on me;   255

If you offend him, I for him defy you.

SIR TOBY.   You, sir! why, what are you?

ANTONIO.   One, sir, that for his love dares yet do more

Than you have heard him brag to you he will.

SIR TOBY.   Nay, if you be an undertaker, I am for you.   260

[They draw]

[Enter OFFICERS.]

FABIAN.   O good Sir Toby, hold! here come the officers.

SIR TOBY.   I'll be with you anon.

VIOLA.   Pray, sir, put your sword up, if you please.

SIR ANDREW.   Marry, will I, sir; and, for that I promis'd you, I'll be as good as my
word; he will bear you easily, and reins well.   265

1 OFFICER.   This is the man; do thy office.

2 OFFICER.   Antonio, I arrest thee at the suit

Of Count Orsino.

ANTONIO.   You do mistake me, sir.

1 OFFICER.   No, sir, no jot; I know your favour well,   270

Though now you have no sea-cap on your head.

Take him away; he knows I know him well.

ANTONIO.   I must obey. [To VIOLA] This comes with seeking you:

But there's no remedy; I shall answer it.

What will you do, now my necessity   275

Makes me to ask you for my purse? It grieves me

Much more for what I cannot do for you

Than what befalls myself. You stand amaz'd;

But be of comfort.

2 OFFICER.   Come, sir, away.   280

ANTONIO.   I must entreat of you some of that money.

VIOLA.   What money, sir?

For the fair kindness you have show'd me here,

And, part, being prompted by your present trouble,

Out of my lean and low ability   285

	I'll lend you something. My having is not much;	
	I'll make division of my present with you:	
	Hold, there's half my coffer.	
ANTONIO.	Will you deny me now?	
	Is't possible that my deserts to you	290
	Can lack persuasion? Do not tempt my misery,	
	Lest that it make me so unsound a man	
	As to upbraid you with those kindnesses	
	That I have done for you.	
VIOLA.	I know of none;	295
	Nor know I you by voice or any feature.	
	I hate ingratitude more in a man	
	Than lying, vainness, babbling, drunkenness,	
	Or any taint of vice whose strong corruption	
	Inhabits our frail blood.	300
ANTONIO.	O heavens themselves!	
2 OFFICER.	Come, sir, I pray you, go.	
ANTONIO.	Let me speak a little. This youth that you see here	
	I snatch'd one half out of the jaws of death,	
	Reliev'd him with such sanctity of love,	305
	And to his image, which methought did promise	
	Most venerable worth, did I devotion.	
1 OFFICER.	What's that to us? The time goes by; away!	
ANTONIO.	But O how vile an idol proves this god!	
	Thou hast, Sebastian, done good feature shame.	310
	In nature there's no blemish but the mind;	
	None can be call'd deform'd but the unkind.	
	Virtue is beauty; but the beauteous evil	
	Are empty trunks, o'erflourish'd by the devil.	
1 OFFICER.	The man grows mad; away with him!	315
	Come, come, sir.	
ANTONIO.	Lead me on.	
	[Exit with OFFICERS.]	
VIOLA.	Methinks his words do from such passion fly	
	That he believes himself; so do not I. Prove true, imagination, O, prove true,	320
	That I, dear brother, be now ta'en for you!	
SIR TOBY.	Come hither, knight; come hither, Fabian; we'll whisper o'er a couplet or two of most sage saws.	
VIOLA.	He nam'd Sebastian. I my brother know	

| | Yet living in my glass; even such and so | 325 |

Yet living in my glass; even such and so 325
In favour was my brother; and he went
Still in this fashion, colour, ornament,
For him I imitate. O, if it prove,
Tempests are kind, and salt waves fresh in love!
[Exit.]

SIR TOBY. A very dishonest paltry boy, and more a coward than a hare: his 330 dishonesty appears in leaving his friend here in necessity and denying him; and for his cowardship, ask Fabian.

FABIAN. A coward, a most devout coward, religious in it.

SIR ANDREW. 'Slid, I'll after him again and beat him.

SIR TOBY. Do; cuff him soundly, but never draw thy sword. 335

SIR ANDREW. And I do not —
[Exit.]

FABIAN. Come, let's see the event.

SIR TOBY. I dare lay any money 'twill be nothing yet.
[Exeunt.]

6.28.15 ACT IV. SCENE I. Before OLIVIA'S house.

[Enter SEBASTIAN and CLOWN.]

CLOWN. Will you make me believe that I am not sent for you?

SEBASTIAN. Go to, go to, thou art a foolish fellow;
Let me be clear of thee.

CLOWN. Well held out, i' faith! No, I do not know you; nor I am not sent to you by my lady, to bid you come speak with her; nor your name is 5 not Master Cesario; nor this is not my nose neither. Nothing that is so is so.

SEBASTIAN. I prithee, vent thy folly somewhere else;
Thou know'st not me.

CLOWN. Vent my folly! He has heard that word of some great man, and now 10 applies it to a fool. Vent my folly! I am afraid this great lubber, the world, will prove a cockney. I prithee now, ungird thy strangeness, and tell me what I shall vent to my lady; shall I vent to her that thou art coming?

SEBASTIAN. I prithee, foolish Greek, depart from me. 15
There's money for thee; if you tarry longer,
I shall give worse payment.

CLOWN. By my troth, thou hast an open hand. These wise men that give fools money get themselves a good report after fourteen years' purchase. 20
[Enter SIR ANDREW, SIR TOBY, and FABIAN.]

SIR ANDREW.	Now, sir, have I met you again? there's for you.
SEBASTIAN.	Why, there's for thee, and there, and there.
	Are all the people mad?
SIR TOBY.	Hold, sir, or I'll throw your dagger o'er the house.
CLOWN.	This will I tell my lady straight. I would not be in some of your 25
	coats for twopence.
	[Exit.]
SIR TOBY.	Come on, sir; hold.
SIR ANDREW.	Nay, let him alone: I'll go another way to work with him; I'll have an
	action of battery against him, if there be any law in Illyria: though I
	struck him first, yet it's no matter for that. 30
SEBASTIAN.	Let go thy hand.
SIR TOBY.	Come, sir, I will not let you go. Come, my young soldier, put up your
	iron: you are well flesh'd; come on.
SEBASTIAN.	I will be free from thee. What wouldst thou now?
	If thou dar'st tempt me further, draw thy sword. 35
SIR TOBY.	What, what? Nay, then I must have an ounce or two of this malapert
	blood from you.
	[Enter OLIVIA.]
OLIVIA.	Hold, Toby; on thy life, I charge thee, hold!
SIR TOBY.	Madam!
OLIVIA.	Will it be ever thus? Ungracious wretch, 40
	Fit for the mountains and the barbarous caves,
	Where manners ne'er were preach'd! Out of my sight!
	Be not offended, dear Cesario.
	Rudesby, be gone!
	[Exeunt SIR TOBY, SIR ANDREW, and FABIAN.]
	I prithee, gentle friend, 45
	Let thy fair wisdom, not thy passion, sway
	In this uncivil and unjust extent
	Against thy peace. Go with me to my house;
	And hear thou there how many fruitless pranks
	This ruffian hath botch'd up, that thou thereby 50
	Mayst smile at this: thou shalt not choose but go;
	Do not deny. Beshrew his soul for me,
	He started one poor heart of mine in thee.
SEBASTIAN.	What relish is in this? how runs the stream?
	Or I am mad, or else this is a dream. 55
	Let fancy still my sense in Lethe steep;
	If it be thus to dream, still let me sleep!

OLIVIA.	Nay, come, I prithee. Would thou'dst be rul'd by me!	
SEBASTIAN.	Madam, I will.	
OLIVIA.	O, say so, and so be!	60
	[Exeunt.]	

6.28.16 ACT IV. SCENE II. OLIVIA'S house.

	[Enter MARIA and CLOWN.]	
MARIA.	Nay, I prithee, put on this gown and this beard; make him believe	
	thou art Sir Topas the curate: do it quickly; I'll call Sir Toby	
	the whilst.	
	[Exit.]	
CLOWN.	Well, I'll put it on, and I will dissemble myself in't; and I would I were	
	the first that ever dissembl'd in such a gown. I am not tall enough	5
	to become the function well, nor lean enough to be thought a good	
	student; but to be said an honest man and a good housekeeper	
	goes as fairly as to say a careful man and a great scholar. The	
	competitors enter.	
	[Enter SIR TOBY and MARIA.]	
SIR TOBY.	Jove bless thee, master parson!	10
CLOWN.	Bonos dies, Sir Toby: for, as the old hermit of Prague, that never	
	saw pen and ink, very wittily said to niece of King Gorboduc, "That	
	that is is"; so I, being master parson, am master parson; for, what is	
	"that" but "that," and "is" but "is"?	
SIR TOBY.	To him, Sir Topas.	15
CLOWN.	What, ho, I say, peace in this prison!	
SIR TOBY.	The knave counterfeits well; a good knave.	
MALVOLIO.	[Within] Who calls there?	
CLOWN.	Sir Topas the curate, who comes to visit Malvolio the lunatic.	
MALVOLIO.	Sir Topas, Sir Topas, good Sir Topas, go to my lady.	20
CLOWN.	Out, hyperbolical fiend! how vexest thou this man! talkest thou	
	nothing but of ladies?	
SIR TOBY.	Well said, master parson.	
MALVOLIO.	Sir Topas, never was man thus wrong'd; good Sir Topas, do not	
	think I am mad: they have laid me here in hideous darkness.	25
CLOWN.	Fie, thou dishonest Satan! I call thee by the most modest terms;	
	for I am one of those gentle ones that will use the devil himself with	
	courtesy. Say'st thou that house is dark?	
MALVOLIO.	As hell, Sir Topas.	

CLOWN.	Why, it hath bay-windows transparent as barricadoes, and the clerestories toward the south north are as lustrous as ebony; and yet complainest thou of obstruction?	30
MALVOLIO.	I am not mad, Sir Topas; I say to you, this house is dark.	
CLOWN.	Madman, thou errest: I say, there is no darkness but ignorance; in which thou art more puzzl'd than the Egyptians in their fog.	35
MALVOLIO.	I say, this house is as dark as ignorance, though ignorance were as dark as hell; and I say, there was never man thus abus'd. I am no more mad than you are; make the trial of it in any constant question.	
CLOWN.	What is the opinion of Pythagoras concerning wild fowl?	
MALVOLIO.	That the soul of our grandam might haply inhabit a bird.	40
CLOWN.	What think'st thou of his opinion?	
MALVOLIO.	I think nobly of the soul, and no way approve his opinion.	
CLOWN.	Fare thee well. Remain thou still in darkness; thou shalt hold th' opinion of Pythagoras ere I will allow of thy wits, and fear to kill a woodcock lest thou dispossess the soul of thy grandam. Fare thee well.	45
MALVOLIO.	Sir Topas, Sir Topas!	
SIR TOBY.	My most exquisite Sir Topas!	
CLOWN.	Nay, I am for all waters.	
MARIA.	Thou mightst have done this without thy beard and gown; he sees thee not.	50
SIR TOBY.	To him in thine own voice, and bring me word how thou find'st him; I would we were well rid of this knavery. If he may be conveniently deliver'd, I would he were, for I am now so far in offence with my niece that I cannot pursue with any safety this sport to the upshot. Come by and by to my chamber.	55
	[Exeunt SIR TOBY and MARIA.]	
CLOWN.	[Singing] Hey, Robin, jolly Robin, Tell me how thy lady does.	
MALVOLIO.	Fool—	
CLOWN.	My lady is unkind, perdy.	
MALVOLIO.	Fool—	60
CLOWN.	Alas, why is she so?	
MALVOLIO.	Fool, I say—	
CLOWN.	She loves another—Who calls, ha?	
MALVOLIO.	Good fool, as ever thou wilt deserve well at my hand, help me to a candle, and pen, ink, and paper; as I am a gentleman, I will live to be thankful to thee for't.	65
CLOWN.	Master Malvolio?	
MALVOLIO.	Ay, good fool.	
CLOWN.	Alas, sir, how fell you besides your five wits?	

MALVOLIO.	Fool, there was never man so notoriously abus'd; I am as well in my 70
	wits, fool, as thou art.
CLOWN.	But as well? then you are mad indeed, if you be no better in your
	wits than a fool.
MALVOLIO.	They have here propertied me; keep me in darkness, send ministers
	to me, asses, and do all they can to face me out of my wits. 75
CLOWN.	Advise you what you say; the minister is here. Malvolio,
	Malvolio, thy wits the heavens restore! endeavour thyself to
	sleep, and leave thy vain bibble babble.
MALVOLIO.	Sir Topas!
CLOWN.	Maintain no words with him, good fellow. Who, I, sir? not I, sir. 80
	God be wi' you, good Sir Topas! Marry, amen. I will, sir, I
	will.
MALVOLIO.	Fool, fool, fool, I say!
CLOWN.	Alas, sir, be patient. What say you, sir? I am shent for speaking to you.
MALVOLIO.	Good fool, help me to some light and some paper. I tell thee, I am 85
	as well in my wits as any man in Illyria.
CLOWN.	Well-a-day that you were, sir!
MALVOLIO.	By this hand, I am. Good fool, some ink, paper, and light; and
	convey what I will set down to my lady. It shall advantage thee more
	than ever the bearing of letter did. 90
CLOWN.	I will help you to't. But tell me true, are you not mad indeed, or do
	you but counterfeit?
MALVOLIO.	Believe me, I am not; I tell thee true.
CLOWN.	Nay, I'll ne'er believe a madman till I see his brains. I will fetch you
	light and paper and ink. 95
MALVOLIO.	Fool, I'll requite it in the highest degree; I prithee, be gone.
CLOWN.	[Singing]

> I am gone, sir,
>> And anon, sir,
> I'll be with you again,
>> In a trice,   100
>> Like to the old Vice,
> Your need to sustain;
>> Who, with dagger of lath,
>> In his rage and his wrath,
> Cries, ah, ha! to the devil: 105
>> Like a mad lad,
>> Pare thy nails, dad;
> Adieu, goodman devil.

[Exit.]

6.28.17 ACT IV. SCENE III. OLIVIA'S garden.

[Enter SEBASTIAN.]

SEBASTIAN. This is the air; that is the glorious sun;
This pearl she gave me, I do feel't and see't;
And though 'tis wonder that enwraps me thus,
Yet 'tis not madness. Where's Antonio, then?
I could not find him at the Elephant: 5
Yet there he was; and there I found this credit,
That he did range the town to seek me out.
His counsel now might do me golden service;
For though my soul disputes well with my sense,
That this may be some error, but no madness, 10
Yet doth this accident and flood of fortune
So far exceed all instance, all discourse,
That I am ready to distrust mine eyes
And wrangle with my reason, that persuades me
To any other trust but that I am mad, 15
Or else the lady's mad; yet if 'twere so,
She could not sway her house, command her followers,
Take and give back affairs and their dispatch
With such a smooth, discreet, and stable bearing
As I perceive she does. There's something in't 20
That is deceivable. But here the lady comes.
[Enter OLIVIA and PRIEST.]

OLIVIA. Blame not this haste of mine. If you mean well,
Now go with me and with this holy man
Into the chantry by. There, before him,
And underneath that consecrated roof, 25
Plight me the full assurance of your faith;
That my most jealous and too doubtful soul
May live at peace. He shall conceal it
Whiles you are willing it shall come to note,
What time we will our celebration keep 30
According to my birth. What do you say?

SEBASTIAN. I'll follow this good man, and go with you;
And, having sworn truth, ever will be true.

OLIVIA. Then lead the way, good father; and heavens so shine
That they may fairly note this act of mine! 35
[Exeunt.]

6.28.18 ACT V. SCENE I. Before OLIVIA's house.

	[Enter CLOWN and FABIAN.]	
FABIAN.	Now, as thou lov'st me, let me see his letter.	
CLOWN.	Good Master Fabian, grant me another request.	
FABIAN.	Any thing.	
CLOWN.	Do not desire to see this letter.	
FABIAN.	This is, to give a dog, and in recompense desire my dog again.	5
	[Enter DUKE, VIOLA, CURIO, and LORDS.]	
DUKE.	Belong you to the Lady Olivia, friends?	
CLOWN.	Ay, sir; we are some of her trappings.	
DUKE.	I know thee well; how dost thou, my good fellow?	
CLOWN.	Truly, sir, the better for my foes and the worse for my friends.	
DUKE.	Just the contrary; the better for thy friends.	10
CLOWN.	No, sir, the worse.	
DUKE.	How can that be?	
CLOWN.	Marry, sir, they praise me and make an ass of me. Now my foes tell me plainly I am an ass: so that by my foes, sir, I profit in the knowledge of myself, and by my friends I am abus'd: so that, conclusions to be as kisses, if your four negatives make your two affirmatives, why, then the worse for my friends and the better for my foes.	15
DUKE.	Why, this is excellent.	
CLOWN.	By my troth, sir, no; though it please you to be one of my friends.	
DUKE.	Thou shalt not be the worse for me; there's gold.	20
CLOWN.	But that it would be double-dealing, sir, I would you could make it another.	
DUKE.	O, you give me ill counsel.	
CLOWN.	Put your grace in your pocket, sir, for this once, and let your flesh and blood obey it.	25
DUKE.	Well, I will be so much a sinner to be a double-dealer; there's another.	
CLOWN.	Primo, secundo, tertio, is a good play; and the old saying is, the third pays for all: the triplex, sir, is a good tripping measure; or the bells of Saint Bennet, sir, may put you in mind; one, two, three.	30
DUKE.	You can fool no more money out of me at this throw; if you will let your lady know I am here to speak with her, and bring her along with you, it may awake my bounty further.	
CLOWN.	Marry, sir, lullaby to your bounty till I come again. I go, sir; but I would not have you to think that my desire of having is the sin of covetousness: but, as you say, sir, let your bounty take a nap, I will awake it anon.	35
	[Exit.]	

VIOLA.	Here comes the man, sir, that did rescue me.
	[Enter ANTONIO and OFFICERS .]
DUKE.	That face of his I do remember well; 40
	Yet, when I saw it last, it was besmear'd
	As black as Vulcan in the smoke of war.
	A baubling vessel was he captain of,
	For shallow draught and bulk unprizable;
	With which such scathful grapple did he make 45
	With the most noble bottom of our fleet
	That very envy and the tongue of loss
	Cried fame and honour on him. What's the matter?
1 OFFICER.	Orsino, this is that Antonio
	That took the Phoenix and her fraught from Candy; 50
	And this is he that did the Tiger board,
	When your young nephew Titus lost his leg.
	Here in the streets, desperate of shame and state,
	In private brabble did we apprehend him.
VIOLA.	He did me kindness, sir; drew on my side; 55
	But in conclusion put strange speech upon me;
	I know not what 'twas but distraction.
DUKE.	Notable pirate! thou salt-water thief!
	What foolish boldness brought thee to their mercies,
	Whom thou, in terms so bloody and so dear, 60
	Hast made thine enemies?
ANTONIO.	Orsino, noble sir,
	Be pleas'd that I shake off these names you give me;
	Antonio never yet was thief or pirate,
	Though, I confess, on base and ground enough, 65
	Orsino's enemy. A witchcraft drew me hither:
	That most ingrateful boy there by your side,
	From the rude sea's enrag'd and foamy mouth
	Did I redeem; a wreck past hope he was.
	His life I gave him, and did thereto ad 70
	My love, without retention or restraint,
	All his in dedication; for his sake
	Did I expose myself, pure for his love,
	Into the danger of this adverse town;
	Drew to defend him when he was beset: 75
	Where being apprehended, his false cunning,
	Not meaning to partake with me in danger,

	Taught him to face me out of his acquaintance,	
	And grew a twenty years removed thing	
	While one would wink; denied me mine own purse,	80
	Which I had recommended to his use	
	Not half an hour before.	
VIOLA.	How can this be?	
DUKE.	When came he to this town?	
ANTONIO.	To-day, my lord; and for three months before,	85
	No interim, not a minute's vacancy,	
	Both day and night did we keep company.	
	[Enter OLIVIA and ATTENDANTS.]	
DUKE.	Here comes the countess; now heaven walks on earth.	
	But for thee, fellow—fellow, thy words are madness;	
	Three months this youth hath tended upon me;	90
	But more of that anon. Take him aside.	
OLIVIA.	What would my lord, but that he may not have,	
	Wherein Olivia may seem serviceable?	
	Cesario, you do not keep promise with me.	
VIOLA.	Madam!	95
DUKE.	Gracious Olivia—	
OLIVIA.	What do you say, Cesario? Good my lord—	
VIOLA.	My lord would speak; my duty hushes me.	
OLIVIA.	If it be aught to the old tune, my lord,	
	It is as fat and fulsome to mine ear	100
	As howling after music.	
DUKE.	Still so cruel?	
OLIVIA.	Still so constant, lord.	
DUKE.	What, to perverseness? you uncivil lady,	
	To whose ingrate and unauspicious altars	105
	My soul the faithfull'st off'rings have breath'd out	
	That e'er devotion tender'd! What shall I do?	
OLIVIA.	Even what it please my lord that shall become him.	
DUKE.	Why should I not, had I the heart to do it,	
	Like to th' Egyptian thief at point of death,	110
	Kill what I love?—a savage jealousy	
	That sometime savours nobly. But hear me this:	
	Since you to non-regardance cast my faith,	
	And that I partly know the instrument	
	That screws me from my true place in your favour,	115
	Live you the marble-breasted tyrant still;	

	But this your minion, whom I know you love,	
	And whom, by heaven I swear, I tender dearly,	
	Him will I tear out of that cruel eye,	
	Where he sits crowned in his master's spite.	120
	Come, boy, with me; my thoughts are ripe in mischief;	
	I'll sacrifice the lamb that I do love,	
	To spite a raven's heart within a dove.	
VIOLA.	And I, most jocund, apt, and willingly,	
	To do you rest, a thousand deaths would die.	125
OLIVIA.	Where goes Cesario?	
VIOLA.	After him I love	
	More than I love these eyes, more than my life,	
	More, by all mores, than ere I shall love wife.	
	If I do feign, you witnesses above,	130
	Punish my life for tainting of my love!	
OLIVIA.	Ay me, detested! how am I beguil'd!	
VIOLA.	Who does beguile you? who does do you wrong?	
OLIVIA.	Hast thou forgot thyself? is it so long?	
	Call forth the holy father.	135
DUKE.	Come, away!	
OLIVIA.	Whither, my lord? Cesario, husband, stay.	
DUKE.	Husband!	
OLIVIA.	Ay, husband! can he that deny?	
DUKE.	Her husband, sirrah!	140
VIOLA.	No, my lord, not I.	
OLIVIA.	Alas, it is the baseness of thy fear	
	That makes thee strangle thy propriety.	
	Fear not, Cesario; take thy fortunes up;	
	Be that thou know'st thou art, and then thou art	145
	As great as that thou fear'st.	
	[Enter PRIEST.]	
	O, welcome, father!	
	Father, I charge thee, by thy reverence,	
	Here to unfold, though lately we intended	
	To keep in darkness what occasion now	150
	Reveals before 'tis ripe, what thou dost know	
	Hath newly pass'd between this youth and me.	
PRIEST.	A contract of eternal bond of love,	
	Confirm'd by mutual joinder of your hands,	
	Attested by the holy close of lips,	155

	Strengthen'd by interchangement of your rings;	
	And all the ceremony of this compact	
	Seal'd in my function, by my testimony;	
	Since when, my watch hath told me, toward my grave	
	I have travell'd but two hours.	160
DUKE.	O thou dissembling cub! what wilt thou be	
	When time hath sow'd a grizzle on thy case?	
	Or will not else thy craft so quickly grow	
	That thine own trip shall be thine overthrow?	
	Farewell, and take her; but direct thy feet	165
	Where thou and I henceforth may never meet.	
VIOLA.	My lord, I do protest—	
OLIVIA.	O, do not swear!	
	Hold little faith, though thou has too much fear.	
	[Enter SIR ANDREW.]	

SIR ANDREW.   For the love of God, a surgeon! Send one presently to Sir Toby.   170

OLIVIA.   What's the matter?

SIR ANDREW.   Has broke my head across and has given Sir Toby a bloody cox-comb too; for the love of God, your help! I had rather than forty pound I were at home.

OLIVIA.   Who has done this, Sir Andrew?   175

SIR ANDREW.   The count's gentleman, one Cesario; we took him for a coward, but he's the very devil incardinate.

DUKE.   My gentleman Cesario?

SIR ANDREW.   'Od's lifelings, here he is! You broke my head for nothing; and that that I did, I was set on to do't by Sir Toby.   180

VIOLA.   Why do you speak to me? I never hurt you.
You drew your sword upon me without cause;
But I bespake you fair, and hurt you not.

SIR ANDREW.   If a bloody coxcomb be a hurt, you have hurt me; I think you set nothing by a bloody coxcomb.   185

[Enter SIR TOBY and CLOWN.]

Here comes Sir Toby halting; you shall hear more: but if he had not been in drink, he would have tickl'd you othergates than he did.

DUKE.   How now, gentleman! how is't with you?

SIR TOBY.   That's all one. Has hurt me, and there's th' end on't. Sot, didst see Dick Surgeon, sot?   190

CLOWN.   O, he's drunk, Sir Toby, an hour agone; his eyes were set at eight i' th' morning.

SIR TOBY.   Then he's a rogue, and a passy measures pavin. I hate a drunken rogue.

OLIVIA.	Away with him! Who hath made this havoc with them?	195
SIR ANDREW.	I'll help you, Sir Toby, because we'll be dress'd together.	
SIR TOBY.	Will you help? an ass-head and a coxcomb and a knave! a thin-fac'd knave, a gull!	
OLIVIA.	Get him to bed, and let his hurt be look'd to.	
	[Exeunt CLOWN, FABIAN, SIR TOBY, and SIR ANDREW.]	
	[Enter SEBASTIAN.]	
SEBASTIAN.	I am sorry, madam, I have hurt your kinsman	200
	But, had it been the brother of my blood,	
	I must have done no less with wit and safety.	
	You throw a strange regard upon me, and by that	
	I do perceive it hath offended you;	
	Pardon me, sweet one, even for the vows	205
	We made each other but so late ago.	
DUKE.	One face, one voice, one habit, and two persons,	
	A natural perspective, that is and is not!	
SEBASTIAN.	Antonio, O my dear Antonio!	
	How have the hours rack'd and tortur'd me,	210
	Since I have lost thee!	
ANTONIO.	Sebastian are you?	
SEBASTIAN.	Fear'st thou that, Antonio?	
ANTONIO.	How have you made division of yourself?	
	An apple cleft in two is not more twin	215
	Than these two creatures. Which is Sebastian?	
OLIVIA.	Most wonderful!	
SEBASTIAN.	Do I stand there? I never had a brother;	
	Nor can there be that deity in my nature,	
	Of here and everywhere. I had a sister,	220
	Whom the blind waves and surges have devour'd.	
	Of charity, what kin are you to me?	
	What countryman? what name? what parentage?	
VIOLA.	Of Messaline: Sebastian was my father;	
	Such a Sebastian was my brother too,	225
	So went he suited to his watery tomb.	
	If spirits can assume both form and suit,	
	You come to fright us.	
SEBASTIAN.	A spirit I am indeed;	
	But am in that dimension grossly clad	230
	Which from the womb I did participate.	
	Were you a woman, as the rest goes even,	

	I should my tears let fall upon your cheek,	
	And say, 'Thrice-welcome, drowned Viola!'	
VIOLA.	My father had a mole upon his brow.	235
SEBASTIAN.	And so had mine.	
VIOLA.	And died that day when Viola from her birth	
	Had numb'red thirteen years.	
SEBASTIAN.	O, that record is lively in my soul!	
	He finished, indeed, his mortal act	240
	That day that made my sister thirteen years.	
VIOLA.	If nothing lets to make us happy both	
	But this my masculine usurp'd attire,	
	Do not embrace me till each circumstance	
	Of place, time, fortune, do cohere and jump	245
	That I am Viola: which to confirm,	
	I'll bring you to a captain in this town,	
	Where lie my maiden weeds; by whose gentle help	
	I was preserv'd to serve this noble count.	
	All the occurrence of my fortune since	250
	Hath been between this lady and this lord.	
SEBASTIAN.	[To OLIVIA] So comes it, lady, you have been mistook;	
	But nature to her bias drew in that.	
	You would have been contracted to a maid;	
	Nor are you therein, by my life, deceiv'd,	255
	You are betroth'd both to a maid and man.	
DUKE.	Be not amaz'd; right noble is his blood.	
	If this be so, as yet the glass seems true,	
	I shall have share in this most happy wreck.	
	[To VIOLA] Boy, thou hast said to me a thousand times	260
	Thou never shouldst love woman like to me.	
VIOLA.	And all those sayings will I over-swear;	
	And all those swearings keep as true in soul	
	As doth that orbed continent the fire	
	That severs day from night.	265
DUKE.	Give me thy hand;	
	And let me see thee in thy woman's weeds.	
VIOLA.	The captain that did bring me first on shore	
	Hath my maid's garments; he, upon some action,	
	Is now in durance, at Malvolio's suit,	270
	A gentleman and follower of my lady's.	
OLIVIA.	He shall enlarge him. Fetch Malvolio hither;	

	And yet, alas, now I remember me,	
	They say, poor gentleman, he's much distract.	
	[Re-enter CLOWN with a letter, and FABIAN.]	
	A most extracting frenzy of mine own	275
	From my remembrance clearly banish'd his.	
	How does he, sirrah?	
CLOWN.	Truly, madam, he holds Belzebub at the stave's end as well as	
	a man in his case may do. Has here writ a letter to you; I should	
	have given't you to-day morning; but as a madman's epistles are	280
	no gospels, so it skills not much when they are deliver'd.	
OLIVIA.	Open't, and read it.	
CLOWN.	Look then to be well edified when the fool delivers the madman.	
	[Reads] By the Lord, madam—	
OLIVIA.	How now! art thou mad?	285
CLOWN.	No, madam, I do but read madness: and your ladyship will have it	
	as it ought to be, you must allow Vox.	
OLIVIA.	Prithee, read i' thy right wits.	
CLOWN.	So I do, madonna; but to read his right wits is to read thus: there	
	fore perpend, my princess, and give ear.	290
OLIVIA.	[To FABIAN] Read it you, sirrah.	
FABIAN.	[Reads] "By the Lord, madam, you wrong me, and the world shall	
	know it; though you have put me into darkness and given your	
	drunken cousin rule over me, yet have I the benefit of my senses	
	as well as your ladyship, I have your own letter that induc'd me to	295
	the semblance I put on; with the which I doubt not but to do myself	
	much right, or you much shame. Think of me as you please. I	
	leave my duty a little unthought of, and speak out of my injury. THE	
	MADLY-US'D MALVOLIO."	
OLIVIA.	Did he write this?	300
CLOWN.	Ay, madam.	
DUKE.	This savours not much of distraction.	
OLIVIA.	See him deliver'd, Fabian; bring him hither.	
	[Exit FABIAN.]	
	My lord, so please you, these things further thought on,	
	To think me as well a sister as a wife,	305
	One day shall crown th' alliance on't, so please you,	
	Here at my house, and at my proper cost.	
DUKE.	Madam, I am most apt t' embrace your offer.	
	[To VIOLA] Your master quits you; and, for your service done him,	
	So much against the mettle of your sex,	310
	So far beneath your soft and tender breeding,	
	And since you call'd me master for so long,	

	Here is my hand; you shall from this time be	
	Your master's mistress.	
OLIVIA.	A sister! you are she.	315
	[Re-enter FABIAN, with MALVOLIO.]	
DUKE.	Is this the madman?	
OLIVIA.	Ay, my lord, this same.	
	How now, Malvolio!	
MALVOLIO.	Madam, you have done me wrong,	
	Notorious wrong.	320
OLIVIA.	Have I, Malvolio? no.	
MALVOLIO.	Lady, you have. Pray you peruse that letter.	
	You must not now deny it is your hand;	
	Write from it, if you can, in hand or phrase;	
	Or say 'tis not your seal, not your invention:	325
	You can say none of this. Well, grant it then;	
	And tell me, in the modesty of honour,	
	Why you have given me such clear lights of favour,	
	Bade me come smiling and cross-garter'd to you,	
	To put on yellow stockings, and to frown	330
	Upon Sir Toby and the lighter people;	
	And, acting this in an obedient hope,	
	Why have you suffer'd me to be imprison'd,	
	Kept in a dark house, visited by the priest,	
	And made the most notorious geck and gull	335
	That e'er invention play'd on? tell me why.	
OLIVIA.	Alas, Malvolio, this is not my writing,	
	Though, I confess, much like the character;	
	But out of question 'tis Maria's hand.	
	And now I do bethink me, it was she	340
	First told me thou wast mad; then cam'st in smiling,	
	And in such forms which here were presuppos'd	
	Upon thee in the letter. Prithee, be content:	
	This practice hath most shrewdly pass'd upon thee,	
	But when we know the grounds and authors of it,	345
	Thou shalt be both the plaintiff and the judge	
	Of thine own cause.	
FABIAN.	Good madam, hear me speak;	
	And let no quarrel nor no brawl to come	
	Taint the condition of this present hour,	350
	Which I have wond'red at. In hope it shall not,	
	Most freely I confess myself and Toby	

Set this device against Malvolio here,

Upon some stubborn and uncourteous parts

We had conceiv'd against him. Maria writ   355

The letter at Sir Toby's great importance;

In recompense whereof he hath married her.

How with a sportful malice it was follow'd

May rather pluck on laughter than revenge;

If that the injuries be justly weigh'd   360

That have on both sides pass'd.

OLIVIA. Alas, poor fool, how have they baffl'd thee!

CLOWN. Why, "some are born great, some achieve greatness, and some
have greatness thrown upon them." I was one, sir, in this interlude;
one Sir Topas, sir; but that's all one. "By the Lord, fool, I am not   365
mad"; but do you remember? "Madam, why laugh you at such
a barren rascal? and you smile not, he's gagg'd": and thus the
whirligig of time brings in his revenges.

MALVOLIO. I'll be reveng'd on the whole pack of you.

[Exit.]

OLIVIA. He hath been most notoriously abus'd.   370

DUKE. Pursue him, and entreat him to a peace.

He hath not told us of the captain yet;

When that is known, and golden time convents,

A solemn combination shall be made

Of our dear souls. Meantime, sweet sister,   375

We will not part from hence. Cesario, come;

For so you shall be, while you are a man;

But, when in other habits you are seen,

Orsino's mistress and his fancy's queen.

[Exeunt all but the CLOWN.]

CLOWN. [Sings]

When that I was and a little tiny boy,   380

With hey, ho, the wind and the rain,

A foolish thing was but a toy,

For the rain it raineth every day.

But when I came to man's estate,

With hey, ho, the wind and the rain,   385

'Gainst knaves and thieves men shut their gate,

For the rain it raineth every day.

But when I came, alas! to wive,

With hey, ho, the wind and the rain,

By swaggering could I never thrive,   390
  For the rain it raineth every day.
But when I came unto my beds,
  With hey, ho, the wind and the rain,
With toss-pots still had drunken heads,
  For the rain it raineth every day.   395
A great while ago the world begun,
  With hey, ho, the wind and the rain,
But that's all one, our play is done,
  And we'll strive to please you every day.
    [Exit.]

Critical Thinking Topics

1. The opening line of *Twelfth Night*, "If music be the food of love, play on," is frequently quoted. However, it is often quoted in a way that gives it a different meaning than its meaning in the play. "Translate" (or put into your own words) the first fifteen lines of the play. What does Duke Orsino feel about love, and how does he compare it to music?

2. Malvolio is the object of deception. Why do Maria and Sir Toby play a prank on Malvolio; what has he done to deserve this trick? Why does Feste (the clown) get involved, and how does the prank escalate?

3. Romantic love serves as a major element of the plot, as we should expect in a comedy by Shakespeare. However, this play is also about the love of sisters for brothers; both Olivia and Viola are mourning a dead brother. How do they each respond to grief? Use specific lines from the play for support.

4. Like all of Shakespeare's plays, *Twelfth Night* contains many words that are no longer current in English or that have taken on very different meanings—for example, in line 14 of the Duke's opening speech in Act I, Scene I, "shapes" means "imagined forms" and "fancy" means "love" (as in "she fancies him"); and in line 84 of Act IV, Scene II, the clown uses the obsolete word "shent," meaning "scolded" or "rebuked." Find about another dozen obsolete or changed words in *Twelfth Night* (two or three from each act), do some research to determine what those words mean in the play, and write up your results.

Writing Topic

Viola/Cesario changes her name and her gender in this comedy. When she first meets Olivia, she states, "I am not what I play." So, if she is not what she pretends to be, who is she? How much does changing outward appearances affect our identity? Explain the importance of names, genders, and/or social roles in establishing how we see ourselves and how others see us. Use specific examples from your own observations for support.

6.29 Sharon E. Cooper, Siriously (A Ten-Minute play) (2017)

CHARACTERS

DARYL, M. early 30s	Teacher, Jackie's boyfriend, African-American
RON, M. late 30s / early 40s	Daryl's friend, Jewish
JACKIE, F. 20s	Daryl's girlfriend, White, loves the holidays
SETTING	A bar in midtown, Manhattan
TIME	New Year's Eve, the present

On New Year's Eve, near midnight, RON sits at the bar, scrolling through his phone. There are sounds of New Year's Eve merriment in the background. DARYL enters, shakes Ron's hand, and they give each other a quick pat on the back.

DARYL   *(rubbing his hands together to warm up)* How long do you think idiots have been standing outside waiting for a freakin' ball to drop? Jeez Louise, sugar, is it cold.

RON   Dude, you're not at school—you can swear. So, where's Jackie?

DARYL   On her way. What do you wanna drink?   5

DARYL heads towards the bar.

RON   Ah, whatever. Budweiser, I guess.

DARYL   This round's on me.

RON   Johnnie Walker Blue Label.

DARYL gives Ron a look and walks away. Ron takes out his phone and talks to it.

RON   Siri, in what year—

The noise from the bar increases, and Ron leans into his phone. Daryl returns with drinks; Ron is still engrossed in his phone. Daryl holds out a bottle of water for Ron.

DARYL   Helllooo?   10

RON   *(referring to the drink)* What the hell?

Daryl points to a blue label on the water bottle.

DARYL   Blue Label.

RON   Ass—it's 1907, by the way.

Daryl hands Ron a beer and drinks the water.

DARYL   What is?

RON   You asked how long the ball's been going down in Times Square.   15

DARYL   No I didn't. I asked how long have people been standing outside *today*.

RON	Oh. *(into the phone)* Siri, how long—	
DARYL	Please don't. Whose stupid idea was it to meet spitting distance from this madness?	
RON	I didn't feel like venturing far away from home tonight.	20
DARYL	Oh, sorry. Right. I heard about you and Lili. That sucks. Sorry I didn't call. You know, holidays. Busy.	
RON	I don't want to talk about it.	
DARYL	I understand.	
RON	It's just the little things, you know? Like she'd ask me if I wanted coffee and I'd say "no" and then she'd ask again. Like didn't I say *no* the first time?	25
DARYL	Oh, well—don't feel like you have to share—	
RON	And she doesn't like my dog. Says he barks too much. He's a dog. That's his job.	30

Daryl nods his head.

RON	I mean, what's not to like about Rufus? And last weekend, she was at my place and was helping me fold. *(Daryl looks confused.)* My socks. She rolls them together like this—*(demonstrates)*—even though she knows I fold them like this *(demonstrates).* How could I be with someone like that? She's clearly sending a message that she wants to change me. Whatever. How did you find out anyway? Did Lili tell Dana and Dana tell Jackie and Jackie tell you?	35
DARYL	No. Lili changed her Facebook status.	
RON	Oh. Really?	
DARYL	I'm sorry it's so hard—	
RON	It's—not—hard. You know what? I'm going to "like" that right now.	40

A moment, as Ron is looking on his phone.

RON (cont.)	Huh. She's in a relationship. Wow, that was fast.	
DARYL	No kidding.	

Ron looks back at his phone and then at Daryl.

| RON | **Jackie** posted on Lili's comment: "Maybe you'll end up walking down the aisle like I'll be **NEXT YEAR**. I knew you could do better." | |

JACKIE enters, more dressed up than the guys. She's brought New Year's Eve noisemakers, hats, etc.

| DARYL | Jackie! | 45 |

Jackie leans past Daryl to show off her ring to Ron.

JACKIE	Look, look, look, look, look, look! *(Ron does. Finally.)* I had to show my mother first. That's where I was. At my mom's. I had to show her before I tweeted and posted.	
	Thirteen people have already liked me, us, me. Aahhh!	
RON	Aaahhhhhh! Wow, that's wow. That's so great. I'm so happy for you two.	50

Jackie plants herself on Daryl's lap.

JACKIE	We are going to Johannesburg!
RON	Oh, okay.
DARYL	For the honeymoon. She's always wanted to go to Africa.
RON	To do a safari or something?
JACKIE	We are going to go to the Apartheid museum. 55
RON	Really?
JACKIE	You have to walk the walk, you know?
RON	No, I don't know.
JACKIE	*(overlapping)* So here's how he proposed. Daryl wrote, "Will you marry me?" on a parachute. His great uncle did that for his great aunt because 60 he was in World War II and was away and was fighting and stuff and came home with a parachute with a proposal on it. So I wake up on Dec. 28, which is my—*(waiting for them to guess)* favorite day of the year because it's smack between Christmas and New Year's—*(to Ron)* I hope that doesn't offend you because you're Jewish—Happy Hanukkah 65 by the way!
RON	Thanks, it was several weeks ago.
JACKIE	*(in her own world)* And there's a small parachute at the foot of the bed and in big black stalker-like letters, it says, "Will you marry me?" Just like that. "Will—you—marry—me?" And even though Daryl didn't serve in a war, 70 it had the same sentiment, you know? The lighting in here is terrible. I'm going to the girls' room to look at my ring.

And she's gone. A moment.

DARYL	Oh, sugar, man, I was going to tell you about the engagement and then you just seemed so devastated about Lili.
RON	I'm not—devastated. 75
DARYL	It's just awkward to be like "Hey, we're engaged" and you're like all alone. Single. By yourself. Without anyone. On New Year's Eve.
RON	I'm good, man. I've got everything I need.

Jackie returns. Daryl hands her a drink.

JACKIE	Ooohhhh, isn't he sweet? So, Ron, it hit me while I was trying to look at my ring in bad lighting that *we*, well mostly Daryl, but *we* were being 80 insensitive about you and Lili.
DARYL	Ron was just telling me that things are going well.
JACKIE	Oh yeah? Dating someone new?
RON	Oh, no, better than that—a new upgrade. I can't get out the door without her. She has a great sense of direction. She has a nice voice; she doesn't 85 contradict me, she doesn't control me. She doesn't act like she's my friend and then stab me in the back.
JACKIE	That's because it's a phone.
DARYL	Yeah, right, a phone can't make up for human contact.
RON	Sometimes I'm checking in with her like a dozen times a day. 90

JACKIE	*(to Daryl)* You used to check in with me more often. *(to Ron)*. He used to call me every day during his lunch break until a slutty substitute became his "friend" and he brushed her boobs by mistake while eating cafeteria food.
DARYL	I thought you were over that.
JACKIE	I was until I brought it up.

95

RON	*(to Daryl)* Why would you volunteer that kind of information?
JACKIE	And ever since then, he wants me to wear these push-up bras—
DARYL	*(overlapping)* It was a gift. You like Victoria's Secret. It didn't have anything—
JACKIE	*(overlapping)* I can't breathe in these things!
DARYL	*(overlapping, to Jackie)* And I told you, I stopped calling because they cut down on part-time staff, and now I have to sit with kids during lunch. I have to work all day at work. I don't just sit around dreaming up riddles and jingles.

100

| JACKIE | **Branding**. This isn't the 1950s. And that's how we're going to buy an apartment, because we're sure as hell not going to do it on a piss-ant teacher's salary. |

105

| RON | Daryl, maybe it's time for you to get an upgrade, too. *(leaning into his phone)* Siri, should Daryl— |
| JACKIE | *(to Ron)* Does your iPhone girlfriend tell you about the thousands of Chinese workers making slave wages and living in squalor so you can spend all day with some simulated female that can help you find the nearest Starbucks? |

110

| RON | No, but if I ask her, "Hey, where are over half of the diamonds in the world mined in war zones to finance insurgencies, she'd be like 'Africa.'" |
| JACKIE | What is wrong with you? |

115

RON	"Lili, I knew you could do better."
JACKIE	That was a private message!
RON	No, apparently, it wasn't!
DARYL	Enough, you two, this is all a bit fudged up.
JACKIE	We are in a bar, for Christ's sakes, not with second graders!

120

| DARYL | You think it's cute that I don't swear. |
| JACKIE | Don't talk to me. |

And in the background we hear: 10, 9, 8, 7, 6, 5, 4, 3, 2, 1! And "Auld Lang Syne."

SIRI says: "Happy New Year."

Jackie scrolls through her phone while Daryl drinks his water and turns away.

Ron, quite content, kisses his phone and continues to scroll through his phone as the lights fade.

Blackout. End of Play.

Source: Sharon E Cooper. "Siriously." Used by permission. For inquiries for any production rights, please contact playwright Sharon E. Cooper, secooper1@yahoo.com or visit her website: www.sharonecooper.com.

Critical Thinking Topics

1. After experiencing this brief glimpse into the lives of Daryl, Ron, and Jackie, do you come away thinking these three people are caring, compassionate friends? Explain why or why not.

2. The playwright specifies that Daryl is in his early 30s and African-American; Ron is in his "late 30s/early 40s" and Jewish; and Jackie is in her 20s and white. Describe how this information impacts your perception of the characters and their interactions.

Writing Topic

Ron, Daryl, and Jackie demonstrate frustration with romantic relationships. Ron implies that a relationship with a function on a smartphone is preferable to human interaction. Using details from both the play and your own observations, discuss the benefits and drawbacks of relationships with synthetic "persons" like the iPhone's Siri.

6.30 Nonfiction

The eight nonfiction pieces in this section, spanning the years from 1861 through 2017, explore topics and issues related to the theme of individual and community identity.

6.31 Sullivan Ballou, Major Sullivan Ballou's Letter to His Wife (July 14, 1861; first published 1986)

During the Civil War, a week before the First Battle of Bull Run, Sullivan Ballou, a major in the Second Rhode Island Volunteers, wrote home to his wife in Smithfield.

Headquarters, Camp Clark
Washington, D.C., July 14, 1861
My Very Dear Wife:

Indications are very strong that we shall move in a few days, perhaps to-morrow. Lest I should not be able to write you again, I feel impelled to write a few lines, that may fall under your eye when I shall be no more.

Our movement may be one of a few days duration and full of pleasure and it may be one of severe conflict and death to me. Not my will, but thine, O God, be done. If it is necessary that I should fall on the battle-field for my country, I am ready. I have no misgivings about, or lack of confidence in, the cause in which I am engaged, and my courage does not halt or falter. I know how strongly American civilization now leans upon the triumph of the government, and how great a debt we owe to those who went before us through the blood and suffering of the Revolution, and I am willing, perfectly willing, to lay down all my joys in this life to help maintain this government, and to pay that debt.

But, my dear wife, when I know, that with my own joys, I lay down nearly all of yours, and replace them in this life with care and sorrows, when, after having eaten for long years the bitter fruit of orphanage myself, I must offer it, as their only sustenance, to my dear little children, is it weak or dishonorable, while the banner of my purpose floats calmly and proudly in the breeze, that my unbounded love for you, my darling wife and children, should struggle in fierce, though useless, contest with my love of country?

I cannot describe to you my feelings on this calm summer night, when two thousand men are sleeping around me, many of them enjoying the last, perhaps, before that of death, and I, suspicious that Death is creeping behind me with his fatal dart, am communing with God, my country and thee.

I have sought most closely and diligently, and often in my breast, for a wrong motive in thus hazarding the happiness of those I loved, and I could not find one. A pure love of my country, and of the principles I have often advocated before the people, and "the name of honor, that I love more than I fear death," have called upon me, and I have obeyed. 5

Sarah, my love for you is deathless. It seems to bind me with mighty cables, that nothing but Omnipotence can break; and yet, my love of country comes over me like a strong wind, and bears me irresistibly on with all those chains, to the battlefield. The memories of all the blissful moments I have spent with you come crowding over me, and I feel most deeply grateful to God and you, that I have enjoyed them so long. And how hard it is for me to give them up, and burn to ashes the hopes of future years, when, God willing, we might still have lived and loved together, and seen our boys grow up to honorable manhood around us.

I know I have but few claims upon Divine Providence, but something whispers to me, perhaps it is the wafted prayer of my little Edgar, that I shall return to my loved ones unharmed. If I do not, my dear Sarah, never forget how much I love you, nor that, when my last breath escapes me on the battle-field, it will whisper your name.

Forgive my many faults, and the many pains I have caused you. How thoughtless, how foolish I have oftentimes been! How gladly would I wash out with my tears, every little spot upon your happiness, and struggle with all the misfortune of this world, to shield you and my children from harm. But I cannot, I must watch you from the spirit land and hover near you, while you buffet the storms with your precious little freight, and wait with sad patience till we meet to part no more.

But, O Sarah, if the dead can come back to this earth, and flit unseen around those they loved, I shall always be near you in the brightest day and the darkest night amidst your happiest scenes and gloomiest hours always, always, and, if the soft breeze fans your cheek, it shall be my breath; or if the cool air cools your throbbing temples, it shall be my spirit passing by.

Sarah, do not mourn me dear; think I am gone, and wait for me, for we shall meet again. 10

As for my little boys, they will grow as I have done, and never know a father's love and care. Little Willie is too young to remember me long, and my blue-eyed Edgar will keep my frolics with him among the dimmest memories of his childhood. Sarah, I have unlimited confidence in your maternal care, and your development of their characters. Tell my two mothers, I call God's blessing upon them. O Sarah, I wait for you there! Come to me, and lead thither my children.

—Sullivan

A week after writing this letter, Major Ballou was killed at the First Battle of Bull Run.
Source: Major Sullivan Ballou's Last Letter to His Wife.

Critical Thinking Topics

1. Major Ballou's letter is not only a poignant expression of his love for his family—his wife Sarah and his two young sons—but also an articulate description of the conflict between his love of family and his love of country. Find the passages that depict this conflict, and examine the figurative language in them. In what specific ways does this language reveal the conflict?

2. Analyze this letter as a Rogerian argument centered on the personal conflict the war creates for Major Ballou. What is Ballou's compromise, or middle-ground, position? (You may want to refer to the discussion of Rogerian argument in Chapter 4.)

3. Imagine a letter like Major Ballou's, but written by a suicide bomber to the husband or wife being left behind—for example, a letter addressed to "Dear Alexander" and signed, "Your loving wife, Mary." Imagine, too, that the writer's plan to detonate explosives on herself in a crowded shopping area the following day is not directly stated in the letter but can only be inferred. How might your response to this letter differ from your response to Major Ballou's letter?

Writing Topic

Reread paragraphs 8–10, focusing on the rhetorical strategies—for example, sentence rhythm, patterns, and lengths; use of figurative language; and use of repetition. Try modeling these paragraphs while casting yourself in the role of one who is writing a letter to an intimate friend to explain your feelings about a difficult choice—for example, whether to leave your hometown to go away to college, or whether to leave the country in order to avoid military service in a war you believe is immoral.

6.32 Scott Russell Sanders, The Men We Carry in Our Minds (1984)

This must be a hard time for women," I say to my friend Anneke. "They have so many paths to choose from, and so many voices calling them."

"I think it's a lot harder for men," she replies.

"How do you figure that?"

"The women I know feel excited, innocent, like crusaders in a just cause. The men I know are eaten up with guilt."

We are sitting at the kitchen table drinking sassafras tea, our hands wrapped   5
around the mugs because this April morning is cool and drizzly. "Like a Dutch morning," Anneke told me earlier. She is Dutch herself, a writer and midwife and peacemaker, with the round face and sad eyes of a woman in a Vermeer painting who might be waiting for the rain to stop, for a door to open. She leans over to sniff a sprig of lilac, pale lavender, that rises from a vase of cobalt blue.

"Women feel such pressure to be everything, do everything," I say. "Career, kids, art, politics. Have their babies and get back to the office a week later. It's as if they're trying to overcome a million years' worth of evolution in one lifetime."

"But we help one another. We don't try to lumber on alone, like so many wounded grizzly bears, the way men do." Anneke sips her tea. I gave her the mug with owls on it, for wisdom. "And we have this deep-down sense that we're in the *right*—we've been held back, passed over, used—while men feel they're in the wrong. Men are the ones who've been discredited, who have to search their souls."

I search my soul. I discover guilty feelings aplenty—toward the poor, the Vietnamese, Native Americans, the whales, an endless list of debts—a guilt in each case that is as bright and unambiguous as a neon sign. But toward women I feel something more confused, a snarl of shame, envy, wary tenderness, and amazement. This muddle troubles me. To hide my unease I say, "You're right, it's tough being a man these days."

"Don't laugh." Anneke frowns at me, mournful-eyed, through the sassafras steam. "I wouldn't be a man for anything. It's much easier being the victim. All the victim has to do is break free. The persecutor has to live with his past."

How deep is that past? I find myself wondering after Anneke has left. How much of 10 an inheritance do I have to throw off? Is it just the beliefs I breathed in as a child? Do I have to scour memory back through father and grandfather? Through St. Paul? Beyond Stonehenge and into the twilit caves? I'm convinced the past we must contend with is deeper even than speech. When I think back on my childhood, on how I learned to see men and women, I have a sense of ancient, dizzying depths. The back roads of Tennessee and Ohio where I grew up were probably closer, in their sexual patterns, to the campsites of Stone Age hunters than to the genderless cities of the future into which we are rushing.

The first men, besides my father, I remember seeing were black convicts and white guards, in the cottonfield across the road from our farm on the outskirts of Memphis. I must have been three or four. The prisoners wore dingy gray-and-black zebra suits, heavy as canvas, sodden with sweat. Hatless, stooped, they chopped weeds in the fierce heat, row after row, breathing the acrid dust of boll-weevil poison. The overseers wore dazzling white shirts and broad shadowy hats. The oiled barrels of their shotguns flashed in the sunlight. Their faces in memory are utterly blank. Of course those men, white and black, have become for me an emblem of racial hatred. But they have also come to stand for the twin poles of my early vision of manhood—the brute toiling animal and the boss.

When I was a boy, the men I knew labored with their bodies. They were marginal farmers, just scraping by, or welders, steelworkers, carpenters; they swept floors, dug ditches, mined coal, or drove trucks, their forearms ropy with muscle; they trained horses, stoked furnaces, built tires, stood on assembly lines wrestling parts onto cars and refrigerators. They got up before light, worked all day long whatever the weather, and when they came home at night they looked as though somebody had been whipping them. In the evenings and on weekends they worked on their own places, tilling gardens that were lumpy with clay, fixing broken-down cars, hammering on houses that were always too drafty, too leaky, too small.

The bodies of the men I knew were twisted and maimed in ways visible and invisible. The nails of their hands were black and split, the hands tattooed with scars. Some had lost fingers. Heavy lifting had given many of them finicky backs and guts weak from hernias. Racing against conveyor belts had given them ulcers. Their ankles and knees ached from years of standing on concrete. Anyone who had worked for long around machines was hard of hearing. They squinted, and the skin of their faces was creased like the leather of old work gloves. There were times, studying them, when I dreaded growing up. Most of them coughed, from dust or cigarettes, and most of them drank cheap wine or whiskey, so their eyes looked bloodshot and bruised. The fathers of my friends always seemed older than the mothers. Men wore out sooner. Only women lived into old age.

As a boy I also knew another sort of men, who did not sweat and break down like mules. They were soldiers, and so far as I could tell they scarcely worked at all. During my early school years we lived on a military base, an arsenal in Ohio, and every day I saw GIs in the guardshacks, on the stoops of barracks, at the wheels of olive drab Chevrolets. The chief fact of their lives was boredom. Long after I left the arsenal I came to recognize the sour smell the soldiers gave off as that of souls in limbo. They were all waiting—for wars, for transfers, for leaves, for promotions, for the end of their hitch— like so many braves waiting for the hunt to begin. Unlike the warriors of older tribes, however, they would have no say about when the battle would start or how it would be waged. Their waiting was broken only when they practiced for war. They fired guns at targets, drove tanks across the churned-up fields of the military reservation, set off bombs in the wrecks of old fighter planes. I knew this was all play. But I also felt certain that when the hour for killing arrived, they would kill. When the real shooting started, many of them would die. This was what soldiers were *for,* just as a hammer was for driving nails.

Warriors and toilers: those seemed, in my boyhood vision, to be the chief destinies   15 for men. They weren't the only destinies, as I learned from having a few male teachers, from reading books, and from watching television. But the men on television—the politicians, the astronauts, the generals, the savvy lawyers, the philosophical doctors, the bosses who gave orders to both soldiers and laborers—seemed as remote and unreal to me as the figures in tapestries. I could no more imagine growing up to become one of these cool, potent creatures than I could imagine becoming a prince.

A nearer and more hopeful example was that of my father, who had escaped from a red-dirt farm to a tire factory, and from the assembly line to the front office. Eventually he dressed in a white shirt and tie. He carried himself as if he had been born to work with his mind. But his body, remembering the earlier years of slogging work, began to give out on him in his fifties, and it quit on him entirely before he turned sixty-five. Even such a partial escape from man's fate as he had accomplished did not seem possible for most of the boys I knew. They joined the Army, stood in line for jobs in the smoky plants, helped build highways. They were bound to work as their fathers had worked, killing themselves or preparing to kill others.

A scholarship enabled me not only to attend college, a rare enough feat in my circle, but even to study in a university meant for the children of the rich. Here I met for the first time young men who had assumed from birth that they would lead lives of comfort and power. And for the first time I met women who told me that men were guilty of having kept all the joys and privileges of the earth for themselves. I was baffled. What privileges? What joys? I thought about the maimed, dismal lives of most of the men back home. What had they stolen from their wives and daughters? The right to go five days a week, twelve months a year, for thirty or forty years to a steel mill or a coal mine? The right to drop bombs and die in war? The right to feel every leak in the roof, every gap in the fence, every cough in the engine, as a wound they must mend? The right to feel, when the lay-off comes or the plant shuts down, not only afraid but ashamed?

I was slow to understand the deep grievances of women. This was because, as a boy, I had envied them. Before college, the only people I had ever known who were interested in art or music or literature, the only ones who read books, the only ones who ever seemed to enjoy a sense of ease and grace were the mothers and daughters. Like the menfolk, they fretted about money, they scrimped and made-do. But, when the pay stopped coming in, they were not the ones who had failed. Nor did they have to go to war, and that seemed to me a blessed fact. By comparison with the narrow, ironclad days of fathers, there was an expansiveness, I thought, in the days of mothers. They went to see neighbors, to shop in town, to run errands at school, at the library, at church. No doubt, had I looked harder at their lives, I would have envied them less. It was not my fate to become a woman, so it was easier for me to see the graces. Few of them held jobs outside the home, and those who did filled thankless roles as clerks and waitresses. I didn't see, then, what a prison a house could be, since houses seemed to me brighter, handsomer places than any factory. I did not realize—because such things were never spoken of—how often women suffered from men's bullying. I did learn about the wretchedness of abandoned wives, single mothers, widows; but I also learned about the wretchedness of lone men. Even then I could see how exhausting it was for a mother to cater all day to the needs of young children. But if I had been asked, as a boy, to choose between tending a baby and tending a machine, I think I would have chosen the baby. (Having now tended both, I know I would choose the baby.)

So I was baffled when the women at college accused me and my sex of having cornered the world's pleasures. I think something like my bafflement has been felt by other boys (and by girls as well) who grew up in dirt-poor farm country, in mining country, in black ghettos, in Hispanic barrios, in the shadows of factories, in Third World nations—any place where the fate of men is as grim and bleak as the fate of women. Toilers and warriors. I realize now how ancient these identities are, how deep the tug they exert on men, the undertow of a thousand generations. The miseries I saw, as a boy, in the lives of nearly all men I continue to see in the lives of many—the body-breaking toil, the tedium, the call to be tough, the humiliating powerlessness, the battle for a living and for territory.

When the women I met at college thought about the joys and privileges of men,   20 they did not carry in their minds the sort of men I had known in my childhood. They thought of their fathers, who were bankers, physicians, architects, stockbrokers, the big wheels of the big cities. These fathers rode the train to work or drove cars that cost more than any of my childhood houses. They were attended from morning to night by female helpers, wives and nurses and secretaries. They were never laid off, never short of cash at month's end, never lined up for welfare. These fathers made decisions that mattered. They ran the world.

The daughters of such men wanted to share in this power, this glory. So did I. They yearned for a say over their future, for jobs worthy of their abilities, for the right to live at peace, unmolested, whole. Yes, I thought, yes yes. The difference between me and these daughters was that they saw me, because of my sex, as destined from birth to become like their fathers, and therefore as an enemy to their desires. But I knew better. I wasn't an enemy, in fact or in feeling. I was an ally. If I had known, then, how to tell them so, would they have believed me? Would they now?

Source: "The Men We Carry in Our Minds" (c) 1984 by Scott Russell Sanders; first published in Milkweed Chronicle, Vol. 5, No. 2 (Spring/Summer 1984)

Critical Thinking Topics

1. Write out at least four assumptions about gender—being a man, being a woman—that Sanders questions in his essay. Reflect on the validity of each one for men today and for women today. What has changed and what has not changed since Sanders was a boy and since 1984, when he wrote this essay? Use examples to elaborate on your reflections.

2. What is an implied claim in Sanders's essay? What sentences in the essay lead you to this conclusion? To what degree is Sanders's argument valid today? Use examples to explain your perspective.

Writing Topics

1. Write creative and critical reading responses to the first ten paragraphs of Sanders's essay; then synthesize the responses into several sentences of commentary and reflection.

2. Anneke argues, "It's much easier being the victim. All the victim has to do is break free. The persecutor has to live with his past." Do you agree? Why or why not? In your response, include examples that relate to gender issues and consider other, non–gender-related victim–persecutor relationships.

6.33 Richard Rodriguez, The Chinese in All of Us: A Mexican American Explores Multiculturalism (1992)

The other day, the phone rang; it was a woman who identified herself as the "talent coordinator" for the "Oprah Winfrey Show." She said Oprah was planning a show on self-hating ethnics. "You know," she confided, "Norwegians who don't want to be Norwegian, Greeks who hate Greek food." Anyway, she said breezily, wouldn't I like to make an appearance?

About 10 years ago I wrote a thin book called *Hunger of Memory*. It was a book about my education, which is to say, a book about my Americanization. I wrote of losses and triumphs. And, in passing, I wrote about two issues particularly, affirmative action and bilingual education.

I was a nay-sayer. I became, because of my book, a notorious figure among the Ethnic Left in America. Consider me the brown Uncle Tom. I am a traitor, a sellout. The Spanish word is *pocho*. A pocho is someone who forgets his true home. (A shame.) A Richard Rodriguez.

Last year, I was being interviewed by Bill Moyers. "Do you consider yourself American or Hispanic?" he asked.

"I think of myself as Chinese," I answered.   5

A smart-aleck answer, but one that is true enough. I live in San Francisco, a city that has become, in my lifetime, predominantly Asian, predominantly Chinese. I am becoming like them. Do not ask me how, it is too early to tell. But it is inevitable, living side by side, that we should become like each other. So think of me as Chinese.

Oh, my critics say: Look at you Mr. Rod-ree-guess. You have lost your culture.

They mean, I think, that I am not my father, which is true enough. I did not grow up in the state of Jalisco, in the western part of Mexico. I grew up here, in this country, amongst you. I am like you.

My critics mean, when they speak of culture, something solid, something intact. You have lost your culture, they say, as though I lost it at the Greyhound bus station. You have lost your culture, as though culture is a coat I took off one warm afternoon and then forgot.

I AM MY CULTURE. Culture is not something opposite us, it is rather something   10
we breathe and sweat and live. My culture? Lucille Ball is my culture. (I love Lucy, after all.) And Michael Jackson. And Benjamin Franklin is my culture. And Elvis Presley and Walter Cronkite. Walt Disney is my culture. The New York Yankees.

My culture is you. You created me; if you don't like it, if I make you uncomfortable now by being too much like you, too bad.

When I was a little boy in Sacramento, California, the son of Mexican immigrant parents, Spanish-speaking mainly, even then, in those years, America came at me. America was everywhere around me. America was in the pace of the traffic lights, the assertion of neon, the slouch of the crowd, the impatience of the fast food counter. America was everywhere.

I recognized America best, in those years, standing outside the culture. I recognized its power, and from the first I knew that it threatened to swallow me up. America did not feel like something to choose or not choose. America felt inevitable.

Truman Capote said somewhere that he never met a true bisexual. He meant, I think, that finally people are one thing or the other.

Well, I must tell you that I have never met a truly bicultural person. Oh, I have met   15
people who speak two languages, and all that. But finally, their allegiance belongs more to one side of the border than the other.

And yet, I believe in multiculturalism—my kind of multiculturalism.

I think the adventure of living in a multi-racial, multi-ethnic America leaves one vulnerable to a variety of cultures, a variety of influences. Consider me, for example, Chinese. I am also Irish.

About 10 years ago, I was going to school in England. One weekend, Aer Lingus, the Irish national airline, was offering a reduced fare to Dublin. I thought, "What a lark— it'd be fun to go off to Ireland for the weekend." Strange thing, once I got off the plane, I suddenly felt myself at home. I knew these people. I recognized their faces and their irony and their wit and their sadness.

I'll tell you why. I was educated by Irish Catholic nuns. They were my first, my most important foreign culture, intruding on my Mexican soul, reshaping my soul with their voices.

Sometime after Dublin, I realized something more about myself: All of my best   20
friends from childhood to now, the people I have been closest to, have been Irish-Americans, Irish Catholics.

How is this possible? How is it possible for a Mexican kid from Sacramento, California, to discover himself to be Irish?

In the orthodox American scheme of things, it is nonsense. America is a Protestant country. A low-church Protestant country. America was founded by Puritans who resisted the notion of the group. The most important founding idea of America was the notion of individualism—your freedom from the group, my freedom from you. A most glamorous idea.

Consider this paradox: The belief we share in common as Americans is the belief that we are separate from one another.

There is already with this paradox implied an important tension, one basic to American experience. Our culture, by which I mean our daily experience, is at war with our ideology, by which I mean our Protestant belief in separateness.

Diversity is our strength, we say. There is not an American president who would   25
say anything else: We are a country made stronger by our individuality, by our differences. Which is, in a way, true. But only partly true.

The other truth, I call it my catholic truth about puritan America, is that America exists. America exists as a culture, a sound, an accent, a walk.

Thousands of hotel clerks in thousands of hotels around the world will tell you that America exists. There is a recognizable type. Here they come, the Americans. Bermuda shorts. High-pitched voices. Too easy familiarity. Big tip, insecure tip. A slap on the back.

And when we ourselves are far from home, when we are in the Hilton lobby in Cairo or in Paris, we, too, recognize one another immediately. Across the crowded hotel lobby Americans find one another immediately, either with relief or with slight, acknowledging embarrassment.

It is only when we are home working alongside one another and living next to one another that we wonder whether America exists. We wonder about our individuality. And we talk about our traditional Protestant virtues. We talk about respecting our diversity.

Nativist politicians are saying these days that maybe we should think twice about   30
allowing non-European immigrants into this country. Can America, after all, sustain such diversity?

Liberal American educators end up echoing the point, in a way. They look at faces like mine and they see only what they call "diversity." They wonder, now, if the purpose of education shouldn't be diversity. We should teach our children about their separate cultures—forget the notion of a common culture.

The other day in Las Vegas I was speaking to a group of high school principals. One man, afterward, came up and told me that his school has changed in recent years. In little more than a decade the student body has changed its color, changed its complexion; the school is no longer black and white, but now suddenly Asian and Hispanic.

This principal smiled and said his school has dropped Black History Month in favor of what he calls, "Newcomers Month."

I think this is absurd. I think this is nonsense.

There isn't an American whose history is not black history. All of us, by virtue of   35
being Americans, share in the history of black America—the oppression, the endurance, the triumph.

Do not speak to me of your diversity. My cultural forefathers are black slaves and black emancipators. I am an American.

America exists. Nothing more will I tell you, can I tell you.

Let me tell you some stories.

A friend of mine—let's call him Michael—tells me he's confused by America. Mike goes to junior high school in San Francisco. His teacher is always telling him to stand up, look up. "Speak up, Michael, we can't hear you! Look at me, Michael!"

Then Michael goes home. His Chinese father is always complaining at home. His   40
Chinese father says that Michael is picking up American ways. "And since when have you started to look your father in the eye?"

America exists, dear Michael.

At the family picnic, the boy listens to his relatives argue and laugh. The spices are as familiar as the jokes. There are arguments about old civil wars and faceless politicians. The family is talking Greek or Chinese or Spanish. The boy grows restless; the boy gets up and wanders away from the family picnic to watch some other boys playing baseball in the distance.

America exists.

My Mexican father looks out at America from the window of his morning newspaper. After all these years in this country, he still doubts that America exists. Look at this place, he says. So many faces. So many colors. So many grandmothers and religions and memories here. This is not a real country. Not a real country like China or Germany or Mexico.

It falls to the son to say, America exists, Papa.   45

There is an unresolved tension between the "I" and the "we." We trust most the "I," though grudgingly we admit the necessity of the "we." The most important communal institution we have is the classroom. We build classrooms, recognize their necessity. But we don't like them.

In the most famous American novel, our greatest book about ourselves, Mark Twain's *Adventures of Huckleberry Finn,* the school marm plays the comic villain. She is always trying to tie down Huck. She tries to make him speak regular. She is always trying to civilize.

We recognize the value of having Huck Finn learn to speak regular, even if we don't like it. And we don't like it. Something in us as Americans forces us to fear the coming of fall, the chill in the woods, the starched shirt, the first day of school.

Let me tell you about my first day of school. I came to the classroom clutching a handful of English. A bilingual child?

The important distinction I want to make here is not between Spanish and English,   50 but between private and public language.

I was the son of working class, immigrant parents. I stress working class. Too often in recent years, we have considered ethnicity and race at the expense of economic standing. Thus, we speak of "minorities" in America and we mean only certain races or so-called "non-white" groups. We use the term minority in a numerical sense. Am I a minority? Well, yes, if we mean that Hispanics generally are "under represented" in American public life. But the term minority is richer as a cultural term. There are certain people in this country who do not imagine themselves to belong to majority society. White. Black. Brown. Most of them are poor. Many of them are uneducated. All of them share a diffidence, a fear, an anxiety about public institutions.

When I walked into the classroom, I was such a minority. I remember the nun wrote my name on the black board: RICHARD RODRIGUEZ. She pronounced it. Then she said, repeat it after me.

It was not that I could not say it. Rather, I would not say it. Why should I? Who was this nun?

She said: Repeat your name after me loud enough so all the boys and girls can understand.

The nun was telling me not just to speak English, but to use language publicly. To   55 speak in a voice loud enough to be heard by strangers. (She was calling me to the first and most crucial lesson of grammar school.)

I was a minority child. It wasn't a question of English versus Spanish. It was a question of public language. I didn't want to speak to *you—los gringos,* boys and girls.

I would not. I could not. I refused to speak up, to look up.

Half a year passed. The nuns worried over me. Speak up, Richard. Stand up, Richard. A year passed. A second year began.

Then one Saturday three nuns appeared at our door. They walked into our house and sat on our sagging blue sofa.

Would it be possible, Mrs. Rodriguez, for you and your husband to use English   60 around the house?

Of course, my mother complied. (What would she not do for her children's public success?)

At first, it seemed a kind of game. We practiced English after dinner. But it was still your language.

Until one other Saturday. I remember my mother and father were speaking Spanish to one another in the kitchen. I did not realize they were speaking Spanish until, the moment they saw me, they switched to English.

I felt pushed away. I remember going over to the sink and turning on the water; standing there dumbly, feeling the water on my hand. I wanted to cry. The water was tepid, then warm, then scalding. I wanted to scream. But I didn't. I turned off the faucet and walked out of the room.

And now you have forgotten how I used to go after school to your house. I used   65 to watch you. I watched television with you, there on the floor. I used to watch the way you laughed. I used to listen to the way you used words. I wanted to swallow you up, to become you. Five-thirty and your mom said, Well, Rickey, we're going to eat in half an hour. Do you want to stay? And I did. I became you.

Something happens to you in the classroom if you are a very good student. You change.

A friend of mine, who went to Bryn Mawr College in the 1950s—when she was the only black student in her class—remembers coming home to North Carolina. She remembers getting off the Greyhound bus. She remembers walking up the sidewalk on the hot early summer day.

When she got home and walked up the five steps of the front porch, her mother was waiting for her behind the screen door.

"I don't want you talkin' white in here," her mother said.

There is a sad story in America about "making it." It is the story of summer vaca-   70 tions. Of no longer being able to speak to one's parents. Of having your Chinese father mock your American ways. ("And since when have you started to look your father in the eye?") It is the story of the girl who learns a different kind of English at school and then is embarrassed to use it at the dinner table.

Bilinguists speak of the necessity of using what they call "family language" in the classroom. If I know anything about education, it is that such a bilingual scheme is bound to fail. Classroom language can never be family language. It is a matter not of different words, but of different contexts.

We don't like to hear such things. We don't like the school marm to change us. We want to believe that August will go on forever and that we can avoid wearing shoes. Huck Finn is America's archetypal bilingual student. He speaks one way—his way, his free way—the school marm wants him to speak another.

As Americans, we must root for Huck.

Americans have lately been searching for a new multi-cultural metaphor for America. We don't like the melting pot. Hispanic Americans particularly have been looking for a new metaphor. Our political coming of age in the late 1960s was accompanied by a stern resistance to the melting pot model of America.

America is a stew. (All of us, presumably chunks of beef in a common broth.)   75

Or America is a mosaic. A Mexican-American bishop recently said that to me. He pointed at a mosaic of the Virgin of Guadalupe. "That is how I think of America," he said. "We are each of us different colors, but united we produce a wonderful, a beautiful effect."

The trouble, I thought to myself, the trouble is that the tiny pieces of glass are static. In our real lives, we are not static.

America is fluid. The best metaphors of America for me are metaphors suggesting fluidity. Our lives melting into one another.

For myself, I like the metaphor of the melting pot. I like it for two reasons.

First, its suggestion of pain—and there is pain. The school teacher can put a som-   80
brero on my head and tell me to feel proud of my heritage, but I know I am becoming a different person than my father. There is pain in the melting pot. Fall in and you are burned.

But there is to the metaphor also a suggestion of alchemy or magic. Fall into the melting pot and you become a new person, changed, like magic, to gold.

Why do we even talk about multiculturalism?

For several reasons, most of them positive. First and foremost is the influence of the great black civil rights movement of the 1950s and 1960s. We are more apt today to recognize the colors of America than perhaps we were several decades ago. On the TV ad, on the football field, in the bank, in a room like this—we have grown used to different shades of America. But that is only to say that we are more apt to be struck by our differences now that we are side by side than in earlier times when segregation legalized separation.

Less positively, the black civil rights movement was undermined by a romantic separatism. Americans were romanced by the moral authority of the outsider, and the benefits of claiming outsider status. White women. Hispanics. Asians. Suddenly, in the 1970s there was a rush to proclaim one's separate status. The benefit was clear: America confronted real social problems. But the decadence also was clear: middle class Americans ended up competing with one another to proclaim themselves society's victims.

The second factor that gives rise to this multicultural preoccupation has recently   85
been the epic migration of non-Europeans into this country.

A friend of mine teaches at a school in Los Angeles where, she says, there are children from 54 language groups. "What possibility is there," she asks, "to teach such a diverse student body anything in common?"

These children do have something in common, however. They may be strangers to Los Angeles, but they are becoming Americans in Los Angeles. That is the beginning.

While I believe in the notion of a common culture, I believe also in the notion of a dynamic culture. Even while America changes the immigrants, the immigrants are changing us. They have always changed us. Assimilation is reciprocal.

Consider American English, for example. It is not British English. The British forced it down our throats, but the language we speak is changed. We speak American here. There are the sighs of German grandmothers and the laughter of Africans in the speech we use. There are in our speech thousands of words imported and brought unregistered through Ellis Island. Swedish words. Yiddish. Italian.

Listen to my voice and you will hear your Lithuanian grandmother. Listen to my   90
American voice and you will hear the echoes of my Chinese neighbors.

Yes, Mr. Bill Moyers, we are all destined to become Chinese.

Source: "The Chinese in All of Us: A Mexican American Explores Multiculturalism" by Richard Rodriguez. Copyright © 1992 by Richard Rodriguez. Reprinted by permission of Georges Borchardt, Inc., on behalf of the author.

Critical Thinking Topics

1. Richard Rodriguez has angered many advocates of bilingual education as well as those arguing for ethnic pride. Identify specific assertions that might stir hostility among these groups and discuss why those assertions might incite such a response.

2. How does Rodriguez make use of personal experience, not only as evidence in support of his assertion, but also in establishing an appeal to *ethos*? How do these appeals affect the persuasiveness of his argument?

3. Consider the metaphors Rodriguez uses in paragraphs 74–81. Is America a melting pot or is it a mosaic? Are the communities or cultures in the United States static or fluid? What have you experienced that helps you answer these questions?

Writing Topic

In what specific ways do you think our society is influenced by ethnic diversity? You might look for examples in food, music, fashion, and language. Are these influences overall beneficial or harmful to society? Write several paragraphs that elaborate on at least four pieces of evidence to support your claim.

6.34 John Hope Franklin, The Train from Hate (1994)

My pilgrimage from racial apprehension—read just plain confusion—to racial tolerance was early and brief. I was 7 years old, and we lived in the all-black town of Rentiesville, Oklahoma. My father had moved to Tulsa where he hoped to have a law practice that would make it possible for him to support his family. Meanwhile, my mother, sister, and I would occasionally make the journey to Checotah, six miles away, to shop for supplies.

One day, we went down, as usual, by railroad. My mother flagged the train and we boarded. It so happened that when the train stopped, the only place we could enter was the coach reserved for white people. We did not take notice of this, and as the train picked up speed, the conductor entered and told us that we would have to move to the "colored" coach. My mother explained that we were not responsible for where the coach stopped and we had no other alternative to climbing aboard and finding seats as soon as possible. She told him that she could not risk the possible injury of her and her children by going to the "colored" coach while the train was moving. The conductor seemed to agree and said that he would signal to the engineer to stop the train. When the train came to a halt, the conductor did not guide us to the coach for African Americans. Instead, he commanded us to leave the train. We had no alternative to stepping off the train into the woods and beginning the trek back to Rentiesville.

As we trudged along, I began to cry. Taking notice of my sadness, my mother sought to comfort me by saying that it was not all that far to Rentiesville. I assured her that I did not mind the walk, but that man, the conductor, was so mean. Why would he not permit us to ride the train to Checotah?

My mother then gave me my first lesson in race relations. She told me that the laws required racial separation, but that they did not, could not, make us inferior in any way. She assured me that the conductor was not superior because he was white, and I was not inferior because I was black. I must always remember that simple fact, she said.

Then she made a statement that is as vivid and clear to me today as the day she uttered it. Under no circumstances, she said, should I be upset or distressed because someone sought to demean me. It took too much energy to hate or even to fight intolerance with one's emotions. She smiled and added that in going home we did not have far to walk.

It would be too much to claim that my mother's calm talk removed a burden from my shoulders. But it is not too much to say that her observations provided a sound basis for my attitudes and conduct from that day to this. At that early age, I had made an important journey. In the future, I remembered that I should not waste my time or energy lamenting the inability of some members of society to take me as I was. Instead, I would use my energies to make me a better person and to distance myself from the perpetrators and purveyors of hate and misunderstanding. I shall always be happy that my mother taught me that the journey to understanding and tolerance was more important than the journey to Checotah.

Source: Franklin, John Hope. "The Train from Hate" from SLAVERY TO FREEDOM: A HISTORY OF NEGRO AMERICANS, 7e by John Hope Franklin. Copyright © 1994 by John Hope Franklin. Reprinted courtesy of John W. Franklin.

Critical Thinking Topics

1. Through his personal experience, Franklin argues for a claim of policy. Write a sentence that expresses that claim.

2. What assumptions underlie the thinking of those who put the mother and her children off that train? Give at least three examples of situations in which some people today hold those same assumptions.

Writing Topic

Think of a time when you as a child witnessed people experiencing an injustice. If you cannot recall any such incidents from real life, think of a comparable situation in a book, movie, or TV show that you experienced as a child. In what ways did the witnessing of injustice change you and/or your views of the world and of other people? What did you learn from the experience? Was the lesson immediate, or did it take years for you to understand it fully?

6.35 Lu Vickers, New Last Words for My Mother: I meant what I said, but I wish I hadn't said it.
(2002)

My mother threatened to kill herself so many times—rifling through the kitchen drawers to find a knife, getting drunk and swallowing pills—that when my brother called to tell me that she and my stepfather had been killed, I assumed it was a double suicide. Or that she killed him, and then killed herself.

My last words to her were "Fuck you." The day before she died was the first time my family had gotten together since my father died the year before. We met at my brother's house in Orlando, and although things started out OK, by the end of the evening Mama started up her usual shit, and I, tired of it all, said the magic words. My stepfather tried to get me to apologize, but I wouldn't. Mama called later and talked to my sister, and

I remember holding the receiver to my ear, listening to her cry, saying she was sorry. I didn't say I was, though. After 21 years of dealing with her, I meant what I said.

She was 48 when she died. It was 1981. She and my stepfather were driving home from Clearwater Beach, drunk, still wearing their swimsuits at midnight, their bare feet grainy with sugary white sand. They ran their light-blue Plymouth under a tractor-trailer, shearing off the top. Both of them were thrown into the weeds on the side of the road. The next day the sheriff handed my brother a brown paper bag with a stiff bloody bikini in it. Instant death, he said, but I knew better. My mother had been aiming for that moment for a long time. She couldn't have chosen a better ending to her story.

Her trajectory began inside the white scalloped edges of a photograph. She flirts with the camera, poses like a beauty queen standing in a small wooden boat on the shore of Lake Seminole, barefoot, hands on hips, head thrown back, a wide and bright smile. Open. She's wearing short shorts and she's conscious: "This is how I want to be remembered; I am as marvelous as Miss America." She gives herself to the camera, maybe to the eyes behind the camera.

I imagine my father before he was my father, smiling at my mother before she was   5
my mother. He has a head full of glossy black hair. Squinting his eyes, bringing her into focus, he snaps this photo of her, thinks of butterflies resting on leaves, camouflaged, right before they are netted, pinned into boxes.

In the next photo, she and my father are leaning against an enormous pine tree near the banks of the Apalachicola River, right on the Georgia-Florida line. He's wearing shoes, thick brown brogans. She isn't. Her long slender feet are posed calendar-girl style. Daddy surrounds her with a bearlike grasp, his arm draped over her shoulder, his big hand pulling her to him. He smooches her ear with his mouth, whispering, "Baby, I love you, I love you so much." I can't remember my father's voice saying those words to my mother, but I know he did. Love her, that is, even if he did forget her birthday later.

Once, he did remember, and he hurt her feelings by buying her one pair of flimsy ladies underwear from the Dollar Store uptown and she wailed that nobody loved her, then threw the underwear in the garbage can beneath our pecan tree. But you can tell he loved her by looking at this photograph, the way his arm circles her, the way he holds her hand. She lets herself be contained, lets him whisper in her ear. This time the camera is peeping; Mama seems almost embarrassed at being watched; her eyes glance toward the ground.

Then there was a photograph taken after Mama had children. May 1962. That's three years after my sister was born. Four children in five years and all of a sudden she's wearing shoes, like she's afraid we're going to tramp on her feet. No more smiling, barefoot Miss America. The photograph is blurry, hazy. Mama's sitting in one of those old-fashioned shell-shaped lawn chairs, scrunched to one side as if she's going to share her seat with someone much smaller than herself. Her hands are clasped on top of her head, her legs crossed. She's smiling but it's a smile tinged with sorrow, the one I become most familiar with.

She sits beneath a tung oil tree, in front of a metal swing set. To her left is a clothesline, diapers fluttering in the breeze. In the corner of the photograph, there are bleary shapes, tiny feet, what seem to be hands. If you squint at this photograph you can almost see one baby helping another baby stand.

The stories I imagine behind those photographs seem as real to me as actual   10
memories. What happened in real real life? The life I experienced? Consider me unreliable. I told my mother to fuck off, after all.

I am sitting in my mother's lap in my cousin Billy's backyard, a garden full of ferns, fountains, birds of paradise. Wind chimes dangle from the branch of a Japanese magnolia. Mama's chin is resting softly against the top of my head. The grass we sit on is so lush and green it's almost blue.

Even though I like sitting in my mother's lap, her chin pressed against the top of my head, my small body folded into hers, I want to get up and walk across that green grass and down the beaten path to the metal pens where my cousin's father, King, raised quail. I liked the smell of birdshit and cornmeal, the brownness of it all, the birds running back and forth in the powdery dirt, the worn wood, the earth beneath my feet.

When I think of that moment, I feel how torn I was between the quail and my mother. Her chin resting on my head was the completion of a circle, her body looped around mine. That circle said "You belong to me." I should've savored the moment, and I suppose I did or I wouldn't have remembered it, but the birds won, and I found myself edging through the azaleas to walk down the path bordered by weeds.

I looped my fingers into the wire pen, stared at the birds' speckled brown feathers as they darted back and forth. I hadn't learned yet to hold on to my mother's happiness while it lasted.

It never lasted long. One morning, completely flustered by trying to get my brothers   15
and sister and I out the door and up the hill to school, she threw my satchel on the floor and started shouting, "I wish I'd never had any of you!" She ran into her bedroom, flung herself onto her bed and started crying uncontrollably.

I remember moving forward to touch her, feeling sick on my stomach, on the verge of tears myself. I don't remember what happened later that day—my father probably came home, set things right. I can't remember leaving the side of her bed. In that memory I stand there, never moving, watching my mother sob into her hands, my heart forever breaking.

My mother was a study in opposites: a classic manic-depressive, full of light and dark. When she wasn't suffering from one of her depressions, she took me and my brothers and sister to the Gulf of Mexico where she wore a bikini and we had picnics and built sand castles and played Goofy Golf.

Back home, she took us out to the country to fly kites. She let us drive down red dirt roads before we were old enough, and took us fishing practically every day during the summer. She once saved a boy from drowning even though she couldn't swim herself, and she managed to laugh about the rattlesnake who'd crawled up under the quilt she sat on while she fished at Lake Seminole.

She would go into the bait store to buy crickets or worms, but she wouldn't answer the door at our house. Once when a favorite teacher of mine came to visit, my mother locked herself in the bedroom and wouldn't come out. Her inability to face people led to my having to go into the drugstore to get refills of the drugs she was addicted to, after my brothers refused to. I died of embarrassment every time.

Gradually, she began drinking, too, and once drunk, she'd climb out of the win-   20
dows and sit hunched over in the dirt beneath the azaleas, not even speaking to us when we begged her to come back into the house.

When she and father weren't home, my sister and I snuck into their bedroom to snoop around. It was silent and still as a church, full of mysteries. My sister and I always dug in the cedar chest to look at the blue jumper Mama'd worn as a baby. In the beginning there were quilts and old pocketbooks, and a blue-and-green silk dress I never saw her wear, couldn't even imagine her wearing. There was a Nazi flag my father said he took from some dead Germans at the end of World War II.

Later, there were surprises, the things my parents hid, revealing they'd changed. We found a dirty-joke book in the closet; another time we found a manual on how to have sex. And then one afternoon, probably the last afternoon we snooped, there was a note in an envelope, a scrawl of words that said "Your wife is having an affair."

I was stung by the sentence, but it wasn't exactly a revelation. I figured she was running around with this black-haired cowboy she worked with. Something was going on. What was confusing was who put the note in the cedar chest. Who would even want to save a scrap like that?

Mama finally left my father and the black-haired cowboy or whoever he was, and moved to Tampa to live with another man. She came to visit me once during this period. She sat in my one-room apartment beneath a poster of flying dykes from the Michigan Womyn's Music Festival, uncomfortable, as if she were visiting a stranger. I sat across the room from her, staring at the shadows the yellow lamplight made on her face.

It wasn't until after she died that I found the note she stuck inside my dictionary that   25
night. "Help me; I need your help," she'd scrawled on a piece of drawing paper. It was strange, finding those words stuck in my dictionary months after she died. It was as if she'd known I'd snooped all those years; as if she were saying, "Here, find this." I kept it, even though it reminded me of how sad she'd been and how little I'd been able to do about it.

After her death, my sister went down south to clean out my stepfather and mother's trailer. As she moved boxes outside, the woman next door came over and shouted at her: "They were nothing but a couple of drunks." In the end, I suppose that's how she appeared. Maybe that's what drove me to tell her to get fucked the day before she died. But that's not how she appears to me now. Maybe it's because I wish I could rewrite my last words to her, have the story end a different way.

Yes, she scared the hell out of me when I was a child. She hurt me. She stole corn from a field in the country, filled the trunk to the brim while I cried, worried she'd get shot. But she also took me to a Jackson County farm to pick hampers of White Acre peas she paid for. She taught me to appreciate the tinny sound of AM country-music radio. She let me drive to Panama City Beach when I was 12 years old. She bought me drawing paper when she thought I wanted to be an artist. She taught me how to bait a hook and how to hold a bream in my hand without getting finned.

I think of her at the oddest moments—when my girlfriend and I travel to Central Florida on back roads and pass one of those rinky-dink horse-riding corrals. I stopped at one of those once with my mother, and still remember the way she looked in the dappled green shadows beneath the trees. I think of her when I go to the Gulf of Mexico or see a stringer full of silver fish, a varnished bamboo fishing pole, paper kites, a car driving down a road with a roostertail of red Georgia dirt blowing up behind it.

I can't remember my mother's voice anymore, how she sounded when she said, "I wish I'd never had you," but I remember how she looked in her white cotton nightgown, leaning over me at night, nibbling words into my ears, Mmmmmmm, I love you. Her breasts brushed against the sheets as she bowed her body over my bed. I remember her smell, the sweet, cherry-almond scent of Jergens Lotion. I can't remember the exact brown of her eyes or how long her eyelashes were or how her lips were shaped, but I can remember how her chin rested on the top of my head, making us a perfect circle, just for a moment.

Source: "This article first appeared in Salon.com, at http://www.Salon.com. An online version remains in the Salon archives. Reprinted with permission."

Critical Thinking Topics

1. Vickers writes, "I imagine my father before he was my father, smiling at my mother before she was my mother." We often think of our parents as our parents, not as individuals with lives beyond their connections to us. Consider someone important to you and describe him or her objectively, with an identity separate from your relationship, as if you were observing from a distance.

2. This nonfiction narrative describes some harsh family interactions. However, this essay also includes powerful images of circles, clothing, nature, and color that balance the pain of reality. Write out two descriptions that you find particularly memorable and explain the symbolism or significance of each description.

Writing Topic

Mental or physical illness can alter people's identity: how they see themselves and how others see them. How does the narrator's mother's depression affect each of them? Do you have any experience of serious ongoing illness in yourself or in someone you know? Can you think of other examples of illness portrayed in literature, movies, or television? You might check out the blog Hyperbole and a Half: Adventures in Depression. Reflect on the difficult situation that such illness can create, and discuss how factors beyond our control can affect the perceptions of our own and others' characters or personalities.

6.36 Robin D. G. Kelley, The People in Me (2003)

"So, what are you?" I don't know how many times people have asked me that. "Are you Puerto Rican? Dominican? Indian or something? You must be mixed." My stock answer has rarely changed: "My mom is from Jamaica but grew up in New York, and my father was from North Carolina but grew up in Boston. Both black."

My family has lived with "the question" for as long as I can remember. We're "exotics," all cursed with "good hair" and strange accents—we don't sound like we from da Souf or the Norwth, and don't have that West Coast-by-way-of-Texas Calabama thang going on. The only one with the real West Indian singsong vibe is my grandmother, who looks even more East Indian than my sisters. Whatever Jamaican patois my mom possessed was pummeled out of her by cruel preteens who never had sensitivity seminars in diversity. The result for us was a nondescript way of talking, walking, and being that made us not black enough, not white enough—just a bunch of not-quite-nappy-headed enigmas.

My mother never fit the "black momma" media image. A beautiful, demure, light brown woman, she didn't drink, smoke, curse, or say things like "Lawd Jesus" or "hallelujah," nor did she cook chitlins or gumbo. A vegetarian, she played the harmonium (a foot-pumped miniature organ), spoke softly with textbook diction, meditated, followed the teachings of Paramahansa Yogananda, and had wild hair like Chaka Khan. She burned incense in our tiny Harlem apartment, sometimes walked the streets barefoot, and, when she could afford it, cooked foods from the East.

To this day, my big sister gets misidentified for Pakistani or Bengali or Ethiopian. (Of course, changing her name from Sheral Anne Kelley to Makani Themba has not helped.) Not long ago, an Oakland cab driver, apparently a Sikh who had immigrated from India, treated my sister like dirt until he discovered that she was not a "scoundrel from Sri Lanka," but a common black American. Talk about ironic. How often are black women spared indignities *because* they are African American?

"What are you?" dogged my little brother more than any of us. He came out look-   5
ing just like his father, who was white. In the black communities of Los Angeles and Pasadena, my baby bro' had to fight his way into blackness, usually winning only when he invited his friends to the house. When he got tired of this, he became what people thought he was—a cool white boy. Today he lives in Tokyo, speaks fluent Japanese, and is happily married to a Japanese woman (who is actually Korean passing as Japanese!). He stands as the perfect example of our mulattoness: a black boy trapped in a white body who speaks English with a slight Japanese accent and has a son who will spend his life confronting "the question."

Although folk had trouble naming us, we were never blanks or aliens in a "black world." We were and are "polycultural," and I'm talking about all peoples in the Western world. It is not skin, hair, walk, or talk that renders black people so diverse. Rather, it is the fact that most of them are products of different "cultures"—living cultures, not dead ones. These cultures live in and through us every day, with almost no self-consciousness about hierarchy or meaning. "Polycultural" works better than "multicultural," which implies that cultures are fixed, discrete entities that exist side by side—a kind of zoological approach to culture. Such a view obscures power relations, but often reifies race and gender differences.

Black people were polycultural from the get-go. Most of our ancestors came to these shores not as Africans, but as Ibo, Yoruba, Hausa, Kongo, Bambara, Mende, Mandingo, and so on. Some of our ancestors came as Spanish, Portuguese, French, Dutch, Irish, English, Italian. And more than a few of us, in North America as well as in the Caribbean and Latin America, have Asian and Native American roots.

Our lines of biological descent are about as pure as O. J.'s blood sample, and our cultural lines of descent are about as mixed up as a pot of gumbo. What we know as "black culture" has always been fluid and hybrid. In Harlem in the late 1960s and 1970s, Nehru suits were as popular—and as "black"—as dashikis, and martial arts films placed Bruce Lee among a pantheon of black heroes that included Walt Frazier of the New York Knicks and Richard Rountree, who played John Shaft in blaxploitation cinema. How do we understand the zoot suit—or the conk—without the pachuco culture of Mexican American youth, or low riders in black communities without Chicanos? How can we discuss black visual artists in the interwar years without reference to the Mexican muralists, or the radical graphics tradition dating back to the late 19th century, or the Latin American artists influenced by surrealism?

Vague notions of "Eastern" religion and philosophy, as well as a variety of Orientalist assumptions, were far more important to the formation of the Lost-Found Nation of

Islam than anything coming out of Africa. And Rastafarians drew many of their ideas from South Asians, from vegetarianism to marijuana, which was introduced into Jamaica by Indians. Major black movements like Garveyism and the African Blood Brotherhood are also the products of global developments. We won't understand these movements until we see them as part of a dialogue with Irish nationalists from the Easter Rebellion, Russian and Jewish émigrés from the 1905 and 1917 revolutions, and Asian socialists like India's M. N. Roy and Japan's Sen. Katayama.

Indeed, I'm not sure we can even limit ourselves to Earth. How do we make sense   10 of musicians Sun Ra, George Clinton, and Lee "Scratch" Perry or, for that matter, the Nation of Islam, when we consider the fact that space travel and notions of intergalactic exchange constitute a key source of their ideas?

So-called "mixed race" children are not the only ones with a claim to multiple heritages. All of us are inheritors of European, African, Native American, and Asian pasts, even if we can't exactly trace our bloodlines to these continents.

To some people that's a dangerous concept. Too many Europeans don't want to acknowledge that Africans helped create so-called Western civilization, that they are both indebted to and descendants of those they enslaved. They don't want to see the world as One—a tiny little globe where people and cultures are always on the move, where nothing stays still no matter how many times we name it. To acknowledge our polycultural heritage and cultural dynamism is not to give up our black identity. It does mean expanding our definition of blackness, taking our history more seriously, and looking at the rich diversity within us with new eyes.

So next time you see me, don't ask where I'm from or what I am, unless you're ready to sit through a long-ass lecture. As singer/songwriter Abbey Lincoln once put it, "I've got some people in me."

Source: Robin D. G. Kelley, "People in Me." Originally published in COLOR LINE MAGAZINE. Copyright © 1999. Used by permission.

Critical Thinking Topics

1. Describe the writer's tone. Point to examples to illustrate your description. Explain how the tone affects you as the reader. Does the tone enhance or detract from the writer's credibility?

2. Find at least two examples of specific images, words, or cultural references with which you are unfamiliar. Take a moment to research information online about those references, and then reread the passages in which the references occur. How has your research enriched your understanding of the passages?

3. The writer claims, "All of us are inheritors of European, African, Native American, and Asian pasts..." (par. 11). Who might find this idea threatening, and why? In contrast, who might argue that polyculturalism is advantageous, and why?

Writing Topics

1. How are aspects of an individual's cultural heritage reflected by the communities with which he or she associates, including online communities? Provide examples to elaborate on your response.

2. "Say it loud. I'm hybrid and I'm proud," poet Andrei Codrescu proclaimed on National Public Radio's *All Things Considered.* Think of polycultural families you know, personally or otherwise—for example, in popular culture. Describe the challenges that these families face. Do you share Kelley's and Codrescu's enthusiasm for the expanded definition of family and heritage reflected in the term "polycultural"? Why or why not?

6.37 Katrina Karkazis and Rebecca Jordan-Young, The Trouble with Too Much T
(2014)

In 2009, the South African middle-distance runner Caster Semenya was barred from competition and obliged to undergo intrusive and humiliating "sex testing" after fellow athletes at the Berlin World Championships questioned her sex. Ms. Semenya was eventually allowed to compete again, but the incident opened the world's eyes to the process of sex testing and the distress it could bring to an athlete who had lived her whole life as a girl. When an endocrinologist, a gynecologist and a psychologist were brought in to determine whether the teenager was really a woman, she simply asserted, "I know who I am."

From 2011, major sports governing bodies, including the International Olympic Committee, the Fédération Internationale de Football Association and the International Association of Athletics Federations, instituted new eligibility rules that were intended to quell the outrage over the handling of the Semenya case. Instead, as recent cases attest, they may have made things worse.

Rather than trying to decide whether an athlete is "really" female, as decades of mandatory sex tests did, the current policy targets women whose bodies produce more testosterone than is typical. If a female athlete's T level is deemed too high, a medical team selected by the sport's governing bodies develops a "therapeutic proposal." This involves either surgery or drugs to lower the hormone level. If doctors can lower the athlete's testosterone to what the governing bodies consider an appropriate level, she may return to competition. If she refuses to cooperate with the investigation or the medical procedures, she is placed under a permanent ban from elite women's sports.

The first evidence of this new policy in action was published last year in The Journal of Clinical Endocrinology and Metabolism. Four female athletes, ages 18 to 21, all from developing countries, were investigated for high testosterone. Three were identified as having atypically high testosterone after undergoing universal doping tests. (They were not suspected of doping: Tests clearly distinguish between doping and naturally occurring testosterone.)

Sports officials (the report does not identify their governing-body affiliation) sent the young women to a medical center in France, where they were put through examinations that included blood tests, genital inspections, magnetic resonance imaging, X-rays and psychosexual history—many of the same invasive procedures Ms. Semenya endured. Since the athletes were all born as girls but also had internal testes that produce unusually high levels of testosterone for a woman, doctors proposed removing the women's gonads and partially removing their clitorises. All four agreed to undergo both procedures; a year later, they were allowed to return to competition.

The doctors who performed the surgeries and wrote the report acknowledged that there was no medical reason for the procedures. Quite simply, these young female athletes were required to have drastic, unnecessary and irreversible medical interventions if they wished to continue in their sports.

Many conditions can lead to naturally high testosterone, including polycystic ovarian syndrome or an ovarian tumor during pregnancy, but women with intersex traits tend to have the highest T levels. And it is these intersex traits that sports authorities want "corrected."

Sports authorities argue that screening for high T levels is needed to keep women's athletics fair, reasoning that testosterone improves performance. Elite male athletes generally outperform women, and this difference has been attributed to men's higher testosterone levels. Ergo, women with naturally high testosterone are thought to have an unfair advantage over other women.

But these assumptions do not match the science. A new study in Clinical Endocrinology fits with other emerging research on the relationship between natural testosterone and performance, especially in elite athletes, which shows that T levels can't predict who will run faster, lift more weight or fight harder to win. The study, of a sample of 693 elite athletes, revealed a significant overlap in testosterone levels among men and women: 16.5 percent of the elite male athletes had testosterone below the lower limit of the so-called male range; nearly 14 percent of the women were above the female range.

This finding undermines the idea that sex-linked performance differences are   10 mainly because of testosterone. The authors suggest that lean body mass, rather than hormone levels, may better explain the performance gap. They also conclude that their research makes the I.O.C.'s testosterone-guided eligibility policy for women "untenable."

Some might argue that the procedures used to lower T levels are simply part of the price athletes must pay to compete at the elite level. But these choices aren't temporary hardships like training far from home or following a rigorous diet. The required drug and surgical treatments are irreversible and medically unjustifiable. Clitoral surgery impairs sexual function and sensation; gonadectomy causes sterility; and hormone-suppressive drugs have side effects with potentially lifelong health risks.

Moreover, the policy places a disproportionate burden on poor women who may have limited career opportunities and are likely to face enormous pressure to submit to these interventions in order to continue their athletic careers. Under the current policies, more and more female athletes with naturally high T levels will be confronted with these harsh choices—and not just at the elite level. The I.O.C. requires that each country's Olympic committee investigate cases of female athletes with high T levels before naming them to national teams. Some countries, like India, now apply such policies to all female athletes, not just those competing internationally.

Barring female athletes with high testosterone levels from competition is a solution to a problem that doesn't exist. Worse, it is pushing young women into a choice they shouldn't have to make: either to accept medically unnecessary interventions with harmful side effects or to give up their future in sports.

Source: From The New York Times, 4/10/2014 © 2014 The New York Times. All rights reserved. Used by permission and protected by the Copyright Laws of the United States. The printing, copying, redistribution, or retransmission of this Content without express written permission is prohibited.

Critical Thinking Topics

1. The writers present an explicit argument centered on a claim of fact. What is the claim, and where in the essay do they present it?

2. On which of the rhetorical appeals—*ethos, logos,* or *pathos*—is the argument primarily based? Point to specific passages as evidence of this appeal. Is the use of this appeal an effective argument strategy? Why or why not?

3. Describe the writers' tone. To what degree does the tone enhance or detract from the writers' credibility?

4. Where in the essay do the writers address opposing arguments? What concessions and or counterarguments do they provide, and how effective are they?

Writing Topic

Before reading this piece, were you aware of the issue of female athletes potentially being barred from competition for having too high testosterone levels? Were the writers successful in awakening or further engaging your interest in the issue? Why or why not? After reading this article, what is your stance on the issue? Do you agree with the authors? Why or why not?

6.38 Laurie Penny, Bots at Work: Men Will Lose the Most Jobs to Robots. That's OK.
(2017)

Robots are coming for our jobs—but not all of our jobs. They're coming, in ever increasing numbers, for a certain kind of work. For farm and factory labor. For construction. For haulage. In other words, blue-collar jobs traditionally done by men.

This is why automation is so much more than an economic problem. It is a cultural problem, an identity problem, and—critically—a gender problem. Millions of men around the world are staring into the lacquered teeth of obsolescence, terrified of losing not only their security but also their source of meaning and dignity in a world that tells them that if they're not rich, they'd better be doing something quintessentially manly for money. Otherwise they're about as much use as a wooden coach-and-four on the freeway.

There's hope for mankind, but it'll be a hard sell. The way we respond to automation will depend very much on what we decide it means to be a man, or a woman, in the awkward adolescence of the 21st century.

Some political rhetoric blames outsourcing and immigration for the decline in "men's work," but automation is a greater threat to these kinds of jobs—and technological progress cannot be stopped at any border. A recent Oxford study predicted that 70 percent of US construction jobs will disappear in the coming decades; 97 percent of those jobs are held by men, and so are 95 percent of the 3.5 million transport and trucking jobs that robots are presently eyeing. That's scary, and it's one reason so many men are expressing their anger and anxiety at home, in the streets, and at the polls.

While all of this is going on, though, there's a counter-phenomenon playing out. As society panics about bricklaying worker droids and self-driving 18-wheelers, jobs traditionally performed by women—in the so-called pink-collar industries, as well as unpaid labor—are still relatively safe, and some are even on the rise. These include childcare. And service. And nursing, which the US Bureau of Labor Statistics predicts will need a million-plus more workers in the next decade.

According to the logic of the free market, when jobs are destroyed in one area of the economy, people will shift to new areas of productivity, acquiring new skills as they travel. So you might imagine that factory workers are becoming nannies. Not exactly. That's because we're talking about "women's work." Women's work is low paid and low status, and men are conditioned to expect better.

But we've all heard of the gender pay gap. The larger issue is the gender work gap—the fact that women around the world do more work for less pay, or no pay at all. (One 2016 UN report estimated that if women's unpaid work were assigned a monetary value, it would constitute up to 40 percent of global GDP.) Technological progress could make this imbalance worse—or it could help us solve the twin crises of labor and care in one go. The problem, as ever, is not one of technology. The problem is with social attitudes, and those can't be updated with the tap of a touchscreen.

Whether or not you believe men are about to go the way of the portable CD player depends entirely on how you define manhood itself. A great many men have been trained over countless generations to associate their self-worth with the performance of tasks that are, in a very real sense, robotic—predictable, repetitive, and emotionless. The trouble is that machines are far better at being predictable, repetitive, and emotionless than human beings. What human beings do better are all the other things: We are better at being adaptable, compassionate, and intuitive; better at doing work that involves actually touching and thinking about one another; better at making art and music that elevates us above the animals— better, in short, at keeping each other alive. We have walled off all that work and declared it mostly women's business, even as exhausted women have begged men to join them.

Some men have already shown a willingness to think about these issues. In Silicon Valley, the hot topic of the day is universal basic income, proposed by quasi-enlightened VC types and tech CEOs as a way of delinking work and wages as robots take over more and more jobs. Feminists have, in fact, been arguing for a basic income for decades as compensation for unpaid domestic labor. Now that men might find themselves with more time to perform household tasks, they're finally starting to listen.

That's frustrating, but it's also fantastic, because it's a first step. Work is work, and as men come to realize that, society as a whole might start valuing pink-collar and unpaid labor more highly and—as men take these jobs and join the call for increased wages—compensating it more fairly. Benefits only multiply. No longer forced to choose between work and family life, more women can remain and thrive in, say, fast-growing STEM fields, increasing the pool of talent and expertise.

Automation doesn't have to make men obsolete, not if they're willing to change their mindset. As long as men aspire to be cogs in an outdated machine, robots may well replace them. But if they have the courage to imagine different lives of service and dignity, and then demand that those lives be made feasible in terms of both hours and pay, automation can help all of us be more human.

Source: Penny, Laurie. Wired (10/2017). Reprinted by permission of The David Higham Agency.

Critical Thinking Topics

1. Laurie Penny's argument includes a number of assumptions, one of the primary elements in argument (as discussed in Chapter 3). Identify three assumptions in Penny's argument and evaluate each one: Are most readers likely to accept the assumption? Why or why not?

2. Identify at least two appeals to *logos* and at least two appeals to *pathos* in Penny's article. Evaluate the persuasive effect of each example. Explain how each strengthens or detracts from the argument's effectiveness.

3. Describe the writer's tone. Using quotations from the article, explain how this tone influences your response to the argument.

4. Penny makes it clear that she has a stance on the topic; her intention is to persuade readers with a different stance to change their thinking. Is there a single sentence that expresses a claim for her argument? If so, write it out. If not, write a sentence of your own to articulate the argument's claim. Which type of claim is it: fact, policy, or value? What does Penny's argument leave you thinking about the topic? If you began with a different stance from the writer, has the writer succeeded in changing your thinking? If so, how? If you began in agreement with the writer's stance, did the article strengthen, detract from, or have little effect on your stance? Explain why.

Writing Topic

Select one assumption in Penny's argument that strikes you as especially bold, if not brash. Write out the assumption and then imagine that Penny is reading her article to an audience, followed by a Q&A. During the Q&A, an audience member challenges Penny on the assumption you selected. Beginning with this challenge, write a debate between Penny and the audience member that evolves into a Rogerian middle-ground agreement. (See Chapter 4 for a discussion of Rogerian argument strategy.)

6.39 Chapter Activities

The series of activities on the following pages invite you to apply the concepts and ideas embodied in the readings and brought out in the critical thinking topics and writing topics throughout this chapter.

6.39.1 Topics for Writing Arguments

1. Puritans came to these shores seeking freedom, yet, ironically, created one of the more restrictive societies in our country's history. Conflicting attitudes toward questions of freedom and conformity, therefore, go back to our very beginnings. Where do you observe or personally encounter those conflicts today? Perhaps you can recall examples of such conflicts dramatized in popular culture—in movies, song lyrics, or TV miniseries. In this chapter, the short stories "The Storm" and "The Foundations of the Earth" and the poems "Much Madness is divinest Sense" and "Crazy Courage" highlight conflicts surrounding questions of freedom and conformity. In those works, what are some of the primary factors underlying these conflicts? Find and critically review three examples that illustrate conflicts between freedom and conformity—examples drawn from firsthand observations and experience, from other works of literature, or from popular culture. Based on this review and keeping in mind your assessment of the primary factors underlying these conflicts, create a claim about such conflicts; to support the claim, draw on evidence from your analyses of the three examples.

2. The concept of "keeping the family name alive" is one of many clichéd notions centered on family. What do you think the idea implies, in terms of the responsibilities of family members? Do most people today concern themselves with the idea, or is it a thing of the past? What do you know about your family history? How is this history shared among family members, and how is it valued? In this chapter, the short story "Beading Lesson," the poems "Lost Sister" and "Lineage," and the nonfiction piece "The People in Me" address the dynamics of the interplay among family tradition, cultural heritage, and individual identity and fulfillment. How do family traditions and cultural legacies contribute to or constrain an individual's identity? Drawing on evidence from at least two literature selections in this chapter and from your own experience and observations, develop an argument centered on a claim of value about an aspect of family heritage and individual identity.

3. In a nation founded and settled by immigrants, we might expect that most individuals would celebrate cultural diversity. However, cultural diversity has given rise to polarizing conflicts within and among communities, conflicts that seem to be as fraught today as in past centuries. Several of the selections in this chapter address aspects of cultural diversity—for example, the poems "Outcast" and "Counting" and the nonfiction pieces "The Chinese in All of Us" and "The People in Me." Reflect on your own observations of celebrations of cultural diversity and of conflicts arising from cultural diversity, and with at least two of these reading selections in mind, propose a constructive approach for addressing conflicts arising from cultural diversity. Imagine yourself speaking to a culturally diverse gathering of people from a community where violent conflicts have broken out between different ethnic groups. How would your approach contribute to resolving the conflicts?

4. "You're right, it's tough being a man these days," Scott Russell Sanders concedes in the opening paragraphs of his nonfiction piece "The Men We Carry in Our Minds." What does *being a man* suggest to you? Likewise, what does *being a woman* suggest? Today, with transgendered individuals beginning to speak out and assert their place in

mainstream society, the lines between genders seem less pronounced, if not dissolving. Or are they? With gender diversity in mind, reflect on your firsthand knowledge, experience, and observations, as well as on two or more of the selections in this chapter, such as the poems "Crazy Courage" and "Boss's Son" and the nonfiction pieces "The Men We Carry in Our Minds," "The Trouble with Too Much T," and "Bots at Work: Men Will Lose the Most Jobs. That's OK." What does it mean to be a man and to be a woman in contemporary society? Are genders becoming more fluid, and should they? Why or why not? Develop an argument essay centered on your perspective on the topic of genders; support your viewpoint with details from your own experience and observations and with analyses of at least two of the selections in this chapter.

5. Look back at your responses to the Prewriting and Discussion tasks at the beginning of this chapter; then, keeping in mind your reading, writing, and discussion experiences related to the chapter's reading selections, reflect on these questions about the themes of individual and community identity:

- How have your ideas and perspectives about those themes been shaped by your experiences?
- Which three reading selections have most influenced your thinking about those themes? How and why?

6.39.2 Taking a Global Perspective: Individuals and Global Online Communities

Facebook, Instagram, Snapchat, Twitter, and a host of other social networking platforms bring people together from around the globe who can form online communities based on shared interests. According to pollster John Zogby, American young adults—in particular, those between the ages of 18 and 29—are "the First Globals...more networked and globally engaged than members of any similar age cohort in American history."[2] What in your view does the notion of "First Globals" mean? Do you participate in online social networking, and if so, have you connected with individuals from multiple other countries? Even if you do not consider yourself to be engaged in global online communities, reflect on the implications of this global connectivity for individuals. What are the positive and negative effects that participating in such communities might have on individuals? For example, with communities instantly available, an individual may have a multitude of allegiances—a diversity of associations that can be both liberating and unsettling. On the one hand, such associations can expose a person to new ideas and information that inspire creative and critical thinking; on the other hand, they can create confusion and disorientation. Based on your critical analysis of the effects of participating in global online communities, create an argument that addresses the impact of these communities on individuals.

---

[2] qtd. in Anne-Marie Slaughter, "America's Edge," *Foreign Affairs* 1 Feb. 2009: n. pag. *Global NewsBank*, NewsBank Online. Web. 16 Mar. 2015.

6.39.3 Collaborating on a Rogerian Argument

For this activity, you will work in small groups to research and write a Rogerian argument on a contemporary issue that has emerged from your exploration of readings in this chapter. The writing topics that follow the readings can help you identify an issue. (See Chapter 4 for a discussion of Rogerian argument and a suggested organizational approach to developing a Rogerian argument essay.) Here are some suggested guidelines for this collaborative activity:

- Identify an issue.
- Divide the research and writing responsibilities as follows:
  - Student one: introduction section
  - Student two: body section, affirmative position
  - Student three: body section, opposing position
  - Student four: conclusion, summation, and middle-ground position

For an effective collaboration, each team member should take responsibility for

- Collecting information related to the issue.
- Completing assigned work on time.
- Listening to and considering the viewpoints of the other team members.

Sample Topic: Immigration Reform

"The New Colossus," a sonnet by American poet Emma Lazarus (1849–1887), is engraved on a plaque in the pedestal of the Statue of Liberty. The poem depicts Lady Liberty as saying, "Give me your tired, your poor,/Your huddled masses yearning to breathe free." Traditionally, the United States has offered immigrants the opportunity to join and contribute to the American community. Many Americans continue to value that tradition; however, since the September 11, 2001, terrorist attacks and in the face of continued threats to internal security, as well as increasing numbers of illegal immigrants, many other Americans have sought to curtail immigration. At the time of this writing (early 2018), President Donald J. Trump has called for the construction of a 1,000-mile wall along the Mexico–United States border. He argues that such a wall is essential to stop the influx of illegal immigrants, who, he claims, endanger citizens and threaten national security. Meanwhile, when it comes to negotiating immigration reform, the U.S. Congress seems to remain paralyzed by partisan divisions. Hanging in the balance are the "dreamers," children and young adults brought to the U.S. illegally by their parents and allowed to remain legally under certain conditions, according to the Obama-era Deferred Action for Childhood Arrivals (DACA). Do some background research on the current status of federal immigration policy and develop a Rogerian argument essay on the issue. What immigration reforms, if any, should be implemented?

6.39.4 Arguing Themes from Literature

1. Both "Not Leaving the House" and "The Gift of the Magi" describe loving families. The family relationships depicted in these works, however, share more than love: they also show a willingness to sacrifice. Using quotations from the texts to support your position, describe how these two works demonstrate the concept of sacrifice.
2. Children's identities are often tightly woven into their connections with family. The speakers in "Lineage" and "Cayenne Warning" and the narrator in "New Last Words for My Mother" all reflect on maternal influences. Compare and contrast the positive and negative effects of the relationships depicted in these works.
3. Reread Katherine Mansfield's "The Garden Party." Do you think that Laura will grow up to accept or reject her family's values and their sense of belonging to an upper class? Use specific examples and quotations from the story to support your viewpoint.

6.39.5 Multimodal Activity: "Never Say Die" Diners

In Judy Grahn's poem "Ella, in a Square Apron, Along Highway 80," Ella, a waitress, frequently fends off the advances of overly friendly customers and probably longs for more defined social barriers in the diner. Meanwhile, many patrons seek a feeling of community in traditional diners like the one in Figure 6.2. The image of the diner resonates widely in American culture, symbolizing optimism, friendship, and connections to strangers.

Figure 6.2

BirchTree/Alamy Stock Photo

Find portrayals of diners in three different media—for example:

- In art—*Nighthawks,* by Edward Hopper; *The Runaway,* by Norman Rockwell.
- In music—"Tom's Diner," by Suzanne Vega.
- In television—*Alice; Happy Days*; Food Network's *Diners, Drive-ins and Dives.*
- In film—*The Equalizer* (2014); *Pulp Fiction* (1994); *The Shape of Water* (2017); *The Kid* (2000); *Diner* (1982).

Compare and contrast how the portrayals in your three examples reflect both individual and community identity.

Chapter 7
Crime and Punishment

At his best, man is the noblest of all animals; separated from
law and justice, he is the worst.

—Aristotle

Aristotle's epigram reminds us that civilized society requires rules, including a system of laws. Our culture values a commitment to justice and to the ideal that no innocent person will be convicted of a crime that he or she did not commit and that those who have committed crimes will be found and convicted, regardless of their position in society. However, reality is often complicated in ways that make it difficult to decide whether a person is truly innocent or guilty and, if guilty, what the punishment should be.

For example, celebrities like Jay Z and civic organizations like Color of Change have argued that the case of rapper Meek Mill illustrates that our justice system is flawed and unfair (Mill has been arrested, released on parole, and then rearrested for violating parole on multiple occasions, with much controversy about the circumstances surrounding his original arrest and conviction and his rearrests). Similarly, the #MeToo movement has tried to ensure that the cases of alleged victims of sexual discrimination, harassment, and assault are treated like other serious criminal cases and that justice is not denied because the accused are influential people favored by society. The complications of seeking justice in real life often send us searching for moral absolutes in pop culture, like superhero movies, illustrating our longing for scenarios in which good ultimately defeats evil.

The idea that people must pay for their transgressions is a prevalent theme in classic literature and popular media. Whether one of Edgar Allen Poe's proud characters takes vengeance on a friend who he feels slighted him, Sherlock Holmes solves a crime and catches the criminal, or Tywin Lannister on HBO's popular series *Game of Thrones* plots the takedown of a political enemy, audiences always seem to have an appetite for watching the guilty receive their just deserts. However, literature often avoids promoting moral absolutes and instead mirrors the complexity of life. Many of the selections in this chapter involve scenarios in which a crime ultimately brings with it a type of punishment—but those who receive the punishment are not necessarily the offenders. Some readers might sympathize with a convicted felon in Flannery O'Connor's "A Good Man Is Hard to Find" or find themselves outraged that a drug company's executives can escape their just deserts, as Barry Meier argues in "Origins of an Epidemic: Purdue Pharma Knew Its Opioids Were Widely Abused." Some might share the bitterness of the speakers in Langston Hughes's "Justice" or Marge Piercy's "What's That Smell in the Kitchen?" We would like to think that justice is always carried out—that those who are right always prevail; however, some of the situations and characters in this chapter's selections might make us doubt whether this desired outcome always occurs and acknowledge that the lines between right and wrong, innocence and guilt, are not always distinct.

7.1 Prewriting and Discussion: Crime and Punishment

1. Read the image in Figure 7.1 creatively and critically. What ideas does it suggest about crime and punishment?
2. Police procedurals are some of the most popular shows on television—for example, *CSI, NCIS, Law and Order, Hawaii Five-0*, and others. Each episode of this type of show follows the same basic formula: crime committed, clues gathered, solution deduced, criminal apprehended. If these shows are so repetitive, why are they so popular—what is the appeal? Support your response by citing specific shows, episodes, and scenes.

Figure 7.1 *Night Patrol*, by Sean Svendsen

'Night Patrol' © Sean Svendsen

3. Is revenge ever justified? Several characters in this chapter's reading selections seek revenge for perceived wrongs. Do you think that revenge is ever justified? If so, explain why and give examples of appropriate circumstances. If no, explain why not and give examples of alternative approaches. Consider examples from your own observations or from the media.

7.2 Fiction

The six short stories in this section, spanning the years 1844 through 1997, explore issues related to the theme of crime and punishment.

7.3 Nathaniel Hawthorne, The Birth-Mark (1844)

In the latter part of the last century there lived a man of science, an eminent proficient in every branch of natural philosophy, who not long before our story opens had made experience of a spiritual affinity more attractive than any chemical one. He had left his laboratory to the care of an assistant, cleared his fine countenance from the furnace smoke, washed the stain of acids from his fingers, and persuaded a beautiful woman to become his wife. In those days when the comparatively recent discovery of electricity and other kindred mysteries of Nature seemed to open paths into the region of miracle, it was not unusual for the love of science to rival the love of woman in its depth and absorbing energy. The higher intellect, the imagination, the spirit, and even the heart might all find their congenial aliment in pursuits which, as some of their ardent votaries believed, would ascend from one step of powerful intelligence to another, until the philosopher should lay his hand on the secret of creative force and perhaps make new worlds for himself. We know not whether Aylmer possessed this degree of faith in man's ultimate control over Nature. He had devoted himself, however, too unreservedly to scientific studies ever to be weaned from them by any second passion. His love for his young wife might prove the stronger of the two; but it could only be by intertwining itself with his love of science, and uniting the strength of the latter to his own.

Such a union accordingly took place, and was attended with truly remarkable consequences and a deeply impressive moral. One day, very soon after their marriage, Aylmer sat gazing at his wife with a trouble in his countenance that grew stronger until he spoke.

"Georgiana," said he, "has it never occurred to you that the mark upon your cheek might be removed?"

"No, indeed," said she, smiling; but perceiving the seriousness of his manner, she blushed deeply. "To tell you the truth it has been so often called a charm that I was simple enough to imagine it might be so."

"Ah, upon another face perhaps it might," replied her husband; "but never on 5 yours. No, dearest Georgiana, you came so nearly perfect from the hand of Nature that this slightest possible defect, which we hesitate whether to term a defect or a beauty, shocks me, as being the visible mark of earthly imperfection."

"Shocks you, my husband!" cried Georgiana, deeply hurt; at first reddening with momentary anger, but then bursting into tears. "Then why did you take me from my mother's side? You cannot love what shocks you!"

To explain this conversation it must be mentioned that in the centre of Georgiana's left cheek there was a singular mark, deeply interwoven, as it were, with the texture and substance of her face. In the usual state of her complexion—a healthy though delicate bloom—the mark wore a tint of deeper crimson, which imperfectly defined its shape amid the surrounding rosiness. When she blushed it gradually became more indistinct, and finally vanished amid the triumphant rush of blood that bathed the whole cheek with its brilliant glow. But if any shifting motion caused her to turn pale there was the mark again, a crimson stain upon the snow, in what Aylmer sometimes deemed an almost fearful distinctness. Its shape bore not a little similarity to the human hand, though of the smallest pygmy size. Georgiana's lovers were wont to say that some fairy at her birth hour had laid her tiny hand upon the infant's cheek, and left this impress there in token of the magic endowments that were to give her such sway over all hearts. Many a desperate swain would have risked life for the privilege of pressing his lips to the mysterious hand. It must not be concealed, however, that the impression wrought by this fairy sign manual varied exceedingly, according to the difference of temperament in the beholders. Some fastidious persons—but they were exclusively of her own sex—affirmed that the bloody hand, as they chose to call it, quite destroyed the effect of Georgiana's beauty, and rendered her countenance even hideous. But it would be as reasonable to say that one of those small blue stains which sometimes occur in the purest statuary marble would convert the Eve of Powers to a monster. Masculine observers, if the birthmark did not heighten their admiration, contented themselves with wishing it away, that the world might possess one living specimen of ideal loveliness without the semblance of a flaw. After his marriage,—for he thought little or nothing of the matter before,—Aylmer discovered that this was the case with himself.

Had she been less beautiful,—if Envy's self could have found aught else to sneer at,—he might have felt his affection heightened by the prettiness of this mimic hand, now vaguely portrayed, now lost, now stealing forth again and glimmering to and fro with every pulse of emotion that throbbed within her heart; but seeing her otherwise so perfect, he found this one defect grow more and more intolerable with every moment of their united lives. It was the fatal flaw of humanity which Nature, in one shape or another, stamps ineffaceably on all her productions, either to imply that they are temporary and finite, or that their perfection must be wrought by toil and pain. The crimson hand expressed the ineludible gripe in which mortality clutches the highest and purest of earthly mould, degrading them into kindred with the lowest, and even with the very brutes, like whom their visible frames return to dust. In this manner, selecting it as the symbol of his wife's liability to sin, sorrow, decay, and death, Aylmer's sombre imagination was not long in rendering the birthmark a frightful object, causing him more trouble and horror than ever Georgiana's beauty, whether of soul or sense, had given him delight.

At all the seasons which should have been their happiest, he invariably and without intending it, nay, in spite of a purpose to the contrary, reverted to this one disastrous topic. Trifling as it at first appeared, it so connected itself with innumerable trains of thought and modes of feeling that it became the central point of all. With the morning twilight Aylmer opened his eyes upon his wife's face and recognized the symbol of imperfection; and when they sat together at the evening hearth his eyes wandered stealthily to her cheek, and beheld, flickering with the blaze of the wood fire, the spectral hand that wrote mortality where he would fain have worshipped. Georgiana soon learned to shudder at his gaze. It needed but a glance with the peculiar expression that his face often wore to change the roses of her cheek into a deathlike paleness, amid which the crimson hand was brought strongly out, like a bass-relief of ruby on the whitest marble.

Late one night when the lights were growing dim, so as hardly to betray the stain   10 on the poor wife's cheek, she herself, for the first time, voluntarily took up the subject.

"Do you remember, my dear Aylmer," said she, with a feeble attempt at a smile, "have you any recollection of a dream last night about this odious hand?"

"None! none whatever!" replied Aylmer, starting; but then he added, in a dry, cold tone, affected for the sake of concealing the real depth of his emotion, "I might well dream of it; for before I fell asleep it had taken a pretty firm hold of my fancy."

"And you did dream of it?" continued Georgiana, hastily; for she dreaded lest a gush of tears should interrupt what she had to say. "A terrible dream! I wonder that you can forget it. Is it possible to forget this one expression? — 'It is in her heart now; we must have it out!' Reflect, my husband; for by all means I would have you recall that dream."

The mind is in a sad state when Sleep, the all-involving, cannot confine her spectres within the dim region of her sway, but suffers them to break forth, affrighting this actual life with secrets that perchance belong to a deeper one. Aylmer now remembered his dream. He had fancied himself with his servant Aminadab, attempting an operation for the removal of the birthmark; but the deeper went the knife, the deeper sank the hand, until at length its tiny grasp appeared to have caught hold of Georgiana's heart; whence, however, her husband was inexorably resolved to cut or wrench it away.

When the dream had shaped itself perfectly in his memory, Aylmer sat in his wife's   15 presence with a guilty feeling. Truth often finds its way to the mind close muffled in robes of sleep, and then speaks with uncompromising directness of matters in regard to which we practise an unconscious self-deception during our waking moments. Until now he had not been aware of the tyrannizing influence acquired by one idea over his mind, and of the lengths which he might find in his heart to go for the sake of giving himself peace.

"Aylmer," resumed Georgiana, solemnly, "I know not what may be the cost to both of us to rid me of this fatal birthmark. Perhaps its removal may cause cureless deformity; or it may be the stain goes as deep as life itself. Again: do we know that there is a possibility, on any terms, of unclasping the firm gripe of this little hand which was laid upon me before I came into the world?"

"Dearest Georgiana, I have spent much thought upon the subject," hastily interrupted Aylmer. "I am convinced of the perfect practicability of its removal."

"If there be the remotest possibility of it," continued Georgiana, "let the attempt be made at whatever risk. Danger is nothing to me; for life, while this hateful mark makes me the object of your horror and disgust, — life is a burden which I would fling down with joy. Either remove this dreadful hand, or take my wretched life! You have deep science. All the world bears witness of it. You have achieved great wonders. Cannot you remove this little, little mark, which I cover with the tips of two small fingers? Is this beyond your power, for the sake of your own peace, and to save your poor wife from madness?"

"Noblest, dearest, tenderest wife," cried Aylmer, rapturously, "doubt not my power. I have already given this matter the deepest thought—thought which might almost have enlightened me to create a being less perfect than yourself. Georgiana, you have led me deeper than ever into the heart of science. I feel myself fully competent to render this dear cheek as faultless as its fellow; and then, most beloved, what will be my triumph when I shall have corrected what Nature left imperfect in her fairest work! Even Pygmalion, when his sculptured woman assumed life, felt not greater ecstasy than mine will be."

"It is resolved, then," said Georgiana, faintly smiling. "And, Aylmer, spare me not, 20 though you should find the birthmark take refuge in my heart at last."

Her husband tenderly kissed her cheek—her right cheek—not that which bore the impress of the crimson hand.

The next day Aylmer apprised his wife of a plan that he had formed whereby he might have opportunity for the intense thought and constant watchfulness which the proposed operation would require; while Georgiana, likewise, would enjoy the perfect repose essential to its success. They were to seclude themselves in the extensive apartments occupied by Aylmer as a laboratory, and where, during his toilsome youth, he had made discoveries in the elemental powers of Nature that had roused the admiration of all the learned societies in Europe. Seated calmly in this laboratory, the pale philosopher had investigated the secrets of the highest cloud region and of the profoundest mines; he had satisfied himself of the causes that kindled and kept alive the fires of the volcano; and had explained the mystery of fountains, and how it is that they gush forth, some so bright and pure, and others with such rich medicinal virtues, from the dark bosom of the earth. Here, too, at an earlier period, he had studied the wonders of the human frame, and attempted to fathom the very process by which Nature assimilates all her precious influences from earth and air, and from the spiritual world, to create and foster man, her masterpiece. The latter pursuit, however, Aylmer had long laid aside in unwilling recognition of the truth—against which all seekers sooner or later stumble—that our great creative Mother, while she amuses us with apparently working in the broadest sunshine, is yet severely careful to keep her own secrets, and, in spite of her pretended openness, shows us nothing but results. She permits us, indeed, to mar, but seldom to mend, and, like a jealous patentee, on no account to make. Now, however, Aylmer resumed these half-forgotten investigations; not, of course, with such hopes or wishes as first suggested them; but because they involved much physiological truth and lay in the path of his proposed scheme for the treatment of Georgiana.

As he led her over the threshold of the laboratory, Georgiana was cold and tremulous. Aylmer looked cheerfully into her face, with intent to reassure her, but was so startled with the intense glow of the birthmark upon the whiteness of her cheek that he could not restrain a strong convulsive shudder. His wife fainted.

"Aminadab! Aminadab!" shouted Aylmer, stamping violently on the floor.

Forthwith there issued from an inner apartment a man of low stature, but bulky 25 frame, with shaggy hair hanging about his visage, which was grimed with the vapors of the furnace. This personage had been Aylmer's underworker during his whole scientific career, and was admirably fitted for that office by his great mechanical readiness, and the skill with which, while incapable of comprehending a single principle, he executed all the details of his master's experiments. With his vast strength, his shaggy hair, his smoky aspect, and the indescribable earthiness that incrusted him, he seemed to represent man's physical nature; while Aylmer's slender figure, and pale, intellectual face, were no less apt a type of the spiritual element.

"Throw open the door of the boudoir, Aminadab," said Aylmer, "and burn a pastil."

"Yes, master," answered Aminadab, looking intently at the lifeless form of Georgiana; and then he muttered to himself, "If she were my wife, I'd never part with that birthmark."

When Georgiana recovered consciousness she found herself breathing an atmosphere of penetrating fragrance, the gentle potency of which had recalled her from her deathlike faintness. The scene around her looked like enchantment. Aylmer had converted those smoky, dingy, sombre rooms, where he had spent his brightest years in recondite pursuits, into a series of beautiful apartments not unfit to be the secluded abode of a lovely woman. The walls were hung with gorgeous curtains, which imparted the combination of grandeur and grace that no other species of adornment can achieve; and as they fell from the ceiling to the floor, their rich and ponderous folds, concealing all angles and straight lines, appeared to shut in the scene from infinite space. For aught Georgiana knew, it might be a pavilion among the clouds. And Aylmer, excluding the sunshine, which would have interfered with his chemical processes, had supplied its place with perfumed lamps, emitting flames of various hue, but all uniting in a soft, impurpled radiance. He now knelt by his wife's side, watching her earnestly, but without alarm; for he was confident in his science, and felt that he could draw a magic circle round her within which no evil might intrude.

"Where am I? Ah, I remember," said Georgiana, faintly; and she placed her hand over her cheek to hide the terrible mark from her husband's eyes.

"Fear not, dearest!" exclaimed he. "Do not shrink from me! Believe me, Georgiana,   30
I even rejoice in this single imperfection, since it will be such a rapture to remove it."

"Oh, spare me!" sadly replied his wife. "Pray do not look at it again. I never can forget that convulsive shudder."

In order to soothe Georgiana, and, as it were, to release her mind from the burden of actual things, Aylmer now put in practice some of the light and playful secrets which science had taught him among its profounder lore. Airy figures, absolutely bodiless ideas, and forms of unsubstantial beauty came and danced before her, imprinting their momentary footsteps on beams of light. Though she had some indistinct idea of the method of these optical phenomena, still the illusion was almost perfect enough to warrant the belief that her husband possessed sway over the spiritual world. Then again, when she felt a wish to look forth from her seclusion, immediately, as if her thoughts were answered, the procession of external existence flitted across a screen. The scenery and the figures of actual life were perfectly represented, but with that bewitching, yet indescribable difference which always makes a picture, an image, or a shadow so much more attractive than the original. When wearied of this, Aylmer bade her cast her eyes upon a vessel containing a quantity of earth. She did so, with little interest at first; but was soon startled to perceive the germ of a plant shooting upward from the soil. Then came the slender stalk; the leaves gradually unfolded themselves; and amid them was a perfect and lovely flower. "It is magical!" cried Georgiana. "I dare not touch it."

"Nay, pluck it," answered Aylmer, — "pluck it, and inhale its brief perfume while you may. The flower will wither in a few moments and leave nothing save its brown seed vessels; but thence may be perpetuated a race as ephemeral as itself."

But Georgiana had no sooner touched the flower than the whole plant suffered a blight, its leaves turning coal-black as if by the agency of fire.

"There was too powerful a stimulus," said Aylmer, thoughtfully.   35

To make up for this abortive experiment, he proposed to take her portrait by a scientific process of his own invention. It was to be effected by rays of light striking upon a polished plate of metal. Georgiana assented; but, on looking at the result, was affrighted to find the features of the portrait blurred and indefinable; while the minute figure of a hand appeared where the cheek should have been. Aylmer snatched the metallic plate and threw it into a jar of corrosive acid.

Soon, however, he forgot these mortifying failures. In the intervals of study and chemical experiment he came to her flushed and exhausted, but seemed invigorated by her presence, and spoke in glowing language of the resources of his art. He gave a history of the long dynasty of the alchemists, who spent so many ages in quest of the universal solvent by which the golden principle might be elicited from all things vile and base. Aylmer appeared to believe that, by the plainest scientific logic, it was altogether within the limits of possibility to discover this long-sought medium; "but," he added, "a philosopher who should go deep enough to acquire the power would attain too lofty a wisdom to stoop to the exercise of it." Not less singular were his opinions in regard to the elixir vitae. He more than intimated that it was at his option to concoct a liquid that should prolong life for years, perhaps interminably; but that it would produce a discord in Nature which all the world, and chiefly the quaffer of the immortal nostrum, would find cause to curse.

"Aylmer, are you in earnest?" asked Georgiana, looking at him with amazement and fear. "It is terrible to possess such power, or even to dream of possessing it."

"Oh, do not tremble, my love," said her husband. "I would not wrong either you or myself by working such inharmonious effects upon our lives; but I would have you consider how trifling, in comparison, is the skill requisite to remove this little hand."

At the mention of the birthmark, Georgiana, as usual, shrank as if a redhot iron had touched her cheek.   40

Again Aylmer applied himself to his labors. She could hear his voice in the distant furnace room giving directions to Aminadab, whose harsh, uncouth, misshapen tones were audible in response, more like the grunt or growl of a brute than human speech. After hours of absence, Aylmer reappeared and proposed that she should now examine his cabinet of chemical products and natural treasures of the earth. Among the former he showed her a small vial, in which, he remarked, was contained a gentle yet most powerful fragrance, capable of impregnating all the breezes that blow across a kingdom. They were of inestimable value, the contents of that little vial; and, as he said so, he threw some of the perfume into the air and filled the room with piercing and invigorating delight.

"And what is this?" asked Georgiana, pointing to a small crystal globe containing a gold-colored liquid. "It is so beautiful to the eye that I could imagine it the elixir of life."

"In one sense it is," replied Aylmer; "or, rather, the elixir of immortality. It is the most precious poison that ever was concocted in this world. By its aid I could apportion the lifetime of any mortal at whom you might point your finger. The strength of the dose would determine whether he were to linger out years, or drop dead in the midst of a breath. No king on his guarded throne could keep his life if I, in my private station, should deem that the welfare of millions justified me in depriving him of it."

"Why do you keep such a terrific drug?" inquired Georgiana in horror.

"Do not mistrust me, dearest," said her husband, smiling; "its virtuous potency is yet greater than its harmful one. But see! here is a powerful cosmetic. With a few drops of this in a vase of water, freckles may be washed away as easily as the hands are cleansed. A stronger infusion would take the blood out of the cheek, and leave the rosiest beauty a pale ghost."   45

"Is it with this lotion that you intend to bathe my cheek?" asked Georgiana, anxiously.

"Oh, no," hastily replied her husband; "this is merely superficial. Your case demands a remedy that shall go deeper."

In his interviews with Georgiana, Aylmer generally made minute inquiries as to her sensations and whether the confinement of the rooms and the temperature of the atmosphere agreed with her. These questions had such a particular drift that Georgiana began to conjecture that she was already subjected to certain physical influences, either breathed in with the fragrant air or taken with her food. She fancied likewise, but it might be altogether fancy, that there was a stirring up of her system—a strange, indefinite sensation creeping through her veins, and tingling, half painfully, half pleasurably, at her heart. Still, whenever she dared to look into the mirror, there she beheld herself pale as a white rose and with the crimson birthmark stamped upon her cheek. Not even Aylmer now hated it so much as she.

To dispel the tedium of the hours which her husband found it necessary to devote to the processes of combination and analysis, Georgiana turned over the volumes of his scientific library. In many dark old tomes she met with chapters full of romance and poetry. They were the works of philosophers of the middle ages, such as Albertus Magnus, Cornelius Agrippa, Paracelsus, and the famous friar who created the prophetic Brazen Head. All these antique naturalists stood in advance of their centuries, yet were imbued with some of their credulity, and therefore were believed, and perhaps imagined themselves to have acquired from the investigation of Nature a power above Nature, and from physics a sway over the spiritual world. Hardly less curious and imaginative were the early volumes of the Transactions of the Royal Society, in which the members, knowing little of the limits of natural possibility, were continually recording wonders or proposing methods whereby wonders might be wrought.

But to Georgiana the most engrossing volume was a large folio from her husband's 50 own hand, in which he had recorded every experiment of his scientific career, its original aim, the methods adopted for its development, and its final success or failure, with the circumstances to which either event was attributable. The book, in truth, was both the history and emblem of his ardent, ambitious, imaginative, yet practical and laborious life. He handled physical details as if there were nothing beyond them; yet spiritualized them all, and redeemed himself from materialism by his strong and eager aspiration towards the infinite. In his grasp the veriest clod of earth assumed a soul. Georgiana, as she read, reverenced Aylmer and loved him more profoundly than ever, but with a less entire dependence on his judgment than heretofore. Much as he had accomplished, she could not but observe that his most splendid successes were almost invariably failures, if compared with the ideal at which he aimed. His brightest diamonds were the merest pebbles, and felt to be so by himself, in comparison with the inestimable gems which lay hidden beyond his reach. The volume, rich with achievements that had won renown for its author, was yet as melancholy a record as ever mortal hand had penned. It was the sad confession and continual exemplification of the shortcomings of the composite man, the spirit burdened with clay and working in matter, and of the despair that assails the higher nature at finding itself so miserably thwarted by the earthly part. Perhaps every man of genius in whatever sphere might recognize the image of his own experience in Aylmer's journal.

So deeply did these reflections affect Georgiana that she laid her face upon the open volume and burst into tears. In this situation she was found by her husband.

"It is dangerous to read in a sorcerer's books," said he with a smile, though his countenance was uneasy and displeased. "Georgiana, there are pages in that volume which I can scarcely glance over and keep my senses. Take heed lest it prove as detrimental to you."

"It has made me worship you more than ever," said she.

"Ah, wait for this one success," rejoined he, "then worship me if you will. I shall deem myself hardly unworthy of it. But come, I have sought you for the luxury of your voice. Sing to me, dearest."

So she poured out the liquid music of her voice to quench the thirst of his spirit. He 55 then took his leave with a boyish exuberance of gayety, assuring her that her seclusion would endure but a little longer, and that the result was already certain. Scarcely had he departed when Georgiana felt irresistibly impelled to follow him. She had forgotten to inform Aylmer of a symptom which for two or three hours past had begun to excite her attention. It was a sensation in the fatal birthmark, not painful, but which induced a restlessness throughout her system. Hastening after her husband, she intruded for the first time into the laboratory.

The first thing that struck her eye was the furnace, that hot and feverish worker, with the intense glow of its fire, which by the quantities of soot clustered above it seemed to have been burning for ages. There was a distilling apparatus in full operation. Around the room were retorts, tubes, cylinders, crucibles, and other apparatus of chemical research. An electrical machine stood ready for immediate use. The atmosphere felt oppressively close, and was tainted with gaseous odors which had been tormented forth by the processes of science. The severe and homely simplicity of the apartment, with its naked walls and brick pavement, looked strange, accustomed as Georgiana had become to the fantastic elegance of her boudoir. But what chiefly, indeed almost solely, drew her attention, was the aspect of Aylmer himself.

He was pale as death, anxious and absorbed, and hung over the furnace as if it depended upon his utmost watchfulness whether the liquid which it was distilling should be the draught of immortal happiness or misery. How different from the sanguine and joyous mien that he had assumed for Georgiana's encouragement!

"Carefully now, Aminadab; carefully, thou human machine; carefully, thou man of clay!" muttered Aylmer, more to himself than his assistant. "Now, if there be a thought too much or too little, it is all over."

"Ho! ho!" mumbled Aminadab. "Look, master! look!"

Aylmer raised his eyes hastily, and at first reddened, then grew paler than ever, on 60 beholding Georgiana. He rushed towards her and seized her arm with a gripe that left the print of his fingers upon it.

"Why do you come hither? Have you no trust in your husband?" cried he, impetuously. "Would you throw the blight of that fatal birthmark over my labors? It is not well done. Go, prying woman, go!"

"Nay, Aylmer," said Georgiana with the firmness of which she possessed no stinted endowment, "it is not you that have a right to complain. You mistrust your wife; you have concealed the anxiety with which you watch the development of this experiment. Think not so unworthily of me, my husband. Tell me all the risk we run, and fear not that I shall shrink; for my share in it is far less than your own."

"No, no, Georgiana!" said Aylmer, impatiently; "it must not be."

"I submit," replied she calmly. "And, Aylmer, I shall quaff whatever draught you bring me; but it will be on the same principle that would induce me to take a dose of poison if offered by your hand."

"My noble wife," said Aylmer, deeply moved, "I knew not the height and depth of   65
your nature until now. Nothing shall be concealed. Know, then, that this crimson hand,
superficial as it seems, has clutched its grasp into your being with a strength of which I
had no previous conception. I have already administered agents powerful enough to do
aught except to change your entire physical system. Only one thing remains to be tried.
If that fail us we are ruined."

"Why did you hesitate to tell me this?" asked she.

"Because, Georgiana," said Aylmer, in a low voice, "there is danger."

"Danger? There is but one danger—that this horrible stigma shall be left upon my
cheek!" cried Georgiana. "Remove it, remove it, whatever be the cost, or we shall both
go mad!"

"Heaven knows your words are too true," said Aylmer, sadly. "And now, dearest,
return to your boudoir. In a little while all will be tested."

He conducted her back and took leave of her with a solemn tenderness which spoke   70
far more than his words how much was now at stake. After his departure Georgiana
became rapt in musings. She considered the character of Aylmer, and did it completer
justice than at any previous moment. Her heart exulted, while it trembled, at his honorable
love—so pure and lofty that it would accept nothing less than perfection nor miserably
make itself contented with an earthlier nature than he had dreamed of. She felt how much
more precious was such a sentiment than that meaner kind which would have borne with
the imperfection for her sake, and have been guilty of treason to holy love by degrading its
perfect idea to the level of the actual; and with her whole spirit she prayed that, for a single
moment, she might satisfy his highest and deepest conception. Longer than one moment
she well knew it could not be; for his spirit was ever on the march, ever ascending, and
each instant required something that was beyond the scope of the instant before.

The sound of her husband's footsteps aroused her. He bore a crystal goblet containing a liquor colorless as water, but bright enough to be the draught of immortality.
Aylmer was pale; but it seemed rather the consequence of a highly-wrought state of
mind and tension of spirit than of fear or doubt.

"The concoction of the draught has been perfect," said he, in answer to Georgiana's look. "Unless all my science have deceived me, it cannot fail."

"Save on your account, my dearest Aylmer," observed his wife, "I might wish to put
off this birthmark of mortality by relinquishing mortality itself in preference to any other
mode. Life is but a sad possession to those who have attained precisely the degree of
moral advancement at which I stand. Were I weaker and blinder it might be happiness.
Were I stronger, it might be endured hopefully. But, being what I find myself, methinks I
am of all mortals the most fit to die."

"You are fit for heaven without tasting death!" replied her husband "But why do we
speak of dying? The draught cannot fail. Behold its effect upon this plant."

On the window seat there stood a geranium diseased with yellow blotches, which   75
had overspread all its leaves. Aylmer poured a small quantity of the liquid upon the soil
in which it grew. In a little time, when the roots of the plant had taken up the moisture,
the unsightly blotches began to be extinguished in a living verdure.

"There needed no proof," said Georgiana, quietly. "Give me the goblet I joyfully
stake all upon your word."

"Drink, then, thou lofty creature!" exclaimed Aylmer, with fervid admiration. "There is
no taint of imperfection on thy spirit. Thy sensible frame, too, shall soon be all perfect."

She quaffed the liquid and returned the goblet to his hand.

"It is grateful," said she with a placid smile. "Methinks it is like water from a heavenly fountain; for it contains I know not what of unobtrusive fragrance and deliciousness. It allays a feverish thirst that had parched me for many days. Now, dearest, let me sleep. My earthly senses are closing over my spirit like the leaves around the heart of a rose at sunset."

She spoke the last words with a gentle reluctance, as if it required almost more 80 energy than she could command to pronounce the faint and lingering syllables. Scarcely had they loitered through her lips ere she was lost in slumber. Aylmer sat by her side, watching her aspect with the emotions proper to a man the whole value of whose existence was involved in the process now to be tested. Mingled with this mood, however, was the philosophic investigation characteristic of the man of science. Not the minutest symptom escaped him. A heightened flush of the cheek, a slight irregularity of breath, a quiver of the eyelid, a hardly perceptible tremor through the frame,—such were the details which, as the moments passed, he wrote down in his folio volume. Intense thought had set its stamp upon every previous page of that volume, but the thoughts of years were all concentrated upon the last.

While thus employed, he failed not to gaze often at the fatal hand, and not without a shudder. Yet once, by a strange and unaccountable impulse he pressed it with his lips. His spirit recoiled, however, in the very act, and Georgiana, out of the midst of her deep sleep, moved uneasily and murmured as if in remonstrance. Again Aylmer resumed his watch. Nor was it without avail. The crimson hand, which at first had been strongly visible upon the marble paleness of Georgiana's cheek, now grew more faintly outlined. She remained not less pale than ever; but the birthmark with every breath that came and went, lost somewhat of its former distinctness. Its presence had been awful; its departure was more awful still. Watch the stain of the rainbow fading out the sky, and you will know how that mysterious symbol passed away.

"By Heaven! it is well-nigh gone!" said Aylmer to himself, in almost irrepressible ecstasy. "I can scarcely trace it now. Success! success! And now it is like the faintest rose color. The lightest flush of blood across her cheek would overcome it. But she is so pale!"

He drew aside the window curtain and suffered the light of natural day to fall into the room and rest upon her cheek. At the same time he heard a gross, hoarse chuckle, which he had long known as his servant Aminadab's expression of delight.

"Ah, clod! ah, earthly mass!" cried Aylmer, laughing in a sort of frenzy, "you have served me well! Matter and spirit—earth and heaven—have both done their part in this! Laugh, thing of the senses! You have earned the right to laugh."

These exclamations broke Georgiana's sleep. She slowly unclosed her eyes and 85 gazed into the mirror which her husband had arranged for that purpose. A faint smile flitted over her lips when she recognized how barely perceptible was now that crimson hand which had once blazed forth with such disastrous brilliancy as to scare away all their happiness. But then her eyes sought Aylmer's face with a trouble and anxiety that he could by no means account for.

"My poor Aylmer!" murmured she.

"Poor? Nay, richest, happiest, most favored!" exclaimed he. "My peerless bride, it is successful! You are perfect!"

"My poor Aylmer," she repeated, with a more than human tenderness, "you have aimed loftily; you have done nobly. Do not repent that with so high and pure a feeling, you have rejected the best the earth could offer. Aylmer, dearest Aylmer, I am dying!"

Alas! it was too true! The fatal hand had grappled with the mystery of life, and was the bond by which an angelic spirit kept itself in union with a mortal frame. As the last crimson tint of the birthmark—that sole token of human imperfection—faded from her cheek, the parting breath of the now perfect woman passed into the atmosphere, and her soul, lingering a moment near her husband, took its heavenward flight. Then a hoarse, chuckling laugh was heard again! Thus ever does the gross fatality of earth exult in its invariable triumph over the immortal essence which, in this dim sphere of half development, demands the completeness of a higher state. Yet, had Aylmer reached a profounder wisdom, he need not thus have flung away the happiness which would have woven his mortal life of the selfsame texture with the celestial. The momentary circumstance was too strong for him; he failed to look beyond the shadowy scope of time, and, living once for all in eternity, to find the perfect future in the present.

Critical Thinking Topics

1. In the story's closing sentence, the narrator tells the reader that Aylmer "failed to look beyond the shadowy scope of time, and, living once for all in eternity, to find the perfect future in the present." Today we are often admonished to live in the moment, to be *present*. Did Marie Curie miss out being *present* while pursuing her life work studying radioactivity? Did Albert Einstein neglect being *in the moment* as he was transforming our understanding of light, gravity and space-time? What might be a reasonable middle ground between finding "the perfect future in the present" and aspiring to achievements such as the creation of new knowledge by devoting oneself "unreservedly to scientific studies"?

2. How does the narrator of the story view Aylmer's belief in himself as a scientist? Identify several short passages that support your response.

3. Spend a few minutes reading some online information about "manslaughter," in particular, the distinction between "voluntary" and "involuntary" manslaughter. Imagine that you are a criminal detective who is investigating Georgiana's death, and it is your duty to recommend to the prosecuting attorney whether or not to have Aylmer arrested and charged with either voluntary or involuntary manslaughter. Using specific details from the story, make a case for your recommendation to the prosecuting attorney.

4. Imagine that Aylmer is standing trial for manslaughter and you are his defense attorney. Using specific details from the story, argue that Georgiana is complicit in the alleged crime.

5. Reflecting on your responses to the previous two topics, discuss your personal opinion on the issue: Did Aylmer commit the crime of manslaughter or not? Why?

Writing Topic

Stem cells have the capacity to develop into various types of cells, such as brain cells or skin cells, which can then be used to repair damaged tissues. Proponents of stem cell research hail its promise for treating conditions such as Alzheimer's disease, diabetes, and heart disease. However, opponents raise ethical concerns because stem cells are derived from nonviable human embryos. In their arguments, some opponents have alluded to "The Birth-Mark," suggesting that it is hubris to probe "the mystery of life," as Aylmer did. In contrast, advocates of the research question those moral qualms when viable human beings' lives are at stake. As is often the case, reasonable and compassionate people disagree, and stem cell research is the subject of vigorous debate among scientists, policymakers, and citizens. Research this topic and develop an argument on the ethics and legality of stem cell research.

7.4 Edgar Allen Poe, The Cask[1] of Amontillado[2] (1846)

The thousand injuries of Fortunato I had borne as I best could, but when he ventured upon insult I vowed revenge. You, who so well know the nature of my soul, will not suppose, however, that gave utterance to a threat. At length I would be avenged; this was a point definitely, settled—but the very definitiveness with which it was resolved precluded the idea of risk. I must not only punish but punish with impunity. A wrong is unredressed when retribution overtakes its redresser. It is equally unredressed when the avenger fails to make himself felt as such to him who has done the wrong.

It must be understood that neither by word nor deed had I given Fortunato cause to doubt my good will. I continued, as was my wont, to smile in his face, and he did not perceive that my smile *now* was at the thought of his immolation.

He had a weak point—this Fortunato—although in other regards he was a man to be respected and even feared. He prided himself on his connoisseurship in wine. Few Italians have the true virtuoso spirit. For the most part their enthusiasm is adopted to suit the time and opportunity, to practice imposture upon the British and Austrian *millionaires*. In painting and gemmary, Fortunato, like his countrymen, was a quack, but in the matter of old wines he was sincere. In this respect I did not differ from him materially;—I was skillful in the Italian vintages myself, and bought largely whenever I could.

It was about dusk, one evening during the supreme madness of the carnival season, that I encountered my friend. He accosted me with excessive warmth, for he had been drinking much. The man wore motley. He had on a tight-fitting parti-striped dress, and his head was surmounted by the conical cap and bells. I was so pleased to see him that I thought I should never have done wringing his hand.

I said to him—"My dear Fortunato, you are luckily met. How remarkably well you are looking to-day. But I have received a pipe of what passes for Amontillado, and I have my doubts." 5

"How?" said he. "Amontillado, A pipe? Impossible! And in the middle of the carnival?"

"I have my doubts," I replied; "and I was silly enough to pay the full Amontillado price without consulting you in the matter. You were not to be found, and I was fearful of losing a bargain."

"Amontillado!"

"I have my doubts."

"Amontillado!" 10

"And I must satisfy them."

"Amontillado!"

---

[1]**Cask** a barrel-shaped container for storing wine or spirits
[2]**Amontillado** a type of wine—a medium dry sherry originally from Spain

"As you are engaged, I am on my way to Luchesi. If any one has a critical turn it is he. He will tell me—"

"Luchesi cannot tell Amontillado from Sherry."

"And yet some fools will have it that his taste is a match for your own."   15

"Come, let us go."

"Whither?"

"To your vaults."

"My friend, no; I will not impose upon your good nature. I perceive you have an engagement. Luchesi—"

"I have no engagement; come."   20

"My friend, no. It is not the engagement, but the severe cold with which I perceive you are afflicted. The vaults are insufferably damp. They are encrusted with nitre."

"Let us go, nevertheless. The cold is merely nothing. Amontillado! You have been imposed upon. And as for Luchesi, he cannot distinguish Sherry from Amontillado."

Thus speaking, Fortunato possessed himself of my arm; and putting on a mask of black silk and drawing a roquelaire[3] closely about my person, I suffered him to hurry me to my palazzo.

There were no attendants at home; they had absconded to make merry in honor of the time. I had told them that I should not return until the morning, and had given them explicit orders not to stir from the house. These orders were sufficient, I well knew, to insure their immediate disappearance, one and all, as soon as my back was turned.

I took from their sconces two flambeaux, and giving one to Fortunato, bowed him   25 through several suites of rooms to the archway that led into the vaults. I passed down a long and winding staircase, requesting him to be cautious as he followed. We came at length to the foot of the descent, and stood together upon the damp ground of the catacombs[4] of the Montresors.

The gait of my friend was unsteady, and the bells upon his cap jingled as he strode.

"The pipe," he said.

"It is farther on," said I; "but observe the white web-work which gleams from these cavern walls."

He turned towards me, and looked into my eyes with two filmy orbs that distilled the rheum[5] of intoxication.

"Nitre?"[6] he asked, at length.   30

"Nitre," I replied. "How long have you had that cough?"

"Ugh! ugh! ugh!—ugh! ugh! ugh!—ugh! ugh! ugh!—ugh! ugh! ugh!—ugh! ugh! ugh!"

My poor friend found it impossible to reply for many minutes.

"It is nothing," he said, at last.

"Come," I said, with decision, "we will go back; your health is precious. You are   35 rich, respected, admired, beloved; you are happy, as once I was. You are a man to be missed. For me it is no matter. We will go back; you will be ill, and I cannot be responsible. Besides, there is Luchesi—"

"Enough," he said; "the cough's a mere nothing; it will not kill me. I shall not die of a cough."

---

[3]**roquelaire** a long coat

[4]**catacombs** underground burial site

[5]**rheum** mucus, indicating presence of a cold

[6]**nitre** potassium nitrate, also known as saltpeter; it's the "white web-work" mentioned above and could cause Fortunato's cough

"True—true," I replied; "and, indeed, I had no intention of alarming you unnecessarily—but you should use all proper caution. A draught of this Medoc will defend us from the damps.

Here I knocked off the neck of a bottle which I drew from a long row of its fellows that lay upon the mould.

"Drink," I said, presenting him the wine.

He raised it to his lips with a leer. He paused and nodded to me familiarly, while his 40 bells jingled.

"I drink," he said, "to the buried that repose around us."

"And I to your long life."

He again took my arm, and we proceeded.

"These vaults," he said, "are extensive."

"The Montresors," I replied, "were a great and numerous family." 45

"I forget your arms."

"A huge human foot d'or, in a field azure; the foot crushes a serpent rampant whose fangs are imbedded in the heel."

"And the motto?"

"*Nemo me impune lacessit.*"[7]

"Good!" he said. 50

The wine sparkled in his eyes and the bells jingled. My own fancy grew warm with the Medoc. We had passed through long walls of piled skeletons, with casks and puncheons intermingling, into the inmost recesses of the catacombs. I paused again, and this time I made bold to seize Fortunato by an arm above the elbow.

"The nitre!" I said; "see, it increases. It hangs like moss upon the vaults. We are below the river's bed. The drops of moisture trickle among the bones. Come, we will go back ere it is too late. Your cough—"

"It is nothing," he said; "let us go on. But first, another draught of the Medoc."

I broke and reached him a flagon of De Grave. He emptied it at a breath. His eyes flashed with a fierce light. He laughed and threw the bottle upwards with a gesticulation I did not understand.

I looked at him in surprise. He repeated the movement—a grotesque one. 55

"You do not comprehend?" he said.

"Not I," I replied.

"Then you are not of the brotherhood."

"How?"

"You are not of the masons." 60

"Yes, yes," I said; "yes, yes."

"You? Impossible! A mason?"

"A mason," I replied.

"A sign," he said, "a sign."

"It is this," I answered, producing from beneath the folds of my roquelaire a trowel. 65

"You jest," he exclaimed, recoiling a few paces. "But let us proceed to the Amontillado."

"Be it so," I said, replacing the tool beneath the cloak and again offering him my arm. He leaned upon it heavily. We continued our route in search of the Amontillado. We passed through a range of low arches, descended, passed on, and descending again,

---

[7]**Translation:** "No one attacks me with impunity!"

arrived at a deep crypt, in which the foulness of the air caused our flambeaux rather to glow than flame.

At the most remote end of the crypt there appeared another less spacious. Its walls had been lined with human remains, piled to the vault overhead, in the fashion of the great catacombs of Paris. Three sides of this interior crypt were still ornamented in this manner. From the fourth side the bones had been thrown down, and lay promiscuously upon the earth, forming at one point a mound of some size. Within the wall thus exposed by the displacing of the bones, we perceived a still interior crypt or recess, in depth about four feet, in width three, in height six or seven. It seemed to have been constructed for no especial use within itself, but formed merely the interval between two of the colossal supports of the roof of the catacombs, and was backed by one of their circumscribing walls of solid granite.

It was in vain that Fortunato, uplifting his dull torch, endeavored to pry into the depth of the recess. Its termination the feeble light did not enable us to see.

"Proceed," I said; "herein is the Amontillado. As for Luchesi—"   70

"He is an ignoramus," interrupted my friend, as he stepped unsteadily forward, while I followed immediately at his heels. In an instant he had reached the extremity of the niche, and finding his progress arrested by the rock, stood stupidly bewildered. A moment more and I had fettered him to the granite. In its surface were two iron staples, distant from each other about two feet, horizontally. From one of these depended a short chain, from the other a padlock. Throwing the links about his waist, it was but the work of a few seconds to secure it. He was too much astounded to resist. Withdrawing the key I stepped back from the recess.

"Pass your hand," I said, "over the wall; you cannot help feeling the nitre. Indeed, it is very damp. Once more let me implore you to return. No? Then I must positively leave you. But I must first render you all the little attentions in my power."

"The Amontillado!" ejaculated my friend, not yet recovered from his astonishment.

"True," I replied; "the Amontillado."

As I said these words I busied myself among the pile of bones of which I have   75 before spoken. Throwing them aside, I soon uncovered a quantity of building stone and mortar. With these materials and with the aid of my trowel, I began vigorously to wall up the entrance of the niche.

I had scarcely laid the first tier of the masonry when I discovered that the intoxication of Fortunato had in a great measure worn off. The earliest indication I had of this was a low moaning cry from the depth of the recess. It was not the cry of a drunken man. There was then a long and obstinate silence. I laid the second tier, and the third, and the fourth; and then I heard the furious vibrations of the chain. The noise lasted for several minutes, during which, that I might hearken to it with the more satisfaction, I ceased my labors and sat down upon the bones. When at last the clanking subsided, I resumed the trowel, and finished without interruption the fifth, the sixth, and the seventh tier. The wall was now nearly upon a level with my breast. I again paused, and holding the flambeaux over the mason-work, threw a few feeble rays upon the figure within.

A succession of loud and shrill screams, bursting suddenly from the throat of the chained form, seemed to thrust me violently back. For a brief moment I hesitated, I trembled. Unsheathing my rapier, I began to grope with it about the recess; but the thought of an instant reassured me. I placed my hand upon the solid fabric of the catacombs, and felt satisfied. I reapproached the wall; I replied to the yells of him who clamored. I re-echoed, I aided, I surpassed them in volume and in strength. I did this, and the clamorer grew still.

It was now midnight, and my task was drawing to a close. I had completed the eighth, the ninth and the tenth tier. I had finished a portion of the last and the eleventh; there remained but a single stone to be fitted and plastered in. I struggled with its weight; I placed it partially in its destined position. But now there came from out the niche a low laugh that erected the hairs upon my head. It was succeeded by a sad voice, which I had difficulty in recognizing as that of the noble Fortunato. The voice said—

"Ha! ha! ha!—he! he! he! —a very good joke, indeed—an excellent jest. We will have many a rich laugh about it at the palazzo—he! he! he!—over our wine—he! he! he!"

"The Amontillado!" I said.   80

"He! he! he!—he! he! he!—yes, the Amontillado. But is it not getting late? Will not they be awaiting us at the palazzo, the Lady Fortunato and the rest? Let us be gone."

"Yes," I said, "let us be gone."

"For the love of God, Montresor!"

"Yes," I said, "for the love of God!"

But to these words I hearkened in vain for a reply. I grew impatient. I called aloud—   85

"Fortunato!"

No answer. I called again—

"Fortunato!"

No answer still. I thrust a torch through the remaining aperture and let it fall within. There came forth in return only a jingling of the bells. My heart grew sick; it was the dampness of the catacombs that made it so. I hastened to make an end of my labor. I forced the last stone into its position; I plastered it up. Against the new masonry I re-erected the old rampart of bones. For the half of a century no mortal has disturbed them. *In pace requiescat!*[8]

Critical Thinking Topics

1. Using specific examples from the story, describe how Montresor manipulates Fortunato to execute his plan of revenge.

2. Fortunato is under the influence of alcohol at the time the story begins. What implied claim could be argued from this story about the influence of alcohol upon the human mind?

Writing Topic

Poe tells "The Cask of Amontillado" from the perspective of a murderer and uses this same technique in several of his other stories, such as "The Black Cat," "The Tell-Tale Heart," and "Berenice." This perspective is also common in songs. Consider "Folsom Prison Blues," by Johnny Cash; "Cell Block Tango" (from the musical *Chicago*); "Wake Up Call," by Maroon 5; "Natural Born Killers," by Dr. Dre; or other songs of your own choosing. Reflect on how Montresor and other narrators rationalize their crimes. Johnny Cash's narrator says that he "shot a man in Reno just to watch him die." The ladies in "Cell Block Tango" argue "he had it coming." Explain the motives of at least three narrators. Can you justify any of these murders? Why or why not?

---

[8]**Translation:** "Rest in peace!"

7.5 Ambrose Bierce, An Occurrence at Owl Creek Bridge (1890)

I

A man stood upon a railroad bridge in northern Alabama, looking down into the swift water twenty feet below. The man's hands were behind his back, the wrists bound with a cord. A rope closely encircled his neck. It was attached to a stout cross-timber above his head and the slack fell to the level of his knees. Some loose boards laid upon the sleepers supporting the metals of the railway supplied a footing for him and his executioners—two private soldiers of the Federal army, directed by a sergeant who in civil life may have been a deputy sheriff. At a short remove upon the same temporary platform was an officer in the uniform of his rank, armed. He was a captain. A sentinel[9] at each end of the bridge stood with his rifle in the position known as "support," that is to say, vertical in front of the left shoulder, the hammer resting on the forearm thrown straight across the chest—a formal and unnatural position, enforcing an erect carriage of the body. It did not appear to be the duty of these two men to know what was occurring at the center of the bridge; they merely blockaded the two ends of the foot planking that traversed it.

Beyond one of the sentinels nobody was in sight; the railroad ran straight away into a forest for a hundred yards, then, curving, was lost to view. Doubtless there was an outpost farther along. The other bank of the stream was open ground—a gentle acclivity topped with a stockade of vertical tree trunks, loopholed for rifles, with a single embrasure through which protruded the muzzle of a brass cannon commanding the bridge. Midway of the slope between bridge and fort were the spectators—a single company of infantry in line, at "parade rest," the butts of the rifles on the ground, the barrels inclining slightly backward against the right shoulder, the hands crossed upon the stock. A lieutenant stood at the right of the line, the point of his sword upon the ground, his left hand resting upon his right. Excepting the group of four at the center of the bridge, not a man moved. The company faced the bridge, staring stonily, motionless. The sentinels, facing the banks of the stream, might have been statues to adorn the bridge. The captain stood with folded arms, silent, observing the work of his subordinates, but making no sign. Death is a dignitary who when he comes announced is to be received with formal manifestations of respect, even by those most familiar with him. In the code of military etiquette silence and fixity are forms of deference.

The man who was engaged in being hanged was apparently about thirty-five years of age. He was a civilian, if one might judge from his habit, which was that of a planter. His features were good—a straight nose, firm mouth, broad forehead, from which his long, dark hair was combed straight back, falling behind his ears to the collar of his well-fitting frock-coat. He wore a mustache and pointed beard, but no whiskers; his eyes were large and dark gray, and had a kindly expression which one would hardly have expected in one whose neck was in the hemp. Evidently this was no vulgar assassin. The liberal military code makes provision for hanging many kinds of persons, and gentlemen are not excluded.

The preparations being complete, the two private soldiers stepped aside and each drew away the plank upon which he had been standing. The sergeant turned to the captain, saluted and placed himself immediately behind that officer, who in turn moved apart one pace. These movements left the condemned man and the sergeant standing on the

---

[9]**sentinel** a sentry—an armed guard who keeps watch

two ends of the same plank, which spanned three of the crossties of the bridge. The end upon which the civilian stood almost, but not quite, reached a fourth. This plank had been held in place by the weight of the captain; it was now held by that of the sergeant. At a signal from the former the latter would step aside, the plank would tilt and the condemned man go down between two ties. The arrangement commended itself to his judgment as simple and effective. His face had not been covered nor his eyes bandaged. He looked a moment at his "unsteadfast footing," then let his gaze wander to the swirling water of the stream racing madly beneath his feet. A piece of dancing driftwood caught his attention and his eyes followed it down the current. How slowly it appeared to move! What a sluggish stream!

He closed his eyes in order to fix his last thoughts upon his wife and children. The   5
water, touched to gold by the early sun, the brooding mists under the banks at some distance down the stream, the fort, the soldiers, the piece of drift—all had distracted him. And now he became conscious of a new disturbance. Striking through the thought of his dear ones was a sound which he would neither ignore nor understand, a sharp, distinct, metallic percussion like the stroke of a blacksmith's hammer upon the anvil; it had the same ringing quality. He wondered what it was, and whether immeasurably distant or near by—it seemed both. Its recurrence was regular, but as slow as the tolling of a death knell. He awaited each stroke with impatience and—he knew not why—apprehension. The intervals of silence grew progressively longer; the delays became maddening. With their greater infrequency the sounds increased in strength and sharpness. They hurt his ear like the thrust of a knife; he feared he would shriek. What he heard was the ticking of his watch.

He unclosed his eyes and saw again the water below him. "If I could free my hands," he thought, "I might throw off the noose and spring into the stream. By diving I could evade the bullets and, swimming vigorously, reach the bank, take to the woods and get away home. My home, thank God, is as yet outside their lines; my wife and little ones are still beyond the invader's farthest advance."

As these thoughts, which have here to be set down in words, were flashed into the doomed man's brain rather than evolved from it the captain nodded to the sergeant. The sergeant stepped aside.

II

Peyton Farquhar was a well-to-do planter, of an old and highly respected Alabama family. Being a slave owner and like other slave owners a politician he was naturally an original secessionist and ardently devoted to the Southern cause. Circumstances of an imperious nature, which it is unnecessary to relate here, had prevented him from taking service with the gallant army that had fought the disastrous campaigns ending with the fall of Corinth,[10] and he chafed under the inglorious restraint, longing for the release of his energies, the larger life of the soldier, the opportunity for distinction. That opportunity, he felt, would come, as it comes to all in war time. Meanwhile he did what he could. No service was too humble for him to perform in aid of the South, no adventure too perilous for him to undertake if consistent with the character of a civilian who was at heart a soldier, and who in good faith and without too much qualification assented to at least a part of the frankly villainous dictum that all is fair in love and war.

One evening while Farquhar and his wife were sitting on a rustic bench near the entrance to his grounds, a gray-clad soldier rode up to the gate and asked for a drink of water. Mrs. Farquhar was only too happy to serve him with her own white hands. While

---

[10]**Corinth** a town in Mississippi; site of a Confederate army defeat in 1862

she was fetching the water her husband approached the dusty horseman and inquired eagerly for news from the front.

"The Yanks are repairing the railroads," said the man, "and are getting ready for   10 another advance. They have reached the Owl Creek bridge, put it in order and built a stockade on the north bank. The commandant has issued an order, which is posted everywhere, declaring that any civilian caught interfering with the railroad, its bridges, tunnels or trains will be summarily hanged. I saw the order."

"How far is it to the Owl Creek bridge?" Farquhar asked.

"About thirty miles."

"Is there no force on this side the creek?"

"Only a picket post half a mile out, on the railroad, and a single sentinel at this end of the bridge."

"Suppose a man—a civilian and student of hanging—should elude the picket   15 post and perhaps get the better of the sentinel," said Farquhar, smiling, "what could he accomplish?"

The soldier reflected. "I was there a month ago," he replied, "I observed that the flood of last winter had lodged a great quantity of driftwood against the wooden pier at this end of the bridge. It is now dry and would burn like tow."

The lady had now brought the water, which the soldier drank. He thanked her ceremoniously, bowed to her husband and rode away. An hour later, after nightfall, he repassed the plantation, going northward in the direction from which he had come. He was a Federal scout.

III

As Peyton Farquhar fell straight downward through the bridge he lost consciousness and was as one already dead. From this state he was awakened—ages later, it seemed to him—by the pain of a sharp pressure upon his throat, followed by a sense of suffocation. Keen, poignant agonies seemed to shoot from his neck downward through every fiber of his body and limbs. These pains appeared to flash along well-defined lines of ramification and to beat with an inconceivably rapid periodicity. They seemed like streams of pulsating fire heating him to an intolerable temperature. As to his head, he was conscious of nothing but a feeling of fullness—of congestion. These sensations were unaccompanied by thought. The intellectual part of his nature was already effaced; he had power only to feel, and feeling was torment. He was conscious of motion. Encompassed in a luminous cloud, of which he was now merely the fiery heart, without material substance, he swung through unthinkable arcs of oscillation, like a vast pendulum. Then all at once, with terrible suddenness, the light about him shot upward with the noise of a loud plash; a frightful roaring was in his ears, and all was cold and dark. The power of thought was restored; he knew that the rope had broken and he had fallen into the stream. There was no additional strangulation; the noose about his neck was already suffocating him and kept the water from his lungs. To die of hanging at the bottom of a river!—the idea seemed to him ludicrous. He opened his eyes in the darkness and saw above him a gleam of light, but how distant, how inaccessible! He was still sinking, for the light became fainter and fainter until it was a mere glimmer. Then it began to grow and brighten, and he knew that he was rising toward the surface—knew it with reluctance, for he was now very comfortable. "To be hanged and drowned," he thought, "that is not so bad; but I do not wish to be shot. No; I will not be shot; that is not fair."

He was not conscious of an effort, but a sharp pain in his wrist apprised him that he was trying to free his hands. He gave the struggle his attention, as an idler might observe the feat of a juggler, without interest in the outcome. What splendid effort!—what magnificent, what superhuman strength! Ah, that was a fine endeavor! Bravo! The cord fell away; his arms parted and floated upward; the hands dimly seen on each side in the growing light. He watched them with new interest as first one and then the other pounced upon the noose at his neck. They tore it away and thrust it fiercely aside, its undulations resembling those of a water-snake. "Put it back, put it back!" He thought he shouted these words to his hands, for the undoing of the noose had been succeeded by the direst pang that he had yet experienced. His neck ached horribly; his brain was on fire; his heart, which had been fluttering faintly, gave a great leap, trying to force itself out at his mouth. His whole body was racked and wrenched with an insupportable anguish! But his disobedient hands gave no heed to the command. They beat the water vigorously with quick, downward strokes, forcing him to the surface. He felt his head emerge; his eyes were blinded by the sunlight; his chest expanded convulsively, and with a supreme and crowning agony his lungs engulfed a great draught of air, which instantly he expelled in a shriek!

He was now in full possession of his physical senses. They were, indeed, preter-   20
naturally keen and alert. Something in the awful disturbance of his organic system had so exalted and refined them that they made record of things never before perceived. He felt the ripples upon his face and heard their separate sounds as they struck. He looked at the forest on the bank of the stream, saw the individual trees, the leaves and the veining of each leaf—saw the very insects upon them: the locusts, the brilliant-bodied flies, the gray spiders stretching their webs from twig to twig. He noted the prismatic colors in all the dewdrops upon a million blades of grass. The humming of the gnats that danced above the eddies of the stream, the beating of the dragon-flies' wings, the strokes of water-spider's legs, like oars which had lifted their boat—all these made audible music. A fish slid along beneath his eyes and he heard the rush of its body parting the water.

He had come to the surface facing down the stream; in a moment the visible world seemed to wheel slowly round, himself the pivotal point, and he saw the bridge, the fort, the soldiers upon the bridge, the captain, the sergeant, the two privates, his executioners. They were in silhouette against the blue sky. They shouted and gesticulated, pointing at him. The captain had drawn his pistol, but did not fire; the others were unarmed. Their movements were grotesque and horrible, their forms gigantic.

Suddenly he heard a sharp report and something struck the water smartly within a few inches of his head, spattering his face with spray. He heard a second report, and saw one of the sentinels with his rifle at his shoulder, a light cloud of blue smoke rising from the muzzle. The man in the water saw the eye of the man on the bridge gazing into his own through the sights of the rifle. He observed that it was a gray eye and remembered having read that gray eyes were keenest, and that all famous marksmen had them. Nevertheless, this one had missed.

A counter-swirl had caught Farquhar and turned him half round; he was again looking into the forest on the bank opposite the fort. The sound of a clear, high voice in a monotonous singsong now rang out behind him and came across the water with a distinctness that pierced and subdued all other sounds, even the beating of the ripples in his ears. Although no soldier, he had frequented camps enough to know the dread significance of that deliberate, drawling, aspirated chant; the lieutenant on shore was taking a part in the morning's work. How coldly and pitilessly—with what an even, calm intonation, presaging, and enforcing tranquility in the men—with what accurately measured intervals fell those cruel words:

"Attention, company! . . . Shoulder arms! . . . Ready! . . . Aim! . . . Fire!"

Farquhar dived—dived as deeply as he could. The water roared in his ears like the   25
voice of Niagara, yet he heard the dulled thunder of the volley and, rising again toward the
surface, met shining bits of metal, singularly flattened, oscillating slowly downward. Some
of them touched him on the face and hands, then fell away, continuing their descent. One
lodged between his collar and neck; it was uncomfortably warm and he snatched it out.

As he rose to the surface, gasping for breath, he saw that he had been a long time
under water; he was perceptibly farther down stream—nearer to safety. The soldiers
had almost finished reloading; the metal ramrods flashed all at once in the sunshine as
they were drawn from the barrels, turned in the air, and thrust into their sockets. The
two sentinels fired again, independently and ineffectually.

The hunted man saw all this over his shoulder; he was now swimming vigorously
with the current. His brain was as energetic as his arms and legs; he thought with the
rapidity of lightning.

"The officer," he reasoned, "will not make that martinet's error a second time. It is
as easy to dodge a volley as a single shot. He has probably already given the command
to fire at will. God help me, I cannot dodge them all!"

An appalling splash within two yards of him was followed by a loud, rushing sound,
diminuendo,[11] which seemed to travel back through the air to the fort and died in an
explosion which stirred the very river to its deeps! A rising sheet of water curved over
him, fell down upon him, blinded him, strangled him! The cannon had taken a hand in
the game. As he shook his head free from the commotion of the smitten water he heard
the deflected shot humming through the air ahead, and in an instant it was cracking and
smashing the branches in the forest beyond.

"They will not do that again," he thought; "the next time they will use a charge of   30
grape.[12] I must keep my eye upon the gun; the smoke will apprise me—the report
arrives too late; it lags behind the missile. That is a good gun."

Suddenly he felt himself whirled round and round—spinning like a top. The water,
the banks, the forests, the now distant bridge, fort and men—all were commingled and
blurred. Objects were represented by their colors only; circular horizontal streaks of
color—that was all he saw. He had been caught in a vortex and was being whirled on
with a velocity of advance and gyration that made him giddy and sick. In a few moments
he was flung upon the gravel at the foot of the left bank of the stream—the southern
bank—and behind a projecting point which concealed him from his enemies. The sudden arrest of his motion, the abrasion of one of his hands on the gravel, restored him,
and he wept with delight. He dug his fingers into the sand, threw it over himself in hand-
fuls and audibly blessed it. It looked like diamonds, rubies, emeralds; he could think of
nothing beautiful which it did not resemble. The trees upon the bank were giant garden
plants; he noted a definite order in their arrangement, inhaled the fragrance of their
blooms. A strange, roseate light shone through the spaces among their trunks and the
wind made in their branches the music of aeolian harps. He had no wish to perfect his
escape—was content to remain in that enchanting spot until retaken.

A whiz and rattle of grapeshot among the branches high above his head roused
him from his dream. The baffled cannoneer had fired him a random farewell. He sprang
to his feet, rushed up the sloping bank, and plunged into the forest.

---

[11]**diminuendo** lessening in intensity of sound
[12]**grape** grapeshot—a cluster of small iron balls fired from a cannon

All that day he traveled, laying his course by the rounding sun. The forest seemed interminable; nowhere did he discover a break in it, not even a woodman's road. He had not known that he lived in so wild a region. There was something uncanny in the revelation.

By nightfall he was fatigued, footsore, famishing. The thought of his wife and children urged him on. At last he found a road which led him in what he knew to be the right direction. It was as wide and straight as a city street, yet it seemed untraveled. No fields bordered it, no dwelling anywhere. Not so much as the barking of a dog suggested human habitation. The black bodies of the trees formed a straight wall on both sides, terminating on the horizon in a point, like a diagram in a lesson in perspective. Overhead, as he looked up through this rift in the wood, shone great golden stars looking unfamiliar and grouped in strange constellations. He was sure they were arranged in some order which had a secret and malign significance. The wood on either side was full of singular noises, among which—once, twice, and again—he distinctly heard whispers in an unknown tongue.

His neck was in pain and lifting his hand to it he found it horribly swollen. He knew that it had a circle of black where the rope had bruised it. His eyes felt congested; he could no longer close them. His tongue was swollen with thirst; he relieved its fever by thrusting it forward from between his teeth into the cold air. How softly the turf had carpeted the untraveled avenue—he could no longer feel the roadway beneath his feet! 35

Doubtless, despite his suffering, he had fallen asleep while walking, for now he sees another scene—perhaps he has merely recovered from a delirium. He stands at the gate of his own home. All is as he left it, and all bright and beautiful in the morning sunshine. He must have traveled the entire night. As he pushes open the gate and passes up the wide white walk, he sees a flutter of female garments; his wife, looking fresh and cool and sweet, steps down from the veranda to meet him. At the bottom of the steps she stands waiting, with a smile of ineffable joy, an attitude of matchless grace and dignity. Ah, how beautiful she is! He springs forward with extended arms. As he is about to clasp her he feels a stunning blow upon the back of the neck; a blinding white light blazes all about him with a sound like the shock of a cannon—then all is darkness and silence!

Peyton Farquhar was dead; his body, with a broken neck, swung gently from side to side beneath the timbers of the Owl Creek bridge.

Critical Thinking Topics

1. Describe your reaction to the short story's ending. Rereading the story, identify and explain details that seem to foreshadow its ending.

2. Examine the story by its sections and describe the narrative tone of each section. How do variations in tone contribute to suggesting a central theme? What is at least one theme in the story? Point to specific details to support your responses.

Writing Topics

1. What does this story imply about the capacity and complexity of the human mind, particularly during times of extreme emotional and/or physical crises?

2. In the first line of Langston Hughes's poem "Justice" (later in this chapter), the speaker asserts, "That Justice is a blind goddess." Reflect on this metaphor in the context of this story.

7.6 Sir Arthur Conan Doyle, The Adventure of the Speckled Band (1892)

On glancing over my notes of the seventy odd cases in which I have during the last eight years studied the methods of my friend Sherlock Holmes, I find many tragic, some comic, a large number merely strange, but none commonplace; for, working as he did rather for the love of his art than for the acquirement of wealth, he refused to associate himself with any investigation which did not tend towards the unusual, and even the fantastic. Of all these varied cases, however, I cannot recall any which presented more singular features than that which was associated with the well-known Surrey family of the Roylotts of Stoke Moran. The events in question occurred in the early days of my association with Holmes, when we were sharing rooms as bachelors in Baker Street. It is possible that I might have placed them upon record before, but a promise of secrecy was made at the time, from which I have only been freed during the last month by the untimely death of the lady to whom the pledge was given. It is perhaps as well that the facts should now come to light, for I have reasons to know that there are widespread rumours as to the death of Dr. Grimesby Roylott which tend to make the matter even more terrible than the truth.

It was early in April in the year '83[13] that I woke one morning to find Sherlock Holmes standing, fully dressed, by the side of my bed. He was a late riser, as a rule, and as the clock on the mantelpiece showed me that it was only a quarter-past seven, I blinked up at him in some surprise, and perhaps just a little resentment, for I was myself regular in my habits.

"Very sorry to knock you up, Watson," said he, "but it's the common lot this morning. Mrs. Hudson has been knocked up, she retorted upon me, and I on you."

"What is it, then—a fire?"

"No, a client. It seems that a young lady has arrived in a considerable state of excitement, who insists upon seeing me. She is waiting now in the sitting-room. Now, when young ladies wander about the metropolis at this hour of the morning, and knock sleepy people up out of their beds, I presume that it is something very pressing which they have to communicate. Should it prove to be an interesting case, you would, I am sure, wish to follow it from the outset. I thought, at any rate, that I should call you and give you the chance."

"My dear fellow, I would not miss it for anything."

I had no keener pleasure than in following Holmes in his professional investigations, and in admiring the rapid deductions, as swift as intuitions, and yet always founded on a logical basis with which he unravelled the problems which were submitted to him. I rapidly threw on my clothes and was ready in a few minutes to accompany my friend down to the sitting-room. A lady dressed in black and heavily veiled, who had been sitting in the window, rose as we entered.

"Good-morning, madam," said Holmes cheerily. "My name is Sherlock Holmes. This is my intimate friend and associate, Dr. Watson, before whom you can speak as freely as before myself. Ha! I am glad to see that Mrs. Hudson has had the good sense to light the fire. Pray draw up to it, and I shall order you a cup of hot coffee, for I observe that you are shivering."

"It is not cold which makes me shiver," said the woman in a low voice, changing her seat as requested.

[13]1883

"What, then?"   10

"It is fear, Mr. Holmes. It is terror." She raised her veil as she spoke, and we could
see that she was indeed in a pitiable state of agitation, her face all drawn and grey, with
restless frightened eyes, like those of some hunted animal. Her features and figure were
those of a woman of thirty, but her hair was shot with premature grey, and her expression was weary and haggard. Sherlock Holmes ran her over with one of his quick, all-
comprehensive glances.

"You must not fear," said he soothingly, bending forward and patting her forearm.

"We shall soon set matters right, I have no doubt. You have come in by train this
morning, I see."

"You know me, then?"

"No, but I observe the second half of a return ticket in the palm of your left glove.   15
You must have started early, and yet you had a good drive in a dog-cart, along heavy
roads, before you reached the station."

The lady gave a violent start and stared in bewilderment at my companion.

"There is no mystery, my dear madam," said he, smiling. "The left arm of your
jacket is spattered with mud in no less than seven places. The marks are perfectly fresh.
There is no vehicle save a dog-cart which throws up mud in that way, and then only
when you sit on the left-hand side of the driver."

"Whatever your reasons may be, you are perfectly correct," said she. "I started
from home before six, reached Leatherhead at twenty past, and came in by the first
train to Waterloo. Sir, I can stand this strain no longer; I shall go mad if it continues.
I have no one to turn to—none, save only one, who cares for me, and he, poor fellow, can be of little aid. I have heard of you, Mr. Holmes; I have heard of you from
Mrs. Farintosh, whom you helped in the hour of her sore need. It was from her that I
had your address. Oh, sir, do you not think that you could help me, too, and at least
throw a little light through the dense darkness which surrounds me? At present it is
out of my power to reward you for your services, but in a month or six weeks I shall
be married, with the control of my own income, and then at least you shall not find me
ungrateful."

Holmes turned to his desk and, unlocking it, drew out a small case-book, which he
consulted.

"Farintosh," said he. "Ah yes, I recall the case; it was concerned with an opal tiara.   20
I think it was before your time, Watson. I can only say, madam, that I shall be happy
to devote the same care to your case as I did to that of your friend. As to reward, my
profession is its own reward; but you are at liberty to defray whatever expenses I may
be put to, at the time which suits you best. And now I beg that you will lay before us
everything that may help us in forming an opinion upon the matter."

"Alas!" replied our visitor, "the very horror of my situation lies in the fact that my
fears are so vague, and my suspicions depend so entirely upon small points, which
might seem trivial to another, that even he to whom of all others I have a right to look
for help and advice looks upon all that I tell him about it as the fancies of a nervous
woman. He does not say so, but I can read it from his soothing answers and averted
eyes. But I have heard, Mr. Holmes, that you can see deeply into the manifold wickedness of the human heart. You may advise me how to walk amid the dangers which
encompass me."

"I am all attention, madam."

"My name is Helen Stoner, and I am living with my stepfather, who is the last sur-vivor of one of the oldest Saxon[14] families in England, the Roylotts of Stoke Moran, on the western border of Surrey."

Holmes nodded his head. "The name is familiar to me," said he.

"The family was at one time among the richest in England, and the estates extended   25 over the borders into Berkshire in the north, and Hampshire in the west. In the last century, however, four successive heirs were of a dissolute and wasteful disposition, and the family ruin was eventually completed by a gambler in the days of the Regency.[15] Nothing was left save a few acres of ground, and the two-hundred-year-old house, which is itself crushed under a heavy mortgage. The last squire dragged out his existence there, living the horrible life of an aristocratic pauper; but his only son, my stepfather, seeing that he must adapt himself to the new conditions, obtained an advance from a relative, which enabled him to take a medical degree and went out to Calcutta,[16] where, by his professional skill and his force of character, he established a large practice. In a fit of anger, however, caused by some robberies which had been perpetrated in the house, he beat his native butler to death and narrowly escaped a capital sentence. As it was, he suffered a long term of imprisonment and afterwards returned to England a morose and disappointed man.

"When Dr. Roylott was in India he married my mother, Mrs. Stoner, the young widow of Major-General Stoner, of the Bengal Artillery. My sister Julia and I were twins, and we were only two years old at the time of my mother's re-marriage. She had a considerable sum of money—not less than 1000 pounds a year—and this she bequeathed to Dr. Roy-lott entirely while we resided with him, with a provision that a certain annual sum should be allowed to each of us in the event of our marriage. Shortly after our return to England my mother died—she was killed eight years ago in a railway accident near Crewe. Dr. Roylott then abandoned his attempts to establish himself in practice in London and took us to live with him in the old ancestral house at Stoke Moran. The money which my mother had left was enough for all our wants, and there seemed to be no obstacle to our happiness.

"But a terrible change came over our stepfather about this time. Instead of making friends and exchanging visits with our neighbours, who had at first been overjoyed to see a Roylott of Stoke Moran back in the old family seat, he shut himself up in his house and seldom came out save to indulge in ferocious quarrels with whoever might cross his path. Violence of temper approaching to mania has been hereditary in the men of the family, and in my stepfather's case it had, I believe, been intensified by his long residence in the tropics. A series of disgraceful brawls took place, two of which ended in the police-court, until at last he became the terror of the village, and the folks would fly at his approach, for he is a man of immense strength, and absolutely uncontrollable in his anger.

"Last week he hurled the local blacksmith over a parapet into a stream, and it was only by paying over all the money which I could gather together that I was able to avert another public exposure. He had no friends at all save the wandering gipsies, and he would give these vagabonds leave to encamp upon the few acres of bramble-covered land which represent the family estate, and would accept in return the hospitality of their tents, wandering away with them sometimes for weeks on end. He has a passion also for Indian animals, which are sent over to him by a correspondent, and he has at this

---

[14]**Saxon** Germanic tribes that settled in Great Britain in the Middle Ages

[15]**Regency** the historical period (1811–1820) when the Prince of Wales ruled for George III due to the latter's mental illness

[16]**Calcutta** now Kolkata—a city in India; India was a British colony from the mid-nineteenth century to the mid-twentieth century

moment a cheetah and a baboon, which wander freely over his grounds and are feared by the villagers almost as much as their master.

"You can imagine from what I say that my poor sister Julia and I had no great pleasure in our lives. No servant would stay with us, and for a long time we did all the work of the house. She was but thirty at the time of her death, and yet her hair had already begun to whiten, even as mine has."

"Your sister is dead, then?" 30

"She died just two years ago, and it is of her death that I wish to speak to you. You can understand that, living the life which I have described, we were little likely to see anyone of our own age and position. We had, however, an aunt, my mother's maiden sister, Miss Honoria Westphail, who lives near Harrow, and we were occasionally allowed to pay short visits at this lady's house. Julia went there at Christmas two years ago, and met there a half-pay major of marines, to whom she became engaged. My stepfather learned of the engagement when my sister returned and offered no objection to the marriage; but within a fortnight of the day which had been fixed for the wedding, the terrible event occurred which has deprived me of my only companion."

Sherlock Holmes had been leaning back in his chair with his eyes closed and his head sunk in a cushion, but he half opened his lids now and glanced across at his visitor.

"Pray be precise as to details," said he.

"It is easy for me to be so, for every event of that dreadful time is seared into my memory. The manor-house is, as I have already said, very old, and only one wing is now inhabited. The bedrooms in this wing are on the ground floor, the sitting-rooms being in the central block of the buildings. Of these bedrooms the first is Dr. Roylott's, the second my sister's, and the third my own. There is no communication between them, but they all open out into the same corridor. Do I make myself plain?"

"Perfectly so." 35

"The windows of the three rooms open out upon the lawn. That fatal night Dr. Roylott had gone to his room early, though we knew that he had not retired to rest, for my sister was troubled by the smell of the strong Indian cigars which it was his custom to smoke. She left her room, therefore, and came into mine, where she sat for some time, chatting about her approaching wedding. At eleven o'clock she rose to leave me, but she paused at the door and looked back. "'Tell me, Helen,' said she, 'have you ever heard anyone whistle in the dead of the night?'" "'Never,' said I.

"'I suppose that you could not possibly whistle, yourself, in your sleep?'

"'Certainly not. But why?'

"'Because during the last few nights I have always, about three in the morning, heard a low, clear whistle. I am a light sleeper, and it has awakened me. I cannot tell where it came from—perhaps from the next room, perhaps from the lawn. I thought that I would just ask you whether you had heard it.'

"'No, I have not. It must be those wretched gipsies in the plantation.' 40

"'Very likely. And yet if it were on the lawn, I wonder that you did not hear it also.'

"'Ah, but I sleep more heavily than you.'

"'Well, it is of no great consequence, at any rate.' She smiled back at me, closed my door, and a few moments later I heard her key turn in the lock."

"Indeed," said Holmes. "Was it your custom always to lock yourselves in at night?"

"Always." 45

"And why?"

"I think that I mentioned to you that the doctor kept a cheetah and a baboon. We had no feeling of security unless our doors were locked."

"I could not sleep that night. A vague feeling of impending misfortune impressed me. My sister and I, you will recollect, were twins, and you know how subtle are the links which bind two souls which are so closely allied. It was a wild night. The wind was howling outside, and the rain was beating and splashing against the windows. Suddenly, amid all the hubbub of the gale, there burst forth the wild scream of a terrified woman. I knew that it was my sister's voice. I sprang from my bed, wrapped a shawl round me, and rushed into the corridor. As I opened my door I seemed to hear a low whistle, such as my sister described, and a few moments later a clanging sound, as if a mass of metal had fallen. As I ran down the passage, my sister's door was unlocked, and revolved slowly upon its hinges. I stared at it horror-stricken, not knowing what was about to issue from it. By the light of the corridor-lamp I saw my sister appear at the opening, her face blanched with terror, her hands groping for help, her whole figure swaying to and fro like that of a drunkard. I ran to her and threw my arms round her, but at that moment her knees seemed to give way and she fell to the ground. She writhed as one who is in terrible pain, and her limbs were dreadfully convulsed. At first I thought that she had not recognised me, but as I bent over her she suddenly shrieked out in a voice which I shall never forget, 'Oh, my God! Helen! It was the band! The speckled band!' There was something else which she would fain have said, and she stabbed with her finger into the air in the direction of the doctor's room, but a fresh convulsion seized her and choked her words. I rushed out, calling loudly for my stepfather, and I met him hastening from his room in his dressing-gown. When he reached my sister's side she was unconscious, and though he poured brandy down her throat and sent for medical aid from the village, all efforts were in vain, for she slowly sank and died without having recovered her consciousness. Such was the dreadful end of my beloved sister."

"One moment," said Holmes, "are you sure about this whistle and metallic sound? Could you swear to it?"

"That was what the county coroner asked me at the inquiry. It is my strong impression that I heard it, and yet, among the crash of the gale and the creaking of an old house, I may possibly have been deceived." 50

"Was your sister dressed?"

"No, she was in her night-dress. In her right hand was found the charred stump of a match, and in her left a match-box."

"Showing that she had struck a light and looked about her when the alarm took place. That is important. And what conclusions did the coroner come to?"

"He investigated the case with great care, for Dr. Roylott's conduct had long been notorious in the county, but he was unable to find any satisfactory cause of death. My evidence showed that the door had been fastened upon the inner side, and the windows were blocked by old-fashioned shutters with broad iron bars, which were secured every night. The walls were carefully sounded, and were shown to be quite solid all round, and the flooring was also thoroughly examined, with the same result. The chimney is wide, but is barred up by four large staples. It is certain, therefore, that my sister was quite alone when she met her end. Besides, there were no marks of any violence upon her."

"How about poison?" 55

"The doctors examined her for it, but without success."

"What do you think that this unfortunate lady died of, then?"

"It is my belief that she died of pure fear and nervous shock, though what it was that frightened her I cannot imagine."

"Were there gipsies in the plantation at the time?"

"Yes, there are nearly always some there."   60

"Ah, and what did you gather from this allusion to a band—a speckled band?"

"Sometimes I have thought that it was merely the wild talk of delirium, sometimes that it may have referred to some band of people, perhaps to these very gipsies in the plantation. I do not know whether the spotted handkerchiefs which so many of them wear over their heads might have suggested the strange adjective which she used."

Holmes shook his head like a man who is far from being satisfied.

"These are very deep waters," said he; "pray go on with your narrative."

"Two years have passed since then, and my life has been until lately lonelier than   65 ever. A month ago, however, a dear friend, whom I have known for many years, has done me the honour to ask my hand in marriage. His name is Armitage—Percy Armitage—the second son of Mr. Armitage, of Crane Water, near Reading.[17] My stepfather has offered no opposition to the match, and we are to be married in the course of the spring. Two days ago some repairs were started in the west wing of the building, and my bedroom wall has been pierced, so that I have had to move into the chamber in which my sister died, and to sleep in the very bed in which she slept. Imagine, then, my thrill of terror when last night, as I lay awake, thinking over her terrible fate, I suddenly heard in the silence of the night the low whistle which had been the herald of her own death. I sprang up and lit the lamp, but nothing was to be seen in the room. I was too shaken to go to bed again, however, so I dressed, and as soon as it was daylight I slipped down, got a dog-cart at the Crown Inn, which is opposite, and drove to Leatherhead, from whence I have come on this morning with the one object of seeing you and asking your advice."

"You have done wisely," said my friend. "But have you told me all?"

"Yes, all."

"Miss Roylott, you have not. You are screening your stepfather."

"Why, what do you mean?"

For answer Holmes pushed back the frill of black lace which fringed the hand that   70 lay upon our visitor's knee. Five little livid spots, the marks of four fingers and a thumb, were printed upon the white wrist.

"You have been cruelly used," said Holmes.

The lady coloured deeply and covered over her injured wrist. "He is a hard man," she said, "and perhaps he hardly knows his own strength."

There was a long silence, during which Holmes leaned his chin upon his hands and stared into the crackling fire.

"This is a very deep business," he said at last. "There are a thousand details which I should desire to know before I decide upon our course of action. Yet we have not a moment to lose. If we were to come to Stoke Moran to-day, would it be possible for us to see over these rooms without the knowledge of your stepfather?"

"As it happens, he spoke of coming into town to-day upon some most important   75 business. It is probable that he will be away all day, and that there would be nothing to disturb you. We have a housekeeper now, but she is old and foolish, and I could easily get her out of the way."

"Excellent. You are not averse to this trip, Watson?"

"By no means."

"Then we shall both come. What are you going to do yourself?"

---

[17]**Reading** a town in England

"I have one or two things which I would wish to do now that I am in town. But I shall return by the twelve o'clock train, so as to be there in time for your coming."

"And you may expect us early in the afternoon. I have myself some small business 80 matters to attend to. Will you not wait and breakfast?"

"No, I must go. My heart is lightened already since I have confided my trouble to you. I shall look forward to seeing you again this afternoon." She dropped her thick black veil over her face and glided from the room.

"And what do you think of it all, Watson?" asked Sherlock Holmes, leaning back in his chair. "It seems to me to be a most dark and sinister business."

"Dark enough and sinister enough."

"Yet if the lady is correct in saying that the flooring and walls are sound, and that the door, window, and chimney are impassable, then her sister must have been undoubtedly alone when she met her mysterious end."

"What becomes, then, of these nocturnal whistles, and what of the very peculiar 85 words of the dying woman?"

"I cannot think."

"When you combine the ideas of whistles at night, the presence of a band of gipsies who are on intimate terms with this old doctor, the fact that we have every reason to believe that the doctor has an interest in preventing his stepdaughter's marriage, the dying allusion to a band, and, finally, the fact that Miss Helen Stoner heard a metallic clang, which might have been caused by one of those metal bars that secured the shutters falling back into its place, I think that there is good ground to think that the mystery may be cleared along those lines."

"But what, then, did the gipsies do?"

"I cannot imagine."

"I see many objections to any such theory." 90

"And so do I. It is precisely for that reason that we are going to Stoke Moran this day. I want to see whether the objections are fatal, or if they may be explained away. But what in the name of the devil!"

The ejaculation had been drawn from my companion by the fact that our door had been suddenly dashed open, and that a huge man had framed himself in the aperture. His costume was a peculiar mixture of the professional and of the agricultural, having a black top-hat, a long frock-coat, and a pair of high gaiters, with a hunting-crop swinging in his hand. So tall was he that his hat actually brushed the cross bar of the doorway, and his breadth seemed to span it across from side to side. A large face, seared with a thousand wrinkles, burned yellow with the sun, and marked with every evil passion, was turned from one to the other of us, while his deep-set, bile-shot eyes, and his high, thin, fleshless nose, gave him somewhat the resemblance to a fierce old bird of prey.

"Which of you is Holmes?" asked this apparition.

"My name, sir; but you have the advantage of me," said my companion quietly.

"I am Dr. Grimesby Roylott, of Stoke Moran." 95

"Indeed, Doctor," said Holmes blandly. "Pray take a seat."

"I will do nothing of the kind. My stepdaughter has been here. I have traced her. What has she been saying to you?"

"It is a little cold for the time of the year," said Holmes.

"What has she been saying to you?" screamed the old man furiously.

"But I have heard that the crocuses promise well," continued my companion imper- 100 turbably. "Ha! You put me off, do you?" said our new visitor, taking a step forward and shaking his hunting-crop. "I know you, you scoundrel! I have heard of you before. You are Holmes, the meddler."

My friend smiled.

"Holmes, the busybody!"

His smile broadened.

"Holmes, the Scotland Yard Jack-in-office!"

Holmes chuckled heartily. "Your conversation is most entertaining," said he.   105

"When you go out close the door, for there is a decided draught."

"I will go when I have said my say. Don't you dare to meddle with my affairs. I know that Miss Stoner has been here. I traced her! I am a dangerous man to fall foul of! See here." He stepped swiftly forward, seized the poker, and bent it into a curve with his huge brown hands.

"See that you keep yourself out of my grip," he snarled, and hurling the twisted poker into the fireplace he strode out of the room.

"He seems a very amiable person," said Holmes, laughing. "I am not quite so bulky, but if he had remained I might have shown him that my grip was not much more feeble than his own." As he spoke he picked up the steel poker and, with a sudden effort, straightened it out again.

"Fancy his having the insolence to confound me with the official detective force! 110 This incident gives zest to our investigation, however, and I only trust that our little friend will not suffer from her imprudence in allowing this brute to trace her. And now, Watson, we shall order breakfast, and afterwards I shall walk down to Doctors' Commons, where I hope to get some data which may help us in this matter."

It was nearly one o'clock when Sherlock Holmes returned from his excursion. He held in his hand a sheet of blue paper, scrawled over with notes and figures.

"I have seen the will of the deceased wife," said he. "To determine its exact meaning I have been obliged to work out the present prices of the investments with which it is concerned. The total income, which at the time of the wife's death was little short of 1100 pounds, is now, through the fall in agricultural prices, not more than 750 pounds. Each daughter can claim an income of 250 pounds, in case of marriage. It is evident, therefore, that if both girls had married, this beauty would have had a mere pittance, while even one of them would cripple him to a very serious extent. My morning's work has not been wasted, since it has proved that he has the very strongest motives for standing in the way of anything of the sort. And now, Watson, this is too serious for dawdling, especially as the old man is aware that we are interesting ourselves in his affairs; so if you are ready, we shall call a cab and drive to Waterloo. I should be very much obliged if you would slip your revolver into your pocket. An Eley's No. 2 is an excellent argument with gentlemen who can twist steel pokers into knots. That and a tooth-brush are, I think, all that we need."

At Waterloo[18] we were fortunate in catching a train for Leatherhead, where we hired a trap[19] at the station inn and drove for four or five miles through the lovely Surrey lanes. It was a perfect day, with a bright sun and a few fleecy clouds in the heavens. The trees and wayside hedges were just throwing out their first green shoots, and the air was full of the pleasant smell of the moist earth. To me at least there was a strange contrast between the sweet promise of the spring and this sinister quest upon which we were

---

[18]**Waterloo** a train station in London, named after the famous 1815 battle near Waterloo, in Belgium, where British-led allied armies commanded by the Duke of Wellington, aided by a Prussian army, defeated the French forces under Napoleon

[19]**trap** a horse-drawn carriage

engaged. My companion sat in the front of the trap, his arms folded, his hat pulled down over his eyes, and his chin sunk upon his breast, buried in the deepest thought. Suddenly, however, he started, tapped me on the shoulder, and pointed over the meadows.

"Look there!" said he.

A heavily timbered park stretched up in a gentle slope, thickening into a grove at   115
the highest point. From amid the branches there jutted out the grey gables and high roof-tree of a very old mansion.

"Stoke Moran?" said he.

"Yes, sir, that be the house of Dr. Grimesby Roylott," remarked the driver.

"There is some building going on there," said Holmes; "that is where we are going."
"There's the village," said the driver, pointing to a cluster of roofs some distance to the left; "but if you want to get to the house, you'll find it shorter to get over this stile, and so by the foot-path over the fields. There it is, where the lady is walking."

"And the lady, I fancy, is Miss Stoner," observed Holmes, shading his eyes. "Yes, I think we had better do as you suggest."

We got off, paid our fare, and the trap rattled back on its way to Leatherhead.   120

"I thought it as well," said Holmes as we climbed the stile, "that this fellow should think we had come here as architects, or on some definite business. It may stop his gossip. Good-afternoon, Miss Stoner. You see that we have been as good as our word."

Our client of the morning had hurried forward to meet us with a face which spoke her joy. "I have been waiting so eagerly for you," she cried, shaking hands with us warmly. "All has turned out splendidly. Dr. Roylott has gone to town, and it is unlikely that he will be back before evening."

"We have had the pleasure of making the doctor's acquaintance," said Holmes, and in a few words he sketched out what had occurred. Miss Stoner turned white to the lips as she listened.

"Good heavens!" she cried, "he has followed me, then."

"So it appears."   125

"He is so cunning that I never know when I am safe from him. What will he say when he returns?"

"He must guard himself, for he may find that there is someone more cunning than himself upon his track. You must lock yourself up from him to-night. If he is violent, we shall take you away to your aunt's at Harrow. Now, we must make the best use of our time, so kindly take us at once to the rooms which we are to examine."

The building was of grey, lichen-blotched stone, with a high central portion and two curving wings, like the claws of a crab, thrown out on each side. In one of these wings the windows were broken and blocked with wooden boards, while the roof was partly caved in, a picture of ruin. The central portion was in little better repair, but the right-hand block was comparatively modern, and the blinds in the windows, with the blue smoke curling up from the chimneys, showed that this was where the family resided. Some scaffolding had been erected against the end wall, and the stone-work had been broken into, but there were no signs of any workmen at the moment of our visit. Holmes walked slowly up and down the ill-trimmed lawn and examined with deep attention the outsides of the windows.

"This, I take it, belongs to the room in which you used to sleep, the centre one to your sister's, and the one next to the main building to Dr. Roylott's chamber?"

"Exactly so. But I am now sleeping in the middle one."   130

"Pending the alterations, as I understand. By the way, there does not seem to be any very pressing need for repairs at that end wall."

"There were none. I believe that it was an excuse to move me from my room."

"Ah! That is suggestive. Now, on the other side of this narrow wing runs the corridor from which these three rooms open. There are windows in it, of course?"

"Yes, but very small ones. Too narrow for anyone to pass through."

"As you both locked your doors at night, your rooms were unapproachable from that 135 side. Now, would you have the kindness to go into your room and bar your shutters?"

Miss Stoner did so, and Holmes, after a careful examination through the open window, endeavoured in every way to force the shutter open, but without success. There was no slit through which a knife could be passed to raise the bar. Then with his lens he tested the hinges, but they were of solid iron, built firmly into the massive masonry.

"Hum!" said he, scratching his chin in some perplexity, "my theory certainly presents some difficulties. No one could pass these shutters if they were bolted. Well, we shall see if the inside throws any light upon the matter."

A small side door led into the whitewashed corridor from which the three bedrooms opened. Holmes refused to examine the third chamber, so we passed at once to the second, that in which Miss Stoner was now sleeping, and in which her sister had met with her fate. It was a homely little room, with a low ceiling and a gaping fireplace, after the fashion of old country-houses. A brown chest of drawers stood in one corner, a narrow white-counterpaned bed in another, and a dressing-table on the left-hand side of the window. These articles, with two small wicker-work chairs, made up all the furniture in the room save for a square of Wilton carpet in the centre. The boards round and the panelling of the walls were of brown, worm-eaten oak, so old and discoloured that it may have dated from the original building of the house. Holmes drew one of the chairs into a corner and sat silent, while his eyes travelled round and round and up and down, taking in every detail of the apartment.

"Where does that bell communicate with?" he asked at last pointing to a thick bell-rope which hung down beside the bed, the tassel actually lying upon the pillow.

"It goes to the housekeeper's room."   140

"It looks newer than the other things?"

"Yes, it was only put there a couple of years ago."

"Your sister asked for it, I suppose?"

"No, I never heard of her using it. We used always to get what we wanted for ourselves."

"Indeed, it seemed unnecessary to put so nice a bell-pull there. You will excuse 145 me for a few minutes while I satisfy myself as to this floor." He threw himself down upon his face with his lens in his hand and crawled swiftly backward and forward, examining minutely the cracks between the boards. Then he did the same with the wood-work with which the chamber was panelled. Finally he walked over to the bed and spent some time in staring at it and in running his eye up and down the wall. Finally he took the bell-rope in his hand and gave it a brisk tug.

"Why, it's a dummy," said he.

"Won't it ring?"

"No, it is not even attached to a wire. This is very interesting. You can see now that it is fastened to a hook just above where the little opening for the ventilator is."

"How very absurd! I never noticed that before."

"Very strange!" muttered Holmes, pulling at the rope. "There are one or two very 150 singular points about this room. For example, what a fool a builder must be to open a ventilator into another room, when, with the same trouble, he might have communicated with the outside air!"

"That is also quite modern," said the lady.

"Done about the same time as the bell-rope?" remarked Holmes.

"Yes, there were several little changes carried out about that time."

"They seem to have been of a most interesting character—dummy bell-ropes, and ventilators which do not ventilate. With your permission, Miss Stoner, we shall now carry our researches into the inner apartment."

Dr. Grimesby Roylott's chamber was larger than that of his step-daughter, but was as plainly furnished. A camp-bed, a small wooden shelf full of books, mostly of a technical character, an armchair beside the bed, a plain wooden chair against the wall, a round table, and a large iron safe were the principal things which met the eye. Holmes walked slowly round and examined each and all of them with the keenest interest. 155

"What's in here?" he asked, tapping the safe.

"My stepfather's business papers."

"Oh! You have seen inside, then?"

"Only once, some years ago. I remember that it was full of papers."

"There isn't a cat in it, for example?" 160

"No. What a strange idea!"

"Well, look at this!" He took up a small saucer of milk which stood on the top of it.

"No; we don't keep a cat. But there is a cheetah and a baboon."

"Ah, yes, of course! Well, a cheetah is just a big cat, and yet a saucer of milk does not go very far in satisfying its wants, I daresay. There is one point which I should wish to determine." He squatted down in front of the wooden chair and examined the seat of it with the greatest attention.

"Thank you. That is quite settled," said he, rising and putting his lens in his pocket. 165 "Hullo! Here is something interesting!"

The object which had caught his eye was a small dog lash hung on one corner of the bed. The lash, however, was curled upon itself and tied so as to make a loop of whipcord.

"What do you make of that, Watson?"

"It's a common enough lash. But I don't know why it should be tied."

"That is not quite so common, is it? Ah, me! It's a wicked world, and when a clever man turns his brains to crime it is the worst of all. I think that I have seen enough now, Miss Stoner, and with your permission we shall walk out upon the lawn."

I had never seen my friend's face so grim or his brow so dark as it was when we 170 turned from the scene of this investigation. We had walked several times up and down the lawn, neither Miss Stoner nor myself liking to break in upon his thoughts before he roused himself from his reverie.

"It is very essential, Miss Stoner," said he, "that you should absolutely follow my advice in every respect."

"I shall most certainly do so."

"The matter is too serious for any hesitation. Your life may depend upon your compliance."

"I assure you that I am in your hands."

"In the first place, both my friend and I must spend the night in your room." 175

Both Miss Stoner and I gazed at him in astonishment.

"Yes, it must be so. Let me explain. I believe that that is the village inn over there?"

"Yes, that is the Crown."

"Very good. Your windows would be visible from there?"

"Certainly." 180

"You must confine yourself to your room, on pretence of a headache, when your step-father comes back. Then when you hear him retire for the night, you must open the shutters of your window, undo the hasp, put your lamp there as a signal to us, and then withdraw quietly with everything which you are likely to want into the room which you used to occupy. I have no doubt that, in spite of the repairs, you could manage there for one night."

"Oh, yes, easily."

"The rest you will leave in our hands."

"But what will you do?"

"We shall spend the night in your room, and we shall investigate the cause of this 185 noise which has disturbed you."

"I believe, Mr. Holmes, that you have already made up your mind," said Miss Stoner, laying her hand upon my companion's sleeve. "Perhaps I have."

"Then, for pity's sake, tell me what was the cause of my sister's death."

"I should prefer to have clearer proofs before I speak."

"You can at least tell me whether my own thought is correct, and if she died from some sudden fright."

"No, I do not think so. I think that there was probably some more tangible cause. 190 And now, Miss Stoner, we must leave you for if Dr. Roylott returned and saw us our journey would be in vain. Good-bye, and be brave, for if you will do what I have told you, you may rest assured that we shall soon drive away the dangers that threaten you."

Sherlock Holmes and I had no difficulty in engaging a bedroom and sitting-room at the Crown Inn. They were on the upper floor, and from our window we could command a view of the avenue gate, and of the inhabited wing of Stoke Moran Manor House. At dusk we saw Dr. Grimesby Roylott drive past, his huge form looming up beside the little figure of the lad who drove him. The boy had some slight difficulty in undoing the heavy iron gates, and we heard the hoarse roar of the doctor's voice and saw the fury with which he shook his clinched fists at him. The trap drove on, and a few minutes later we saw a sudden light spring up among the trees as the lamp was lit in one of the sitting-rooms.

"Do you know, Watson," said Holmes as we sat together in the gathering darkness, "I have really some scruples as to taking you to-night. There is a distinct element of danger."

"Can I be of assistance?"

"Your presence might be invaluable."

"Then I shall certainly come." 195

"It is very kind of you."

"You speak of danger. You have evidently seen more in these rooms than was visible to me."

"No, but I fancy that I may have deduced a little more. I imagine that you saw all that I did."

"I saw nothing remarkable save the bell-rope, and what purpose that could answer I confess is more than I can imagine."

"You saw the ventilator, too?" 200

"Yes, but I do not think that it is such a very unusual thing to have a small opening between two rooms. It was so small that a rat could hardly pass through."

"I knew that we should find a ventilator before ever we came to Stoke Moran."

"My dear Holmes!"

"Oh, yes, I did. You remember in her statement she said that her sister could smell Dr. Roylott's cigar. Now, of course that suggested at once that there must be a communication between the two rooms. It could only be a small one, or it would have been remarked upon at the coroner's inquiry. I deduced a ventilator."

"But what harm can there be in that?" 205

"Well, there is at least a curious coincidence of dates. A ventilator is made, a cord is hung, and a lady who sleeps in the bed dies. Does not that strike you?"

"I cannot as yet see any connection."

"Did you observe anything very peculiar about that bed?"

"No."

"It was clamped to the floor. Did you ever see a bed fastened like that before?" 210

"I cannot say that I have."

"The lady could not move her bed. It must always be in the same relative position to the ventilator and to the rope—or so we may call it, since it was clearly never meant for a bell-pull."

"Holmes," I cried, "I seem to see dimly what you are hinting at. We are only just in time to prevent some subtle and horrible crime."

"Subtle enough and horrible enough. When a doctor does go wrong he is the first of criminals. He has nerve and he has knowledge. Palmer and Pritchard were among the heads of their profession. This man strikes even deeper, but I think, Watson, that we shall be able to strike deeper still. But we shall have horrors enough before the night is over; for goodness' sake let us have a quiet pipe and turn our minds for a few hours to something more cheerful."

About nine o'clock the light among the trees was extinguished, and all was dark in 215 the direction of the Manor House. Two hours passed slowly away, and then, suddenly, just at the stroke of eleven, a single bright light shone out right in front of us.

"That is our signal," said Holmes, springing to his feet; "it comes from the middle window."

As we passed out he exchanged a few words with the landlord, explaining that we were going on a late visit to an acquaintance, and that it was possible that we might spend the night there. A moment later we were out on the dark road, a chill wind blowing in our faces, and one yellow light twinkling in front of us through the gloom to guide us on our sombre errand.

There was little difficulty in entering the grounds, for unrepaired breaches gaped in the old park wall. Making our way among the trees, we reached the lawn, crossed it, and were about to enter through the window when out from a clump of laurel bushes there darted what seemed to be a hideous and distorted child, who threw itself upon the grass with writhing limbs and then ran swiftly across the lawn into the darkness.

"My God!" I whispered; "did you see it?"

Holmes was for the moment as startled as I. His hand closed like a vice upon my 220 wrist in his agitation. Then he broke into a low laugh and put his lips to my ear.

"It is a nice household," he murmured. "That is the baboon."

I had forgotten the strange pets which the doctor affected. There was a cheetah, too; perhaps we might find it upon our shoulders at any moment. I confess that I felt easier in my mind when, after following Holmes' example and slipping off my shoes, I found myself inside the bedroom. My companion noiselessly closed the shutters, moved the lamp onto the table, and cast his eyes round the room. All was as we had seen it in the daytime. Then creeping up to me and making a trumpet of his hand, he whispered into my ear again so gently that it was all that I could do to distinguish the words:

"The least sound would be fatal to our plans."

I nodded to show that I had heard.

"We must sit without light. He would see it through the ventilator."

I nodded again.

"Do not go asleep; your very life may depend upon it. Have your pistol ready in case we should need it. I will sit on the side of the bed, and you in that chair."

I took out my revolver and laid it on the corner of the table.

Holmes had brought up a long thin cane, and this he placed upon the bed beside him. By it he laid the box of matches and the stump of a candle. Then he turned down the lamp, and we were left in darkness.

How shall I ever forget that dreadful vigil? I could not hear a sound, not even the drawing of a breath, and yet I knew that my companion sat open-eyed, within a few feet of me, in the same state of nervous tension in which I was myself. The shutters cut off the least ray of light, and we waited in absolute darkness.

From outside came the occasional cry of a night-bird, and once at our very window a long drawn catlike whine, which told us that the cheetah was indeed at liberty. Far away we could hear the deep tones of the parish clock, which boomed out every quarter of an hour. How long they seemed, those quarters! Twelve struck, and one and two and three, and still we sat waiting silently for whatever might befall.

Suddenly there was the momentary gleam of a light up in the direction of the ventilator, which vanished immediately, but was succeeded by a strong smell of burning oil and heated metal. Someone in the next room had lit a dark-lantern. I heard a gentle sound of movement, and then all was silent once more, though the smell grew stronger. For half an hour I sat with straining ears. Then suddenly another sound became audible—a very gentle, soothing sound, like that of a small jet of steam escaping continually from a kettle. The instant that we heard it, Holmes sprang from the bed, struck a match, and lashed furiously with his cane at the bell-pull.

"You see it, Watson?" he yelled. "You see it?"

But I saw nothing. At the moment when Holmes struck the light I heard a low, clear whistle, but the sudden glare flashing into my weary eyes made it impossible for me to tell what it was at which my friend lashed so savagely. I could, however, see that his face was deadly pale and filled with horror and loathing. He had ceased to strike and was gazing up at the ventilator when suddenly there broke from the silence of the night the most horrible cry to which I have ever listened. It swelled up louder and louder, a hoarse yell of pain and fear and anger all mingled in the one dreadful shriek. They say that away down in the village, and even in the distant parsonage, that cry raised the sleepers from their beds. It struck cold to our hearts, and I stood gazing at Holmes, and he at me, until the last echoes of it had died away into the silence from which it rose.

"What can it mean?" I gasped.

"It means that it is all over," Holmes answered. "And perhaps, after all, it is for the best. Take your pistol, and we will enter Dr. Roylott's room."

With a grave face he lit the lamp and led the way down the corridor. Twice he struck at the chamber door without any reply from within. Then he turned the handle and entered, I at his heels, with the cocked pistol in my hand.

It was a singular sight which met our eyes. On the table stood a dark-lantern with the shutter half open, throwing a brilliant beam of light upon the iron safe, the door of which was ajar. Beside this table, on the wooden chair, sat Dr. Grimesby Roylott clad in a long grey dressing-gown, his bare ankles protruding beneath, and his feet thrust into red heelless Turkish slippers. Across his lap lay the short stock with the long lash which we had noticed during the day. His chin was cocked upward and his eyes were fixed in a dreadful, rigid stare at the corner of the ceiling. Round his brow he had a peculiar yellow band, with brownish speckles, which seemed to be bound tightly round his head. As we entered he made neither sound nor motion.

"The band! The speckled band!" whispered Holmes.

I took a step forward. In an instant his strange headgear began to move, and there   240
reared itself from among his hair the squat diamond-shaped head and puffed neck of a loathsome serpent.

"It is a swamp adder!" cried Holmes; "the deadliest snake in India. He has died within ten seconds of being bitten. Violence does, in truth, recoil upon the violent, and the schemer falls into the pit which he digs for another. Let us thrust this creature back into its den, and we can then remove Miss Stoner to some place of shelter and let the county police know what has happened."

As he spoke he drew the dog-whip swiftly from the dead man's lap, and throwing the noose round the reptile's neck he drew it from its horrid perch and, carrying it at arm's length, threw it into the iron safe, which he closed upon it.

Such are the true facts of the death of Dr. Grimesby Roylott, of Stoke Moran. It is not necessary that I should prolong a narrative which has already run to too great a length by telling how we broke the sad news to the terrified girl, how we conveyed her by the morning train to the care of her good aunt at Harrow, of how the slow process of official inquiry came to the conclusion that the doctor met his fate while indiscreetly playing with a dangerous pet. The little which I had yet to learn of the case was told me by Sherlock Holmes as we travelled back next day.

"I had," said he, "come to an entirely erroneous conclusion which shows, my dear Watson, how dangerous it always is to reason from insufficient data. The presence of the gipsies, and the use of the word 'band,' which was used by the poor girl, no doubt, to explain the appearance which she had caught a hurried glimpse of by the light of her match, were sufficient to put me upon an entirely wrong scent. I can only claim the merit that I instantly reconsidered my position when, however, it became clear to me that whatever danger threatened an occupant of the room could not come either from the window or the door. My attention was speedily drawn, as I have already remarked to you, to this ventilator, and to the bell-rope which hung down to the bed.

The discovery that this was a dummy, and that the bed was clamped to the floor,   245
instantly gave rise to the suspicion that the rope was there as a bridge for something passing through the hole and coming to the bed. The idea of a snake instantly occurred to me, and when I coupled it with my knowledge that the doctor was furnished with a supply of creatures from India, I felt that I was probably on the right track. The idea of using a form of poison which could not possibly be discovered by any chemical test was just such a one as would occur to a clever and ruthless man who had had an Eastern training. The rapidity with which such a poison would take effect would also, from his point of view, be an advantage. It would be a sharp-eyed coroner, indeed, who could distinguish the two little dark punctures which would show where the poison fangs had done their work. Then I thought of the whistle. Of course he must recall the snake before the morning light revealed it to the victim. He had trained it, probably by the use of the milk which we saw, to return to him when summoned. He would put it through this ventilator at the hour that he thought best, with the certainty that it would crawl down the rope and land on the bed. It might or might not bite the occupant, perhaps she might escape every night for a week, but sooner or later she must fall a victim.

"I had come to these conclusions before ever I had entered his room. An inspection of his chair showed me that he had been in the habit of standing on it, which of course would be necessary in order that he should reach the ventilator. The sight of the safe, the saucer of milk, and the loop of whipcord were enough to finally dispel any doubts which may have remained. The metallic clang heard by Miss Stoner was obviously caused by her stepfather hastily closing the door of his safe upon its terrible occupant. Having once made up my mind, you know the steps which I took in order to put the matter to the proof. I heard the creature hiss as I have no doubt that you did also, and I instantly lit the light and attacked it."

"With the result of driving it through the ventilator."

"And also with the result of causing it to turn upon its master at the other side.

Some of the blows of my cane came home and roused its snakish temper, so that it flew upon the first person it saw. In this way I am no doubt indirectly responsible for Dr. Grimesby Roylott's death, and I cannot say that it is likely to weigh very heavily upon my conscience."

Critical Thinking Topics

1. What role does Doctor Watson play in this story? What is the effect of the story's being told in first person from his point of view? Is he a reliable narrator? Why or why not?

2. We associate Sherlock Holmes with intelligence and insight, but he also works hard to solve a crime. Give details from the story to illustrate his method and work ethic.

3. Why does Miss Stoner seek the help of Sherlock Holmes? How does her position illustrate the role of women in Victorian England?

Writing Topics

1. Why does Sherlock Holmes first suspect the "gipsies" (more properly referred to as the Romani people)? What does this tell us about their position in that society? How might this story connect to current issues like racial profiling? Conduct some research and give examples to make the connection.

2. The villain dies at the end of this story, and Holmes believes that he is "indirectly responsible for Dr. Grimesby Roylott's death." Holmes then states that Dr. Roylott's death will not "weigh very heavily upon [his] conscience." Do you agree that Holmes is responsible for Dr. Roylott's death? Could Holmes have avoided another death by taking a different approach to solving the crime? Explain your responses.

7.7 Flannery O'Connor, A Good Man Is Hard to Find (1955)

The grandmother didn't want to go to Florida. She wanted to visit some of her connections in east Tennessee and she was seizing at every chance to change Bailey's mind. Bailey was the son she lived with, her only boy. He was sitting on the edge of his chair at the table, bent over the orange sports section of the *Journal*. "Now look here, Bailey," she said, "see here, read this," and she stood with one hand on her thin hip and the other rattling the newspaper at his bald head. "Here this fellow that calls himself The Misfit is aloose from the Federal Pen and headed toward Florida and you read here what it says he did to these people. Just you read it. I wouldn't take my children in any direction with a criminal like that aloose in it. I couldn't answer to my conscience if I did."

Bailey didn't look up from his reading so she wheeled around then and faced the children's mother, a young woman in slacks, whose face was as broad and innocent as a cabbage and was tied around with a green head-kerchief that had two points on the top like rabbit's ears. She was sitting on the sofa, feeding the baby his apricots out of a jar. "The children have been to Florida before," the old lady said. "You all ought to take them somewhere else for a change so they would see different parts of the world and be broad. They never have been to east Tennessee."

The children's mother didn't seem to hear her but the eight-year-old boy, John Wesley, a stocky child with glasses, said, "If you don't want to go to Florida, why dontcha stay at home?" He and the little girl, June Star, were reading the funny papers on the floor.

"She wouldn't stay at home to be queen for a day," June Star said without raising her yellow head.

"Yes and what would you do if this fellow, The Misfit, caught you?" the grand-   5
mother asked.

"I'd smack his face," John Wesley said.

"She wouldn't stay at home for a million bucks," June Star said. "Afraid she'd miss something. She has to go everywhere we go."

"All right, Miss," the grandmother said. "Just remember that the next time you want me to curl your hair."

June Star said her hair was naturally curly.

The next morning the grandmother was the first one in the car, ready to go. She   10
had her big black valise that looked like the head of a hippopotamus in one corner, and underneath it she was hiding a basket with Pitty Sing, the cat, in it. She didn't intend for the cat to be left alone in the house for three days because he would miss her too much and she was afraid he might brush against one of her gas burners and accidentally asphyxiate himself. Her son, Bailey, didn't like to arrive at a motel with a cat.

She sat in the middle of the back seat with John Wesley and June Star on either side of her. Bailey and the children's mother and the baby sat in front and they left Atlanta at eight forty-five with the mileage on the car at 55890. The grandmother wrote this down because she thought it would be interesting to say how many miles they had been when they got back. It took them twenty minutes to reach the outskirts of the city.

The old lady settled herself comfortably, removing her white cotton gloves and putting them up with her purse on the shelf in front of the back window. The children's mother still had on slacks and still had her head tied up in a green kerchief, but the grandmother had on a navy blue straw sailor hat with a bunch of white violets on the brim and a navy blue dress with a small white dot in the print. Her collars and cuffs were white organdy trimmed with lace and at her neckline she had pinned a purple spray of cloth violets containing a sachet. In case of an accident, anyone seeing her dead on the highway would know at once that she was a lady.

She said she thought it was going to be a good day for driving, neither too hot nor too cold, and she cautioned Bailey that the speed limit was fifty-five miles an hour and that the patrolmen hid themselves behind billboards and small clumps of trees and sped out after you before you had a chance to slow down. She pointed out interesting details of the scenery: Stone Mountain; the blue granite that in some places came up to both sides of the highway; the brilliant red clay banks slightly streaked with purple; and the various crops that made rows of green lace-work on the ground. The trees were full of silver-white sunlight and the meanest of them sparkled. The children were reading comic magazines and their mother had gone back to sleep.

"Let's go through Georgia fast so we won't have to look at it much," John Wesley said.

"If I were a little boy," said the grandmother, "I wouldn't talk about my native state   15 that way. Tennessee has the mountains and Georgia has the hills."

"Tennessee is just a hillbilly dumping ground," John Wesley said, "and Georgia is a lousy state too."

"You said it," June Star said.

"In my time," said the grandmother, folding her thin veined fingers, "children were more respectful of their native states and their parents and everything else. People did right then. Oh look at the cute little pickaninny!" she said and pointed to a Negro child standing in the door of a shack. "Wouldn't that make a picture, now?" she asked and they all turned and looked at the little Negro out of the back window. He waved

"He didn't have any britches on," June Star said.

"He probably didn't have any," the grandmother explained. "Little niggers in the   20 country don't have things like we do. If I could paint, I'd paint that picture," she said.

The children exchanged comic books.

The grandmother offered to hold the baby and the children's mother passed him over the front seat to her. She set him on her knee and bounced him and told him about the things they were passing. She rolled her eyes and screwed up her mouth and stuck her leathery thin face into his smooth bland one. Occasionally he gave her a faraway smile. They passed a large cotton field with five or six graves fenced in the middle of it, like a small island. "Look at the graveyard!" the grandmother said, pointing it out. "That was the old family burying ground. That belonged to the plantation."

"Where's the plantation?" John Wesley asked.

"Gone With the Wind" said the grandmother. "Ha. Ha."

When the children finished all the comic books they had brought, they opened the   25 lunch and ate it. The grandmother ate a peanut butter sandwich and an olive and would not let the children throw the box and the paper napkins out the window. When there was nothing else to do they played a game by choosing a cloud and making the other two guess what shape it suggested. John Wesley took one the shape of a cow and June Star guessed a cow and John Wesley said, no, an automobile, and June Star said he didn't play fair, and they began to slap each other over the grandmother.

The grandmother said she would tell them a story if they would keep quiet. When she told a story, she rolled her eyes and waved her head and was very dramatic. She said once when she was a maiden lady she had been courted by a Mr. Edgar Atkins Teagarden from Jasper, Georgia. She said he was a very good-looking man and a gentleman and that he brought her a watermelon every Saturday afternoon with his initials cut in it, E. A. T. Well, one Saturday, she said, Mr. Teagarden brought the watermelon and there was nobody at home and he left it on the front porch and returned in his buggy to Jasper, but she never got the watermelon, she said, because a nigger boy ate it when he saw the initials, E. A. T. ! This story tickled John Wesley's funny bone and he giggled and giggled but June Star didn't think it was any good. She said she wouldn't marry a man that just brought her a watermelon on Saturday. The grandmother said she would have done well to marry Mr. Teagarden because he was a gentleman and had bought Coca-Cola stock when it first came out and that he had died only a few years ago, a very wealthy man.

They stopped at The Tower for barbecued sandwiches. The Tower was a part stucco and part wood filling station and dance hall set in a clearing outside of Timothy. A fat man named Red Sammy Butts ran it and there were signs stuck here and there on the building and for miles up and down the highway saying, TRY RED SAMMY'S FAMOUS BARBECUE. NONE LIKE FAMOUS RED SAMMY'S! RED SAM! THE FAT BOY WITH THE HAPPY LAUGH. A VETERAN! RED SAMMY'S YOUR MAN!

Red Sammy was lying on the bare ground outside The Tower with his head under a truck while a gray monkey about a foot high, chained to a small chinaberry tree, chattered nearby. The monkey sprang back into the tree and got on the highest limb as soon as he saw the children jump out of the car and run toward him.

Inside, The Tower was a long dark room with a counter at one end and tables at the other and dancing space in the middle. They all sat down at a board table next to the nickelodeon and Red Sam's wife, a tall burnt-brown woman with hair and eyes lighter than her skin, came and took their order. The children's mother put a dime in the machine and played "The Tennessee Waltz," and the grandmother said that tune always made her want to dance. She asked Bailey if he would like to dance but he only glared at her. He didn't have a naturally sunny disposition like she did and trips made him nervous. The grandmother's brown eyes were very bright. She swayed her head from side to side and pretended she was dancing in her chair. June Star said play something she could tap to so the children's mother put in another dime and played a fast number and June Star stepped out onto the dance floor and did her tap routine.

"Ain't she cute?" Red Sam's wife said, leaning over the counter. "Would you like to   30 come be my little girl?"

"No I certainly wouldn't," June Star said. "I wouldn't live in a broken-down place like this for a million bucks!" and she ran back to the table.

"Ain't she cute?" the woman repeated, stretching her mouth politely.

"Aren't you ashamed?" hissed the grandmother.

Red Sam came in and told his wife to quit lounging on the counter and hurry up with these people's order. His khaki trousers reached just to his hip bones and his stomach hung over them like a sack of meal swaying under his shirt. He came over and sat down at a table nearby and let out a combination sigh and yodel. "You can't win," he said. "You can't win," and he wiped his sweating red face off with a gray handkerchief. "These days you don't know who to trust," he said. "Ain't that the truth?"

"People are certainly not nice like they used to be," said the grandmother.   35

"Two fellers come in here last week," Red Sammy said, "driving a Chrysler. It was a old beat-up car but it was a good one and these boys looked all right to me. Said they worked at the mill and you know I let them fellers charge the gas they bought? Now why did I do that?"

"Because you're a good man!" the grandmother said at once.

"Yes'm, I suppose so," Red Sam said as if he were struck with this answer.

His wife brought the orders, carrying the five plates all at once without a tray, two in each hand and one balanced on her arm. "It isn't a soul in this green world of God's that you can trust," she said. "And I don't count nobody out of that, not nobody," she repeated, looking at Red Sammy.

"Did you read about that criminal, The Misfit, that's escaped?" asked the   40 grandmother.

"I wouldn't be a bit surprised if he didn't attack this place right here," said the woman. "If he hears about it being here, I wouldn't be none surprised to see him. If he hears it's two cent in the cash register, I wouldn't be at all surprised if he . . ."

"That'll do," Red Sam said. "Go bring these people their Co'-Colas," and the woman went off to get the rest of the order.

"A good man is hard to find," Red Sammy said. "Everything is getting terrible. I remember the day you could go off and leave your screen door unlatched. Not no more."

He and the grandmother discussed better times. The old lady said that in her opinion Europe was entirely to blame for the way things were now. She said the way Europe acted you would think we were made of money and Red Sam said it was no use talking about it, she was exactly right. The children ran outside into the white sunlight and looked at the monkey in the lacy chinaberry tree. He was busy catching fleas on himself and biting each one carefully between his teeth as if it were a delicacy.

They drove off again into the hot afternoon. The grandmother took cat naps and woke up every few minutes with her own snoring. Outside of Toombsboro she woke up and recalled an old plantation that she had visited in this neighborhood once when she was a young lady. She said the house had six white columns across the front and that there was an avenue of oaks leading up to it and two little wooden trellis arbors on either side in front where you sat down with your suitor after a stroll in the garden. She recalled exactly which road to turn off to get to it. She knew that Bailey would not be willing to lose any time looking at an old house, but the more she talked about it, the more she wanted to see it once again and find out if the little twin arbors were still standing. "There was a secret panel in this house," she said craftily, not telling the truth but wishing that she were, "and the story went that all the family silver was hidden in it when Sherman came through but it was never found . . ."

"Hey!" John Wesley said. "Let's go see it! We'll find it! We'll poke all the woodwork and find it! Who lives there? Where do you turn off at? Hey Pop, can't we turn off there?"

"We never have seen a house with a secret panel!" June Star shrieked. "Let's go to the house with the secret panel! Hey Pop, can't we go see the house with the secret panel!"

"It's not far from here, I know," the grandmother said. "It wouldn't take over twenty minutes."

Bailey was looking straight ahead. His jaw was as rigid as a horseshoe. "No," he said.

The children began to yell and scream that they wanted to see the house with the secret panel. John Wesley kicked the back of the front seat and June Star hung over her mother's shoulder and whined desperately into her ear that they never had any fun even on their vacation, that they could never do what THEY wanted to do. The baby began to scream and John Wesley kicked the back of the seat so hard that his father could feel the blows in his kidney.

"All right!" he shouted and drew the car to a stop at the side of the road. "Will you all shut up? Will you all just shut up for one second? If you don't shut up, we won't go anywhere."

"It would be very educational for them," the grandmother murmured.

"All right," Bailey said, "but get this: this is the only time we're going to stop for anything like this. This is the one and only time."

45

50

"The dirt road that you have to turn down is about a mile back," the grandmother directed. "I marked it when we passed."

"A dirt road," Bailey groaned.

After they had turned around and were headed toward the dirt road, the grandmother   55
recalled other points about the house, the beautiful glass over the front doorway and the candle-lamp in the hall. John Wesley said that the secret panel was probably in the fireplace.

"You can't go inside this house," Bailey said. "You don't know who lives there."

"While you all talk to the people in front, I'll run around behind and get in a window," John Wesley suggested.

"We'll all stay in the car," his mother said.

They turned onto the dirt road and the car raced roughly along in a swirl of pink dust. The grandmother recalled the times when there were no paved roads and thirty miles was a day's journey. The dirt road was hilly and there were sudden washes in it and sharp curves on dangerous embankments. All at once they would be on a hill, looking down over the blue tops of trees for miles around, then the next minute, they would be in a red depression with the dust-coated trees looking down on them.

"This place had better turn up in a minute," Bailey said, "or I'm going to turn   60
around."

The road looked as if no one had traveled on it in months.

"It's not much farther," the grandmother said and just as she said it, a horrible thought came to her. The thought was so embarrassing that she turned red in the face and her eyes dilated and her feet jumped up, upsetting her valise in the corner. The instant the valise moved, the newspaper top she had over the basket under it rose with a snarl and Pitty Sing, the cat, sprang onto Bailey's shoulder.

The children were thrown to the floor and their mother, clutching the baby, was thrown out the door onto the ground; the old lady was thrown into the front seat. The car turned over once and landed right-side-up in a gulch off the side of the road. Bailey remained in the driver's seat with the cat gray-striped with a broad white face and an orange nose clinging to his neck like a caterpillar.

As soon as the children saw they could move their arms and legs, they scrambled out of the car, shouting, "We've had an ACCIDENT!" The grandmother was curled up under the dashboard, hoping she was injured so that Bailey's wrath would not come down on her all at once. The horrible thought she had had before the accident was that the house she had remembered so vividly was not in Georgia but in Tennessee.

Bailey removed the cat from his neck with both hands and flung it out the window   65
against the side of a pine tree. Then he got out of the car and started looking for the children's mother. She was sitting against the side of the red gutted ditch, holding the screaming baby, but she only had a cut down her face and a broken shoulder. "We've had an ACCIDENT!" the children screamed in a frenzy of delight.

"But nobody's killed," June Star said with disappointment as the grandmother limped out of the car, her hat still pinned to her head but the broken front brim standing up at a jaunty angle and the violet spray hanging off the side. They all sat down in the ditch, except the children, to recover from the shock. They were all shaking.

"Maybe a car will come along," said the children's mother hoarsely.

"I believe I have injured an organ," said the grandmother, pressing her side, but no one answered her. Bailey's teeth were clattering. He had on a yellow sport shirt with bright blue parrots designed in it and his face was as yellow as the shirt. The grandmother decided that she would not mention that the house was in Tennessee.

The road was about ten feet above and they could see only the tops of the trees on the other side of it. Behind the ditch they were sitting in there were more woods, tall and dark and deep. In a few minutes they saw a car some distance away on top of a hill, coming slowly as if the occupants were watching them. The grandmother stood up and waved both arms dramatically to attract their attention. The car continued to come on slowly, disappeared around a bend and appeared again, moving even slower, on top of the hill they had gone over. It was a big black battered hearselike automobile. There were three men in it.

It came to a stop just over them and for some minutes, the driver looked down 70 with a steady expressionless gaze to where they were sitting, and didn't speak. Then he turned his head and muttered something to the other two and they got out. One was a fat boy in black trousers and a red sweat shirt with a silver stallion embossed on the front of it. He moved around on the right side of them and stood staring, his mouth partly open in a kind of loose grin. The other had on khaki pants and a blue striped coat and a gray hat pulled down very low, hiding most of his face. He came around slowly on the left side. Neither spoke.

The driver got out of the car and stood by the side of it, looking down at them. He was an older man than the other two. His hair was just beginning to gray and he wore silver-rimmed spectacles that gave him a scholarly look. He had a long creased face and didn't have on any shirt or undershirt. He had on blue jeans that were too tight for him and was holding a black hat and a gun. The two boys also had guns.

"We've had an ACCIDENT!" the children screamed.

The grandmother had the peculiar feeling that the bespectacled man was someone she knew. His face was as familiar to her as if she had known him all her life but she could not recall who he was. He moved away from the car and began to come down the embankment, placing his feet carefully so that he wouldn't slip. He had on tan and white shoes and no socks, and his ankles were red and thin. "Good afternoon," he said. "I see you all had you a little spill."

"We turned over twice!" said the grandmother.

"Oncet," he corrected. "We seen it happen. Try their car and see will it run, Hiram," 75 he said quietly to the boy with the gray hat.

"What you got that gun for?" John Wesley asked. "Whatcha gonna do with that gun?"

"Lady," the man said to the children's mother, "would you mind calling them children to sit down by you? Children make me nervous. I want all you all to sit down right together there where you're at."

"What are you telling US what to do for?" June Star asked.

Behind them the line of woods gaped like a dark open mouth. "Come here," said their mother.

"Look here now," Bailey began suddenly, "we're in a predicament! We're in . . ." 80

The grandmother shrieked. She scrambled to her feet and stood staring. "You're The Misfit!" she said. "I recognized you at once!"

"Yes'm," the man said, smiling slightly as if he were pleased in spite of himself to be known, "but it would have been better for all of you, lady, if you hadn't of reckernized me."

Bailey turned his head sharply and said something to his mother that shocked even the children. The old lady began to cry and The Misfit reddened.

"Lady," he said, "don't you get upset. Sometimes a man says things he don't mean. I don't reckon he meant to talk to you thataway."

"You wouldn't shoot a lady, would you?" the grandmother said and removed a   85
clean handkerchief from her cuff and began to slap at her eyes with it.

The Misfit pointed the toe of his shoe into the ground and made a little hole and
then covered it up again. "I would hate to have to," he said.

"Listen," the grandmother almost screamed, "I know you're a good man. You don't
look a bit like you have common blood. I know you must come from nice people!"

"Yes ma'm," he said, "finest people in the world." When he smiled he showed a
row of strong white teeth. "God never made a finer woman than my mother and my
daddy's heart was pure gold," he said. The boy with the red sweat shirt had come
around behind them and was standing with his gun at his hip. The Misfit squatted down
on the ground. "Watch them children, Bobby Lee," he said. "You know they make me
nervous." He looked at the six of them huddled together in front of him and he seemed
to be embarrassed as if he couldn't think of anything to say. "Ain't a cloud in the sky,"
he remarked, looking up at it. "Don't see no sun but don't see no cloud neither."

"Yes, it's a beautiful day," said the grandmother. "Listen," she said, "you shouldn't
call yourself The Misfit because I know you're a good man at heart. I can just look at
you and tell."

"Hush!" Bailey yelled. "Hush! Everybody shut up and let me handle this!" He was   90
squatting in the position of a runner about to sprint forward but he didn't move.

"I pre-chate that, lady," The Misfit said and drew a little circle in the ground with the
butt of his gun.

"It'll take a half a hour to fix this here car," Hiram called, looking over the raised
hood of it.

"Well, first you and Bobby Lee get him and that little boy to step over yonder with
you," The Misfit said, pointing to Bailey and John Wesley. "The boys want to ask you
something," he said to Bailey. "Would you mind stepping back in them woods there
with them?"

"Listen," Bailey began, "we're in a terrible predicament! Nobody realizes what this
is," and his voice cracked. His eyes were as blue and intense as the parrots in his shirt
and he remained perfectly still.

The grandmother reached up to adjust her hat brim as if she were going to the   95
woods with him but it came off in her hand. She stood staring at it and after a second
she let it fall on the ground. Hiram pulled Bailey up by the arm as if he were assisting an
old man. John Wesley caught hold of his father's hand and Bobby Lee followed. They
went off toward the woods and just as they reached the dark edge, Bailey turned and
supporting himself against a gray naked pine trunk, he shouted, "I'll be back in a minute, Mamma, wait on me!"

"Come back this instant!" his mother shrilled but they all disappeared into the
woods.

"Bailey Boy!" the grandmother called in a tragic voice but she found she was looking at The Misfit squatting on the ground in front of her. "I just know you're a good man,"
she said desperately. "You're not a bit common!"

"Nome, I ain't a good man," The Misfit said after a second as if he had considered
her statement carefully, "but I ain't the worst in the world neither. My daddy said I was a
different breed of dog from my brothers and sisters. 'You know,' Daddy said, 'it's some
that can live their whole life out without asking about it and it's others has to know why
it is, and this boy is one of the latters. He's going to be into everything!'" He put on his
black hat and looked up suddenly and then away deep into the woods as if he were

embarrassed again. "I'm sorry I don't have on a shirt before you ladies," he said, hunching his shoulders slightly. "We buried our clothes that we had on when we escaped and we're just making do until we can get better. We borrowed these from some folks we met," he explained.

"That's perfectly all right," the grandmother said. "Maybe Bailey has an extra shirt in his suitcase."

"I'll look and see terrectly," The Misfit said.   100

"Where are they taking him?" the children's mother screamed.

"Daddy was a card himself," The Misfit said. "You couldn't put anything over on him. He never got in trouble with the Authorities though. Just had the knack of handling them."

"You could be honest too if you'd only try," said the grandmother. "Think how wonderful it would be to settle down and live a comfortable life and not have to think about somebody chasing you all the time."

The Misfit kept scratching in the ground with the butt of his gun as if he were thinking about it. "Yes'm, somebody is always after you," he murmured.

The grandmother noticed how thin his shoulder blades were just behind his hat 105 because she was standing up looking down on him. "Do you ever pray?" she asked.

He shook his head. All she saw was the black hat wiggle between his shoulder blades. "Nome," he said.

There was a pistol shot from the woods, followed closely by another. Then silence. The old lady's head jerked around. She could hear the wind move through the tree tops like a long satisfied insuck of breath. "Bailey Boy!" she called.

"I was a gospel singer for a while," The Misfit said. "I been most everything. Been in the arm service both land and sea, at home and abroad, been twict married, been an undertaker, been with the railroads, plowed Mother Earth, been in a tornado, seen a man burnt alive onct," and he looked up at the children's mother and the little girl who were sitting close together, their faces white and their eyes glassy; "I even seen a woman flogged," he said.

"Pray, pray," the grandmother began, "pray, pray . . ."

"I never was a bad boy that I remember of," The Misfit said in an almost dreamy 110 voice, "but somewheres along the line I done something wrong and got sent to the penitentiary. I was buried alive," and he looked up and held her attention to him by a steady stare.

"That's when you should have started to pray," she said. "What did you do to get sent to the penitentiary that first time?"

"Turn to the right, it was a wall," The Misfit said, looking up again at the cloudless sky. "Turn to the left, it was a wall. Look up it was a ceiling, look down it was a floor. I forget what I done, lady. I set there and set there, trying to remember what it was I done and I ain't recalled it to this day. Oncet in a while, I would think it was coming to me, but it never come."

"Maybe they put you in by mistake," the old lady said vaguely.

"Nome," he said. "It wasn't no mistake. They had the papers on me."

"You must have stolen something," she said.   115

The Misfit sneered slightly. "Nobody had nothing I wanted," he said. "It was a head-doctor at the penitentiary said what I had done was kill my daddy but I known that for a lie. My daddy died in nineteen ought nineteen of the epidemic flu and I never had a thing to do with it. He was buried in the Mount Hopewell Baptist churchyard and you can go there and see for yourself."

"If you would pray," the old lady said, "Jesus would help you."

"That's right," The Misfit said.

"Well then, why don't you pray?" she asked trembling with delight suddenly.

"I don't want no hep," he said. "I'm doing all right by myself."   120

Bobby Lee and Hiram came ambling back from the woods. Bobby Lee was dragging a yellow shirt with bright blue parrots in it.

"Throw me that shirt, Bobby Lee," The Misfit said. The shirt came flying at him and landed on his shoulder and he put it on. The grandmother couldn't name what the shirt reminded her of. "No, lady," The Misfit said while he was buttoning it up, "I found out the crime don't matter. You can do one thing or you can do another, kill a man or take a tire off his car, because sooner or later you're going to forget what it was you done and just be punished for it."

The children's mother had begun to make heaving noises as if she couldn't get her breath. "Lady," he asked, "would you and that little girl like to step off yonder with Bobby Lee and Hiram and join your husband?"

"Yes, thank you," the mother said faintly. Her left arm dangled helplessly and she was holding the baby, who had gone to sleep, in the other. "Hep that lady up, Hiram," The Misfit said as she struggled to climb out of the ditch, "and Bobby Lee, you hold onto that little girl's hand."

"I don't want to hold hands with him," June Star said. "He reminds me of a pig."   125

The fat boy blushed and laughed and caught her by the arm and pulled her off into the woods after Hiram and her mother.

Alone with The Misfit, the grandmother found that she had lost her voice. There was not a cloud in the sky nor any sun. There was nothing around her but woods. She wanted to tell him that he must pray. She opened and closed her mouth several times before anything came out. Finally she found herself saying, "Jesus. Jesus," meaning, Jesus will help you, but the way she was saying it, it sounded as if she might be cursing.

"Yes'm," The Misfit said as if he agreed. "Jesus thown everything off balance. It was the same case with Him as with me except He hadn't committed any crime and they could prove I had committed one because they had the papers on me. Of course," he said, "they never shown me my papers. That's why I sign myself now. I said long ago, you get you a signature and sign everything you do and keep a copy of it. Then you'll know what you done and you can hold up the crime to the punishment and see do they match and in the end you'll have something to prove you ain't been treated right. I call myself The Misfit," he said, "because I can't make what all I done wrong fit what all I gone through in punishment."

There was a piercing scream from the woods, followed closely by a pistol report. "Does it seem right to you, lady, that one is punished a heap and another ain't punished at all?"

"Jesus!" the old lady cried. "You've got good blood! I know you wouldn't shoot a   130 lady! I know you come from nice people! Pray! Jesus, you ought not to shoot a lady. I'll give you all the money I've got!"

"Lady," The Misfit said, looking beyond her far into the woods, "there never was a body that give the undertaker a tip."

There were two more pistol reports and the grandmother raised her head like a parched old turkey hen crying for water and called, "Bailey Boy, Bailey Boy!" as if her heart would break.

"Jesus was the only One that ever raised the dead," The Misfit continued, "and He shouldn't have done it. He thown everything off balance. If He did what He said, then it's nothing for you to do but throw away everything and follow Him, and if He didn't, then it's nothing for you to do but enjoy the few minutes you got left the best way you can by killing somebody or burning down his house or doing some other meanness to him. No pleasure but meanness," he said and his voice had become almost a snarl.

"Maybe He didn't raise the dead," the old lady mumbled, not knowing what she was saying and feeling so dizzy that she sank down in the ditch with her legs twisted under her.

"I wasn't there so I can't say He didn't," The Misfit said. "I wisht I had of been there," 135 he said, hitting the ground with his fist. "It ain't right I wasn't there because if I had of been there I would of known. Listen lady," he said in a high voice, "if I had of been there I would of known and I wouldn't be like I am now." His voice seemed about to crack and the grandmother's head cleared for an instant. She saw the man's face twisted close to her own as if he were going to cry and she murmured, "Why you're one of my babies. You're one of my own children!" She reached out and touched him on the shoulder. The Misfit sprang back as if a snake had bitten him and shot her three times through the chest. Then he put his gun down on the ground and took off his glasses and began to clean them.

Hiram and Bobby Lee returned from the woods and stood over the ditch, looking down at the grandmother who half sat and half lay in a puddle of blood with her legs crossed under her like a child's and her face smiling up at the cloudless sky.

Without his glasses, The Misfit's eyes were red-rimmed and pale and defenseless-looking. "Take her off and thow her where you thown the others," he said, picking up the cat that was rubbing itself against his leg.

"She was a talker, wasn't she?" Bobby Lee said, sliding down the ditch with a yodel.

"She would of been a good woman," The Misfit said, "if it had been somebody there to shoot her every minute of her life."

"Some fun!" Bobby Lee said. 140

"Shut up, Bobby Lee," The Misfit said. "It's no real pleasure in life."

Source: O'Connor, Flannery: "A Good Man is Hard to Find" from A GOOD MAN IS HARD TO FIND AND OTHER STORIES by Flannery O'Connor. Copyright © 1953 by Flannery O'Connor. Reprinted by permission of Houghton Mifflin Harcourt Publishing Company. All rights reserved.

Critical Thinking Topics

1. Look back at The Tower scene and consider the role of the monkey (par. 28 and 44). Other than providing scenic detail, what symbolic meanings does the monkey suggest?

2. The short story's title appears in paragraph 43, when Red Sammy opines, "A good man is hard to find." Towards the end of the story, the title, in part, is echoed as the grandmother attempts to convince The Misfit that he is "a good man": "I know you're a good man" (par. 87). Examine and explain the implications of the title, as the story progresses. Do you think the grandmother believes that The Misfit is a good man? Why or why not? How do you think the grandmother defines "a good man"?

3. What does The Misfit mean at the end of the story when he says that the grandmother would have been a good woman if someone could have been there to shoot her every day? What happened between those two characters at the end?

Look closely at the last exchange between The Misfit and the grandmother (par. 127 and following). Do you think the grandmother has experienced a flash of insight? If so, what might it be? Had she, as The Misfit suggests, become "a good woman"? How do you think The Misfit defines "a good woman"?

Writing Topic

The Misfit says that his father died of the flu, but he also states that he was imprisoned for murdering his father. Is it possible that he was wrongfully imprisoned? Could his jail time have turned him into a "misfit"? Explain why or why not.

7.8 Brady Udall, He Becomes Deeply and Famously Drunk (1997)

I am a cowboy. There are others in this outfit who prefer to call themselves ranch hands or just "hands," maybe they think *cowboy* is a little too flamboyant for this day and age, who knows, but shit, I herd cows, I vaccinate, brand, dehorn and castrate cows, more often than not I smell exactly like a cow—I am a cowboy. I've been at this for nine months now and I figure I've earned the right to call myself whatever in God's name I please.

I am two months shy of eighteen years old, I'm covered with freckles and am quite good-looking if I can believe what the girls tell me. I am also a natural loudmouth which has caused me no end of grief and misery. Pretty much all my life I've been hearing the same thing: take it easy, Archie, put a lid on it Archie, pipe the hell down. You hear this enough it gets on your nerves.

One of the good things about this kind of work: I can really let loose, talking and shouting and singing—at the top of my lungs if I want to and out in the brush there's no one to give a hooey but the cows. Something about my voice scares the cows, some of them are terrified of me, I swear it, when they hear me they get this rolling wild look in their eyes and start to running and climbing all over each other. My horse, Loaf, gets annoyed by all my talking and singing and every once in awhile she'll reach back and bite the hell out of my leg. I don't mind, I just hit her back, a good sock on the side of the head, and she won't try anything like that again for at least a couple weeks.

Before I came to work here I had this idea that A & C Ranch would be this big beautiful spread, full of rivers and green rolling hills, like that TV show Big Valley. I imagined myself as Heath Barkley, riding around on a shiny roan, wearing a vest and a silk scarf, smoking a long cigarillo and shooting bad guys lurking in the bushes. The actual ranch, I was sorry to learn, is plain and relatively small: fifteen hundred acres of overgrazed scrub land that can't support more than two hundred head at any one time. Mr. Platt, who is richer and more of a recluse than God, has his thousand-head herd spread out all over the place, on at least fourteen other pieces of land between here and the Navajo reservation, most of it government-owned. The sad truth is we spend more time zipping around in our pickup trucks than we do on our good and noble horses.

Today, for instance, we've got to go up around Sell's Pasture, a good forty-five minute drive, to fix a busted windmill, a rickety fifty-footer that is a horror to climb. Of course it will be me, the new guy, climbing to the top of the damn thing, risking my neck and reputation. It's about five in the morning and I'm in the shower, singing the jingles to every TV commercial I can think of. Richard bangs on the bathroom door and shouts, "Archie, keep it down in there! Got-damn!"

This is exactly what I'm talking about. I can't even take a shower without somebody having an opinion about it. Richard is one of the hands, he and I share a trailer out here on the ranch. He is the oldest of us, the veteran, and apparently his job is to keep an eye on me. Richard is short and middle-aged and one of these days I'm going to pick up his scrawny little body and break it over my knee if he is not careful. This morning Richard woke me up at five a.m. the way he does every morning, by shouting right in my ear, Come to, you candy corn son of a bitch! He learned this particular wake-up call in the Army and inflicts it on me each and every day. This kind of thing makes Richard feel like the big enchilada, so I let him get away with it.

I yodel about six more jingles and then towel off and walk into the kitchen for a piece of toast, and Ted, the foreman, is there explaining to Richard how he wants to do things today. Ted lives in the old ranch house up on the hill with his wife and little girl. He had some serious childhood ailment and now he's got a lumpy oversized head and hearing aids strapped to his big loose ears.

"Change of plans," Ted says to me. "I'm taking Richard with me to help bring in the heifers from Copper Springs. I want you to pick up Jesus and get that windmill fixed. Take your time and fix it right. Take all day if you have to."

"And put some pants on," Richard says. Richard absolutely hates my guts because I am bigger, younger, handsomer, and a hell of a lot smarter than he is.

I lift up the towel and show him my bare butt: one of the attributes women enjoy most about me. I sing a line from "Moon Over Georgia" in a girlish falsetto and do a few softshoe shuffles on the kitchen linoleum. 10

Richard just sits there, red-faced, shoveling plain oatmeal into his mouth, unable to come up with anything to say. He is one of these literal types who simply cannot comprehend sarcasm or humor of any sort. He reaches over and grabs the Volume A encyclopedia from the kitchen counter and begins studying it, his nose inches from the page. About six months ago Richard decided that he was going to get himself educated. Instead of wasting all that time and money on a college education, he decided to read the 'entire Encyclopedia Brittanica, the whole blasted thing, from A to Z.

Richard is terribly proud of himself for coming up with a way to become a genius and a scholar for only $99.95 in twelve easy monthly installments. Problem is, it's been over half a year now and Richard is only about a third of the way through the first volume. He is now an authority on aardvarks, acupuncture, and John Adams, but he'll be collecting social security before he could tell you what a zygote is.

I go back to the laundry room and take Doug off his perch. He acts happy to see me, bobs his head and hunches his shoulders. I get a piece of dog kibble from a bag in the cupboard and he snatches it out of my hand so quick you'd think he's dying of starvation.

Doug is an eight year-old male turkey vulture. Because he doesn't get much exercise, he's a little overweight, but he is a good bird, and I've become attached to him; some nights when he has trouble sleeping, I'll take him to bed with me and hold him against my chest until he gets drowsy enough to go to sleep perched on my bedpost. He used to belong to one R. L. Ledbetter, who worked for Mr. Platt and lived in this trailer with Richard until one early morning a couple of years ago when R.L. got run over by a garbage truck crossing the road. R.L. had worked for a few years as a rodeo clown and used Doug (short for Douglas Fairbanks) in one of his acts. In this rodeo act, R.L. would act like he got shot by a villain, and Doug would come flying in out of nowhere, land on his chest and start picking at him. R.L. trained Doug to do this by hiding a Corn Nut somewhere on his person and Doug would go picking around until he found it, R.L. squirming and cringing whenever Doug got too near his crotch. Apparently rodeo crowds found this hilarious.

Even though Richard doesn't enjoy Doug's company all that much, he is convinced 15 he can teach Doug to talk. Sometimes I'll come home and find Richard at the kitchen table, with Doug perched on the back of a chair and Richard saying something like, "Come on, Doug, say 'bazooka.' Ba-zoo-ka." And Doug sitting there mum as a fence post, watching barn swallows buzzing past the window. Richard says he read somewhere that vultures have the same vocal apparatus as parrots, and with enough persistence he thinks Doug could become a talking vulture. So far, Doug hasn't said a word.

I go back into my room where I put on jeans, a T-shirt—it's going to be a hot son of a bitch out there today—and a pair of workboots. I have to wear these run-of-the-mill clodhoppers because I've yet to find a pair of cowboy boots that will fit my splayed feet. When I go outside and fire up the old Ford the sun is just coming up and long shadows stretch out under the sage and creosote. I let the engine run for a minute, then I lay on the accelerator like Richard Petty in his prime, spraying dust and gravel everywhere, and head out on Witchicume Road, on my way to pick up Jesus.

I came out to the A & C to get my life turned around. My mother made the arrangements, did all the sweet-talking to get me out here and her theory goes something like this: you take your loudmouth juvenile delinquent with bad table manners, stick him out in the middle of nowhere, bust his balls with honest hard labor, and maybe, just maybe, he will turn out to be the upstanding citizen you hoped for all along. I'm pretty certain the folks out here weren't all that hot to hire a city kid with no ranch experience and a history with the law, but Ted was an old acquaintance of my father, and finally he gave in.

The truth is I've always wanted to come back, always harbored secret desires about strapping on the chaps and riding fences. I was born only forty miles from here, in Holbrook, and I lived on the ranch the first four and a half years of my life until my father was killed and my mother took me to live in Stillwater, Oklahoma, her hometown. My father was the ranch foreman and we lived in the old house where Ted and his family live now. Even though I can't remember anything at all about living here, I did some work on this ranch, in my own way, all those years ago. My mother told me that the winter I turned four, my father would take me out on the feed runs, put the old International into compound and let me steer, kneeling on the seat, while he stood in the back, breaking bales and pitching hay to the cows standing in the snow.

In Oklahoma I spent my energy talking too much, getting into fights, drinking booze, smashing mailboxes, pretty much being obnoxious however and wherever I could. I have something wrong with me, something bad inside that builds up until I have to let it out by talking, shouting, raging, letting it all loose, even if there is no one there to listen. (I even thrash and holler in my sleep sometimes—one more thing Richard holds against me.) But there are times when the only way I can get back to feeling normal again is by beating the shit out of someone who may not even deserve it, or by destroying something, it doesn't really matter what. When I feel this way, I get to punching or smashing or kicking and I can feel this blackness pouring out of me and I just keep going, it's a great feeling, just letting go, flailing away, until I feel empty and clean again. I've hurt some people and wrecked a lot of perfectly innocent cars, dishware, phone booths, electronic goods, what have you. Even though a lot of my teachers called me gifted (over and over again: unlimited potential! a diamond in the rough!), I never finished high school because they finally kicked me out once and for all. I've been arrested for battery, disorderly conduct, theft, vandalism, disturbing the peace, assaulting a police officer. I've been on probation since I was eleven years old.

I've seen therapists, psychiatrists, clergymen, even a hypnotist. My mother had   20 high hopes for the hypnotist, but for some reason in my second session with the poor old guy I came out of my trance and sucker-punched him a good one right in the face. I don't remember doing it, only remember waking up and seeing him sitting on the carpet, his nose spattered on his face like a piece of rotten watermelon.

I have a probation officer, Ms. Condley, who calls Ted every week to make sure I haven't busted anyone's lip or committed an act of debauchery. Ms. Condley calls me every week, too, and asks me about my feelings, about my dreams and aspirations, it's all very sensitive, but she never says goodbye without reminding me that if I break my probation, if I slip up even a little, get even a little drunk or involve myself in some minor fisticuffs, I'll be sent off to boot camp and won't get out till I'm twenty-nine. So far I have been able to keep my ass clean. My only serious difficulty is keeping myself from beating the day-lights out of Richard.

A few weeks before I moved back out here I went to the public library and stole the only book I could find on cowboys. I wanted to get some general how-to information (how to put on a saddle, how to make a lasso, how to mount a horse) so that when I got here I wouldn't look like a complete fool. The book didn't give tips or anything like that, it was just a lot of quaint old bullshit about the cowboys of yore. I read the whole thing anyway. Under a pen and ink drawing of a couple of dirty cowpunchers weaving down Main Street, arm in arm, clutching half-empty whiskey bottles, was this caption:

After a mythic cattle drive or a bone-wearying spring roundup, the cowboy, looking for release and diversion, commonly finds his way to the nearest saloon where he becomes deeply and famously drunk.

I remember this because it describes to a T my father and the way he died. Like the cowboys in the picture, he liked to celebrate after a big job by getting himself good and hammered. It was his only vice and the one thing my mother could not stand about him. The day he died, they had finished getting the herd down off the mountain for the winter (nearly a two-week job) and he went into town to throw a few down with his crew at the Sure Seldom. He was two solid hours into his drinking when Calfred Pulsipher, a piece-of-shit well-digger with a lazy eyeball, came around to pick a fight. Calfred and my father had been good friends in their younger years, but Calfred had carried a grudge against my father ever since he lost his starting quarterback job to him on the Salado Wildcats eight-man football team. Apparently, Calfred said some terrible things about my mother, right there in front of my father's crew—sick, perverted things—and finally my father invited Calfred outside to settle it. Calfred went outside first and in the thirty seconds or so it took my drunk father to find the door, Calfred had time to pick up an industrial jack from the back of his pickup. When my father stepped out into the cold night air, ready to whip Calfred's sorry ass and be done with it, Calfred brought down the jack full force, right on top of his head. My father went down, stayed face down in the gravel for a minute or so, dead still, and suddenly got up punching with everything he had, as if the blow not only sobered him up but also lit a fire under his ass. He got some fine licks in on Calfred before one of the sheriff's deputies came and arrested them both.

Even though my father's head had stopped bleeding, the sheriff wanted to call the   25
ambulance in from Round Valley (there was no doctor in Salado in those days) but my
father kept assuring everyone he was feeling fine, all he needed was a few more drinks
to get rid of the headache he was having. In the end, the sheriff stuck them both in the
same jail cell to sleep off their drunk. Some time that night in that puke-smelling cell full
of drunks and no-goods and bums, my father died of bleeding in the brain, his head
resting on the lap of Calfred Pulsipher, the man who killed him.

Out here in Arizona, Jesus is my only real friend. He is a tiny wetback, barely five feet
tall with his boots on and even though he's lived on American soil for over two decades
his English is as piss-poor as if he showed up here last Christmas. He has star-quality
teeth and likes to keep his hair coifed and oiled with one curl hanging down on his forehead in the manner of old time movie actors. He's worked for Mr. Platt off and on for a
good many years and while the others here resented me, pissed on me for being young
and ignorant, enjoyed watching me make a fool of myself, Jesus helped me out from the
start, taking time to show how to dally a rope, say, or throw a calf for branding.

Right now Jesus is explaining, in his own way, why he doesn't like people calling him a Mexican. He doesn't consider himself a Mexican at all, he says, because he
is actually a full-blooded Yaqui Indian and very proud of it, a direct descendant of the
Aztecs, who were, according to him, the most proud and powerful nation the world
ever saw. And who, according to him, had it not been for malaria, typhoid and other
white-man plagues, would have kicked some Spaniard ass.

"I'm not eh-Spanish," he says, thumping his chest like a little brown Tarzan. "I'm
Yaqui."

"It's not *eh*-Spanish," I say. "That's not how you say it. You got to get your S's right.
She sells seashells by the sea shore. Okay, I'm going to say a word and you repeat.
Snoopy."

"Eh-Snoopy," Jesus says.   30

"Sssssnoopy," I say.

"Ehhhhh-snoopy," Jesus says.

"Ah shit," I say.

"Ah shit," says Jesus, proud of himself for making such great advancement in the
language.

The guy truly is hopeless. Since he has done so much for me, I figured the least I   35
could do was help him polish his English, but now, after nine months of correcting his
pronunciation and word order, he hasn't improved a bit.

"Why don't you want to be an American?" I say. "All you have to do is get your
green card, you've lived here long enough. Then you won't have to run from the border
patrol any more."

"American?" Jesus says, a look of disgust twisting his wide brown face. "America-
nos fat pigs, you know, honk honk."

"I'm fat, is that what you're saying?"

Jesus lifts up my T-shirt to have a look. He nods gravely. "Maybe," he says.

We stop for gas and coffee at Sud Baker's, a little eatery/truck stop. Once we've   40
finished off our eggs and sausage, and with Jesus taking forever in the john, I pick up a
loose copy of the local paper, The Apache County Sentinel, and there, right on the front
page is that son of a bitch Calfred Pulsipher himself. It looks like an old wedding picture:
Calfred's got these ridiculous lambchop sideburns and a thick polyester tie and one of

his eyes, his left one, seems to be looking at the mole on his forehead while the other is pointed straight ahead. A fat woman, Calfred's wife, I guess, is sitting next to him, all dressed up. Underneath the picture it reads, *The Pulsipher children would like to congratulate Calfred and Erma on the occasion of their twenty-fifth wedding anniversary.*

A trembling starts in my stomach and moves out to my arms and hands. When I first got here I tried to look up Calfred's name in the phone book and when I couldn't find it, I convinced myself that he was dead or had moved away to Alaska. I thought I wouldn't have to worry about him anymore.

A secret: since I was five years old I have been a murderer in my heart. I've tortured, mutilated, torn, skewered, beaten, killed Calfred Pulsipher ten thousand times over. I've burned his house down, kidnapped his children, cut the head off his dog. I've dreamed, time and again, about being there that night at the Sure Seldom. In my dreams I've stopped him from killing my father in various ways, perforating him with an ice pick, shotgunning him in the gut, beating him bloody with a chain. I even made plans, back when I was twelve or thirteen and crazed with puberty, for stealing a car and a big-ass case of dynamite and coming all the way out here and blowing him into the outer reaches of space.

Growing up, I used to read a lot, mostly Zane Grey and Louis L'Amour, and in those books if someone killed a member of your family or a even a friend, it was pretty much your duty to pay the son of a bitch back. It's what anyone who had any courage or sense of justice did; it's what cowboys did. It's what my father would have done.

My father's name was Quinn. He was a big man with a barrel chest, curly red hair, a missing front tooth—everybody loved him. He lost the tooth to the back hoof of an Appaloosa gelding and he never got it fixed because he thought the hole in his face made him look friendlier. He was an excellent golfer (ten handicap), liked old blues music, and had a deep-seated fear of bees. Although I was a kid, not much more than a toddler when he died, I know all kinds of things—facts, stories, anecdotes—about him. After my mother took me away to Stillwater, friends would call or sometimes stop in and they'd tell me things my father used to do, the kind of man he was. I remember a few of the visitors, usually it would be a man in Wranglers, alone, or maybe with a frizzy-haired woman with big earrings, and always they'd say things like, *Oh my God, he looks just like Quinn, doesn't he?* Or, *Listen there, he's even got Quinn's voice.* And without fail my mother would break down and have to leave the room.

My mother, I think, went certifiably crazy during the year after my father's death. Nobody really knows about this except me, because I was the only one who got to witness all the lunatic things she did. One of my clearest memories is of my mother, just a few days after we'd moved to Stillwater, running outside in only her underwear as a stranger's car pulled up to the curb, hysterical and shouting, "I knew he'd come back, oh my God, you're back! Look Archie, Daddy's home!" Or the time she ripped through the house, clearing out cupboards and cabinets, trashing the attic, sure my father was there because she could smell his English Leather cologne.

Finally, she went to see a doctor who introduced her to the wonderful world of pills. It's a world she's been living in ever since.

Now, out here on the ranch, I'm always finding reminders of him. A few weeks ago, I was down near the mud pond just south of the big house, mending fence with Richard when I found the letter Q carved deep into one of the anchor posts near the dam. It's kind of a tradition out here for the person that builds a fence to carve his initial into the final anchor post and I knew without a doubt it was my father that had done it. I imagined him there in the very spot I was standing, his shirt off, his big round shoulders covered with sweat, making cracks with his crew and grinning that gap-toothed grin while he cut his first initial into the thick cedar post with a buck knife.

By the time Jesus and I get to Sell's Pasture it is already upwards of ninety degrees and with the white sun burning into everything it feels like we're moving across the surface of Venus. After we pull off the highway, I have to guide the truck over three or four miles of a rutted two-track, me and Jesus bouncing all over the seat, the stiff sagebrush on the truck's underside like fingernails on a chalkboard. On our way over to the windmill Jesus notices a bad case of pinkeye on a Hereford calf. By the time he's got the medicine kit from the glove compartment, run the calf down on foot, lassoed it, thrown it to the ground and begun to doctor the eye, all the time keeping one eye on the calf's very pissed-off mother, I've climbed the ladder up to the platform and am doing my best to dismantle the windmill head and see what the problem is.

The windmill stopped working only a few days ago, so the galvanized holding tank is still half full of algae-green water and a few mangy cows are hanging around to check out what's going on. They don't have anything better to do, blinking those big dull eyes. I'll tell you one thing about cows: they're dumb-asses. They're so dumb it's hard to understand how stupid they really are.

Once in awhile I'll look down and see a metallic flash in the green water—huge shaggy   50
goldfish and carp they put in the tanks to keep the algae down. These things grow to be as big as poodles and they swim around flapping their tails like they own the tank.

About a hundred yards away, over next to a juniper tree, Jesus struggles to keep the bawling calf down while performing the delicate work of injecting medicine directly into its eyeball with a syringe. I shout encouragements from up on my perch and Jesus grunts and hisses and calls the calf a bigtime donkey turd. By the time he's done he's sweating, covered with dust, the calf has crapped green pudding all over his pearl-buttoned shirt and what's worse, it's not even ten o'clock in the morning. He walks up to the holding tank, slings his hat like a Frisbee, sheds the rest of his clothes and steps in, the thick water closing around him. He slides down so that his head is just above water, still as a turtle on a rock.

I am banging away with my Vise-Grips at a stuck bolt, trying to loosen it, when I miss the bolt completely. My momentum throws me off balance, the whole windmill shifting underneath me, and I slip sideways off the side of the platform. I grab one of the supports to keep myself from falling, but my legs are dangling out from under me and with my White Mule work gloves on I can't get a good grip on the smooth, two-inch pipe. My hands begin to slide and my stomach curls up on itself and I look down past my feet and try to figure out the best way to fall without snapping my spine. Below me, Jesus leaps out of the tank, naked as a newborn, the huge fish writhing and bucking in the swampy water, and begins scrambling up the metal scaffolding, his wet hands and feet causing him to slip and flail and clutch.

I start bellowing, a loud panicked sound like a heifer giving birth, which causes all the cows in sight to spook and set off sprinting for the safety of the trees. Somehow I hold out, yelling the whole time, until Jesus reaches the platform from the other side and grabs my belt and with the strength of a man twice his size hauls me up.

I lie on my back for a minute staring at the blank sky and listening to my heart thumping so hard it sounds like bones are popping in my chest. Above me Jesus is standing there all goose-pimply with this huge grin on his face, as if my near-death experience has made his day. He keeps shaking his head; he just can't get over it. "Arshie hanging, feet kicking, help, help!" Jesus says, pantomiming the whole incident. "Arshie shouting like woman, ooooooha!, every cow runs away."

I get up and try to grab him but he ducks out of the way and cowers at the corner of the platform, mocking me, covering his head with his hands. "Big fat Americano scaring me. Oh boy," he says.

I stop going after him; I'm still a little nervous about one of us falling off this thing, and then I notice that Jesus has the biggest pecker I've ever seen. I get a good look at it and there's no doubt — I've been in a lot of locker rooms and seen quite a few, but this one takes the cake.

"That's a considerable pecker you've got there," I tell him, keeping a good grip on one of the supports.

He looks down at it, lifts it up with his hand like it's a vegetable he's considering purchasing at the supermarket. "Oh mama," he says.

He picks up the Vise-Grips, goes right to work on the stuck bolt, and starts lamenting that his wife took his kids to visit relatives down in Mexico and it's been two long weeks since his *pendejo* saw any action. He begins to croon some mournful Sonoran ballad, using the Vise-Grips like a microphone, and for some reason it seems perfectly appropriate that he is nude and fifty feet in the air.

We get the head dismantled and find that the windmill needs nothing more than new suction leathers. In no time at all we've got the thing fixed, put back together, and I've joined Jesus down in the cow tank.

The inside of the tank is as slimy as frog innards and the huge fish curl around my stomach and legs and I still haven't decided whether the whole sensation is disgusting or kind of pleasant. We sit there for awhile and even though the windmill has been fixed, there is no wind to speak of and the big fan is completely still and useless as before. This kind of silence drives me crazy and I bear it for as long as I can until I ask the question I've been waiting to ask somebody for nine months: "You know who Calfred Pulsipher is?"

Jesus, who appeared to be falling asleep, sits up and looks right at me, but he only shrugs and mumbles something I can't understand.

"What?" I say.

"Nada, nada," he says.

"Do you know him?"

"Pool-see-fur," Jesus says, rolling the word across his tongue. I don't mind Jesus screwing around with me but sometimes he drives me nuts.

"Come on, you Mexican," I say. "Does he live around here?"

"Oh, he live around somewhere."

"Where?"

Now he's giving me that sly half grin that Latin males everywhere are famous for. "Why you want to know?"

Since I've been here I haven't talked about Calfred Pulsipher or my father with anyone and now that I have, it feels like I've betrayed myself in some way. Even though I'm pretty sure everybody on the ranch knows my situation, not one of them has ever mentioned it, and that's the way I like it.

We look at each other across the tank, Jesus waiting for an answer and me not ready to give it.

Finally a mangy Hereford, either a very brave or a very stupid one, comes strolling right up to the tank to have a drink. Jesus hollers at the cow, calling it some of the most vile words in the English language and his pronunciation is absolutely perfect.

I didn't believe I could actually *enjoy* ranch work. I've heard some of the hands complain about certain kinds of work, mostly jobs that require getting down out of the saddle, but I pretty much love it all: branding, clearing ditches, building fence, irrigating. I love hauling hay, throwing those bales around as if they have *offended* me. I don't even mind getting up before the crack of dawn, even if I have to do it with Richard the army general barking in my ear. I like the way the world feels empty at that time of day; it seems as if you are the only one alive, early in the morning when you're up before everybody else and you can step out into the low light with your cup of coffee and hear a horse chewing grass from two hundred yards away.

Every day you get something new thrown at you; I mean, one thing I've never 75 been around here is bored. You work all day, so busy sweating and busting your ass that you don't even have time to think; you go and go and go until you look up and notice the sun is nearly down and it's time to pack it in. There's nothing as nice as that ride home; the truck rumbling loosey-goosey down the road with a mind of its own, the radio hissing out Mexican trumpets, that sweet aching tiredness settling deep in your joints. You go home and fix yourself some dinner and even though it's nothing more than chili out of a can and a tube of instant biscuits it's the best damned meal you've ever had.

The only thing that will ruin a day like this is getting a call from my mother. My mother calls once or twice a week to make sure I'm caught up on all her problems. A few days ago she called me just as we were getting in from a day of calving out heifers to tell me that she had broken up with her boyfriend.

"Archie?" she said. "Archie? Are you there, honey?" Her voice was as highpitched as a train whistle.

"I'm right here," I said.

Suddenly she began to weep and I knew immediately that she had taken too many of one pill or had mixed some up that weren't supposed to be mixed. She was speaking in that hysterical little-girl voice that I remember hearing so much after my father was killed.

"He left me, Arch, he's gone." She was practically shrieking. I didn't know who the 80 hell she was talking about. I was able to piece together that her current boyfriend, a hot tub salesman named Chet, had decided to go back to his ex-wife in Florida. I told her I was sure she'd be able to find another boyfriend in a day or two.

"I miss you honey," she cried. "I want to see you. You're the only one left."

A number of times she's called me, trying to get me to come home, even though she herself is the one that did what was necessary to get me out here. One particularly bad night a couple of months ago she accused me of abandoning her, just as my father had done. Every time I talk to her it breaks the spell; I'm not Archie the cowboy anymore, but Archie the delinquent with his afflicted mother and dead father, with all his crimes against society. Honest, it makes me feel like crap.

Good thing that's a feeling that doesn't last long. I can hang up the phone, go to bed, sleep like a dead man, give Richard a hundred-watt smile when he rousts me out of bed, ready to get out on the open range and make those cows pay.

I've just come into town from shoveling about three tons of cowshit out at the loading corrals and now I'm here in a bar called Whirly Burly's (the guy at the door didn't card me; because of my six-four frame and five-o'clock shadow I haven't been carded since I was fourteen). I've decided to go through with it, I won't wait any longer: I'm going to locate Calfred Pulsipher and let him have it. I figured the natural place to look for him would be a bar; the man was a full-time drunk and I doubt he's changed his ways. But, I have to admit, this doesn't seem the kind of place you'd find somebody like Calfred Pulsipher, full as it is with a bunch of yahoos dressed up like they're waiting to audition for *Oklahoma!*

As I search the crowd, looking for something like the face I saw in the paper, I have   85
this heavy, sick feeling in my gut. What if I do see him? What am I going to do? I've thought a lot about this, especially in the past few days, I've gone over and over it in my mind. My plan is simple and just: I'll do it to him the way he did it to my father: I'll pick a fight. I will *make* him fight me. The only difference is I won't need to use a forty-pound jack to finish him off.

But what about afterwards? Don't think I haven't considered that. Calfred Pulsipher killed my father and wasn't even given a trial. An autopsy was done and they said they could not infallibly trace the bleeding to any of the blows he received. Small town, bogus bullshit. My mother kept all the newspaper clippings and they tell the whole story; the way they saw it, two good old boys got drunk, had a bit of a scuffle, and one of them had the misfortune of getting killed. Sending somebody to jail wouldn't make anything better, would it? Why make a bad situation worse?

Just thinking about it makes my blood go lava-hot and I want to grab the chair I'm in and start smashing things and people. Even if I get thrown in the clink, even if they send me there forever, I've got to go through with it. I owe it to my father. I owe it to my mother and to myself. It's the one thing I want to get right in this fucked-up life of mine.

I sip my Dr. Pepper and watch people pushing through the big swinging wooden doors and each time I get this needle-jab of dread in my chest, thinking it might be him, but it's only these assholes in their creased blue jeans. Honest, I'd like to line them up and whale the shit out of them, one by one, just for practice. And this music they all listen to. I may like the cowboy life but nobody says I have to listen to their music.

Everyone starts clearing chairs and lining up to do these ridiculous syncopated honky-tonk dance steps. Even though I smell like the end of civilization and I'm not wearing Tony Lamas and a shiny belt buckle the size of a dessert plate, a few of these swivel-hipped cowgirls with moisture in their cleavages come up and ask me to dance. I put on my best smile and politely decline; I have a lot on my mind.

I sit there and watch the clumps of young men crowded together, slamming beers   90
and cat-calling the women, and for the first time since I've been in Arizona I feel lonely and a little homesick, sitting here by myself in a bar roaring with people having a good time.

Before going home I hit the remaining bars in Salado, all four of them, but there is not a sign of Calfred Pulsipher. When I drag my ass back to the trailer it's nearly one a.m. and I can see through the window that Richard, clad in camouflage-style long johns, has fallen asleep in his recliner with the Volume A encyclopedia nestled in his groin. I know he is waiting up for me; he wants to be the one to catch me when I slip up.

I'm tired but I don't feel like dealing with Richard, so I take a walk up the hill toward the ranch house. Though I hadn't meant to, I end up standing on the front lawn of the house, looking up at the dark windows, thinking: I used to live in this house. It is white, two-storied and has a wide covered porch with a built-in swinging love seat. In the nine months I've been here I've never stepped foot in this house, never really had any desire to, until now.

I walk around the place a couple of times, tripping over a Big Wheel, nearly falling into one of those plastic baby-pools, and finally I decide—what can it hurt?—to take a look inside. The only first-floor window I can find that doesn't have the shades drawn is back behind a thick mass of bushes. I use a breast-stroke swimming motion to claw my way in and find myself looking into what is probably the family room: pictures on the wall, a cowhide couch, a grandfather clock, a collection of old Coca-Cola bottles on the mantel. Everything is dark and shadowed, but I try to imagine what the room would look like in the light of day, what my mother—a young, pretty version—might have looked like sitting on the couch, or my father over in the corner, winding the clock.

I strain, I try, but nothing; I can't seem to jog a single memory. Then, just as I'm pulling myself out of the bushes, I hear something behind me and there's Ted in nothing but boxer shorts and unlaced running shoes holding a .22 pistol. His legs and chest are the color of mayonnaise.

"Hey," he says, squinting. He's not wearing his glasses and I can tell he doesn't   95 know who I am—I think about making a break for it. Finally, I whisper, "Ted, it's Archie."

Ted fiddles with one of his hearing aids and says, "Archie?"

"Couldn't sleep," I say. "I'm out for a walk."

"Is there something wrong?" Ted says. "Something you need to talk about?"

I think of the questions I would love to ask Ted: *What was my father like when you knew him? Do we really have the same looks, the same way of talking? When you moved into the house did it smell like English Leather?* But I keep my mouth shut.

Ted looks at me for a minute, as if he's trying to make some kind of decision, and   100 then he says, "That Miss Condley woman called tonight. She tried calling over to your place but you weren't there all night. She was pretty upset."

"Shit," I say. I'd completely forgotten it was Tuesday, the day Ms. Condley calls every week.

"Five o'clock's a bitch, Archie," Ted says, turning around to go inside. "I'd get to bed if I was you."

On my way to the trailer a wave of exhaustion hits me and I can barely put one foot in front of the other. Careful not to wake Richard, I check in on Doug who is pacing the floor of the laundry room like an expectant father, back and forth, back and forth, no doubt full of worries of his own—an insomniac if there ever was one. I pick him up and take him to bed with me. I lie under the covers and hold him tight against my chest— this kind of pressure calms him for some reason—and pretty soon he's making this gurgling noise in the back of his throat, almost like the purring of a cat. When he's good and relaxed I put him up on the bedpost where he hunkers right down and nods off. Crazy as it sounds, it comforts me to have him there, above me in the dark while I sleep.

Instead of lounging on the couch watching Cheers after work, I'm driving hellbent-for-leather in a lavender Oldsmobile packed with illegal aliens. My blood is hopped up with adrenaline and I'm doing well over seventy with an old Mexican woman asleep in my lap.

This all started last night after surveying the bars and my little run-in with Ted. I   105 barely got to sleep and the next thing I knew there was Jesus, right in my bedroom, tugging on my big toe. "Arshie," he whispered. "Wake it up."

I could tell right away something was the matter; instead of that what-the-hell grin he always wears, his face was pinched and worried. And what's more, he'd once vowed never to step foot in a residence which housed a "big dirty-shit buzzard," as he put it. But here he was.

He jabbered in a mixture of English and Spanish and finally I got the gist of the problem; his family was stuck at the border. Jesus' wife and kids go down to visit family once or twice a year and they've always had someone, a contact, who would arrange for them to get across the border, bribe the right people, and drive them up to Salado. Now apparently, that contact had disappeared and the family was waiting at the border down near Nogales; Jesus had made arrangements for them to get across but there was nobody to pick them up. Jesus himself couldn't risk going; not only did he not have a driver's license (if he was stopped on the highway he'd end up on the other side of the border, too), he was supposed to go with Ted to the livestock auction in Albuquerque.

He pulled a fist-sized wad of money out of his pocket. "I pay big cash."

I pushed the wad away and told him he was insulting me with his money. What was a favor between friends? Jesus eyed me like he thought I was crazy, then began outlining what he wanted me to do.

My work today involved digging out several cattle guards and I worked like a man 110 on fire to get done early. I finished by four o'clock, drove the Ford home, and there was the '72 Oldsmobile sitting out in front of the trailer just as Jesus said it would be. He had borrowed the car from his Aunt Lourdes, and I figured it would be an inconspicuous looking vehicle, but this one looked like a pimp/drug pusher special. The damn thing was about as long as your average school bus and *purple.*

It drove like a champ, though. It's a four-hour drive down to Nogales but I made it in just under three, the huge rosary on the rearview mirror clacking against the windshield the whole way. By the time I got there it was just getting dark and starting to drizzle. I had no trouble finding the spot Jesus described to me; about eight miles west of Nogales a small utility road runs parallel to the twelve-foot border fence, which is intersected by some railroad tracks. Above the tracks two red warning lights cast their glow over everything, making you feel like you're in hell.

I had assumed that the family would be there, already across, but the place was as quiet and empty as the rest of the desert. I could hear coyotes shouting at each other off in the distance.

I sat there a good hour, seeing nothing, hearing nothing but the coyotes, getting more worried by the minute. With the racket the coyotes were making, and the perfect stillness of everything else, along with the red glow of the lights, I got paranoid. I was scared, I'll admit it. I wanted to fire up that long purple machine and get the hell away. On the way down I'd worried about getting back in time for Ms. Condley to call; since she missed me last night I knew she would be calling tonight, and being out of the house again would look suspicious. But now I was simply spooked about getting caught; it's not something I've checked on, but transporting illegal aliens is most likely a felony and would land me in some serious shit.

I got out of the car, pacing around in the mud, stopping to listen once in a while, until I heard what sounded like a car motor out in the dark. I strained my ears and after awhile I heard voices that sounded like they were coming from the other side of the fence. About a hundred yards off, in a shallow ravine, I saw movement. I crept closer and could just make out somebody working on the fence with what looked like a pair of wire-cutters.

I counted ten people coming under, a few of them children. When I agreed to pick 115
up Jesus' family, I thought he meant his wife and kids, not the whole bunch. They all
started off in the opposite direction from me, lugging shopping sacks full of belongings.
It was obvious they could not see me so I flashed my headlights to let them know where
I was. Immediately someone swore in Spanish and everyone began running towards
the car, shouting and bumping into each other. About halfway to the car, one of the
kids, apparently spooked and bewildered by this whole affair, peeled off to the left and
began running helter-skelter through the brush. I went after him, using a little cowboy
geometry; when going after a steer you don't pursue him directly, you estimate where
his path will take him and you head out for that point. The kid, however, didn't cooperate, zigzagging like a rabbit under fire, with me high-stepping it through the mud behind
him, clown-like.

By the time I was able to corral the kid and carry him back to the car, everyone had
most of their belongings stuffed into the trunk, themselves jammed in the car, and some
old lady was at the wheel, cranking the key and gunning the accelerator. I convinced her
to scoot over and let me take the controls, and just as we started out, a pair of headlights with a search beam on top came over a hill about half a mile away. Who knows, it
could have been some redneck out spotlighting deer, but at that moment I was sure the
border patrol, the FBI and CIA were all bearing down on us. Everyone shouted at once
and the grandma put up a high-pitched wail, the kind you hear at third-world funerals.
The car fishtailed in the mud and lumbered over clumps of cactus and mesquite; I kept
the lights off so I had no idea where I was going. I'm a veteran of chases like these,
but this time I was scared out of my mind, pretty much like everybody else in the car.
Somebody in back prayed to the Virgin Mary, the kids screamed, Grandma wailed, and
for once in my life I kept perfectly quiet.

It didn't take long for my eyes to adjust to the darkness and pretty soon I found
myself on a washboard dirt road heading god-knows-where. A couple of times we saw
headlights, way off in the distance, which made the Grandma start up her wail, inducing
the kids in back to commence their crying again.

But now, after about a half hour of searching, we've got ourselves back on the
highway and everybody seems to have calmed. Grandma is so relaxed she's snoring
like a lumber-jack. By the time we make it to Salado, it's near midnight and pretty much
everybody in the car except me is asleep. When I pull into Jesus' front yard, I can see
him sitting under the old basketball hoop, his hands clamped together between his
legs. I pull to a stop, shut off the engine and suddenly it's chaos again, people shouting
and trying to untangle themselves, babies crying, Grandma giving orders.

As I help pull belongings out of the trunk I watch Jesus gather his two daughters
and little son, hugging them, not willing to let go even though they are already squirming
to get away. I know this is a common scene, a father being reunited with his kids, but
for some reason, standing there in the dark of the other side of the car, I have to turn
away. I look in the other direction, out at the lights of town, until Jesus comes up behind
me and gives me a good whack on the back, saying, "Tank you, Arshie, very good,"
and holding a hand over his heart.

He invites me inside, but his tiny house is already overflowing with people, so I ask 120
him if I can take the Oldsmobile out for a drive. I've only had a couple hours of sleep in
the last two days but I don't feel like going back to the trailer. Jesus says no problem,
take the car to Las Vegas if you want.

I drive into Salado and stop at Burly's; I feel like talking to someone, blowing off a little steam, but the place is nearly empty tonight. Only a few old-timers sit at the bar, bending down to their shot glasses like birds drinking from a puddle. I take a table near the back and I sit there alone for a minute. I keep seeing that scene with Jesus and his kids and I feel so clenched and jumpy it's like I'm going to explode. So when the bartender calls over the bar, asking what do I want, without much hesitation I call back, "Shot of Jim Beam."

When the drink comes, I look at it for a minute before I lift it to my mouth. It's been less than a year since I had a drink, but the stuff scorches my throat like it's my first time ever. I sip the whiskey, swishing it around, and by the time I'm halfway finished with my second shot I've decided—it's almost like a revelation—that tonight is the night I'm going to take care of Calfred Pulsipher. I could wait around forever for him to come out of hiding, checking the bars, looking under every hat at the gas station and grocery store, or I could have some real-man balls and go directly to him.

Suddenly I can't stay a minute longer in that place, not even for a few more drinks, so I drop some money on the table, get into the car, and stop in at the Circle K for a six-pack. Then I'm on my way back to Jesus' house.

When I get there, the house is entirely dark. I figured everybody would still be up, celebrating or something, but the place is quiet as a tomb. Without meaning to I pound so hard on the door the whole house shakes.

I see a teenage girl—one of my passengers earlier tonight—peek through the win- 125 dow and then Jesus comes out, pants unzipped, shirt on inside-out. I can smell the damp scent of sex on him and there's no doubt I've just broken up the long awaited reunion with his wife. He's in there putting that big pecker of his to good use and along comes Archie in the middle of the night to break things up.

I feel stupid and guilty, but I'm not going to let that stop me. "Jesus," I say, "I'm real sorry but I need you to tell me where Calfred Pulsipher lives."

"Ah?" Jesus says, peering out at me.

"I need to know where Calfred Pulsipher lives. Please."

"Now? You going there now?"

"Right now." 130

Jesus sighs, shouts back something inside to his wife, closes the door and steps outside next to me.

"Why you going there?" he says.

"All you have to do is tell me where."

"Come on," Jesus says, walking barefoot across the gravel and bullheads. He gets in his work truck and says, "I bring you."

I try to tell him that he only needs to give me directions, but he shakes his head, 135 revs the engine, and says, "Come in."

I feel like cockroach shit for taking advantage of him like this, doing him a favor and then asking one in return right off the bat, ruining his night and everything. I try to tell him this on the way but he waves his hand at me without looking my way. I break one of the beers off the six-pack and hand it to him and he tosses it right out the window.

We're on the highway for a couple of miles before Jesus turns off on a tiny dirt road I've never noticed before. It's barely a cow track, full of mudholes and melon-sized boulders. Jesus keeps the truck on a straight course, heedless of the obstacles, and the truck jounces and rocks like a boat in high seas. I tear off one of the beers for myself; the whiskey I drank at Burly's hardly did a thing for me, and I know I'll need to be good and whacked-out to get through this whole thing, but the beer tastes sour and watery, and with all the bouncing around this truck is doing, I'm this close to throwing up all over the floor. So I chuck the remainder of the six-pack out the window, as far as it will go, and watch the cans jump and spray among the bushes. After what seems like miles of bump and rattle, Jesus turns again on another dirt road and suddenly stops.

"What's wrong?" I say.

"Here," he says.

I look around, seeing nothing but brush and slab-sided buttes, and then I notice the shell of an old Buick sitting back off the road about thirty yards, and behind that, in the night-shadows of an old cottonwood, is a house no bigger than a rich man's bathroom. I look back at Jesus, who's staring out the windshield, and get out of the truck.

Walking toward that house it's like I'm a ghost, floating, nothing but air. I can't feel   140
my feet touch the ground. I try not to think about what I'm doing, what I'm going to do. Once I'm within ten feet or so I can see that the house is a ramshackle adobe affair, mud showing through holes in the stucco. Somebody has done their best to make the place look nice, the tiny, half-dead lawn cluttered with ceramic elves, ducks whose wings spin when the wind blows, birdbaths and plastic sunflowers.

I step up on the porch and give the screen door three good raps. A long, sick minute passes before I hear someone shuffling along the floor. The porch light clicks on, the door opens toward me and somebody leans half into the light.

It takes me a moment to recognize Calfred Pulsipher. Instead of the young man in the newspaper picture, or the even younger man I've seen in my father's old yearbooks, this Calfred Pulsipher looks like he belongs in an old folk's home. His hair is thin and colorless, his back bowed, his skin papery and stained with coffee-colored blotches. An oxygen tube, strapped around his head, feeds into both his nostrils. He's pulling a wheeled tank behind him with one hand and in the other he's holding a rusty sawed-off shotgun, pointed at my stomach.

The light blinds him for a moment and he squints at me, bracing the screen door with his elbow. We stand there like that, two feet apart, staring at each other, until his eyes suddenly go wide, his mouth opens slowly, forming a circle, and he says, "Oh."

The gun slides out of his hand, bouncing off the threshold and clattering against the oxygen tank.

I can't do anything but look from his right eye, which is locked on me, burning and   145
wet, to his left, which is swiveling around in his head like a thing that's got a mind of its own. His brows are pushed up and together and his mouth is opening and closing without any sound.

He takes one stumbling step toward me, arms out. One of his knees buckles under him and he grabs my shirt, pulling himself back up, leaning into me, reaching up and putting his arms around my shoulders. I can feel his whiskers on my neck and I don't know if the strong, bitter smell of alcohol is coming from him or me. He holds his head against my collarbone, moving it back and forth, saying, "Oh, oh."

It would be so easy, all I would have to do is return his embrace, crush him in my arms until his bones cracked and his worthless lungs gave out. But I can't do it. I can't. My whole body feels numb and my hands are at my sides, as heavy and useless as hub caps.

He hangs on me like that, until Jesus steps out of the shadows and pulls me away. Jesus leads me back towards the truck and I make it only ten steps or so until I fall forward, my whole body gone limp with shame and relief. I catch myself with my hands and begin coughing into the dirt, it's like there are chunks of black matter dislodging themselves from deep inside, stuff that has been there forever is coming up, and I can't stop, my stomach heaving, and I begin to weep. I can't remember ever crying in my entire life, but I'm making up for it now, my sinuses burning with tears, my throat constricting on me, and I go like that, hacking and retching, unable to breathe, until I vomit violently into a clump of sagebrush.

Jesus stands over me, his hand on my back, and he says quietly, "Come on, Archie. Get it up."

He wipes off my mouth with his shirt, helps me to my feet, and with his arm locked 150 in mine, we start again for the truck. I look back and the last thing I see is Calfred Pulsipher still standing in the light, like a man caught in the bright beam of a spaceship.

The ride home is nothing more than a dense fog moving past, and when we get back to the trailer Doug is in the front room, waddling around in the dark like some deformed duck, picking crumbs off the carpet. Jesus kicks him out of the way, and Doug goes flapping toward the kitchen, a few black feathers coming loose. Jesus sits me down on the couch and asks me if I want him to stay with me. I tell him to get his ass on home where his wife is waiting for him to finish the job he'd started and he is out the door in a heartbeat.

Richard appears in his bedroom doorway, wearing his camo-pajamas, his hair smashed against one side of his head. "Hey, Ms. Condley called again," he says. "Sounds like you're in a little trouble."

"Ms. Condley can go to hell," I say, not caring whether Richard notices my puffy eyes or the thickness in my voice. "And so can you, for that matter."

Once Richard retreats to his room, I go and get Doug, who is sulking under the kitchen table, and take him outside. The sky has cleared and the stars are shining down and even though I've slept only a few minutes in the past few days, even though I'm exhausted and weak, there is still something inside me that needs to be released; I want to open up my lungs and shout like a maniac, wake everyone for miles. Instead, I take Doug in the crook of my arm and walk up the hill past the ranch house, which is glowing a faint, moonlit blue, all the way down to the mud pond where a few steers are standing around, rubbing their heads together. It's become such a bright night there's no difficulty at all in finding the anchor post, the one with my father's initial. I squat down next to that post and bite into it, hard, right near the Q. I bite so hard the muscles in my jaw begin to burn and I come away with a taste in my mouth of wood and salt and dust. I stand up, holding Doug close, looking down at the indentations my teeth made and a feeling of pride and certainty rises up in me. There is no doubt in my mind: this is my place, it's where I belong, and I'm here to stay.

Source: "He Becomes Deeply and Famously Drunk", from LETTING LOOSE THE HOUNDS: Stories by Brady Udall. Copyright © 1997 by Brady Udall. Used by permission of W. W. Norton & Company, Inc.

Critical Thinking Topics

1. The story centers on the concept of revenge. Considering only details from Archie's life, develop a claim about vengeance that is implied by the story. What details from the story led you to create this claim? Do you believe this claim—that is, do your own observations lead you to support the claim or to qualify it or deny it? Elaborate with firsthand examples.

2. Describe the friendship between Archie and Jesus. What qualities of each character seem to draw them together?

3. Given the facts of his life, Jesus might have been an angry character; however, he clearly is a positive force in Archie's life. Is it possible to argue that Jesus is the hero of this story? If so, explain why, and if not, explain why not.

Writing Topic

Archie's drive for revenge originates in a concept he gained from reading westerns: "It's what anyone who had any courage or sense of justice did; it's what cowboys did" (par. 43). How is Archie's quest for revenge admirable and, at the same time, destructive? What alternative path might Archie have followed?

7.9 Poetry

The eight poems in this section, spanning the years 1767 through 2003, explore issues related to the theme of crime and punishment.

7.10 A Few Lines on Magnus Mode, Richard Hodges & J. Newington Clark
(1767 broadside)

A few LINES on
Magnus Mode, Richard Hodges & J. Newington Clark.
Who are Sentenc'd to stand one Hour in the
Pillory at Charlestown;
To have one of their EARS cut off, and to be Whipped 20 Stripes at the public   5
Whipping Post, for making and passing Counterfeit DOLLARS, &c.

BEHOLD the villains rais'd on high!
(The Post they've got attracts the eye:)
Both Jews and Gentiles all appear
To see them stand exalted here;   10
Both rich and poor, both young and old,
The dirty slut, the common scold:
What multitudes do them surround,
Many as bad as can be found.
And to encrease their sad disgrace   15
Throw rotten eggs into their face,
And pelt them fore with dirt and stones,
Nay, if they could wou'd break their bones.
Their malice to such height arise,
Who knows but they'll put out their eyes: 20
But pray consider what you do
While thus expos'd to public view.
Justice has often done its part,
And made the guilty rebels smart;
But they went on did still rebel,   25
And seem'd to storm the gates of hell.
To no good counsel would they hear;

But now each one must loose an EAR,
And they although against their will
Are forc'd to chew this bitter pill;   30
And this day brings the villains hence
To suffer for their late offense;
They on th' Pillory stand in view:
A warning sirs to me and you!
The drunkards song, the harlots scorn,   35
Reproach of some as yet unborn.
But now the Post they're forc'd to hug,
But loath to take that nauseous drug
Which brings the blood from out their veins
And marks their back with purple stains.   40

From their disgrace, now warning take,
And never do your ruin make
By stealing, or unlawful ways;
(If you would live out all your days)
But keep secure from Theft and Pride;   45
Strive to have virtue on your side.
Despise the harlot's flattering airs,
And hate her ways, avoid her snares;
Keep clear from Sin of every kind,
And then you'll have true peace of Mind.   50

Critical Thinking Topics

1. Look back at the last five lines of the poem, where the writer wants to leave
the reader with the poem's strongest message. In this case, the writer urges
the reader to "Despise the harlot's flattering airs,/And hate her ways, avoid
her snares." Rhetorically, the end of a piece of writing is considered the
emphatic place, whether it is in a sentence, a paragraph, a chapter, or a poem.
The poem is generally about crime, using counterfeiting as an example, so
why did the writer switch to talking about harlots in the closing lines?

2. Do some research on public pillorying as it was used in colonial America.
What sorts of crimes were punished in this way, and what sorts of punishments at the pillory were endured? Do you think such punishments fit the
crimes? Explain your response.

Writing Topic

In this poem, the audience plays a role in pillorying: The crowd throws rotten
eggs and stones at the convicted criminals. Not so long ago, there were public
hangings in this country. What was behind the idea of public humiliation and
public execution? Why do we no longer do this? Should we return to public
humiliation for criminals—for example, should we require convicted drunken
drivers to attach a large sign on their cars advertising their transgressions?
Write an argument advocating or opposing the idea of public humiliation for
criminals.

7.11 A. E. Housman, The Use and Abuse of Toads (1919)

As into the garden Elizabeth ran
Pursued by the just indignation of Ann,
She trod on an object that lay in her road,
She trod on an object that looked like a toad.

It looked like a toad, and it looked so because   5
A toad was the actual object it was;
And after supporting Elizabeth's tread
It looked like a toad that was visibly dead.

Elizabeth, leaving her footprint behind,
Continued her flight on the wings of the wind,   10
And Ann in her anger was heard to arrive
At the toad that was not any longer alive.

She was heard to arrive, for the firmament rang
With the sound of a scream and the noise of a bang,
As her breath on the breezes she broadly bestowed   15
And fainted away on Elizabeth's toad.

Elizabeth, saved by the sole of her boot,
Escaped her insensible sister's pursuit;
And if ever hereafter she irritates Ann,
She will tread on a toad if she possibly can.   20

Critical Thinking Topics

1. What evidence in the poem suggests that Elizabeth has wronged Ann in some way? Speculate on what Elizabeth might have done to warrant Ann's anger.
2. What is the difference between Ann's and Elizabeth's reactions to the toad that was and is no more? What do their reactions reveal about their personalities?
3. Though this poem reads like children's poetry in its subject matter, rhythm, and rhyme, what details in the poem are more sophisticated? What is the effect of this juxtaposition of simplicity and sophistication?

Writing Topic

One possible theme of this poem is sibling rivalry or, more specifically, the ability of those we know best to provoke us, intentionally or not. How might we protect ourselves from this kind of provocation? How might such provocations affect our relationships? Have you ever been the victim or the perpetrator of such a provocation? If you have, what was the outcome? If you have not, think of another example from a work of literature, a movie, or other media, and describe the provocation and its aftermath.

7.12 D. H. Lawrence, Snake
(1921)

A snake came to my water-trough
On a hot, hot day, and I in pyjamas for the heat,
To drink there.

In the deep, strange-scented shade of the great dark carob tree
I came down the steps with my pitcher   5
And must wait, must stand and wait, for there he was at the trough before me.

He reached down from a fissure in the earth-wall in the gloom
And trailed his yellow-brown slackness soft-bellied down, over the edge of the stone trough
And rested his throat upon the stone bottom,
And where the water had dripped from the tap, in a small clearness,   10
He sipped with his straight mouth,
Softly drank through his straight gums, into his slack long body,
Silently.

Someone was before me at my water-trough,
And I, like a second-comer, waiting.   15

He lifted his head from his drinking, as cattle do,
And looked at me vaguely, as drinking cattle do,
And flickered his two-forked tongue from his lips, and mused a moment,
And stooped and drank a little more,
Being earth-brown, earth-golden from the burning bowels of the earth   20
On the day of Sicilian July, with Etna smoking.

The voice of my education said to me
He must be killed,
For in Sicily the black, black snakes are innocent, the gold are venomous.

And voices in me said, If you were a man   25
You would take a stick and break him now, and finish him off.

But must I confess how I liked him,
How glad I was he had come like a guest in quiet, to drink at my water-trough
And depart peaceful, pacified, and thankless,
Into the burning bowels of this earth?   30

Was it cowardice, that I dared not kill him?
Was it perversity, that I longed to talk to him?
Was it humility, to feel honoured?
I felt so honoured.

And yet those voices: 35
If you were not afraid you would kill him!

And truly I was afraid, I was most afraid,
But even so, honoured still more
That he should seek my hospitality
From out the dark door of the secret earth.   40

He drank enough
And lifted his head, dreamily, as one who has drunken,
And flickered his tongue like a forked night on the air, so black,
Seeming to lick his lips,
And looked around like a god, unseeing, into the air,   45
And slowly turned his head,
And slowly, very slowly, as if thrice adream,
Proceeded to draw his slow length curving round
And climb again the broken bank of my wall-face.

And as he put his head into that dreadful hole,   50
And as he slowly drew up, snake-easing his shoulders, and entered further,
A sort of horror, a sort of protest against his withdrawing into that horrid black hole,
Deliberately going into the blackness, and slowly drawing himself after,
Overcame me now his back was turned.

I looked round, I put down my pitcher,   55
I picked up a clumsy log
And threw it at the water-trough with a clatter.

I think it did not hit him,
But suddenly that part of him that was left behind convulsed in undignified haste,
Writhed like lightning, and was gone   60
Into the black hole, the earth-lipped fissure in the wall-front,
At which, in the intense still noon, I stared with fascination.

And immediately I regretted it.
I thought how paltry, how vulgar, what a mean act!
I despised myself and the voices of my accursed human education.   65

And I thought of the albatross,
And I wished he would come back, my snake.

For he seemed to me again like a king,
Like a king in exile, uncrowned in the underworld,
Now due to be crowned again.   70

And so, I missed my chance with one of the lords
Of life.
And I have something to expiate;
A pettiness.

Critical Thinking Topics

1. The speaker mentions that he feels "honoured" that the snake should seek "hospitality" at the water trough (38–39). He later compares the snake to "the albatross" (66), undoubtedly alluding to the albatross in Samuel Taylor Coleridge's *The Rime of the Ancient Mariner*. Research the laws of hospitality, and read Coleridge's poem; consider the connection in that poem between the image of the albatross and the idea of hospitality. How are these motifs connected to the snake?

2. The speaker compares the snake to a cow in how it drinks water. Later in the poem, the speaker draws a parallel between the snake and royalty. What do you think is the purpose of these comparisons?

Writing Topic

Snakes are often viewed as symbols of danger and evil. The speaker struggles with conflicting reactions to the snake: his respect for the creature and his urge to kill it. As the snake goes back into its hole, the speaker throws a log at it. He regrets this act of undeserved violence and remarks that he despises himself and the voices of his "accursed human education" (65). This suggests that the act of throwing the log was culturally conditioned and not an expression of the speaker's true character. Describe instances where you have observed other people allowing societal expectations to dictate unfair reactions to their fellow creatures.

7.13 Don Marquis, A Communication from Archy the Cockroach (1922)

I was talking to a moth
the other evening
he was trying to break into
an electric light bulb
and fry himself on the wires   5
why do you fellows
pull this stunt I asked him because
it is the conventional
thing for moths or why
if that had been an uncovered   10
candle instead of an electric
light bulb you would
now be a small unsightly cinder
have you no sense
plenty of it he answered   15
but at times we get tired
of using it
we get bored with the routine
and crave beauty
and excitement   20
fire is beautiful
and we know that if we get
too close it will kill us
but what does that matter
it is better to be happy   25
for a moment
and be burned up with beauty
than to live a long time
and be bored all the while

so we wad all our life up   30
into one little roll
and then we shoot the roll
that is what life is for
it is better to be a part of beauty
for one instant and then cease to   35
exist than to exist forever
and never be a part of beauty
our attitude toward life
is come easy go easy
we are like human beings   40
used to be before they became
too civilized to enjoy themselves
and before I could argue him
out of his philosophy
he went and immolated himself   45
on a patent cigar lighter
I do not agree with him
myself I would rather have
half the happiness and twice
the longevity   50
but at the same time I wish
there was something I wanted
as badly as he wanted to fry himself
archy

Critical Thinking Topics

1. The moth says, "we are like human beings/used to be before they became/too civilized to enjoy themselves" (40–42). However, he offers no evidence in support of this claim that humans at one time followed the example of his own life and death. Provide several examples of past or present human behavior—from real life or from literature or other media—to support the moth's claim.

2. Can you think of ways that humans, much like the moth, attempt "to break into an electric light bulb and fry" themselves? What are some examples of life lessons that many people have to learn painfully?

3. List key points that the moth and the cockroach present in support of their respective positions. From your perspective, who presents the more compelling argument? Explain your response.

Writing Topics

1. Select another insect or other animal and, as Marquis has done with the moth, write out phrases or sentences in the insect's or animal's voice articulating its attitude toward life.

2. Is taking a life-threatening risk a harmless act if it endangers no one but yourself? Some might argue that individuals who put themselves at extreme risk—for example, by participating in dangerous sports or daredevil

adventures—are considering neither the nonphysical damages that they might cause to others, such as family and friends, nor the potential financial damages of rescue efforts. Offer your ideas and reflections on this topic.

7.14 Langston Hughes, Justice (1932)

That Justice is a blind goddess
Is a thing to which we black are wise:
Her bandage hides two festering sores
That once perhaps were eyes

Source: Hughes, Langston. The Golden Stair Press (1932).

Critical Thinking Topics

1. The representation of justice as Lady Justice—blindfolded and holding a sword and a balance scale—dates back to ancient Rome. By focusing on the blindfold, what ironical statement is Hughes making?
2. Why do you think Justice has been depicted as female and a goddess? How might a male representation alter your interpretation of the image?

Writing Topic

The poem's publication date (1932) is several decades prior to the civil rights movement of the 1960s and 1970s. To what extent is the poem's message relevant today? Can you think of other specific groups—in addition to "we black"—who might view Justice's bandage as hiding "two festering sores"? Elaborate on your response with examples.

7.15 Marge Piercy, What's That Smell in the Kitchen? (1982)

All over America women are burning dinners.
It's lamb chops in Peoria; it's haddock
In Providence; it's steak in Chicago;
tofu delight in Big Sur; red
rice and beans in Dallas.   5
All over American women are burning
food they're supposed to bring with calico
smile on platters glittering like wax.
Anger sputters in her brainpan, confined
but spewing out missiles of hot fat.   10
Carbonized despair presses like a clinker
From a barbecue against the back of her eyes.
If she wants to grill anything, it's
her husband over a slow fire.
If she wants to serve him anything   15

it's a dead rat with a bomb in its belly
ticking like the heart of an insomniac.
Her life is cooked and digested
nothing but leftovers in Tupperware.
Look, she says, once I was roast duck   20
on your platter with parsley but now I am Spam
Burning dinner is not incompetence but war.

Source: "What's That Smell in the Kitchen?" By Marge Piercy. Copyright © 1982 by Marge Piercy. From CIR-
CLES ON THE WATER, Alfred A. Knopf. Used by permission of the Wallace Literary Agency. Used by permission
of Alfred A. Knopf, an imprint of the Knopf Doubleday Publishing Group, a division of Penguin Random House
LLC. All rights reserved.

Critical Thinking Topics

1. Select three or more vivid images from the poem and describe the implications of each—for example, what ideas and emotions does the image arouse?
2. In closing, the speaker declares, "Burning dinner is not incompetence but
   war." How do you interpret that assertion—war on whom, and why? What
   is gained and what is lost by waging war in such situations?

Writing Topic

Imagine yourself in the role of the husband. How would you respond? What
concessions and/or counterarguments could you present?

7.16 Etheridge Knight, Hard Rock Returns to Prison from the Hospital for the Criminal Insane (1986)

Hard Rock/was/"known not to take no shit
From nobody," and he had the scars to prove it:
Split purple lips, lumped ears, welts above
His yellow eyes, and one long scar that cut
Across his temple and plowed through a thick   5
Canopy of kinky hair.

The WORD/was/that Hard Rock wasn't a mean nigger
Anymore, that the doctors had bored a hole in his head,
Cut out part of his brain, and shot electricity
Through the rest. When they brought Hard Rock back,   10
Handcuffed and chained, he was turned loose,
Like a freshly gelded stallion, to try his new status.
And we all waited and watched, like indians at a corral,
To see if the WORD was true.

As we waited we wrapped ourselves in the cloak   15
Of his exploits: "Man, the last time, it took eight
Screws to put him in the Hole." "Yeah, remember when he
Smacked the captain with his dinner tray?" "He set
The record for time in the Hole—67 straight days!"

"Ol Hard Rock! man, that's one crazy nigger."   20
And then the jewel of a myth that Hard Rock had once bit
A screw on the thumb and poisoned him with syphilitic spit.

The testing came, to see if Hard Rock was really tame.
A hillbilly called him a black son of a bitch
And didn't lose his teeth, a screw who knew Hard Rock   25
From before shook him down and barked in his face.
And Hard Rock did *nothing*. Just grinned and looked silly,
His eyes empty like knot holes in a fence.

And even after we discovered that it took Hard Rock
Exactly 3 minutes to tell you his first name,   30
We told ourselves that he had just wised up,
Was being cool; but we could not fool ourselves for long,
And we turned away, our eyes on the ground. Crushed.
He had been our Destroyer, the doer of things   '
We dreamed of doing but could not bring ourselves to do,   35
The fears of years, like a biting whip,
Had cut grooves too deeply across our backs.

Source: Knight, Etheridge, "Hard Rock Returns To Prison From The Hospital For The Criminal Insane" from THE ESSENTIAL ETHERIDGE KNIGHT, by Etheridge Knight, © 1986. Reprinted by permission of the University of Pittsburgh Press.

Critical Thinking Topics

1. How does the poem's speaker appeal to *pathos?*
2. Describe the speaker and assess his *ethos.*
3. How does this poem affect your attitude toward or feelings about prisoners?

Writing Topic

The surgical procedure that Hard Rock was forced to undergo is no longer allowed; however, solitary confinement is still used in some prisons as a punishment for misbehavior or even—in maximum-security, or supermax, prisons—as the nearly permanent condition of imprisonment. Do some research on solitary confinement in U.S. prisons today. Based on your research, write a *claim of policy* on the use of solitary confinement in prisons. Provide at least three supporting points for your claim and at least one concession and one refutation.

7.17 Robert Johnson, Police line: do not cross (2003)

Bright yellow bands
bind the black night
corralling chaos
containing confusion
communicating in cold chorus   5
-

Caution, stand back, stay clear
something terrible has happened here
Lights, sirens, suits
action, but too little,
too late   10
too bad.
Lines have been crossed
lives have been lost
long before the police
were called to the scene.   15
It'll take more than tape
to staunch the blood
bind the wounds
make us whole
when we can't   20
police ourselves.

Source: Reprinted by permission of the author.

Critical Thinking Topics

1. Read the poem out loud. How is the sound of this poem built upon repetition? Explain how sound adds to the effect of the poem.
2. The lines of the poem are short, sometimes merely phrases. How do these short lines make an impact that might be lost in longer, more narrative descriptions?

Writing Topic

The poem chastises us—the readers—because we cannot "police ourselves." Yet how is that possible? If I live in a rough neighborhood, can I go into the street and tell the mugger or the thief, "Please do not behave this way"? Or say, "Please Mr. Gangster, don't shoot anyone in this neighborhood." Or does "police ourselves" suggest we should each "police" our own self, as opposed to policing each other? An effective argument closes with a call to action. What exactly do you think the writer would have us do?

7.18 Drama

The early-twentieth-century play in this section explores topics and issues related to the theme of crime and punishment.

7.19 Susan Glaspell, Trifles
(1916)

George Henderson (County Attorney)
Henry Peters (Sheriff)
Lewis Hale, A Neighboring Farmer
Mrs. Peters
Mrs. Hale

Scene: *The kitchen is the now abandoned farmhouse of* John Wright, *a gloomy kitchen, and left without having been put in order—unwashed pans under the sink, a loaf of bread outside the bread-box, a dish-towel on the table—other signs of incompleted work. At the rear the outer door opens and the* Sheriff *comes in followed by the* County Attorney *and* Hale. *The* Sheriff *and* Hale *are men in middle life, the* County Attorney *is a young man; all are much bundled up and go at once to the stove. They are followed by the two women—the* Sheriff's *wife first; she is a slight wiry woman, a thin nervous face.* Mrs. Hale *is larger and would ordinarily be called more comfortable looking, but she is disturbed now and looks fearfully about as she enters. The women have come in slowly, and stand close together near the door.*

COUNTY ATTORNEY:	(*rubbing his hands*) This feels good. Come up to the fire, ladies.
MRS. PETERS:	(*after taking a step forward*) I'm not—cold.
SHERIFF:	(*unbuttoning his overcoat and stepping away from the stove as if to mark the beginning of official business*) Now, Mr. Hale, before we move things about, you explain to Mr. Henderson just what you saw when you came here yesterday morning.
COUNTY ATTORNEY:	By the way, has anything been moved? Are things just as you left them yesterday?
SHERIFF:	(*looking about*) It's just the same. When it dropped below zero last night I thought I'd better send Frank out this morning to make a fire for us—no use getting pneumonia with a big case on, but I told him not to touch anything except the stove—and you know Frank.
COUNTY ATTORNEY:	Somebody should have been left here yesterday.
SHERIFF:	Oh—yesterday. When I had to send Frank to Morris Center for that man who went crazy—I want you to know I had my hands full yesterday. I knew you could get back from Omaha by today and as long as I went over everything here myself—
COUNTY ATTORNEY:	Well, Mr. Hale, tell just what happened when you came here yesterday morning.
HALE:	Harry and I had started to town with a load of potatoes. We came along the road from my place and as I got here I said, 'I'm going to see if I can't get John Wright to go in with me on a party telephone.' I spoke to Wright about it once before and he put me off, saying folks talked too much anyway, and all he asked was peace and quiet—I guess you know about how much he talked himself; but I thought maybe if I went to the house and talked about it before his wife, though I said to Harry that I didn't know as what his wife wanted made much difference to John—
COUNTY ATTORNEY:	Let's talk about that later, Mr. Hale. I do want to talk about that, but tell now just what happened when you got to the house.
HALE:	I didn't hear or see anything; I knocked at the door, and still it was all quiet inside. I knew they must be up, it was past eight

o'clock. So I knocked again, and I thought I heard somebody   35
say, 'Come in.' I wasn't sure, I'm not sure yet, but I opened
the door—this door (*indicating the door by which the two
women are still standing*) and there in that rocker—(*pointing
to it*) sat Mrs. Wright.
> (*They all look at the rocker.*)

COUNTY ATTORNEY: What—was she doing?   40

HALE: She was rockin' back and forth. She had her apron in her
hand and was kind of—pleating it.

COUNTY ATTORNEY: And how did she—look?

HALE: Well, she looked queer.

COUNTY ATTORNEY: How do you mean—queer?   45

HALE: Well, as if she didn't know what she was going to do next.
And kind of done up.

COUNTY ATTORNEY: How did she seem to feel about your coming?

HALE: Why, I don't think she minded—one way or other. She
didn't pay much attention. I said, 'How do, Mrs. Wright it's   50
cold, ain't it?' And she said, 'Is it?'—and went on kind of
pleating at her apron. Well, I was surprised; she didn't ask me
to come up to the stove, or to set down, but just sat there, not
even looking at me, so I said, 'I want to see John.' And then
she—laughed. I guess you would call it a laugh. I thought of 55
Harry and the team outside, so I said a little sharp: 'Can't I see
John?' 'No', she says, kind o' dull like. 'Ain't he home?' says
I. 'Yes', says she, 'he's home'. 'Then why can't I see him?'
I asked her, out of patience. 'Cause he's dead', says she.
'*Dead*?' says I. She just nodded her head, not getting a bit   60
excited, but rockin' back and forth. 'Why—where is he?' says
I, not knowing what to say. She just pointed upstairs—like that
(*himself pointing to the room above*) I got up, with the idea
of going up there. I walked from there to here—then I says,
'Why, what did he die of?' 'He died of a rope round his neck',   65
says she, and just went on pleatin' at her apron. Well, I went
out and called Harry. I thought I might—need help. We went
upstairs and there he was lyin'—

COUNTY ATTORNEY: I think I'd rather have you go into that upstairs, where
you can point it all out. Just go on now with the rest   70
of the story.

HALE: Well, my first thought was to get that rope off. It looked . . .
(*stops, his face twitches*) . . . but Harry, he went up to him,
and he said, 'No, he's dead all right, and we'd better not
touch anything.' So we went back down stairs. She was still   75
sitting that same way. 'Has anybody been notified?' I asked.
'No', says she unconcerned. 'Who did this, Mrs. Wright?' said
Harry. He said it business-like—and she stopped pleatin' of her

apron. 'I don't know', she says. 'You don't *know*?' says Harry. 'No', says she. 'Weren't you sleepin' in the bed with him?' says Harry. 'Yes', says she, 'but I was on the inside'. 'Somebody slipped a rope round his neck and strangled him and you didn't wake up?' says Harry. 'I didn't wake up', she said after him. We must 'a looked as if we didn't see how that could be, for after a minute she said, 'I sleep sound'. Harry was going to ask her more questions but I said maybe we ought to let her tell her story first to the coroner, or the Sheriff, so Harry went fast as he could to Rivers' place, where there's a telephone. 80

85

COUNTY ATTORNEY: And what did Mrs. Wright do when she knew that you had gone for the coroner? 90

HALE: She moved from that chair to this one over here (*pointing to a small chair in the corner*) and just sat there with her hands held together and looking down. I got a feeling that I ought to make some conversation, so I said I had come in to see if John wanted to put in a telephone, and at that she started to laugh, and then she stopped and looked at me—scared, (*the* County Attorney, *who has had his notebook out, makes a note*) I dunno, maybe it wasn't scared. I wouldn't like to say it was. Soon Harry got back, and then Dr. Lloyd came, and you, Mr. Peters, and so I guess that's all I know that you don't. 95

100

COUNTY ATTORNEY: (*looking around*) I guess we'll go upstairs first—and then out to the barn and around there, (*to the* Sheriff) You're convinced that there was nothing important here—nothing that would point to any motive.

SHERIFF: Nothing here but kitchen things. 105
> (*The* County Attorney, *after again looking around the kitchen, opens the door of a cupboard closet. He gets up on a chair and looks on a shelf. Pulls his hand away, sticky.*)

COUNTY ATTORNEY: Here's a nice mess.
> (*The women draw nearer.*)

MRS. PETERS: (*to the other woman*) Oh, her fruit; it did freeze, (*to the* LAWYER) She worried about that when it turned so cold. She said the fire'd go out and her jars would break.

SHERIFF: Well, can you beat the women! Held for murder and worryin' about her preserves. 110

COUNTY ATTORNEY: I guess before we're through she may have something more serious than preserves to worry about.

HALE: Well, women are used to worrying over trifles.
> (*The two women move a little closer together.*)

COUNTY ATTORNEY: (*with the gallantry of a young politician*) And yet, for all their worries, what would we do without the ladies? (*the women do not unbend. He goes to the sink, takes a dipperful of water from the pail and pouring it into a basin, washes his hands. Starts to wipe them on the roller-towel, turns it for a cleaner* 115

	place) Dirty towels! (*kicks his foot against the pans under the sink*) Not much of a housekeeper, would you say, ladies?	120
MRS HALE:	(*stiffly*) There's a great deal of work to be done on a farm.	
COUNTY ATTORNEY:	To be sure. And yet (*with a little bow to her*) I know there are some Dickson county farmhouses which do not have such roller towels. (*He gives it a pull to expose its length again.*)	125
MRS HALE:	Those towels get dirty awful quick. Men's hands aren't always as clean as they might be.	
COUNTY ATTORNEY:	Ah, loyal to your sex, I see. But you and Mrs. Wright were neighbors. I suppose you were friends, too.	
MRS HALE:	(*shaking her head*) I've not seen much of her of late years. I've not been in this house—it's more than a year.	130
COUNTY ATTORNEY:	And why was that? You didn't like her?	
MRS HALE:	I liked her all well enough. Farmers' wives have their hands full, Mr. Henderson. And then—	
COUNTY ATTORNEY:	Yes—?	135
MRS HALE:	(*looking about*) It never seemed a very cheerful place.	
COUNTY ATTORNEY:	No—it's not cheerful. I shouldn't say she had the homemaking instinct.	
MRS HALE:	Well, I don't know as Wright had, either.	
COUNTY ATTORNEY:	You mean that they didn't get on very well?	140
MRS HALE:	No, I don't mean anything. But I don't think a place'd be any cheerfuller for John Wright's being in it.	
COUNTY ATTORNEY:	I'd like to talk more of that a little later. I want to get the lay of things upstairs now. (*He goes to the left, where three steps lead to a stair door.*)	145
SHERIFF:	I suppose anything Mrs. Peters does'll be all right. She was to take in some clothes for her, you know, and a few little things. We left in such a hurry yesterday.	
COUNTY ATTORNEY:	Yes, but I would like to see what you take, Mrs. Peters, and keep an eye out for anything that might be of use to us.	150
MRS. PETERS:	Yes, Mr. Henderson. (*The women listen to the men's steps on the stairs, then look about the kitchen.*)	
MRS HALE:	I'd hate to have men coming into my kitchen, snooping around and criticizing. (*She arranges the pans under sink which the* LAWYER *had shoved out of place.*)	
MRS. PETERS:	Of course it's no more than their duty.	
MRS HALE:	Duty's all right, but I guess that deputy Sheriff that came out to make the fire might have got a little of this on. (*gives the roller towel a pull*) Wish I'd thought of that sooner. Seems	155

mean to talk about her for not having things slicked up when she had to come away in such a hurry.

MRS. PETERS: (*who has gone to a small table in the left rear corner of the room, and lifted one end of a towel that covers a pan*) She had bread set. (*Stands still.*) 160

MRS HALE: (*eyes fixed on a loaf of bread beside the bread-box, which is on a low shelf at the other side of the room. Moves slowly toward it*) She was going to put this in there, (*picks up loaf, then abruptly drops it. In a manner of returning to familiar things*) It's a shame about her fruit. I wonder if it's all gone. (*gets up on the chair and looks*) I think there's some here that's all right, Mrs. Peters. Yes—here; (*holding it toward the window*) this is cherries, too. (*looking again*) I declare I believe that's the only one. (*gets down, bottle in her hand. Goes to the sink and wipes it off on the outside*) She'll feel awful bad after all her hard work in the hot weather. I remember the afternoon I put up my cherries last summer. 165 170

> (*She puts the bottle on the big kitchen table, center of the room. With a sigh, is about to sit down in the rocking-chair. Before she is seated realizes what chair it is; with a slow look at it, steps back. The chair which she has touched rocks back and forth.*)

MRS. PETERS: Well, I must get those things from the front room closet, (*she goes to the door at the right, but after looking into the other room, steps back*) You coming with me, Mrs. Hale? You could help me carry them. 175

> (*They go in the other room; reappear,* Mrs. Peters *carrying a dress and skirt,* Mrs. Hale *following with a pair of shoes.*)

MRS. PETERS: My, it's cold in there.

> (*She puts the clothes on the big table, and hurries to the stove.*)

MRS HALE: (*examining the skirt*) Wright was close. I think maybe that's why she kept so much to herself. She didn't even belong to the Ladies Aid. I suppose she felt she couldn't do her part, and then you don't enjoy things when you feel shabby. She used to wear pretty clothes and be lively, when she was Minnie Foster, one of the town girls singing in the choir. But that—oh, that was thirty years ago. This all you as to take in? 180 185

MRS. PETERS: She said she wanted an apron. Funny thing to want, for there isn't much to get you dirty in jail, goodness knows. But I suppose just to make her feel more natural. She said they was in the top drawer in this cupboard. Yes, here. And then her little shawl that always hung behind the door. (*opens stair door and looks*) Yes, here it is. 190

> (*Quickly shuts door leading upstairs.*)

MRS HALE:	(*abruptly moving toward her*) Mrs. Peters?
MRS. PETERS:	Yes, Mrs. Hale? 195
MRS HALE:	Do you think she did it?
MRS. PETERS:	(*in a frightened voice*) Oh, I don't know.
MRS HALE:	Well, I don't think she did. Asking for an apron and her little shawl. Worrying about her fruit.
MRS. PETERS:	(*starts to speak, glances up, where footsteps are heard in the* 200 *room above. In a low voice*) Mr. Peters says it looks bad for her. Mr. Henderson is awful sarcastic in a speech and he'll make fun of her sayin' she didn't wake up.
MRS HALE:	Well, I guess John Wright didn't wake when they was slipping that rope under his neck. 205
MRS. PETERS:	No, it's strange. It must have been done awful crafty and still. They say it was such a—funny way to kill a man, rigging it all up like that.
MRS HALE:	That's just what Mr. Hale said. There was a gun in the house. He says that's what he can't understand. 210
MRS. PETERS:	Mr. Henderson said coming out that what was needed for the case was a motive; something to show anger, or— sudden feeling.
MRS HALE:	(*who is standing by the table*) Well, I don't see any signs of an-ger around here, (*she puts her hand on the dish towel which lies* 215 *on the table, stands looking down at table, one half of which is clean, the other half messy*) It's wiped to here, (*makes a move as if to finish work, then turns and looks at loaf of bread outside the breadbox. Drops towel. In that voice of coming back to familiar things.*) Wonder how they are finding things upstairs. I hope she 220 had it a little more red-up up there. You know, it seems kind of sneaking. Locking her up in town and then coming out here and trying to get her own house to turn against her!
MRS. PETERS:	But Mrs. Hale, the law is the law.
MRS HALE:	I s'pose 'tis, (*unbuttoning her coat*) Better loosen up your 225 things, Mrs. Peters. You won't feel them when you go out.
	(Mrs. Peters *takes off her fur tippet, goes to hang it on hook at back of room, stands looking at the under part of the small corner table*.)
MRS. PETERS:	She was piecing a quilt.
	(*She brings the large sewing basket and they look at the bright pieces.*)
MRS HALE:	It's log cabin pattern. Pretty, isn't it? I wonder if she was goin' to quilt it or just knot it?
	(*Footsteps have been heard coming down the stairs.* The Sheriff enters followed by HALE and the County Attorney.)

SHERIFF:	They wonder if she was going to quilt it or just knot it! 230
	(The men laugh, the women look abashed.)
COUNTY ATTORNEY:	*(rubbing his hands over the stove)* Frank's fire didn't do much up there, did it? Well, let's go out to the barn and get that cleared up.
	(The men go outside.)
MRS HALE:	*(resentfully)* I don't know as there's anything so strange, our takin' up our time with little things while we're waiting for 235 them to get the evidence. *(she sits down at the big table smoothing out a block with decision)* I don't see as it's anything to laugh about.
MRS. PETERS:	*(apologetically)* Of course they've got awful important things on their minds. 240
	(Pulls up a chair and joins Mrs. Hale at the table.)
MRS HALE:	*(examining another block)* Mrs. Peters, look at this one. Here, this is the one she was working on, and look at the sewing! All the rest of it has been so nice and even. And look at this! It's all over the place! Why, it looks as if she didn't know what she was about! 245
	(After she has said this they look at each other, then start to glance back at the door. After an instant Mrs. Hale has pulled at a knot and ripped the sewing.)
MRS. PETERS:	Oh, what are you doing, Mrs. Hale?
MRS HALE:	*(mildly)* Just pulling out a stitch or two that's not sewed very good. *(threading a needle)* Bad sewing always made me fidgety.
MRS. PETERS:	*(nervously)* I don't think we ought to touch things. 250
MRS HALE:	I'll just finish up this end. *(suddenly stopping and leaning forward)* Mrs.Peters?
MRS. PETERS:	Yes, Mrs. Hale?
MRS HALE:	What do you suppose she was so nervous about?
MRS. PETERS:	Oh—I don't know. I don't know as she was nervous. I some- 255 times sew awful queer when I'm just tired. (Mrs. Hale *starts to say something, looks at* Mrs. Peters, *then goes on sewing)* Well I must get these things wrapped up. They may be through sooner than we think, *(putting apron and other things together)* I wonder where I can find a piece of paper, and string. 260
MRS HALE:	In that cupboard, maybe.
MRS. PETERS:	*(looking in cupboard)* Why, here's a bird-cage, *(holds it up)* Did she have a bird, Mrs. Hale?
MRS HALE:	Why, I don't know whether she did or not—I've not been here for so long. There was a man around last year selling 265

	canaries cheap, but I don't know as she took one; maybe she did. She used to sing real pretty herself.	
MRS. PETERS:	(*glancing around*) Seems funny to think of a bird here. But she must have had one, or why would she have a cage? I wonder what happened to it.	270
MRS HALE:	I s'pose maybe the cat got it.	
MRS. PETERS:	No, she didn't have a cat. She's got that feeling some people have about cats—being afraid of them. My cat got in her room and she was real upset and asked me to take it out.	
MRS HALE:	My sister Bessie was like that. Queer, ain't it?	275
MRS. PETERS:	(*examining the cage*) Why, look at this door. It's broke. One hinge is pulled apart.	
MRS HALE:	(*looking too*) Looks as if someone must have been rough with it.	
MRS. PETERS:	Why, yes.	280
	(*She brings the cage forward and puts it on the table.*)	
MRS HALE:	I wish if they're going to find any evidence they'd be about it. I don't like this place.	
MRS. PETERS:	But I'm awful glad you came with me, Mrs. Hale. It would be lonesome for me sitting here alone.	
MRS HALE:	It would, wouldn't it? (*dropping her sewing*) But I tell you what I do wish, Mrs. Peters. I wish I had come over sometimes when *she* was here. I—(*looking around the room*)—wish I had.	285
MRS. PETERS:	But of course you were awful busy, Mrs. Hale—your house and your children.	
MRS HALE:	I could've come. I stayed away because it weren't cheerful—and that's why I ought to have come. I—I've never liked this place. Maybe because it's down in a hollow and you don't see the road. I dunno what it is, but it's a lonesome place and always was. I wish I had come over to see Minnie Foster sometimes. I can see now—(*shakes her head*)	290 295
MRS. PETERS:	Well, you mustn't reproach yourself, Mrs. Hale. Somehow we just don't see how it is with other folks until—something comes up.	
MRS HALE:	Not having children makes less work—but it makes a quiet house, and Wright out to work all day, and no company when he did come in. Did you know John Wright, Mrs. Peters?	300
MRS. PETERS:	Not to know him; I've seen him in town. They say he was a good man.	
MRS HALE:	Yes—good; he didn't drink, and kept his word as well as most, I guess, and paid his debts. But he was a hard man, Mrs. Peters. Just to pass the time of day with him—(*shivers*) Like a raw wind that gets to the bone, (*pauses, her eye falling on the cage*) I should think she would 'a wanted a bird. But what do you suppose went with it?	305

MRS. PETERS:	I don't know, unless it got sick and died.
	(She reaches over and swings the broken door, swings it again, both women watch it.)
MRS HALE:	You weren't raised round here, were you? (*Mrs. Peters shakes her head*) You didn't know—her?
MRS. PETERS:	Not till they brought her yesterday.
MRS HALE:	She—come to think of it, she was kind of like a bird herself— real sweet and pretty, but kind of timid and—fluttery. How— she—did—change. (*silence; then as if struck by a happy thought and relieved to get back to everyday things*) Tell you what, Mrs. Peters, why don't you take the quilt in with you? It might take up her mind.
MRS. PETERS:	Why, I think that's a real nice idea, Mrs. Hale. There couldn't possibly be any objection to it, could there? Now, just what would I take? I wonder if her patches are in here—and her things. (*They look in the sewing basket.*)
MRS HALE:	Here's some red. I expect this has got sewing things in it. (*brings out a fancy box*) What a pretty box. Looks like something somebody would give you. Maybe her scissors are in here. (*Opens box. Suddenly puts her hand to her nose*) Why—(Mrs. Peters *bends nearer, then turns her face away*) There's something wrapped up in this piece of silk.
MRS. PETERS:	Why, this isn't her scissors.
MRS HALE:	(*lifting the silk*) Oh, Mrs. Peters—it's—
	(Mrs. Peters *bends closer.*)
MRS. PETERS:	It's the bird.
MRS HALE:	(*jumping up*) But, Mrs. Peters—look at it! It's neck! Look at its neck! It's all—other side *to*.
MRS. PETERS:	Somebody—wrung—its—neck.
	(Their eyes meet. A look of growing comprehension, of horror. Steps are heard outside. MRS. HALE *slips box under quilt pieces, and sinks into her chair. Enter* Sheriff *and* County Attorney. Mrs. Peters *rises.)*
COUNTY ATTORNEY:	(*as one turning from serious things to little pleasantries*) Well ladies, have you decided whether she was going to quilt it or knot it?
MRS. PETERS:	We think she was going to—knot it.
COUNTY ATTORNEY:	Well, that's interesting, I'm sure. (*seeing the birdcage*) Has the bird flown?
MRS HALE:	(*putting more quilt pieces over the box*) We think the—cat got it.
COUNTY ATTORNEY:	(*preoccupied*) Is there a cat?
	(Mrs. Hale *glances in a quick covert way at Mrs. Peters.*)
MRS. PETERS:	Well, not now. They're superstitious, you know. They leave.

310

315

320

325

330

335

340

COUNTY ATTORNEY: (*to* Sheriff Peters, *continuing an interrupted conversation*) No   345
sign at all of anyone having come from the outside. Their
own rope. Now let's go up again and go over it piece by
piece. (*they start upstairs*) It would have to have been
someone who knew just the—

> (Mrs. Peters *sits down. The two women sit there not looking*
> *at one another, but as if peering into something and at the*
> *same time holding back. When they talk now it is in the*
> *manner of feeling their way over strange ground, as if afraid of*
> *what they are saying, but as if they can not help saying it.*)

MRS HALE: She liked the bird. She was going to bury it in that pretty box.   350

MRS. PETERS: (*in a whisper*) When I was a girl—my kitten—there was a
boy took a hatchet, and before my eyes—and before I could
get there—(*covers her face an instant*) If they hadn't held me
back I would have—(*catches herself, looks upstairs where*
steps are heard, falters weakly)—hurt him.   355

MRS HALE: (*with a slow look around her*) I wonder how it would seem
never to have had any children around. (*pause*) No, Wright
wouldn't like the bird—a thing that sang. She used to sing.
He killed that, too.

MRS. PETERS: (*moving uneasily*) We don't know who killed the bird.   360

MRS HALE: I knew John Wright.

MRS. PETERS: It was an awful thing was done in this house that night, Mrs.
Hale. Killing a man while he slept, slipping a rope around his
neck that choked the life out of him.

MRS HALE: His neck. Choked the life out of him.   365

> (*Her hand goes out and rests on the bird-cage.*)

MRS. PETERS: (*with rising voice*) We don't know who killed him. We don't
know.

MRS HALE: (*her own feeling not interrupted*) If there'd been years and
years of nothing, then a bird to sing to you, it would be
awful—still, after the bird was still.   370

MRS. PETERS: (*something within her speaking*) I know what stillness is.
When we homesteaded in Dakota, and my first baby died—
after he was two years old, and me with no other then—

MRS HALE: (*moving*) How soon do you suppose they'll be through,
looking for the evidence?   375

MRS. PETERS: I know what stillness is. (*pulling herself back*) The law has got
to punish crime, Mrs. Hale.

MRS HALE: (*not as if answering that*) I wish you'd seen Minnie Foster
when she wore a white dress with blue ribbons and stood
up there in the choir and sang. (*a look around the room*) Oh,   380
I *wish* I'd come over here once in a while! That was a crime!
That was a crime! Who's going to punish that?

MRS. PETERS:	(*looking upstairs*) We mustn't—take on.
MRS HALE:	I might have known she needed help! I know how things can be—for women. I tell you, it's queer, Mrs. Peters. We live 385 close together and we live far apart. We all go through the same things—it's all just a different kind of the same thing. (*brushes her eyes, noticing the bottle of fruit, reaches out for it*) If I was you, I wouldn't tell her her fruit was gone. Tell her it *ain't*. Tell her it's all right. Take this in to prove it to her. She— 390 she may never know whether it was broke or not.
MRS. PETERS:	(*takes the bottle, looks about for something to wrap it in; takes petticoat from the clothes brought from the other room, very nervously begins winding this around the bottle. In a false voice*) My, it's a good thing the men couldn't hear us. 395 Wouldn't they just laugh! Getting all stirred up over a little thing like a—dead canary. As if that could have anything to do with—with—wouldn't they *laugh*!
	(*The men are heard coming down stairs.*)
MRS HALE:	(*under her breath*) Maybe they would—maybe they wouldn't.
COUNTY ATTORNEY:	No, Peters, it's all perfectly clear except a reason for doing 400 it. But you know juries when it comes to women. If there was some definite thing. Something to show—something to make a story about—a thing that would connect up with this strange way of doing it—
	(*The women's eyes meet for an instant. Enter Hale from outer door.*)
HALE:	Well, I've got the team around. Pretty cold out there. 405
COUNTY ATTORNEY:	I'm going to stay here a while by myself. (*to the* Sheriff) You can send Frank out for me, can't you? I want to go over everything. I'm not satisfied that we can't do better.
SHERIFF:	Do you want to see what Mrs. Peters is going to take in?
	(*The* Lawyer *goes to the table, picks up the apron, laughs.*)
COUNTY ATTORNEY:	Oh, I guess they're not very dangerous things the ladies have 410 picked out. (*Moves a few things about, disturbing the quilt pieces which cover the box. Steps back*) No, Mrs. Peters doesn't need supervising. For that matter, a Sheriff's wife is married to the law. Ever think of it that way, Mrs. Peters?
MRS. PETERS:	Not—just that way. 415
SHERIFF:	(*chuckling*) Married to the law. (*moves toward the other room*) I just want you to come in here a minute, George. We ought to take a look at these windows.
COUNTY ATTORNEY:	(*scoffingly*) Oh, windows!
SHERIFF:	We'll be right out, Mr. Hale. 420
	(Hale *goes outside. The* Sheriff *follows the* County Attorney *into the other room. Then* Mrs. Hale *rises, hands*

> tight together, looking intensely at Mrs. Peters, *whose
> eyes make a slow turn, finally meeting* Mrs. Hale's. *A
> moment* Mrs. Hale *holds her, then her own eyes point
> the way to where the box is concealed. Suddenly* Mrs.
> Peters *throws back quilt pieces and tries to put the box
> in the bag she is wearing. It is too big. She opens box,
> starts to take bird out, cannot touch it, goes to pieces,
> stands there helpless. Sound of a knob turning in the
> other room.* Mrs. Hale *snatches the box and puts it in
> the pocket of her big coat. Enter* County Attorney *and*
> Sheriff.)

COUNTY ATTORNEY: (*facetiously*) Well, Henry, at least we found out that she was not going to quilt it. She was going to—what is it you call it, ladies?

MRS HALE: (*her hand against her pocket*) We call it—knot it, Mr. Henderson.   425
(CURTAIN)

Critical Thinking Topics

1. What assumptions do the men make about the women? Explain how these assumptions relate to the title of the play.
2. Toward the end of the play, the County Attorney declares, "For that matter, a Sheriff's wife is married to the law. Ever think of it that way, Mrs. Peters?" At the beginning of the play, Mrs. Peters defends the men as they conduct their search for evidence. What events in the play and what memories cause her to shift her loyalties and to sympathize with Minnie Wright?
3. Minnie Wright's character never appears in the play. We only hear about her situation through the accounts of the other characters—primarily, her neighbor Mrs. Hale's account. Citing specific details, explain how Minnie Wright's character is depicted.

Writing Topics

1. Mrs. Hale and Mrs. Peters conceal evidence from the authorities. Which is their greater responsibility, to protect Minnie or to obey the law? Choose a position and develop an argument for it.
2. By the end of the play, it is evident that Minnie Wright murdered her husband. Should she come forward and confess? If she were to stand trial for murder and you were her defense attorney, what closing argument might you present to the jurors? If you were the prosecuting attorney, what closing argument might you present? If you were one of the jurors, would you vote for a verdict of guilty or not guilty? Why?

7.20 Nonfiction

The six nonfiction pieces in this section, spanning the years from 1597 through 2018, explore topics and issues related to the theme of crime and punishment.

7.21 Francis Bacon, Of Revenge (1597)

Revenge is a kind of wild justice, which the more man's nature runs to, the more ought law to weed it out. For as for the first wrong, it doth but offend the law, but the revenge of that wrong putteth the law out of office. Certainly in taking revenge, a man is but even with his enemy, but in passing it over, he is superior, for it is a prince's part to pardon. And Solomon, I am sure, saith, "It is the glory of a man to pass by an offense." That which is past is gone and irrevocable, and wise men have enough to do with things present and to come; therefore they do but trifle with themselves that labor in past matters. There is no man doth a wrong for the wrong's sake, but thereby to purchase himself profit, or pleasure, or honor, or the like. Therefore why should I be angry with a man for loving himself better than me? And if any man should do wrong merely out of ill nature, why, yet it is but like the thorn or briar, which prick and scratch because they can do no other. The most tolerable sort of revenge is for those wrongs which there is no law to remedy, but then let a man take heed the revenge be such as there is no law to punish; else a man's enemy is still beforehand, and it is two for one. Some, when they take revenge, are desirous the party should know whence it cometh. This the more generous. For the delight seemeth to not be so much in doing the hurt as in making the party repent. But base and crafty cowards are like the arrow that flieth in the dark. Cosmus, duke of Florence, had a desperate saying against perfidious or neglecting friends, as if those wrongs were unpardonable: "You shall read," saith he, "that we are commanded to forgive our enemies; but you never read that we are commanded to forgive our friends." But yet the spirit of Job was in better tune: "Shall we," saith he, "take good at God's hands, and not be content to take evil also?" And so of friends in a proportion. This is certain, that a man that studieth revenge keeps his own wounds green, which otherwise would heal and do well. Public revenges are for the most part fortunate, as that for the death of Caesar, for the death of Pertinax, for the death of Henry the Third of France, and many more. But in private revenges it is not so. Nay rather, vindictive persons live the life of witches, who, as they are mischievous, so end they unfortunate.

Critical Thinking Topics

1. What does Bacon believe about the character of someone who does not seek revenge?
2. Bacon argues that a person who does seek vengeance is more generous if the revenge is not anonymous. Would you agree with him? Why or why not?

Writing Topic

Bacon tells us that "vindictive persons live the life of witches, who, as they are mischievous, so end they unfortunate." He also claims, "This is certain, that a man that studieth revenge keeps his own wounds green, which otherwise would heal and do well." No doubt Bacon takes the high ground when it comes to vengeance on his fellow man. Why do some people who agree in theory with Bacon's ideals not practice them? What is it about human nature that drives people to desire to "get even"? Using examples from your own observations or from popular culture, reflect on ways in which our culture encourages revengeful behavior.

7.22 George G. Vest, Eulogy of the Dog[20]
(September 23, 1870—Warrensburg, Missouri)

Gentlemen of the jury. The best friend a man has in the world may turn against him and become his enemy. His son or daughter whom he has reared with loving care may prove ungrateful. Those who are nearest and dearest to us, those whom we trust with our happiness and our good name, may become traitors to their faith. The money that a man has he may lose. It flies away from him perhaps when he needs it most. A man's reputation may be sacrificed in a moment of ill-considered action. The people who are prone to fall on their knees to do us honor when success is with us may be the first to throw the stone of malice when failure settles its cloud upon our heads. The one absolutely unselfish friend that a man can have in this selfish world, the one that never deserts him, the one that never proves ungrateful or treacherous, is the dog.

Gentlemen of the jury, a man's dog stands by him in prosperity and in poverty, in health and in sickness. He will sleep on the cold ground when the wintry winds blow and the snow drives fiercely, if only he can be near his master's side. He will kiss the hand that has no food to offer, he will lick the wounds and sores that come in encounter with the roughness of the world. He guards the sleep of his pauper master as if he were a prince.

When all other friends desert, he remains. When riches take wings and reputation falls to pieces, he is as constant in his love as the sun in its journey through the heavens. If fortune drives the master forth an outcast into the world, friendless and homeless, the faithful dog asks no higher privilege than that of accompanying him, to guard him against danger, to fight against his enemies. And when the last scene of all comes, and death takes his master in its embrace and his body is laid in the cold ground, no matter if all other friends pursue their way, there by his graveside will the noble dog be found, his head between his paws and his eyes sad but open, in alert watchfulness, faithful and true, even unto death.

Critical Thinking Topics

1. Which rhetorical appeal or appeals (*logos, ethos, pathos*) are most prevalent in Vest's speech? Offer examples.

2. Vest clearly implies that the loyalty of canine companions far surpasses the loyalty of fellow human beings. Do you agree with this claim? Why or why not?

Writing Topics

1. Vest's speech is actually the closing argument he presented as an attorney in a famous Missouri court case. Research the details of the case—a civil suit—and its outcome. Was justice served—that is, did the jury reach a fair verdict? If you had been on the jury, how would you have voted? Why?

---

[20]U.S. Congress, Senate, *Congressional Record*, 101st Cong., 2d sess., pp. S4823–24 (daily edition).

2. Imagine yourself as the attorney opposing Vest in this case. What counterarguments could you make to attempt to win the jury over to your client's side?

7.23 George Orwell, A Hanging (1931)

It was in Burma, a sodden morning of the rains. A sickly light, like yellow tinfoil, was slanting over the high walls into the jail yard. We were waiting outside the condemned cells, a row of sheds fronted with double bars, like small animal cages. Each cell measured about ten feet by ten and was quite bare within except for a plank bed and a pot for drinking water. In some of them brown, silent men were squatting at the inner bars, with their blankets draped round them. These were the condemned men, due to be hanged within the next week or two.

One prisoner had been brought out of his cell. He was a Hindu, a puny wisp of a man, with a shaven head and vague liquid eyes. He had a thick, sprouting mustache, absurdly too big for his body, rather like the mustache of a comic man on the films. Six tall Indian warders were guarding him and getting him ready for the gallows. Two of them stood by with rifles and fixed bayonets, while the others handcuffed him, passed a chain through his handcuffs and fixed it to their belts, and lashed his arms tight to his sides. They crowded very close about him, with their hands always on him in a careful, caressing grip, as though all the while feeling him to make sure he was there. It was like men handling a fish which is still alive and may jump back into the water. But he stood quite unresisting, yielding his arms limply to the ropes, as though he hardly noticed what was happening.

Eight o'clock struck and a bugle call, desolately thin in the wet air, floated from the distant barracks. The superintendent of the jail, who was standing apart from the rest of us, moodily prodding the gravel with his stick, raised his head at the sound. He was an army doctor, with a gray toothbrush mustache and a gruff voice. "For God's sake, hurry up, Francis," he said irritably. "The man ought to have been dead by this time. Aren't you ready yet?"

Francis, the head jailer, a fat Dravidian in a white drill suit and gold spectacles, waved his black hand. "Yes sir, yes sir," he bubbled. "All iss satisfactorily prepared. The hangman iss waiting. We shall proceed."

"Well, quick march, then. The prisoners can't get their breakfast till this job's over."   5

We set out for the gallows. Two warders marched on either side of the prisoner, with their rifles at the slope; two others marched close against him, gripping him by arm and shoulder, as though at once pushing and supporting him. The rest of us, magistrates and the like, followed behind. Suddenly, when we had gone ten yards, the procession stopped short without any order or warning. A dreadful thing had happened—a dog, come goodness knows whence, had appeared in the yard. It came bounding among us with a loud volley of barks and leapt round up wagging its whole body, wild with glee at finding so many human beings together. It was a large woolly dog, half Airedale, half pariah. For a moment it pranced around us, and then, before anyone could stop it, it had made a dash for the prisoner, and jumping up tried to lick his face. Everybody stood aghast, too taken aback even to grab the dog.

"Who let that bloody brute in here?" said the superintendent angrily. "Catch it, someone!"

A warder detached from the escort charged clumsily after the dog, but it danced and gamboled just out of his reach, taking everything as part of the game. A young Eurasian jailer picked up a handful of gravel and tried to stone the dog away, but it dodged the stones and came after us again. Its yaps echoed from the jail walls. The prisoner, in the grasp of the two warders, looked on incuriously, as though this was another formality of the hanging. It was several minutes before someone managed to catch the dog. Then we put my handkerchief through its collar and moved off once more, with the dog still straining and whimpering.

It was about forty yards to the gallows. I watched the bare brown back of the prisoner marching in front of me. He walked clumsily with his bound arms, but quite steadily, with that bobbing gait of the Indian who never straightens his knees. At each step his muscles slid neatly into place, the lock of hair on his scalp danced up and down, his feet printed themselves on the wet gravel. And once, in spite of the men who gripped him by each shoulder, he stepped lightly aside to avoid a puddle on the path.

It is curious; but till that moment I had never realized what it means to destroy   10 a healthy, conscious man. When I saw the prisoner step aside to avoid the puddle, I saw the mystery, the unspeakable wrongness, of cutting a life short when it is in full tide. This man was not dying, he was alive just as we are alive. All the organs of his body were working—bowels digesting food, skin renewing itself, nails growing, tissues forming—all toiling away in solemn foolery. His nails would still be growing when he stood on the drop, when he was falling through the air with a tenth-of-a-second to live. His eyes saw the yellow gravel and the gray walls, and his brain still remembered, foresaw, reasoned—even about puddles. He and we were a party of men walking together, seeing, hearing, feeling, understanding the same world; and in two minutes, with a sudden snap, one of us would be gone—one mind less, one world less.

The gallows stood in a small yard, separate from the main grounds of the prison, and overgrown with tall prickly weeds. It was a brick erection like three sides of a shed, with planking on top, and above that two beams and a crossbar with the rope dangling. The hangman, a gray-haired convict in the white uniform of the prison, was waiting beside his machine. He greeted us with a servile crouch as we entered. At a word from Francis the two warders, gripping the prisoner more closely than ever, half led, half pushed him to the gallows and helped him clumsily up the ladder. Then the hangman climbed up and fixed the rope round the prisoner's neck.

We stood waiting, five yards away. The warders had formed in a rough circle round the gallows. And then, when the noose was fixed, the prisoner began crying out to his god. It was a high, reiterated cry of "Ram! Ram! Ram! Ram!" not urgent and fearful like a prayer or cry for help, but steady, rhythmical, almost like the tolling of a bell. The dog answered the sound with a whine. The hangman, still standing on the gallows, produced a small cotton bag like a flour bag and drew it down over the prisoner's face. But the sound, muffled by the cloth, still persisted, over and over again: "Ram! Ram! Ram! Ram! Ram!"

The hangman climbed down and stood ready, holding the lever. Minutes seemed to pass. The steady, muffled crying from the prisoner went on and on, "Ram! Ram! Ram!" never faltering for an instant. The superintendent, his head on his chest, was slowly poking the ground with his stick; perhaps he was counting the cries, allowing the prisoner a fixed number—fifty, perhaps, or a hundred. Everyone had changed color. The Indians had gone gray like bad coffee, and one or two of the bayonets were wavering. We looked at the lashed, hooded man on the drop, and listened to his cries—each cry another second of life; the same thought was in all our minds; oh, kill him quickly, get it over, stop that abominable noise!

Suddenly the superintendent made up his mind. Throwing up his head he made a swift motion with his stick. "Chalo!" he shouted almost fiercely.

There was a clanking noise, and then dead silence. The prisoner had vanished, 15 and the rope was twisting on itself. I let go of the dog, and it galloped immediately to the back of the gallows; but when it got there it stopped short, barked, and then retreated into a corner of the yard, where it stood among the weeds, looking timorously out at us. We went round the gallows to inspect the prisoner's body. He was dangling with his toes pointed straight downwards, very slowly revolving, as dead as a stone.

The superintendent reached out with his stick and poked the bare brown body; it oscillated slightly. "*He's* all right," said the superintendent. He backed out from under the gallows, and blew out a deep breath. The moody look had gone out of his face quite suddenly. He glanced at his wristwatch. "Eight minutes past eight. Well, that's all for this morning, thank God."

The warders unfixed bayonets and marched away. The dog, sobered and conscious of having misbehaved itself, slipped after them. We walked out of the gallows yard, past the condemned cells with their waiting prisoners, into the big central yard of the prison. The convicts, under the command of warders armed with lathis,[21] were already receiving their breakfast. They squatted in long rows, each man holding a tin pannikin,[22] while two warders with buckets marched around ladling out rice; it seemed quite a homely, jolly scene, after the hanging. An enormous relief had come upon us now that the job was done. One felt an impulse to sing, to break into a run, to snigger. All at once everyone began chattering gaily.

The Eurasian boy walking beside me nodded towards the way we had come, with a knowing smile: "Do you know sir, our friend (he meant the dead man) when he heard his appeal had been dismissed, he pissed on the floor of his cell. From fright. Kindly take one of my cigarettes, sir. Do you not admire my new silver case, sir? From the boxwallah,[23] two rupees eight annas. Classy European style."

Several people laughed—at what, nobody seemed certain.

Francis was walking by the superintendent, talking garrulously: "Well, sir, all has 20 passed off with the utmost satisfactoriness. It was all finished—flick! Like that. It iss not always so—oah, no! I have known cases where the doctor wass obliged to go beneath the gallows and pull the prisoner's legs to ensure decease. Most disagreeable!"

"Wriggling about, eh? That's bad," said the superintendent.

"Ach, sir, it iss worse when they become refractory! One man, I recall, clung to the bars of hiss cage when we went to take him out. You will scarcely credit, sir, that it took six warders to dislodge him, three pulling at each leg. We reasoned with him, 'My dear fellow,' we said, 'think of all the pain and trouble you are causing to us!' But no, he would not listen! Ach, he wass very troublesome!"

I found that I was laughing quite loudly. Everyone was laughing. Even the superintendent grinned in a tolerant way. "You'd better all come out and have a drink," he said quite genially. "I've got a bottle of whiskey in the car. We could do with it."

We went through the big double gates of the prison into the road. "Pulling at his legs!" exclaimed a Burmese magistrate suddenly, and burst into a loud chuckling. We all began laughing again. At that moment Francis' anecdote seemed extraordinarily

---

[21]**lathis** police club
[22]**pannikin** metal cup
[23]**boxwallah** a vendor who sold from boxes on the streets of India

funny. We all had a drink together, native and European alike, quite amicably. The dead man was a hundred yards away.

Source: Orwell, George. "A Hanging" from A COLLECTION OF ESSAYS by George Orwell. Copyright © 1950 by Sonia Brownell Orwell. Reprinted by permission of Houghton Mifflin Harcourt Publishing Company. All rights reserved.

Critical Thinking Topics

1. The powers of law and order have structured this execution perfectly, and all the details of the process seem so right, so correct. What small event allows Orwell to see past all the trappings of justice being carried out?

2. Why do some observers sing, snigger, and laugh at the end? Surely an execution cannot be humorous. Explain these strange reactions.

Writing Topic

Orwell cannot disconnect himself from the shared humanity between the condemned man and himself: "It is curious; but till that moment I had never realized what it means to destroy a healthy, conscious man. When I saw the prisoner step aside to avoid the puddle, I saw the mystery, the unspeakable wrongness, of cutting a life short when it is in full tide. This man was not dying, he was alive just as we are alive" (par. 10). In your opinion, how are people able to separate themselves from their work duties when those duties clash with their own personal value systems? Have you ever been in a circumstance—for example, on a job or in school—that made you uncomfortable about violating your own value system? If so, how did you handle the situation? If not, think of another person—real or fictional—who, like Orwell, had to deal with this type of situation, and describe how that person handled it.

7.24 Edward Abbey, Eco-Defense
(1985)

If a stranger batters your door down with an axe, threatens your family and yourself with deadly weapons, and proceeds to loot your home of whatever he wants, he is committing what is universally recognized—by law and in common morality—as a crime. In such a situation the householder has both the right and the obligation to defend himself, his family, and his property by whatever means are necessary. This right and this obligation is universally recognized, justified, and praised by all civilized human communities. Self-defense against attack is one of the basic laws not only of human society but of life itself, not only of human life but of all life.

   The American wilderness, what little remains, is now undergoing exactly such an assault. With bulldozer, earth mover, chainsaw, and dynamite the international timber, mining, and beef industries are invading our public lands—property of all Americans—bashing their way into our forests, mountains, and rangelands and looting them for everything they can get away with. This for the sake of short-term profits in the corporate sector and multimillion-dollar annual salaries for the three-piece-suited gangsters (MBA—Harvard, Yale, University of Tokyo, et alia) who control and manage these bandit enterprises. Cheered on, naturally, by *Time*, *Newsweek*, and *The Wall Street Journal*, actively encouraged, inevitably, by those jellyfish government agencies that are supposed to *protect* the public lands, and as always aided and abetted in every way possible by the compliant politicians of our Western states, such as Babbitt, DeConcini, Goldwater, McCain, Hatch, Garn, Simms, Hansen, Andrus, Wallop, Domenici and Co. Inc.—who would sell the graves of their mothers if there's a quick buck in the deal, over or under the table, what do they care.

Representative government in the United States has broken down. Our legislators do not represent the public, the voters, or even those who voted for them but rather the commercial industrial interests that finance their political campaigns and control the organs of communication—the TV, the newspapers, the billboards, the radio. Politics is a game for the rich only. Representative government in the USA represents money, not people, and therefore has forfeited our allegiance and moral support. We owe it nothing but the taxation it extorts from us under threats of seizure of property, imprisonment, or in some cases already, when resisted, a violent death by gunfire.

Such is the nature and structure of the industrial megamachine (in Lewis Mumford's term) which is now attacking the American wilderness. That wilderness is our ancestral home, the primordial homeland of all living creatures including the human, and the present final dwelling place of such noble beings as the grizzly bear, the mountain lion, the eagle and the condor, the moose and the elk and the pronghorn antelope, the redwood tree, the yellow pine, the bristlecone pine, and yes, why not say it?—the streams, waterfalls, rivers, the very bedrock itself of our hills, canyons, deserts, mountains. For many of us, perhaps for most of us, the wilderness is more our home than the little stucco boxes, wallboard apartments, plywood trailer-houses, and cinderblock condominiums in which the majority are now confined by the poverty of an overcrowded industrial culture.

And if the wilderness is our true home, and if it is threatened with invasion, pillage, and destruction—as it certainly is—then we have the right to defend that home, as we would our private quarters, by whatever means are necessary. (An Englishman's home is his castle; the American's home is his favorite forest, river, fishing stream, her favorite mountain or desert canyon, his favorite swamp or woods or lake.) We have the right to resist and we have the obligation; not to defend that which we love would be dishonorable. The majority of the American people have demonstrated on every possible occasion that they support the ideal of wilderness preservation; even our politicians are forced by popular opinion to *pretend* to support the idea; as they have learned, a vote against wilderness is a vote against their own reelection. We are justified then in defending our homes—our private home and our public home—not only by common law and common morality but also by common belief. We are the majority; they—the powerful—are in the minority.

How best defend our homes? Well, that is a matter of the strategy, tactics, and technique which eco-defense is all about.

What is eco-defense? Eco-defense means fighting back. Eco-defense means sabotage. Eco-defense is risky but sporting; unauthorized but fun; illegal but ethically imperative. Next time you enter a public forest scheduled for chainsaw massacre by some timber corporation and its flunkies in the US Forest Service, carry a hammer and a few pounds of 60-penny nails in your creel, saddlebag, game bag, backpack, or picnic basket. Spike those trees; you won't hurt them; they'll be grateful for the protection; and you may save the forest. Loggers hate nails. My Aunt Emma back in West Virginia has been enjoying this pleasant exercise for years. She swears by it. It's good for the trees, it's good for the woods, and it's good for the human soul. Spread the word.

5

Source: Reprinted by permission of Don Congdon Associates, Inc. Copyright © 1985 by Edward Abbey.

Critical Thinking Topics

1. Abbey describes enemies who threaten the environment as "three-piece-suited gangsters." In fact, Abbey often resorts to name-calling in his brief argument. Cite at least two other examples of name-calling and explain how this tactic weakens or strengthens the writer's argument.

2. The writer's argument turns on an analogy: We have the right and the obligation to defend our homes. The wilderness is our home. We therefore have the right and obligation to defend the wilderness. Is this a valid analogy or an example of false analogy (one of the logical fallacies discussed in Chapter 3)? Explain your answer.

3. Identify three or more assumptions in Abbey's argument, and explain why each is or is not valid (a valid assumption is one that is likely to be shared by a broad range of readers).

Writing Topic

Abbey openly calls for spiking trees, an illegal practice that can lead to serious bodily injury among loggers. He asks you, the reader, to willfully violate the law in an act of civil disobedience. Similarly, a number of environmental organizations today practice and sometimes advocate civil disobedience. For example, Greenpeace boats illegally disrupt whaling and fishing activities; PETA members block hunters; and the Animal Liberation Front has burned veterinary labs. Think of a cause—preferably, an actual cause, but otherwise, an imagined one—for which you would consider breaking the law. Argue with evidence that this cause would justify civil disobedience. Then think of a cause for which people have actually engaged in civil disobedience (such as one of the causes mentioned above or some other cause), and construct an argument, with evidence, that the civil disobedience was not justified.

7.25 Peter J. Henning, Determining a Punishment That Fits the Crime (2016)

One of the vexing issues in white-collar crime is figuring out the appropriate sentence for someone who usually has an otherwise spotless record and poses no physical threat to the community. Recent cases show how hard it is to determine a just punishment for defendants who have so much going for them yet engaged in criminal conduct.

Andrew Caspersen, sentenced last Friday to four years in prison, seemed like the epitome of a success story. Described by a headline in *The New York Times* as a Wall Street scion, he came from a wealthy family and, armed with an Ivy League education, held a position at the private equity firm Park Hill Group that put him near the upper reaches of financial power.

Then he threw it all away by bilking family and friends out of more than $38 million—and was seeking more when he was arrested in March—to finance wildly speculative options trades that ultimately failed. At the sentencing hearing, Mr. Caspersen's lawyer portrayed the fraud as the product of a gambling addiction that drove his client to keep betting more and more on the market until he was broke.

Unlike those who commit street crimes, white-collar offenders are much more likely to be members of the middle class, and possibly even among the economic elite like Mr. Caspersen. They have the resources to present a sympathetic picture of their life while claiming that violations of the law were just aberrations from an otherwise exemplary life.

These offenders can often serve up a variety of reasons to explain, and perhaps   5 diminish, their violations. Thus, Mr. Caspersen claimed that his gambling addiction fueled the trading that led to the fraud, not ordinary greed that would make it palatable to impose a harsher sentence.

In federal fraud cases, the sentencing guidelines are the starting point for determining the appropriate punishment. They put great weight on the amount of the loss caused by a defendant, or the intended gain from the misconduct. This can lead to sentences of a decade or more.

For example, insider trading convictions led to prison terms of 11 years for the former hedge fund manager Raj Rajaratnam and 12 years for the former lawyer Matthew Kluger for crimes that had little direct impact on investors but led to outsize gains for the defendants and those who traded on their information.

Jed S. Rakoff, the judge for the Federal District Court for the Southern District of New York who sentenced Mr. Caspersen, has been a frequent critic of the numerical focus of the sentencing guidelines, once calling for them to be scrapped in a speech to white-collar defense lawyers. He described the Justice Department's recommendation of a sentence of more than 15 years for Mr. Caspersen based on the amount he took from investors as "absurd" because of the overemphasis on numerical calculations that ignore the factors leading to criminal conduct.

Federal judges are not bound to follow the guidelines, and often vary from them, especially in white-collar cases in which defendants can present a number of reasons they are not the typical offender who should receive a prison term.

The issue is what excuses are appropriate for a judge to consider in determining   10 the right punishment for the crime. Figuring out the appropriate sentence requires consideration of multiple competing interests, not the least of which is the message sent to the general public about how this type of criminal should be treated.

In Mr. Caspersen's case, Judge Rakoff agreed that he was afflicted with an addiction to gambling, but said it was just one factor in the sentence because "it was a fraud that involved the deception of people who had a lot of faith in the defendant." By giving a four-year prison term, the judge took a position somewhere in between what the government wanted and the defense was hoping for—a common occurrence.

A sentencing scheduled for Wednesday before Judge Rakoff will present another issue that arises frequently in white-collar sentencing: How much should the loss of prestige and income by the white-collar offender be a factor in mitigating a sentence?

Paul Thompson pleaded guilty to helping manipulate the London Interbank Offered Rate, or Libor, while he was a trader at Rabobank, working with other defendants to push the rate to help the bank's positions.

In a memorandum submitted to Judge Rakoff, his lawyer pointed to the impact of his conviction, that he "has lost his job, his career, his reputation, and, despite decades of sacrifice and hard work, he is unlikely to work in his chosen profession ever again." In asking for probation, the lawyer argued that manipulating Libor submissions "was widespread, condoned and well-known throughout the industry," so that the punishment he "has already suffered has been harsh."

The Justice Department appears torn by what is an appropriate sentence in a case   15
like this in which the financial harm is difficult to measure. It recommended that he receive at least a year in prison, yet told Judge Rakoff that "beyond his participation in the scheme at hand, however, all available evidence suggests that Mr. Thompson is fundamentally a decent person." Should that kind of person be required to spend time in a federal prison?

Convictions always have an impact on both defendants and their families, whether it be a white-collar case or a street crime. Judges are fearful of imposing a light sentence on those who look more like them because it would foster the perception that offenders with greater wealth and social standing can expect better treatment in the criminal justice system. So the argument that a defendant has already paid a price for a violation rarely gains much traction.

What judges really want to hear is an expression of contrition, word that the defendant is sorry for any harm caused while promising never to engage in such misconduct again. For those who plead guilty, like Mr. Caspersen and Mr. Thompson, the acknowledgment of guilt puts them in a much better position with the court because they can avoid the perception of trying to get away with something or planning the next crime.

Bridget Anne Kelly and Bill Baroni, former aides to Governor Chris Christie of New Jersey who were convicted last Friday for their role in shutting access lanes to the George Washington Bridge as political payback for a New Jersey mayor who did not endorse the governor's re-election effort in 2013, are in a difficult position when their sentencing occurs next year. By testifying that they did nothing wrong and continuing to proclaim their innocence, they are now locked into a position that prevents them from acknowledging that their conduct was illegal and asking for leniency.

Under the sentencing guidelines, the two defendants could easily face a recommended prison term of more than four years for the corruption charges. Prosecutors may ask the court to find they committed perjury by testifying that they were unaware of any scheme to engage in misconduct on behalf of the governor, which could push the potential punishment even higher.

They have suffered the same loss of their career and social status as Mr. Caspersen   20
and Mr. Thompson, but by going to trial, any claim they might make that they have "suffered enough already" is likely to fall on deaf ears.

Sentencing is certainly an art, not a science, despite the attempt at precision in the loss calculations in the sentencing guidelines. Judges are left with making a decision based on what they see in the defendant in front of them, in the hope that the punishment will be perceived as fair. Like it or not, that is the system we have, even if it leaves the public unsatisfied with a penalty that can be considered too lenient—or too harsh.

Source: From The New York Times, 11/8/2016 © 2016 The New York Times. All rights reserved. Used by permission and protected by the Copyright Laws of the United States. The printing, copying, redistribution, or retransmission of this Content without express written permission is prohibited.

Critical Thinking Topics

1. The writer uses examples to help the reader understand the challenges judges face in sentencing white-collar criminals. State those challenges in your own words.

2. Henning provides detailed examples in his piece, but in the end, has he created an argument? Does he reveal an implicit bias on the subject? If you think he does, state what you think his bias is, and identify specific words or phrases that reveal it. If, in your view, he has maintained an objective stance, what do you think he achieves by doing so?

Writing Topic

Wells Fargo Bank has been fined a billion dollars for defrauding millions of customers by setting up false accounts in their names. The car companies Volkswagen and Porsche have been found to have defrauded their customers by falsifying emissions testing. Do some research on the three cases. Did any of the people in management positions who oversaw the frauds go to jail or endure any other punishment that you would consider commensurate with their crimes? Using examples, explain your position on the outcome of these cases.

7.26 Barry Meier, Origins of an Epidemic: Purdue Pharma Knew Its Opioids Were Widely Abused (2018)

Purdue Pharma, the company that planted the seeds of the opioid epidemic through its aggressive marketing of OxyContin, has long claimed it was unaware of the powerful opioid painkiller's growing abuse until years after it went on the market.

But a copy of a confidential Justice Department report shows that federal prosecutors investigating the company found that Purdue Pharma knew about "significant" abuse of OxyContin in the first years after the drug's introduction in 1996 and concealed that information.

Company officials had received reports that the pills were being crushed and snorted; stolen from pharmacies; and that some doctors were being charged with selling prescriptions, according to dozens of previously undisclosed documents that offer a detailed look inside Purdue Pharma. But the drug maker continued "in the face of this knowledge" to market OxyContin as less prone to abuse and addiction than other prescription opioids, prosecutors wrote in 2006.

Based on their findings after a four-year investigation, the prosecutors recommended that three top Purdue Pharma executives be indicted on felony charges, including conspiracy to defraud the United States, that could have sent the men to prison if convicted.

But top Justice Department officials in the George W. Bush administration did not support the move, said four lawyers who took part in those discussions or were briefed about them. Instead, the government settled the case in 2007.

Prosecutors found that the company's sales representatives used the words "street value," "crush," or "snort" in 117 internal notes recording their visits to doctors or other medical professionals from 1997 through 1999.

The 120-page report also cited emails showing that Purdue Pharma's owners, members of the wealthy Sackler family, were sent reports about abuse of OxyContin and another company opioid, MS Contin.

"We have in fact picked up references to abuse of our opioid products on the internet," Purdue Pharma's general counsel, Howard R. Udell, wrote in early 1999 to another company official. That same year, prosecutors said, company officials learned of a call to a pharmacy describing "OxyContin as the hottest thing on the street—forget Vicodin."

Mr. Udell and other company executives testified in Congress and elsewhere that the drug maker did not learn about OxyContin's growing abuse until early 2000, when the United States attorney in Maine issued an alert. Today, Purdue Pharma, which is based in Stamford, Conn., maintains that position.

The episode remains relevant as lawmakers and regulators struggle to stem a mounting epidemic that involves both prescription opioids and, increasingly, illegal opioid compounds like heroin and counterfeit forms of fentanyl. President Trump has declared the problem a public health emergency.   10

Over the past two decades, more than 200,000 people have died in the United States from overdoses involving prescription opioids. States and cities continue to file a wave of lawsuits against Purdue Pharma and other opioid manufacturers and distributors.

A spokesman for Purdue Pharma, Robert Josephson, declined to comment on the allegations in the report but said the company was involved in efforts to address opioid abuse.

"Suggesting that activities that last occurred more than 16 years ago are responsible for today's complex and multifaceted opioid crisis is deeply flawed," he said in a statement.

In 2007, Purdue Pharma pleaded guilty to a felony charge of "misbranding" Oxy-Contin while marketing the drug by misrepresenting, among other things, its risk of addiction and potential to be abused. Three executives — the company's chief executive, Michael Friedman; its top medical officer, Dr. Paul D. Goldenheim; and Mr. Udell, who died in 2013 — each pleaded guilty to a misdemeanor "misbranding" charge that solely held them liable as Purdue Pharma's "responsible" executives and did not accuse them of wrongdoing. The company and the executives paid a combined $634.5 million in fines and the men were required to perform community service.

The head of the Justice Department's criminal division at the time, Alice S. Fisher, did not respond to emails seeking comment about the decision not to pursue indictments. That decision followed meetings with a Purdue Pharma defense team whose advisers included Rudolph W. Giuliani, a onetime United States attorney and former New York mayor. Mr. Giuliani, who was then regarded as a potential Republican presidential candidate, is now a legal adviser to Mr. Trump.   15

The Justice Department hailed the settlement as a victory. But several former government officials said the decision not to bring more serious charges and air the evidence prosecutors had gathered meant that a critical chance to slow the trajectory of the opioid epidemic was lost.

"It would have been a turning point," said Terrance Woodworth, a former Drug Enforcement Administration official who investigated Purdue Pharma in the early 2000s. "It would have sent a message to the entire drug industry."

Prosecutors did not accuse any Sackler family members of wrongdoing. But they wrote that Richard Sackler was told in 1999 while he was president of Purdue Pharma about discussions in internet chat rooms where drug abusers described snorting OxyContin, which contains oxycodone, a powerful narcotic. Other family members, including Raymond and Mortimer Sackler, the drug maker's founders, were sent reports about the abuse of OxyContin's predecessor drug, a long-acting form of morphine sold as MS Contin, the report said.

A spokesman for Sackler family members involved with the company, Linden Zakula, declined to comment. Richard Sackler, who is now a director of Purdue Pharma, also declined to comment.

The three executives, who prosecutors described as reporting directly to the Sack-   20
lers, have always asserted they had done nothing wrong and had moved quickly to address the drug's growing abuse after they became aware of it in 2000.

"Everyone was taken by surprise by what happened," Dr. Goldenheim testified in 2001. "We launched OxyContin in 1996, and for the first four years on the market, we did not hear of any particular problem."

A Powerful Marketing Claim

When the Food and Drug Administration approved OxyContin in late 1995, the agency permitted Purdue Pharma to make a unique claim for it — that its long-acting formulation was "believed to reduce" its appeal to drug abusers compared with shorter-acting painkillers like Percocet and Vicodin.

The F.D.A. decision was not based on findings from clinical trials, but a theory that drug abusers favored shorter-acting painkillers because the narcotic they contained was released faster and so produced a quicker "hit."

Purdue Pharma viewed the agency's decision as "so valuable" that it could serve as OxyContin's "principal selling tool," an internal 1995 company report shows. The drugmaker admitted in 2007, when confronted with evidence gathered by prosecutors, that it trained sales representative to tell doctors that OxyContin was less addictive and prone to abuse than competing opioids, claims beyond the one approved by the F.D.A.

But even as Purdue Pharma aggressively promoted OxyContin as safer, pros-   25
ecutors wrote, it soon learned that drug abusers were seeking out OxyContin and its other long-acting opioid, MS Contin. The reason: They had far higher narcotic levels than standard, shorter-acting painkillers, and could be snorted or injected intravenously.

In May 1996, five months after OxyContin's approval, Richard Sackler and Mr. Udell were sent an older medical journal article describing how drug abusers were extracting morphine from MS Contin tablets in order to inject the drug, prosecutors reported. A Purdue Pharma scientist researched the issue and sent his findings to several Sacklers, the government report states.

"I found MS Contin mentioned a couple of times on the internet underground drug culture scene," the researcher wrote in that 1996 email. "Most of it was mentioned in the context of MS Contin as a morphine source."

By the following year, prosecutors wrote, Purdue Pharma learned that drug addicts in Australia and New Zealand were abusing MS Contin and Dr. Goldenheim was sent an article from American Family Physician, a publication, about the ease of extracting morphine from MS Contin.

Then in 1998, as OxyContin's marketing campaign was taking off, Purdue Pharma learned of a medical journal study that appeared to undercut its central message — that OxyContin, as a long-acting opioid, had less appeal to drug abusers.

In the study, which was published in The Journal of the Canadian Medical   30 Association, researchers from the University of British Columbia in Vancouver interviewed local drug dealers and abusers to learn what legal drugs sold for on the black market. They found that MS Contin commanded the highest price of any prescription opioid with a 30-milligram tablet that cost $1 at a pharmacy bringing up to $40 on the street.

In an accompanying editorial, a Canadian physician, Dr. Brian Goldman, wrote that the findings turned thinking about the supposed safety of long-acting opioids like OxyContin on its head by showing that drug abusers "coveted" such drugs.

"This should ring alarm bells," Dr. Goldman, who was then a paid speaker for Purdue Pharma, wrote in the editorial.

Purdue Pharma did not send the Canadian study to the F.D.A. or tell its sales representatives about it. Instead, one sales official testified later to a federal grand jury that the company gave him an older survey to show doctors that had concluded that drug abusers were not attracted to time-release opioids.

Mr. Josephson, the Purdue Pharma spokesman, said it was not required to tell the F.D.A. about the Canadian study or editorial. He added that the company did not consider the small study's results significant because it was already known that morphine could be abused.

However, in March 1998, a few months before the study's publication, Mr. Udell,   35 the chief counsel, sent seven members of the Sackler family a memo titled "MS Contin Abuse," described by prosecutors as containing articles from Vancouver-area newspapers about the drug's abuse there and the price MS Contin was bringing on the street.

Two years later, as OxyContin's abuse publicly exploded in early 2000, a Purdue Pharma executive described in an email to Mr. Friedman, the chief executive, how he was reminded of what he had seen earlier managing MS Contin sales in the Midwest.

"I received this kind of news on MS Contin, all the time and from everywhere," the company's vice-president of marketing, Mark Alfonso, wrote in June 2000. "Some pharmacies would not even stock MS Contin for fear they would be robbed. In Wisconsin, Minnesota and Oklahoma, we had physicians indicted for prescribing too much MS Contin."

Mr. Friedman's response, prosecutors reported, was to forward that email to Mr. Udell with a question: "You want all this chat on email?"

"We Have a Credibility Problem"

By 1997, Purdue Pharma was also aware that OxyContin was becoming a popular topic online, according to one email cited in the prosecution report previously published in Fortune magazine. As sales of the drug began to boom, prosecutors found, so did the number of reports the company received about abuse, addiction and crimes connected to the drug.

During one brief period in 1999, they reported, company officials learned from 40 articles in small-town newspapers and other sources that a doctor in Pennsylvania had stopped writing prescriptions for OxyContin because patients eager to get more of the drug were getting arrested for altering them; that a Connecticut man had been arrested for trying to illegally purchase OxyContin; that a man in Massachusetts had told the police that he preferred crushing the drug because it worked better "if he sniffs it;" and that a pharmacy in Maryland had been robbed of OxyContin.

"I continue to see OxyContin increase in abuse with our doctor shoppers and sellers," a drug investigator near Cincinnati wrote in a message that was forwarded to Mr. Udell, prosecutors reported.

Mark Ross, a former company sales representative, testified during a grand jury appearance that after he warned a manager that one doctor's office was filled with drug seekers he was told his job was to sell drugs, not to determine if a "doctor was a drug pusher," according to a summary of his testimony in the report.

A sales representative in Jacksonville, Fla., also questioned the company's claim that OxyContin had less abuse potential after the arrest of a doctor there on charges of illegally prescribing the opioid and other drugs, an email cited by prosecutors shows.

"I feel like we have a credibility problem with our product," the sales representative, Jim Speed, wrote in a 1999 email.

By late 1999, other doctors had been arrested nationwide on similar charges. But 45 when one Purdue Pharma executive, Dr. J. David Haddox, suggested after the arrest in Jacksonville that the company adopt a crisis-response plan, Mr. Friedman responded that he did not think such action was needed, prosecutors wrote.

"I simply do not want us to overreact to this specific story," he wrote, according to prosecutors. "This has not been a repetitive pattern or something new."

Settlement Talks Begin

In mid-2006, prosecutors notified Purdue Pharma and the three executives about the charges they planned to seek. Over a two-day meeting in September, a high-profile team of defense lawyers rebutted those allegations and argued that the government's case would collapse when tested in court, according to lawyers present. They also presented evidence which they said proved that the executives were unaware of significant OxyContin abuse before early 2000.

The prosecutors and their boss, the United States attorney for the Western District of Virginia, John L. Brownlee, were not swayed.

In late September 2006, the recommendations for indictments were forwarded to Justice Department headquarters in Washington. A few weeks later, defense lawyers representing Purdue Pharma and the executives met with top Justice Department officials to again make their case.

Top officials such as Ms. Fisher, the head of the department's criminal division, 50 soon made it clear that they did not support the indictments, former government lawyers said. Talks to resolve the case through a plea bargain began.

"We made a presentation of evidence and advocacy to DOJ without having seen the prosecution memo," a defense lawyer, Andrew Good, who represented Dr. Goldenheim, said in a statement. "No charge of false testimony or concealment of abuse was brought because none of that happened." Mr. Friedman did not respond to requests seeking comment.

Mr. Brownlee, the United States attorney, later testified that he believed the misdemeanor charges against the executives were "appropriate" given the evidence. But former government officials said he was upset by the department's decision not to support more serious charges.

A former Drug Enforcement Administration official, Joseph Rannazzisi, said Mr. Brownlee told him that the decision had left him with little choice but to settle the case because his small team of prosecutors faced being overwhelmed by Purdue Pharma's unlimited resources.

"He told me he was outgunned," Mr. Rannazzisi said. Mr. Brownlee, who is now in private practice, declined to comment.

At a court hearing held in 2007 to approve the settlement, a prosecutor who had 55 worked on the case, Randy Ramseyer, said the misdemeanor pleas by the three officials would send a message to drug industry executives that they faced being held "to a higher standard."

But drug companies continued to flood areas rife with drug abuse with more opioids. Starting in 2007, the year of the settlement, distributors of prescription drugs sent enough pain pills to West Virginia over a five-year period to supply every man, woman and child there with 433 of them, according to a report in the Charleston Gazette-Mail.

Source: Barry Meier, Origins of an Epidemic: Purdue Pharma Knew Its Opioids Were Widely Abused May 29, 2018, https://www.nytimes.com/2018/05/29/health/purdue-opioids-oxycontin.html?nl=top-stories&nlid=55891 406ries&ref=cta, The New York Times Company

---

Critical Thinking Topics

1. The article's title and its opening paragraph reveal the writer's claim: Barry Meier believes Purdue Pharma executives are partly responsible for the opioid epidemic that has swept through the United States over the last twenty years, an epidemic that had claimed more than 200,000 lives at the time the article was written (par. 11). Meier then proceeds to lay out his case for the claim. Analyze and evaluate his use of different types of evidence and of different rhetorical appeals (see Chapter 3 for discussion of evidence and rhetorical appeals):

   - Identify three examples each of at least two types of evidence. Explain how effective each example is in supporting Meier's claim.
   - On which rhetorical appeal—*ethos*, *logos*, or *pathos*—does Meier most strongly rely? Identify three examples of this appeal and evaluate each example's effectiveness. Identify an example of each of the other two appeals and evaluate the effectiveness of each.

2. Describe the tone of Meier's writing. Explain how tone influences your response to his argument. How does it enhance or weaken the argument's persuasiveness? Use examples to elaborate.

3. Evaluate the overall effectiveness of Meier's argument. Did he make his case? Why or why not? What does his argument leave you thinking? Discuss your viewpoint on Pharma Purdue executives' culpability. Should they be held accountable? If so, why, and if not, why not?

Writing Topic

On March 1, 2018, as he convened an opioid summit at the White House, President Donald J. Trump announced, "Together, we will face this challenge as a national family with conviction, with unity, and with a commitment to love and support our neighbors in times of dire need. Working together, we will defeat this opioid epidemic." And, as Meier's article reports, "President Trump has declared the opioid crisis a public health emergency" (par. 10). Do some research on the opioid epidemic. Where does the epidemic stand today? What actions have been implemented to address the public health emergency? What seems to be working, and what is not? What are some actions that you would advocate to end the epidemic? And what role, if any, should the criminal justice system have?

7.27 Chapter Activities

The series of activities on the following pages invite you to apply the concepts and ideas embodied in the readings and brought out in the critical thinking topics and writing topics throughout this chapter.

7.27.1 Topics for Writing Arguments

1. For most of us, the desire to get even—to make someone who has wronged us suffer— is instinctive. The question is, how do we respond to that instinctive urge? If we do not act on it, will it grow into an obsession that deepens and festers? Such seems to be Archie's experience in Brady Udall's short story in this chapter, "He Becomes Deeply and Famously Drunk." Will carrying out an act of revenge provide satisfaction and closure or bring on regret and guilt? In "Of Revenge" (also in this chapter), sixteenth-century philosopher Francis Bacon asserts, "Revenge is a kind of wild justice, which the more man's nature runs to it, the more the law ought to weed it out," implying that we need the rule of law to tame our instinct to seek revenge. What do you deem to be an acceptable response to the urge for revenge, and what do you consider to be an unacceptable response? In answering this question, reflect on Archie's experience in Udall's story and on examples from your own experiences and observations; also consider examples from history, in other literature, or in popular culture. Develop an argument on the concept of revenge by creating a claim of value and supporting it with extended analyses of three or more examples.

2. Commit a crime and you will be punished. This statement involves the implicit assumption that punishment—commonly meted out as a prison sentence—not only teaches the perpetrator a lesson but also serves to deter the perpetrator and others from committing more

crimes. But is this assumption valid? Consider this statement by Philadelphia district attorney Larry Krasner in a 2018 interview: "We have a country that seems to be, even now, unaware of the fact that it is the most incarcerated country in the world. . . we have had a 500 percent increase in incarceration nationally over a period of a few decades, and yet we find ourselves basically not safer." (Figure 7.2 supports Krasner's statement about the U.S. incarceration rate.) Also consider how The Misfit, in Flannery O' Connor's short story in this chapter, "A Good Man Is Hard to Find," suggests that punishment is no deterrent to crime. The Misfit is a fictional character, but how representative might he be of real-life criminals who have served time in prison? Do some research on the question of whether punishment deters crime, including finding some statistics on crime rates, incarceration rates, and recidivism rates (a recidivist is someone who commits more crimes after having been caught and punished for previous crimes). How effective is the prison system at rehabilitation—that is, which is more common: that criminals become law-abiding people after imprisonment or that they commit further crimes? Develop an argument centered on the effectiveness of incarceration as a means of reducing crime; create a claim and provide evidence based on analyses of the information you have gathered.

3. In Flannery O'Connor's short story in this chapter, "A Good Man Is Hard to Find," The Misfit tells the grandmother he was sent to the penitentiary, "buried alive," for killing his father, a crime he believes he did not commit: "My daddy died in nineteen ought nineteen of the epidemic flu and I never had a thing to do with it" (par. 117). The story makes it clear that The Misfit, even if innocent of his father's murder, is nevertheless a murderer many times over, so his imprisonment for his father's murder could still be seen as a just outcome. In real life, in contrast, there is no doubt that completely innocent people are sometimes convicted of crimes, as indicated by the many cases in

Figure 7.2 Incarceration rates in selected countries, 2015 (per 100,000 population)[24]

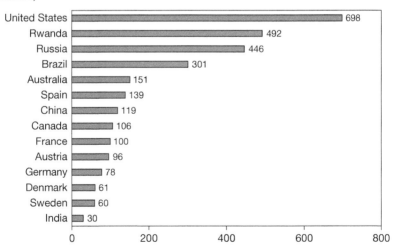

which forensic DNA analysis has led to the exoneration of wrongfully convicted persons (at the time of this writing, more than 350 convicted prisoners have been exonerated through the use of DNA evidence, including at least 20 prisoners on death row). DNA forensics have become a valuable tool for detectives in criminal investigations, not only in exonerating wrongfully convicted persons but also in apprehending the "right" person and securing a conviction. Consider, for example, the April 2018 case of the suspect arrested as the notorious Golden State Killer, Joseph James DeAngelo, a 72-year-old former police officer. DeAngelo was charged with at least eight murders and thought to be responsible for numerous rapes and burglaries in California between 1976 and 1986. However, the case triggered controversy centered on privacy and ethical issues because a public genealogy database was used to identify DeAngelo. Research this case and at least two other criminal cases in which DNA forensics was used either to find the guilty or to exonerate the innocent. Based on your research, create a claim of policy on the use of DNA forensics, considering privacy and ethical issues and the issue of ensuring that justice is carried out. Support your claim with details from the cases you examined.

4. Look back at your responses to the Prewriting and Discussion tasks at the beginning of this chapter; then, keeping in mind your reading, writing, and discussion experiences related to the chapter's reading selections, reflect on these questions about the themes of crime and punishment:

   - How have your ideas and perspectives about those themes been shaped by those experiences?
   - Which three reading selections have most influenced your thinking about those themes? How and why?

7.27.2 Taking a Global Perspective: Gun Control Laws and Mass Shootings

Following the news of yet another mass shooting, the gun control debate in the United States seems to escalate and then, inevitably, to fade out. However, the February 14, 2018, shooting at Marjory Stoneman High School in Parkland, Florida, in which 17 people were killed, may finally lead to a different outcome. The student-led March for Our Lives, on March 24, 2018, calling for stricter gun control laws, mobilized hundreds of thousands of people, not only across the United States, but around the world. Do some research to find out in which countries mass shootings are most problematic, in terms of the number of incidents and the number of casualties, and how those countries approach gun control. Is there a clear relationship between the seriousness of the problem in a given country, the prevalence of guns in that country (see Figure 7.3), and that country's approach to gun control? Develop an argument about ways in which other differences between countries might also account for differences in the prevalence of mass shootings. The argument should include a claim related to the question of whether gun control laws could effectively cut back on mass shootings in the United States.

Figure 7.3 Prevalence of civilian guns, by country

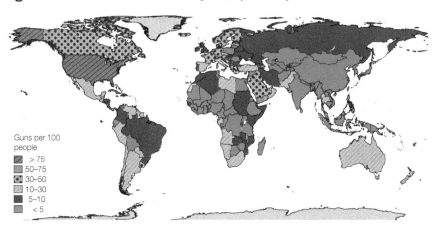

Guns per 100 people
- > 75
- 50–75
- 30–50
- 10–30
- 5–10
- < 5

SOURCE: 'Data from Small Arms Survey 2007; Map Created by R. Gloucester, derived from blank map created by Frank Bennett'

7.27.3 Collaborating on a Rogerian Argument

For this activity, you will work in small groups to research and write a Rogerian argument on a contemporary issue that has emerged from your exploration of readings in this chapter. The writing topics that follow the readings can help you identify an issue. (See Chapter 4 for a discussion of Rogerian argument and a suggested organizational approach to developing a Rogerian argument essay.) Here are some suggested guidelines for this collaborative activity:

- Identify an issue.
- Divide the research and writing responsibilities as follows:
  - Student one: introduction section
  - Student two: body section, affirmative position
  - Student three: body section, opposing position
  - Student four: conclusion, summation, and middle-ground position

  For an effective collaboration, each team member should take responsibility for
- Collecting information related to the issue.
- Completing assigned work on time.
- Listening to and considering the viewpoints of the other team members.

Sample Topic: Implicit Bias Training for Police

> March 2018: *Stephon Clark, a 22-year-old unarmed black man, shot and killed by two Sacramento police officers.*

> April 2018: *Two black men, waiting at Starbucks for a meeting with a friend, handcuffed and arrested by Philadelphia police officers.*

News reports like these seem to have become regular fare in recent years. And with the ubiquity of social media platforms, one need not be tuned into mainstream news outlets to learn about such incidents. For example, within hours of the arrest of the two men at the

Philadelphia Starbucks, a Starbucks customer's video of the incident had gone viral (https://www.youtube.com/watch?v=9fBOQCfx6xc).

Not surprisingly, anger and outrage, as well as fear and distrust of law enforcement officers, have been ignited around the country, especially within communities of color. Protests have spilled onto the streets, and people, nonwhite and white, have charged that the disproportionate rate at which black men are arrested and are the victims of police shootings demonstrates racial bias.

At the time of this writing, law enforcement agencies around the country have been taking steps to address the issue, including by giving police officers implicit bias training. This type of training is designed to make individuals aware of their automatic associations between groups of people and stereotypes about those groups, associations that can lead to biased behavior even when the individual is not overtly prejudiced. The premise behind such training is that we all make such associations—those of which we are aware are explicit biases, and those of which we are not aware are implicit biases. In the case of persons in law enforcement roles, implicit biases can be especially harmful, if not lethal. In an April 2018 interview, Clarence Cox, president of the National Organization of Black Law Enforcement (NOBLE), called for implicit bias training to be mandated for police departments around the country. However, others have questioned the validity of such training, claiming that the science behind the concept is weak and suggesting that it needs further study and testing. While conceding that data on the program's effectiveness were lacking, Cox said he had witnessed the successes of approaches including implicit bias training at the local level, notably among New Orleans police.

Conduct some research on implicit bias training and the results of its implementation—for example, in the Los Angeles and New York City police departments. If you think that implicit bias training should be mandated nationally, as Cox advocates, explain why, using specific examples from your research. If you do not think that such training is useful (or is not the complete solution) in helping ensure that police officers interact fairly with people of color, what other approaches or policies do you think should be implemented? Explain why.

7.27.4 Arguing Themes from Literature

1. Sherlock Holmes, a nineteenth-century creation of Sir Arthur Conan Doyle's, is also a hero in contemporary popular culture, portrayed by actors such as Robert Downey, Jr., and Benedict Cumberbatch. However, Sherlock Holmes is a flawed hero. Look up the concept of an antihero and Joseph Campbell's concept of a hero's journey. How does Holmes compare to other heroes or antiheroes?

2. People often make the assumption that, in some way, wrongdoers will pay for their misdeeds. Consider two short stories in this chapter, Flannery O'Connor's "A Good Man Is Hard to Find" and Edgar Allen Poe's "The Cask of Amontillado." In each story, we are given a glimpse into the life of a character who suffers death. Do you think that the grandmother and Fortunato are wrongdoers who get what they deserve, or are they innocent victims of circumstances? For each of these characters, use evidence from the story to argue either that the character is facing a judgment day of her or his own making or that the character would be more accurately cast in the role of innocent victim.

3. George Orwell's "A Hanging" is a work of nonfiction, whereas Ambrose Bierce's "An Occurrence at Owl Creek Bridge" is fiction, yet these two pieces (both are in this chapter) have similar narratives. Besides the method of execution (hanging), what are the similarities between these pieces of literature, and what are the differences? For example, do you see similarities among the reactions and emotions of the condemned men and the

executioners in the two works? Explain your response with details from each piece.

4. In this chapter, both Susan Glaspell's play *Trifles* and Marge Piercy's poem "What's That Smell in the Kitchen?" highlight examples of vigilante domestic justice. Do you sympathize with Mrs. Wright and/or with the speaker in Piercy's poem? For each woman:
   - If you think the woman was wronged, explain how, and explain why you think her recourse to vigilantism was or was not justified.
   - If you do not think the woman was wronged, explain why, and explain another course of action she could have taken.

7.27.5 Multimodal Activity: The Many Faces of Justice

Langston Hughes's poem "Justice" (in this chapter) centers on the ancient Roman representation of Lady Justice, which often graces courthouses and attorneys' offices. The representation typically includes three attributes, a blindfold, a sword, and a balance scale (see Figure 7.4). Spend a few moments writing about the implications of each item in depicting justice. Then consider justice as you see it meted out today—through firsthand encounters and in popular culture and news media. With these reflections in mind, create a collage to represent what, in your view, are the many faces of justice seen in today's world. Construct your collage out of photographs; excerpts from news reports, song lyrics, or literature; and images from video clips, movies, or other media.

Figure 7.4 Lady Justice

© Gorosi/Shutterstock

Chapter 8
Power and Responsibility

"With great power, comes great responsibility," Peter Parker's Uncle Ben warns Peter in the 2002 film *Spider-Man*. Admirable superheroes like Spider-Man are familiar from comics and movies—they often come from humble beginnings, unexpectedly acquire their powers, and learn to wield those powers to protect and serve others. Such individuals, however, are not only found in fiction—there are many real-life "superheroes," ordinary individuals who have overcome adversity, acquired power (even if it be the power of a public voice), and used that power responsibly to help others. For example, after the February 2018 mass shooting at Marjory Stoneman Douglas High School, in Parkland, Florida, in which 17 people were killed, Parkland students inspired and led a vigorous nationwide movement advocating stricter gun control laws, a movement still going strong at the time of this writing.

Why are heroes like these—both "super" and "ordinary"—widely admired? Perhaps, in part, we admire them because we see them—consciously or unconsciously—in contrast to childhood bullies at school who used their intimidating physical or social power without responsibility and without compassion. And perhaps, in part, we admire them because we see them in contrast to those bullies who, today, use online tools to intimidate or belittle others, whether through body shaming or by instigating rumors and exploiting gossip. All of us, both as children and as adults, have witnessed the abuse of power by individuals who seek to influence and control others for their own gain.

In literature and in pop culture, the abuse of power is a prevalent theme, one we readily recognize in classic works such as *Hamlet, Pride and Prejudice,* and the essays of Martin Luther King, Jr., as well as in works such as the *Avengers* and *Star Wars* films and the books and films of the Harry Potter franchise.

Even though the abuse of power creates striking drama, we must remember that people with power can, and often do, act responsibly by using their position for the good of others. Former President Jimmy Carter has used his power not only to work for world peace but also to build houses for Habitat for Humanity and to raise funds to help eradicate diseases. The wives of U.S. presidents—most recently, Melania Trump and Michelle Obama—have frequently used their position both to educate children and to inspire them to pursue their goals.

Many artists and athletes also have used their power constructively and responsibly. Musicians Dolly Parton and J Cole seek to improve the education of children. Parton ships a new book every month to each participant in her Imagination Library initiative, which has grown to the point where she now shares over one million books per month. Cole began the Dreamville Foundation to provide support for children through writing contests, book clubs, and materials for school. Former New York Yankee shortstop Derek Jeter created the Turn 2 Foundation, which has donated over $18 million to programs that help young people turn away from drugs and alcohol.

In this chapter, you will read a variety of works focusing on power and the responsibility that comes with it. In Ed Vega's short story "Spanish Roulette," a young man feels he must use his power to act responsibly even though those actions may well cost him his life. In Maxine Kumin's poem "Woodchucks," a woman illustrates how easy it can be to justify the abuse of power. And in Lisa Lewis's essay "Why We Still Allow Bullying to Flourish in Kids' Sports," the author expresses serious concerns regarding the potential effects of bullying and power imbalance on child athletes. Whether on the playground, online, or in public affairs, standing up to bullies always comes at a cost, but as writers in Chapter 8 show us, failing to confront those who abuse their power comes at an even greater price.

8.1 Prewriting and Discussion: Power and Responsibility

1. Read the image in Figure 8.1 creatively and critically. What ideas does it suggest about power and responsibility?
2. What do people mean when they talk about power? Focus on a particular context, such as local or state government, family, schools, or the community.

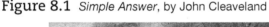

Figure 8.1 *Simple Answer*, by John Cleaveland

John Cleaveland, Morris Museum of Art

Who has power and who does not—and why? Is power related to money? To social status or education? To experience?

3. What is our responsibility? Write for a few minutes about responsibility. What responsibility do we as individuals have to our families, friends, organizations, communities, and nation? Use examples to elaborate on your response.

8.2 Fiction

The eight short stories in this section, spanning the years 1820 through 2014, explore issues related to the theme of power and responsibility.

8.3 Washington Irving, The Legend of Sleepy Hollow (1820)

Found among the papers of the late Diedrich Knickerbocker

A pleasing land of drowsy head it was,
Of dreams that wave before the half-shut eye;
And of gay castles in the clouds that pass,
Forever flushing round a summer sky.—*Castle of Indolence*

In the bosom of one of those spacious coves which indent the eastern shore of the Hudson, at that broad expansion of the river denominated by the ancient Dutch navigators the Tappan Zee, and where they always prudently shortened sail and implored the protection of St. Nicholas when they crossed, there lies a small market town or rural port, which by some is called Greensburgh, but which is more generally and properly known by the name of Tarry Town. This name was given, we are told, in former days, by the good housewives of the adjacent country, from the inveterate propensity of their husbands to linger about the village tavern on market days. Be that as it may, I do not vouch for the fact, but merely advert to it, for the sake of being precise and authentic. Not far from this village, perhaps about two miles, there is a little valley or rather lap of land among high hills, which is one of the quietest places in the whole world. A small brook glides through it, with just murmur enough to lull one to repose; and the occasional whistle of a quail or tapping of a woodpecker is almost the only sound that ever breaks in upon the uniform tranquillity.

I recollect that, when a stripling, my first exploit in squirrel-shooting was in a grove of tall walnut-trees that shades one side of the valley. I had wandered into it at noontime, when all nature is peculiarly quiet, and was startled by the roar of my own gun, as it broke the Sabbath stillness around and was prolonged and reverberated by the angry echoes. If ever I should wish for a retreat whither I might steal from the world and its distractions, and dream quietly away the remnant of a troubled life, I know of none more promising than this little valley.

From the listless repose of the place, and the peculiar character of its inhabitants, who are descendants from the original Dutch settlers, this sequestered glen has long been known by the name of SLEEPY HOLLOW, and its rustic lads are called the Sleepy

Hollow Boys throughout all the neighboring country. A drowsy, dreamy influence seems to hang over the land, and to pervade the very atmosphere. Some say that the place was bewitched by a High German doctor, during the early days of the settlement; others, that an old Indian chief, the prophet or wizard of his tribe, held his powwows there before the country was discovered by Master Hendrick Hudson. Certain it is, the place still continues under the sway of some witching power, that holds a spell over the minds of the good people, causing them to walk in a continual reverie. They are given to all kinds of marvellous beliefs, are subject to trances and visions, and frequently see strange sights, and hear music and voices in the air. The whole neighborhood abounds with local tales, haunted spots, and twilight superstitions; stars shoot and meteors glare oftener across the valley than in any other part of the country, and the nightmare, with her whole nine-fold, seems to make it the favorite scene of her gambols.

The dominant spirit, however, that haunts this enchanted region, and seems to be commander-in-chief of all the powers of the air, is the apparition of a figure on horseback, without a head. It is said by some to be the ghost of a Hessian trooper, whose head had been carried away by a cannon-ball, in some nameless battle during the Revolutionary War, and who is ever and anon seen by the country folk hurrying along in the gloom of night, as if on the wings of the wind. His haunts are not confined to the valley, but extend at times to the adjacent roads, and especially to the vicinity of a church at no great distance. Indeed, certain of the most authentic historians of those parts, who have been careful in collecting and collating the floating facts concerning this spectre, allege that the body of the trooper having been buried in the churchyard, the ghost rides forth to the scene of battle in nightly quest of his head, and that the rushing speed with which he sometimes passes along the Hollow, like a midnight blast, is owing to his being belated, and in a hurry to get back to the churchyard before daybreak.

Such is the general purport of this legendary superstition, which has furnished 5 materials for many a wild story in that region of shadows; and the spectre is known at all the country firesides, by the name of the Headless Horseman of Sleepy Hollow.

It is remarkable that the visionary propensity I have mentioned is not confined to the native inhabitants of the valley, but is unconsciously imbibed by every one who resides there for a time. However wide awake they may have been before they entered that sleepy region, they are sure, in a little time, to inhale the witching influence of the air, and begin to grow imaginative, to dream dreams, and see apparitions.

I mention this peaceful spot with all possible laud, for it is in such little retired Dutch valleys, found here and there embosomed in the great State of New York, that population, manners, and customs remain fixed, while the great torrent of migration and improvement, which is making such incessant changes in other parts of this restless country, sweeps by them unobserved. They are like those little nooks of still water, which border a rapid stream, where we may see the straw and bubble riding quietly at anchor, or slowly revolving in their mimic harbor, undisturbed by the rush of the passing current. Though many years have elapsed since I trod the drowsy shades of Sleepy Hollow, yet I question whether I should not still find the same trees and the same families vegetating in its sheltered bosom.

In this by-place of nature there abode, in a remote period of American history, that is to say, some thirty years since, a worthy wight of the name of Ichabod Crane, who sojourned, or, as he expressed it, "tarried," in Sleepy Hollow, for the purpose of instructing the children of the vicinity. He was a native of Connecticut, a State which supplies the Union with pioneers for the mind as well as for the forest, and sends forth yearly its legions of frontier woodmen and country schoolmasters. The cognomen of Crane was not inapplicable to his person. He was tall, but exceedingly lank, with narrow shoulders, long arms and legs, hands that dangled a mile out of his sleeves, feet that might have served for shovels, and his whole frame most loosely hung together. His head was small, and flat at top, with huge ears, large green glassy eyes, and a long snipe nose, so that it looked like a weather-cock perched upon his spindle neck to tell which way the wind blew. To see him striding along the profile of a hill on a windy day, with his clothes bagging and fluttering about him, one might have mistaken him for the genius of famine descending upon the earth, or some scarecrow eloped from a cornfield.

His schoolhouse was a low building of one large room, rudely constructed of logs; the windows partly glazed, and partly patched with leaves of old copybooks. It was most ingeniously secured at vacant hours, by a withe twisted in the handle of the door, and stakes set against the window shutters; so that though a thief might get in with perfect ease, he would find some embarrassment in getting out,—an idea most probably borrowed by the architect, Yost Van Houten, from the mystery of an eelpot. The schoolhouse stood in a rather lonely but pleasant situation, just at the foot of a woody hill, with a brook running close by, and a formidable birch-tree growing at one end of it. From hence the low murmur of his pupils' voices, conning over their lessons, might be heard in a drowsy summer's day, like the hum of a beehive; interrupted now and then by the authoritative voice of the master, in the tone of menace or command, or, peradventure, by the appalling sound of the birch, as he urged some tardy loiterer along the flowery path of knowledge. Truth to say, he was a conscientious man, and ever bore in mind the golden maxim, "Spare the rod and spoil the child." Ichabod Crane's scholars certainly were not spoiled.

I would not have it imagined, however, that he was one of those cruel potentates 10 of the school who joy in the smart of their subjects; on the contrary, he administered justice with discrimination rather than severity; taking the burden off the backs of the weak, and laying it on those of the strong. Your mere puny stripling, that winced at the least flourish of the rod, was passed by with indulgence; but the claims of justice were satisfied by inflicting a double portion on some little tough wrong-headed, broad-skirted Dutch urchin, who sulked and swelled and grew dogged and sullen beneath the birch. All this he called "doing his duty by their parents;" and he never inflicted a chastisement without following it by the assurance, so consolatory to the smarting urchin, that "he would remember it and thank him for it the longest day he had to live."

When school hours were over, he was even the companion and playmate of the larger boys; and on holiday afternoons would convoy some of the smaller ones home, who happened to have pretty sisters, or good housewives for mothers, noted for the comforts of the cupboard. Indeed, it behooved him to keep on good terms with his pupils. The revenue arising from his school was small, and would have been scarcely sufficient to furnish him with daily bread, for he was a huge feeder, and, though lank, had the dilating powers of an anaconda; but to help out his maintenance, he was, according to country custom in those parts, boarded and lodged at the houses of the farmers whose children he instructed. With these he lived successively a week at a time, thus going the rounds of the neighborhood, with all his worldly effects tied up in a cotton handkerchief.

That all this might not be too onerous on the purses of his rustic patrons, who are apt to consider the costs of schooling a grievous burden, and schoolmasters as mere drones, he had various ways of rendering himself both useful and agreeable. He assisted the farmers occasionally in the lighter labors of their farms, helped to make hay, mended the fences, took the horses to water, drove the cows from pasture, and cut wood for the winter fire. He laid aside, too, all the dominant dignity and absolute sway with which he lorded it in his little empire, the school, and became wonderfully gentle and ingratiating. He found favor in the eyes of the mothers by petting the children, particularly the youngest; and like the lion bold, which whilom so magnanimously the lamb did hold, he would sit with a child on one knee, and rock a cradle with his foot for whole hours together.

In addition to his other vocations, he was the singing-master of the neighborhood, and picked up many bright shillings by instructing the young folks in psalmody. It was a matter of no little vanity to him on Sundays, to take his station in front of the church gallery, with a band of chosen singers; where, in his own mind, he completely carried away the palm from the parson. Certain it is, his voice resounded far above all the rest of the congregation; and there are peculiar quavers still to be heard in that church, and which may even be heard half a mile off, quite to the opposite side of the millpond, on a still Sunday morning, which are said to be legitimately descended from the nose of Ichabod Crane. Thus, by divers little makeshifts, in that ingenious way which is commonly denominated "by hook and by crook," the worthy pedagogue got on tolerably enough, and was thought, by all who understood nothing of the labor of headwork, to have a wonderfully easy life of it.

The schoolmaster is generally a man of some importance in the female circle of a rural neighborhood; being considered a kind of idle, gentlemanlike personage, of vastly superior taste and accomplishments to the rough country swains, and, indeed, inferior in learning only to the parson. His appearance, therefore, is apt to occasion some little stir at the tea-table of a farmhouse, and the addition of a supernumerary dish of cakes or sweetmeats, or, peradventure, the parade of a silver teapot. Our man of letters, therefore, was peculiarly happy in the smiles of all the country damsels. How he would figure among them in the churchyard, between services on Sundays; gathering grapes for them from the wild vines that overran the surrounding trees; reciting for their amusement all the epitaphs on the tombstones; or sauntering, with a whole bevy of them, along the banks of the adjacent millpond; while the more bashful country bumpkins hung sheepishly back, envying his superior elegance and address.

From his half-itinerant life, also, he was a kind of travelling gazette, carrying the whole budget of local gossip from house to house, so that his appearance was always greeted with satisfaction. He was, moreover, esteemed by the women as a man of great erudition, for he had read several books quite through, and was a perfect master of Cotton Mather's "History of New England Witchcraft," in which, by the way, he most firmly and potently believed.

He was, in fact, an odd mixture of small shrewdness and simple credulity. His appetite for the marvellous, and his powers of digesting it, were equally extraordinary; and both had been increased by his residence in this spell-bound region. No tale was too gross or monstrous for his capacious swallow. It was often his delight, after his school was dismissed in the afternoon, to stretch himself on the rich bed of clover bordering the little brook that whimpered by his schoolhouse, and there con over old Mather's direful tales, until the gathering dusk of evening made the printed page a mere mist before his eyes. Then, as he wended his way by swamp and stream and awful woodland, to the farmhouse where he happened to be quartered, every sound of nature, at that witching hour, fluttered his excited imagination,—the moan of the whip-poor-will from the hillside, the boding cry of the tree toad, that harbinger of storm, the dreary hooting of the screech owl, or the sudden rustling in the thicket of birds frightened from their roost. The fireflies, too, which sparkled most vividly in the darkest places, now and then startled him, as one of uncommon brightness would stream across his path; and if, by chance, a huge blockhead of a beetle came winging his blundering flight against him, the poor varlet was ready to give up the ghost, with the idea that he was struck with a witch's token. His only resource on such occasions, either to drown thought or drive away evil spirits, was to sing psalm tunes and the good people of Sleepy Hollow, as they sat by their doors of an evening, were often filled with awe at hearing his nasal melody, "in linked sweetness long drawn out," floating from the distant hill, or along the dusky road.

Another of his sources of fearful pleasure was to pass long winter evenings with the old Dutch wives, as they sat spinning by the fire, with a row of apples roasting and spluttering along the hearth, and listen to their marvellous tales of ghosts and goblins, and haunted fields, and haunted brooks, and haunted bridges, and haunted houses, and particularly of the headless horseman, or Galloping Hessian of the Hollow, as they sometimes called him. He would delight them equally by his anecdotes of witchcraft, and of the direful omens and portentous sights and sounds in the air, which prevailed in the earlier times of Connecticut; and would frighten them woefully with speculations upon comets and shooting stars; and with the alarming fact that the world did absolutely turn round, and that they were half the time topsy-turvy!

But if there was a pleasure in all this, while snugly cuddling in the chimney corner of a chamber that was all of a ruddy glow from the crackling wood fire, and where, of course, no spectre dared to show its face, it was dearly purchased by the terrors of his subsequent walk homewards. What fearful shapes and shadows beset his path, amidst the dim and ghastly glare of a snowy night! With what wistful look did he eye every trembling ray of light streaming across the waste fields from some distant window! How often was he appalled by some shrub covered with snow, which, like a sheeted spectre, beset his very path! How often did he shrink with curdling awe at the sound of his own steps on the frosty crust beneath his feet; and dread to look over his shoulder, lest he should behold some uncouth being tramping close behind him! And how often was he thrown into complete dismay by some rushing blast, howling among the trees, in the idea that it was the Galloping Hessian on one of his nightly scourings!

All these, however, were mere terrors of the night, phantoms of the mind that walk in darkness; and though he had seen many spectres in his time, and been more than once beset by Satan in divers shapes, in his lonely perambulations, yet daylight put an end to all these evils; and he would have passed a pleasant life of it, in despite of the Devil and all his works, if his path had not been crossed by a being that causes more perplexity to mortal man than ghosts, goblins, and the whole race of witches put together, and that was—a woman.

Among the musical disciples who assembled, one evening in each week, to   20 receive his instructions in psalmody, was Katrina Van Tassel, the daughter and only child of a substantial Dutch farmer. She was a blooming lass of fresh eighteen; plump as a partridge; ripe and melting and rosy-cheeked as one of her father's peaches, and universally famed, not merely for her beauty, but her vast expectations. She was withal a little of a coquette, as might be perceived even in her dress, which was a mixture of ancient and modern fashions, as most suited to set off her charms. She wore the ornaments of pure yellow gold, which her great-great-grandmother had brought over from Saardam; the tempting stomacher of the olden time, and withal a provokingly short petticoat, to display the prettiest foot and ankle in the country round.

Ichabod Crane had a soft and foolish heart towards the sex; and it is not to be wondered at that so tempting a morsel soon found favor in his eyes, more especially after he had visited her in her paternal mansion. Old Baltus Van Tassel was a perfect picture of a thriving, contented, liberal-hearted farmer. He seldom, it is true, sent either his eyes or his thoughts beyond the boundaries of his own farm; but within those everything was snug, happy and well-conditioned. He was satisfied with his wealth, but not proud of it; and piqued himself upon the hearty abundance, rather than the style in which he lived. His stronghold was situated on the banks of the Hudson, in one of those green, sheltered, fertile nooks in which the Dutch farmers are so fond of nestling. A great elm tree spread its broad branches over it, at the foot of which bubbled up a spring of the softest and sweetest water, in a little well formed of a barrel; and then stole sparkling away through the grass, to a neighboring brook, that babbled along among alders and dwarf willows. Hard by the farmhouse was a vast barn, that might have served for a church; every window and crevice of which seemed bursting forth with the treasures of the farm; the flail was busily resounding within it from morning to night; swallows and martins skimmed twittering about the eaves; and rows of pigeons, some with one eye turned up, as if watching the weather, some with their heads under their wings or buried in their bosoms, and others swelling, and cooing, and bowing about their dames, were enjoying the sunshine on the roof. Sleek unwieldy porkers were grunting in the repose and abundance of their pens, from whence sallied forth, now and then, troops of sucking pigs, as if to snuff the air. A stately squadron of snowy geese were riding in an adjoining pond, convoying whole fleets of ducks; regiments of turkeys were gobbling through the farmyard, and Guinea fowls fretting about it, like ill-tempered housewives, with their peevish, discontented cry. Before the barn door strutted the gallant cock, that pattern of a husband, a warrior and a fine gentleman, clapping his burnished wings and crowing in the pride and gladness of his heart, — sometimes tearing up the earth with his feet, and then generously calling his ever-hungry family of wives and children to enjoy the rich morsel which he had discovered.

The pedagogue's mouth watered as he looked upon this sumptuous promise of luxurious winter fare. In his devouring mind's eye, he pictured to himself every roasting-pig running about with a pudding in his belly, and an apple in his mouth; the pigeons were snugly put to bed in a comfortable pie, and tucked in with a coverlet of crust; the geese were swimming in their own gravy; and the ducks pairing cosily in dishes, like snug married couples, with a decent competency of onion sauce. In the porkers he saw carved out the future sleek side of bacon, and juicy relishing ham; not a turkey but he beheld daintily trussed up, with its gizzard under its wing, and, peradventure, a necklace of savory sausages; and even bright chanticleer himself lay sprawling on his back, in a side dish, with uplifted claws, as if craving that quarter which his chivalrous spirit disdained to ask while living.

As the enraptured Ichabod fancied all this, and as he rolled his great green eyes over the fat meadow lands, the rich fields of wheat, of rye, of buckwheat, and Indian corn, and the orchards burdened with ruddy fruit, which surrounded the warm tenement of Van Tassel, his heart yearned after the damsel who was to inherit these domains, and his imagination expanded with the idea, how they might be readily turned into cash, and the money invested in immense tracts of wild land, and shingle palaces in the wilderness. Nay, his busy fancy already realized his hopes, and presented to him the blooming Katrina, with a whole family of children, mounted on the top of a wagon loaded with household trumpery, with pots and kettles dangling beneath; and he beheld himself bestriding a pacing mare, with a colt at her heels, setting out for Kentucky, Tennessee, — or the Lord knows where!

When he entered the house, the conquest of his heart was complete. It was one of those spacious farmhouses, with high-ridged but lowly sloping roofs, built in the style handed down from the first Dutch settlers; the low projecting eaves forming a piazza along the front, capable of being closed up in bad weather. Under this were hung flails, harness, various utensils of husbandry, and nets for fishing in the neighboring river. Benches were built along the sides for summer use; and a great spinning-wheel at one end, and a churn at the other, showed the various uses to which this important porch might be devoted. From this piazza the wondering Ichabod entered the hall, which formed the centre of the mansion, and the place of usual residence. Here rows of resplendent pewter, ranged on a long dresser, dazzled his eyes. In one corner stood a huge bag of wool, ready to be spun; in another, a quantity of linsey-woolsey just from the loom; ears of Indian corn, and strings of dried apples and peaches, hung in gay festoons along the walls, mingled with the gaud of red peppers; and a door left ajar gave him a peep into the best parlor, where the claw-footed chairs and dark mahogany tables shone like mirrors; andirons, with their accompanying shovel and tongs, glistened from their covert of asparagus tops; mock-oranges and conch-shells decorated the mantelpiece; strings of various-colored birds eggs were suspended above it; a great ostrich egg was hung from the centre of the room, and a corner cupboard, knowingly left open, displayed immense treasures of old silver and well-mended china.

From the moment Ichabod laid his eyes upon these regions of delight, the peace of   25 his mind was at an end, and his only study was how to gain the affections of the peerless daughter of Van Tassel. In this enterprise, however, he had more real difficulties than generally fell to the lot of a knight-errant of yore, who seldom had anything but giants, enchanters, fiery dragons, and such like easily conquered adversaries, to contend with and had to make his way merely through gates of iron and brass, and walls of adamant to the castle keep, where the lady of his heart was confined; all which he achieved as easily as a man would carve his way to the centre of a Christmas pie; and then the lady gave him her hand as a matter of course. Ichabod, on the contrary, had to win his way to the heart of a country coquette, beset with a labyrinth of whims and caprices, which were forever presenting new difficulties and impediments; and he had to encounter a host of fearful adversaries of real flesh and blood, the numerous rustic admirers, who beset every portal to her heart, keeping a watchful and angry eye upon each other, but ready to fly out in the common cause against any new competitor.

Among these, the most formidable was a burly, roaring, roystering blade, of the name of Abraham, or, according to the Dutch abbreviation, Brom Van Brunt, the hero of the country round, which rang with his feats of strength and hardihood. He was broad-shouldered and double-jointed, with short curly black hair, and a bluff but not unpleasant countenance, having a mingled air of fun and arrogance. From his Herculean frame and great powers of limb he had received the nickname of BROM BONES, by which he was universally known. He was famed for great knowledge and skill in horsemanship, being as dexterous on horseback as a Tartar. He was foremost at all races and cock fights; and, with the ascendancy which bodily strength always acquires in rustic life, was the umpire in all disputes, setting his hat on one side, and giving his decisions with an air and tone that admitted of no gainsay or appeal. He was always ready for either a fight or a frolic; but had more mischief than ill-will in his composition; and with all his overbearing roughness, there was a strong dash of waggish good humor at bottom. He had three or four boon companions, who regarded him as their model, and at the head of whom he scoured the country, attending every scene of feud or merriment for miles round. In cold weather he was distinguished by a fur cap, surmounted with a flaunting fox's tail; and when the folks at a country gathering descried this well-known crest at a distance, whisking about among a squad of hard riders, they always stood by for a squall. Sometimes his crew would be heard dashing along past the farmhouses at midnight, with whoop and halloo, like a troop of Don Cossacks; and the old dames, startled out of their sleep, would listen for a moment till the hurry-scurry had clattered by, and then exclaim, "Ay, there goes Brom Bones and his gang!" The neighbors looked upon him with a mixture of awe, admiration, and good-will; and, when any madcap prank or rustic brawl occurred in the vicinity, always shook their heads, and warranted Brom Bones was at the bottom of it.

This rantipole hero had for some time singled out the blooming Katrina for the object of his uncouth gallantries, and though his amorous toyings were something like the gentle caresses and endearments of a bear, yet it was whispered that she did not altogether discourage his hopes. Certain it is, his advances were signals for rival candidates to retire, who felt no inclination to cross a lion in his amours; insomuch, that when his horse was seen tied to Van Tassel's paling, on a Sunday night, a sure sign that his master was courting, or, as it is termed, "sparking," within, all other suitors passed by in despair, and carried the war into other quarters.

Such was the formidable rival with whom Ichabod Crane had to contend, and, considering all things, a stouter man than he would have shrunk from the competition, and a wiser man would have despaired. He had, however, a happy mixture of pliability and perseverance in his nature; he was in form and spirit like a supple-jack—yielding, but tough; though he bent, he never broke; and though he bowed beneath the slightest pressure, yet, the moment it was away—jerk!—he was as erect, and carried his head as high as ever.

To have taken the field openly against his rival would have been madness; for he was not a man to be thwarted in his amours, any more than that stormy lover, Achilles. Ichabod, therefore, made his advances in a quiet and gently insinuating manner. Under cover of his character of singing-master, he made frequent visits at the farmhouse; not that he had anything to apprehend from the meddlesome interference of parents, which is so often a stumbling-block in the path of lovers. Balt Van Tassel was an easy indulgent soul; he loved his daughter better even than his pipe, and, like a reasonable man and an excellent father, let her have her way in everything. His notable little wife, too, had enough to do to attend to her housekeeping and manage her poultry; for, as she sagely observed, ducks and geese are foolish things, and must be looked after, but girls can take care of themselves. Thus, while the busy dame bustled about the house, or plied her spinning-wheel at one end of the piazza, honest Balt would sit smoking his evening pipe at the other, watching the achievements of a little wooden warrior, who, armed with a sword in each hand, was most valiantly fighting the wind on the pinnacle of the barn. In the mean time, Ichabod would carry on his suit with the daughter by the side of the spring under the great elm, or sauntering along in the twilight, that hour so favorable to the lover's eloquence.

I profess not to know how women's hearts are wooed and won. To me they have   30 always been matters of riddle and admiration. Some seem to have but one vulnerable point, or door of access; while others have a thousand avenues, and may be captured in a thousand different ways. It is a great triumph of skill to gain the former, but a still greater proof of generalship to maintain possession of the latter, for man must battle for his fortress at every door and window. He who wins a thousand common hearts is therefore entitled to some renown; but he who keeps undisputed sway over the heart of a coquette is indeed a hero. Certain it is, this was not the case with the redoubtable Brom Bones; and from the moment Ichabod Crane made his advances, the interests of the former evidently declined: his horse was no longer seen tied to the palings on Sunday nights, and a deadly feud gradually arose between him and the preceptor of Sleepy Hollow.

Brom, who had a degree of rough chivalry in his nature, would fain have carried matters to open warfare and have settled their pretensions to the lady, according to the mode of those most concise and simple reasoners, the knights-errant of yore, — by single combat; but Ichabod was too conscious of the superior might of his adversary to enter the lists against him; he had overheard a boast of Bones, that he would "double the schoolmaster up, and lay him on a shelf of his own schoolhouse;" and he was too wary to give him an opportunity. There was something extremely provoking in this obstinately pacific system; it left Brom no alternative but to draw upon the funds of rustic waggery in his disposition, and to play off boorish practical jokes upon his rival. Ichabod became the object of whimsical persecution to Bones and his gang of rough riders. They harried his hitherto peaceful domains; smoked out his singing school by stopping up the chimney; broke into the schoolhouse at night, in spite of its formidable fastenings of withe and window stakes, and turned everything topsy-turvy, so that the poor schoolmaster began to think all the witches in the country held their meetings there. But what was still more annoying, Brom took all opportunities of turning him into ridicule in presence of his mistress, and had a scoundrel dog whom he taught to whine in the most ludicrous manner, and introduced as a rival of Ichabod's, to instruct her in psalmody.

In this way matters went on for some time, without producing any material effect on the relative situations of the contending powers. On a fine autumnal afternoon, Ichabod, in pensive mood, sat enthroned on the lofty stool from whence he usually watched all the concerns of his little literary realm. In his hand he swayed a ferule, that sceptre of despotic power; the birch of justice reposed on three nails behind the throne, a constant terror to evil doers, while on the desk before him might be seen sundry contraband articles and prohibited weapons, detected upon the persons of idle urchins, such as half-munched apples, popguns, whirligigs, fly-cages, and whole legions of rampant little paper gamecocks. Apparently there had been some appalling act of justice recently inflicted, for his scholars were all busily intent upon their books, or slyly whispering behind them with one eye kept upon the master; and a kind of buzzing stillness reigned throughout the schoolroom. It was suddenly interrupted by the appearance of a negro in tow-cloth jacket and trowsers, a round-crowned fragment of a hat, like the cap of Mercury, and mounted on the back of a ragged, wild, half-broken colt, which he managed with a rope by way of halter. He came clattering up to the school door with an invitation to Ichabod to attend a merry-making or "quilting frolic," to be held that evening at Mynheer Van Tassel's; and having delivered his message with that air of importance, and effort at fine language, which a negro is apt to display on petty embassies of the kind, he dashed over the brook, and was seen scampering away up the hollow, full of the importance and hurry of his mission.

All was now bustle and hubbub in the late quiet schoolroom. The scholars were hurried through their lessons without stopping at trifles; those who were nimble skipped over half with impunity, and those who were tardy had a smart application now and then in the rear, to quicken their speed or help them over a tall word. Books were flung aside without being put away on the shelves, inkstands were overturned, benches thrown down, and the whole school was turned loose an hour before the usual time, bursting forth like a legion of young imps, yelping and racketing about the green in joy at their early emancipation.

The gallant Ichabod now spent at least an extra half hour at his toilet, brushing and furbishing up his best, and indeed only suit of rusty black, and arranging his locks by a bit of broken looking-glass that hung up in the schoolhouse. That he might make his appearance before his mistress in the true style of a cavalier, he borrowed a horse from the farmer with whom he was domiciliated, a choleric old Dutchman of the name of Hans Van Ripper, and, thus gallantly mounted, issued forth like a knight-errant in quest of adventures. But it is meet I should, in the true spirit of romantic story, give some account of the looks and equipments of my hero and his steed. The animal he bestrode was a broken-down plow-horse, that had outlived almost everything but its viciousness. He was gaunt and shagged, with a ewe neck, and a head like a hammer; his rusty mane and tail were tangled and knotted with burs; one eye had lost its pupil, and was glaring and spectral, but the other had the gleam of a genuine devil in it. Still he must have had fire and mettle in his day, if we may judge from the name he bore of Gunpowder. He had, in fact, been a favorite steed of his master's, the choleric Van Ripper, who was a furious rider, and had infused, very probably, some of his own spirit into the animal; for, old and broken-down as he looked, there was more of the lurking devil in him than in any young filly in the country.

Ichabod was a suitable figure for such a steed. He rode with short stirrups, which 35 brought his knees nearly up to the pommel of the saddle; his sharp elbows stuck out like grasshoppers'; he carried his whip perpendicularly in his hand, like a sceptre, and as his horse jogged on, the motion of his arms was not unlike the flapping of a pair of wings. A small wool hat rested on the top of his nose, for so his scanty strip of forehead might be called, and the skirts of his black coat fluttered out almost to the horse's tail. Such was the appearance of Ichabod and his steed as they shambled out of the gate of Hans Van Ripper, and it was altogether such an apparition as is seldom to be met with in broad daylight.

It was, as I have said, a fine autumnal day; the sky was clear and serene, and nature wore that rich and golden livery which we always associate with the idea of abundance. The forests had put on their sober brown and yellow, while some trees of the tenderer kind had been nipped by the frosts into brilliant dyes of orange, purple, and scarlet. Streaming files of wild ducks began to make their appearance high in the air; the bark of the squirrel might be heard from the groves of beech and hickory-nuts, and the pensive whistle of the quail at intervals from the neighboring stubble field.

The small birds were taking their farewell banquets. In the fullness of their revelry, they fluttered, chirping and frolicking from bush to bush, and tree to tree, capricious from the very profusion and variety around them. There was the honest cock robin, the favorite game of stripling sportsmen, with its loud querulous note; and the twittering blackbirds flying in sable clouds; and the golden-winged woodpecker with his crimson crest, his broad black gorget, and splendid plumage; and the cedar bird, with its red-tipt wings and yellow-tipt tail and its little monteiro cap of feathers; and the blue jay, that noisy coxcomb, in his gay light blue coat and white underclothes, screaming and chattering, nodding and bobbing and bowing, and pretending to be on good terms with every songster of the grove.

As Ichabod jogged slowly on his way, his eye, ever open to every symptom of culinary abundance, ranged with delight over the treasures of jolly autumn. On all sides he beheld vast store of apples; some hanging in oppressive opulence on the trees; some gathered into baskets and barrels for the market; others heaped up in rich piles for the cider-press. Farther on he beheld great fields of Indian corn, with its golden ears peeping from their leafy coverts, and holding out the promise of cakes and hasty-pudding; and the yellow pumpkins lying beneath them, turning up their fair round bellies to the sun, and giving ample prospects of the most luxurious of pies; and anon he passed the fragrant buckwheat fields breathing the odor of the beehive, and as he beheld them, soft anticipations stole over his mind of dainty slapjacks, well buttered, and garnished with honey or treacle, by the delicate little dimpled hand of Katrina Van Tassel.

Thus feeding his mind with many sweet thoughts and "sugared suppositions," he journeyed along the sides of a range of hills which look out upon some of the goodliest scenes of the mighty Hudson. The sun gradually wheeled his broad disk down in the west. The wide bosom of the Tappan Zee lay motionless and glassy, excepting that here and there a gentle undulation waved and prolonged the blue shadow of the distant mountain. A few amber clouds floated in the sky, without a breath of air to move them. The horizon was of a fine golden tint, changing gradually into a pure apple green, and from that into the deep blue of the mid-heaven. A slanting ray lingered on the woody crests of the precipices that overhung some parts of the river, giving greater depth to the dark gray and purple of their rocky sides. A sloop was loitering in the distance, dropping slowly down with the tide, her sail hanging uselessly against the mast; and as the reflection of the sky gleamed along the still water, it seemed as if the vessel was suspended in the air.

It was toward evening that Ichabod arrived at the castle of the Heer Van Tassel, 40 which he found thronged with the pride and flower of the adjacent country. Old farmers, a spare leathern-faced race, in homespun coats and breeches, blue stockings, huge shoes, and magnificent pewter buckles. Their brisk, withered little dames, in close-crimped caps, long-waisted short gowns, homespun petticoats, with scissors and pincushions, and gay calico pockets hanging on the outside. Buxom lasses, almost as antiquated as their mothers, excepting where a straw hat, a fine ribbon, or perhaps a white frock, gave symptoms of city innovation. The sons, in short square-skirted coats, with rows of stupendous brass buttons, and their hair generally queued in the fashion of the times, especially if they could procure an eel-skin for the purpose, it being esteemed throughout the country as a potent nourisher and strengthener of the hair.

Brom Bones, however, was the hero of the scene, having come to the gathering on his favorite steed Daredevil, a creature, like himself, full of mettle and mischief, and which no one but himself could manage. He was, in fact, noted for preferring vicious animals, given to all kinds of tricks which kept the rider in constant risk of his neck, for he held a tractable, well-broken horse as unworthy of a lad of spirit.

Fain would I pause to dwell upon the world of charms that burst upon the enraptured gaze of my hero, as he entered the state parlor of Van Tassel's mansion. Not those of the bevy of buxom lasses, with their luxurious display of red and white; but the ample charms of a genuine Dutch country tea-table, in the sumptuous time of autumn. Such heaped up platters of cakes of various and almost indescribable kinds, known only to experienced Dutch housewives! There was the doughty doughnut, the tender oly koek, and the crisp and crumbling cruller; sweet cakes and short cakes, ginger cakes and honey cakes, and the whole family of cakes. And then there were apple pies, and peach pies, and pumpkin pies; besides slices of ham and smoked beef; and moreover delectable dishes of preserved plums, and peaches, and pears, and quinces; not to mention broiled shad and roasted chickens; together with bowls of milk and cream, all mingled higgledy-piggledy, pretty much as I have enumerated them, with the motherly teapot sending up its clouds of vapor from the midst—Heaven bless the mark! I want breath and time to discuss this banquet as it deserves, and am too eager to get on with my story. Happily, Ichabod Crane was not in so great a hurry as his historian, but did ample justice to every dainty.

He was a kind and thankful creature, whose heart dilated in proportion as his skin was filled with good cheer, and whose spirits rose with eating, as some men's do with drink. He could not help, too, rolling his large eyes round him as he ate, and chuckling with the possibility that he might one day be lord of all this scene of almost unimaginable luxury and splendor. Then, he thought, how soon he'd turn his back upon the old schoolhouse; snap his fingers in the face of Hans Van Ripper, and every other niggardly patron, and kick any itinerant pedagogue out of doors that should dare to call him comrade!

Old Baltus Van Tassel moved about among his guests with a face dilated with content and good humor, round and jolly as the harvest moon. His hospitable attentions were brief, but expressive, being confined to a shake of the hand, a slap on the shoulder, a loud laugh, and a pressing invitation to "fall to, and help themselves."

And now the sound of the music from the common room, or hall, summoned to   45 the dance. The musician was an old gray-headed negro, who had been the itinerant orchestra of the neighborhood for more than half a century. His instrument was as old and battered as himself. The greater part of the time he scraped on two or three strings, accompanying every movement of the bow with a motion of the head; bowing almost to the ground, and stamping with his foot whenever a fresh couple were to start.

Ichabod prided himself upon his dancing as much as upon his vocal powers. Not a limb, not a fibre about him was idle; and to have seen his loosely hung frame in full motion, and clattering about the room, you would have thought St. Vitus himself, that blessed patron of the dance, was figuring before you in person. He was the admiration of all the negroes; who, having gathered, of all ages and sizes, from the farm and the neighborhood, stood forming a pyramid of shining black faces at every door and window, gazing with delight at the scene, rolling their white eyeballs, and showing grinning rows of ivory from ear to ear. How could the flogger of urchins be otherwise than animated and joyous? The lady of his heart was his partner in the dance, and smiling graciously in reply to all his amorous oglings; while Brom Bones, sorely smitten with love and jealousy, sat brooding by himself in one corner.

When the dance was at an end, Ichabod was attracted to a knot of the sager folks, who, with Old Van Tassel, sat smoking at one end of the piazza, gossiping over former times, and drawing out long stories about the war.

This neighborhood, at the time of which I am speaking, was one of those highly favored places which abound with chronicle and great men. The British and American line had run near it during the war; it had, therefore, been the scene of marauding and infested with refugees, cowboys, and all kinds of border chivalry. Just sufficient time had elapsed to enable each storyteller to dress up his tale with a little becoming fiction, and, in the indistinctness of his recollection, to make himself the hero of every exploit.

There was the story of Doffue Martling, a large blue-bearded Dutchman, who had nearly taken a British frigate with an old iron nine-pounder from a mud breastwork, only that his gun burst at the sixth discharge. And there was an old gentleman who shall be nameless, being too rich a mynheer to be lightly mentioned, who, in the battle of White Plains, being an excellent master of defence, parried a musket-ball with a small sword, insomuch that he absolutely felt it whiz round the blade, and glance off at the hilt; in proof of which he was ready at any time to show the sword, with the hilt a little bent. There were several more that had been equally great in the field, not one of whom but was persuaded that he had a considerable hand in bringing the war to a happy termination.

But all these were nothing to the tales of ghosts and apparitions that succeeded.   50 The neighborhood is rich in legendary treasures of the kind. Local tales and superstitions thrive best in these sheltered, long-settled retreats; but are trampled under foot by the shifting throng that forms the population of most of our country places. Besides, there is no encouragement for ghosts in most of our villages, for they have scarcely had time to finish their first nap and turn themselves in their graves, before their surviving friends have travelled away from the neighborhood; so that when they turn out at night to walk their rounds, they have no acquaintance left to call upon. This is perhaps the reason why we so seldom hear of ghosts except in our long-established Dutch communities.

The immediate cause, however, of the prevalence of supernatural stories in these parts, was doubtless owing to the vicinity of Sleepy Hollow. There was a contagion in the very air that blew from that haunted region; it breathed forth an atmosphere of dreams and fancies infecting all the land. Several of the Sleepy Hollow people were present at Van Tassel's, and, as usual, were doling out their wild and wonderful legends. Many dismal tales were told about funeral trains, and mourning cries and wailings heard and seen about the great tree where the unfortunate Major André was taken, and which stood in the neighborhood. Some mention was made also of the woman in white, that haunted the dark glen at Raven Rock, and was often heard to shriek on winter nights before a storm, having perished there in the snow. The chief part of the stories, however, turned upon the favorite spectre of Sleepy Hollow, the Headless Horseman, who had been heard several times of late, patrolling the country; and, it was said, tethered his horse nightly among the graves in the churchyard.

The sequestered situation of this church seems always to have made it a favorite haunt of troubled spirits. It stands on a knoll, surrounded by locust-trees and lofty elms, from among which its decent, whitewashed walls shine modestly forth, like Christian purity beaming through the shades of retirement. A gentle slope descends from it to a silver sheet of water, bordered by high trees, between which, peeps may be caught at the blue hills of the Hudson. To look upon its grass-grown yard, where the sunbeams seem to sleep so quietly, one would think that there at least the dead might rest in peace. On one side of the church extends a wide woody dell, along which raves a large brook among broken rocks and trunks of fallen trees. Over a deep black part of the stream, not far from the church, was formerly thrown a wooden bridge; the road that led to it, and the bridge itself, were thickly shaded by overhanging trees, which cast a gloom about it, even in the daytime; but occasioned a fearful darkness at night. Such was one of the favorite haunts of the Headless Horseman, and the place where he was most frequently encountered. The tale was told of old Brouwer, a most heretical disbeliever in ghosts, how he met the Horseman returning from his foray into Sleepy Hollow, and was obliged to get up behind him; how they galloped over bush and brake, over hill and swamp, until they reached the bridge; when the Horseman suddenly turned into a skeleton, threw old Brouwer into the brook, and sprang away over the tree-tops with a clap of thunder.

This story was immediately matched by a thrice marvellous adventure of Brom Bones, who made light of the Galloping Hessian as an arrant jockey. He affirmed that on returning one night from the neighboring village of Sing Sing, he had been overtaken by this midnight trooper; that he had offered to race with him for a bowl of punch, and should have won it too, for Daredevil beat the goblin horse all hollow, but just as they came to the church bridge, the Hessian bolted, and vanished in a flash of fire.

All these tales, told in that drowsy undertone with which men talk in the dark, the countenances of the listeners only now and then receiving a casual gleam from the glare of a pipe, sank deep in the mind of Ichabod. He repaid them in kind with large extracts from his invaluable author, Cotton Mather, and added many marvellous events that had taken place in his native State of Connecticut, and fearful sights which he had seen in his nightly walks about Sleepy Hollow.

The revel now gradually broke up. The old farmers gathered together their families 55 in their wagons, and were heard for some time rattling along the hollow roads, and over the distant hills. Some of the damsels mounted on pillions behind their favorite swains, and their light-hearted laughter, mingling with the clatter of hoofs, echoed along the silent woodlands, sounding fainter and fainter, until they gradually died away,—and the late scene of noise and frolic was all silent and deserted. Ichabod only lingered behind, according to the custom of country lovers, to have a tête-à-tête with the heiress; fully convinced that he was now on the high road to success. What passed at this interview I will not pretend to say, for in fact I do not know. Something, however, I fear me, must have gone wrong, for he certainly sallied forth, after no very great interval, with an air quite desolate and chapfallen. Oh, these women! these women! Could that girl have been playing off any of her coquettish tricks? Was her encouragement of the poor pedagogue all a mere sham to secure her conquest of his rival? Heaven only knows, not I! Let it suffice to say, Ichabod stole forth with the air of one who had been sacking a henroost, rather than a fair lady's heart. Without looking to the right or left to notice the scene of rural wealth, on which he had so often gloated, he went straight to the stable, and with several hearty cuffs and kicks roused his steed most uncourteously from the comfortable quarters in which he was soundly sleeping, dreaming of mountains of corn and oats, and whole valleys of timothy and clover.

It was the very witching time of night that Ichabod, heavy-hearted and crestfallen, pursued his travels homewards, along the sides of the lofty hills which rise above Tarry Town, and which he had traversed so cheerily in the afternoon. The hour was as dismal as himself. Far below him the Tappan Zee spread its dusky and indistinct waste of waters, with here and there the tall mast of a sloop, riding quietly at anchor under the land. In the dead hush of midnight, he could even hear the barking of the watchdog from the opposite shore of the Hudson; but it was so vague and faint as only to give an idea of his distance from this faithful companion of man. Now and then, too, the long-drawn crowing of a cock, accidentally awakened, would sound far, far off, from some farmhouse away among the hills—but it was like a dreaming sound in his ear. No signs of life occurred near him, but occasionally the melancholy chirp of a cricket, or perhaps the guttural twang of a bullfrog from a neighboring marsh, as if sleeping uncomfortably and turning suddenly in his bed.

All the stories of ghosts and goblins that he had heard in the afternoon now came crowding upon his recollection. The night grew darker and darker; the stars seemed to sink deeper in the sky, and driving clouds occasionally hid them from his sight. He had never felt so lonely and dismal. He was, moreover, approaching the very place where many of the scenes of the ghost stories had been laid. In the centre of the road stood an enormous tulip-tree, which towered like a giant above all the other trees of the neighborhood, and formed a kind of landmark. Its limbs were gnarled and fantastic, large enough to form trunks for ordinary trees, twisting down almost to the earth, and rising again into the air. It was connected with the tragical story of the unfortunate André, who had been taken prisoner hard by; and was universally known by the name of Major André's tree. The common people regarded it with a mixture of respect and superstition, partly out of sympathy for the fate of its ill-starred namesake, and partly from the tales of strange sights, and doleful lamentations, told concerning it.

As Ichabod approached this fearful tree, he began to whistle; he thought his whistle was answered; it was but a blast sweeping sharply through the dry branches. As he approached a little nearer, he thought he saw something white, hanging in the midst of the tree: he paused and ceased whistling but, on looking more narrowly, perceived that it was a place where the tree had been scathed by lightning, and the white wood laid bare. Suddenly he heard a groan—his teeth chattered, and his knees smote against the saddle: it was but the rubbing of one huge bough upon another, as they were swayed about by the breeze. He passed the tree in safety, but new perils lay before him.

About two hundred yards from the tree, a small brook crossed the road, and ran into a marshy and thickly-wooded glen, known by the name of Wiley's Swamp. A few rough logs, laid side by side, served for a bridge over this stream. On that side of the road where the brook entered the wood, a group of oaks and chestnuts, matted thick with wild grape-vines, threw a cavernous gloom over it. To pass this bridge was the severest trial. It was at this identical spot that the unfortunate André was captured, and under the covert of those chestnuts and vines were the sturdy yeomen concealed who surprised him. This has ever since been considered a haunted stream, and fearful are the feelings of the schoolboy who has to pass it alone after dark.

As he approached the stream, his heart began to thump; he summoned up, 60 however, all his resolution, gave his horse half a score of kicks in the ribs, and attempted to dash briskly across the bridge; but instead of starting forward, the perverse old animal made a lateral movement, and ran broadside against the fence. Ichabod, whose fears increased with the delay, jerked the reins on the other side, and kicked lustily with the contrary foot: it was all in vain; his steed started, it is true, but it was only to plunge to the opposite side of the road into a thicket of brambles and alder bushes. The schoolmaster now bestowed both whip and heel upon the starveling ribs of old Gunpowder, who dashed forward, snuffling and snorting, but came to a stand just by the bridge, with a suddenness that had nearly sent his rider sprawling over his head. Just at this moment a plashy tramp by the side of the bridge caught the sensitive ear of Ichabod. In the dark shadow of the grove, on the margin of the brook, he beheld something huge, misshapen and towering. It stirred not, but seemed gathered up in the gloom, like some gigantic monster ready to spring upon the traveller.

The hair of the affrighted pedagogue rose upon his head with terror. What was to be done? To turn and fly was now too late; and besides, what chance was there of escaping ghost or goblin, if such it was, which could ride upon the wings of the wind? Summoning up, therefore, a show of courage, he demanded in stammering accents, "Who are you?" He received no reply. He repeated his demand in a still more agitated voice. Still there was no answer. Once more he cudgelled the sides of the inflexible Gunpowder, and, shutting his eyes, broke forth with involuntary fervor into a psalm tune. Just then the shadowy object of alarm put itself in motion, and with a scramble and a bound stood at once in the middle of the road. Though the night was dark and dismal, yet the form of the unknown might now in some degree be ascertained. He appeared to be a horseman of large dimensions, and mounted on a black horse of powerful frame. He made no offer of molestation or sociability, but kept aloof on one side of the road, jogging along on the blind side of old Gunpowder, who had now got over his fright and waywardness.

Ichabod, who had no relish for this strange midnight companion, and bethought himself of the adventure of Brom Bones with the Galloping Hessian, now quickened his steed in hopes of leaving him behind. The stranger, however, quickened his horse to an equal pace. Ichabod pulled up, and fell into a walk, thinking to lag behind,—the other did the same. His heart began to sink within him; he endeavored to resume his psalm tune, but his parched tongue clove to the roof of his mouth, and he could not utter a stave. There was something in the moody and dogged silence of this pertinacious companion that was mysterious and appalling. It was soon fearfully accounted for. On mounting a rising ground, which brought the figure of his fellow-traveller in relief against the sky, gigantic in height, and muffled in a cloak, Ichabod was horror-struck on perceiving that he was headless!—but his horror was still more increased on observing that the head, which should have rested on his shoulders, was carried before him on the pommel of his saddle! His terror rose to desperation; he rained a shower of kicks and blows upon Gunpowder, hoping by a sudden movement to give his companion the slip; but the spectre started full jump with him. Away, then, they dashed through thick and thin; stones flying and sparks flashing at every bound. Ichabod's flimsy garments fluttered in the air, as he stretched his long lank body away over his horse's head, in the eagerness of his flight.

They had now reached the road which turns off to Sleepy Hollow; but Gunpowder, who seemed possessed with a demon, instead of keeping up it, made an opposite turn, and plunged headlong downhill to the left. This road leads through a sandy hollow shaded by trees for about a quarter of a mile, where it crosses the bridge famous in goblin story; and just beyond swells the green knoll on which stands the whitewashed church.

As yet the panic of the steed had given his unskilful rider an apparent advantage in the chase, but just as he had got half way through the hollow, the girths of the saddle gave way, and he felt it slipping from under him. He seized it by the pommel, and endeavored to hold it firm, but in vain; and had just time to save himself by clasping old Gunpowder round the neck, when the saddle fell to the earth, and he heard it trampled under foot by his pursuer. For a moment the terror of Hans Van Ripper's wrath passed across his mind,—for it was his Sunday saddle; but this was no time for petty fears; the goblin was hard on his haunches; and (unskilful rider that he was!) he had much ado to maintain his seat; sometimes slipping on one side, sometimes on another, and some-times jolted on the high ridge of his horse's backbone, with a violence that he verily feared would cleave him asunder.

An opening in the trees now cheered him with the hopes that the church bridge   65 was at hand. The wavering reflection of a silver star in the bosom of the brook told him that he was not mistaken. He saw the walls of the church dimly glaring under the trees beyond. He recollected the place where Brom Bones's ghostly competitor had disap-peared. "If I can but reach that bridge," thought Ichabod, "I am safe." Just then he heard the black steed panting and blowing close behind him; he even fancied that he felt his hot breath. Another convulsive kick in the ribs, and old Gunpowder sprang upon the bridge; he thundered over the resounding planks; he gained the opposite side; and now Ichabod cast a look behind to see if his pursuer should vanish, according to rule, in a flash of fire and brimstone. Just then he saw the goblin rising in his stirrups, and in the very act of hurling his head at him. Ichabod endeavored to dodge the horrible missile, but too late. It encountered his cranium with a tremendous crash,—he was tumbled headlong into the dust, and Gunpowder, the black steed, and the goblin rider, passed by like a whirlwind.

The next morning the old horse was found without his saddle, and with the bridle under his feet, soberly cropping the grass at his master's gate. Ichabod did not make his appearance at breakfast; dinner-hour came, but no Ichabod. The boys assembled at the schoolhouse, and strolled idly about the banks of the brook; but no school-master. Hans Van Ripper now began to feel some uneasiness about the fate of poor Ichabod, and his saddle. An inquiry was set on foot, and after diligent investigation they came upon his traces. In one part of the road leading to the church was found the saddle trampled in the dirt; the tracks of horses' hoofs deeply dented in the road, and evidently at furious speed, were traced to the bridge, beyond which, on the bank of a broad part of the brook, where the water ran deep and black, was found the hat of the unfortunate Ichabod, and close beside it a shattered pumpkin.

The brook was searched, but the body of the schoolmaster was not to be discov-ered. Hans Van Ripper as executor of his estate, examined the bundle which contained all his worldly effects. They consisted of two shirts and a half; two stocks for the neck; a pair or two of worsted stockings; an old pair of corduroy small-clothes; a rusty razor; a book of psalm tunes full of dog's-ears; and a broken pitch-pipe. As to the books and furniture of the schoolhouse, they belonged to the community, excepting Cotton Mather's "History of Witchcraft," a "New England Almanac," and a book of dreams and fortune-telling; in which last was a sheet of foolscap much scribbled and blotted in several fruitless attempts to make a copy of verses in honor of the heiress of Van Tassel. These magic books and the poetic scrawl were forthwith consigned to the flames by Hans Van Ripper; who, from that time forward, determined to send his children no more to school, observing that he never knew any good come of this same reading and writing. Whatever money the schoolmaster possessed, and he had received his quarter's pay but a day or two before, he must have had about his person at the time of his disappearance.

The mysterious event caused much speculation at the church on the following Sunday. Knots of gazers and gossips were collected in the churchyard, at the bridge, and at the spot where the hat and pumpkin had been found. The stories of Brouwer, of Bones, and a whole budget of others were called to mind; and when they had diligently considered them all, and compared them with the symptoms of the present case, they shook their heads, and came to the conclusion that Ichabod had been carried off by the Galloping Hessian. As he was a bachelor, and in nobody's debt, nobody troubled his head any more about him; the school was removed to a different quarter of the hollow, and another pedagogue reigned in his stead.

It is true, an old farmer, who had been down to New York on a visit several years after, and from whom this account of the ghostly adventure was received, brought home the intelligence that Ichabod Crane was still alive; that he had left the neighborhood partly through fear of the goblin and Hans Van Ripper, and partly in mortification at having been suddenly dismissed by the heiress; that he had changed his quarters to a distant part of the country; had kept school and studied law at the same time; had been admitted to the bar; turned politician; electioneered; written for the newspapers; and finally had been made a justice of the Ten Pound Court. Brom Bones, too, who, shortly after his rival's disappearance conducted the blooming Katrina in triumph to the altar, was observed to look exceedingly knowing whenever the story of Ichabod was related, and always burst into a hearty laugh at the mention of the pumpkin; which led some to suspect that he knew more about the matter than he chose to tell.

The old country wives, however, who are the best judges of these matters, main-   70
tain to this day that Ichabod was spirited away by supernatural means; and it is a favorite story often told about the neighborhood round the winter evening fire. The bridge became more than ever an object of superstitious awe; and that may be the reason why the road has been altered of late years, so as to approach the church by the border of the millpond. The schoolhouse being deserted soon fell to decay, and was reported to be haunted by the ghost of the unfortunate pedagogue and the plowboy, loitering homeward of a still summer evening, has often fancied his voice at a distance, chanting a melancholy psalm tune among the tranquil solitudes of Sleepy Hollow.

POSTSCRIPT.
FOUND IN THE HANDWRITING OF MR. KNICKERBOCKER.

The preceding tale is given almost in the precise words in which I heard it related at a Corporation meeting at the ancient city of Manhattoes, at which were present many of its sagest and most illustrious burghers. The narrator was a pleasant, shabby, gentlemanly old fellow, in pepper-and-salt clothes, with a sadly humourous face, and one whom I strongly suspected of being poor–he made such efforts to be entertaining. When his story was concluded, there was much laughter and approbation, particularly from two or three deputy aldermen, who had been asleep the greater part of the time. There was, however, one tall, dry-looking old gentleman, with beetling eyebrows, who maintained a grave and rather severe face throughout, now and then folding his arms, inclining his head, and looking down upon the floor, as if turning a doubt over in his mind. He was one of your wary men, who never laugh but upon good grounds–when they have reason and law on their side. When the mirth of the rest of the company had subsided, and silence was restored, he leaned one arm on the elbow of his chair, and sticking the other akimbo, demanded, with a slight, but exceedingly sage motion of the head, and contraction of the brow, what was the moral of the story, and what it went to prove?

The story-teller, who was just putting a glass of wine to his lips, as a refreshment after his toils, paused for a moment, looked at his inquirer with an air of infinite deference, and, lowering the glass slowly to the table, observed that the story was intended most logically to prove–

"That there is no situation in life but has its advantages and pleasures–provided we will but take a joke as we find it:

"That, therefore, he that runs races with goblin troopers is likely to have rough riding of it.

"Ergo, for a country schoolmaster to be refused the hand of a Dutch heiress is a   75
certain step to high preferment in the state."

The cautious old gentleman knit his brows tenfold closer after this explanation, being sorely puzzled by the ratiocination of the syllogism, while, methought, the one in pepper-and-salt eyed him with something of a triumphant leer. At length he observed that all this was very well, but still he thought the story a little on the extravagant–there were one or two points on which he had his doubts.

"Faith, sir," replied the story-teller, "as to that matter, I don't believe one-half of it myself." D. K.

THE END.

Critical Thinking Topics

1. Reflecting upon Ichabod Crane's interest in Katrina Van Tassel, do you think he is motivated primarily by lust/love or by desire for power? Use details from the story to support your position.

2. Brom Bones is depicted as having great strength and physical ability, whereas Ichabod Crane is painted as primarily intellectual. In what ways do these characterizations promote or inhibit the characters' feeling of power?

3. Watch a portion of the well-known 1949 Disney animated version of this classic American short story. How effectively (or ineffectively) do the animators characterize Brom Bones and Ichabod Crane? Do the animated versions match your impression of the characters' personalities and physical features? Why or why not? Use specific examples from the both the story and the film.

Writing Topic

Whether it was tales of witches or the Headless Horseman, the Sleepy Hollow community believed and perpetuated its supernatural stories. In what ways has superstition influenced actual historical figures? In what ways does superstition play a part in the lives of twenty-first-century Americans? Is superstition still a powerful force in our lives? Support your response with specific examples.

8.4 Alphonse Daudet, The Last Lesson
(1870)

I started for school very late that morning and was in great dread of a scolding, especially because M. Hamel had said that he would question us on participles, and I did not know the first word about them. For a moment I thought of running away and spending the day out-of-doors. It was so warm, so bright! The birds were chirping at the edge of the woods; and in the open field back of the saw-mill the Prussian soldiers were drilling. It was all much more tempting than the rule for participles, but I had the strength to resist, and hurried off to school.

When I passed the town hall there was a crowd in front of the bulletin board. For the last two years all our bad news had come from there—the lost battles, the draft, the orders of the commanding officer—and I thought to myself, without stopping:

"What can be the matter now?"

Then, as I hurried by as fast as I could go, the blacksmith, Wachter, who was there, with his apprentice, reading the bulletin, called after me:

"Don't go so fast, bub; you'll get to your school in plenty of time!"   5

I thought he was making fun of me, and reached M. Hamel's little garden all out of breath.

Usually, when school began, there was a great bustle, which could be heard out in the street, the opening and closing of desks, lessons repeated in unison, very loud, with our hands over our ears to understand better, and the teacher's great ruler rapping on the table. But now it was all so still! I had counted on the commotion to get to my desk without being seen; but, of course, that day everything had to be as quiet as Sunday morning. Through the window I saw my classmates, already in their places, and M. Hamel walking up and down with his terrible iron ruler under his arm. I had to open the door and go in before everybody. You can imagine how I blushed and how frightened I was.

But nothing happened, M. Hamel saw me and said very kindly:

"Go to your place quickly, little Franz. We were beginning without you."

I jumped over the bench and sat down at my desk. Not till then, when I had got a   10
little over my fright, did I see that our teacher had on his beautiful green coat, his frilled shirt, and the little black silk cap, all embroidered, that he never wore except on inspection and prize days. Besides, the whole school seemed so strange and solemn. But the thing that surprised me most was to see, on the back benches that were always empty, the village people sitting quietly like ourselves; old Hauser, with his three-cornered hat, the former mayor, the former postmaster, and several others besides. Everybody looked sad; and Hauser had brought an old primer, thumbed at the edges, and he held it open on his knees with his great spectacles lying across the pages.

While I was wondering about it all, M. Hamel mounted his chair, and, in the same grave and gentle tone which he had used to me, said:

"My children, this is the last lesson I shall give you. The order has come from Berlin to teach only German in the schools of Alsace and Lorraine. The new master comes tomorrow. This is your last French lesson. I want you to be very attentive."

What a thunder-clap these words were to me!

Oh, the wretches; that was what they had put up at the town hall!

My last French lesson! Why, I hardly knew how to write! I should never learn any   15
more! I must stop there, then! Oh, how sorry I was for not learning my lessons, for

seeking birds' eggs, or going sliding on the Saar! My books, that had seemed such a nuisance a while ago, so heavy to carry, my grammar, and my history of the saints, were old friends now that I couldn't give up. And M. Hamel, too; the idea that he was going away, that I should never see him again, made me forget all about his ruler and how cranky he was.

Poor man! It was in honor of this last lesson that he had put on his fine Sunday-clothes, and now I understood why the old men of the village were sitting there in the back of the room. It was because they were sorry, too, that they had not gone to school more. It was their way of thanking our master for his forty years of faithful service and of showing their respect for the country that was theirs no more.

While I was thinking of all this, I heard my name called. It was my turn to recite. What would I not have given to be able to say that dreadful rule for the participle all through, very loud and clear, and without one mistake? But I got mixed up on the first words and stood there, holding on to my desk, my heart beating, and not daring to look up. I heard M. Hamel say to me:

"I won't scold you, little Franz; you must feel bad enough. See how it is! Every day we have said to ourselves: 'Bah! I've plenty of time. I'll learn it tomorrow.' And now you see where we've come out. Ah, that's the great trouble with Alsace; she puts off learning till tomorrow. Now those fellows out there will have the right to say to you: 'How is it; you pretend to be Frenchmen, and yet you can neither speak nor write your own language?' But you are not the worst, poor little Franz. We've all a great deal to reproach ourselves with.

"Your parents were not anxious enough to have you learn. They preferred to put you to work on a farm or at the mills, so as to have a little more money. And I? I've been to blame also. Have I not often sent you to water my flowers instead of learning your lessons? And when I wanted to go fishing, did I not just give you a holiday?"

Then, from one thing to another, M. Hamel went on to talk of the French language,   20 saying that it was the most beautiful language in the world—the clearest, the most logical; that we must guard it among us and never forget it, because when a people are enslaved, as long as they hold fast to their language it is as if they had the key to their prison. Then he opened a grammar and read us our lesson. I was amazed to see how well I understood it. All he said seemed so easy, so easy! I think, too, that I had never listened so carefully, and that he had never explained everything with so much patience. It seemed almost as if the poor man wanted to give us all he knew before going away, and to put it all into our heads at one stroke.

After the grammar, we had a lesson in writing. That day M. Hamel had new copies for us, written in a beautiful round hand: France, Alsace, France, Alsace. They looked like little flags floating everywhere in the schoolroom, hung from the rod at the top of our desks. You ought to have seen how everyone set to work, and how quiet it was! The only sound was the scratching of the pens over the paper. Once some beetles flew in; but nobody paid any attention to them, not even the littlest ones, who worked right on tracing their fishhooks, as if that was French, too. On the roof the pigeons cooed very low, and I thought to myself:

"Will they make them sing in German, even the pigeons?"

Whenever I looked up from my writing I saw M. Hamel sitting motionless in his chair and gazing first at one thing, then at another, as if he wanted to fix in his mind just how everything looked in that little schoolroom. Fancy! For forty years he had been there in the same place, with his garden outside the window and his class in front of him, just like that. Only the desks and benches had been worn smooth; the walnut trees in the garden were taller, and the hop vine, that he had planted himself twined about the windows to the roof. How it must have broken his heart to leave it all, poor man; to hear his sister moving about in the room above, packing their trunks! For they must leave the country next day.

But he had the courage to hear every lesson to the very last. After the writing, we had a lesson in history, and then the babies chanted their ba, be, bi, bo, bu. Down there at the back of the room old Hauser had put on his spectacles and, holding his primer in both hands, spelled the letters with them. You could see that he, too, was crying; his voice trembled with emotion, and it was so funny to hear him that we all wanted to laugh and cry. Ah, how well I remember it, that last lesson!

All at once the church clock struck twelve. Then the Angelus. At the same moment   25
the trumpets of the Prussians, returning from drill, sounded under our windows. M. Hamel stood up, very pale, in his chair. I never saw him look so tall.

"My friends," said he, "I—I—" But something choked him. He could not go on.

Then he turned to the blackboard, took a piece of chalk, and, bearing down with all his might, he wrote as large as he could:

"Vive la France!"

Then he stopped and leaned his head against the wall, and, without a word, he made a gesture to us with his hand:

"School is dismissed—you may go."   30

Critical Thinking Topics

1. What is the significance of the title, "The Last Lesson"? Clearly, the teacher is offering his last formal lesson, but is there another last lesson he is imparting? What might that lesson be? Identify at least two passages that support your conclusion and explain how they do so.

2. The Prussians occupied the French regions of Alsace and Lorraine during the Franco-Prussian War (1870–1871; note that "The Last Lesson" dates from 1870). In this story the occupiers have dictated that only German will be taught in the schools. The demands of dictatorial power are usually met, but along with compliance comes hostility. It is likely that very few of us have experienced life under a military dictatorship; however, we may have observed or experienced similar forms of power being exercised in family or work environments. Analyze such a situation you have observed or experienced, or read about or seen in a film. In your analysis, explore these questions: Were the demands met? Did the demands create hostility? Were the long-term results satisfactory or unsatisfactory, and in what ways?

Writing Topic

When the occupying army enforces lessons in German only, everyone regrets not studying French as they should have. *Sometimes we must lose something in order to appreciate it.* That is a tough lesson for anyone—in a sense, it is always the last lesson on the particular subject. Have you lost or been threatened with the loss of something you perhaps took for granted and in retrospect came to appreciate? Maybe it was an opportunity or a friendship, maybe a person or a tradition. Use the italicized sentence above as an opening claim and write an argument of several paragraphs using your experience as evidence.

8.5 Edith Wharton, The Choice
(1916)

I

Stilling, that night after dinner, had surpassed himself. He always did, Wrayford reflected, when the small fry from Highfield came to dine. He, Cobham Stilling, who had to find his bearings and keep to his level in the big heedless ironic world of New York, dilated and grew vast in the congenial medium of Highfield. The Red House was the biggest house of the Highfield summer colony, and Cobham Stilling was its biggest man. No one else within a radius of a hundred miles (on a conservative estimate) had as many horses, as many greenhouses, as many servants, and assuredly no one else had three motors and a motorboat for the lake.

The motorboat was Stilling's latest hobby, and he rode—or steered—it in and out of the conversation all the evening, to the obvious edification of everyone present save his wife and his visitor, Austin Wrayford. The interest of the latter two who, from opposite ends of the drawing room, exchanged a fleeting glance when Stilling again launched his craft on the thin current of the talk—the interest of Mrs. Stilling and Wrayford had already lost its edge by protracted contact with the subject.

But the dinner guests—the Rector, Mr. Swordsley, his wife Mrs. Swordsley, Lucy and Agnes Granger, their brother Addison, and young Jack Emmerton from Harvard— were all, for divers reasons, stirred to the proper pitch of feeling. Mr. Swordsley, no doubt, was saying to himself: "If my good parishioner here can afford to buy a motorboat, in addition to all the other expenditures which an establishment like this must entail, I certainly need not scruple to appeal to him again for a contribution for our Galahad Club." The Granger girls, meanwhile, were evoking visions of lakeside picnics, not unadorned with the presence of young Mr. Emmerton; while that youth himself speculated as to whether his affable host would let him, when he came back on his next vacation, "learn to run the thing himself"; and Mr. Addison Granger, the elderly bachelor brother of the volatile Lucy and Agnes, mentally formulated the precise phrase in which, in his next letter to his cousin Professor Spildyke of the University of East Latmos, he should allude to "our last delightful trip in my old friend Cobham Stilling's ten thousand dollar motor launch"—for East Latmos was still in that primitive stage of culture on which five figures impinge.

Isabel Stilling, sitting beside Mrs. Swordsley, her head slightly bent above the needlework with which on these occasions it was her old-fashioned habit to employ herself—Isabel also had doubtless her reflections to make. As Wrayford leaned back in his corner and looked at her across the wide flower-filled drawing room he noted, first of all—for the how many hundredth time?—the play of her hands above the embroidery frame, the shadow of the thick dark hair on her forehead, the listless droops of the lids over her somewhat full grey eyes. He noted all this with a conscious deliberateness of enjoyment, taking in unconsciously, at the same time, the particular quality in her attitude, in the fall of her dress and the turn of her head, which had set her for him, from the first day, in a separate world; then he said to himself: "She is certainly thinking: 'Where on earth will Cobham get the money to pay for it?'"

Stilling, cigar in mouth and thumbs in his waistcoat pockets, was impressively   5
perorating from his usual dominant position on the hearthrug.

"I said: 'If I have the thing at all, I want the best that can be got.' That's my way, you know, Swordsley; I suppose I'm what you'd call fastidious. Always was, about every-thing, from cigars to wom—" his eye met the apprehensive glance of Mrs. Swordsley, who looked like her husband with his clerical coat cut slightly lower "—so I said: 'If I have the thing at all, I want the best that can be got.' Nothing makeshift for me, no sec-ond best. I never cared for the cheap and showy. I always say frankly to a man: 'If you can't give me a first-rate cigar, for the Lord's sake let me smoke my own.'" He paused to do so. "Well, if you have my standards, you can't buy a thing in a minute. You must look round, compare, select. I found there were lots of motorboats on the market, just as there's lots of stuff called champagne. But I said to myself: 'Ten to one there's only one fit to buy, just as there's only one champagne fit for a gentleman to drink.' Argued like a lawyer, eh, Austin?" He tossed this to Wrayford. "Take me for one of your own trade, wouldn't you? Well, I'm not such a fool as I look. I suppose you fellows who are tied to the treadmill—excuse me, Swordsley, but work's work, isn't it?—I suppose you think a man like me has nothing to do but take it easy: loll through life like a woman. By George, sir, I'd like either of you to see the time it takes—I won't say the *brains*—but just the time it takes to pick out a good motorboat. Why, I went—"

Mrs. Stilling set her embroidery frame noiselessly on the table at her side, and turned her head toward Wrayford. "Would you mind ringing for the tray?"

The interruption helped Mrs. Swordsley to waver to her feet. "I'm afraid we ought really to be going; my husband has an early service tomorrow."

Her host intervened with a genial protest. "Going already? Nothing of the sort! Why, the night's still young, as the poet says. Long way from here to the rectory? Nonsense! In our little twenty-horse car we do it in five minutes—don't we, Belle? Ah, you're walk-ing, to be sure—" Stilling's indulgent gesture seemed to concede that, in such a case, allowances must be made, and that he was the last man not to make them. "Well, then, Swordsley—" He held out a thick red hand that seemed to exude beneficence, and the clergyman, pressing it, ventured to murmur a suggestion.

"What, that Galahad Club again? Why, I thought my wife—Isabel, didn't we—No?   10
Well, it must have been my mother, then. Of course, you know, anything my good mother gives is—well—virtually—You haven't asked her? Sure? I could have sworn; I get so many of these appeals. And in these times, you know, we have to go cautiously. I'm sure you recognize that yourself, Swordsley. With my obligations—here now, to show you don't bear malice, have a brandy and soda before you go. Nonsense, man! This brandy isn't liquor, it's liqueur. I picked it up last year in London—last of a famous lot from Lord St. Oswyn's cellar. Laid down here, it stood me at—Eh?" he broke off as his wife moved toward him. "Ah, yes, of course. Miss Lucy, Miss Agnes—a drop of soda water? Look here, Addison, you won't refuse my tipple, I know. Well, take a cigar, at any rate, Swordsley. And, by the way, I'm afraid you'll have to go round the long way by the avenue tonight. Sorry, Mrs. Swordsley, but I forgot to tell them to leave the gate into the lane unlocked. Well, it's a jolly night, and I dare say you won't mind the extra turn along the lake. And, by Jove! If the moon's out, you'll have a glimpse of the motorboat. She's moored just out beyond our boathouse; and it's a privilege to look at her, I can tell you!"

The dispersal of his guests carried Stilling out into the hall, where his pleasantries reverberated under the oak rafters while the Granger girls were being muffled for the drive and the carriages summoned from the stables.

By a common impulse Mrs. Stilling and Wrayford had moved together toward the fireplace, which was hidden by a tall screen from the door into the hall. Wrayford leaned his elbow against the mantelpiece, and Mrs. Stilling stood beside him, her clasped hands hanging down before her.

"Have you anything more to talk over with him?" she asked.

"No. We wound it all up before dinner. He doesn't want to talk about it any more than he can help."

"It's so bad?"   15

"No; but this time he's got to pull up."

She stood silent, with lowered lids. He listened a moment, catching Stilling's farewell shout; then he moved a little nearer, and laid his hand on her arm.

"In an hour?"

She made an imperceptible motion of assent.

"I'll tell you about it then. The key's as usual?"   20

She signed another "Yes" and walked away with her long drifting step as her husband came in from the hall. He went up to the tray and poured himself out a tall glass of brandy and soda.

"The weather is turning queer—black as pitch. I hope the Swordsleys won't walk into the lake—involuntary immersion, eh? He'd come out a Baptist, I suppose. What'd the Bishop do in such a case? There's a problem for a lawyer, my boy!"

He clapped his hand on Wrayford's thin shoulder and then walked over to his wife, who was gathering up her embroidery silks and dropping them into her workbag. Stilling took her by the arms and swung her playfully about so that she faced the lamp-light.

"What's the matter with you tonight?"

"The matter?" she echoed, coloring a little, and standing very straight in her desire   25
not to appear eager to shrink from his touch.

"You never opened your lips. Left me the whole job of entertaining those blessed people. Didn't she, Austin?"

Wrayford laughed and lit a cigarette.

"There! You see even Austin noticed it. What's the matter, I say? Aren't they good enough for you? I don't say they're particularly exciting; but, hang it! I like to ask them here—I like to give people pleasure."

"I didn't mean to be dull," said Isabel.

"Well, you must learn to make an effort. Don't treat people as if they weren't in the   30
room just because they don't happen to amuse you. Do you know what they'll think? They'll think it's because you've got a bigger house and more money than they have. Shall I tell you something? My mother said she'd noticed the same thing in you lately. She said she sometimes felt you looked down on her for living in a small house. Oh, she was half joking, of course; but you see you do give people that impression. I can't understand treating any one in that way. The more I have myself, the more I want to make other people happy."

Isabel gently freed herself and laid the workbag on her embroidery frame. "I have a headache; perhaps that made me stupid. I'm going to bed." She turned toward Wrayford and held out her hand. "Good night."

"Good night," he answered, opening the door for her.

When he turned back into the room, his host was pouring himself a third glass of brandy and soda.

"Here, have a nip, Austin? Gad, I need it badly, after the shaking up you gave me this afternoon." Stilling laughed and carried his glass to the hearth, where he took up his usual commanding position. "Why the deuce don't you drink something? You look as glum as Isabel. One would think you were the chap that had been hit by this business."

Wrayford threw himself into the chair from which Mrs. Stilling had lately risen. It was   35 the one she usually sat in, and to his fancy a faint scent of her clung to it. He leaned back and looked up at Stilling.

"Want a cigar?" the latter continued. "Shall we go into the den and smoke?"

Wrayford hesitated. "If there's anything more you want to ask me about—"

"Gad, no! I had full measure and running over this afternoon. The deuce of it is, I don't see where the money's all gone to. Luckily I've got plenty of nerve; I'm not the kind of man to sit down and snivel because I've been touched in Wall Street."

Wrayford got to his feet again. "Then, if you don't want me, I think I'll go up to my room and put some finishing touches to a brief before I turn in. I must get back to town tomorrow afternoon."

"All right, then." Stilling set down his empty glass, and held out his hand with a   40 tinge of alacrity. "Good night, old man."

They shook hands, and Wrayford moved toward the door.

"I say, Austin—stop a minute!" his host called after him. Wrayford turned, and the two men faced each other across the hearthrug. Stilling's eyes shifted uneasily.

"There's one thing more you can do for me before you leave. Tell Isabel about that loan; explain to her that she's got to sign a note for it."

Wrayford, in his turn, flushed slightly. "You want me to tell her?"

"Hang it! I'm softhearted—that's the worst of me." Stilling moved toward the tray, and   45 lifted the brandy decanter. "And she'll take it better from you; she'll *have* to take it from you. She's proud. You can take her out for a row tomorrow morning—look here, take her out in the motor launch if you like. I meant to have a spin in it myself; but if you'll tell her—"

Wrayford hesitated. "All right, I'll tell her."

"Thanks a lot, my dear fellow. And you'll make her see it wasn't my fault, eh? Women are awfully vague about money, and she'll think it's all right if you back me up."

Wrayford nodded. "As you please."

"And, Austin—there's just one more thing. You needn't say anything to Isabel about the other business—I mean about my mother's securities."

"Ah?" said Wrayford, pausing.   50

Stilling shifted from one foot to the other. "I'd rather put that to the old lady myself. I can make it clear to her. She idolizes me, you know—and, hang it! I've got a good record. Up to now, I mean. My mother's been in clover since I married; I may say she's been my first thought. And I don't want her to hear of this beastly business from Isabel. Isabel's a little harsh at times—and of course this isn't going to make her any easier to live with."

"Very well," said Wrayford.

Stilling, with a look of relief, walked toward the window which opened on the terrace. "Gad! what a queer night! Hot as the kitchen range. Shouldn't wonder if we had a squall before morning. I wonder if that infernal skipper took in the launch's awnings before he went home."

Wrayford stopped with his hand on the door. "Yes, I saw him do it. She's shipshape for the night."

"Good! That saves me a run down to the shore."   55

"Good night, then," said Wrayford.

"Good night, old man. You'll tell her?"

"I'll tell her."

"And mum about my mother!" his host called after him.

II

The darkness had thinned a little when Wrayford scrambled down the steep path to the   60
shore. Though the air was heavy the threat of a storm seemed to have vanished, and now and then the moon's edge showed above a torn slope of cloud.

But in the thick shrubbery about the boathouse the darkness was still dense, and Wrayford had to strike a match before he could find the lock and insert his key. He left the door unlatched, and groped his way in. How often he had crept into this warm pine-scented obscurity, guiding himself by the edge of the bench along the wall, and hearing the soft lap of water through the gaps in the flooring! He knew just where one had to duck one's head to avoid the two canoes swung from the rafters, and just where to put his hand on the latch of the farther door that led to the broad balcony above the lake.

The boathouse represented one of Stilling's abandoned whims. He had built it some seven years before, and for a time it had been the scene of incessant nautical exploits. Stilling had rowed, sailed, paddled indefatigably, and all Highfield had been impressed to bear him company, and to admire his versatility. Then motors had come in, and he had forsaken aquatic sports for the flying chariot. The canoes of birch bark and canvas had been hoisted to the roof, the sailboat had rotted at her moorings, and the movable floor of the boathouse, ingeniously contrived to slide back on noiseless runners, had laid undisturbed through several seasons. Even the key of the boathouse had been mislaid—by Isabel's fault, her husband said—and the locksmith had to be called in to make a new one when the purchase of the motorboat made the lake once more the center of Stilling's activity.

As Wrayford entered he noticed that a strange oily odor over-powered the usual scent of dry pine wood; and at the next step his foot struck an object that rolled noisily across the boards. He lighted another match, and found he had overturned a can of grease which the boatman had no doubt been using to oil the runners of the sliding floor.

Wrayford felt his way down the length of the boathouse, and softly opening the balcony door looked out on the lake. A few yards away, he saw the launch lying at anchor in the veiled moonlight; and just below him, on the black water, was the dim outline of the skiff which the boatman kept to paddle out to her. The silence was so intense that Wrayford fancied he heard a faint rustling in the shrubbery on the high bank behind the boathouse, and the crackle of gravel on the path descending to it.

He closed the door again and turned back into the darkness; and as he did so the   65
other door, on the land side, swung inward, and he saw a figure in the dim opening. Just enough light entered through the round holes above the respective doors to reveal Mrs. Stilling's cloaked outline, and to guide her to him as he advanced. But before they met she stumbled and gave a little cry.

"What is it?" he exclaimed.

"My foot caught; the floor seemed to give way under me. Ah, of course"—she bent down in the darkness—"I saw the men oiling it this morning."

Wrayford caught her by the arm. "Do take care! It might be dangerous if it slid too easily. The water's deep under here."

"Yes; the water's very deep. I sometimes wish—" She leaned against him without finishing her sentence, and he put both arms about her.

"Hush!" he said, his lips to hers.   70

Suddenly she threw her head back and seemed to listen.

"What's the matter? What do you hear?"

"I don't know." He felt her trembling. "I'm not sure this place is as safe as it used to be—"

Wrayford held her to him reassuringly. "But the boatman sleeps down at the village; and who else should come here at this hour?"

"Cobham might. He thinks of nothing but the launch."   75

"He won't tonight. I told him I'd seen the skipper put her shipshape, and that satisfied him."

"Ah—he did think of coming, then?"

"Only for a minute, when the sky looked so black half an hour ago, and he was afraid of a squall. It's clearing now, and there's no danger."

He drew her down on the bench, and they sat a moment or two in silence, her hands in his. Then she said: "You'd better tell me."

Wrayford gave a faint laugh. "Yes, I suppose I had. In fact, he asked me to."   80

"He asked you to?"

"Yes."

She uttered an exclamation of contempt. "He's afraid!"

Wrayford made no reply, and she went on: "I'm not. Tell me everything, please."

"Well, he's chucked away a pretty big sum again—"   85

"How?"

"He says he doesn't know. He's been speculating, I suppose. The madness of making him your trustee!"

She drew her hands away. "You know why I did it. When we married I didn't want to put him in the false position of the man who contributes nothing and accepts everything; I wanted people to think the money was partly his."

"I don't know what you've made people think; but you've been eminently successful in one respect. *He* thinks it's all his—and he loses it as if it were."

"There are worse things. What was it that he wished you to tell me?"   90

"That you've got to sign another promissory note—for fifty thousand this time."

"Is that all?"

Wrayford hesitated; then he said: "Yes—for the present."

She sat motionless, her head bent, her hand resting passively in his.

He leaned nearer. "What did you mean just now, by worse things?"   95

She hesitated. "Haven't you noticed that he's been drinking a great deal lately?"

"Yes; I've noticed."

They were both silent; then Wrayford broke out, with sudden vehemence: "And yet you won't—"

"Won't?"

"Put an end to it. Good God! Save what's left of your life."   100

She made no answer, and in the stillness the throb of the water underneath them sounded like the beat of a tormented heart.

"Isabel—" Wrayford murmured. He bent over to kiss her. "Isabel! I can't stand it! Listen—"

"No; no. I've thought of everything. There's the boy—the boy's fond of him. He's not a bad father."

"Except in the trifling matter of ruining his son."

"And there's his poor old mother. He's a good son, at any rate; he'd never hurt her. 105 And I know her. If I left him, she'd never take a penny of my money. What she has of her own is not enough to live on; and how could he provide for her? If I put him out of doors, I should be putting his mother out too."

"You could arrange that—there are always ways."

"Not for her! She's proud. And then she believes in him. Lots of people believe in him, you know. It would kill her if she ever found out."

Wrayford made an impatient movement. "It will kill you if you stay with him to prevent her finding out."

She laid her other hand on his: "Not while I have you."

"Have me? In this way?"   110

"In any way."

"My poor girl—poor child!"

"Unless you grow tired—unless your patience gives out."

He was silent, and she went on insistently: "Don't you suppose I've thought of that too—foreseen it?"

"Well—and then?" he exclaimed.   115

"I've accepted that too."

He dropped her hands with a despairing gesture. "Then, indeed, I waste my breath!"

She made no answer, and for a time they sat silent again, a little between them. At length he asked: "You're not crying?"

"No."

"I can't see your face, it's grown so dark."   120

"Yes. The storm must be coming." She made a motion as if to rise.

He drew close and put his arm about her. "Don't leave me yet. You know I must go tomorrow." He broke off with a laugh. "I'm to break the news to you tomorrow morning, by the way; I'm to take you out in the motor launch and break it to you." He dropped her hands and stood up. "Good God! How can I go and leave you here with him?"

"You've done it often."

"Yes; but each time it's more damnable. And then I've always had a hope—"

She rose also. "Give it up! Give it up!"   125

"You've none, then, yourself?"

She was silent, drawing the folds of her cloak about her.

"None—none?" he insisted.

He had to bend his head to hear her answer. "Only one!"

"What, my dearest? What?"   130

"Don't touch me! That he may die!"

They drew apart again, hearing each other's quick breathing through the darkness.

"You wish that too?" he said.

"I wish it always—every day, every hour, every moment!" She paused, and then let the words break from her. "You'd better know it; you'd better know the worst of me. I'm not the saint you suppose; the duty I do is poisoned by the thoughts I think. Day by day, hour by hour, I wish him dead. When he goes out I pray for something to happen; when he comes back I say to myself: 'Are you here again?' When I hear of people being killed in accidents, I think: 'Why wasn't he there?' When I read the death notices in the paper I say: 'So-and-so was just his age.' When I see him taking such care of his health and his diet—as he does, you know, except when he gets reckless and begins to drink too much—when I see him exercising and resting, and eating only certain things, and weighing himself, and feeling his muscles, and boasting that he hasn't gained a pound, I think of the men who die from overwork, or who throw their lives away for some great object, and I say to myself: 'What can kill a man who thinks only of himself?' And night after night I keep myself from going to sleep for fear I may dream that he's dead. When I dream that, and wake and find him there it's worse than ever—"

She broke off with a sob, and the loud lapping of the water under the floor was like   135
the beat of a rebellious heart.

"There, you know the truth!" she said.

He answered after a pause: "People do die."

"Do they?" She laughed. "Yes—in happy marriages!"

They were silent again, and Isabel turned, feeling her way toward the door. As she did so, the profound stillness was broken by the sound of a man's voice trolling out unsteadily the refrain of a music-hall song.

The two in the boathouse darted toward each other with a simultaneous move-   140
ment, clutching hands as they met.

"He's coming!" Isabel said.

Wrayford disengaged his hands.

"He may only be out for a turn before he goes to bed. Wait a minute. I'll see." He felt his way to the bench, scrambled up on it, and stretching his body forward managed to bring his eyes in line with the opening above the door.

"It's as black as pitch. I can't see anything."

The refrain rang out nearer.   145

"Wait! I saw something twinkle. There it is again. It's his cigar. It's coming this way—down the path."

There was a long rattle of thunder through the stillness.

"It's the storm!" Isabel whispered. "He's coming to see about the launch."

Wrayford dropped noiselessly from the bench and she caught him by the arm.

"Isn't there time to get up the path and slip under the shrubbery?"   150

"No, he's in the path now. He'll be here in two minutes. He'll find us."

He felt her hand tighten on his arm.

"You must go in the skiff, then. It's the only way."

"And let him find you? And hear my oars? Listen—there's something I must say."

She flung her arms about him and pressed her face to his.   155

"Isabel, just now I didn't tell you everything. He's ruined his mother—taken everything of hers too. And he's got to tell her; it can't be kept from her."

She uttered an incredulous exclamation and drew back.

"Is this the truth? Why didn't you tell me before?"

"He forbade me. You were not to know."

Close above them, in the shrubbery, Stilling warbled: 160

"Nita, Juanita,
Ask thy soul if we must part!"

Wrayford held her by both arms. "Understand this—if he comes in, he'll find us. And if there's a row you'll lose your boy."

She seemed not to hear him. "You—you—you—he'll kill you!" she exclaimed.

Wrayford laughed impatiently and released her, and she stood shrinking against the wall, her hands pressed to her breast. Wrayford straightened himself and she felt that he was listening intently. Then he dropped to his knees and laid his hands against the boards of the sliding floor. It yielded at once, as if with a kind of evil alacrity; and at their feet they saw, under the motionless solid night, another darker night that moved and shimmered. Wrayford threw himself back against the opposite wall, behind the door.

A key rattled in the lock, and after a moment's fumbling the door swung open. Wrayford and Isabel saw a man's black bulk against the obscurity. It moved a step, lurched forward, and vanished out of sight. From the depths beneath them there came a splash and a long cry.

"Go! go!" Wrayford cried out, feeling blindly for Isabel in the blackness.   165

"Oh—" she cried, wrenching herself away from him.

He stood still a moment, as if dazed; then she saw him suddenly plunge from her side, and heard another splash far down, and a tumult in the beaten water.

In the darkness she cowered close to the opening, pressing her face over the edge, and crying out the name of each of the two men in turn. Suddenly she began to see: the obscurity was less opaque, as if a faint moon pallor diluted it. Isabel vaguely discerned the two shapes struggling in the black pit below her; once she saw the gleam of a face. She glanced up desperately for some means of rescue, and caught sight of the oars ranged on brackets against the walls. She snatched the nearest, bent over the opening, and pushed the oar down into the blackness, crying out her husband's name.

The clouds had swallowed the moon again, and she could see nothing below her; but she still heard tumult in the beaten water.

"Cobham! Cobham!" she screamed.   170

As if in answer, she felt a mighty clutch on the oar, a clutch that strained her arms to the breaking point as she tried to brace her knees against the runners on the sliding floor.

"Hold on! Hold on! Hold on!" a voice gasped out from below; and she held on, with racked muscles, with bleeding palms, with eyes straining from their sockets, and a heart that tugged at her as the weight was tugging at the oar.

Suddenly the weight relaxed, and the oar slipped up through her lacerated hands. She felt a wet body scrambling over the edge of the opening, and Stilling's voice, raucous and strange, groaned out, close to her: "God! I thought I was done for."

He staggered to his knees, coughing and sputtering, and the water dripped on her from his streaming clothes.

She flung herself down, again, straining over the pit. Not a sound came up from it. 175

"Austin! Austin! Quick! Another oar!" she shrieked.

Stilling gave a cry. "My God! Was it Austin? What in hell—Another oar? No, no; untie the skiff, I tell you. But it's no use. Nothing's any use. I felt him lose hold as I came up."

After that she was conscious of nothing till, hours later, as it appeared to her, she became dimly aware of her husband's voice, high, hysterical and important, haranguing a group of scared lantern-struck faces that had sprung up mysteriously about them in the night.

"Poor Austin! Poor Wrayford . . . terrible loss to me . . . mysterious dispensation. Yes, I do feel gratitude—miraculous escape—but I wish old Austin could have known that I was saved!"

Critical Thinking Topics

1. When considering the title, do you think Isabel made a conscious choice as to whose life she saved at the end of the story? Explain how details from the story lead you to this conclusion.

2. The story's title, "The Choice," refers to Isabel's conscious or unconscious choice at the conclusion of the story, but to what other choices do you think the title refers? In formulating an answer, consider fully the motivations of Cobham Stilling, Isabel Stilling, and Austin Wrayford.

3. The Stillings are a powerful couple, and Isabel Stilling is a powerful woman. Using specific passages from the story, describe what makes them powerful as a couple and as individuals. Is this power appealing to Austin Wrayford? Is it appealing to the reading audience? Why or why not?

Writing Topic

Write an epilogue to "The Choice," picking up where Wharton's story ends. Offer insight into the ramifications, if any, the Stilling couple will face following the drowning of Austin Wrayford. How will they explain his death? Will they be investigated? Do you think the couple has the clout to hide from the community the true reason the three of them converged on the boathouse on a dark night as a storm moved into Highfield? Knowing what you do of Isabel and Cobham, do you think the Stilling marriage will survive?

8.6 Tim O'Brien, The Things They Carried (1990)

First Lieutenant Jimmy Cross carried letters from a girl named Martha, a junior at Mount Sebastian College in New Jersey. They were not love letters, but Lieutenant Cross was hoping, so he kept them folded in plastic at the bottom of his rucksack. In the late afternoon, after a day's march, he would dig his foxhole, wash his hands under a canteen, unwrap the letters, hold them with the tips of his fingers, and spend the last hour of light pretending. He would imagine romantic camping trips into the White Mountains in New Hampshire. He would sometimes taste the envelope flaps, knowing her tongue had been there. More than anything, he wanted Martha to love him as he loved her, but the letters were mostly chatty, elusive on the matter of love. She was a virgin, he was almost sure. She was an English major at Mount Sebastian, and she wrote beautifully about her professors and roommates and midterm exams, about her respect for Chaucer and her great affection for Virginia Woolf. She often quoted lines of poetry; she never mentioned the war, except to say, Jimmy, take care of yourself. The letters weighed 10 ounces.

They were signed Love, Martha, but Lieutenant Cross understood that Love was only a way of signing and did not mean what he sometimes pretended it meant. At dusk, he would carefully return the letters to his rucksack. Slowly, a bit distracted, he would get up and move among his men, checking the perimeter, then at full dark he would return to his hole and watch the night and wonder if Martha was a virgin.

The things they carried were largely determined by necessity. Among the necessities or near-necessities were P-38 can openers, pocket knives, heat tabs, wristwatches, dog tags, mosquito repellent, chewing gum, candy, cigarettes, salt tablets, packets of Kool-Aid, lighters, matches, sewing kits, Military Payment Certificates, C rations, and two or three canteens of water. Together, these items weighed between 15 and 20 pounds, depending upon a man's habits or rate of metabolism. Henry Dobbins, who was a big man, carried extra rations; he was especially fond of canned peaches in heavy syrup over pound cake. Dave Jensen, who practiced field hygiene, carried a toothbrush, dental floss, and several hotel-sized bars of soap he'd stolen on R&R in Sydney, Australia. Ted Lavender, who was scared, carried tranquilizers until he was shot in the head outside the village of Than Khe in mid-April. By necessity, and because it was SOP, they all carried steel helmets that weighed 5 pounds including the liner and camouflage cover. They carried the standard fatigue jackets and trousers. Very few carried underwear. On their feet they carried jungle boots—2.1 pounds—and Dave Jensen carried three pairs of socks and a can of Dr. Scholl's foot powder as a precaution against trench foot. Until he was shot, Ted Lavender carried six or seven ounces of premium dope, which for him was a necessity. Mitchell Sanders, the RTO, carried condoms. Norman Bowker carried a diary. Rat Kiley carried comic books. Kiowa, a devout Baptist, carried an illustrated New Testament that had been presented to him by his father, who taught Sunday school in Oklahoma City, Oklahoma. As a hedge against bad times, however, Kiowa also carried his grandmother's distrust of the white man, his grandfather's old hunting hatchet. Necessity dictated. Because the land was mined and booby-trapped, it was SOP for each man to carry a steelcentered, nylon-covered flak jacket, which weighed 6.7 pounds, but which on hot days seemed much heavier. Because you could die so quickly, each man carried at least one large compress bandage, usually in the helmet band for easy access. Because the nights were cold, and because the monsoons were wet, each carried a green plastic poncho that could be used as a raincoat or groundsheet or makeshift tent. With its quilted liner, the poncho weighed almost two pounds, but it was worth every ounce. In April, for instance, when Ted Lavender was shot, they used his poncho to wrap him up, then to carry him across the paddy, then to lift him into the chopper that took him away.

They were called legs or grunts.

To carry something was to hump it, as when Lieutenant Jimmy Cross humped his love for Martha up the hills and through the swamps. In its intransitive form, to hump meant to walk, or to march, but it implied burdens far beyond the intransitive.

Almost everyone humped photographs. In his wallet, Lieutenant Cross carried two photographs of Martha. The first was a Kodacolor snapshot signed Love, though he knew better. She stood against a brick wall. Her eyes were gray and neutral, her lips slightly open as she stared straight-on at the camera. At night, sometimes, Lieutenant Cross wondered who had taken the picture, because he knew she had boyfriends, because he loved her so much, and because he could see the shadow of the picture-taker spreading out against the brick wall. The second photograph had been clipped from the 1968 Mount Sebastian yearbook. It was an action shot—women's volleyball—and Martha was bent horizontal to the floor, reaching, the palms of her hands in sharp focus, the tongue taut, the expression frank and competitive. There was no visible sweat. She wore white gym shorts. Her legs, he thought, were almost certainly the legs of a virgin, dry and without hair, the left knee cocked and carrying her entire weight, which was just over one hundred pounds. Lieutenant Cross remembered touching that left knee. A dark theater, he remembered, and the movie was *Bonnie and Clyde,* and Martha wore a tweed skirt, and during the final scene, when he touched her knee, she turned and looked at him in a sad, sober way that made him pull his hand back, but he would always remember the feel of the tweed skirt and the knee beneath it and the sound of the gunfire that killed Bonnie and Clyde, how embarrassing it was, how slow and oppressive. He remembered kissing her good night at the dorm door. Right then, he thought, he should've done something brave. He should've carried her up the stairs to her room and tied her to the bed and touched that left knee all night long. He should've risked it. Whenever he looked at the photographs, he thought of new things he should've done.

What they carried was partly a function of rank, partly of field specialty.

As a first lieutenant and platoon leader, Jimmy Cross carried a compass, maps, code books, binoculars, and a. 45-caliber pistol that weighed 2.9 pounds fully loaded. He carried a strobe light and the responsibility for the lives of his men.

As an RTO, Mitchell Sanders carried the PRC-25 radio, a killer, 26 pounds with its battery.

As a medic, Rat Kiley carried a canvas satchel filled with morphine and plasma and malaria tablets and surgical tape and comic books and all the things a medic must carry, including M&M's for especially bad wounds, for a total weight of nearly 20 pounds.

As a big man, therefore a machine gunner, Henry Dobbins carried the M-60 which 10 weighed 23 pounds unloaded, but which was almost always loaded. In addition, Dobbins carried between 10 and 15 pounds of ammunition draped in belts across his chest and shoulders.

As PFCs or Spec 4s, most of them were common grunts and carried the standard M-16 gas-operated assault rifle. The weapon weighed 7.5 pounds unloaded, 8.2 pounds with its full 20-round magazine. Depending on numerous factors, such as topography and psychology, the riflemen carried anywhere from 12 to 20 magazines, usually in cloth bandoliers, adding on another 8.4 pounds at minimum, 14 pounds at maximum. When it was available, they also carried M-16 maintenance gear—rods and steel brushes and swabs and tubes of LSA oil—all of which weighed about a pound. Among the grunts, some carried the M-79 grenade launcher, 5.9 pounds unloaded, a reasonably light weapon except for the ammunition, which was heavy. A single round weighed 10 ounces. The typical load was 25 rounds. But Ted Lavender, who was scared, carried 34 rounds when he was shot and killed outside Than Khe, and he went down under an exceptional burden, more than 20 pounds of ammunition, plus the flak jacket and helmet and rations and water and toilet paper and tranquilizers and all the rest, plus the unweighed fear. He was dead weight. There was no twitching or flopping. Kiowa, who saw it happen, said it was like watching a rock fall, or a big sandbag or something—just boom, then down—not like the movies where the dead guy rolls around and does fancy spins and goes ass over teakettle—not like that, Kiowa said, the poor bastard just flat-fuck fell. Boom. Down. Nothing else. It was a bright morning in mid-April. Lieutenant Cross felt the pain. He blamed himself. They stripped off Lavender's canteens and ammo, all the heavy things, and Rat Kiley said the obvious, the guy's dead, and Mitchell Sanders used his radio to report one U.S. KIA and to request a chopper. Then they wrapped Lavender in his poncho. They carried him out to a dry paddy, established security, and sat smoking the dead man's dope until the chopper came. Lieutenant Cross kept to himself. He pictured Martha's smooth young face, thinking he loved her more than anything, more than his men, and now Ted Lavender was dead because he loved her so much and could not stop thinking about her. When the dustoff arrived, they carried Lavender aboard. Afterward they burned Than Khe. They marched until dusk, then dug their holes, and that night Kiowa kept explaining how you had to be there, how fast it was, how the poor guy just dropped like so much concrete. Boom-down, he said. Like cement.

In addition to the three standard weapons—the M-60, M-16, and M-79—they carried whatever presented itself, or whatever seemed appropriate as a means of killing or staying alive. They carried catch-as-catch-can. At various times, in various situations, they carried M-14s and CAR-15s and Swedish Ks and grease guns and captured AK-47s and Chi-Coms and RPGs and Simonov carbines and black market Uzis "and .38-caliber" Smith & Wesson handguns and 66 mm LAWs and shotguns and silencers and blackjacks and bayonets and C-4 plastic explosives. Lee Strunk carried a slingshot; a weapon of last resort, he called it. Mitchell Sanders carried brass knuckles. Kiowa carried his grandfather's feathered hatchet. Every third or fourth man carried a Claymore antipersonnel mine—3.5 pounds with its firing device. They all carried fragmentation grenades—14 ounces each. They all carried at least one M-18 colored smoke grenade—24 ounces. Some carried CS or tear gas grenades. Some carried white phosphorus grenades. They carried all they could bear, and then some, including a silent awe for the terrible power of the things they carried.

In the first week of April, before Lavender died, Lieutenant Jimmy Cross received a good-luck charm from Martha. It was a simple pebble, an ounce at most. Smooth to the touch, it was a milky white color with flecks of orange and violet, oval-shaped, like a miniature egg. In the accompanying letter, Martha wrote that she had found the pebble on the Jersey shoreline, precisely where the land touched water at high tide, where things came together but also separated. It was this separate-but-together quality, she wrote, that had inspired her to pick up the pebble and to carry it in her breast pocket for several days, where it seemed weightless, and then to send it through the mail, by air, as a token of her truest feelings for him. Lieutenant Cross found this romantic. But he wondered what her truest feelings were, exactly, and what she meant by separate-but-together. He wondered how the tides and waves had come into play on that afternoon along the Jersey shoreline when Martha saw the pebble and bent down to rescue it from geology. He imagined bare feet. Martha was a poet, with the poet's sensibilities, and her feet would be brown and bare, the toenails unpainted, the eyes chilly and somber like the ocean in March, and though it was painful, he wondered who had been with her that afternoon. He imagined a pair of shadows moving along the strip of sand where things came together but also separated. It was phantom jealousy, he knew, but he couldn't help himself. He loved her so much. On the march, through the hot days of early April, he carried the pebble in his mouth, turning it with his tongue, tasting sea salt and moisture. His mind wandered. He had difficulty keeping his attention on the war. On occasion he would yell at his men to spread out the column, to keep their eyes open, but then he would slip away into daydreams, just pretending, walking barefoot along the Jersey shore, with Martha, carrying nothing. He would feel himself rising. Sun and waves and gentle winds, all love and lightness.

What they carried varied by mission.

When a mission took them to the mountains, they carried mosquito netting, 15 machetes, canvas tarps, and extra bug juice.

If a mission seemed especially hazardous, or if it involved a place they knew to be bad, they carried everything they could. In certain heavily mined AOs, where the land was dense with Toe Poppers and Bouncing Betties, they took turns humping a 28-pound mine detector. With its headphones and big sensing plate, the equipment was a stress on the lower back and shoulders, awkward to handle, often useless because of the shrapnel in the earth, but they carried it anyway, partly for safety, partly for the illusion of safety.

On ambush, or other night missions, they carried peculiar little odds and ends. Kiowa always took along his New Testament and a pair of moccasins for silence. Dave Jensen carried night-sight vitamins high in carotene. Lee Strunk carried his slingshot; ammo, he claimed, would never be a problem. Rat Kiley carried brandy and M&M's candy. Until he was shot, Ted Lavender carried the starlight scope, which weighed 6.3 pounds with its aluminum carrying case. Henry Dobbins carried his girlfriend's pantyhose wrapped around his neck as a comforter. They all carried ghosts. When dark came, they would move out single file across the meadows and paddies to their ambush coordinates, where they would quietly set up the Claymores and lie down and spend the night waiting.

Other missions were more complicated and required special equipment. In mid-April, it was their mission to search out and destroy the elaborate tunnel complexes in the Than Khe area south of Chu Lai. To blow the tunnels, they carried one-pound blocks of pentrite high explosives, four blocks to a man, 68 pounds in all. They carried wiring, detonators, and battery-powered clackers. Dave Jensen carried earplugs. Most often, before blowing the tunnels, they were ordered by higher command to search them, which was considered bad news, but by and large they just shrugged and carried out orders. Because he was a big man, Henry Dobbins was excused from tunnel duty. The others would draw numbers. Before Lavender died there were 17 men in the platoon, and whoever drew the number 17 would strip off his gear and crawl in headfirst with a flashlight and Lieutenant Cross's .45-caliber pistol. The rest of them would fan out as security. They would sit down or kneel, not facing the hole, listening to the ground beneath them, imagining cobwebs and ghosts, whatever was down there—the tunnel walls squeezing in—how the flashlight seemed impossibly heavy in the hand and how it was tunnel vision in the very strictest sense, compression in all ways, even time, and how you had to wiggle in—ass and elbows—a swallowed-up feeling—and how you found yourself worrying about odd things: Will your flashlight go dead? Do rats carry rabies? If you screamed, how far would the sound carry? Would your buddies hear it? Would they have the courage to drag you out? In some respects, though not many, the waiting was worse than the tunnel itself. Imagination was a killer.

On April 16, when Lee Strunk drew the number 17, he laughed and muttered something and went down quickly. The morning was hot and very still. Not good, Kiowa said. He looked at the tunnel opening, then out across a dry paddy toward the village of Than Khe. Nothing moved. No clouds or birds or people. As they waited, the men smoked and drank Kool-Aid, not talking much, feeling sympathy for Lee Strunk but also feeling the luck of the draw. You win some, you lose some, said Mitchell Sanders, and sometimes you settle for a rain check. It was a tired line and no one laughed.

Henry Dobbins ate a tropical chocolate bar. Ted Lavender popped a tranquilizer   20
and went off to pee.

After five minutes, Lieutenant Jimmy Cross moved to the tunnel, leaned down, and examined the darkness. Trouble, he thought—a cave-in maybe. And then suddenly, without willing it, he was thinking about Martha. The stresses and fractures, the quick collapse, the two of them buried alive under all that weight. Dense, crushing love. Kneeling, watching the hole, he tried to concentrate on Lee Strunk and the war, all the dangers, but his love was too much for him, he felt paralyzed, he wanted to sleep inside her lungs and breathe her blood and be smothered. He wanted her to be a virgin and not a virgin, all at once. He wanted to know her. Intimate secrets: Why poetry? Why so sad? Why that grayness in her eyes? Why so alone? Not lonely, just alone—riding her bike across campus or sitting off by herself in the cafeteria—even dancing, she danced alone—and it was the aloneness that filled him with love. He remembered telling her that one evening. How she nodded and looked away. And how, later, when he kissed her, she received the kiss without returning it, her eyes wide open, not afraid, not a virgin's eyes, just flat and uninvolved.

Lieutenant Cross gazed at the tunnel. But he was not there. He was buried with Martha under the white sand at the Jersey shore. They were pressed together, and the pebble in his mouth was her tongue. He was smiling. Vaguely, he was aware of how quiet the day was, the sullen paddies, yet he could not bring himself to worry about matters of security. He was beyond that. He was just a kid at war, in love. He was twenty-four years old. He couldn't help it.

A few moments later Lee Strunk crawled out of the tunnel. He came up grinning, filthy but alive. Lieutenant Cross nodded and closed his eyes while the others clapped Strunk on the back and made jokes about rising from the dead.

Worms, Rat Kiley said. Right out of the grave. Fuckin' zombie.

The men laughed. They all felt great relief.   25

Spook city, said Mitchell Sanders.

Lee Strunk made a funny ghost sound, a kind of moaning, yet very happy, and right then, when Strunk made that high happy moaning sound, when we went *Ahhooooo*, right then Ted Lavender was shot in the head on his way back from peeing. He lay with his mouth open. The teeth were broken. There was a swollen black bruise under his left eye. The cheekbone was gone. Oh shit, Rat Kiley said, the guy's dead. The guy's dead, he kept saying, which seemed profound—the guy's dead. I mean really.

The things they carried were determined to some extent by superstition. Lieutenant Cross carried his good-luck pebble. Dave Jensen carried a rabbit's foot. Norman Bowker, otherwise a very gentle person, carried a thumb that had been presented to him as a gift by Mitchell Sanders. The thumb was dark brown, rubbery to the touch, and weighed four ounces at most. It had been cut from a VC corpse, a boy of fifteen or sixteen. They'd found him at the bottom of an irrigation ditch, badly burned, flies in his mouth and eyes. The boy wore black shorts and sandals. At the time of his death he had been carrying a pouch of rice, a rifle and three magazines of ammunition.

You want my opinion, Mitchell Sanders said, there's a definite moral here.

He put his hand on the dead boy's wrist. He was quiet for a time, as if counting 30 a pulse, then he patted the stomach, almost affectionately, and used Kiowa's hunting hatchet to remove the thumb.

Henry Dobbins asked what the moral was.

Moral?

You know. *Moral.*

Sanders wrapped the thumb in toilet paper and handed it across to Norman Bowker. There was no blood. Smiling, he kicked the boy's head, watched the flies scatter, and said, It's like with that old TV show—Paladin. Have gun, will travel.

Henry Dobbins thought about it. 35

Yeah, well, he finally said. I don't see no moral.

There it *is,* man.

Fuck off.

They carried USO stationery and pencils and pens. They carried Sterno, safety pins, trip flares, signal flares, spools of wire, razor blades, chewing tobacco, liberated joss sticks and statuettes of the smiling Buddha, candles, grease pencils, *The Stars and Stripes,* fingernail clippers, Psy Ops leaflets, bush hats, bolos, and much more. Twice a week, when the resupply choppers came in, they carried hot chow in green mermite cans and large canvas bags filled with iced beer and soda pop. They carried plastic water containers, each with a two-gallon capacity. Mitchell Sanders carried a set of starched tiger fatigues for special occasions. Henry Dobbins carried Black Flag insecticide. Dave Jensen carried empty sandbags that could be filled at night for added protection. Lee Strunk carried tanning lotion. Some things they carried in common. Taking turns, they carried the big PRC-77 scrambler radio, which weighed 30 pounds with its battery. They shared the weight of memory. They took up what others could no longer bear. Often, they carried each other, the wounded or weak. They carried infections. They carried chess sets, basketballs, Vietnamese-English dictionaries, insignia of rank, Bronze Stars and Purple Hearts, plastic cards imprinted with the Code of Conduct. They carried diseases, among them malaria and dysentery. They carried lice and ringworm and leeches and paddy algae and various rots and molds. They carried the land itself—Vietnam, the place, the soil—a powdery orange-red dust that covered their boots and fatigues and faces. They carried the sky. The whole atmosphere, they carried it, the humidity, the monsoons, the stink of fungus and decay, all of it, they carried gravity. They moved like mules. By daylight they took sniper fire, at night they were mortared, but it was not battle, it was just the endless march, village to village, without purpose, nothing won or lost. They marched for the sake of the march. They plodded along slowly, dumbly, leaning forward against the heat, unthinking, all blood and bone, simple grunts, soldiering with their legs, toiling up the hills and down into the paddies and across the rivers and up again and down, just humping, one step and then the next and then another, but no volition, no will, because it was automatic, it was anatomy, and the war was entirely a matter of posture and carriage, the hump was everything, a kind of inertia, a kind of emptiness, a dullness of desire and intellect and conscience and hope and human sensibility. Their principles were in their feet. Their calculations were biological. They had no sense of strategy or mission. They searched the villages without knowing what to look for, not caring, kicking over jars of rice, frisking children and old men, blowing tunnels, sometimes setting fires and sometimes not, then forming up and moving on to the next village, then other villages, where it would always be the same. They carried their own lives. The pressures were enormous. In the heat of early afternoon, they would remove their helmets and flak jackets, walking bare, which was dangerous but which helped ease the strain. They would often discard things along the route of march. Purely for comfort, they would throw away rations, blow their Claymores and grenades, no matter, because by nightfall the resupply choppers would arrive with more of the same, then a day or two later still more, fresh watermelons and crates of ammunition and sunglasses and woolen sweaters—the resources were stunning—sparklers for the Fourth of July, colored eggs for Easter—it was the great American war chest—the fruits of science, the smokestacks, the canneries, the arsenals at Hartford, the Minnesota forests, the machine shops, the vast fields of corn and wheat—they carried like freight trains; they carried it on their backs and shoulders—and for all the ambiguities of Vietnam, all the mysteries and unknowns, there was at least the single abiding certainty that they would never be at a loss for things to carry.

After the chopper took Lavender away, Lieutenant Jimmy Cross led his men into the village of Than Khe. They burned everything. They shot chickens and dogs, they trashed the village well, they called in artillery and watched the wreckage, then they marched for several hours through the hot afternoon, and then at dusk, while Kiowa explained how Lavender died, Lieutenant Cross found himself trembling. 40

He tried not to cry. With his entrenching tool, which weighed five pounds, he began digging a hole in the earth.

He felt shame. He hated himself. He had loved Martha more than his men, and as a consequence Lavender was now dead, and this was something he would have to carry like a stone in his stomach for the rest of the war.

All he could do was dig. He used his entrenching tool like an ax, slashing, feeling both love and hate, and then later, when it was full dark, he sat at the bottom of his foxhole and wept. It went on for a long while. In part, he was grieving for Ted Lavender, but mostly it was for Martha, and for himself, because she belonged to another world, which was not quite real, and because she was a junior at Mount Sebastian College in New Jersey, a poet and a virgin and uninvolved, and because he realized she did not love him and never would.

Like cement, Kiowa whispered in the dark. I swear to God—boom, down. Not a word.

I've heard this, said Norman Bowker. 45

A pisser, you know? Still zipping himself up. Zapped while zipping.

All right, fine. That's enough.

Yeah, but you had to see it, the guy just—

I *heard,* man. Cement. So why not shut the fuck *up?*

Kiowa shook his head sadly and glanced over at the hole where Lieutenant Jimmy Cross sat watching the night. The air was thick and wet. A warm dense fog had settled over the paddies and there was the stillness that precedes rain. 50

After a time Kiowa sighed.

One thing for sure, he said. The lieutenant's in some deep hurt. I mean that crying jag—the way he was carrying on—it wasn't fake or anything, it was real heavy-duty hurt. The man cares.

Sure, Norman Bowker said.

Say what you want, the man does care.

We all got problems.   55

Not Lavender.

No, I guess not, Bowker said. Do me a favor, though.

Shut up?

That's a smart Indian. Shut up.

Shrugging, Kiowa pulled off his boots. He wanted to say more, just to lighten up   60
his sleep, but instead he opened his New Testament and arranged it beneath his head as a pillow. The fog made things seem hollow and unattached. He tried not to think about Ted Lavender, but then he was thinking how fast it was, no drama, down and dead, and how it was hard to feel anything except surprise. It seemed unchristian. He wished he could find some great sadness, or even anger, but the emotion wasn't there and he couldn't make it happen. Mostly he felt pleased to be alive. He liked the smell of the New Testament under his cheek, the leather and ink and paper and glue, whatever the chemicals were. He liked hearing the sounds of night. Even his fatigue, it felt fine, the stiff muscles and the prickly awareness of his own body, a floating feeling. He enjoyed not being dead. Lying there, Kiowa admired Lieutenant Jimmy Cross's capacity for grief. He wanted to share the man's pain, he wanted to care as Jimmy Cross cared. And yet when he closed his eyes, all he could think was Boom-down, and all he could feel was the pleasure of having his boots off and the fog curling in around him and the damp soil and the Bible smells and the plush comfort of night.

After a moment Norman Bowker sat up in the dark.

What the hell, he said. You want to talk, *talk*. Tell it to me.

Forget it.

No, man, go on. One thing I hate, it's a silent Indian.

For the most part they carried themselves with poise, a kind of dignity. Now and   65
then, however, there were times of panic, when they squealed or wanted to squeal but couldn't, when they twitched and made moaning sounds and covered their heads and said Dear Jesus and flopped around on the earth and fired their weapons blindly and cringed and sobbed and begged for the noise to stop and went wild and made stupid promises to themselves and to God and to their mothers and fathers, hoping not to die. In different ways, it happened to all of them. Afterward, when the firing ended, they would blink and peek up. They would touch their bodies, feeling shame, then quickly hiding it. They would force themselves to stand. As if in slow motion, frame by frame, the world would take on the old logic—absolute silence, then the wind, then sunlight, then voices. It was the burden of being alive. Awkwardly, the men would reassemble themselves, first in private, then in groups, becoming soldiers again. They would repair the leaks in their eyes. They would check for casualties, call in dust-offs, light cigarettes, try to smile, clear their throats and spit and begin cleaning their weapons. After a time someone would shake his head and say. No lie, I almost shit my pants, and someone else would laugh, which meant it was bad, yes, but the guy had obviously not shit his pants, it wasn't that bad, and in any case nobody would ever do such a thing and then

go ahead and talk about it. They would squint into the dense, oppressive sunlight. For a few moments, perhaps, they would fall silent, lighting a joint and tracking its passage from man to man, inhaling, holding in the humiliation. Scary stuff, one of them might say. But then someone else would grin or flick his eyebrows and say, Roger-dodger, almost cut me a new asshole, *almost.*

There were numerous such poses. Some carried themselves with a sort of wistful resignation, others with pride or stiff soldierly discipline or good humor or macho zeal. They were afraid of dying but they were even more afraid to show it.

They found jokes to tell.

They used a hard vocabulary to contain the terrible softness. *Greased* they'd say. *Offed, lit up, zapped while zipping.* It wasn't cruelty, just stage presence. They were actors. When someone died, it wasn't quite dying, because in a curious way it seemed scripted, and because they had their lines mostly memorized, irony mixed with tragedy, and because they called it by other names, as if to encyst and destroy the reality of death itself. They kicked corpses. They cut off thumbs. They talked grunt lingo. They told stories about Ted Lavender's supply of tranquilizers, how the poor guy didn't feel a thing, how incredibly tranquil he was.

There's a moral here, said Mitchell Sanders.

They were waiting for Lavender's chopper, smoking the dead man's dope.   70

The moral's pretty obvious, Sanders said, and winked. Stay away from drugs. No joke, they'll ruin your day every time.

Cute, said Henry Dobbins.

Mind blower, get it? Talk about wiggy. Nothing left, just blood and brains.

They made themselves laugh.

There it is, they'd say. Over and over—there it is, my friend, there it is—as if the   75
repetition itself were an act of poise, a balance between crazy and almost crazy, knowing without going, there it is, which meant be cool, let it ride, because Oh yeah man, you can't change what can't be changed, there it is, there it absolutely and positively and fucking well *is.*

They were tough.

They carried all the emotional baggage of men who might die. Grief, terror, love, longing—these were intangibles, but the intangibles had their own mass and specific gravity, they had tangible weight. They carried shameful memories. They carried the common secret of cowardice barely restrained, the instinct to run or freeze or hide, and in many respects this was the heaviest burden of all, for it could never be put down, it required perfect balance and perfect posture. They carried their reputations. They carried the soldier's greatest fear, which was the fear of blushing. Men killed, and died, because they were embarrassed not to. It was what had brought them to the war in the first place, nothing positive, no dream of glory or honor, just to avoid the blush of dishonor. They died so as not to die of embarrassment. They crawled into tunnels and walked point and advanced under fire. Each morning, despite the unknowns, they made their legs move. They endured. They kept humping. They did not submit to the obvious alternative, which was simply to close the eyes and fall. So easy, really. Go limp and tumble to the ground and let the muscles unwind and not speak and not bulge until your buddies picked you up and lifted you into the chopper that would roar and dip its nose and carry you off to the world. A mere matter of falling, yet no one ever fell. It was not courage, exactly; the object was not valor. Rather, they were too frightened to be cowards.

By and large they carried these things inside, maintaining the masks of composure. They sneered at sick call. They spoke bitterly about guys who had found release by shooting off their own toes or fingers. Pussies, they'd say. Candy-asses. It was fierce, mocking talk, with only a trace of envy or awe, but even so the image played itself out behind their eyes.

They imagined the muzzle against flesh. So easy: squeeze the trigger and blow away a toe. They imagined it. They imagined the quick, sweet pain, then the evacuation to Japan, then a hospital with warm beds and cute geisha nurses.

And they dreamed of freedom birds. 80

At night, on guard, staring into the dark, they were carried away by jumbo jets. They felt the rush of takeoff. *Gone!* they yelled. And then velocity—wings and engines—a smiling stewardess—but it was more than a plane, it was a real bird, a big sleek silver bird with feathers and talons and high screeching. They were flying. The weights fell off; there was nothing to bear. They laughed and held on tight, feeling the cold slap of wind and altitude, soaring, thinking *It's over, I'm gone!*—they were naked, they were light and free—it was all lightness, bright and fast and buoyant, light as light, a helium buzz in the brain, a giddy bubbling in the lungs as they were taken up over the clouds and the war, beyond duty, beyond gravity and mortification and global entanglements—*Sin loi!* they yelled. *I'm sorry, motherfuckers, but I'm out of it, I'm goofed, I'm on a space cruise, I'm gone!*—and it was a restful, unencumbered sensation, just riding the light waves, sailing that big silver freedom bird over the mountains and oceans, over America, over the farms and great sleeping cities and cemeteries and highways and the golden arches of McDonald's, it was flight, a kind of fleeing, a kind of falling, falling higher and higher, spinning off the edge of the earth and beyond the sun and through the vast, silent vacuum where there were no burdens and where everything weighed exactly nothing—*Gone!* they screamed. *I'm sorry but I'm gone!*—and so at night, not quite dreaming, they gave themselves over to lightness, they were carried, they were purely borne.

On the morning after Ted Lavender died, First Lieutenant Jimmy Cross crouched at the bottom of his foxhole and burned Martha's letters. Then he burned the two photographs. There was a steady rain falling, which made it difficult, but he used heat tabs and Sterno to build a small fire, screening it with his body, holding the photographs over the tight blue flame with the tips of his fingers.

He realized it was only a gesture. Stupid, he thought. Sentimental, too, but mostly just stupid.

Lavender was dead. You couldn't burn the blame.

Besides, the letters were in his head. And even now, without photographs, Lieuten- 85 ant Cross could see Martha playing volleyball in her white gym shorts and yellow T-shirt. He could see her moving in the rain.

When the fire died out, Lieutenant Cross pulled his poncho over his shoulders and ate breakfast from a can.

There was no great mystery, he decided.

In those burned letters Martha had never mentioned the war, except to say, Jimmy, take care of yourself. She wasn't involved. She signed the letters Love, but it wasn't love, and all the fine lines and technicalities did not matter. Virginity was no longer an issue. He hated her. Yes, he did. He hated her. Love, too, but it was a hard, hating kind of love.

The morning came up wet and blurry. Everything seemed part of everything else, the fog and Martha and the deepening rain.

He was a soldier, after all.   90

Half smiling, Lieutenant Jimmy Cross took out his maps. He shook his head hard, as if to clear it, then bent forward and began planning the day's march. In ten minutes, or maybe twenty, he would rouse the men and they would pack up and head west, where the maps showed the country to be green and inviting. They would do what they had always done. The rain might add some weight, but otherwise it would be one more day layered upon all the other days.

He was realistic about it. There was that new hardness in his stomach. He loved her but he hated her.

No more fantasies, he told himself.

Henceforth, when he thought about Martha, it would be only to think that she belonged elsewhere. He would shut down the daydreams. This was not Mount Sebastian, it was another world, where there were no pretty poems or midterm exams, a place where men died because of carelessness and gross stupidity. Kiowa was right. Boomdown, and you were dead, never partly dead.

Briefly, in the rain, Lieutenant Cross saw Martha's gray eyes gazing back at him.   95

He understood.

It was very sad, he thought. The things men carried inside. The things men did or felt they had to do.

He almost nodded at her, but didn't.

Instead he went back to his maps. He was now determined to perform his duties firmly and without negligence. It wouldn't help Lavender, he knew that, but from this point on he would comport himself as an officer. He would dispose of his good-luck pebble. Swallow it, maybe, or use Lee Strunk's slingshot, or just drop it along the trail. On the march he would impose strict field discipline. He would be careful to send out flank security, to prevent straggling or bunching up, to keep his troops moving at the proper pace and at the proper interval. He would insist on clean weapons. He would confiscate the remainder of Lavender's dope. Later in the day, perhaps, he would call the men together and speak to them plainly. He would accept the blame for what had happened to Ted Lavender. He would be a man about it. He would look them in the eyes, keeping his chin level, and he would issue the new SOPs in a calm, impersonal tone of voice, a lieutenant's voice, leaving no room for argument or discussion. Commencing immediately, he'd tell them, they would no longer abandon equipment along the route of march. They would police up their acts. They would get their shit together, and keep it together, and maintain it neatly and in good working order.

He would not tolerate laxity. He would show strength, distancing himself.   100

Among the men there would be grumbling, of course, and maybe worse, because their days would seem longer and their loads heavier, but Lieutenant Jimmy Cross reminded himself that his obligation was not to be loved but to lead. He would dispense with love; it was not now a factor. And if anyone quarreled or complained, he would simply tighten his lips and arrange his shoulders in the correct command posture. He might give a curt little nod. Or he might not. He might just shrug and say, Carry on, then they would saddle up and form into a column and move out toward the villages west of Than Khe.

Source: "The Things They Carried" from THE THINGS THEY CARRIED by Tim O'Brien © 1990 by Tim O'Brien. Reprinted by permission of Houghton Mifflin Harcourt Publishing Company. All rights reserved.

Critical Thinking Topics

1. Throughout the short story, the words of the title are a steady refrain: "The things they carried were largely determined by necessity" (par. 2); "They carried all they could bear, and then some, including a silent awe for the terrible power of the things they carried" (par. 12); "they all carried ghosts" (par. 17). List at least 10 different kinds of "things" the men carry. Describe how these "things" shape your response to the individual men, in particular, when juxtaposed with some of their unsavory, even brutish actions.

2. As the leader of his platoon, young Lieutenant Jimmy Cross bears the heavy burden of power over and responsibility for his men. He blames himself for Ted Lavender's death. To what degree do you believe Cross is responsible? Explain your answer.

3. Despite its terrible consequences, war is sometimes remembered as a time of bonding and friendship like no other. What is there in such a horrible situation that could make soldiers recall it with longing? In addition to combat experiences, identify at least one other situation that is likely to foster a special bond among soldiers.

4. Reread the passage that begins, "They moved like mules" and concludes with "a dullness of desire and intellect and conscience and hope and human sensibility" (par. 39). Write a three-part response to the passage:
   • Creative reading response;
   • Critical reading response; and,
   • Synthesis of creative and critical responses.
   (See Chapter 2 for discussion and examples of these types of responses.)

Writing Topic

Reread Wilfred Owen's poem *"Dulce et Decorum Est"* in Chapter 3. In O'Brien's story, find images and other details that support Owen's rejection of what he calls "The old Lie": *"Dulce et decorum est/Pro patria mori."* Based on these images and details, create a free-form poem that also concludes by rejecting the same "old Lie."

8.7 Lucia Berlin, A Manual for Cleaning Women (1990)

42–PIEDMONT. Slow bus to Jack London Square. Maids and old ladies. I sat next to an old blind woman who was reading Braille, her finger gliding across the page, slow and quiet, line after line. It was soothing to watch, reading over her shoulder. The woman got off at Twenty-ninth, where all the letters have fallen from the sign NATIONAL PRODUCTS BY THE BLIND except for BLIND.

Twenty-ninth is my stop too, but I have to go all the way downtown to cash Mrs. Jessel's check. If she pays me with a check one more time I'll quit. Besides she never has any change for carfare. Last week I went all the way to the bank with my own quarter and she had forgotten to sign the check.

She forgets everything, even her ailments. As I dust I collect them and put them on her desk. 10 AM. NAUSEEA (sp) on a piece of paper on the mantel. DIARREEA on the drainboard. DIZZY POOR MEMORY on the kitchen stove. Mostly she forgets if she took her phenobarbital or not, or that she has already called me twice at home to ask if she did, where her ruby ring is, etc.

She follows me from room to room, saying the same things over and over. I'm going as cuckoo as she is. I keep saying I'll quit but I feel sorry for her. I'm the only person she has to talk to. Her husband is a lawyer, plays golf and has a mistress. I don't think Mrs. Jessel knows this, or remembers. Cleaning women know everything.

Cleaning women do steal. Not the things the people we work for are so nervous   5
about. It is the superfluity that finally gets to you. We don't want the change in the little ashtrays.

Some lady at a bridge party somewhere started the rumor that to test the honesty of a cleaning woman you leave little rosebud ashtrays around with loose change in them, here and there. My solution to this is to always add a few pennies, even a dime.

The minute I get to work I first check out where the watches are, the rings, the gold lamé evening purses. Later when they come running in all puffy and red-faced I just coolly say, "Under your pillow, behind the avocado toilet." All I really steal is sleeping pills, saving up for a rainy day.

Today I stole a bottle of Spice Islands sesame seeds. Mrs. Jessel rarely cooks. When she does she makes Sesame Chicken. The recipe is pasted inside the spice cupboard. Another copy is in the stamp and string drawer and another in her address book. Whenever she orders chicken, soy sauce, and sherry she orders another bottle of sesame seeds. She has fifteen bottles of sesame seeds. Fourteen now.

At the bus stop I sat on the curb. Three other maids, black in white uniforms, stood above me. They are old friends, have worked on Country Club Road for years. At first we were all mad . . . the bus was two minutes early and we missed it. Damn. He knows the maids are always there, that the 42–PIEDMONT only runs once an hour.

I smoked while they compared booty. Things they took . . . nail polish, perfume,   10
toilet paper. Things they were given . . . one-earrings, twenty hangers, torn bras.

(Advice to cleaning women: Take everything that your lady gives you and say Thank you. You can leave it on the bus, in the crack.)

To get into the conversation I showed them my bottle of sesame seeds. They roared with laughter. "Oh, child! Sesame seeds?" They asked me how come I've worked for Mrs. Jessel so long. Most women can't handle her for more than three times. They asked if it is true she has one hundred and forty pairs of shoes. Yes, but the bad part is that most of them are identical.

The hour passed pleasantly. We talked about all the ladies we each work for. We laughed, not without bitterness.

I'm not easily accepted by most old-time cleaning women. Hard to get cleaning jobs too, because I'm "educated." Sure as hell can't find any other jobs right now. Learned to tell the ladies right away that my alcoholic husband just died, leaving me and the four kids. I had never worked before, raising the children and all.

43–SHATTUCK–BERKELEY. The benches that say SATURATION ADVERTISING   15
are soaking wet every morning. I asked a man for a match and he gave me the pack. SUICIDE PREVENTION. They were the dumb kind with the striker on the back. Better safe than sorry.

Across the street the woman at SPOTLESS CLEANERS was sweeping her sidewalk. The sidewalks on either side of her fluttered with litter and leaves. It is autumn now, in Oakland.

Later that afternoon, back from cleaning at Horwitz's, the SPOTLESS sidewalk was covered with leaves and garbage again. I dropped my transfer on it. I always get a transfer. Sometimes I give them away, usually I just hold them.

Ter used to tease me about how I was always holding things all the time.

"Say, Maggie May, ain't nothing in this world you can hang on to. 'Cept me, maybe."

One night on Telegraph I woke up to feel him closing a Coors fliptop into my palm.   20 He was smiling down at me. Terry was a young cowboy, from Nebraska. He wouldn't go to foreign movies. I just realized it's because he couldn't read fast enough.

Whenever Ter read a book, rarely—he would rip each page off and throw it away. I would come home, to where the windows were always open or broken and the whole room would be swirling with pages, like Safeway lot pigeons.

33–BERKELEY EXPRESS. The 33 got lost! The driver overshot the turn at SEARS for the freeway. Everybody was ringing the bell as, blushing, he made a left on Twenty-seventh. We ended up stuck in a dead end. People came to their windows to see the bus. Four men got out to help him back out between the parked cars on the narrow street. Once on the freeway he drove about eighty. It was scary. We all talked together, pleased by the event.

Linda's today.

(Cleaning women: As a rule, never work for friends. Sooner or later they resent you because you know so much about them. Or else you'll no longer like them, because you do.)

But Linda and Bob are good, old friends. I feel their warmth even though they   25 aren't there. Come and blueberry jelly on the sheets. Racing forms and cigarette butts in the bathroom. Notes from Bob to Linda: "Buy some smokes and take the car . . . dooh-dah dooh-dah." Drawings by Andrea with Love to Mom. Pizza crusts. I clean their coke mirror with Windex.

It is the only place I work that isn't spotless to begin with. It's filthy in fact. Every Wednesday I climb the stairs like Sisyphus into their living room where it always looks like they are in the middle of moving.

I don't make much money with them because I don't charge by the hour, no car-fare. No lunch for sure. I really work hard. But I sit around a lot, stay very late. I smoke and read *The New York Times*, porno books, *How to Build a Patio Roof*. Mostly I just look out the window at the house next door, where we used to live. 2129½ Russell Street. I look at the tree that grows wooden pears Ter used to shoot at. The wooden fence glistens with BBs. The BEKINS sign that lit our bed at night. I miss Ter and I smoke. You can't hear the trains during the day.

40–TELEGRAPH. MILLHAVEN CONVALESCENT HOME. Four old women in wheelchairs staring filmily out into the street. Behind them, at the nurses' station, a beautiful black girl dances to "I Shot the Sheriff." The music is loud, even to me, but the old women can't hear it at all. Beneath them, on the sidewalk, is a crude sign: TUMOR INSTITUTE 1:30.

The bus is late. Cars drive by. Rich people in cars never look at people on the street, at all. Poor ones always do . . . in fact it sometimes seems they're just driving around, looking at people on the street. I've done that. Poor people wait a lot. Welfare, unemployment lines, laundromats, phone booths, emergency rooms, jails, etc.

As everyone waited for the 40 we looked into the window of MILL AND ADDIE'S LAUNDRY. Mill was born in a mill in Georgia. He was lying down across five washing machines, installing a huge TV set above them. Addie made silly pantomimes for us, how the TV would never hold up. Passersby stopped to join us watching Mill. All of us were reflected in the television, like a Man on the Street show.

Down the street is a big black funeral at FOUCHÉ'S. I used to think the neon sign said "Touché," and would always imagine death in a mask, his point at my heart.

I have thirty pills now, from Jessel, Burns, Mcintyre, Horwitz, and Blum. These people I work for each have enough uppers or downers to put a Hell's Angel away for twenty years.

18–PARK–MONTCLAIR. Downtown Oakland. A drunken Indian knows me by now, always says, "That's the way the ball bounces, sugar."

At Park Boulevard a blue County Sheriff's bus with the windows boarded up. Inside are about twenty prisoners on their way to arraignment. The men, chained together, move sort of like a crew team in their orange jumpsuits. With the same camaraderie, actually. It is dark inside the bus. Reflected in the window is the traffic light. Yellow WAIT WAIT. Red STOP STOP.

A long sleepy hour up into the affluent foggy Montclair hills. Just maids on the bus. Beneath Zion Lutheran church is a big black-and-white sign that says WATCH OUT FOR FALLING ROCKS. Every time I see it I laugh out loud. The other maids and the driver turn around and stare at me. It is a ritual by now. There was a time when I used to automatically cross myself when I passed a Catholic church. Maybe I stopped because people in buses always turned around and stared. I still automatically say a Hail Mary, silently, whenever I hear a siren. This is a nuisance because I live on Pill Hill in Oakland, next to three hospitals.

At the foot of the Montclair hills women in Toyotas wait for their maids to get off the bus. I always get a ride up Snake Road with Mamie and her lady who says, "My don't we look pretty in that frosted wig, Mamie, and me in my tacky paint clothes." Mamie and I smoke.

Women's voices always rise two octaves when they talk to cleaning women or cats.

(Cleaning women: As for cats . . . never make friends with cats, don't let them play with the mop, the rags. The ladies will get jealous. Never, however, knock cats off of chairs. On the other hand, always make friends with dogs, spend five or ten minutes scratching Cherokee or Smiley when you first arrive. Remember to close the toilet seats. Furry, jowly drips.)

The Blums. This is the weirdest place I work, the only beautiful house. They are both psychiatrists. They are marriage counselors with two adopted "preschoolers."

(Never work in a house with "preschoolers." Babies are great. You can spend hours looking at them, holding them. But the older ones . . . you get shrieks, dried Cheerios, accidents hardened and walked on in the Snoopy pajama foot.)

(Never work for psychiatrists, either. You'll go crazy. I could tell *them* a thing or two . . . Elevator shoes?)

Dr. Blum, the male one, is home sick again. He has asthma, for crissake. He stands around in his bathrobe, scratching a pale hairy leg with his slipper.

Oh ho ho ho, Mrs. Robinson. He has over two thousand dollars' worth of stereo equipment and five records. Simon and Garfunkel, Joni Mitchell, and three Beatles.

He stands in the doorway to the kitchen, scratching the other leg now. I make sultry Mr. Clean mop-swirls away from him into the breakfast nook while he asks me why I chose this particular line of work.

"I figure it's either guilt or anger," I drawl. 45

"When the floor dries may I make myself a cup of tea?"

"Oh, look, just go sit down. I'll bring you some tea. Sugar or honey?"

"Honey. If it isn't too much trouble. And lemon if it . . ."

"Go sit down." I take him tea.

Once I brought Natasha, four years old, a black sequined blouse. For dress-up. 50 Ms. Dr. Blum got furious and hollered that it was sexist. For a minute I thought she was accusing me of trying to seduce Natasha. She threw the blouse into the garbage. I retrieved it later and wear it now, sometimes, for dress-up.

(Cleaning women: You will get a lot of liberated women. First stage is a CR group; second stage is a cleaning woman; third, divorce.)

The Blums have a lot of pills, a plethora of pills. She has uppers, he has downers. Mr. Dr. Blum has belladonna pills. I don't know what they do but I wish it was my name.

One morning I heard him say to her, in the breakfast nook, "Let's do something spontaneous today, take the kids to go fly a kite!"

My heart went out to him. Part of me wanted to rush in like the maid in the back of *Saturday Evening Post*. I make great kites, know good places in Tilden for wind. There is no wind in Montclair. The other part of me turned on the vacuum so I couldn't hear her reply. It was pouring rain outside.

The playroom was a wreck. I asked Natasha if she and Todd actually played with 55 all those toys. She told me when it was Monday she and Todd got up and dumped them, because I was coming. "Go get your brother," I said.

I had them working away when Ms. Dr. Blum came in. She lectured me about interference and how she refused to "lay any guilt or duty trips" on her children. I listened, sullen. As an afterthought she told me to defrost the refrigerator and clean it with ammonia and vanilla.

Ammonia and vanilla? It made me stop hating her. Such a simple thing. I could see she really did want a homey home, didn't want guilt or duty trips laid on her children. Later on that day I had a glass of milk and it tasted like ammonia and vanilla.

40–TELEGRAPH–BERKELEY. MILL AND ADDIE'S LAUNDRY. Addie is alone in the laundromat, washing the huge plate glass window. Behind her, on top of a washer is an enormous fish head in a plastic bag. Lazy blind eyes. A friend, Mr. Walker, brings them fish heads for soup. Addie makes immense circles of flurry white on the glass. Across the street, at St. Luke's nursery, a child thinks she is waving at him. He waves back, making the same swooping circles. Addie stops, smiles, waves back for real. My bus comes. Up Telegraph toward Berkeley. In the window of the MAGIC WAND BEAUTY PARLOR there is an aluminum foil star connected to a fly-swatter. Next door is an orthopedic shop with two supplicating hands and a leg.

Ter refused to ride buses. The people depressed him, sitting there. He liked Greyhound stations though. We used to go to the ones in San Francisco and Oakland. Mostly Oakland, on San Pablo Avenue. Once he told me he loved me because I was like San Pablo Avenue.

He was like the Berkeley dump. I wish there was a bus to the dump. We went 60 there when we got homesick for New Mexico. It is stark and windy and gulls soar like nighthawks in the desert. You can see the sky all around you and above you. Garbage trucks thunder through dust-billowing roads. Gray dinosaurs.

I can't handle you being dead, Ter. But you know that.

It's like the time at the airport, when you were about to get on the caterpillar ramp for Albuquerque.

"Oh, shit. I can't go. You'll never find the car."

"Watcha gonna do when I'm gone, Maggie?" you kept asking over and over, the other time, when you were going to London.

"I'll do macramé, punk."   65

"Whatcha gonna do when I'm gone, Maggie?"

"You really think I need you that bad?"

"Yes," you said. A simple Nebraska statement.

My friends say I am wallowing in self-pity and remorse. Said I don't see anybody anymore. When I smile, my hand goes involuntarily to my mouth.

I collect sleeping pills. Once we made a pact . . . if things weren't okay by 1976   70 we were going to have a shoot-out at the end of the Marina. You didn't trust me, said I would shoot you first and run, or shoot myself first, whatever. I'm tired of the bargain, Ter.

58–COLLEGE–ALAMEDA. Old Oakland ladies all go to Hink's department store in Berkeley. Old Berkeley ladies go to Capwell's department store in Oakland. Everyone on this bus is young and black or old and white, including the drivers. The old white drivers are mean and nervous, especially around Oakland Tech High School. They're always jolting the bus to a stop, hollering about smoking and radios. They lurch and stop with a bang, knocking the old white ladies into posts. The old ladies' arms bruise, instantly.

The young black drivers go fast, sailing through yellow lights at Pleasant Valley Road. Their buses are loud and smoky but they don't lurch.

Mrs. Burke's house today. Have to quit her, too. Nothing ever changes. Nothing is ever dirty. I can't understand why I am there at all. Today I felt better. At least I understood about the thirty Lancers Rosé Wine bottles. There were thirty-one. Apparently yesterday was their anniversary. There were two cigarette butts in his ashtray (not just his one), one wineglass (she doesn't drink), and my new rosé bottle. The bowling trophies had been moved, slightly. Our life together.

She taught me a lot about housekeeping. Put the toilet paper in so it comes out from under. Only open the Comet tab to three holes instead of six. Waste not, want not. Once, in a fit of rebellion, I ripped the tab completely off and accidentally spilled Comet all down the inside of the stove. A mess.

(Cleaning women: Let them know you are thorough. The first day put all the fur-   75 niture back wrong . . . five to ten inches off, or facing the wrong way. When you dust, reverse the Siamese cats, put the creamer to the left of the sugar. Change the tooth-brushes all around.)

My masterpiece in this area was when I cleaned the top of Mrs. Burke's refrigerator. She sees everything, but if I hadn't left the flashlight on she would have missed the fact that I scoured and re-oiled the waffle iron, mended the geisha girl, and washed the flashlight as well.

Doing everything wrong not only reassures them you are thorough, it gives them a chance to be assertive and a "boss." Most American women are very uncomfortable about having servants. They don't know what to do while you are there. Mrs. Burke does things like recheck her Christmas card list and iron last year's wrapping paper. In August.

Try to work for Jews or blacks. You get lunch. But mostly Jewish and black women respect work, the work you do, and also they are not at all ashamed of spending the entire day doing absolutely nothing. They are paying *you*, right?

The Christian Eastern Stars are another story. So they won't feel guilty always try to be doing something they never would do. Stand on the stove to clean an exploded Coca-Cola off the ceiling. Shut yourself inside the glass shower. Shove all the furniture, including the piano, against the door. They would never do that, besides, they can't get in.

Thank God they always have at least one TV show that they are addicted to. I flip   80
the vacuum on for half an hour (a soothing sound), lie down under the piano with an Endust rag clutched in my hand, just in case. I just lie there and hum and think. I refused to identify your body, Ter, which caused a lot of hassle. I was afraid I would hit you for what you did. Died.

Burke's piano is what I do last before I leave. Bad part about that is the only music on it is "The Marine Hymn." I always end up marching to the bus stop "From the Halls of Monte-zu-u-ma . . ."

58–COLLEGE–BERKELEY. A mean old white driver. It's raining, late, crowded, cold. Christmas is a bad time for buses. A stoned hippy girl shouted, "Let me off this fuckin' bus!" "Wait for the designated stop!" the driver shouted back. A fat woman, a cleaning woman, vomited down the front seat onto people's galoshes and my boot. The smell was foul and several people got off at the next stop, when she did. The driver stopped at the Arco station on Alcatraz, got a hose to clean it up but of course just ran it all into the back and made things wetter. He was red-faced and furious, ran the next light, endangering us all, the man next to me said.

At Oakland Tech about twenty students with radios waited behind a badly crippled man. Welfare is next door to Tech. As the man got on the bus, with much difficulty, the driver said, "OH JESUS CHRIST" and the man looked surprised.

Burke's again. No changes. They have ten digital clocks and they all have the same right time. The day I quit I'll pull all the plugs.

I finally did quit Mrs. Jessel. She kept on paying me with a check and once she called   85
me four times in one night. I called her husband and told him I had mononucleosis. She forgot I quit, called me last night to ask if she had looked a little paler to me. I miss her.

A new lady today. A real lady.

(I never think of myself as a cleaning lady, although that's what they call you, their lady or their girl.)

Mrs. Johansen. She is Swedish and speaks English with a great deal of slang, like Filipinos.

The first thing she said to me, when she opened the door, was "HOLY MOSES!"

"Oh. Am I too early?"   90

"Not at all, my dear."

She took the stage. An eighty-year-old Glenda Jackson. I was bowled over. (See, I'm talking like her already.) Bowled over in the foyer.

In the foyer, before I even took off my coat, Ter's coat, she explained to me the event of her life.

Her husband, John, died six months ago. She had found it hard, most of all, to sleep. She started putting together picture puzzles. (She gestured toward the card table in the living room, where Jefferson's Monticello was almost finished, a gaping protozoan hole, top right.)

One night she got so stuck with her puzzle she didn't go to sleep at all. She forgot,   95 actually forgot to sleep! Or eat to boot, matter of fact. She had supper at eight in the morning. She took a nap then, woke up at two, had breakfast at two in the afternoon and went out and bought another puzzle.

When John was alive it was Breakfast 6, Lunch 12, Dinner 6. I'll tell the cockeyed world times have changed.

"No, dear, you're not too early," she said. "I might just pop off to bed at any moment."

I was still standing there, hot, gazing into my new lady's radiant sleepy eyes, waiting for talk of ravens.

All I had to do was wash windows and vacuum the carpet. But, before vacuuming the carpet, to find a puzzle piece. Sky with a little bit of maple. I know it is missing.

It was nice on the balcony, washing windows. Cold, but the sun was on my back.   100 Inside she sat at her puzzle. Enraptured, but striking a pose nevertheless. She must have been very lovely.

After the windows came the task of looking for the puzzle piece. Inch by inch in the green shag carpet, cracker crumbs, rubber bands from the *Chronicle*. I was delighted, this was the best job I ever had. She didn't "give a hoot" if I smoked or not so I just crawled around on the floor and smoked, sliding my ashtray with me.

I found the piece, way across the room from the puzzle table. It was sky, with a little bit of maple.

"I found it!" she cried, "I knew it was missing!"

"*I* found it!" I cried.

Then I could vacuum, which I did as she finished the puzzle with a sigh. As I was   105 leaving I asked her when she thought she might need me again.

"Who knows?" she said.

"Well . . . anything goes," I said, and we both laughed. Ter, I don't want to die at all, actually.

40–TELEGRAPH. Bus stop outside the laundry. MILL AND ADDIE'S is crowded with people waiting for machines, but festive, like waiting for a table. They stand, chatting at the window drinking green cans of Sprite. Mill and Addie mingle like genial hosts, making change. On the TV the Ohio State band plays the national anthem. Snow flurries in Michigan.

It is a cold, clear January day. Four sideburned cyclists turn up at the corner at Twenty-ninth like a kite string. A Harley idles at the bus stop and some kids wave at the rasty rider from the bed of a '50 Dodge pickup truck. I finally weep.

Source: "A Manual for Cleaning Women" from A MANUAL FOR CLEANING WOMEN by Lucia Berlin. Copyright © 2015 by the Literary Estate of Lucia Berlin LP. Reprinted by permission of Farrar, Straus and Giroux.

Critical Thinking Topics

1. Throughout the short story, the narrator, a cleaning woman, offers advice to fellow cleaning women. Select three or more of the tips and explain how each empowers a cleaning woman in her relationship with her employer.

2. Describe the shifting tones of the narrator's voice. Identify details or brief passages that illustrate these variations in tone. Does one tone seem to predominate? Explain.

3. More than halfway into the story, the narrator introduces Ter: "Ter refused to ride buses" (par. 59). What emotional power does Ter hold over the narrator? Explain the significance of the closing line, "I finally weep."

Writing Topic

We commonly assume that an employer is in a position of power over his or her employee. In what ways does this story challenge that assumption? Based on your own experiences and observation or on examples from fiction or the news media (but not from this short story), describe a situation in which people in subservient positions shift the balance of power in their own favor by subverting the power of those above them.

8.8 Ed Vega, Spanish Roulette (1991)

Sixto Andrade snapped the gun open and shut several times and then spun the cylinder, intrigued by the kaleidoscopic pattern made by the empty chambers. He was fascinated by the blue-black color of the metal, but more so by the almost toy-like quality of the small weapon. As the last rays of sunlight began their retreat from the four-room tenement flat, Sixto once again snapped the cylinder open and began loading the gun. It pleased him that each brass and lead projectile fit easily into each one of the chambers and yet would not fall out. When he had finished inserting the last of the bullets, he again closed the cylinder and, enjoying the increased weight of the gun, pointed it at the ceiling and pulled back the hammer.

"What's the piece for, man?"

Sixto had become so absorbed in the gun that he did not hear Willie Collazo, with whom he shared the apartment, come in. His friend's question came at him suddenly, the words intruding into the world he had created since the previous weekend.

"Nothing," he said, lowering the weapon.

"What do you mean, 'nothing'?" said Willie. "You looked like you were ready to play   5
Russian roulette when I came in, bro."

"No way, man," said Sixto, and as he had been shown by Tommy Ramos, he let the hammer fall back gently into place. "It's called Spanish roulette," he added, philosophically.

Willie's dark face broke into a wide grin and his eyes, just as if he were playing his congas, laughed before he did. "No kidding, man," he said. "You taking up a new line of work? I know things are rough but sticking up people and writing poetry don't go together."

Sixto put the gun on the table, tried to smile but couldn't, and recalled the last time he had read at the cafe on Sixth Street. Willie had played behind him, his hands making the drums sing a background to his words. "I gotta take care of some business, Willie," he said, solemnly, and, turning back to his friend, walked across the worn linoleum to the open window of the front room.

"Not like that, *panita*," Willie said as he followed him.

"Family stuff, bro." 10

"Who?"

"My sister," Sixto said without turning.

"Mandy?"

Sixto nodded, his small body taut with the anger he had felt when Mandy had finished telling him of the attack. He looked out over the street four flights below and fought an urge to jump. It was one solution but not *the* solution. Despairingly, he shook his head at the misery below: burned out buildings, torched by landlords because it was cheaper than fixing them; empty lots, overgrown with weeds and showing the ravages of life in the neighborhood. On the sidewalk, the discarded refrigerator still remained as a faceless sentinel standing guard over the lot, its door removed too late to save the little boy from Avenue B. He had been locked in it half the day while his mother, going crazy with worry, searched the streets so that by the time she saw the blue-faced child, she was too far gone to understand what it all meant.

He tried to cheer himself up by focusing his attention on the children playing in front 15 of the open fire hydrant, but could not. The twilight rainbow within the stream of water, which they intermittently shot up in the air to make it cascade in a bright arc of white against the asphalt, was an illusion, *un engaño,* a poetic image of his childhood created solely to contrast his despair. He thought again of the crushed innocence on his sister's face and his blood felt like sand as it ran in his veins.

"You want to talk about it?" asked Willie.

"No, man," Sixto replied. "I don't."

Up the street, in front of the *bodega,* the old men were already playing dominoes and drinking beer. Sixto imagined them joking about each other's weaknesses, always, he thought ironically, with respect. They had no worries. Having lived a life of service to that which now beckoned him, they could afford to be light-hearted. It was as if he had been programmed early on for the task now facing him. He turned slowly, wiped an imaginary tear from his eyes and recalled his father's admonition about crying: *"Usted es un machito y los machos no lloran,* machos don't cry." How old had he been? Five or six, no more. He had fallen in the playground and cut his lip. His father's friends had laughed at the remark, but he couldn't stop crying and his father had shaken him. *"Le dije que usted no es una chancleta. ¡Apréndalo bien!"* "You are not a girl, understand that once and for all!"

Concerned with Sixto's mood, once again Willie tried drawing him out. *"Coño,* bro, she's only fifteen," he said. *"¿Qué pasó?"*

The gentleness and calm which Sixto so much admired had faded from Willie's 20 face and now mirrored his own anguish. It was wrong to involve his friend but perhaps that was part of it. Willie was there to test his resolve. He had been placed there by fate to make sure the crime did not go unpunished. In the end, when it came to act, he'd have only his wits and manhood.

"It's nothing, bro," Sixto replied, walking back into the kitchen. "I told you, family business. Don't worry about it."

"Man, don't be like that."

There was no injury in Willie's voice and as if someone had suddenly punched him in the stomach to obtain a confession, the words burst out of Sixto.

"Un tipo la mangó en el rufo, man. Some dude grabbed her. You happy now?"

"Where?" Willie asked, knowing that uttering the words was meaningless. "In the 25 projects?"

"Yeah, last week. She got let out of school early and he grabbed her in the elevator and brought her up to the roof."

"And you kept it all in since you came back from your Mom's Sunday night?"

"What was I supposed to do, man? Go around broadcasting that my sister got took off?"

"I'm sorry, Sixto. You know I don't mean it like that."

"I know, man. I know."   30

"Did she know the guy? *Un cocolo,* right? A black dude. They're the ones that go for that stuff."

"No, man. It wasn't no *cocolo.*"

"But she knew him."

"Yeah, you know. From seeing him around the block. *Un bonitillo,* man. Pretty dude that deals coke and has a couple of women hustling for him. A dude named Lino."

"*¿Bien blanco?* Pale dude with Indian hair like yours?"   35

"Yeah, that's the guy."

"Drives around in a gold Camaro, right?"

"Yeah, I think so." Willie nodded several times and then shook his head.

"He's Shorty Pardo's cousin, right?" Sixto knew about the family connection but hadn't wanted to admit it until now.

"So?" he said, defiantly.   40

"Those people are crazy, bro," said Willie.

"I know."

"They've been dealing *tecata* up there in El Barrio since forever, man. Even the Italians stay clear of them, they're so crazy."

"That doesn't mean nothing to me," said Sixto, feeling his street manhood, the bravado which everyone develops growing up in the street, surfacing. Bad talk was the antidote to fear and he wasn't immune to it. "I know how crazy they are, but I'm gonna tell you something. I don't care who the dude is. I'm gonna burn him. Gonna set his heart on fire with that piece."

"Hey, go easy, *panita,*" said Willie. "Be cool, bro. I know how you feel but that   45
ain't gonna solve nothing. You're an artist, man. You know that? A poet. And a playwright. You're gonna light up Broadway one of these days." Willie was suddenly silent as he reflected on his words. He sat down on one of the kitchen chairs and lowered his head. After a few moments he looked up and said: "Forget what I said, man. I don't know what I'm talking about. I wouldn't know what to do if that happened to one of the women in my family. I probably would've done the dude in by now. I'm sorry I said anything. I just don't wanna see you messed up. And I'm not gonna tell you to go to the cops, either."

Sixto did not answer Willie. They both knew going to the police would serve no purpose. As soon as the old man found out, he'd beat her for not protecting herself. It would become a personal matter, as if it had been he who had submitted. He'd rant and rave about short skirts and lipstick and music and then compare everything to the way things were on the island and his precious hometown, his beloved Cacimar, like it was the center of the universe and the place where all the laws governing the human race had been created. But Sixto had nothing to worry about. He was different from his father. He was getting an education, had been enlightened to truth and beauty and knew about equality and justice. Hell, he was a new man, forged out of steel and concrete, not old banana leaves and coconuts. And yet, he wanted to strike back and was sick to his stomach because he wanted Lino Quintana in front of him, on his knees, begging for mercy. He'd smoke a couple of joints and float back uptown to the Pardo's turf and then blast away at all of them like he was the Lone Ranger.

He laughed sarcastically at himself and thought that in the end he'd probably back down, allow the matter to work itself out and let Mandy live with the scar for the rest of her life. And he'd tell himself that rape was a common thing, even in families, and that people went on living and working and making babies like a bunch of zombies, like somebody's puppets without ever realizing who was pulling the strings. It was all crazy. You were born and tagged with a name: Rodríguez, Mercado, Torres, Cartagena, Pantoja, Maldonado, Sandoval, Ballester, Nieves, Carmona. All of them, funny-ass Spanish names. And then you were told to speak English and be cool because it was important to try and get over by imitating the Anglo-Saxon crap, since that's where all the money and success were to be found. Nobody actually came out and said it, but it was written clearly in everything you saw, printed boldly between the lines of books, television, movies, advertising. And at the place where you got your love, your mother's milk, your rice and beans, you were told to speak Spanish and be respectful and defend your honor and that of the women around you.

"I'm gonna burn him, Willie," Sixto repeated. "Gonna burn him right in his *güevos.* Burn him right there in his balls so he can feel the pain before I blow him away and let God deal with him. He'll understand, man, because I don't." Sixto felt the dizzying anger blind him for a moment. "*Coño,* man, she was just fifteen," he pleaded, as if Willie could absolve him of his sin before it had been committed. "I have to do it, man. She was just a kid. *Una nena,* man. A little innocent girl who dug Latin music and danced only with her girlfriends at home and believed all the nonsense about purity and virginity, man. And now this son of a bitch went and did it to her. *Le hizo el daño.*"

That's what women called it. That damage. And it was true. Damaged goods. He didn't want to believe it but that's how he felt. In all his educated, enlightened splendor, that's how he felt. Like she had been rendered untouchable, her femaleness soiled and smeared forever. Like no man would want to love her, knowing what had happened. The whole thing was so devastating that he couldn't imagine what it was like to be a woman. If they felt even a little of what he was experiencing, it was too much. And he, her own brother, already talking as if she were dead. That's how bad it was. Like she was a memory.

"I'm gonna kill him, Willie," said Sixto once more, pounding on the wall. "*¿Lo mato, coño! Lo mato, lo mato,*" he repeated the death threat over and over in a frenzy. Willie stood up and reached for his arm but Sixto pulled roughly away. "It's cool, man," he said, and put his opened hands in front of him. "I'm all right. Everything's cool." 50

"Slow down," Willie pleaded. "Slow down."

"You're right, man. I gotta slow down." Sixto sat down but before long was up again. "Man, I couldn't sleep the last couple of nights. I kept seeing myself wearing the shame the rest of my life. I gave myself every excuse in the book. I even prayed, Willie. Me, a spic from the streets of the Big Apple, hip and slick, writing my *jíbaro* poetry; *saliéndome las palabras de las entrañas; inventando foquin mundos* like a god; like *foquin* Juracán pitching lightning bolts at the people to wake them from their stupor, man. Wake them up from their lethargy and their four-hundred-year-old sleep of self-induced tyranny, you know?"

"I understand, man."

"Willie, man, I wanted my words to thunder, to shake the earth *pa' que la gente le pida a Yuquiyú que los salve.*"

"And it's gonna be that way, bro. You're the poet, man. The voice."   55

"And me praying. Praying, man. And not to Yuquiyú but to some distorted European idea. I'm messed up, bro. Really messed up. Writing all this jive poetry that's supposed to incite the people to take up arms against the oppressor and all the while my heart is dripping with feelings of love and brotherhood and peace like some programmed puppet, Willie."

"I hear you."

"I mean, I bought all that stuff, man. All that liberal American jive. I bought it. I marched against the war in Vietnam, against colonialism and capitalism, and for the Chicano brothers cracking their backs in the fields, marched till my feet were raw, and every time I saw lettuce or grapes, I saw poison. And man, it felt right, Willie."

"It was a righteous cause, man."

"And I marched for the independence of the island, of Puerto Rico, Willie: *de*   60
Portorro, de Borinquen, la buena, la sagrada, el terruño, madre de todos nosotros; bendita seas entre todas las mujeres y bendito sea el fruto de tu vientre pelú. I marched for the land of our people and it felt right."

"It is right, man."

"You know, once and for all I had overcome all the anger of being a colonized person without a country and my culture being swallowed up, digested and thrown back up so you can't even recognize what it's all about. I had overcome all the craziness and could stand above it; I could look down on the brothers and sisters who took up arms in '50 and '54 when I wasn't even a fantasy in my pop's mind, man. I could stand above all of them, even the ones with their bombs now. I could pay tribute to them with words but still judge them crazy. And it was okay. It felt right to wear two faces, to go back and forth from poetic fury to social condescension or whatever you wanna call it. I thought I had it beat with the education and the poetry and opening up my heart like some long-haired, brown-skinned hippy. And now this. I'm a hypocrite, man."

Like the water from the open fire hydrant, the words had rushed out of him. And yet he couldn't say exactly what it was that troubled him about the attack on his sister, couldn't pinpoint what it was that made his face hot and his blood race angrily in his veins. Willie, silenced by his own impotence, sat looking at him. He knew he could neither urge him on nor discourage him and inevitably he would have to stand aside and let whatever was to happen run its course. His voice almost a whisper, he said, "It's okay, Sixto. I know how it feels. Just let the pain come out, man. Just let it out. Cry if you have to."

But the pain would never leave him. Spics weren't Greeks and the word katharsis had no meaning in private tragedy. Sixto's mind raced back into time, searching for an answer, knowing, even as it fled like a wounded animal seeking refuge from its tormentors, that it was an aimless search. It was like running a maze. Like the rats in the psychology films and the puzzles in the children's section of weekend newspapers. One followed a path with a pencil until he came to a dead end, then retraced his steps. Thousands of years passed before him in a matter of minutes.

The Tainos: a peaceful people, some history books said. No way, he thought. They   65
fought the Spaniards, drowned them to test their immortality. And their *caciques* were as fierce and as brave as Crazy Horse or Geronimo. Proud chiefs they were. Jumacao, Daguao, Yaureibo, Caguax, Agueybaná, Mabodamaca, Aymamón, Urayoán, Orocobix,

Guarionex all fought the Spaniards with all they had... *guasábara*... *guasábara*... *guas ábara*... their battle cry echoing through the hills like an eerie phantom; they fought their horses and dogs; they fought their swords and guns and when there was no other recourse, rather than submitting, they climbed sheer cliffs and, holding their children to their breasts, leapt into the sea.

And the blacks: *los negros,* whose blood and heritage he carried. They didn't submit to slavery but escaped and returned to conduct raids against the oppressors, so that the whole *negrito lindo* business, so readily accepted as a term of endearment, was a joke, an appeasement on the part of the Spaniards. The *bombas* and *bembas* and *ginganbó* and their all night dances and *oraciones* to Changó: warrior men of the Jelofe, Mandingo, Mende, Yoruba, Dahomey, Ashanti, Ibo, Fante, Baule and Congro tribes, choosing battle over slavery.

And the Spaniards: certainly not a peaceful people. For centuries they fought each other and then branched out to cross the sea and slaughter hundreds of thousands of Indians, leaving an indelible mark on entire civilizations, raping and pillaging and gutting the earth of its riches, so that when it was all done and they laid in a drunken stupor four hundred years later, their pockets empty, they rose again to fight themselves in civil war.

And way back, way back before El Cid Campeador began to wage war: The Moors. *Los moros*... *alhambra, alcázar, alcohol, almohada, alcade, alboroto*... NOISE... CRIES OF WAR... A thousand years the maze traveled and it led to a dead end with dark men atop fleet Arabian stallions, dark men, both in visage and intent, raising their scimitars against those dishonoring their house... they had invented algebra and Arabic numbers and it all added up to war... there was no other way...

"I gotta kill him, bro," Sixto heard himself say. "I gotta. Otherwise I'm as good as dead." One had to live with himself and that was the worst part of it; he had to live with the knowledge and that particular brand of cowardice that eroded the mind and destroyed one's soul. And it wasn't so much that his sister had been wronged. He'd seen that. The injury came from not retaliating. He was back at the beginning. Banana leaves and coconuts and machete duels at sundown. Just like his father and his *jíbaro* values. For even if the aggressor never talked, even if he never mentioned his act to another soul for whatever reason, there was still another person, another member of the tribe, who could single him out in a crowd and say to himself: "That one belongs to me and so does his sister."

Sixto tried to recall other times when his manhood had been challenged, but it seemed   70 as if everything had happened long ago and hadn't been important: kid fights over mention of his mother, rights of ownership of an object, a place in the hierarchy of the block, a word said of his person, a lie, a bump by a stranger on a crowded subway train—nothing ever going beyond words or at worst, a sudden shoving match quickly broken up by friends.

But this was different. His brain was not functioning properly, he thought. He tried watching himself, tried to become an observer, the impartial judge of his actions. Through a small opening in his consciousness, he watched the raging battle. His heart called for the blood of the enemy and his brain urged him to use caution. There was no thought of danger, for in that region of struggle, survival meant not so much escaping with his life, but conquering fear and regaining his honor.

Sixto picked up the gun and studied it once more. He pushed the safety to make sure it was locked and placed the gun between the waistband of his pants and the flesh of his stomach. The cold metal sent slivers of ice running down his legs. It was a pleasant sensation, much as if a woman he had desired for some time had suddenly let him know, in an unguarded moment, that intimacy was possible between them. Avoiding Willie's eyes, he walked around the kitchen, pulled out his shirt and let it hang out over his pants. It was important that he learn to walk naturally and reduce his self-consciousness about the weapon. But it was his mind working tricks again. Nobody would notice. The idea was to act calmly. That's what everyone said: the thieves, the cheap stickup men who mugged old people and taxi drivers; the burglars who, like vultures, watched the movement of a family until certain that they were gone, swooped down and cleaned out the apartment, even in the middle of the day; the check specialists, who studied mailboxes as if they were bank vaults so they could break them open and steal welfare checks or fat letters from the island on the chance they might contain money orders or cash. They all said it. Even the young gang kids said it. Don't act suspiciously. Act as if you were going about your business.

Going to shoot someone was like going to work. That was it. He'd carry his books and nobody would suspect that he was carrying death. He laughed inwardly at the immense joke. He'd once seen a film in which Robert Mitchum, posing as a preacher, had pulled a derringer out of a Bible in the final scene. Why not. He'd hollow out his Western Civilization text and place the gun in it. It was his duty. The act was a way of surviving, of earning what was truly his. Whether a pay check or an education, it meant nothing without self-respect.

But the pieces of the puzzle did not fit and Sixto sat down dejectedly. He let his head fall into his hands and for a moment thought he would cry. Willie said nothing and Sixto waited, listening, the void of silence becoming larger and larger, expanding so that the sounds of the street, a passing car, the excitement of a child, the rushing water from the open hydrant, a mother's window warning retreated, became fainter and seemed to trim the outer edges of the nothingness within the silence. He could hear his own breathing and the beating of his heart and still he waited.

And then slowly, as if waking from a refreshing sleep, Sixto felt himself grow calmer   75
and a pleasant coldness entered his body as heart and mind finally merged and became tuned to his mission. He smiled at the feeling and knew he had gone through the barrier of doubt and fear which had been erected to protect him from himself, to make sure he did not panic at the last moment. War had to be similar. He had heard the older men, the ones who had survived Vietnam, talk about it. Sonny Maldonado with his plastic foot, limping everywhere he went, quiet and unassuming, talked about going through a doorway and into a quiet room where one died a little and then came out again, one's mind alive but the rest of the body already dead to the upcoming pain.

It had finally happened, he thought. There was no anger or regret, no rationalizations concerning future actions. No more justifications or talk about honor and dignity. Instead, Sixto perceived the single objective coldly. There was neither danger nor urgency in carrying out the sentence and avenging the wrong. It seemed almost too simple. If it took years he knew the task would be accomplished. He would study the habits of his quarry, chart his every movement, and one day he'd strike. He would wait in a deserted hallway some late night, calmly walk out of the shadows, only his right index finger and his brain connected and say: "How you doing, Lino?" and his voice alone would convey the terrible message. Sixto smiled to himself and saw, as in a slow motion cinematic shot, his mind's ghost delicately squeeze the trigger repeatedly, the small animal muzzle of the gun following Lino Quintana's body as it fell slowly and hit the floor, the muscles of his victim's face twitching and life ebbing away forever. It happened all the time and no one was ever discovered.

Sixto laughed, almost too loudly. He took the gun out from under his shirt and placed it resolutely on the table. "I gotta think some more, man," he said. "That's crazy rushing into the thing. You wanna beer, Willie?"

Willie was not convinced of his friend's newly found calm. Reluctantly, he accepted the beer. He watched Sixto and tried to measure the depth of his eyes. They had become strangely flat, the glint of trust in them absent. It was as if a thin, opaque veil had been sewn over the eyes to mask Sixto's emotions. He felt helpless but said nothing. He opened the beer and began mourning the loss. Sixto was right, he thought. It was Spanish roulette. Spics were born and the cylinder spun. When it stopped one was handed the gun and, without looking, had to bring it to one's head, squeeze the trigger and take his chances.

The belief was pumped into the bloodstream, carved into the flesh through generations of strife, so that being was the enactment of a ritual rather than the beginning of a new life. One never knew his own reactions until faced with Sixto's dilemma. And yet the loss would be too great, the upcoming grief too profound and the ensuing suffering eternal. The violence would be passed on to another generation to be displayed as an invisible coat of arms, much as Sixto's answer had come to him as a relic. His friend would never again look at the world with wonder, and poetry would cease to spring from his heart. If he did write, the words would be guarded, careful, full of excuses and apologies for living. Willie started to raise the beer in a toast but thought better of it and set the can on the table.

"Whatever you do, bro," he said, "be careful."   80

"Don't worry, man," Sixto replied. "I got the thing under control." He laughed once again and suddenly his eyes were ablaze with hatred. He picked up the gun, stuck it back into his pants and stood up. "No good, man," he said, seemingly to himself, and rushed out, slamming the door of the apartment behind him.

Beyond the sound of the door, Willie could hear the whirring cylinder as it began to slow down, each minute click measuring the time before his friend had to raise the weapon to his head and kill part of himself.

Source: "Spanish Roulette" is reprinted with permission from the publisher of "Short Fiction of Hispanic Writers of the United States" by Edgardo Vega (©1993 Arte Publico Press – University of Houston).

Critical Thinking Topics

1. Sixto feels the need to take revenge—an-eye-for-an-eye justice—so strongly that he is prepared to accept any and all consequences of his actions, including the very real possibility of his death. Research this simple concept of justice, an eye for an eye. Do you sympathize with Sixto? Why or why not? Would you support his decision? Why or why not?

2. In what ways do modern societies actively discourage an-eye-for-an-eye justice? If Sixto carries out his revenge and lives to be arrested and tried for murder, how do you think a jury would decide on his case? Explain your answer.

Writing Topic

Assuming Willie would argue against the primitive concept of justice that drives Sixto, write a dialogue between the two men in which each states his side of the argument. Further, imagine yourself as a third-party mediator. Consider how you might construct a Rogerian argument resolution (conclusion) to the conflict in this story. (See Chapter 4 for a discussion of Rogerian argument strategy.)

8.9 Mark Spragg, A Boy's Work (1999)

"Your horse is wire-cut." My father has pulled up to the corrals with a four-horse trailer. This is his second and last load. The rest of the horses have been left on winter pasture. The snow still lies in dirty, humped drifts around the buildings and in the timber. The grass has just started to work up through the smear of gray, gauzelike mold that has spread under the winter's snowcover. Our Forest Service grazing lease won't begin for several weeks. Any horses we have on the place will have to be fed hay. Hay is expensive.

"My horse?"

"You have so many you can't remember which one?"

"They all belong to you."

He steps to the back of the trailer. He turns with one hand on the trailer's gate. He   5
looks tired, hungry. "The horse you rode last summer and fall," he says.

"Socks?"

"I think riding a single animal every day of your life allows you some privileges."

He swings the trailer's gate open and backs out a big sorrel gelding and hands me its halterrope, stepping into the trailer again and turning out a black we call Bird.

"Don't let Bird get by you," he shouts from inside the trailer.

"Wire-cut a little, or a lot?" Bird trails his leadrope, holding his head to the side,   10
careful not to step on the thing. I catch up the leadrope.

My father steps the third horse out of the trailer. We have spring bear hunters coming in on the weekend and need just enough transportation to get us all back and forth to the bait-ground.

"I mean he tried to cut a hoof off." I'm following the horse he leads, bringing the other two with me.

"With what?" I know it doesn't really matter.

"With a wire gate. Some asshole left it open on the ground and Socks got in it. I found him when I was gathering these. He worked himself loose of the gate but the damage had been done."

"He's at the vet's."   15

"His leg's gangrenous." He pauses just inside the corrals. He turns his horse into the corrals and looks back over a shoulder at me. He's looping the leadrope over the halter's headstall. "I hope you've just gotten hard of hearing. You were a good deal brighter when I left this morning."

"You killed him?"

He takes the two other horses from me. His hat is pulled down. I don't get a good look at his eyes. He speaks softly. "He's in the trailer," he says.

When I step in the trailer I can smell him. It is the smell of something that has died in the sun. A hopeless odor that brings memories of road-killed deer and elk—flies, gums drawn back over yellowing teeth. He nickers softly and I move to his head. He's gaunt. His winter coat is shedding in large, uneven gouts. I run a hand along his side, my fingers tracing the cage of his ribs. There are sprigs of dried weed tangled in his tail and mane. I untie his leadrope and lead him from the trailer. Every time he steps with his right front foot his shoulder sinks as though he's stepping into a hole. Outside the trailer my father lights a cigarette.

"Put him in with the others and spill some grain for them." 20

"Why?"

"Because I told you to."

"He's not going to get any better."

The cigarette smoke rises and holds against the brim of my father's hat. "No," he says, "he's not going to get any better."

There is more light out of the trailer. I can see that Socks's leg is swollen badly. 25 From his hoof to his shoulder the skin has split in several weeping slices. His pastern is as thick as his forearm should be and blackened, crusted with dried blood. When he takes a step the heel of his foot flops loose and snaps back up against the pastern. It makes a sucking sound, and then a click.

My father speaks with the cigarette in the corner of his mouth.

He's latching the trailer. "I'd give a lot to get my hands on the son of a bitch who was in such a hurry he couldn't close a gate."

"I don't feel very well."

"You're going to feel worse."

He drops his cigarette at the toe of his boot and methodically grinds it out. He 30 doesn't look up when he speaks, "I've got to be in town tomorrow or I wouldn't ask you."

"I've got school."

"If you think you need to go to school your mother can run you down the valley after lunch."

My father is looking up at me now. He's pulling on a pair of yellow cloth gloves.

"You could have killed him in town," I tell him. "If you didn't have a gun you could have borrowed one." A knot of panic rises in my chest like some small, waking animal clawing its way out of hibernation.

"I want him baited." 35

"Bear-baited?"

"We don't exactly have the kind of money to kill a usable horse. Everything else'll make it until this fall. Kind of looks like Socks volunteered, don't you think?"

I do not, but I'm part of the family and this is part of our work. I'm fifteen. Old enough to be asked. We bait horses for bear, allowing their corpses to ripen, hoping they will attract an otherwise elusive grizzly. Our hunters fire from a blind at the bear that feeds on the dead horse.

I stand staring at my father's boots. They are worn down to the same color as the soil. Socks lips the collar of my denim jacket. His breath feels warm and moist against my neck. This is the first time I've been prompted to draw any conclusions about sport. The horses we have baited in the past were derelict, their teeth gone, ready to die. I have never before connected sorrow with our family's business.

"Where?" I don't look up. 40

"That little meadow up Kitty Creek. Where we killed the big boar two springs ago. It's close; there's no creeks to cross. If he's alive in the morning you might get him up there."

I nod. I'm not sure there is enough light left for my father to see the movement of my head.

"I'm sorry about this," he says. "You have your supper?"

"Elk roast."

"Your mother make a dessert?" 45

"Just canned pears."

"Ask your brother for a hand if you think you need it."

"I'll be fine."

"This won't be the hardest thing you'll ever do. You believe me?"

"Not yet."   50

"I'll see you tomorrow."

I listen to his footfalls grow fainter as he walks away from me. It is dark enough now that I can't distinguish his outline. But I feel the heat of him leave. The night seems to drop ten degrees. I get Socks in the round corral, away from the other horses, heap a coffee can with oats and pour them in his trough, make sure he has clean water. For a while I stand in the dark and listen to him chew—a blunted, rhythmic rasp: the sound of pack rats at work in a hay loft. And a single owl hooting periodically, well rested watching us with its wide night eyes.

When I pass my parents' cabin I can see my father at the supper table. He still wears his neckerchief. His hair is so short it hasn't needed to be combed, his sleeves are rolled above his elbows, the brown hair on his white forearms catching in the light. My mother sits across from him at the table. She sips coffee from a mug my brother has made her as a school project and nods as my father speaks. She grimaces. I step back from the light the window throws to watch them. Their conversation is locked away from me, inside with the light. I do not hear their words. I can hear the creek, and the pine needles under my boots when I shift my weight. The air is warning away from winter. It tastes of pine and sage. I can smell the sap risen in the aspen. I wait until my father is done with his meal and walk in the night to the cabin where I live with my brother.

"What's the capital of Romania?" he asks.

"I don't know."   55

My brother sits at a desk by the gas heater in our cabin. There is just the one room with a closet-sized bathroom that we keep closed off in the winters. The plumbing isn't buried, and the pipes would freeze if not drained. My parents live in a slightly larger cabin just down the creek. It has a well pit dug under the kitchen floor, and their bathroom is capable of running water year-round. We use their tub and toilet. It makes for regular bowel movements. When we have to piss we piss over the railing of our own cabin, writing patterns in the drifted snow.

"Bucharest?" My brother still has not found the answer.

"I said I didn't know."

"It makes a difference."

He's thirteen, a year and a half younger, and smarter than me. He's bent over a   60
report that is due the next day. We don't have television and only get a country western station—KOMA, in Oklahoma City—if we stay up past midnight, flag the antenna with tin foil, and one of us stands by the radio holding the antenna's tip. We read because my father has books, thousands of them. We are not a family that goes on vacation. We are a family that makes the ninety-mile round trip to town once a month for supplies. My brother and I use books when we want to leave Wyoming. We wear out an atlas every three years. I sit on my bed and open the big rectangular book of maps on my lap.

"It's Bucharest," I tell him.

My brother looks up at me and smiles. His eyes tell me that we will go there someday. To Romania. The two of us, when we are men. He winks. He has eyes that are capable of recognizing us anywhere on the planet.

I get undressed and under my quilts. I watch his head bob to the rhythm of his writing and close my eyes. When he goes to bed, when he says good night, I lie with my eyes closed and pretend to sleep. He turns off the light, and I sink into the darkness. I can hear the purr and sputter of Libby Creek outside the cabin. The gas heater ticks and groans.

I imagine the panic and pain that must have sizzled through the horse. Apparently, my horse. Socks. I see the strand of wire wrapped above his hoof, barbed, working with the efficiency of a primitive chainsaw, working faster the harder he struggled. I wonder how long he suffered before he got free of the snare. I wonder if he felt relief, or if he looked down at his hoof and knew that he was ruined. I twist under my bedding and cannot sleep.

Sometime in the middle of the night I get up and kneel by my bed. The linoleum is   65
cold, damp; it feels like the flesh of something old and dead. I sweep an arm under the bed until I find the rifle wrapped in an army-surplus blanket and pull it to me. Its blued, steel barrel is as cold as an unburied pipe.

I set the desk lamp on the floor so I won't wake my brother and fill the rifle's magazine with shells, bolt them back out, wipe them on the front of my T-shirt, reload, and close the action. I lean the gun by the door and get back into bed. I can't get warm. I feel as cold as the linoleum, as the rifle barrel, as the job I must somehow do in the morning. I think of slipping into bed with my brother but know I will wake him. I love the sound of his even breathing while he sleeps. I clench my teeth and concentrate on the rhythms of my brother's breath. I pray to hold firmly, in one whole piece, until it is light. Before dawn I dress in the dark, take up the gun, and start for the corrals.

My parents' cabin is dark. I stand at a window and squint in at the dining table. The hour before dawn seems to me always the coldest of the night. My eyes water, and I flex and fist my fingers against the seams of my leather workgloves. Inside the cabin a propane heater softly illuminates a corner of the room. Yellowed shadows struggle against a line of hanging work coats. A brown-and-white cat named Monk is balled on the seat of a fabric-covered chair. The rifle slips loose from where I have tucked it against my arm, and I heft its weight back into my body and move away.

I stop again where the corrals meet the side of the barn. I listen. I am fond of the sound of horses in the night. The lifting of feet. Stamping. The clicking of their iron shoes against rock. They mouth one another's withers and rear and squeal and whirl and shuffle and cough and stand and snort. There is the combined rumblings of each individual gut. They sound larger than they are. The air tastes of horses, ripples as though come alive with their good-hearted strength and stamina.

I give Socks a half can of oats, break the skim of ice that has formed on the water trough, and catch Bird to ride. I saddle him under the lights of the tackshed, speaking to him softly. It is the first time he's been touched in seven months. He watches every move I make rolling his eyes until the whites show, mouthing the bridle's bit. When I make the final pull on the latigo, the seat of the saddle rises as though I've shoved the oat can under the skirt of its back. Bird's ready to fire. Ready to bust the night-chill out of his bones.

I turn him in a tight circle several times and while he pivots through the last turn   70
I step into the stirrup and let his momentum swing me securely into the saddle. He stands absolutely still for just one breath, snorts, and starts to buck. He's never been very fancy in his tantrums, and I manage to keep his head pulled up and out of the

rhythm of his clumsy plunges. The crow hopping stops as abruptly as it has begun, and he steps out stiffly, as though only now come fully awake. I spur him into a trot for the quarter mile down to the mailbox and back and step off. He stands like a gentleman, his ears up and alert. I slide the rifle into the saddle scabbard. The horizon has just started to lighten. Bird and I can still see our breaths in the morning air, but our blood is hot. I return quickly to the corrals and halter Socks.

Socks has never offered to buck. He's fourteen and has given me nothing but work. He's a rangy bay whose legs run white from his knees down. Without being bred for it he's naturally gaited and one of the smartest horses about terrain I've ever ridden. He studies the ground like some horses study cows. He moves with the same sure ease over loose scree, through downed timber, in fast water, over open ground. If I give him his head after dark he invariably brings me home, stepping in the same prints he's made on the ride out. As one of our hands has said about him, he's the kind of horse that comes early and stays late. I can hardly look back at him as he haltingly follows Bird and me. A step, a pause to gather his weight in his hindquarters, a step. At times he groans so mournfully that I turn in the saddle, prepared to watch him die. The waking knot of panic comes alive again in my gut, rises in my throat. I swallow. My throat burns, my mouth tastes of copper.

I've expected Bird to be impatient and fight the bit for the whole trip, but perhaps there is a communion between animals that I do not understand. I wonder if they find a community in one another's miseries. Bird walks as though he is picking his way through a field littered with cactus and broken stone. He looks back so often that I have to continually rein him back onto the trail. When Socks's breaths come in rasps Bird stops completely, refuses to move, stands with his head hanging low, as though listening.

Traveling the three miles to the bait-ground takes us four hours. By the time we get to the little meadow where I intend to kill him, Socks is almost dead. His eyes appear glazed, as though grown over with bluish cataracts. He sways as he stands. The swelling has spread to his shoulder and chest, and he wheezes without the effort of moving. I pray he is so deeply in shock that he has forgotten he is a horse, forgotten the taste of clear water. I think that a lesser horse could not have made this trip to be killed. A lesser horse would have died tangled in the wire. I feel he has made the effort for me.

I tie Bird in the trees and walk quickly back to Socks and unsnap his halter and let it drop. I'm in a hurry. There is a chance that he can endure more. I know that I cannot. I chamber a shell, sight quickly, and stop his struggle before he can respond to the sound of metal slipping against metal. He falls, kicks once, and is still. The gunshot's report echoes against the opposite side of the valley. A magpie starts up and will not stop his squawking.

The shot and the immediate presence of death spikes through Bird like a lightning strike. He circles the tree where I have tied him, snorting, glaring into the middle distance of every direction, sawing against his leadrope. I drop the empty halter by him as I pass and keep walking through the spare timber. When I get into the creek it is over my knees and my boots fill with the icy water. And then I am out and struggling up a sharp embankment and into a nest of pine boughs heaped around and over the crude pole frame that acts as our blind.

A thick downfall keeps the whole affair held against the hillside, and there is the noise of Kitty Creek to further separate it from the meadow. If there is a breeze it reliably

75

sweeps down this tight drainage and holds the hunter's scent away from the bait. It is a fine place to sit and raise a rifle and kill a bear.

I stare at the reddish brown mound seventy-five yards in front of me. I have killed Socks in a good place. Close to the timber that borders the meadow. A bear will feel safe in his approach. Far enough into the meadow that a hunter will have a good shot. And then I remember that I should have cut a window in his gut. Sawed through his hair and opened him to decay. A sore that coyotes and ravens can worry. A place that will help him rot. My father will be disappointed. I think of my father's disappointment and remember the ruined leg. The smell of the leg will attract a bear. Socks has gotten a head start at decay. I have an excuse. I wonder suddenly why I am not crying. I think a boy would cry. I think maybe I have begun to be a man. I feel only quietly blunt, and desperate. I feel as though I want to stand and run, but do not have the strength. I tighten my chest to exhale, and suck at the air to reinflate. Again, and then again. My eyes water, but the breathing helps. It is my only weapon against the release of the thing that struggles inside me. A small fight. I fear that if I allow myself to empty I will be filled only with the regret of what I have just done.

I look down at the rifle that lies across my knees and think of the bear hunters that pay us for this. They come every spring and fall. Usually from the East. More recently from the Midwest and South. Professional men. Lawyers, executives, doctors. Not bad men. But men who believe in trophy. They are hard men to respect. In hunting camp they drink every night. They stagger out of the dining tent and fall to their knees and vomit and wipe their mouths on the tails of the new shirts they have bought for hunting bear. In the mornings they suffer the shits. When they are drunk they tell us about fucking their wives. They tell us about fucking women who are not their wives. They tell us about fucking the men they are in business with. Not all of them. But the drunks and the braggarts are the ones I remember. Every fall I sit behind the woodstove in the tent and watch them. They only look my way to ask for a dipper of water, or to send me to their sleeping tents for cigarettes. I do not think of them as men. I think of them as big, loud Scouts—overweight and balding children. I imagine that they come to us to earn a bear badge. Not to kill something ordinary that can be eaten, but to kill something extraordinary that is capable of eating them.

I slump against the hillside and look up into the scatter of sunlight through the pines. I think of our hunters' nervousness in this and other blinds where I've sat with them. When it rains they smell of excitement and they smell of fear. They ask what it is like to kill a bear. They ask how others have done the thing. To the sounds that magnify with the dusk they ask in a tight whisper. "What is that? Is there something out there?" There is no whiskey in the blind. And I am not just a boy sitting behind a stove. Now I am a boy who's watched bears die, and they have not.

I tell them that seeing a bear for the first time is like hearing a rattlesnake for the first   80
time. I tell them that there will be no mistake. Sometimes a man moans. Most men just sit and stare. A few smile a terrible smile. They are the ones we do not accept back. There are limits to any profession.

My father tells our hunters to take out the ball of the shoulder with the first shot so that the bear cannot charge. Simple instructions to ruin bone and flesh. He tells them to never shoot at the head, that a grizzly's skull will deflect their bullet. I have no way of knowing if they remember. Some make good shots. Others fire wildly. Some bear are wounded, and we track them and kill them up close where they have curled to die. Some fall where they feed, across the body of the horse. A few have healed themselves, tracked us, become wilder and more dangerous.

My immediate future looms suddenly and vividly real. Within a week a bear can be killed here. That bear might die atop the body of the horse I have just shot. Socks. The skinning of the bear will fall to me. I think that perhaps I might then cry. I promise myself to try. Cry while I twist and lever one dead thing away from the other. Cry while I strip the furred skin away from its flesh. I think of the rank smell, the maggots, the blood gone dark and thick. If it is a boar and the hunter knows the peculiar anatomies of animals, there will be the matter of the bone around which the bear's penis grows. Bear bone. Dick bone. Joke bone. The hunter will want that solid bone. I will knife the muscle away and scrape the thing clean. And then I will take the rolled hide up in my arms. The horses will shy in apprehension as I approach them. The hide will be heavier than it appears, and it will stink. A packhorse might snap its leadrope and run wildly into the timber.

The hide will be made into a rug. The rug will be mounted against a wall. I have just killed a horse so that a man can display the hair of an animal in his den. We often receive pictures of a bear hide nailed to a wall. The hunter stands in front of the thing holding a drink, his legs wide, smiling, looking as though he will be called to dinner shortly. Sometimes his wife poses with him. I have often wondered what ultimately happens to those trophies. I imagine them older, dusty, lackluster, insect ridden, making their way to garage sales, or into trunks littered with mothballs. I imagine them as a gift to a favorite son. I imagine them as proof that a man came West and had an adventure.

In the years that my family has guided hunters we've killed two or three bears each spring, and again in the fall. No one has been mauled. The deck seems stacked. I flex my feet against the insteps of my wet boots. I have just killed a horse and my only punishment is cold feet.

My father has loaned me his copy of the Lewis and Clark journals. I have read that   85
when they traveled through parts of Montana they flanked their party on both sides with several men who did nothing but kill bear who posed some threat. I look up again at Socks's brown body. I do not think that a bear will come here to harm me. I think that a bear will come to eat a dead horse. Because he is hungry. I do not think that he will brag about the thing to his sow. If he knows he is in jeopardy it will not excite him, make the meal more tantalizing. He will run. Or he will not show himself at all. I wonder about the bears who come and are killed. I think that their souls must be disappointed to be killed by a thing who does not even have a solid bone in its penis.

I run my thumb along the length of the rifle's barrel and think that there are boys who play baseball. Boys who ride bicycles, not horses. Boys who complain about having to mow a yard. I have a friend in town who watches a television show titled Zorro. He practices snapping a small whip and longs to own a sword.

In the magazines my father gets each month I've read that there are boys who do not go to school because they have none. Hundreds of thousands of boys who starve. Boys who beg. Boys who spend their days in prayer. I have traced the outlines of their countries with a finger, holding the atlas open on my lap. And I know that someday I will no longer be a boy. Someday I will be a man, perhaps with a son of my own.

I rewade the creek and sit on the bank and empty the water from my boots. Bird has settled and nickers as I approach. The day has warmed. Squirrels chatter. Ravenshadow occasionally blots the trail before us as we move home. It feels good to have something alive and warm beneath me. Bird's ears are pricked, his gait loose, he seems alert to every movement. He stops unexpectedly on the bridge over the Shoshone and stares down into the water. I strain to see if there is a moose, or otter, or fisherman. There is nothing. Only sunlight on water. I smile and feel ashamed that light makes me happy. I tap Bird's sides with my spurs, and he moves ahead. It takes us less than an hour to return to the corrals.

There is a note from my mother tacked to their cabin door telling me that she has had to help a friend who lives farther up the valley. That I will find enough in the refrigerator for a sandwich. That she loves me. I eat and then strip and soak in their tub, half napping. I dream that I run wild in a forest. It is a common dream. My feet grip the earth with certainty. The earth yearns for my touch, arches against me. I lie down upon the soil to feel its care for me, and imagine that I am recognized, that I am held dear. I think that I will fall in love with a girl who is raised on this same wilderness. I do not think I will fall in love with a girl from a city. And then I come fully awake and sit up in a tub of tepid water. I stare at a clock on the shelf by the sink. It is almost four. The yellows and golds in the pine walls catch and hold the afternoon light. It will be summer in six weeks and there will be water in all the cabins, and I will move into the bunkhouse with the older cowboys.

I'm in the tackshed oiling saddles when my father comes home. He has picked up   90
my brother from school, and my brother runs ahead of him and stands shuffling in the doorway of the building. He carries his books and when he can think of nothing to say opens one and stares at the page as though he needs to find out what next to do. He is worried. He wonders if we have grown apart in a day. If I am less a boy, and he more alone.

"How was your report?" I ask him.

"It was great." He snaps the book shut and smiles. "Thompson's Labrador had pups."

"Did you see them?"

"No. Dad says we can go down this weekend. Pete says he's saving us the one that came out with the cord wrapped around its neck." Relief shows on his face. I am still his brother.

My father joins him in the doorway. They lean into its separate jambs and watch me   95
work the neat's-foot into the leather.

"He tell you about the dog you're going to get?"

"This weekend."

We all nod.

"You got an early start this morning," my father says.

I look up from my work. "I'm not good at waiting," I say.   100

"I can understand that," he tells me. "I'm no good at it myself." He lights a cigarette, and we watch the smoke mute and slide in the last slanting light of the day.

Source: Mark Spragg, "A Boy's Work" from WHERE RIVERS CHANGE DIRECTIONS, 1999. Used by permission of Nancy Stauffer Associates.

Critical Thinking Topics

1. Rich with sensory details, the short story depicts a setting and lifestyle that are likely to be far removed from most contemporary readers. Identify three or more vivid depictions and discuss whether each helps bridge the gap

between you as reader and the setting and situation, or whether it widens the gap. Explain why.

2. The father tells his son, "I think riding a single animal every day of your life allows you some privileges" (par. 7), and then he charges his son with the job of shooting Socks. He also tells his son, "This won't be the hardest thing you'll ever do" (par. 49). What lessons might the father be implicitly imparting to his son? How is he empowering his son?

3. Early on, the fifteen-year-old narrator says, "This is the first time I've been prompted to draw any conclusions about sport. . . . I have never connected sorrow with our family business" (par. 39). By the end of the story, what conclusions has the narrator drawn, and why? In connecting "sorrow with our family business," explain how he seems to be taking on a sense of responsibility for the activity that comprises the business.

Writing Topic

The family business centers on the sport of "trophy hunting," which has a long history of controversy. Some decry the "sport" as unethical and morally irresponsible, while others claim the sport supports local communities and helps to preserve endangered species. What viewpoint on trophy hunting is implicitly argued in this short story? Research and analyze the opposing and supporting positions on trophy hunting. Based on your analysis, do you oppose or support the sport? Or is there a Rogerian argument (a middle-ground position) you would advocate? In either case, explain why.

8.10 Virgil Suárez, Bombardment (2014)

When I close my eyes, I see the ropes.

Ropes hanging from the paneled ceiling. Ropes and their round metal necks to signify to the climber this is the limit, as far as you can go. This is a gym in Henry T Gage Junior High School in Los Angeles, California. This is circa 1974.

When I close my eyes I see the braided mesh wire between the glass panes high up on the gym windows where ash and sepia-colored pigeons flock to roost.

When I close my eyes I see the crow, there to steal another pigeon's egg, breaking it open between its own claws, tasting the yolk, looking down at us.

It squawks twice, then takes off with the broken egg in clenched claws.   5

When I close my eyes I see each letter in the word *bombardment* fall from the rafters down to the bleachers. A bee's buzz around the basketball score-keeper. The 'o' of our mouths when Mr. Stupen barks at us to pick teams, knowing how it is going to go.

Lil' Ruben and Ratboy Marcos choose their own team of homeboys—they, of course, are to be shirts, though they sometimes wanted to be skins to show off their Virgin of Guadalupe tattoos on their pectorals, shoulders or arms.

When I close my eyes I hear the 'm' stutter of Benny who always plays on our team, the skins, *los carneritos*, as they call us for *carne*, and he goes down first. Last time he went to the clinic with a bruised rib that hurt like a motherfucker. He believes that once a rib breaks you have less luck in life. Maybe so, Benny. Maybe so.

One time, Chempo, the meanest of them all, got his nose broken. B is for ball. Bad ball. For its heavy, dark weight that bruises the skin where the ball makes contact with our bodies.

A is for the assholes who gang up against us, allow to do so by the lack of supervi-   10
sion by the fucked-up gym teachers. Mr. Stupen, bless his masochist heart, never once looked in on us after be blew his whistle to signal the beginning of the 50-minute bout.

'May the last man standing win,' he'd say, turn around, and leave for a smoke or a nap, or, rumor had it, spy on the girls in the locker room through a peep hole in his office.

When I close my eyes I see the 'R' of his striped referee shirt.

Stinky Watson, the only white kid on the team, likes to spit loogies into our faces. He spits them like bullets. After each spit, he works the mouth and tongue, saving up some more saliva.

'M' is for *mierda*, for what I always said when I found two or three of Watson's spits in my hair. Though I never liked to shower at school, I would have to. I hated it the sound Watson made as he hocked up another one.

When I close my eyes I see the entanglements of flesh, how one boy falls on   15
the ground and then there'd be a pile-up. Who didn't believe in the story of Humpty Dumpty, the little egg that fell off the fence and fell apart? You could almost hear the extinction of breath from the victim.

All of us moved back at the start of the game. If there were rules, they were not fol-lowed as the homeboys ganged up against us, one by one, drawing us away from the walls to the center of the court where they could take better aim with the bombardment ball and nail us on our backs.

'T' is for the hollow *thuck-thuck* of that ball hitting our flesh.

'*Pinches cabrones*,' Ramirez, the Mexican, would say. He was made crazy at school by bombardment.

When he and his family crossed the Rio Grande, bombardment wasn't the school activity he had in mind. He said he'd much rather work in the factories, and he did. A year after they broke his arm, he left school. We never heard from or saw Ramirez again. We need you now, Ramirez. Where are you?

There are three Cubans on the skins team and we bonded. We fight back. I stop   20
fighting after they take me down one day and tie me up with the climbing ropes. I believe they will hang me. And if they hang me, I will not ever have to do this again. And they hang me all right, but all they do is line up and throw the ball at my body as hard as they can.

I hang there and they taunt me. A couple miss, and most of the blows come down below the waist. I cover my groin and my head as I try to guess which way the ball is coming at me.

Fifty minutes lasts an eternity. I can hear the sound of my own heart beating between my burning ears. If there is blood coursing through my veins, it is like the Alm-endares River of my childhood in Cuba gushing after a downpour.

When that bell rings, Mr. Stupen never even bothers to come back and blow the whistle, so the gangsters run at us, stampede us with their kicks, wild-thrown punches. They snap their moist-with-sweat, stinky shirts at us.

They claw and tear through our shirts, ripping them off our waists, taking the good ones and keeping them.

Thank God we didn't share lockers with any of them. Us, the recent arrivals from 25
Cuba, Mexico (Tijuana), Salvador, Nicaragua… we're all wetbacks. Nobody wants us
for locker partners. Shit, that's what they call us. The skin shits.

'Wetback skins,' someone shouts and then there are the whistles to signify the
bomb-ball's drop.

This is warfare. A ball rains down from the I-beam rafters. The *thuds* of the ball hitting our bodies echoes ad infinitum, loud enough to see the pigeons, sparrows, crows
aflutter. They are our only audience. Our only witnesses. I say they are the choir in some
Greek drama.

When I close my eyes I see the heavy ball falling from the sky.

'*WacHale!*' someone shouts. 'Take cover!'

In my nightmares there's more than one ball. They rain down upon us, knocking us 30
to the ground, breaking our bones.

Nobody ever speaks about this.

We hide our bruised limbs as best as we could. From our families. From our parents. 'What's that?' my father will say looking at a bruise on my arm peeking through
my t-shirt sleeve. 'Nothing,' I say.

Most of us are twelve, thirteen, fourteen—we don't have to show our bodies to
anyone. 'Why are you limping?' my mother wants to know. 'Shoes,' I tell her. 'A little
tight.'

The bruises bloom and darken our skins, spilled ink in water, a flowering right
underneath our epidermis where the hurt sends shockwaves to our brain, our hearts.

When we close our eyes we see our broken souls. 35

When we close our eyes we see the scoreboard and how much we are behind,
how much we are losing, how much harder we have to try to keep from going down for
good.

When we close our eyes we see nothing but the purple and yellow of our cowardice. How, though we keep getting up and dusting our hands off, we keep getting
pushed down, ground by a stranger's heel, our cheeks to the hard earth, our ears
tuned to the muted sound of some poor sap somewhere moaning about a nosebleed,
a broken finger, a fistful of hair missing.

Thuck-thud, thuck-thud, when we close our eyes we can still hear the most frightening of sounds: a bombardment ball rolling across an empty gymnasium court floor,
coming to a final rest under put-away bleachers.

We hear ourselves crying, 'Stay close, stay together, stay…'

What is the sound of such a big ball whizzing by you, thrown with deliberate speed, 40
with deliberate maliciousness?

What is the sound of that ball, that ball, hitting your rib cage, knocking the wind out
of you? Or hitting the back of your head and knocking you down and out, teeth ground
into the wood of the floor?

How does your blood taste as you tilt your head up to keep it from trickling down
your mouth and chin? It's blood-in-the-water mentality—one drop and they see your
weakness. They'll set upon you and beat you to a pulp.

You don't want to let them know your hurt, your pains and aches, the throbbing
between your ears. It's a matter of time, you think. It's only a matter of time before
something happens and all this fades away.

Nowhere to run, or hide. Stand up straight. Find out your next move.

Move! 45

Now keep your eyes closed to pretend this heavy, scuffed ball is never going to find you.

Source: Suarez, Virgil. "Bombardment." C&R Press acknowledges the use of Virgil Suarez's "Bombardment" from THE SOVIET CIRCUS AND OTHER STORIES.

Critical Thinking Topics

1. Though "Bombardment" is set in 1974, in what ways do the experiences mentioned by the narrator parallel those of current middle and high school students? Further, how do they extend today to the experiences of students who belong to ethnic minorities?

2. What do you make of the following line from the short story: "He believes that once a rib breaks you have less luck in life. Maybe so, Benny. Maybe so" (par. 8). What inferences might you make about Benny's life experiences and how they correlate with this statement? What do you think about the narrator's reflection on the matter ("Maybe so, Benny. Maybe so")?

3. The narrator never tells his parents the truth about the bruises and other marks on his body. What is your opinion about why he withholds the truth? How is his choice an assertion of power?

Writing Topic

Do you recall being bullied in middle or high school or witnessing classmates being bullied? Have you read or seen real or fictional accounts of bullying? Relay your experiences and observations. In doing so, reflect on why bullying persists as a problem in our society. What does the persistence of bullying reveal about human nature? How can we empower bullying victims, including victims of cyberbullying?

8.11 Poetry

The ten poems in this section, spanning the years from 1673 through 1995, explore topics and issues related to the theme of power and responsibility.

8.12 John Milton, When I Consider How My Light Is Spent (1673)

When I consider how my light is spent,
Ere half my days, in this dark world and wide,
And that one Talent which is death to hide
Lodged with me useless, though my Soul more bent
To serve therewith my Maker, and present   5
My true account, lest he returning chide;
"Doth God exact day-labour, light denied?"
I fondly ask. But patience, to prevent
That murmur, soon replies, "God doth not need
Either man's work or his own gifts; who best   10

Bear his mild yoke, they serve him best. His state
Is Kingly. Thousands at his bidding speed
And post o'er Land and Ocean without rest:
They also serve who only stand and wait."

Critical Thinking Topics

1. The speaker of this poem is reflecting on the frustrations associated with his blindness. The word "light" is used twice in the poem and the word "dark" once. What are the associations with each of these usages?

2. Personification (giving abstract concepts or inanimate objects human qualities) plays an important role in this poem. What is personified and what is the significance of this personification?

Writing Topic

Milton was blind when he composed this poem, in which the speaker is frustrated that his blindness prevents him from fully serving God. Yet Milton also wrote his masterpiece *Paradise Lost* while blind. Describe the theme of "When I Consider How My Light Is Spent," especially in connection to living with a disability. How does the speaker come to accept his blindness? How might this acceptance apply to the struggles of people with disabilities today, and what does such acceptance imply about society's responsibility to provide support?

8.13 Rainer Maria Rilke, The Panther (1907)

— Translated from the German by Stephen Mitchell

His vision, from the constantly passing bars,
has grown so weary that it cannot hold
anything else. It seems to him there are
a thousand bars; and behind the bars, no world.

As he paces in cramped circles, over and over,   5
the movement of his powerful soft strides
is like a ritual dance around a center
in which a mighty will stands paralyzed.

Only at times, the curtain of the pupils
lifts, quietly—. An image enters in,   10
rushes down through the tensed, arrested muscles,
plunges into the heart and is gone.

Source: "The Panther," translation copyright © 1982 by Stephen Mitchell; from SELECTED POETRY OF RAINER MARIA RILKE by Rainer Maria Rilke, translated by Stephen Mitchell. Used by permission of Random House, an imprint and division of Penguin Random House LLC. All rights reserved. Used by permission of Stephen Mitchell.

Critical Thinking Topics

1. On which of the rhetorical appeals (*ethos, logos,* or *pathos*) does the poet rely? Find examples of the appeal and explain their effect on you as reader.
2. What value assumptions about animals are suggested? Explain how these values factor into the debate over the use of animals for medical research.
3. Reread the closing four lines. What "image" do you think the panther sees? What does the last line suggest? Consider what the poem might be suggesting about the value of the panther's life. Based on those considerations, write an implied claim for the poem.

Writing Topic

Today's zoos do not enclose large animals in small cages, as in "The Panther," but usually keep them in habitats modeled after their native habitats. From the zoo visitor's perspective, the animals roam freely. Yet some animal welfare groups claim that, regardless of the environment, it is unethical to remove animals from their native habitats and keep them captive. However, advocates of zoos argue that animal research and breeding opportunities at zoos contribute to species' viability and that zoos bring people in contact with animals, thus fostering support for their preservation. If you have visited a zoo, what can you recall about your experience? Conduct some research on the debate over zoos. Develop a claim of policy on the issue of whether zoos should exist; list at least four supporting points for your position, along with at least one concession and one refutation.

8.14 Robert Frost, Mending Wall (1914)

Something there is that doesn't love a wall,
That sends the frozen-ground-swell under it,
And spills the upper boulders in the sun;
And makes gaps even two can pass abreast.
The work of hunters is another thing: 5
I have come after them and made repair
Where they have left not one stone on a stone,
But they would have the rabbit out of hiding,
To please the yelping dogs. The gaps I mean,
No one has seen them made or heard them made,   10
But at spring mending-time we find them there.
I let my neighbour know beyond the hill;
And on a day we meet to walk the line
And set the wall between us once again.
We keep the wall between us as we go.   15
To each the boulders that have fallen to each.
And some are loaves and some so nearly balls

We have to use a spell to make them balance:
"Stay where you are until our backs are turned!"
We wear our fingers rough with handling them.   20
Oh, just another kind of out-door game,
One on a side. It comes to little more:
There where it is we do not need the wall:
He is all pine and I am apple orchard.
My apple trees will never get across   25
And eat the cones under his pines, I tell him.
He only says, "Good fences make good neighbours."
Spring is the mischief in me, and I wonder
If I could put a notion in his head:
"Why do they make good neighbours? Isn't it   30
Where there are cows? But here there are no cows.
Before I built a wall I'd ask to know
What I was walling in or walling out,
And to whom I was like to give offence.
Something there is that doesn't love a wall,   35
That wants it down." I could say "Elves" to him,
But it's not elves exactly, and I'd rather
He said it for himself. I see him there
Bringing a stone grasped firmly by the top
In each hand, like an old-stone savage armed.   40
He moves in darkness as it seems to me,
Not of woods only and the shade of trees.
He will not go behind his father's saying,
And he likes having thought of it so well
He says again, "Good fences make good neighbours."   45

Critical Thinking Topics

1. Cite lines from the poem in which the speaker is appealing to *logos* in order to argue against the stone wall separating him from his neighbor.

2. Compare the speaker's attitude toward the wall with the attitude of the neighbor. Which do you favor, and why? In your response, consider the speaker's and the neighbor's different views about the power exerted by the wall and their different views about their responsibility to uphold or oppose that power.

Writing Topics

1. Homeowners are increasingly choosing to live securely and homogeneously in gated communities, perhaps because they view this as a way to revive the virtues and values of small towns—where one can go next door to borrow a cup of sugar and where children can ride their bikes without direct supervision. Others claim that gated communities increase social segregation and widen the chasm between the haves and the have-nots. Do you think gated communities illustrate the idea that "good fences make

good neighbors"? Or do they arouse something in you that "doesn't love a wall"? Write an argument supporting or opposing the establishment of gated communities.

2. Immigration is a divisive topic of discussion in the United States; some of that discussion has focused on building walls. When a country chooses to exert its power by walling people out, what is gained and what is lost?

8.15 Claude McKay, America (1919)

Although she feeds me bread of bitterness,
And sinks into my throat her tiger's tooth,
Stealing my breath of life, I will confess
I love this cultured hell that tests my youth!
Her vigor flows like tides into my blood, 5
Giving me strength erect against her hate.
Her bigness sweeps my being like a flood.
Yet as a rebel fronts a king in state,
I stand within her walls with not a shred
Of terror, malice, not a word of jeer. 10
Darkly I gaze into the days ahead,
And see her might and granite wonders there,
Beneath the touch of Time's unerring hand,
Like priceless treasures sinking in the sand.

Critical Thinking Topics

1. Look online for the sonnet "Ozymandias," by Percy Bysshe Shelley, and read it, paying particular attention to the last five lines. Then reread the last four lines of Claude McKay's "America." At the heart of Shelley's poem is the irony of pride, a concept that appears often in the Bible—for example, "Pride goes before destruction, and a haughty spirit before a fall" (Proverbs 16:18). It is not difficult to imagine that Shelley had this Bible verse in mind when he wrote "Ozymandias." How does the verse also apply to McKay's "America"?

2. In line 4, McKay's speaker proclaims, "I love this cultured hell that tests my youth!" Look up the word "ambiguity" in the Glossary (and see the discussion of ambiguity in Chapter 2). Identify other lines in the poem that create ambiguity regarding this line, and explain how each does so.

Writing Topic

Consider the current political and social climate in the United States. Are you more optimistic or pessimistic about the future of the country? If you could facilitate one positive political or social change in our country, what would it be? Explain with details and examples to show why such a change is needed. Also, suggest specific steps that you and others could advocate in order to realize this change.

8.16 Langston Hughes, Democracy (1949)

Democracy will not come
Today, this year
Nor ever
Through compromise and fear.

I have as much right   5
As the other fellow has
To stand
On my two feet
And own the land.

I tire so of hearing people say,   10
Let things take their course.
Tomorrow is another day.
I do not need my freedom when I'm dead.
I cannot live on tomorrow's bread.

Freedom   15
Is a strong seed
Planted
In a great need.
I live here, too.
I want freedom   20
Just as you.

Source: Hughes, Langston. "Democracy" from THE COLLECTED POEMS OF LANGSTON HUGHES by Langston Hughes, edited by Arnold Rampersad with David Roessell, Associate Editor, copyright © 1994 by The Estate of Langston Hughes. Used by permission of Alfred A. Knopf, a division of Random House, Inc. and by permission of Harold Ober Associates Incorporated.

Critical Thinking Topics

1. Describe the speaker's argument supporting the need for democracy. What is his claim and how does he support this claim?
2. The speaker references "the other fellow" and "people" in this poem. Who might they be? How might their experience differ from the speaker's? Support your perspective with specific examples.

Writing Topic

Consider the statement made by the first four lines of the poem "Democracy." Does democracy remain unrealized in the contemporary United States? *Either* argue that the country has made great strides toward democracy since 1949, the date of the poem, *or* argue that while some movement toward democracy has happened in the past seventy years, much that is undemocratic remains as it was. To avoid making generalizations, use specific examples to support your claim.

8.17 Maxine Kumin, Woodchucks (1972)

Gassing the woodchucks didn't turn out right.
The knockout bomb from the Feed and Grain Exchange
was featured as merciful, quick at the bone
and the case we had against them was airtight,
both exits shoehorned shut with puddingstone,   5
but they had a sub-sub-basement out of range.

Next morning they turned up again, no worse
for the cyanide than we for our cigarettes
and state-store Scotch, all of us up to scratch.
They brought down the marigolds as a matter of course   10
and then took over the vegetable patch
nipping the broccoli shoots, beheading the carrots.

The food from our mouths, I said, righteously thrilling
to the feel of the .22, the bullets' neat noses.
I, a lapsed pacifist fallen from grace   15
puffed with Darwinian pieties for killing,
now drew a bead on the little woodchuck's face.
He died down in the everbearing roses.

Ten minutes later I dropped the mother. She
flipflopped in the air and fell, her needle teeth   20
still hooked in a leaf of early Swiss chard.
Another baby next. O one-two-three
the murderer inside me rose up hard,
the hawkeye killer came on stage forthwith.

There's one chuck left. Old wily fellow, he keeps   25
me cocked and ready day after day after day.
All night I hunt his humped-up form. I dream
I sight along the barrel in my sleep.
If only they'd all consented to die unseen
gassed underground the quiet Nazi way.   30

Source: Kumin, Maxine. From "Our Ground Time Here Will Be Brief."

Critical Thinking Topics

1. Examine the tone of Kumin's poem. Select an adjective that you think best describes that tone, and use specific words and phrases from the poem to support your choice of that adjective.

2. The poet uses the phrase "puffed with Darwinian pieties for killing" (line 16). What are "Darwinian pieties" and what does she mean by this phrase?

Writing Topic

Look at the last two lines of the poem—"If only" what? If the woodchucks had died out of sight in gas chambers, what difference would that make? During Nazi rule in Germany, millions of Jews were systematically murdered, along with millions of other people such as the Romani, the sick and disabled, homosexuals, and political opposition groups. If you had been an "average working person" in Germany during the time of these genocides and had heard rumors of them, what would have been your response? Would you have felt relieved that, even if the rumors were true, it was all taking place out of sight and you could go about your everyday life without thinking much about it? Would you have felt a responsibility to determine whether the rumors were true and, if they were, to risk your life by taking a stand against such horrors? Or would your reaction have been somewhere in between—if so, where, and why?

8.18 Louise Erdrich, Dear John Wayne[1] (1984)

August and the drive-in picture is packed.
We lounge on the hood of the Pontiac
surrounded by the slow-burning spirals they sell
at the window, to vanquish the hordes of mosquitoes.
Nothing works. They break through the smoke screen for blood.   5

Always the lookout spots the Indian first,
spread north to south, barring progress.
The Sioux or some other Plains bunch
in spectacular columns, ICBM missiles[2],
feathers bristling in the meaningful sunset.   10

The drum breaks. There will be no parlance.
Only the arrows whining, a death-cloud of nerves
swarming down on the settlers
who die beautifully, tumbling like dust weeds
into the history that brought us all here   15
together: this wide screen beneath the sign of the bear.

The sky fills, acres of blue squint and eye
that the crowd cheers. His face moves over us,
a thick cloud of vengeance, pitted
like the land that was once flesh. Each rut,   20
each scar makes a promise: *It is*

---

[1] John Wayne was an American movie actor (1907–1979) who often starred in Westerns. He died of cancer.

[2] ICBM stands for "intercontinental ballistic missile"; ICBMs were developed in the 1950s for long-range delivery of nuclear warheads.

not over, this fight, not as long as you resist.
Everything we see belongs to us.

A few laughing Indians fall over the hood
slipping in the hot spilled butter.   25
The eye sees a lot, John, but the heart is so blind.
Death makes us owners of nothing.
He smiles, a horizon of teeth
the credits reel over, and then the white fields

again blowing in the true-to-life dark.   30
The dark films over everything.
We get into the car
scratching our mosquito bites, speechless and small
as people are when the movie is done.
 We are back in our skins.   35

How can we help but keep hearing his voice,
the flip side of the sound track, still playing:
Come on, boys, we got them
where we want them, drunk, running.
They'll give us what we want, what we need.   40
Even his disease was the idea of taking everything.
Those cells, burning, doubling, splitting out of their skins.

Source: "Dear John Wayne" by Louise Erdrich, from THAT'S WHAT SHE SAID: A COLLECTION OF CONTEMPORARY FICTION AND POETRY BY NATIVE AMERICAN WOMEN. Copyright © 1984 by Louise Erdrich. Reprinted with permission of The Wylie Agency LLC.

Critical Thinking Topics

1. The speaker writes as the collective "we." Who are "we"? Why is the poet empowering this "we" with a voice?

2. In lines 21–23 and 38–40, italics denote the actor John Wayne's voice. What is Wayne's message to his audience, both on-screen and off? To whom is the actor presuming to speak off-screen? Does this audience include the "we" you identified in the first question? Why or why not?

3. In lines 26–27, italics denote the speaker's voice. What is the speaker's message? Addressed specifically to "John," the speaker also invokes the collective "us." What is the purpose of using the all-inclusive "we" or "us"?

4. The reference to mosquitoes in lines 4–5 is juxtaposed with the image of the "arrows whining . . . swarming down . . ." (12–13). The mosquito imagery is extended after the movie concludes and as the poem is ending (32–35). What theme is suggested by the mosquito imagery?

5. The poet includes at least one other striking juxtaposition, the different images of "skins" (lines 35 and 42). Explain the significance of this juxtaposition.

Writing Topic

The poet titles the poem as though it were a letter to John Wayne and, in lines 14–16, writes, "tumbling like dust weeds/into the history that brought us here/together: this wide screen beneath the sign of the bear." Research the symbol of the bear in Native American culture. What part of Native American history is the poet attempting to reveal? Also, do some research on contemporary Native Americans' lifestyle and socioeconomic status. To what degree have Native Americans succeeded in maintaining their cultural heritage? Should the federal government take more responsibility for aiding Native Americans in this endeavor? Why or why not?

8.19 Martín Espada, Bully (1990)

Boston, Massachusetts, 1987

In the school auditorium,
the Theodore Roosevelt statue
is nostalgic
for the Spanish-American War,
each fist lonely for a saber   5
or the reins of anguish-eyed horses,
or a podium to clatter with speeches
glorying in the malaria of conquest.

But now the Roosevelt school
is pronounced Hernández.   10
Puerto Rico has invaded Roosevelt
with its army of Spanish-singing children
in the hallways,
brown children devouring
the stockpiles of the cafeteria,   15
children painting Taíno ancestors
that leap naked across murals.

Roosevelt is surrounded
by all the faces
he ever shoved in eugenic spite   20
and cursed as mongrels, skin of one race,
hair and cheekbones of another.

Once Marines tramped
from the newsreel of his imagination;
now children plot to spray graffiti   25
in parrot-brilliant colors

across the Victorian mustache
and monocle.

Source: From REBELLION IS THE CIRCLE OF A LOVER'S HANDS/Rebelión es el giro de manos del amante. Copyright © by Martín Espada. Translation Copyright © by Camilo Perez-Bustillo and Martín Espada. First printed in 1990 by Curbstone Press. Used by permission of the author.

Critical Thinking Topics

1. What is the speaker's implied claim of value about Theodore Roosevelt? Explain how three or more details from the poem provide evidence for this claim.

2. On which rhetorical appeal (*ethos, logos,* or *pathos*) does the speaker base his argument? Is this an effective persuasive strategy? Why or why not?

3. Find examples of connotation in the poem (if you are not sure what "connotation" means, look it up in a dictionary). Explain how these word usages contribute to or detract from the poem's argument.

Writing Topics

1. Assume the role of Theodore Roosevelt's defender. Do some research and write a rebuttal to the poem's argument.

2. President Theodore Roosevelt (1901–1909) created the term "bully pulpit," still a fairly common term, but also commonly misunderstood. Research the term's origin and what it means. How is the poem's title ironic? (Refer to a dictionary for a definition of "irony.") Do some online research to find a recent or current example of the use of "bully pulpit." Is the term used in its original sense in this example? Explain your response.

8.20 Gwendolyn Brooks, The Mother (1991)

Abortions will not let you forget.
You remember the children you got that you did not get,
The damp small pulps with a little or with no hair,
The singers and workers that never handled the air.
You will never neglect or beat   5
Them, or silence or buy with a sweet.
You will never wind up the sucking-thumb
Or scuttle off ghosts that come.
You will never leave them, controlling your luscious sigh,
Return for a snack of them, with gobbling mother-eye.   10

I have heard in the voices of the wind the voices of my dim killed children.
I have contracted. I have eased
My dim dears at the breasts they could never suck.
I have said, Sweets, if I sinned, if I seized
Your luck   15

And your lives from your unfinished reach,
If I stole your births and your names,
Your straight baby tears and your games,
Your stilted or lovely loves, your tumults, your marriages, aches, and your deaths,
If I poisoned the beginnings of your breaths,   20
Believe that even in my deliberateness I was not deliberate.
Though why should I whine,
Whine that the crime was other than mine?—
Since anyhow you are dead.
Or rather, or instead,   25
You were never made.

But that too, I am afraid,
Is faulty: oh, what shall I say, how is the truth to be said?
You were born, you had body, you died.
It is just that you never giggled or planned or cried.   30
Believe me, I loved you all.
Believe me, I knew you, though faintly, and I loved, I loved you
All.

Source: Brooks, Gwendolyn: "The Mother" from BLACKS by Gwendolyn Brooks. Copyright (c) 1991 by Gwendolyn Brooks. Reprinted by Consent of Brooks Permissions.

Critical Thinking Topics

1. Beginning with line 21, whenever the speaker says "Believe…," she seems to be sorting through her conscience in trying to articulate "the truth." How do you interpret lines 21–33? How is the speaker judging herself as "the mother"? What is your perspective on this mother (the speaker), and what leads you to that viewpoint?

2. What is the effect of repetition in the poem's closing stanza? Whom is the speaker trying to convince, and why?

3. Examine this poem as an argument. What is its implied claim? What evidence in the poem supports your statement of the claim?

4. Assess the speaker's *ethos*. For example, do you think she is accepting responsibility for her actions, or is she rationalizing them? What details in the poem lead you to that conclusion?

Writing Topic

Abortion has long been, and no doubt will continue to be, a deeply divisive and passionately debated issue. In the decades since the U.S. Supreme Court's 1973 decision in *Roe v. Wade*, affirming women's right to abortion, various state legislatures have passed laws aimed at limiting this right—for example, by requiring that minors have parental consent to an abortion. Research state laws on abortions for minors and parental consent. Based on your examination of the various laws, develop a proposal for a federal law on abortions for minors that you would advocate. Include three or more supporting points and at least one concession and one refutation.

8.21 Naomi Shihab Nye, Famous (1995)

The river is famous to the fish.

The loud voice is famous to silence,
which knew it would inherit the earth
before anybody said so.

The cat sleeping on the fence is famous to the birds   5
watching him from the birdhouse.

The tear is famous, briefly, to the cheek.

The idea you carry close to your bosom
is famous to your bosom.

The boot is famous to the earth,   10
more famous than the dress shoe,
which is famous only to floors.
The bent photograph is famous to the one who carries it
and not at all famous to the one who is pictured.

I want to be famous to shuffling men   15
who smile while crossing streets,
sticky children in grocery lines,
famous as the one who smiled back.

I want to be famous in the way a pulley is famous,
or a buttonhole, not because it did anything spectacular,   20
but because it never forgot what it could do.

Source: Nye, Naomi Shihab. "Famous" from WORDS UNDER THE WORDS: Selected Poems. Copyright (c) 1995. By permission of the author, Naomi Shihab Nye, 2018.

Critical Thinking Topics

1. What is Nye's implied claim about evaluating the concept of "famous"?
2. In a culture that glorifies celebrity, what are some typical images that society attaches to fame? What definition of "famous" do these images suggest? How do these images contrast with the images that Nye uses in her poem and with the definition suggested by those images?

Writing Topic

Compare and contrast Nye's viewpoint on what "famous" means and the viewpoint projected by popular culture. Consider, too, what values you think should be associated with being famous. Based on your comparisons and considerations, write your own argument for defining "famous," and describe the attributes that should be connected with fame. Include specific examples to support your viewpoint.

8.22 Drama

The late-nineteenth-century play in this section explores topics and issues related to the theme of power and responsibility.

8.23 Oscar Wilde, An Ideal Husband (1895)

THE PERSONS OF THE PLAY

THE EARL OF CAVERSHAM, K.G.
VISCOUNT GORING, his Son
SIR ROBERT CHILTERN, Bart., Under-Secretary for Foreign Affairs
VICOMTE DE NANJAC, Attaché at the French Embassy in London
MR. MONTFORD
MASON, Butler to Sir Robert Chiltern
PHIPPS, Lord Goring's Servant
JAMES, Footman
HAROLD, Footman
LADY CHILTERN
LADY MARKBY
THE COUNTESS OF BASILDON
MRS. MARCHMONT
MISS MABEL CHILTERN, Sir Robert Chiltern's Sister
MRS. CHEVELEY

THE SCENES OF THE PLAY

ACT I. The Octagon Room in Sir Robert Chiltern's House in Grosvenor Square.
ACT II. Morning-room in Sir Robert Chiltern's House.
ACT III. The Library of Lord Goring's House in Curzon Street.
ACT IV. Same as Act II.
TIME: The Present.
PLACE: London.

The action of the play is completed within twenty-four hours.

8.23.1 ACT I

SCENE
The octagon room at Sir Robert Chiltern's house in Grosvenor Square.
[The room is brilliantly lighted and full of guests. At the top of the staircase stands LADY CHILTERN, a woman of grave Greek beauty, about twenty-seven years

of age. She receives the guests as they come up. Over the well of the staircase hangs a great chandelier with wax lights, which illumine a large eighteenth-century French tapestry—representing the Triumph of Love, from a design by Boucher—that is stretched on the staircase wall. On the right is the entrance to the music-room. The sound of a string quartette is faintly heard. The entrance on the left leads to other reception-rooms. MRS. MARCHMONT and LADY BASILDON, two very pretty women, are seated together on a Louis Seize sofa. They are types of exquisite fragility. Their affectation of manner has a delicate charm. Watteau would have loved to paint them.]

MRS. MARCHMONT:	Going on to the Hartlocks' to-night, Margaret?	
LADY BASILDON:	I suppose so. Are you?	
MRS. MARCHMONT:	Yes. Horribly tedious parties they give, don't they?	
LADY BASILDON:	Horribly tedious! Never know why I go. Never know why I go anywhere.	5
MRS. MARCHMONT:	I come here to be educated	
LADY BASILDON:	Ah! I hate being educated!	
MRS. MARCHMONT:	So do I. It puts one almost on a level with the commercial classes, doesn't it? But dear Gertrude Chiltern is always telling me that I should have some serious purpose in life. So I come here to try to find one.	10
LADY BASILDON:	[Looking round through her lorgnette.] I don't see anybody here to-night whom one could possibly call a serious purpose. The man who took me in to dinner talked to me about his wife the whole time.	15
MRS. MARCHMONT:	How very trivial of him!	
LADY BASILDON:	Terribly trivial! What did your man talk about?	
MRS. MARCHMONT:	About myself.	
LADY BASILDON:	[Languidly.] And were you interested?	
MRS. MARCHMONT:	[Shaking her head.] Not in the smallest degree.	20
LADY BASILDON:	What martyrs we are, dear Margaret!	
MRS. MARCHMONT:	[Rising.] And how well it becomes us, Olivia!	
	[They rise and go towards the music-room. The VICOMTE DE NANJAC, a young attaché known for his neckties and his Anglomania, approaches with a low bow, and enters into conversation.]	25
MASON:	[Announcing guests from the top of the staircase.] Mr. and Lady Jane Barford. Lord Caversham.	
	[Enter LORD CAVERSHAM, an old gentleman of seventy, wearing the riband and star of the Garter. A fine Whig type. Rather like a portrait by Lawrence.]	30
LORD CAVERSHAM:	Good evening, Lady Chiltern! Has my good-for-nothing young son been here?	
LADY CHILTERN:	[Smiling.] I don't think Lord Goring has arrived yet.	

MABEL CHILTERN:	[Coming up to LORD CAVERSHAM.] Why do you call Lord Goring good-for-nothing?	35
	[MABEL CHILTERN is a perfect example of the English type of prettiness, the apple-blossom type. She has all the fragrance and freedom of a flower. There is ripple after ripple of sunlight in her hair, and the little mouth, with its parted lips, is expectant, like the mouth of a child. She has the fascinating tyranny of youth, and the astonishing courage of innocence. To sane people she is not reminiscent of any work of art. But she is really like a Tanagra statuette, and would be rather annoyed if she were told so.]	40
		45
LORD CAVERSHAM:	Because he leads such an idle life.	
MABEL CHILTERN:	How can you say such a thing? Why, he rides in the Row at ten o'clock in the morning, goes to the Opera three times a week, changes his clothes at least five times a day, and dines out every night of the season. You don't call that leading an idle life, do you?	50
LORD CAVERSHAM:	[Looking at her with a kindly twinkle in his eyes.]	
	You are a very charming young lady!	
MABEL CHILTERN:	How sweet of you to say that, Lord Caversham! Do come to us more often. You know we are always at home on Wednesdays, and you look so well with your star!	55
LORD CAVERSHAM:	Never go anywhere now. Sick of London Society. Shouldn't mind being introduced to my own tailor; he always votes on the right side. But object strongly to being sent down to dinner with my wife's milliner. Never could stand Lady Caversham's bonnets.	60
MABEL CHILTERN:	Oh, I love London Society! I think it has immensely improved. It is entirely composed now of beautiful idiots and brilliant lunatics. Just what Society should be.	
LORD CAVERSHAM:	Hum! Which is Goring? Beautiful idiot, or the other thing?	65
MABEL CHILTERN:	[Gravely.] I have been obliged for the present to put Lord Goring into a class quite by himself. But he is developing charmingly!	
LORD CAVERSHAM:	Into what?	
MABEL CHILTERN:	[With a little curtsey.] I hope to let you know very soon, Lord Caversham!	70
MASON:	[Announcing guests.] Lady Markby. Mrs. Cheveley.	
	[Enter LADY MARKBY and MRS. CHEVELEY. LADY MARKBY is a pleasant, kindly, popular woman, with gray hair à la marquise and good lace.]	75
	[MRS. CHEVELEY, who accompanies her, is tall and rather slight. Lips very thin and highly-coloured, a line of scarlet on a pallid face. Venetian red hair, aquiline nose, and long throat. Rouge accentuates the natural paleness	

of her complexion. Gray-green eyes that move restlessly.   80
She is in heliotrope, with diamonds. She looks rather like
an orchid, and makes great demands on one's curiosity.
In all her movements she is extremely graceful. A work of
art, on the whole, but showing the influence of too many
schools.]   85

LADY MARKBY: Good evening, dear Gertrude! So kind of you to let me
bring my friend, Mrs. Cheveley. Two such charming
women should know each other!

LADY CHILTERN: [Advances towards MRS. CHEVELEY with a sweet smile.
Then suddenly stops, and bows rather distantly.] I think   90
Mrs. Cheveley and I have met before. I did not know she
had married a second time.

LADY MARKBY: [Genially.] Ah, nowadays people marry as often as they
can, don't they? It is most fashionable. [To DUCHESS OF
MARYBOROUGH.] Dear Duchess, and how is the Duke?   95
Brain still weak, I suppose? Well, that is only to be expected, is it not? His good father was just the same. There
is nothing like race, is there?

MRS. CHEVELEY: [Playing with her fan.] But have we really met before, Lady
Chiltern? I can't remember where. I have been out of Eng-   100
land for so long.

LADY CHILTERN: We were at school together, Mrs. Cheveley.

MRS. CHEVELEY: [Superciliously.] Indeed? I have forgotten all about my school-
days. I have a vague impression that they were detestable.

LADY CHILTERN: [Coldly.] I am not surprised!   105

MRS. CHEVELEY: [In her sweetest manner.] Do you know, I am quite looking
forward to meeting your clever husband, Lady Chiltern.
Since he has been at the Foreign Office, he has been so
much talked of in Vienna. They actually succeed in spelling
his name right in the newspapers. That in itself is fame, on   110
the continent.

LADY CHILTERN: I hardly think there will be much in common between you
and my husband, Mrs. Cheveley! [Moves away.]

VICOMTE DE NANJAC: Ah! chere Madame, queue surprise! I have not seen you
since Berlin!   115

MRS. CHEVELEY: Not since Berlin, Vicomte. Five years ago!

VICOMTE DE NANJAC: And you are younger and more beautiful than ever. How
do you manage it?

MRS. CHEVELEY: By making it a rule only to talk to perfectly charming
people like yourself.   120

VICOMTE DE NANJAC: Ah! you flatter me. You butter me, as they say here.

MRS. CHEVELEY: Do they say that here? How dreadful of them!

VICOMTE DE NANJAC: Yes, they have a wonderful language. It should be more
widely known.

[SIR ROBERT CHILTERN enters. A man of forty, but looking somewhat younger. Clean-shaven, with finely-cut features, dark-haired and dark-eyed. A personality of mark. Not popular—few personalities are. But intensely admired by the few, and deeply respected by the many. The note of his manner is that of perfect distinction, with a slight touch of pride. One feels that he is conscious of the success he has made in life. A nervous temperament, with a tired look. The firmly-chiselled mouth and chin contrast strikingly with the romantic expression in the deep-set eyes. The variance is suggestive of an almost complete separation of passion and intellect, as though thought and emotion were each isolated in its own sphere through some violence of will-power. There is nervousness in the nostrils, and in the pale, thin, pointed hands. It would be inaccurate to call him picturesque. Picturesqueness cannot survive the House of Commons. But Vandyck would have liked to have painted his head.]

SIR ROBERT CHILTERN: Good evening, Lady Markby! I hope you have brought Sir John with you?

LADY MARKBY: Oh! I have brought a much more charming person than Sir John. Sir John's temper since he has taken seriously to politics has become quite unbearable. Really, now that the House of Commons is trying to become useful, it does a great deal of harm.

SIR ROBERT CHILTERN: I hope not, Lady Markby. At any rate we do our best to waste the public time, don't we? But who is this charming person you have been kind enough to bring to us?

LADY MARKBY: Her name is Mrs. Cheveley! One of the Dorsetshire Cheveleys, I suppose. But I really don't know. Families are so mixed nowadays. Indeed, as a rule, everybody turns out to be somebody else.

SIR ROBERT CHILTERN: Mrs. Cheveley? I seem to know the name.

LADY MARKBY: She has just arrived from Vienna.

SIR ROBERT CHILTERN: Ah! yes. I think I know whom you mean.

LADY MARKBY: Oh! she goes everywhere there, and has such pleasant scandals about all her friends. I really must go to Vienna next winter. I hope there is a good chef at the Embassy.

SIR ROBERT CHILTERN: If there is not, the Ambassador will certainly have to be recalled. Pray point out Mrs. Cheveley to me. I should like to see her.

LADY MARKBY: Let me introduce you. [To MRS. CHEVELEY.] My dear, Sir Robert Chiltern is dying to know you!

SIR ROBERT CHILTERN: [Bowing.] Every one is dying to know the brilliant Mrs. Cheveley. Our attaches at Vienna write to us about nothing else.

MRS. CHEVELEY:	Thank you, Sir Robert. An acquaintance that begins with 170 a compliment is sure to develop into a real friendship. It starts in the right manner. And I find that I know Lady Chil- tern already.
SIR ROBERT CHILTERN:	Really?
MRS. CHEVELEY:	Yes. She has just reminded me that we were at school 175 together. I remember it perfectly now. She always got the good conduct prize. I have a distinct recollection of Lady Chiltern always getting the good conduct prize!
SIR ROBERT CHILTERN:	[Smiling.] And what prizes did you get, Mrs. Cheveley?
MRS. CHEVELEY:	My prizes came a little later on in life. I don't think any of 180 them were for good conduct. I forget!
SIR ROBERT CHILTERN:	I am sure they were for something charming!
MRS. CHEVELEY:	I don't know that women are always rewarded for being charming. I think they are usually punished for it! Certainly, more women grow old nowadays through the faithfulness 185 of their admirers than through anything else! At least that is the only way I can account for the terribly haggard look of most of your pretty women in London!
SIR ROBERT CHILTERN:	What an appalling philosophy that sounds! To attempt to classify you, Mrs. Cheveley, would be an impertinence. 190 But may I ask, at heart, are you an optimist or a pessimist? Those seem to be the only two fashionable religions left to us nowadays.
MRS. CHEVELEY:	Oh, I'm neither. Optimism begins in a broad grin, and Pes- simism ends with blue spectacles. Besides, they are both 195 of them merely poses.
SIR ROBERT CHILTERN:	You prefer to be natural?
MRS. CHEVELEY:	Sometimes. But it is such a very difficult pose to keep up.
SIR ROBERT CHILTERN:	What would those modern psychological novelists, of whom we hear so much, say to such a theory as that? 200
MRS. CHEVELEY:	Ah! the strength of women comes from the fact that psy- chology cannot explain us. Men can be analysed, women . . . merely adored.
SIR ROBERT CHILTERN:	You think science cannot grapple with the problem of women? 205
MRS. CHEVELEY:	Science can never grapple with the irrational. That is why it has no future before it, in this world.
SIR ROBERT CHILTERN:	And women represent the irrational.
MRS. CHEVELEY:	Well-dressed women do.
SIR ROBERT CHILTERN:	[With a polite bow.] I fear I could hardly agree with you 210 there. But do sit down. And now tell me, what makes you leave your brilliant Vienna for our gloomy London—or perhaps the question is indiscreet?

MRS. CHEVELEY:	Questions are never indiscreet. Answers sometimes are.
SIR ROBERT CHILTERN:	Well, at any rate, may I know if it is politics or pleasure? 215
MRS. CHEVELEY:	Politics are my only pleasure. You see nowadays it is not fashionable to flirt till one is forty, or to be romantic till one is forty-five, so we poor women who are under thirty, or say we are, have nothing open to us but politics or philanthropy. And philanthropy seems to me to have become simply the 220 refuge of people who wish to annoy their fellow-creatures. I prefer politics. I think they are more . . . becoming!
SIR ROBERT CHILTERN:	A political life is a noble career!
MRS. CHEVELEY:	Sometimes. And sometimes it is a clever game, Sir Robert. And sometimes it is a great nuisance. 225
SIR ROBERT CHILTERN:	Which do you find it?
MRS. CHEVELEY:	I? A combination of all three. [Drops her fan.]
SIR ROBERT CHILTERN:	[Picks up fan.] Allow me!
MRS. CHEVELEY:	Thanks.
SIR ROBERT CHILTERN:	But you have not told me yet what makes you honour 230 London so suddenly. Our season is almost over.
MRS. CHEVELEY:	Oh! I don't care about the London season! It is too matrimonial. People are either hunting for husbands, or hiding from them. I wanted to meet you. It is quite true. You know what a woman's curiosity is. Almost as great as 235 a man's! I wanted immensely to meet you, and . . . to ask you to do something for me.
SIR ROBERT CHILTERN:	I hope it is not a little thing, Mrs. Cheveley. I find that little things are so very difficult to do.
MRS. CHEVELEY:	[After a moment's reflection.] No, I don't think it is quite a 240 little thing.
SIR ROBERT CHILTERN:	I am so glad. Do tell me what it is.
MRS. CHEVELEY:	Later on. [Rises.] And now may I walk through your beautiful house? I hear your pictures are charming. Poor Baron Arnheim—you remember the Baron?—used to tell me you 245 had some wonderful Corots.
SIR ROBERT CHILTERN:	[With an almost imperceptible start.] Did you know Baron Arnheim well?
MRS. CHEVELEY:	[Smiling.] Intimately. Did you?
SIR ROBERT CHILTERN:	At one time. 250
MRS. CHEVELEY:	Wonderful man, wasn't he?
SIR ROBERT CHILTERN:	[After a pause.] He was very remarkable, in many ways.
MRS. CHEVELEY:	I often think it such a pity he never wrote his memoirs. They would have been most interesting.
SIR ROBERT CHILTERN:	Yes: he knew men and cities well, like the old Greek. 255
MRS. CHEVELEY:	Without the dreadful disadvantage of having a Penelope waiting at home for him.

MASON:	Lord Goring.
	[Enter LORD GORING. Thirty-four, but always says he is younger. A well-bred, expressionless face. He is clever, but would not like to be thought so. A flawless dandy, he would be annoyed if he were considered romantic. He plays with life, and is on perfectly good terms with the world. He is fond of being misunderstood. It gives him a post of vantage.]	260
SIR ROBERT CHILTERN:	Good evening, my dear Arthur! Mrs. Cheveley, allow me to introduce to you Lord Goring, the idlest man in London.	265
MRS. CHEVELEY:	I have met Lord Goring before.
LORD GORING:	[Bowing.] I did not think you would remember me, Mrs. Cheveley.
MRS. CHEVELEY:	My memory is under admirable control. And are you still a bachelor?	270
LORD GORING:	I . . . believe so.
MRS. CHEVELEY:	How very romantic!
LORD GORING:	Oh! I am not at all romantic. I am not old enough. I leave romance to my seniors.	275
SIR ROBERT CHILTERN:	Lord Goring is the result of Boodle's Club, Mrs. Cheveley.
MRS. CHEVELEY:	He reflects every credit on the institution.
LORD GORING:	May I ask are you staying in London long?
MRS. CHEVELEY:	That depends partly on the weather, partly on the cooking, and partly on Sir Robert.	280
SIR ROBERT CHILTERN:	You are not going to plunge us into a European war, I hope?
MRS. CHEVELEY:	There is no danger, at present!
	[She nods to LORD GORING, with a look of amuse-ment in her eyes, and goes out with SIR ROBERT CHILTERN. LORD GORING saunters over to MABEL CHILTERN.]	285
MABEL CHILTERN:	You are very late!
LORD GORING:	Have you missed me?
MABEL CHILTERN:	Awfully!	290
LORD GORING:	Then I am sorry I did not stay away longer. I like being missed.
MABEL CHILTERN:	How very selfish of you!
LORD GORING:	I am very selfish.
MABEL CHILTERN:	You are always telling me of your bad qualities, Lord Goring.	295
LORD GORING:	I have only told you half of them as yet, Miss Mabel!
MABEL CHILTERN:	Are the others very bad?
LORD GORING:	Quite dreadful! When I think of them at night I go to sleep at once.
MABEL CHILTERN:	Well, I delight in your bad qualities. I wouldn't have you part with one of them.	300

LORD GORING:	How very nice of you! But then you are always nice. By the way, I want to ask you a question, Miss Mabel. Who brought Mrs. Cheveley here? That woman in heliotrope, who has just gone out of the room with your brother? 305
MABEL CHILTERN:	Oh, I think Lady Markby brought her. Why do you ask?
LORD GORING:	I haven't seen her for years, that is all.
MABEL CHILTERN:	What an absurd reason!
LORD GORING:	All reasons are absurd. 310
MABEL CHILTERN:	What sort of a woman is she?
LORD GORING:	Oh! a genius in the daytime and a beauty at night!
MABEL CHILTERN:	I dislike her already.
LORD GORING:	That shows your admirable good taste.
VICOMTE DE NANJAC:	[Approaching.] Ah, the English young lady is the drag- 315 on of good taste, is she not? Quite the dragon of good taste.
LORD GORING:	So the newspapers are always telling us.
VICOMTE DE NANJAC:	I read all your English newspapers. I find them so amusing.
LORD GORING:	Then, my dear Nanjac, you must certainly read between 320 the lines.
VICOMTE DE NANJAC:	I should like to, but my professor objects. [To MABEL CHILTERN.] May I have the pleasure of escorting you to the music-room, Mademoiselle?
MABEL CHILTERN:	[Looking very disappointed.] Delighted, Vicomte, quite 325 delighted! [Turning to LORD GORING.] Aren't you coming to the music-room?
LORD GORING:	Not if there is any music going on, Miss Mabel.
MABEL CHILTERN:	[Severely.] The music is in German. You would not understand it. [Goes out with the VICOMTE DE NANJAC. LORD 330 CAVERSHAM comes up to his son.]
LORD CAVERSHAM:	Well, sir! what are you doing here? Wasting your life as usual! You should be in bed, sir. You keep too late hours! I heard of you the other night at Lady Rufford's dancing till four o'clock in the morning! 335
LORD GORING:	Only a quarter to four, father.
LORD CAVERSHAM:	Can't make out how you stand London Society. The thing has gone to the dogs, a lot of damned nobodies talking about nothing.
LORD GORING:	I love talking about nothing, father. It is the only thing I 340 know anything about.
LORD CAVERSHAM:	You seem to me to be living entirely for pleasure.
LORD GORING:	What else is there to live for, father? Nothing ages like happiness.

LORD CAVERSHAM:	You are heartless, sir, very heartless!	345
LORD GORING:	I hope not, father. Good evening, Lady Basildon!	
LADY BASILDON:	[Arching two pretty eyebrows.] Are you here? I had no idea you ever came to political parties!	
LORD GORING:	I adore political parties. They are the only place left to us where people don't talk politics.	350
LADY BASILDON:	I delight in talking politics. I talk them all day long. But I can't bear listening to them. I don't know how the unfortunate men in the House stand these long debates.	
LORD GORING:	By never listening.	
LADY BASILDON:	Really?	355
LORD GORING:	[In his most serious manner.] Of course. You see, it is a very dangerous thing to listen. If one listens one may be convinced; and a man who allows himself to be convinced by an argument is a thoroughly unreasonable person.	
LADY BASILDON:	Ah! that accounts for so much in men that I have never understood, and so much in women that their husbands never appreciate in them!	360
MRS. MARCHMONT:	[With a sigh.] Our husbands never appreciate anything in us. We have to go to others for that!	
LADY BASILDON:	[Emphatically.] Yes, always to others, have we not?	365
LORD GORING:	[Smiling.] And those are the views of the two ladies who are known to have the most admirable husbands in London.	
MRS. MARCHMONT:	That is exactly what we can't stand. My Reginald is quite hopelessly faultless. He is really unendurably so, at times! There is not the smallest element of excitement in knowing him.	370
LORD GORING:	How terrible! Really, the thing should be more widely known!	
LADY BASILDON:	Basildon is quite as bad; he is as domestic as if he was a bachelor.	
MRS. MARCHMONT:	[Pressing LADY BASILDON'S hand.] My poor Olivia! We have married perfect husbands, and we are well punished for it.	375
LORD GORING:	I should have thought it was the husbands who were punished.	
MRS. MARCHMONT:	[Drawing herself up.] Oh, dear no! They are as happy as possible! And as for trusting us, it is tragic how much they trust us.	380
LADY BASILDON:	Perfectly tragic!	
LORD GORING:	Or comic, Lady Basildon?	
LADY BASILDON:	Certainly not comic, Lord Goring. How unkind of you to suggest such a thing!	385

MRS. MARCHMONT:	I am afraid Lord Goring is in the camp of the enemy, as usual. I saw him talking to that Mrs. Cheveley when he came in.
LORD GORING:	Handsome woman, Mrs. Cheveley!
LADY BASILDON:	[Stiffly.] Please don't praise other women in our presence. 390 You might wait for us to do that!
LORD GORING:	I did wait.
MRS. MARCHMONT:	Well, we are not going to praise her. I hear she went to the Opera on Monday night, and told Tommy Rufford at supper that, as far as she could see, London Society was 395 entirely made up of dowdies and dandies.
LORD GORING:	She is quite right, too. The men are all dowdies and the women are all dandies, aren't they?
MRS. MARCHMONT:	[After a pause.] Oh! do you really think that is what Mrs. Cheveley meant? 400
LORD GORING:	Of course. And a very sensible remark for Mrs. Cheveley to make, too.
	[Enter MABEL CHILTERN. She joins the group.]
MABEL CHILTERN:	Why are you talking about Mrs. Cheveley? Everybody is talking about Mrs. Cheveley! Lord Goring says—what 405 did you say, Lord Goring, about Mrs. Cheveley? Oh! I remember, that she was a genius in the daytime and a beauty at night.
LADY BASILDON:	What a horrid combination! So very unnatural!
MRS. MARCHMONT:	[In her most dreamy manner.] I like looking at geniuses, 410 and listening to beautiful people.
LORD GORING:	Ah! that is morbid of you, Mrs. Marchmont!
MRS. MARCHMONT:	[Brightening to a look of real pleasure.] I am so glad to hear you say that. Marchmont and I have been married for seven years, and he has never once told me that I was 415 morbid. Men are so painfully unobservant!
LADY BASILDON:	[Turning to her.] I have always said, dear Margaret, that you were the most morbid person in London.
MRS. MARCHMONT:	Ah! but you are always sympathetic, Olivia!
MABEL CHILTERN:	Is it morbid to have a desire for food? I have a great 420 desire for food. Lord Goring, will you give me some supper?
LORD GORING:	With pleasure, Miss Mabel. [Moves away with her.]
MABEL CHILTERN:	How horrid you have been! You have never talked to me the whole evening! 425
LORD GORING:	How could I? You went away with the child-diplomatist.
MABEL CHILTERN:	You might have followed us. Pursuit would have been only polite. I don't think I like you at all this evening!
LORD GORING:	I like you immensely.

MABEL CHILTERN:	Well, I wish you'd show it in a more marked way! [They go downstairs.]	430
MRS. MARCHMONT:	Olivia, I have a curious feeling of absolute faintness. I think I should like some supper very much. I know I should like some supper.	
LADY BASILDON:	I am positively dying for supper, Margaret!	435
MRS. MARCHMONT:	Men are so horribly selfish, they never think of these things.	
LADY BASILDON:	Men are grossly material, grossly material!	
	[The VICOMTE DE NANJAC enters from the music-room with some other guests. After having carefully examined all the people present, he approaches LADY BASILDON.]	440
VICOMTE DE NANJAC:	May I have the honour of taking you down to supper, Comtesse?	
LADY BASILDON:	[Coldly.] I never take supper, thank you, Vicomte. [The VICOMTE is about to retire. LADY BASILDON, seeing this, rises at once and takes his arm.] But I will come down with you with pleasure.	445
VICOMTE DE NANJAC:	I am so fond of eating! I am very English in all my tastes.	
LADY BASILDON:	You look quite English, Vicomte, quite English.	
	[They pass out. MR. MONTFORD, a perfectly groomed young dandy, approaches MRS. MARCHMONT.]	450
MR. MONTFORD:	Like some supper, Mrs. Marchmont?	
MRS. MARCHMONT:	[Languidly.] Thank you, Mr. Montford, I never touch supper. [Rises hastily and takes his arm.] But I will sit beside you, and watch you.	
MR. MONTFORD:	I don't know that I like being watched when I am eating!	455
MRS. MARCHMONT:	Then I will watch some one else.	
MR. MONTFORD:	I don't know that I should like that either.	
MRS. MARCHMONT:	[Severely.] Pray, Mr. Montford, do not make these painful scenes of jealousy in public!	
	[They go downstairs with the other guests, passing SIR ROBERT CHILTERN and MRS. CHEVELEY, who now enter.]	460
SIR ROBERT CHILTERN:	And are you going to any of our country houses before you leave England, Mrs. Cheveley?	
MRS. CHEVELEY:	Oh, no! I can't stand your English house-parties. In England people actually try to be brilliant at breakfast. That is so dreadful of them! Only dull people are brilliant at breakfast. And then the family skeleton is always reading family prayers. My stay in England really depends on you, Sir Robert. [Sits down on the sofa.]	465
SIR ROBERT CHILTERN:	[Taking a seat beside her.] Seriously?	470
MRS. CHEVELEY:	Quite seriously. I want to talk to you about a great political and financial scheme, about this Argentine Canal Company, in fact.	

SIR ROBERT CHILTERN: What a tedious, practical subject for you to talk about, Mrs. Cheveley!

MRS. CHEVELEY: Oh, I like tedious, practical subjects. What I don't like are tedious, practical people. There is a wide difference. Besides, you are interested, I know, in International Canal schemes. You were Lord Radley's secretary, weren't you, when the Government bought the Suez Canal shares?

SIR ROBERT CHILTERN: Yes. But the Suez Canal was a very great and splendid undertaking. It gave us our direct route to India. It had imperial value. It was necessary that we should have control. This Argentine scheme is a commonplace Stock Exchange swindle.

MRS. CHEVELEY: A speculation, Sir Robert! A brilliant, daring speculation.

SIR ROBERT CHILTERN: Believe me, Mrs. Cheveley, it is a swindle. Let us call things by their proper names. It makes matters simpler. We have all the information about it at the Foreign Office. In fact, I sent out a special Commission to inquire into the matter privately, and they report that the works are hardly begun, and as for the money already subscribed, no one seems to know what has become of it. The whole thing is a second Panama, and with not a quarter of the chance of success that miserable affair ever had. I hope you have not invested in it. I am sure you are far too clever to have done that.

MRS. CHEVELEY: I have invested very largely in it.

SIR ROBERT CHILTERN: Who could have advised you to do such a foolish thing?

MRS. CHEVELEY: Your old friend—and mine.

SIR ROBERT CHILTERN: Who?

MRS. CHEVELEY: Baron Arnheim.

SIR ROBERT CHILTERN: [Frowning.] Ah! yes. I remember hearing, at the time of his death, that he had been mixed up in the whole affair.

MRS. CHEVELEY: It was his last romance. His last but one, to do him justice.

SIR ROBERT CHILTERN: [Rising.] But you have not seen my Corots yet. They are in the music-room. Corots seem to go with music, don't they? May I show them to you?

MRS. CHEVELEY: [Shaking her head.] I am not in a mood to-night for silver twilights, or rose-pink dawns. I want to talk business. [Motions to him with her fan to sit down again beside her.]

SIR ROBERT CHILTERN: I fear I have no advice to give you, Mrs. Cheveley, except to interest yourself in something less dangerous. The success of the Canal depends, of course, on the attitude of England, and I am going to lay the report of the Commissioners before the House to-morrow night.

MRS. CHEVELEY: That you must not do. In your own interests, Sir Robert, to say nothing of mine, you must not do that.

SIR ROBERT CHILTERN:	[Looking at her in wonder.] In my own interests? My dear Mrs. Cheveley, what do you mean? [Sits down beside her.] 520
MRS. CHEVELEY:	Sir Robert, I will be quite frank with you. I want you to withdraw the report that you had intended to lay before the House, on the ground that you have reasons to believe that the Commissioners have been prejudiced or misinformed, or something. Then I want you to say a few words 525 to the effect that the Government is going to reconsider the question, and that you have reason to believe that the Canal, if completed, will be of great international value. You know the sort of things ministers say in cases of this kind. A few ordinary platitudes will do. In modern life nothing 530 produces such an effect as a good platitude. It makes the whole world kin. Will you do that for me?
SIR ROBERT CHILTERN:	Mrs. Cheveley, you cannot be serious in making me such a proposition!
MRS. CHEVELEY:	I am quite serious. 535
SIR ROBERT CHILTERN:	[Coldly.] Pray allow me to believe that you are not.
MRS. CHEVELEY:	[Speaking with great deliberation and emphasis.] Ah! but I am. And if you do what I ask you, I . . . will pay you very handsomely!
SIR ROBERT CHILTERN:	Pay me! 540
MRS. CHEVELEY:	Yes.
SIR ROBERT CHILTERN:	I am afraid I don't quite understand what you mean.
MRS. CHEVELEY:	[Leaning back on the sofa and looking at him.] How very disappointing! And I have come all the way from Vienna in order that you should thoroughly understand me. 545
SIR ROBERT CHILTERN:	I fear I don't.
MRS. CHEVELEY:	[In her most nonchalant manner.] My dear Sir Robert, you are a man of the world, and you have your price, I suppose. Everybody has nowadays. The drawback is that most people are so dreadfully expensive. I know 550 I am. I hope you will be more reasonable in your terms.
SIR ROBERT CHILTERN:	[Rises indignantly.] If you will allow me, I will call your carriage for you. You have lived so long abroad, Mrs. Cheveley, that you seem to be unable to realise that you are talking to an English gentleman. 555
MRS. CHEVELEY:	[Detains him by touching his arm with her fan, and keeping it there while she is talking.] I realise that I am talking to a man who laid the foundation of his fortune by selling to a Stock Exchange speculator a Cabinet secret.
SIR ROBERT CHILTERN:	[Biting his lip.] What do you mean? 560
MRS. CHEVELEY:	[Rising and facing him.] I mean that I know the real origin of your wealth and your career, and I have got your letter, too.
SIR ROBERT CHILTERN:	What letter?

MRS. CHEVELEY:	[Contemptuously.] The letter you wrote to Baron Arnheim, when you were Lord Radley's secretary, telling the Baron to buy Suez Canal shares—a letter written three days before the Government announced its own purchase.
SIR ROBERT CHILTERN:	[Hoarsely.] It is not true.
MRS. CHEVELEY:	You thought that letter had been destroyed. How foolish of you! It is in my possession.
SIR ROBERT CHILTERN:	The affair to which you allude was no more than a speculation. The House of Commons had not yet passed the bill; it might have been rejected.
MRS. CHEVELEY:	It was a swindle, Sir Robert. Let us call things by their proper names. It makes everything simpler. And now I am going to sell you that letter, and the price I ask for it is your public support of the Argentine scheme. You made your own fortune out of one canal. You must help me and my friends to make our fortunes out of another!
SIR ROBERT CHILTERN:	It is infamous, what you propose—infamous!
MRS. CHEVELEY:	Oh, no! This is the game of life as we all have to play it, Sir Robert, sooner or later!
SIR ROBERT CHILTERN:	I cannot do what you ask me.
MRS. CHEVELEY:	You mean you cannot help doing it. You know you are standing on the edge of a precipice. And it is not for you to make terms. It is for you to accept them. Supposing you refuse—
SIR ROBERT CHILTERN:	What then?
MRS. CHEVELEY:	My dear Sir Robert, what then? You are ruined, that is all! Remember to what a point your Puritanism in England has brought you. In old days nobody pretended to be a bit better than his neighbours. In fact, to be a bit better than one's neighbour was considered excessively vulgar and middle-class. Nowadays, with our modern mania for morality, every one has to pose as a paragon of purity, incorruptibility, and all the other seven deadly virtues—and what is the result? You all go over like ninepins—one after the other. Not a year passes in England without somebody disappearing. Scandals used to lend charm, or at least interest, to a man—now they crush him. And yours is a very nasty scandal. You couldn't survive it. If it were known that as a young man, secretary to a great and important minister, you sold a Cabinet secret for a large sum of money, and that that was the origin of your wealth and career, you would be hounded out of public life, you would disappear completely. And after all, Sir Robert, why should you sacrifice your entire future rather than deal diplomatically with your enemy? For the moment I am your enemy. I admit it! And I am much stronger than you are. The big battalions are on my side. You have a splendid

565

570

575

580

585

590

595

600

605

position, but it is your splendid position that makes you 610
so vulnerable. You can't defend it! And I am in attack. Of
course I have not talked morality to you. You must admit
in fairness that I have spared you that. Years ago you did a
clever, unscrupulous thing; it turned out a great success.
You owe to it your fortune and position. And now you have 615
got to pay for it. Sooner or later we have all to pay for what
we do. You have to pay now. Before I leave you to-night,
you have got to promise me to suppress your report, and
to speak in the House in favour of this scheme.

SIR ROBERT CHILTERN: What you ask is impossible. 620

MRS. CHEVELEY: You must make it possible. You are going to make it possible. Sir Robert, you know what your English newspapers
are like. Suppose that when I leave this house I drive down
to some newspaper office, and give them this scandal and
the proofs of it! Think of their loathsome joy, of the delight 625
they would have in dragging you down, of the mud and
mire they would plunge you in. Think of the hypocrite with
his greasy smile penning his leading article, and arranging
the foulness of the public placard.

SIR ROBERT CHILTERN: Stop! You want me to withdraw the report and to make a 630
short speech stating that I believe there are possibilities in
the scheme?

MRS. CHEVELEY: [Sitting down on the sofa.] Those are my terms.

SIR ROBERT CHILTERN: [In a low voice.] I will give you any sum of money you want.

MRS. CHEVELEY: Even you are not rich enough, Sir Robert, to buy back your 635
past. No man is.

SIR ROBERT CHILTERN: I will not do what you ask me. I will not.

MRS. CHEVELEY: You have to. If you don't . . . [Rises from the sofa.]

SIR ROBERT CHILTERN: [Bewildered and unnerved.] Wait a moment! What did you
propose? You said that you would give me back my letter, 640
didn't you?

MRS. CHEVELEY: Yes. That is agreed. I will be in the Ladies' Gallery
to-morrow night at half-past eleven. If by that time—and
you will have had heaps of opportunity—you have made
an announcement to the House in the terms I wish, I shall 645
hand you back your letter with the prettiest thanks, and
the best, or at any rate the most suitable, compliment I can
think of. I intend to play quite fairly with you. One should
always play fairly . . . when one has the winning cards. The
Baron taught me that . . . amongst other things. 650

SIR ROBERT CHILTERN: You must let me have time to consider your proposal.

MRS. CHEVELEY: No; you must settle now!

SIR ROBERT CHILTERN: Give me a week—three days!

MRS. CHEVELEY: Impossible! I have got to telegraph to Vienna to-night.

SIR ROBERT CHILTERN:	My God! what brought you into my life?	655
MRS. CHEVELEY:	Circumstances. [Moves towards the door.]	
SIR ROBERT CHILTERN:	Don't go. I consent. The report shall be withdrawn. I will arrange for a question to be put to me on the subject.	
MRS. CHEVELEY:	Thank you. I knew we should come to an amicable agreement. I understood your nature from the first. I analysed you, though you did not adore me. And now you can get my carriage for me, Sir Robert. I see the people coming up from supper, and Englishmen always get romantic after a meal, and that bores me dreadfully.	660
	[Exit SIR ROBERT CHILTERN.]	665
	[Enter Guests, LADY CHILTERN, LADY MARKBY, LORD CAVERSHAM, LADY BASILDON, MRS. MARCHMONT, VICOMTE DE NANJAC, MR. MONTFORD.]	
LADY MARKBY:	Well, dear Mrs. Cheveley, I hope you have enjoyed yourself. Sir Robert is very entertaining, is he not?	670
MRS. CHEVELEY:	Most entertaining! I have enjoyed my talk with him immensely.	
LADY MARKBY:	He has had a very interesting and brilliant career. And he has married a most admirable wife. Lady Chiltern is a woman of the very highest principles, I am glad to say. I am a little too old now, myself, to trouble about setting a good example, but I always admire people who do. And Lady Chiltern has a very ennobling effect on life, though her dinner-parties are rather dull sometimes. But one can't have everything, can one? And now I must go, dear. Shall I call for you to-morrow?	675

680 |
MRS. CHEVELEY:	Thanks.	
LADY MARKBY:	We might drive in the Park at five. Everything looks so fresh in the Park now!	
MRS. CHEVELEY:	Except the people!	
LADY MARKBY:	Perhaps the people are a little jaded. I have often observed that the Season as it goes on produces a kind of softening of the brain. However, I think anything is better than high intellectual pressure. That is the most unbecoming thing there is. It makes the noses of the young girls so particularly large. And there is nothing so difficult to marry as a large nose; men don't like them. Good-night, dear! [To LADY CHILTERN.] Good-night, Gertrude! [Goes out on LORD CAVERSHAM'S arm.]	685

690 |
MRS. CHEVELEY:	What a charming house you have, Lady Chiltern! I have spent a delightful evening. It has been so interesting getting to know your husband.	695
LADY CHILTERN:	Why did you wish to meet my husband, Mrs. Cheveley?	
MRS. CHEVELEY:	Oh, I will tell you. I wanted to interest him in this Argentine Canal scheme, of which I dare say you have heard. And I	

	found him most susceptible, — susceptible to reason, I mean. A rare thing in a man. I converted him in ten minutes. He is going to make a speech in the House tomorrow night in favour of the idea. We must go to the Ladies' Gallery and hear him! It will be a great occasion!	700
LADY CHILTERN:	There must be some mistake. That scheme could never have my husband's support.	705
MRS. CHEVELEY:	Oh, I assure you it's all settled. I don't regret my tedious journey from Vienna now. It has been a great success. But, of course, for the next twenty-four hours the whole thing is a dead secret.	710
LADY CHILTERN:	[Gently.] A secret? Between whom?	
MRS. CHEVELEY:	[With a flash of amusement in her eyes.] Between your husband and myself.	
SIR ROBERT CHILTERN:	[Entering.] Your carriage is here, Mm Cheveley!	
MRS. CHEVELEY:	Thanks! Good evening, Lady Chiltern! Good-night, Lord Goring! I am at Claridge's. Don't you think you might leave a card?	715
LORD GORING:	If you wish it, Mrs. Cheveley!	
MRS. CHEVELEY:	Oh, don't be so solemn about it, or I shall be obliged to leave a card on you. In England I suppose that would hardly be considered EN REGLE. Abroad, we are more civilised. Will you see me down, Sir Robert? Now that we have both the same interests at heart we shall be great friends, I hope! [Sails out on SIR ROBERT CHIL-TERN'S arm. LADY CHILTERN goes to the top of the staircase and looks down at them as they descend. Her expression is troubled. After a little time she is joined by some of the guests, and passes with them into another reception-room.]	720 725
MABEL CHILTERN:	What a horrid woman!	730
LORD GORING:	You should go to bed, Miss Mabel.	
MABEL CHILTERN:	Lord Goring!	
LORD GORING:	My father told me to go to bed an hour ago. I don't see why I shouldn't give you the same advice. I always pass on good advice. It is the only thing to do with it. It is never of any use to oneself.	735
MABEL CHILTERN:	Lord Goring, you are always ordering me out of the room. I think it most courageous of you. Especially as I am not going to bed for hours. [Goes over to the sofa.] You can come and sit down if you like, and talk about anything in the world, except the Royal Academy, Mrs. Cheveley, or novels in Scotch dialect. They are not improving subjects. [Catches sight of something that is lying on the sofa half hidden by the cushion.] What is	740

	this? Some one has dropped a diamond brooch! Quite beautiful, isn't it? [Shows it to him.] I wish it was mine, but Gertrude won't let me wear anything but pearls, and I am thoroughly sick of pearls. They make one look so plain, so good and so intellectual. I wonder whom the brooch belongs to.	745
		750
LORD GORING:	I wonder who dropped it.	
MABEL CHILTERN:	It is a beautiful brooch.	
LORD GORING:	It is a handsome bracelet.	
MABEL CHILTERN:	It isn't a bracelet. It's a brooch.	
LORD GORING:	It can be used as a bracelet. [Takes it from her, and, pulling out a green letter-case, puts the ornament carefully in it, and replaces the whole thing in his breast-pocket with the most perfect sang froid.]	755
MABEL CHILTERN:	What are you doing?	
LORD GORING:	Miss Mabel, I am going to make a rather strange request to you.	760
MABEL CHILTERN:	[Eagerly.] Oh, pray do! I have been waiting for it all the evening.	
LORD GORING:	[Is a little taken aback, but recovers himself.] Don't mention to anybody that I have taken charge of this brooch. Should any one write and claim it, let me know at once.	765
MABEL CHILTERN:	That is a strange request.	
LORD GORING:	Well, you see I gave this brooch to somebody once, years ago.	
MABEL CHILTERN:	You did?	770
LORD GORING:	Yes.	
	[LADY CHILTERN enters alone. The other guests have gone.]	
MABEL CHILTERN:	Then I shall certainly bid you good-night. Good-night, Gertrude! [Exit.]	775
LADY CHILTERN:	Good-night, dear! [To LORD GORING.] You saw whom Lady Markby brought here to-night?	
LORD GORING:	YES. It was an unpleasant surprise. What did she come here for?	
LADY CHILTERN:	Apparently to try and lure Robert to uphold some fraudulent scheme in which she is interested. The Argentine Canal, in fact.	780
LORD GORING:	She has mistaken her man, hasn't she?	
LADY CHILTERN:	She is incapable of understanding an upright nature like my husband's!	785
LORD GORING:	Yes. I should fancy she came to grief if she tried to get Robert into her toils. It is extraordinary what astounding mistakes clever women make.	

LADY CHILTERN:	I don't call women of that kind clever. I call them stupid!	
LORD GORING:	Same thing often. Good-night, Lady Chiltern!	790
LADY CHILTERN:	Good-night!	
	[Enter SIR ROBERT CHILTERN.]	
SIR ROBERT CHILTERN:	My dear Arthur, you are not going? Do stop a little!	
LORD GORING:	Afraid I can't, thanks. I have promised to look in at the Hartlocks'. I believe they have got a mauve Hungarian band that plays mauve Hungarian music. See you soon. Good-bye! [Exit.]	795
SIR ROBERT CHILTERN:	How beautiful you look to-night, Gertrude!	
LADY CHILTERN:	Robert, it is not true, is it? You are not going to lend your support to this Argentine speculation? You couldn't!	800
SIR ROBERT CHILTERN:	[Starting.] Who told you I intended to do so?	
LADY CHILTERN:	That woman who has just gone out, Mrs. Cheveley, as she calls herself now. She seemed to taunt me with it. Robert, I know this woman. You don't. We were at school together. She was untruthful, dishonest, an evil influence on every one whose trust or friendship she could win. I hated, I despised her. She stole things, she was a thief. She was sent away for being a thief. Why do you let her influence you?	805
SIR ROBERT CHILTERN:	Gertrude, what you tell me may be true, but it happened many years ago. It is best forgotten! Mrs. Cheveley may have changed since then. No one should be entirely judged by their past.	810
LADY CHILTERN:	[Sadly.] One's past is what one is. It is the only way by which people should be judged.	815
SIR ROBERT CHILTERN:	That is a hard saying, Gertrude!	
LADY CHILTERN:	It is a true saying, Robert. And what did she mean by boasting that she had got you to lend your support, your name, to a thing I have heard you describe as the most dishonest and fraudulent scheme there has ever been in political life?	820
SIR ROBERT CHILTERN:	[Biting his lip.] I was mistaken in the view I took. We all may make mistakes.	
LADY CHILTERN:	But you told me yesterday that you had received the report from the Commission, and that it entirely condemned the whole thing.	825
SIR ROBERT CHILTERN:	[Walking up and down.] I have reasons now to believe that the Commission was prejudiced, or, at any rate, misinformed. Besides, Gertrude, public and private life are different things. They have different laws, and move on different lines.	830
LADY CHILTERN:	They should both represent man at his highest. I see no difference between them.	

SIR ROBERT CHILTERN:	[Stopping.] In the present case, on a matter of practical politics, I have changed my mind. That is all.	835
LADY CHILTERN:	All!	
SIR ROBERT CHILTERN:	[Sternly.] Yes!	
LADY CHILTERN:	Robert! Oh! it is horrible that I should have to ask you such a question—Robert, are you telling me the whole truth?	
SIR ROBERT CHILTERN:	Why do you ask me such a question?	840
LADY CHILTERN:	[After a pause.] Why do you not answer it?	
SIR ROBERT CHILTERN:	[Sitting down.] Gertrude, truth is a very complex thing, and politics is a very complex business. There are wheels within wheels. One may be under certain obligations to people that one must pay. Sooner or later in political life one has to compromise. Every one does.	845
LADY CHILTERN:	Compromise? Robert, why do you talk so differently to-night from the way I have always heard you talk? Why are you changed?	850
SIR ROBERT CHILTERN:	I am not changed. But circumstances alter things.	
LADY CHILTERN:	Circumstances should never alter principles!	
SIR ROBERT CHILTERN:	But if I told you—	
LADY CHILTERN:	What?	
SIR ROBERT CHILTERN:	That it was necessary, vitally necessary?	855
LADY CHILTERN:	It can never be necessary to do what is not honourable. Or if it be necessary, then what is it that I have loved! But it is not, Robert; tell me it is not. Why should it be? What gain would you get? Money? We have no need of that! And money that comes from a tainted source is a degradation. Power? But power is nothing in itself. It is power to do good that is fine—that, and that only. What is it, then? Robert, tell me why you are going to do this dishonourable thing!	860
SIR ROBERT CHILTERN:	Gertrude, you have no right to use that word. I told you it was a question of rational compromise. It is no more than that.	865
LADY CHILTERN:	Robert, that is all very well for other men, for men who treat life simply as a sordid speculation; but not for you, Robert, not for you. You are different. All your life you have stood apart from others. You have never let the world soil you. To the world, as to myself, you have been an ideal always. Oh! be that ideal still. That great inheritance throw not away—that tower of ivory do not destroy. Robert, men can love what is beneath them—things unworthy, stained, dishonoured. We women worship when we love; and when we lose our worship, we lose everything. Oh! don't kill my love for you, don't kill that!	870 875

SIR ROBERT CHILTERN:	Gertrude!
LADY CHILTERN:	I know that there are men with horrible secrets in their lives—men who have done some shameful thing, and who in some critical moment have to pay for it, by doing some other act of shame—oh! don't tell me you are such as they are! Robert, is there in your life any secret dishonour or disgrace? Tell me, tell me at once, that—
SIR ROBERT CHILTERN:	That what?
LADY CHILTERN:	[Speaking very slowly.] That our lives may drift apart.
SIR ROBERT CHILTERN:	Drift apart?
LADY CHILTERN:	That they may be entirely separate. It would be better for us both.
SIR ROBERT CHILTERN:	Gertrude, there is nothing in my past life that you might not know.
LADY CHILTERN:	I was sure of it, Robert, I was sure of it. But why did you say those dreadful things, things so unlike your real self? Don't let us ever talk about the subject again. You will write, won't you, to Mrs. Cheveley, and tell her that you cannot support this scandalous scheme of hers? If you have given her any promise you must take it back, that is all!
SIR ROBERT CHILTERN:	Must I write and tell her that?
LADY CHILTERN:	Surely, Robert! What else is there to do?
SIR ROBERT CHILTERN:	I might see her personally. It would be better.
LADY CHILTERN:	You must never see her again, Robert. She is not a woman you should ever speak to. She is not worthy to talk to a man like you. No; you must write to her at once, now, this moment, and let your letter show her that your decision is quite irrevocable!
SIR ROBERT CHILTERN:	Write this moment!
LADY CHILTERN:	Yes.
SIR ROBERT CHILTERN:	But it is so late. It is close on twelve.
LADY CHILTERN:	That makes no matter. She must know at once that she has been mistaken in you—and that you are not a man to do anything base or underhand or dishonourable. Write here, Robert. Write that you decline to support this scheme of hers, as you hold it to be a dishonest scheme. Yes—write the word dishonest. She knows what that word means. [SIR ROBERT CHILTERN sits down and writes a letter. His wife takes it up and reads it.] Yes; that will do. [Rings bell.] And now the envelope. [He writes the envelope slowly. Enter MASON.] Have this letter sent at once to Claridge's Hotel. There is no answer. [Exit MASON. LADY CHILTERN kneels down beside her husband, and puts her arms around him.]

880

885

890

895

900

905

910

915

920

	Robert, love gives one an instinct to things. I feel to-night that I have saved you from something that might have been a danger to you, from something that might have made men honour you less than they do. I don't think you realise sufficiently, Robert, that you have brought into the political life of our time a nobler atmosphere, a finer attitude towards life, a freer air of purer aims and higher ideals—I know it, and for that I love you, Robert.	925 930
SIR ROBERT CHILTERN:	Oh, love me always, Gertrude, love me always!	
LADY CHILTERN:	I will love you always, because you will always be worthy of love. We needs must love the highest when we see it! [Kisses him and rises and goes out.]	935
	[SIR ROBERT CHILTERN walks up and down for a moment; then sits down and buries his face in his hands. The Servant enters and begins pulling out the lights. SIR ROBERT CHILTERN looks up.]	
SIR ROBERT CHILTERN:	Put out the lights, Mason, put out the lights!	940
	[The Servant puts out the lights. The room becomes almost dark. The only light there is comes from the great chandelier that hangs over the staircase and illumines the tapestry of the Triumph of Love.]	
	ACT DROP	945

8.23.2 Act II

SCENE

Morning-room at Sir Robert Chiltern's house.

[LORD GORING, dressed in the height of fashion, is lounging in an armchair. SIR ROBERT CHILTERN is standing in front of the fireplace. He is evidently in a state of great mental excitement and distress. As the scene progresses he paces nervously up and down the room.]

LORD GORING:	My dear Robert, it's a very awkward business, very awkward indeed. You should have told your wife the whole thing. Secrets from other people's wives are a necessary luxury in modern life. So, at least, I am always told at the club by people who are bald enough to know better. But no man should have a secret from his own wife. She invariably finds it out. Women have a wonderful instinct about things. They can discover everything except the obvious.	 5
SIR ROBERT CHILTERN:	Arthur, I couldn't tell my wife. When could I have told her? Not last night. It would have made a life-long separation between us, and I would have lost the love of the one woman in the world I worship, of the only woman who has ever stirred love within me. Last night it would have	10

	been quite impossible. She would have turned from me in 15 horror . . . in horror and in contempt.
LORD GORING:	Is Lady Chiltern as perfect as all that?
SIR ROBERT CHILTERN:	Yes; my wife is as perfect as all that.
LORD GORING:	[Taking off his left-hand glove.] What a pity! I beg your par- don, my dear fellow, I didn't quite mean that. But if what 20 you tell me is true, I should like to have a serious talk about life with Lady Chiltern.
SIR ROBERT CHILTERN:	It would be quite useless.
LORD GORING:	May I try?
SIR ROBERT CHILTERN:	Yes; but nothing could make her alter her views. 25
LORD GORING:	Well, at the worst it would simply be a psychological ex- periment.
SIR ROBERT CHILTERN:	All such experiments are terribly dangerous.
LORD GORING:	Everything is dangerous, my dear fellow. If it wasn't so, life wouldn't be worth living. . . . Well, I am bound to say that I 30 think you should have told her years ago.
SIR ROBERT CHILTERN:	When? When we were engaged? Do you think she would have married me if she had known that the origin of my fortune is such as it is, the basis of my career such as it is, and that I had done a thing that I suppose most men 35 would call shameful and dishonourable?
LORD GORING:	[Slowly.] Yes; most men would call it ugly names. There is no doubt of that.
SIR ROBERT CHILTERN:	[Bitterly.] Men who every day do something of the same kind themselves. Men who, each one of them, have worse 40 secrets in their own lives.
LORD GORING:	That is the reason they are so pleased to find out other people's secrets. It distracts public attention from their own.
SIR ROBERT CHILTERN:	And, after all, whom did I wrong by what I did? No one. 45
LORD GORING:	[Looking at him steadily.] Except yourself, Robert.
SIR ROBERT CHILTERN:	[After a pause.] Of course I had private information about a certain transaction contemplated by the Government of the day, and I acted on it. Private information is practically the source of every large modern fortune. 50
LORD GORING:	[Tapping his boot with his cane.] And public scandal invari- ably the result.
SIR ROBERT CHILTERN:	[Pacing up and down the room.] Arthur, do you think that what I did nearly eighteen years ago should be brought up against me now? Do you think it fair that a man's 55 whole career should be ruined for a fault done in one's boyhood almost? I was twenty-two at the time, and I had the double misfortune of being well-born and poor, two

	unforgiveable things nowadays. Is it fair that the folly, the sin of one's youth, if men choose to call it a sin, should wreck a life like mine, should place me in the pillory, should shatter all that I have worked for, all that I have built up. Is it fair, Arthur?	60
LORD GORING:	Life is never fair, Robert. And perhaps it is a good thing for most of us that it is not.	65
SIR ROBERT CHILTERN:	Every man of ambition has to fight his century with its own weapons. What this century worships is wealth. The God of this century is wealth. To succeed one must have wealth. At all costs one must have wealth.	
LORD GORING:	You underrate yourself, Robert. Believe me, without wealth you could have succeeded just as well.	70
SIR ROBERT CHILTERN:	When I was old, perhaps. When I had lost my passion for power, or could not use it. When I was tired, worn out, disappointed. I wanted my success when I was young. Youth is the time for success. I couldn't wait.	75
LORD GORING:	Well, you certainly have had your success while you are still young. No one in our day has had such a brilliant success. Under-Secretary for Foreign Affairs at the age of forty—that's good enough for any one, I should think.	
SIR ROBERT CHILTERN:	And if it is all taken away from me now? If I lose everything over a horrible scandal? If I am hounded from public life?	80
LORD GORING:	Robert, how could you have sold yourself for money?	
SIR ROBERT CHILTERN:	[Excitedly.] I did not sell myself for money. I bought success at a great price. That is all.	
LORD GORING:	[Gravely.] Yes; you certainly paid a great price for it. But what first made you think of doing such a thing?	85
SIR ROBERT CHILTERN:	Baron Arnheim.	
LORD GORING:	Damned scoundrel!	
SIR ROBERT CHILTERN:	No; he was a man of a most subtle and refined intellect. A man of culture, charm, and distinction. One of the most intellectual men I ever met.	90
LORD GORING:	Ah! I prefer a gentlemanly fool any day. There is more to be said for stupidity than people imagine. Personally I have a great admiration for stupidity. It is a sort of fellow-feeling, I suppose. But how did he do it? Tell me the whole thing.	95
SIR ROBERT CHILTERN:	[Throws himself into an armchair by the writing-table.] One night after dinner at Lord Radley's the Baron began talking about success in modern life as something that one could reduce to an absolutely definite science. With that wonderfully fascinating quiet voice of his he expounded to us the most terrible of all philosophies, the philosophy of power, preached to us the most marvellous	100

of all gospels, the gospel of gold. I think he saw the
 effect he had produced on me, for some days afterwards 105
he wrote and asked me to come and see him. He was
living then in Park Lane, in the house Lord Woolcomb has
now. I remember so well how, with a strange smile on his
pale, curved lips, he led me through his wonderful picture
gallery, showed me his tapestries, his enamels, his jew- 110
els, his carved ivories, made me wonder at the strange
loveliness of the luxury in which he lived; and then told
me that luxury was nothing but a background, a painted
scene in a play, and that power, power over other men,
power over the world, was the one thing worth having, 115
the one supreme pleasure worth knowing, the one joy
one never tired of, and that in our century only the rich
possessed it.

LORD GORING: [With great deliberation.] A thoroughly shallow creed.

SIR ROBERT CHILTERN: [Rising.] I didn't think so then. I don't think so now. Wealth 120
has given me enormous power. It gave me at the very
outset of my life freedom, and freedom is everything. You
have never been poor, and never known what ambition
is. You cannot understand what a wonderful chance the
Baron gave me. Such a chance as few men get. 125

LORD GORING: Fortunately for them, if one is to judge by results. But tell
me definitely, how did the Baron finally persuade you to—
well, to do what you did?

SIR ROBERT CHILTERN: When I was going away he said to me that if I ever could
give him any private information of real value he would 130
make me a very rich man. I was dazed at the prospect he
held out to me, and my ambition and my desire for power
were at that time boundless. Six weeks later certain private
documents passed through my hands.

LORD GORING: [Keeping his eyes steadily fixed on the carpet.] State docu- 135
ments?

SIR ROBERT CHILTERN: Yes. [LORD GORING sighs, then passes his hand across
his forehead and looks up.]

LORD GORING: I had no idea that you, of all men in the world, could have
been so weak, Robert, as to yield to such a temptation as 140
Baron Arnheim held out to you.

SIR ROBERT CHILTERN: Weak? Oh, I am sick of hearing that phrase. Sick of using
it about others. Weak? Do you really think, Arthur, that it
is weakness that yields to temptation? I tell you that there
are terrible temptations that it requires strength, strength 145
and courage, to yield to. To stake all one's life on a
single moment, to risk everything on one throw, whether
the stake be power or pleasure, I care not—there is no
weakness in that. There is a horrible, a terrible courage.

	I had that courage. I sat down the same afternoon and wrote Baron Arnheim the letter this woman now holds. He made three-quarters of a million over the transaction	150
LORD GORING:	And you?	
SIR ROBERT CHILTERN:	I received from the Baron 110,000 pounds.	
LORD GORING:	You were worth more, Robert.	155
SIR ROBERT CHILTERN:	No; that money gave me exactly what I wanted, power over others. I went into the House immediately. The Baron advised me in finance from time to time. Before five years I had almost trebled my fortune. Since then everything that I have touched has turned out a success. In all things connected with money I have had a luck so extraordinary that sometimes it has made me almost afraid. I remember having read somewhere, in some strange book, that when the gods wish to punish us they answer our prayers.	160 165
LORD GORING:	But tell me, Robert, did you never suffer any regret for what you had done?	
SIR ROBERT CHILTERN:	No. I felt that I had fought the century with its own weapons, and won.	
LORD GORING:	[Sadly.] You thought you had won.	170
SIR ROBERT CHILTERN:	I thought so. [After a long pause.] Arthur, do you despise me for what I have told you?	
LORD GORING:	[With deep feeling in his voice.] I am very sorry for you, Robert, very sorry indeed.	
SIR ROBERT CHILTERN:	I don't say that I suffered any remorse. I didn't. Not remorse in the ordinary, rather silly sense of the word. But I have paid conscience money many times. I had a wild hope that I might disarm destiny. The sum Baron Arnheim gave me I have distributed twice over in public charities since then.	175 180
LORD GORING:	[Looking up.] In public charities? Dear me! what a lot of harm you must have done, Robert!	
SIR ROBERT CHILTERN:	Oh, don't say that, Arthur; don't talk like that!	
LORD GORING:	Never mind what I say, Robert! I am always saying what I shouldn't say. In fact, I usually say what I really think. A great mistake nowadays. It makes one so liable to be misunderstood. As regards this dreadful business, I will help you in whatever way I can. Of course you know that.	185
SIR ROBERT CHILTERN:	Thank you, Arthur, thank you. But what is to be done? What can be done?	190
LORD GORING:	[Leaning back with his hands in his pockets.] Well, the English can't stand a man who is always saying he is in the right, but they are very fond of a man who admits that he has been in the wrong. It is one of the best things in	

them. However, in your case, Robert, a confession would   195
not do. The money, if you will allow me to say so, is . . .
awkward. Besides, if you did make a clean breast of the
whole affair, you would never be able to talk morality again.
And in England a man who can't talk morality twice a week
to a large, popular, immoral audience is quite over as a   200
serious politician. There would be nothing left for him as
a profession except Botany or the Church. A confession
would be of no use. It would ruin you.

SIR ROBERT CHILTERN: It would ruin me. Arthur, the only thing for me to do now is
to fight the thing out.   205

LORD GORING: [Rising from his chair.] I was waiting for you to say that,
Robert. It is the only thing to do now. And you must begin
by telling your wife the whole story.

SIR ROBERT CHILTERN: That I will not do.

LORD GORING: Robert, believe me, you are wrong.   210

SIR ROBERT CHILTERN: I couldn't do it. It would kill her love for me. And now about
this woman, this Mrs. Cheveley. How can I defend myself
against her? You knew her before, Arthur, apparently.

LORD GORING: Yes.

SIR ROBERT CHILTERN: Did you know her well?   215

LORD GORING: [Arranging his necktie.] So little that I got engaged to be
married to her once, when I was staying at the Tenbys'.
The affair lasted for three days . . . nearly.

SIR ROBERT CHILTERN: Why was it broken off?

LORD GORING: [Airily.] Oh, I forget. At least, it makes no matter. By the   220
way, have you tried her with money? She used to be con-
foundedly fond of money.

SIR ROBERT CHILTERN: I offered her any sum she wanted. She refused.

LORD GORING: Then the marvellous gospel of gold breaks down sometimes. The rich can't do everything, after all.   225

SIR ROBERT CHILTERN: Not everything. I suppose you are right. Arthur, I feel that
public disgrace is in store for me. I feel certain of it. I never
knew what terror was before. I know it now. It is as if a
hand of ice were laid upon one's heart. It is as if one's
heart were beating itself to death in some empty hollow.   230

LORD GORING: [Striking the table.] Robert, you must fight her. You must
fight her.

SIR ROBERT CHILTERN: But how?

LORD GORING: I can't tell you how at present. I have not the smallest idea.
But every one has some weak point. There is some flaw in   235
each one of us. [Strolls to the fireplace and looks at himself
in the glass.] My father tells me that even I have faults.
Perhaps I have. I don't know.

SIR ROBERT CHILTERN:	In defending myself against Mrs. Cheveley, I have a right to use any weapon I can find, have I not?	240
LORD GORING:	[Still looking in the glass.] In your place I don't think I should have the smallest scruple in doing so. She is thoroughly well able to take care of herself.	
SIR ROBERT CHILTERN:	[Sits down at the table and takes a pen in his hand.] Well, I shall send a cipher telegram to the Embassy at Vienna, to inquire if there is anything known against her. There may be some secret scandal she might be afraid of.	245
LORD GORING:	[Settling his buttonhole.] Oh, I should fancy Mrs. Cheveley is one of those very modern women of our time who find a new scandal as becoming as a new bonnet, and air them both in the Park every afternoon at five-thirty. I am sure she adores scandals, and that the sorrow of her life at present is that she can't manage to have enough of them.	250
SIR ROBERT CHILTERN:	[Writing.] Why do you say that?	255
LORD GORING:	[Turning round.] Well, she wore far too much rouge last night, and not quite enough clothes. That is always a sign of despair in a woman.	
SIR ROBERT CHILTERN:	[Striking a bell.] But it is worth while my wiring to Vienna, is it not?	260
LORD GORING:	It is always worth while asking a question, though it is not always worth while answering one. [Enter MASON.]	
SIR ROBERT CHILTERN:	Is Mr. Trafford in his room?	
MASON:	Yes, Sir Robert.	265
SIR ROBERT CHILTERN:	[Puts what he has written into an envelope, which he then carefully closes.] Tell him to have this sent off in cipher at once. There must not be a moment's delay.	
MASON:	Yes, Sir Robert.	
SIR ROBERT CHILTERN:	Oh! just give that back to me again. [Writes something on the envelope. MASON then goes out with the letter.]	270
SIR ROBERT CHILTERN:	She must have had some curious hold over Baron Arnheim. I wonder what it was.	
LORD GORING:	[Smiling.] I wonder.	
SIR ROBERT CHILTERN:	I will fight her to the death, as long as my wife knows nothing.	275
LORD GORING:	[Strongly.] Oh, fight in any case—in any case.	
SIR ROBERT CHILTERN:	[With a gesture of despair.] If my wife found out, there would be little left to fight for. Well, as soon as I hear from Vienna, I shall let you know the result. It is a chance, just a chance, but I believe in it. And as I fought the age with its own weapons, I will fight her with her weapons. It is only fair, and she looks like a woman with a past, doesn't she?	280

LORD GORING:	Most pretty women do. But there is a fashion in pasts just as there is a fashion in frocks. Perhaps Mrs. Cheveley's past is merely a slightly DECOLLETE one, and they are excessively popular nowadays. Besides, my dear Robert, I should not build too high hopes on frightening Mrs. Cheveley. I should not fancy Mrs. Cheveley is a woman who would be easily frightened. She has survived all her creditors, and she shows wonderful presence of mind.
SIR ROBERT CHILTERN:	Oh! I live on hopes now. I clutch at every chance. I feel like a man on a ship that is sinking. The water is round my feet, and the very air is bitter with storm. Hush! I hear my wife's voice.
	[Enter LADY CHILTERN in walking dress.]
LADY CHILTERN:	Good afternoon, Lord Goring!
LORD GORING:	Good afternoon, Lady Chiltern! Have you been in the Park?
LADY CHILTERN:	No; I have just come from the Woman's Liberal Association, where, by the way, Robert, your name was received with loud applause, and now I have come in to have my tea. [To LORD GORING.] You will wait and have some tea, won't you?
LORD GORING:	I'll wait for a short time, thanks.
LADY CHILTERN:	I will be back in a moment. I am only going to take my hat off.
LORD GORING:	[In his most earnest manner.] Oh! please don't. It is so pretty. One of the prettiest hats I ever saw. I hope the Woman's Liberal Association received it with loud applause.
LADY CHILTERN:	[With a smile.] We have much more important work to do than look at each other's bonnets, Lord Goring.
LORD GORING:	Really? What sort of work?
LADY CHILTERN:	Oh! dull, useful, delightful things, Factory Acts, Female Inspectors, the Eight Hours' Bill, the Parliamentary Franchise. . . . Everything, in fact, that you would find thoroughly uninteresting.
LORD GORING:	And never bonnets?
LADY CHILTERN:	[With mock indignation.] Never bonnets, never!
	[LADY CHILTERN goes out through the door leading to her boudoir.]
SIR ROBERT CHILTERN:	[Takes LORD GORING'S hand.] You have been a good friend to me, Arthur, a thoroughly good friend.
LORD GORING:	I don't know that I have been able to do much for you, Robert, as yet. In fact, I have not been able to do anything for you, as far as I can see. I am thoroughly disappointed with myself.

285

290

295

300

305

310

315

320

325

SIR ROBERT CHILTERN:	You have enabled me to tell you the truth. That is something. The truth has always stifled me.
LORD GORING:	Ah! the truth is a thing I get rid of as soon as possible! 330 Bad habit, by the way. Makes one very unpopular at the club . . . with the older members. They call it being conceited. Perhaps it is.
SIR ROBERT CHILTERN:	I would to God that I had been able to tell the truth . . . to live the truth. Ah! that is the great thing in life, to live the 335 truth. [Sighs, and goes towards the door.] I'll see you soon again, Arthur, shan't I?
LORD GORING:	Certainly. Whenever you like. I'm going to look in at the Bachelors' Ball to-night, unless I find something better to do. But I'll come round to-morrow morning. If you should 340 want me to-night by any chance, send round a note to Curzon Street.
SIR ROBERT CHILTERN:	Thank you.
	[As he reaches the door, LADY CHILTERN enters from her boudoir.] 345
LADY CHILTERN:	You are not going, Robert?
SIR ROBERT CHILTERN:	I have some letters to write, dear.
LADY CHILTERN:	[Going to him.] You work too hard, Robert. You seem never to think of yourself, and you are looking so tired.
SIR ROBERT CHILTERN:	It is nothing, dear, nothing. [He kisses her and goes out.] 350
LADY CHILTERN:	[To LORD GORING.] Do sit down. I am so glad you have called. I want to talk to you about . . . well, not about bonnets, or the Woman's Liberal Association. You take far too much interest in the first subject, and not nearly enough in the second. 355
LORD GORING:	You want to talk to me about Mrs. Cheveley?
LADY CHILTERN:	Yes. You have guessed it. After you left last night I found out that what she had said was really true. Of course I made Robert write her a letter at once, withdrawing his promise. 360
LORD GORING:	So he gave me to understand.
LADY CHILTERN:	To have kept it would have been the first stain on a career that has been stainless always. Robert must be above reproach. He is not like other men. He cannot afford to do what other men do. [She looks at LORD GORING, who remains 365 silent.] Don't you agree with me? You are Robert's greatest friend. You are our greatest friend, Lord Goring. No one, except myself, knows Robert better than you do. He has no secrets from me, and I don't think he has any from you.
LORD GORING:	He certainly has no secrets from me. At least I don't 370 think so.

LADY CHILTERN:	Then am I not right in my estimate of him? I know I am right. But speak to me frankly.
LORD GORING:	[Looking straight at her.] Quite frankly?
LADY CHILTERN:	Surely. You have nothing to conceal, have you?
LORD GORING:	Nothing. But, my dear Lady Chiltern, I think, if you will allow me to say so, that in practical life—
LADY CHILTERN:	[Smiling.] Of which you know so little, Lord Goring—
LORD GORING:	Of which I know nothing by experience, though I know something by observation. I think that in practical life there is something about success, actual success, that is a little unscrupulous, something about ambition that is unscrupulous always. Once a man has set his heart and soul on getting to a certain point, if he has to climb the crag, he climbs the crag; if he has to walk in the mire—
LADY CHILTERN:	Well?
LORD GORING:	He walks in the mire. Of course I am only talking generally about life.
LADY CHILTERN:	[Gravely.] I hope so. Why do you look at me so strangely, Lord Goring?
LORD GORING:	Lady Chiltern, I have sometimes thought that . . . perhaps you are a little hard in some of your views on life. I think that . . . often you don't make sufficient allowances. In every nature there are elements of weakness, or worse than weakness. Supposing, for instance, that—that any public man, my father, or Lord Merton, or Robert, say, had, years ago, written some foolish letter to some one . . .
LADY CHILTERN:	What do you mean by a foolish letter?
LORD GORING:	A letter gravely compromising one's position. I am only putting an imaginary case.
LADY CHILTERN:	Robert is as incapable of doing a foolish thing as he is of doing a wrong thing.
LORD GORING:	[After a long pause.] Nobody is incapable of doing a foolish thing. Nobody is incapable of doing a wrong thing.
LADY CHILTERN:	Are you a Pessimist? What will the other dandies say? They will all have to go into mourning.
LORD GORING:	[Rising.] No, Lady Chiltern, I am not a Pessimist. Indeed I am not sure that I quite know what Pessimism really means. All I do know is that life cannot be understood without much charity, cannot be lived without much charity. It is love, and not German philosophy, that is the true explanation of this world, whatever may be the explanation of the next. And if you are ever in trouble, Lady Chiltern, trust me absolutely, and I will help you in every way I can. If you ever want me, come to me for my assistance, and you shall have it. Come at once to me.

LADY CHILTERN:	[Looking at him in surprise.] Lord Goring, you are talking quite seriously. I don't think I ever heard you talk seriously before.	
LORD GORING:	[Laughing.] You must excuse me, Lady Chiltern. It won't occur again, if I can help it.	420
LADY CHILTERN:	But I like you to be serious.	
	[Enter MABEL CHILTERN, in the most ravishing frock.]	
MABEL CHILTERN:	Dear Gertrude, don't say such a dreadful thing to Lord Goring. Seriousness would be very unbecoming to him. Good afternoon Lord Goring! Pray be as trivial as you can.	425
LORD GORING:	I should like to, Miss Mabel, but I am afraid I am . . . a little out of practice this morning; and besides, I have to be go ing now.	430
MABEL CHILTERN:	Just when I have come in! What dreadful manners you have! I am sure you were very badly brought up.	
LORD GORING:	I was.	
MABEL CHILTERN:	I wish I had brought you up!	
LORD GORING:	I am so sorry you didn't.	435
MABEL CHILTERN:	It is too late now, I suppose.	
LORD GORING:	[Smiling.] I am not so sure.	
MABEL CHILTERN:	Will you ride to-morrow morning?	
LORD GORING:	Yes, at ten.	
MABEL CHILTERN:	Don't forgot.	440
LORD GORING:	Of course I shan't. By the way, Lady Chiltern, there is no list of your guests in THE MORNING POST of to-day. It has apparently been crowded out by the County Council, or the Lambeth Conference, or something equally boring. Could you let me have a list? I have a particular reason for asking you.	445
LADY CHILTERN:	I am sure Mr. Trafford will be able to give you one.	
LORD GORING:	Thanks, so much.	
MABEL CHILTERN:	Tommy is the most useful person in London.	
	LORD GORING: [Turning to her.] And who is the most ornamental?	450
MABEL CHILTERN:	[Triumphantly.] I am.	
LORD GORING:	How clever of you to guess it! [Takes up his hat and cane.] Good-bye, Lady Chiltern! You will remember what I said to you, won't you?	455
LADY CHILTERN:	Yes; but I don't know why you said it to me.	
LORD GORING:	I hardly know myself. Good-bye, Miss Mabel!	
MABEL CHILTERN:	[With a little moue of disappointment.] I wish you were not going. I have had four wonderful adventures this morning; four and a half, in fact. You might stop and listen to some of them.	460

LORD GORING:	How very selfish of you to have four and a half! There won't be any left for me.
MABEL CHILTERN:	I don't want you to have any. They would not be good for you.
LORD GORING:	That is the first unkind thing you have ever said to me. How charmingly you said it! Ten to-morrow.
MABEL CHILTERN:	Sharp.
LORD GORING:	Quite sharp. But don't bring Mr. Trafford.
MABEL CHILTERN:	[With a little toss of the head.] Of course I shan't bring Tommy Trafford. Tommy Trafford is in great disgrace.
LORD GORING:	I am delighted to hear it. [Bows and goes out.]
MABEL CHILTERN:	Gertrude, I wish you would speak to Tommy Trafford.
LADY CHILTERN:	What has poor Mr. Trafford done this time? Robert says he is the best secretary he has ever had.
MABEL CHILTERN:	Well, Tommy has proposed to me again. Tommy really does nothing but propose to me. He proposed to me last night in the music-room, when I was quite unprotected, as there was an elaborate trio going on. I didn't dare to make the smallest repartee, I need hardly tell you. If I had, it would have stopped the music at once. Musical people are so absurdly unreasonable. They always want one to be perfectly dumb at the very moment when one is longing to be absolutely deaf. Then he proposed to me in broad daylight this morning, in front of that dreadful statue of Achilles. Really, the things that go on in front of that work of art are quite appalling. The police should interfere. At luncheon I saw by the glare in his eye that he was going to propose again, and I just managed to check him in time by assuring him that I was a bimetallist. Fortunately I don't know what bimetallism means. And I don't believe anybody else does either. But the observation crushed Tommy for ten minutes. He looked quite shocked. And then Tommy is so annoying in the way he proposes. If he proposed at the top of his voice, I should not mind so much. That might produce some effect on the public. But he does it in a horrid confidential way. When Tommy wants to be romantic he talks to one just like a doctor. I am very fond of Tommy, but his methods of proposing are quite out of date. I wish, Gertrude, you would speak to him, and tell him that once a week is quite often enough to propose to any one, and that it should always be done in a manner that attracts some attention.
LADY CHILTERN:	Dear Mabel, don't talk like that. Besides, Robert thinks very highly of Mr. Trafford. He believes he has a brilliant future before him.

465

470

475

480

485

490

495

500

505

MABEL CHILTERN:	Oh! I wouldn't marry a man with a future before him for anything under the sun.
LADY CHILTERN:	Mabel!
MABEL CHILTERN:	I know, dear. You married a man with a future, didn't you? But then Robert was a genius, and you have a noble, self- 510 sacrificing character. You can stand geniuses. I have no, character at all, and Robert is the only genius I could ever bear. As a rule, I think they are quite impossible. Geniuses talk so much, don't they? Such a bad habit! And they are always thinking about themselves, when I want them to be 515 thinking about me. I must go round now and rehearse at Lady Basildon's. You remember, we are having tableaux, don't you? The Triumph of something, I don't know what! I hope it will be triumph of me. Only triumph I am really interested in at present. [Kisses LADY CHILTERN and 520 goes out; then comes running back.] Oh, Gertrude, do you know who is coming to see you? That dreadful Mrs. Cheveley, in a most lovely gown. Did you ask her?
LADY CHILTERN:	[Rising.] Mrs. Cheveley! Coming to see me? Impossible!
MABEL CHILTERN:	I assure you she is coming upstairs, as large as life and not 525 nearly so natural.
LADY CHILTERN:	You need not wait, Mabel. Remember, Lady Basildon is expecting you.
MABEL CHILTERN:	Oh! I must shake hands with Lady Markby. She is delight ful. I love being scolded by her. 530
	[Enter MASON.]
MASON:	Lady Markby. Mrs. Cheveley.
	[Enter LADY MARKBY and MRS. CHEVELEY.]
LADY CHILTERN:	[Advancing to meet them.] Dear Lady Markby, how nice of you to come and see me! [Shakes hands with her, and 535 bows somewhat distantly to MRS. CHEVELEY.] Won't you sit down, Mrs. Cheveley?
MRS. CHEVELEY:	Thanks. Isn't that Miss Chiltern? I should like so much to know her.
LADY CHILTERN:	Mabel, Mrs. Cheveley wishes to know you. 540
	[MABEL CHILTERN gives a little nod.]
MRS. CHEVELEY:	[Sitting down.] I thought your frock so charming last night, Miss Chiltern. So simple and . . . suitable.
MABEL CHILTERN:	Really? I must tell my dressmaker. It will be such a surprise to her. Good-bye, Lady Markby! 545
LADY MARKBY:	Going already?
MABEL CHILTERN:	I am so sorry but I am obliged to. I am just off to rehearsal. I have got to stand on my head in some tableaux.
LADY MARKBY:	On your head, child? Oh! I hope not. I believe it is most un- healthy. [Takes a seat on the sofa next LADY CHILTERN.] 550

MABEL CHILTERN:	But it is for an excellent charity: in aid of the Undeserving, the only people I am really interested in. I am the secretary, and Tommy Trafford is treasurer.
MRS. CHEVELEY:	And what is Lord Goring?
MABEL CHILTERN:	Oh! Lord Goring is president. 555
MRS. CHEVELEY:	The post should suit him admirably, unless he has deteriorated since I knew him first.
LADY MARKBY:	[Reflecting.] You are remarkably modern, Mabel. A little too modern, perhaps. Nothing is so dangerous as being too modern. One is apt to grow old-fashioned quite suddenly. I 560 have known many instances of it
MABEL CHILTERN:	What a dreadful prospect!
LADY MARKBY:	Ah! my dear, you need not be nervous. You will always be as pretty as possible. That is the best fashion there is, and the only fashion that England succeeds in setting. 565
MABEL CHILTERN:	[With a curtsey.] Thank you so much, Lady Markby, for England . . . and myself. [Goes out.]
LADY MARKBY:	[Turning to LADY CHILTERN.] Dear Gertrude, we just called to know if Mrs. Cheveley's diamond brooch has been found.
LADY CHILTERN:	Here? 570
MRS. CHEVELEY:	Yes. I missed it when I got back to Claridge's, and I thought I might possibly have dropped it here.
LADY CHILTERN:	I have heard nothing about it. But I will send for the butler and ask. [Touches the bell.]
MRS. CHEVELEY:	Oh, pray don't trouble, Lady Chiltern. I dare say I lost it at 575 the Opera, before we came on here.
LADY MARKBY:	Ah yes, I suppose it must have been at the Opera. The fact is, we all scramble and jostle so much nowadays that I wonder we have anything at all left on us at the end of an evening. I know myself that, when I am coming back from 580 the Drawing Room, I always feel as if I hadn't a shred on me, except a small shred of decent reputation, just enough to prevent the lower classes making painful observations through the windows of the carriage. The fact is that our Society is terribly over-populated. Really, some one should 585 arrange a proper scheme of assisted emigration. It would do a great deal of good.
MRS. CHEVELEY:	I quite agree with you, Lady Markby. It is nearly six years since I have been in London for the Season, and I must say Society has become dreadfully mixed. One sees the 590 oddest people everywhere.
LADY MARKBY:	That is quite true, dear. But one needn't know them. I'm sure I don't know half the people who come to my house. Indeed, from all I hear, I shouldn't like to.
	[Enter MASON.] 595

LADY CHILTERN:	What sort of a brooch was it that you lost, Mrs. Cheveley?
MRS. CHEVELEY:	A diamond snake-brooch with a ruby, a rather large ruby.
LADY MARKBY:	I thought you said there was a sapphire on the head, dear?
MRS. CHEVELEY:	[Smiling.] No, Lady Markby—a ruby. 600
LADY MARKBY:	[Nodding her head.] And very becoming, I am quite sure.
LADY CHILTERN:	Has a ruby and diamond brooch been found in any of the rooms this morning, Mason?
MASON:	No, my lady.
MRS. CHEVELEY:	It really is of no consequence, Lady Chiltern. I am so sorry 605 to have put you to any inconvenience.
LADY CHILTERN:	[Coldly.] Oh, it has been no inconvenience. That will do, Mason. You can bring tea. [Exit MASON.]
LADY MARKBY:	Well, I must say it is most annoying to lose anything. I 610 remember once at Bath, years ago, losing in the Pump Room an exceedingly handsome cameo bracelet that Sir John had given me. I don't think he has ever given me anything since, I am sorry to say. He has sadly degener- ated. Really, this horrid House of Commons quite ruins our 615 husbands for us. I think the Lower House by far the great- est blow to a happy married life that there has been since that terrible thing called the Higher Education of Women was invented.
LADY CHILTERN:	Ah! it is heresy to say that in this house, Lady Markby. 620 Robert is a great champion of the Higher Education of Women, and so, I am afraid, am I.
MRS. CHEVELEY:	The higher education of men is what I should like to see. Men need it so sadly.
LADY MARKBY:	They do, dear. But I am afraid such a scheme would be 625 quite unpractical. I don't think man has much capacity for development. He has got as far as he can, and that is not far, is it? With regard to women, well, dear Gertrude, you belong to the younger generation, and I am sure it is all right if you approve of it. In my time, of course, we were 630 taught not to understand anything. That was the old sys- tem, and wonderfully interesting it was. I assure you that the amount of things I and my poor dear sister were taught not to understand was quite extraordinary. But modern women understand everything, I am told. 635
MRS. CHEVELEY:	Except their husbands. That is the one thing the modern woman never understands.
LADY MARKBY:	And a very good thing too, dear, I dare say. It might break up many a happy home if they did. Not yours, I need hardly say, Gertrude. You have married a pattern husband. 640

	I wish I could say as much for myself. But since Sir John has taken to attending the debates regularly, which he never used to do in the good old days, his language has become quite impossible. He always seems to think that he is addressing the House, and consequently whenever he discusses the state of the agricultural labourer, or the Welsh Church, or something quite improper of that kind, I am obliged to send all the servants out of the room. It is not pleasant to see one's own butler, who has been with one for twenty-three years, actually blushing at the side-board, and the footmen making contortions in corners like persons in circuses. I assure you my life will be quite ruined unless they send John at once to the Upper House. He won't take any interest in politics then, will he? The House of Lords is so sensible. An assembly of gentlemen. But in his present state, Sir John is really a great trial. Why, this morning before breakfast was half over, he stood up on the hearthrug, put his hands in his pockets, and appealed to the country at the top of his voice. I left the table as soon as I had my second cup of tea, I need hardly say. But his violent language could be heard all over the house! I trust, Gertrude, that Sir Robert is not like that.	645 650 655 660
LADY CHILTERN:	But I am very much interested in politics, Lady Markby. I love to hear Robert talk about them.	
LADY MARKBY:	Well, I hope he is not as devoted to Blue Books as Sir John is. I don't think they can be quite improving reading for any one.	665
MRS. CHEVELEY:	[Languidly.] I have never read a Blue Book. I prefer books . . . in yellow covers.	
LADY MARKBY:	[Genially unconscious.] Yellow is a gayer colour, is it not? I used to wear yellow a good deal in my early days, and would do so now if Sir John was not so painfully personal in his observations, and a man on the question of dress is always ridiculous, is he not?	670
MRS. CHEVELEY:	Oh, no! I think men are the only authorities on dress.	675
LADY MARKBY:	Really? One wouldn't say so from the sort of hats they wear? would one? [The butler enters, followed by the footman. Tea is set on a small table close to LADY CHILTERN.]	
LADY CHILTERN:	May I give you some tea, Mrs. Cheveley?	680
MRS. CHEVELEY:	Thanks. [The butler hands MRS. CHEVELEY a cup of tea on a salver.]	
LADY CHILTERN:	Some tea, Lady Markby?	
LADY MARKBY:	No thanks, dear. [The servants go out.] The fact is, I have promised to go round for ten minutes to see poor Lady	685

Brancaster, who is in very great trouble. Her daughter, quite a well-brought-up girl, too, has actually become engaged to be married to a curate in Shropshire. It is very sad, very sad indeed. I can't understand this modern mania for curates. In my time we girls saw them, of course, running about the place like rabbits. But we never took any notice of them, I need hardly say. But I am told that nowadays country society is quite honeycombed with them. I think it most irreligious. And then the eldest son has quarrelled with his father, and it is said that when they meet at the club Lord Brancaster always hides himself behind the money article in *The Times*. However, I believe that is quite a common occurrence nowadays and that they have to take in extra copies of *The Times* at all the clubs in St. James's Street; there are so many sons who won't have anything to do with their fathers, and so many fathers who won't speak to their sons. I think myself, it is very much to be regretted.

690

695

700

MRS. CHEVELEY: So do I. Fathers have so much to learn from their sons nowadays.

LADY MARKBY: Really, dear? What? 705

MRS. CHEVELEY: The art of living. The only really Fine Art we have produced in modern times.

LADY MARKBY: [Shaking her head.] Ah! I am afraid Lord Brancaster knew a good deal about that. More than his poor wife ever did. [Turning to LADY CHILTERN.] You know Lady Brancaster, don't you, dear? 710

LADY CHILTERN: Just slightly. She was staying at Langton last autumn, when we were there.

LADY MARKBY: Well, like all stout women, she looks the very picture of happiness, as no doubt you noticed. But there are many tragedies in her family, besides this affair of the curate. Her own sister, Mrs. Jekyll, had a most unhappy life; through no fault of her own, I am sorry to say. She ultimately was so broken-hearted that she went into a convent, or on to the operatic stage, I forget which. No; I think it was decorative art-needlework she took up. I know she had lost all sense of pleasure in life. [Rising.] And now, Gertrude, if you will allow me, I shall leave Mrs. Cheveley in your charge and call back for her in a quarter of an hour. Or perhaps, dear Mrs. Cheveley, you wouldn't mind waiting in the carriage while I am with Lady Brancaster. As I intend it to be a visit of condolence, I shan't stay long. 715

720

725

MRS. CHEVELEY: [Rising.] I don't mind waiting in the carriage at all, provided there is somebody to look at one.

LADY MARKBY: Well, I hear the curate is always prowling about the house. 730

MRS. CHEVELEY:	I am afraid I am not fond of girl friends.
LADY CHILTERN:	[Rising.] Oh, I hope Mrs. Cheveley will stay here a little. I should like to have a few minutes' conversation with her.
MRS. CHEVELEY:	How very kind of you, Lady Chiltern! Believe me, nothing would give me greater pleasure. 735
LADY MARKBY:	Ah! no doubt you both have many pleasant reminiscences of your schooldays to talk over together. Good-bye, dear Gertrude! Shall I see you at Lady Bonar's to-night? She has discovered a wonderful new genius. He does . . . nothing at all, I believe. That is a great comfort, is it not? 740
LADY CHILTERN:	Robert and I are dining at home by ourselves to-night, and I don't think I shall go anywhere afterwards. Robert, of course, will have to be in the House. But there is nothing interesting on.
LADY MARKBY:	Dining at home by yourselves? Is that quite prudent? Ah, 745 I forgot, your husband is an exception. Mine is the general rule, and nothing ages a woman so rapidly as having married the general rule. [Exit LADY MARKBY.]
MRS. CHEVELEY:	Wonderful woman, Lady Markby, isn't she? Talks more and says less than anybody I ever met. She is made to 750 be a public speaker. Much more so than her husband, though he is a typical Englishman, always dull and usually violent.
LADY CHILTERN:	[Makes no answer, but remains standing. There is a pause. Then the eyes of the two women meet. LADY CHILTERN 755 looks stern and pale. MRS. CHEVELEY seems rather amused.] Mrs. Cheveley, I think it is right to tell you quite frankly that, had I known who you really were, I should not have invited you to my house last night.
MRS. CHEVELEY:	[With an impertinent smile.] Really? 760
LADY CHILTERN:	I could not have done so.
MRS. CHEVELEY:	I see that after all these years you have not changed a bit, Gertrude.
LADY CHILTERN:	I never change.
MRS. CHEVELEY:	[Elevating her eyebrows.] Then life has taught you nothing? 765
LADY CHILTERN:	It has taught me that a person who has once been guilty of a dishonest and dishonourable action may be guilty of it a second time, and should be shunned.
MRS. CHEVELEY:	Would you apply that rule to every one?
LADY CHILTERN:	Yes, to every one, without exception. 770
MRS. CHEVELEY:	Then I am sorry for you, Gertrude, very sorry for you.
LADY CHILTERN:	You see now, I was sure, that for many reasons any further acquaintance between us during your stay in London is quite impossible?

MRS. CHEVELEY:	[Leaning back in her chair.] Do you know, Gertrude, I don't mind your talking morality a bit. Morality is simply the attitude we adopt towards people whom we personally dislike. You dislike me. I am quite aware of that. And I have always detested you. And yet I have come here to do you a service.	775 780
LADY CHILTERN:	[Contemptuously.] Like the service you wished to render my husband last night, I suppose. Thank heaven, I saved him from that.	
MRS. CHEVELEY:	[Starting to her feet.] It was you who made him write that insolent letter to me? It was you who made him break his promise?	785
LADY CHILTERN:	Yes.	
MRS. CHEVELEY:	Then you must make him keep it. I give you till to-morrow morning—no more. If by that time your husband does not solemnly bind himself to help me in this great scheme in which I am interested—	790
LADY CHILTERN:	This fraudulent speculation—	
MRS. CHEVELEY:	Call it what you choose. I hold your husband in the hollow of my hand, and if you are wise you will make him do what I tell him.	795
LADY CHILTERN:	[Rising and going towards her.] You are impertinent. What has my husband to do with you? With a woman like you?	
MRS. CHEVELEY:	[With a bitter laugh.] In this world like meets with like. It is because your husband is himself fraudulent and dishonest that we pair so well together. Between you and him there are chasms. He and I are closer than friends. We are enemies linked together. The same sin binds us.	800
LADY CHILTERN:	How dare you class my husband with yourself? How dare you threaten him or me? Leave my house. You are unfit to enter it. [SIR ROBERT CHILTERN enters from behind. He hears his wife's last words, and sees to whom they are addressed. He grows deadly pale.]	805
MRS. CHEVELEY:	Your house! A house bought with the price of dishonour. A house, everything in which has been paid for by fraud. [Turns round and sees SIR ROBERT CHILTERN.] Ask him what the origin of his fortune is! Get him to tell you how he sold to a stockbroker a Cabinet secret. Learn from him to what you owe your position.	810
LADY CHILTERN:	It is not true! Robert! It is not true!	815
MRS. CHEVELEY:	[Pointing at him with outstretched finger.] Look at him! Can he deny it? Does he dare to?	
SIR ROBERT CHILTERN:	Go! Go at once. You have done your worst now.	

MRS. CHEVELEY:	My worst? I have not yet finished with you, with either of you. I give you both till to-morrow at noon. If by then you 820 don't do what I bid you to do, the whole world shall know the origin of Robert Chiltern.
	[SIR ROBERT CHILTERN strikes the bell. Enter MASON.]
SIR ROBERT CHILTERN:	Show Mrs. Cheveley out.
	[MRS. CHEVELEY starts; then bows with somewhat exag- 825 gerated politeness to LADY CHILTERN, who makes no sign of response. As she passes by SIR ROBERT CHILTERN, who is standing close to the door, she pauses for a moment and looks him straight in the face. She then goes out, followed by the servant, who closes the door after him. The 830 husband and wife are left alone. LADY CHILTERN stands like some one in a dreadful dream. Then she turns round and looks at her husband. She looks at him with strange eyes, as though she were seeing him for the first time.]
LADY CHILTERN:	You sold a Cabinet secret for money! You began your life 835 with fraud! You built up your career on dishonour! Oh, tell me it is not true! Lie to me! Lie to me! Tell me it is not true!
SIR ROBERT CHILTERN:	What this woman said is quite true. But, Gertrude, listen to me. You don't realise how I was tempted. Let me tell you the whole thing. [Goes towards her.] 840
LADY CHILTERN:	Don't come near me. Don't touch me. I feel as if you had soiled me for ever. Oh! what a mask you have been wearing all these years! A horrible painted mask! You sold yourself for money. Oh! a common thief were better. You put yourself up to sale to the highest bidder! You were 845 bought in the market. You lied to the whole world. And yet you will not lie to me.
SIR ROBERT CHILTERN:	[Rushing towards her.] Gertrude! Gertrude!
LADY CHILTERN:	[Thrusting him back with outstretched hands.] No, don't speak! Say nothing! Your voice wakes terrible memories— 850 memories of things that made me love you—memories of words that made me love you—memories that now are horrible to me. And how I worshipped you! You were to me something apart from common life, a thing pure, noble, honest, without stain. The world seemed to me finer 855 because you were in it, and goodness more real because you lived. And now—oh, when I think that I made of a man like you my ideal! the ideal of my life!
SIR ROBERT CHILTERN:	There was your mistake. There was your error. The error all women commit. Why can't you women love us, faults and 860 all? Why do you place us on monstrous pedestals? We have all feet of clay, women as well as men; but when we men love women, we love them knowing their weaknesses, their

follies, their imperfections, love them all the more, it may be, for that reason. It is not the perfect, but the imperfect, who have need of love. It is when we are wounded by our own hands, or by the hands of others, that love should come to cure us—else what use is love at all? All sins, except a sin against itself, Love should forgive. All lives, save loveless lives, true Love should pardon. A man's love is like that. It is wider, larger, more human than a woman's. Women think that they are making ideals of men. What they are making of us are false idols merely. You made your false idol of me, and I had not the courage to come down, show you my wounds, tell you my weaknesses. I was afraid that I might lose your love, as I have lost it now. And so, last night you ruined my life for me—yes, ruined it! What this woman asked of me was nothing compared to what she offered to me. She offered security, peace, stability. The sin of my youth, that I had thought was buried, rose up in front of me, hideous, horrible, with its hands at my throat. I could have killed it for ever, sent it back into its tomb, destroyed its record, burned the one witness against me. You prevented me. No one but you, you know it. And now what is there before me but public disgrace, ruin, terrible shame, the mockery of the world, a lonely dishonoured life, a lonely dishonoured death, it may be, some day? Let women make no more ideals of men! Let them not put them on alters and bow before them, or they may ruin other lives as completely as you—you whom I have so wildly loved—have ruined mine! [He passes from the room. LADY CHILTERN rushes towards him, but the door is closed when she reaches it. Pale with anguish, bewildered, helpless, she sways like a plant in the water. Her hands, outstretched, seem to tremble in the air like blossoms in the mind. Then she flings herself down beside a sofa and buries her face. Her sobs are like the sobs of a child.]

865

870

875

880

885

890

895

ACT DROP

8.23.3 Act III

SCENE

The Library in Lord Goring's house. An Adam room. On the right is the door leading into the hall. On the left, the door of the smoking-room. A pair of folding doors at the back open into the drawing-room. The fire is` lit. Phipps, the butler, is arranging some newspapers on the writing-table. The distinction of Phipps is his impassivity. He has been termed by enthusiasts the Ideal Butler. The Sphinx is not so incommunicable. He is a mask with a manner. Of his intellectual or emotional life, history knows nothing. He represents the dominance of form.

[Enter LORD GORING in evening dress with a buttonhole. He is wearing a silk hat and Inverness cape. White-gloved, he carries a Louis Seize cane. His are all the delicate fopperies of Fashion. One sees that he stands in immediate relation to modern life, makes it indeed, and so masters it. He is the first well-dressed philosopher in the history of thought.]

LORD GORING:	Got my second buttonhole for me, Phipps?
PHIPPS:	Yes, my lord. [Takes his hat, cane, and cape, and presents new buttonhole on salver.]
LORD GORING:	Rather distinguished thing, Phipps. I am the only person of the smallest importance in London at present who wears a buttonhole. 5
PHIPPS:	Yes, my lord. I have observed that.
LORD GORING:	[Taking out old buttonhole.] You see, Phipps, Fashion is what one wears oneself. What is unfashionable is what other people wear. 10
PHIPPS:	Yes, my lord.
LORD GORING:	Just as vulgarity is simply the conduct of other people.
PHIPPS:	Yes, my lord.
LORD GORING:	[Putting in a new buttonhole.] And falsehoods the truths of other people. 15
PHIPPS:	Yes, my lord.
LORD GORING:	Other people are quite dreadful. The only possible society is oneself.
PHIPPS:	Yes, my lord.
LORD GORING:	To love oneself is the beginning of a lifelong romance, Phipps. 20
PHIPPS:	Yes, my lord.
LORD GORING:	[Looking at himself in the glass.] Don't think I quite like this buttonhole, Phipps. Makes me look a little too old. Makes me almost in the prime of life, eh, Phipps? 25
PHIPPS:	I don't observe any alteration in your lordship's appearance.
LORD GORING:	You don't, Phipps?
PHIPPS:	No, my lord.
LORD GORING:	I am not quite sure. For the future a more trivial buttonhole, Phipps, on Thursday evenings. 30
PHIPPS:	I will speak to the florist, my lord. She has had a loss in her family lately, which perhaps accounts for the lack of triviality your lordship complains of in the buttonhole.
LORD GORING:	Extraordinary thing about the lower classes in England— they are always losing their relations. 35
PHIPPS:	Yes, my lord! They are extremely fortunate in that respect.
LORD GORING:	[Turns round and looks at him. PHIPPS remains impassive.] Hum! Any letters, Phipps?

PHIPPS:	Three, my lord. [Hands letters on a salver.]
LORD GORING:	[Takes letters.] Want my cab round in twenty minutes. 40
PHIPPS:	Yes, my lord. [Goes towards door.]
LORD GORING:	[Holds up letter in pink envelope.] Ahem! Phipps, when did this letter arrive?
PHIPPS:	It was brought by hand just after your lordship went to the club. 45
LORD GORING:	That will do. [Exit PHIPPS.] Lady Chiltern's handwriting on Lady Chiltern's pink notepaper. That is rather curious. I thought Robert was to write. Wonder what Lady Chiltern has got to say to me? [Sits at bureau and opens letter, and reads it.] 'I want you. I trust you. I am coming to you. 50 Gertrude.' [Puts down the letter with a puzzled look. Then takes it up, and reads it again slowly.] 'I want you. I trust you. I am coming to you.' So she has found out every-thing! Poor woman! Poor woman! [Pulls out watch and looks at it.] But what an hour to call! Ten o'clock! I shall 55 have to give up going to the Berkshires. However, it is always nice to be expected, and not to arrive. I am not ex-pected at the Bachelors', so I shall certainly go there. Well, I will make her stand by her husband. That is the only thing for her to do. That is the only thing for any woman 60 to do. It is the growth of the moral sense in women that makes marriage such a hopeless, one-sided institution. Ten o'clock. She should be here soon. I must tell Phipps I am not in to any one else. [Goes towards bell]
	[Enter PHIPPS.] 65
PHIPPS:	Lord Caversham.
LORD GORING:	Oh, why will parents always appear at the wrong time? Some extraordinary mistake in nature, I suppose. [Enter LORD CAVERSHAM.] Delighted to see you, my dear father. [Goes to meet him.] 70
LORD CAVERSHAM:	Take my cloak off.
LORD GORING:	Is it worth while, father?
LORD CAVERSHAM:	Of course it is worth while, sir. Which is the most comfort-able chair?
LORD GORING:	This one, father. It is the chair I use myself, when I have 75 visitors.
LORD CAVERSHAM:	Thank ye. No draught, I hope, in this room?
LORD GORING:	No, father.
LORD CAVERSHAM:	[Sitting down.] Glad to hear it. Can't stand draughts. No draughts at home. 80
LORD GORING:	Good many breezes, father.
LORD CAVERSHAM:	Eh? Eh? Don't understand what you mean. Want to have a serious conversation with you, sir.

LORD GORING:	My dear father! At this hour?
LORD CAVERSHAM:	Well, sir, it is only ten o'clock. What is your objection to the hour? I think the hour is an admirable hour! 85
LORD GORING:	Well, the fact is, father, this is not my day for talking seriously. I am very sorry, but it is not my day.
LORD CAVERSHAM:	What do you mean, sir?
LORD GORING:	During the Season, father, I only talk seriously on the first 90 Tuesday in every month, from four to seven.
LORD CAVERSHAM:	Well, make it Tuesday, sir, make it Tuesday.
LORD GORING:	But it is after seven, father, and my doctor says I must not have any serious conversation after seven. It makes me talk in my sleep. 95
LORD CAVERSHAM:	Talk in your sleep, sir? What does that matter? You are not married.
LORD GORING:	No, father, I am not married.
LORD CAVERSHAM:	Hum! That is what I have come to talk to you about, sir. You have got to get married, and at once. Why, when I 100 was your age, sir, I had been an inconsolable widower for three months, and was already paying my addresses to your admirable mother. Damme, sir, it is your duty to get married. You can't be always living for pleasure. Every man of position is married nowadays. Bachelors are not 105 fashionable any more. They are a damaged lot. Too much is known about them. You must get a wife, sir. Look where your friend Robert Chiltern has got to by probity, hard work, and a sensible marriage with a good woman. Why don't you imitate him, sir? Why don't you take him for your 110 model?
LORD GORING:	I think I shall, father.
LORD CAVERSHAM:	I wish you would, sir. Then I should be happy. At present I make your mother's life miserable on your account. You are heartless, sir, quite heartless 115
LORD GORING:	I hope not, father.
LORD CAVERSHAM:	And it is high time for you to get married. You are thirty-four years of age, sir.
LORD GORING:	Yes, father, but I only admit to thirty-two—thirty-one and a half when I have a really good buttonhole. This buttonhole 120 is not . . . trivial enough.
LORD CAVERSHAM:	I tell you you are thirty-four, sir. And there is a draught in your room, besides, which makes your conduct worse. Why did you tell me there was no draught, sir? I feel a draught, sir, I feel it distinctly. 125
LORD GORING:	So do I, father. It is a dreadful draught. I will come and see you to-morrow, father. We can talk over anything you like. Let me help you on with your cloak, father.

LORD CAVERSHAM:	No, sir; I have called this evening for a definite purpose, and I am going to see it through at all costs to my health or yours. Put down my cloak, sir.	130
LORD GORING:	Certainly, father. But let us go into another room. [Rings bell.] There is a dreadful draught here. [Enter PHIPPS.] Phipps, is there a good fire in the smoking-room?	
PHIPPS:	Yes, my lord.	135
LORD GORING:	Come in there, father. Your sneezes are quite heartrending.	
LORD CAVERSHAM:	Well, sir, I suppose I have a right to sneeze when I choose?	
LORD GORING:	[Apologetically.] Quite so, father. I was merely expressing sympathy.	
LORD CAVERSHAM:	Oh, damn sympathy. There is a great deal too much of that sort of thing going on nowadays.	140
LORD GORING:	I quite agree with you, father. If there was less sympathy in the world there would be less trouble in the world.	
LORD CAVERSHAM:	[Going towards the smoking-room.] That is a paradox, sir. I hate paradoxes.	145
LORD GORING:	So do I, father. Everybody one meets is a paradox nowadays. It is a great bore. It makes society so obvious.	
LORD CAVERSHAM:	[Turning round, and looking at his son beneath his bushy eyebrows.] Do you always really understand what you say, sir?	
LORD GORING:	[After some hesitation.] Yes, father, if I listen attentively.	150
LORD CAVERSHAM:	[Indignantly.] If you listen attentively! . . . Conceited young puppy! [Goes off grumbling into the smoking-room. PHIPPS enters.]	
LORD GORING:	Phipps, there is a lady coming to see me this evening on particular business. Show her into the drawing-room when she arrives. You understand?	155
PHIPPS:	Yes, my lord.	
LORD GORING:	It is a matter of the gravest importance, Phipps.	
PHIPPS:	I understand, my lord.	
LORD GORING:	No one else is to be admitted, under any circumstances.	160
PHIPPS:	I understand, my lord. [Bell rings.]	
LORD GORING:	Ah! that is probably the lady. I shall see her myself. [Just as he is going towards the door LORD CAVERSHAM enters from the smoking-room.]	
LORD CAVERSHAM:	Well, sir? am I to wait attendance on you?	165
LORD GORING:	[Considerably perplexed.] In a moment, father. Do excuse me. [LORD CAVERSHAM goes back.] Well, remember my instructions, Phipps—into that room.	
PHIPPS:	Yes, my lord.	
	[LORD GORING goes into the smoking-room. HAROLD, the footman shows MRS. CHEVELEY in. Lamia-like, she	170

is in green and silver. She has a cloak of black satin, lined with dead rose-leaf silk.] HAROLD. What name, madam?

MRS. CHEVELEY: [To PHIPPS, who advances towards her.] Is Lord Goring not here? I was told he was at home?   175

PHIPPS: His lordship is engaged at present with Lord Caversham, madam. [Turns a cold, glassy eye on HAROLD, who at once retires.]

MRS. CHEVELEY: [To herself.] How very filial!

PHIPPS: His lordship told me to ask you, madam, to be kind   180
enough to wait in the drawing-room for him. His lordship will come to you there.

MRS. CHEVELEY: [With a look of surprise.] Lord Goring expects me?

PHIPPS: Yes, madam.

MRS. CHEVELEY: Are you quite sure?   185

PHIPPS: His lordship told me that if a lady called I was to ask her to wait in the drawing-room. [Goes to the door of the drawing-room and opens it.] His lordship's directions on the subject were very precise.

MRS. CHEVELEY: [To herself] How thoughtful of him! To expect the unex-   190
pected shows a thoroughly modern intellect. [Goes to-wards the drawing-room and looks in.] Ugh! How dreary a bachelor's drawing-room always looks. I shall have to alter all this. [PHIPPS brings the lamp from the writing-table.] No, I don't care for that lamp. It is far too glaring. Light   195
some candles.

PHIPPS: [Replaces lamp.] Certainly, madam.

MRS. CHEVELEY: I hope the candles have very becoming shades.

PHIPPS: We have had no complaints about them, madam, as yet. [Passes into the drawing-room and begins to light the   200
candles.]

MRS. CHEVELEY: [To herself.] I wonder what woman he is waiting for to-night. It will be delightful to catch him. Men always look so silly when they are caught. And they are always being caught. [Looks about room and approaches the writing-table.]   205
What a very interesting room! What a very interesting picture! Wonder what his correspondence is like. [Takes up letters.] Oh, what a very uninteresting correspondence! Bills and cards, debts and dowagers! Who on earth writes to him on pink paper? How silly to write on pink paper! It looks   210
like the beginning of a middle-class romance. Romance should never begin with sentiment. It should begin with science and end with a settlement. [Puts letter down, then takes it up again.] I know that handwriting. That is Gertrude Chiltern's. I remember it perfectly. The ten commandments   215
in every stroke of the pen, and the moral law all over the

	page. Wonder what Gertrude is writing to him about? Something horrid about me, I suppose. How I detest that woman! [Reads it.] 'I trust you. I want you. I am coming to you. Gertrude.' 'I trust you. I want you. I am coming to you.' [A look of triumph comes over her face. She is just about to steal the letter, when PHIPPS comes in.]	220
PHIPPS:	The candles in the drawing-room are lit, madam, as you directed.	
MRS. CHEVELEY:	Thank you. [Rises hastily and slips the letter under a large silver-cased blotting-book that is lying on the table.]	225
PHIPPS:	I trust the shades will be to your liking, madam. They are the most becoming we have. They are the same as his lordship uses himself when he is dressing for dinner.	
MRS. CHEVELEY:	[With a smile.] Then I am sure they will be perfectly right.	230
PHIPPS:	[Gravely.] Thank you, madam.	
	[MRS. CHEVELEY goes into the drawing-room. PHIPPS closes the door and retires. The door is then slowly opened, and MRS. CHEVELEY comes out and creeps stealthily towards the writing-table. Suddenly voices are heard from the smoking-room. MRS. CHEVELEY grows pale, and stops. The voices grow louder, and she goes back into the drawing-room, biting her lip.]	235
	[Enter LORD GORING and LORD CAVERSHAM.]	
LORD GORING:	[Expostulating.] My dear father, if I am to get married, surely you will allow me to choose the time, place, and person? Particularly the person.	240
LORD CAVERSHAM:	[Testily.] That is a matter for me, sir. You would probably make a very poor choice. It is I who should be consulted, not you. There is property at stake. It is not a matter for affection. Affection comes later on in married life.	245
LORD GORING:	Yes. In married life affection comes when people thoroughly dislike each other, father, doesn't it? [Puts on LORD CAVERSHAM'S cloak for him.]	
LORD CAVERSHAM:	Certainly, sir. I mean certainly not, sir. You are talking very foolishly to-night. What I say is that marriage is a matter for common sense.	250
LORD GORING:	But women who have common sense are so curiously plain, father, aren't they? Of course I only speak from hearsay.	255
LORD CAVERSHAM:	No woman, plain or pretty, has any common sense at all, sir. Common sense is the privilege of our sex.	
LORD GORING:	Quite so. And we men are so self-sacrificing that we never use it, do we, father?	
LORD CAVERSHAM:	I use it, sir. I use nothing else.	260
LORD GORING:	So my mother tells me.	

LORD CAVERSHAM:	It is the secret of your mother's happiness. You are very heartless, sir, very heartless.	
LORD GORING:	I hope not, father. [Goes out for a moment. Then returns, looking rather put out, with SIR ROBERT CHILTERN.]	265
SIR ROBERT CHILTERN:	My dear Arthur, what a piece of good luck meeting you on the doorstep! Your servant had just told me you were not at home. How extraordinary!	
LORD GORING:	The fact is, I am horribly busy to-night, Robert, and I gave orders I was not at home to any one. Even my father had a comparatively cold reception. He complained of a draught the whole time.	270
SIR ROBERT CHILTERN:	Ah! you must be at home to me, Arthur. You are my best friend. Perhaps by to-morrow you will be my only friend. My wife has discovered everything.	275
LORD GORING:	Ah! I guessed as much!	
SIR ROBERT CHILTERN:	[Looking at him.] Really! How?	
LORD GORING:	[After some hesitation.] Oh, merely by something in the expression of your face as you came in. Who told her?	
SIR ROBERT CHILTERN:	Mrs. Cheveley herself. And the woman I love knows that I began my career with an act of low dishonesty, that I built up my life upon sands of shame—that I sold, like a common huckster, the secret that had been intrusted to me as a man of honour. I thank heaven poor Lord Radley died without knowing that I betrayed him. I would to God I had died before I had been so horribly tempted, or had fallen so low. [Burying his face in his hands.]	280 285
LORD GORING:	[After a pause.] You have heard nothing from Vienna yet, in answer to your wire?	
SIR ROBERT CHILTERN:	[Looking up.] Yes; I got a telegram from the first secretary at eight o'clock to-night.	290
LORD GORING:	Well?	
SIR ROBERT CHILTERN:	Nothing is absolutely known against her. On the contrary, she occupies a rather high position in society. It is a sort of open secret that Baron Arnheim left her the greater portion of his immense fortune. Beyond that I can learn nothing.	295
LORD GORING:	She doesn't turn out to be a spy, then?	
SIR ROBERT CHILTERN:	Oh! spies are of no use nowadays. Their profession is over. The newspapers do their work instead.	
LORD GORING:	And thunderingly well they do it.	300
SIR ROBERT CHILTERN:	Arthur, I am parched with thirst. May I ring for something? Some hock and seltzer?	
LORD GORING:	Certainly. Let me. [Rings the bell.]	
SIR ROBERT CHILTERN:	Thanks! I don't know what to do, Arthur, I don't know what to do, and you are my only friend. But what a friend you are— the one friend I can trust. I can trust you absolutely, can't I?	305

	[Enter PHIPPS.]	
LORD GORING:	My dear Robert, of course. Oh! [To PHIPPS.] Bring some hock and seltzer.	
PHIPPS:	Yes, my lord.	310
LORD GORING:	And Phipps!	
PHIPPS:	Yes, my lord.	
LORD GORING:	Will you excuse me for a moment, Robert? I want to give some directions to my servant.	
SIR ROBERT CHILTERN:	Certainly.	315
LORD GORING:	When that lady calls, tell her that I am not expected home this evening. Tell her that I have been suddenly called out of town. You understand?	
PHIPPS:	The lady is in that room, my lord. You told me to show her into that room, my lord.	320
LORD GORING:	You did perfectly right. [Exit PHIPPS.] What a mess I am in. No; I think I shall get through it. I'll give her a lecture through the door. Awkward thing to manage, though.	
SIR ROBERT CHILTERN:	Arthur, tell me what I should do. My life seems to have crumbled about me. I am a ship without a rudder in a night without a star.	325
LORD GORING:	Robert, you love your wife, don't you?	
SIR ROBERT CHILTERN:	I love her more than anything in the world. I used to think ambition the great thing. It is not. Love is the great thing in the world. There is nothing but love, and I love her. But I am defamed in her eyes. I am ignoble in her eyes. There is a wide gulf between us now. She has found me out, Arthur, she has found me out.	330
LORD GORING:	Has she never in her life done some folly—some indiscretion—that she should not forgive your sin?	335
SIR ROBERT CHILTERN:	My wife! Never! She does not know what weakness or temptation is. I am of clay like other men. She stands apart as good women do—pitiless in her perfection—cold and stern and without mercy. But I love her, Arthur. We are childless, and I have no one else to love, no one else to love me. Perhaps if God had sent us children she might have been kinder to me. But God has given us a lonely house. And she has cut my heart in two. Don't let us talk of it. I was brutal to her this evening. But I suppose when sinners talk to saints they are brutal always. I said to her things that were hideously true, on my side, from my stand-point, from the standpoint of men. But don't let us talk of that.	340 345
LORD GORING:	Your wife will forgive you. Perhaps at this moment she is forgiving you. She loves you, Robert. Why should she not forgive?	350

SIR ROBERT CHILTERN:	God grant it! God grant it! [Buries his face in his hands.] But there is something more I have to tell you, Arthur. [Enter PHIPPS with drinks.]	
PHIPPS:	[Hands hock and seltzer to SIR ROBERT CHILTERN.] Hock and seltzer, sir.	355
SIR ROBERT CHILTERN:	Thank you.	
LORD GORING:	Is your carriage here, Robert?	
SIR ROBERT CHILTERN:	No; I walked from the club.	
LORD GORING:	Sir Robert will take my cab, Phipps.	
PHIPPS:	Yes, my lord. [Exit.]	360
LORD GORING:	Robert, you don't mind my sending you away?	
SIR ROBERT CHILTERN:	Arthur, you must let me stay for five minutes. I have made up my mind what I am going to do to-night in the House. The debate on the Argentine Canal is to begin at eleven. [A chair falls in the drawing-room.] What is that?	365
LORD GORING:	Nothing.	
SIR ROBERT CHILTERN:	I heard a chair fall in the next room. Some one has been listening.	
LORD GORING:	No, no; there is no one there.	
SIR ROBERT CHILTERN:	There is some one. There are lights in the room, and the door is ajar. Some one has been listening to every secret of my life. Arthur, what does this mean?	370
LORD GORING:	Robert, you are excited, unnerved. I tell you there is no one in that room. Sit down, Robert.	
SIR ROBERT CHILTERN:	Do you give me your word that there is no one there?	375
LORD GORING:	Yes.	
SIR ROBERT CHILTERN:	Your word of honour? [Sits down.]	
LORD GORING:	Yes.	
SIR ROBERT CHILTERN:	[Rises.] Arthur, let me see for myself.	
LORD GORING:	No, no.	380
SIR ROBERT CHILTERN:	If there is no one there why should I not look in that room? Arthur, you must let me go into that room and satisfy myself. Let me know that no eavesdropper has heard my life's secret. Arthur, you don't realise what I am going through.	
LORD GORING:	Robert, this must stop. I have told you that there is no one in that room—that is enough.	385
SIR ROBERT CHILTERN:	[Rushes to the door of the room.] It is not enough. I insist on going into this room. You have told me there is no one there, so what reason can you have for refusing me?	
LORD GORING:	For God's sake, don't! There is some one there. Some one whom you must not see.	390
SIR ROBERT CHILTERN:	Ah, I thought so!	
LORD GORING:	I forbid you to enter that room.	

SIR ROBERT CHILTERN:	Stand back. My life is at stake. And I don't care who is there. I will know who it is to whom I have told my secret and my shame. [Enters room.] 395
LORD GORING:	Great heavens! his own wife!
	[SIR ROBERT CHILTERN comes back, with a look of scorn and anger on his face.]
SIR ROBERT CHILTERN:	What explanation have you to give me for the presence of that woman here? 400
LORD GORING:	Robert, I swear to you on my honour that that lady is stainless and guiltless of all offence towards you.
SIR ROBERT CHILTERN:	She is a vile, an infamous thing!
LORD GORING:	Don't say that, Robert! It was for your sake she came here. 405 It was to try and save you she came here. She loves you and no one else.
SIR ROBERT CHILTERN:	You are mad. What have I to do with her intrigues with you? Let her remain your mistress! You are well suited to each other. She, corrupt and shameful—you, false as a 410 friend, treacherous as an enemy even—
LORD GORING:	It is not true, Robert. Before heaven, it is not true. In her presence and in yours I will explain all.
SIR ROBERT CHILTERN:	Let me pass, sir. You have lied enough upon your word of honour. 415
	[SIR ROBERT CHILTERN goes out. LORD GORING rushes to the door of the drawing-room, when MRS. CHEVELEY comes out, looking radiant and much amused.]
MRS. CHEVELEY:	[With a mock curtsey] Good evening, Lord Goring!
LORD GORING:	Mrs. Cheveley! Great heavens! . . . May I ask what you 420 were doing in my drawing-room?
MRS. CHEVELEY:	Merely listening. I have a perfect passion for listening through keyholes. One always hears such wonderful things through them.
LORD GORING:	Doesn't that sound rather like tempting Providence? 425
MRS. CHEVELEY:	Oh! surely Providence can resist temptation by this time. [Makes a sign to him to take her cloak off, which he does.]
LORD GORING:	I am glad you have called. I am going to give you some good advice.
MRS. CHEVELEY:	Oh! pray don't. One should never give a woman anything 430 that she can't wear in the evening.
LORD GORING:	I see you are quite as wilful as you used to be.
MRS. CHEVELEY:	Far more! I have greatly improved. I have had more experience.
LORD GORING:	Too much experience is a dangerous thing. Pray have a 435 cigarette. Half the pretty women in London smoke cigarettes. Personally I prefer the other half.

MRS. CHEVELEY:	Thanks. I never smoke. My dressmaker wouldn't like it, and a woman's first duty in life is to her dressmaker, isn't it? What the second duty is, no one has as yet discovered. 440
LORD GORING:	You have come here to sell me Robert Chiltern's letter, haven't you?
MRS. CHEVELEY:	To offer it to you on conditions. How did you guess that?
LORD GORING:	Because you haven't mentioned the subject. Have you got it with you? 445
MRS. CHEVELEY:	[Sitting down.] Oh, no! A well-made dress has no pockets.
LORD GORING:	What is your price for it?
MRS. CHEVELEY:	How absurdly English you are! The English think that a cheque-book can solve every problem in life. Why, my dear Arthur, I have very much more money than you have, 450 and quite as much as Robert Chiltern has got hold of. Money is not what I want.
LORD GORING:	What do you want then, Mrs. Cheveley?
MRS. CHEVELEY:	Why don't you call me Laura?
LORD GORING:	I don't like the name. 455
MRS. CHEVELEY:	You used to adore it.
LORD GORING:	Yes: that's why. [MRS. CHEVELEY motions to him to sit down beside her. He smiles, and does so.]
MRS. CHEVELEY:	Arthur, you loved me once.
LORD GORING:	Yes. 460
MRS. CHEVELEY:	And you asked me to be your wife.
LORD GORING:	That was the natural result of my loving you.
MRS. CHEVELEY:	And you threw me over because you saw, or said you saw, poor old Lord Mortlake trying to have a violent flirtation with me in the conservatory at Tenby. 465
LORD GORING:	I am under the impression that my lawyer settled that matter with you on certain terms . . . dictated by yourself.
MRS. CHEVELEY:	At that time I was poor; you were rich.
LORD GORING:	Quite so. That is why you pretended to love me.
MRS. CHEVELEY:	[Shrugging her shoulders.] Poor old Lord Mortlake, who 470 had only two topics of conversation, his gout and his wife! I never could quite make out which of the two he was talking about. He used the most horrible language about them both. Well, you were silly, Arthur. Why, Lord Mortlake was never anything more to me than an amusement. One 475 of those utterly tedious amusements one only finds at an English country house on an English country Sunday. I don't think any one at all morally responsible for what he or she does at an English country house.
LORD GORING:	Yes. I know lots of people think that. 480
MRS. CHEVELEY:	I loved you, Arthur.

LORD GORING:	My dear Mrs. Cheveley, you have always been far too clever to know anything about love.	
MRS. CHEVELEY:	I did love you. And you loved me. You know you loved me; and love is a very wonderful thing. I suppose that when a man has once loved a woman, he will do anything for her, except continue to love her? [Puts her hand on his.]	485
LORD GORING:	[Taking his hand away quietly.] Yes: except that.	
MRS. CHEVELEY:	[After a pause.] I am tired of living abroad. I want to come back to London. I want to have a charming house here. I want to have a salon. If one could only teach the English how to talk, and the Irish how to listen, society here would be quite civilised. Besides, I have arrived at the romantic stage. When I saw you last night at the Chilterns', I knew you were the only person I had ever cared for, if I ever have cared for anybody, Arthur. And so, on the morning of the day you marry me, I will give you Robert Chiltern's letter. That is my offer. I will give it to you now, if you promise to marry me.	490 495
LORD GORING:	Now?	
MRS. CHEVELEY:	[Smiling.] To-morrow.	500
LORD GORING:	Are you really serious?	
MRS. CHEVELEY:	Yes, quite serious.	
LORD GORING:	I should make you a very bad husband.	
MRS. CHEVELEY:	I don't mind bad husbands. I have had two. They amused me immensely.	505
LORD GORING.	You mean that you amused yourself immensely, don't you?	
MRS. CHEVELEY:	What do you know about my married life?	
LORD GORING:	Nothing: but I can read it like a book.	
MRS. CHEVELEY:	What book?	
LORD GORING:	[Rising.] The Book of Numbers.	510
MRS. CHEVELEY:	Do you think it is quite charming of you to be so rude to a woman in your own house?	
LORD GORING:	In the case of very fascinating women, sex is a challenge, not a defence.	
MRS. CHEVELEY:	I suppose that is meant for a compliment. My dear Arthur, women are never disarmed by compliments. Men always are. That is the difference between the two sexes.	515
LORD GORING:	Women are never disarmed by anything, as far as I know them.	
MRS. CHEVELEY:	[After a pause.] Then you are going to allow your greatest friend, Robert Chiltern, to be ruined, rather than marry some one who really has considerable attractions left. I thought you would have risen to some great height of self-sacrifice, Arthur. I think you should. And the rest of your life you could spend in contemplating your own perfections.	520 530

LORD GORING:	Oh! I do that as it is. And self-sacrifice is a thing that should be put down by law. It is so demoralising to the people for whom one sacrifices oneself. They always go to the bad.
MRS. CHEVELEY:	As if anything could demoralise Robert Chiltern! You seem to forget that I know his real character. 535
LORD GORING:	What you know about him is not his real character. It was an act of folly done in his youth, dishonourable, I admit, shameful, I admit, unworthy of him, I admit, and therefore . . . not his true character.
MRS. CHEVELEY:	How you men stand up for each other! 540
LORD GORING:	How you women war against each other!
MRS. CHEVELEY:	[Bitterly.] I only war against one woman, against Gertrude Chiltern. I hate her. I hate her now more than ever.
LORD GORING:	Because you have brought a real tragedy into her life, I suppose. 545
MRS. CHEVELEY:	[With a sneer.] Oh, there is only one real tragedy in a woman's life. The fact that her past is always her lover, and her future invariably her husband.
LORD GORING:	Lady Chiltern knows nothing of the kind of life to which you are alluding. 550
MRS. CHEVELEY:	A woman whose size in gloves is seven and three-quarters never knows much about anything. You know Gertrude has always worn seven and three-quarters? That is one of the reasons why there was never any moral sympathy between us. . . . Well, Arthur, I suppose this romantic 555 interview may be regarded as at an end. You admit it was romantic, don't you? For the privilege of being your wife I was ready to surrender a great prize, the climax of my diplomatic career. You decline. Very well. If Sir Robert doesn't uphold my Argentine scheme, I expose him. *Voile tout.* 560
LORD GORING:	You mustn't do that. It would be vile, horrible, infamous.
MRS. CHEVELEY:	[Shrugging her shoulders.] Oh! don't use big words. They mean so little. It is a commercial transaction. That is all. There is no good mixing up sentimentality in it. I offered to sell Robert Chiltern a certain thing. If he won't pay me my 565 price, he will have to pay the world a greater price. There is no more to be said. I must go. Good-bye. Won't you shake hands?
LORD GORING:	With you? No. Your transaction with Robert Chiltern may pass as a loathsome commercial transaction of a loath- 570 some commercial age; but you seem to have forgotten that you came here to-night to talk of love, you whose lips desecrated the word love, you to whom the thing is a book closely sealed, went this afternoon to the house of one of the most noble and gentle women in the world to degrade 575

	her husband in her eyes, to try and kill her love for him, to put poison in her heart, and bitterness in her life, to break her idol, and, it may be, spoil her soul. That I cannot forgive you. That was horrible. For that there can be no forgiveness.	580
MRS. CHEVELEY:	Arthur, you are unjust to me. Believe me, you are quite unjust to me. I didn't go to taunt Gertrude at all. I had no idea of doing anything of the kind when I entered. I called with Lady Markby simply to ask whether an ornament, a jewel, that I lost somewhere last night, had been found at the Chilterns'. If you don't believe me, you can ask Lady Markby. She will tell you it is true. The scene that occurred happened after Lady Markby had left, and was really forced on me by Gertrude's rudeness and sneers. I called, oh!—a little out of malice if you like—but really to ask if a diamond brooch of mine had been found. That was the origin of the whole thing.	585 590
LORD GORING:	A diamond snake-brooch with a ruby?	
MRS. CHEVELEY:	Yes. How do you know?	
LORD GORING:	Because it is found. In point of fact, I found it myself, and stupidly forgot to tell the butler anything about it as I was leaving. [Goes over to the writing-table and pulls out the drawers.] It is in this drawer. No, that one. This is the brooch, isn't it? [Holds up the brooch.]	595
MRS. CHEVELEY:	Yes. I am so glad to get it back. It was . . . a present.	600
LORD GORING:	Won't you wear it?	
MRS. CHEVELEY:	Certainly, if you pin it in. [LORD GORING suddenly clasps it on her arm.] Why do you put it on as a bracelet? I never knew it could be worn as a bracelet.	
LORD GORING:	Really?	605
MRS. CHEVELEY:	[Holding out her handsome arm.] No; but it looks very well on me as a bracelet, doesn't it?	
LORD GORING:	Yes; much better than when I saw it last.	
MRS. CHEVELEY:	When did you see it last?	
LORD GORING:	[Calmly.] Oh, ten years ago, on Lady Berkshire, from whom you stole it.	610
MRS. CHEVELEY:	[Starting.] What do you mean?	
LORD GORING:	I mean that you stole that ornament from my cousin, Mary Berkshire, to whom I gave it when she was married. Suspicion fell on a wretched servant, who was sent away in disgrace. I recognised it last night. I determined to say nothing about it till I had found the thief. I have found the thief now, and I have heard her own confession.	615
MRS. CHEVELEY:	[Tossing her head.] It is not true.	

LORD GORING:	You know it is true. Why, thief is written across your face at this moment. 620
MRS. CHEVELEY:	I will deny the whole affair from beginning to end. I will say that I have never seen this wretched thing, that it was never in my possession.
	[MRS. CHEVELEY tries to get the bracelet off her arm, but 625 fails. LORD GORING looks on amused. Her thin fingers tear at the jewel to no purpose. A curse breaks from her.]
LORD GORING:	The drawback of stealing a thing, Mrs. Cheveley, is that one never knows how wonderful the thing that one steals is. You can't get that bracelet off, unless you know where 630 the spring is. And I see you don't know where the spring is. It is rather difficult to find.
MRS. CHEVELEY:	You brute! You coward! [She tries again to unclasp the bracelet, but fails.]
LORD GORING:	Oh! don't use big words. They mean so little. 635
MRS. CHEVELEY:	[Again tears at the bracelet in a paroxysm of rage, with inarticulate sounds. Then stops, and looks at LORD GORING.] What are you going to do?
LORD GORING:	I am going to ring for my servant. He is an admirable servant. Always comes in the moment one rings for him. 640 When he comes I will tell him to fetch the police.
MRS. CHEVELEY:	[Trembling.] The police? What for?
LORD GORING:	To-morrow the Berkshires will prosecute you. That is what the police are for.
MRS. CHEVELEY:	[Is now in an agony of physical terror. Her face is distorted. 645 Her mouth awry. A mask has fallen from her. She is, for the moment, dreadful to look at.] Don't do that. I will do anything you want. Anything in the world you want.
LORD GORING:	Give me Robert Chiltern's letter.
MRS. CHEVELEY:	Stop! Stop! Let me have time to think. 650
LORD GORING:	Give me Robert Chiltern's letter.
MRS. CHEVELEY:	I have not got it with me. I will give it to you to-morrow.
LORD GORING:	You know you are lying. Give it to me at once. [MRS. CHEVELEY pulls the letter out, and hands it to him. She is horribly pale.] This is it? 655
MRS. CHEVELEY:	[In a hoarse voice.] Yes.
LORD GORING:	[Takes the letter, examines it, sighs, and burns it with the lamp.] For so well-dressed a woman, Mrs. Cheveley, you have moments of admirable common sense. I congratulate you.
MRS. CHEVELEY:	[Catches sight of LADY CHILTERN'S letter, the cover 660 of which is just showing from under the blotting-book.] Please get me a glass of water.

LORD GORING:	Certainly. [Goes to the corner of the room and pours out a glass of water. While his back is turned MRS. CHEVELEY steals LADY CHILTERN'S letter. When 665 LORD GORING returns the glass she refuses it with a gesture.]
MRS. CHEVELEY:	Thank you. Will you help me on with my cloak?
LORD GORING:	With pleasure. [Puts her cloak on.]
MRS. CHEVELEY:	Thanks. I am never going to try to harm Robert Chiltern again. 670
LORD GORING:	Fortunately you have not the chance, Mrs. Cheveley.
MRS. CHEVELEY:	Well, if even I had the chance, I wouldn't. On the contrary, I am going to render him a great service.
LORD GORING:	I am charmed to hear it. It is a reformation.
MRS. CHEVELEY:	Yes. I can't bear so upright a gentleman, so honourable 675 an English gentleman, being so shamefully deceived, and so—
LORD GORING:	Well?
MRS. CHEVELEY:	I find that somehow Gertrude Chiltern's dying speech and confession has strayed into my pocket. 680
LORD GORING:	What do you mean?
MRS. CHEVELEY:	[With a bitter note of triumph in her voice.] I mean that I am going to send Robert Chiltern the love-letter his wife wrote to you to-night.
LORD GORING:	Love-letter? 685
MRS. CHEVELEY:	[Laughing.] 'I want you. I trust you. I am coming to you. Gertrude.'
	[LORD GORING rushes to the bureau and takes up the envelope, finds it empty, and turns round.]
LORD GORING:	You wretched woman, must you always be thieving? Give 690 me back that letter. I'll take it from you by force. You shall not leave my room till I have got it.
	[He rushes towards her, but MRS. CHEVELEY at once puts her hand on the electric bell that is on the table. The bell sounds with shrill reverberations, and PHIPPS 695 enters.]
MRS. CHEVELEY:	[After a pause.] Lord Goring merely rang that you should show me out. Good-night, Lord Goring! [Goes out followed by PHIPPS. Her face is illumined with evil triumph. There is joy in her eyes. Youth seems to have come back to her. 700 Her last glance is like a swift arrow. LORD GORING bites his lip, and lights a cigarette.]

ACT DROPS

8.23.4 Act IV

SCENE

Same as Act II.

[LORD GORING is standing by the fireplace with his hands in his pockets. He is looking rather bored.]

LORD GORING:	[Pulls out his watch, inspects it, and rings the bell.] It is a great nuisance. I can't find any one in this house to talk to. And I am full of interesting information. I feel like the latest edition of something or other.
	[Enter servant.] 5
JAMES:	Sir Robert is still at the Foreign Office, my lord.
LORD GORING:	Lady Chiltern not down yet?
JAMES:	Her ladyship has not yet left her room. Miss Chiltern has just come in from riding.
LORD GORING:	[To himself.] Ah! that is something. 10
JAMES:	Lord Caversham has been waiting some time in the library for Sir Robert. I told him your lordship was here.
LORD GORING:	Thank you! Would you kindly tell him I've gone?
JAMES:	[Bowing.] I shall do so, my lord.
	[Exit servant.] 15
LORD GORING:	Really, I don't want to meet my father three days running. It is a great deal too much excitement for any son. I hope to goodness he won't come up. Fathers should be neither seen nor heard. That is the only proper basin for family life. Mothers are different. Mothers are darlings. [Throws himself 20 down into a chair, picks up a paper and begins to read it.]
	[Enter LORD CAVERSHAM.]
LORD CAVERSHAM:	Well, sir, what are you doing here? Wasting your time as usual, I suppose?
LORD GORING:	[Throws down paper and rises.] My dear father, when one 25 pays a visit it is for the purpose of wasting other people's time, not one's own.
LORD CAVERSHAM:	Have you been thinking over what I spoke to you about last night?
LORD GORING:	I have been thinking about nothing else. 30
LORD CAVERSHAM:	Engaged to be married yet?
LORD GORING:	[Genially.] Not yet: but I hope to be before lunch-time.
LORD CAVERSHAM:	[Caustically.] You can have till dinner-time if it would be of any convenience to you.
LORD GORING:	Thanks awfully, but I think I'd sooner be engaged before 35 lunch.

LORD CAVERSHAM:	Humph! Never know when you are serious or not.
LORD GORING:	Neither do I, father.
	[A pause.]
LORD CAVERSHAM:	I suppose you have read THE TIMES this morning? 40
LORD GORING:	[Airily.] THE TIMES? Certainly not. I only read *The Morning Post*. All that one should know about modern life is where the Duchesses are; anything else is quite demoralising.
LORD CAVERSHAM:	Do you mean to say you have not read *The Times* leading article on Robert Chiltern's career? 45
LORD GORING:	Good heavens! No. What does it say?
LORD CAVERSHAM:	What should it say, sir? Everything complimentary, of course. Chiltern's speech last night on this Argentine Canal scheme was one of the finest pieces of oratory ever delivered in the House since Canning. 50
LORD GORING:	Ah! Never heard of Canning. Never wanted to. And did . . . did Chiltern uphold the scheme?
LORD CAVERSHAM:	Uphold it, sir? How little you know him! Why, he denounced it roundly, and the whole system of modern political finance. This speech is the turning-point in his career, 55 as *The Times* points out. You should read this article, sir. [Opens *The Times*.] 'Sir Robert Chiltern . . . most rising of our young statesmen . . . Brilliant orator . . . Unblemished career . . . Well-known integrity of character . . . Represents what is best in English public life . . . Noble contrast 60 to the lax morality so common among foreign politicians.' They will never say that of you, sir.
LORD GORING:	I sincerely hope not, father. However, I am delighted at what you tell me about Robert, thoroughly delighted. It shows he has got pluck. 65
LORD CAVERSHAM:	He has got more than pluck, sir, he has got genius.
LORD GORING:	Ah! I prefer pluck. It is not so common, nowadays, as genius is.
LORD CAVERSHAM:	I wish you would go into Parliament.
LORD GORING:	My dear father, only people who look dull ever get into the 70 House of Commons, and only people who are dull ever succeed there.
LORD CAVERSHAM:	Why don't you try to do something useful in life?
LORD GORING:	I am far too young.
LORD CAVERSHAM:	[Testily.] I hate this affectation of youth, sir. It is a great deal 75 too prevalent nowadays.
LORD GORING:	Youth isn't an affectation. Youth is an art.
LORD CAVERSHAM:	Why don't you propose to that pretty Miss Chiltern?
LORD GORING:	I am of a very nervous disposition, especially in the morning. 80

LORD CAVERSHAM:	I don't suppose there is the smallest chance of her accepting you.
LORD GORING:	I don't know how the betting stands to-day.
LORD CAVERSHAM:	If she did accept you she would be the prettiest fool in England. 85
LORD GORING:	That is just what I should like to marry. A thoroughly sensible wife would reduce me to a condition of absolute idiocy in less than six months.
LORD CAVERSHAM:	You don't deserve her, sir.
LORD GORING:	My dear father, if we men married the women we de- 90 served, we should have a very bad time of it.
	[Enter MABEL CHILTERN.]
MABEL CHILTERN:	Oh! . . . How do you do, Lord Caversham? I hope Lady Caversham is quite well?
LORD CAVERSHAM:	Lady Caversham is as usual, as usual. 95
LORD GORING:	Good morning, Miss Mabel!
MABEL CHILTERN:	[Taking no notice at all of LORD GORING, and address- ing herself exclusively to LORD CAVERSHAM.] And Lady Caversham's bonnets . . . are they at all better?
LORD CAVERSHAM:	They have had a serious relapse, I am sorry to say. 100
LORD GORING:	Good morning, Miss Mabel!
MABEL CHILTERN:	[To LORD CAVERSHAM.] I hope an operation will not be necessary.
LORD CAVERSHAM:	[Smiling at her pertness.] If it is, we shall have to give Lady Caversham a narcotic. Otherwise she would never consent 105 to have a feather touched.
LORD GORING:	[With increased emphasis.] Good morning, Miss Mabel!
MABEL CHILTERN:	[Turning round with feigned surprise.] Oh, are you here? Of course you understand that after your breaking your appointment I am never going to speak to 110 you again.
LORD GORING:	Oh, please don't say such a thing. You are the one person in London I really like to have to listen to me.
MABEL CHILTERN:	Lord Goring, I never believe a single word that either you or I say to each other. 115
LORD CAVERSHAM:	You are quite right, my dear, quite right . . . as far as he is concerned, I mean.
MABEL CHILTERN:	Do you think you could possibly make your son behave a little better occasionally? Just as a change.
LORD CAVERSHAM:	I regret to say, Miss Chiltern, that I have no influence at 120 all over my son. I wish I had. If I had, I know what I would make him do.
MABEL CHILTERN:	I am afraid that he has one of those terribly weak natures that are not susceptible to influence.

LORD CAVERSHAM:	He is very heartless, very heartless.	125
LORD GORING:	It seems to me that I am a little in the way here.	
MABEL CHILTERN:	It is very good for you to be in the way, and to know what people say of you behind your back.	
LORD GORING:	I don't at all like knowing what people say of me behind my back. It makes me far too conceited.	130
LORD CAVERSHAM:	After that, my dear, I really must bid you good morning.	
MABEL CHILTERN:	Oh! I hope you are not going to leave me all alone with Lord Goring? Especially at such an early hour in the day.	
LORD CAVERSHAM:	I am afraid I can't take him with me to Downing Street. It is not the Prime Minster's day for seeing the unemployed. [Shakes hands with MABEL CHILTERN, takes up his hat and stick, and goes out, with a parting glare of indignation at LORD GORING.]	135
MABEL CHILTERN:	[Takes up roses and begins to arrange them in a bowl on the table.] People who don't keep their appointments in the Park are horrid.	140
LORD GORING:	Detestable.	
MABEL CHILTERN:	I am glad you admit it. But I wish you wouldn't look so pleased about it.	
LORD GORING:	I can't help it. I always look pleased when I am with you.	145
MABEL CHILTERN:	[Sadly.] Then I suppose it is my duty to remain with you?	
LORD GORING:	Of course it is.	
MABEL CHILTERN:	Well, my duty is a thing I never do, on principle. It always depresses me. So I am afraid I must leave you.	
LORD GORING:	Please don't, Miss Mabel. I have something very particular to say to you.	150
MABEL CHILTERN:	[Rapturously.] Oh! is it a proposal?	
LORD GORING:	[Somewhat taken aback.] Well, yes, it is—I am bound to say it is.	
MABEL CHILTERN:	[With a sigh of pleasure.] I am so glad. That makes the second to-day.	155
LORD GORING:	[Indignantly.] The second to-day? What conceited ass has been impertinent enough to dare to propose to you before I had proposed to you?	
MABEL CHILTERN:	Tommy Trafford, of course. It is one of Tommy's days for proposing. He always proposes on Tuesdays and Thursdays, during the Season.	160
LORD GORING:	You didn't accept him, I hope?	
MABEL CHILTERN:	I make it a rule never to accept Tommy. That is why he goes on proposing. Of course, as you didn't turn up this morning, I very nearly said yes. It would have been an excellent lesson both for him and for you if I had. It would have taught you both better manners.	165

LORD GORING:	Oh! bother Tommy Trafford. Tommy is a silly little ass. I love you.
MABEL CHILTERN:	I know. And I think you might have mentioned it before. I am sure I have given you heaps of opportunities.
LORD GORING:	Mabel, do be serious. Please be serious.
MABEL CHILTERN:	Ah! that is the sort of thing a man always says to a girl before he has been married to her. He never says it afterwards.
LORD GORING:	[Taking hold of her hand.] Mabel, I have told you that I love you. Can't you love me a little in return?
MABEL CHILTERN:	You silly Arthur! If you knew anything about . . . anything, which you don't, you would know that I adore you. Every one in London knows it except you. It is a public scandal the way I adore you. I have been going about for the last six months telling the whole of society that I adore you. I wonder you consent to have anything to say to me. I have no character left at all. At least, I feel so happy that I am quite sure I have no character left at all.
LORD GORING:	[Catches her in his arms and kisses her. Then there is a pause of bliss.] Dear! Do you know I was awfully afraid of being refused!
MABEL CHILTERN:	[Looking up at him.] But you never have been refused yet by anybody, have you, Arthur? I can't imagine any one refusing you.
LORD GORING:	[After kissing her again.] Of course I'm not nearly good enough for you, Mabel.
MABEL CHILTERN:	[Nestling close to him.] I am so glad, darling. I was afraid you were.
LORD GORING:	[After some hesitation.] And I'm . . . I'm a little over thirty.
MABEL CHILTERN:	Dear, you look weeks younger than that.
LORD GORING:	[Enthusiastically.] How sweet of you to say so! . . . And it is only fair to tell you frankly that I am fearfully extravagant.
MABEL CHILTERN:	But so am I, Arthur. So we're sure to agree. And now I must go and see Gertrude.
LORD GORING:	Must you really? [Kisses her.]
MABEL CHILTERN:	Yes.
LORD GORING:	Then do tell her I want to talk to her particularly. I have been waiting here all the morning to see either her or Robert.
MABEL CHILTERN:	Do you mean to say you didn't come here expressly to propose to me?
LORD GORING:	[Triumphantly.] No; that was a flash of genius.
MABEL CHILTERN:	Your first.
LORD GORING:	[With determination.] My last.

170

175

180

185

190

195

200

205

210

MABEL CHILTERN:	I am delighted to hear it. Now don't stir. I'll be back in five minutes. And don't fall into any temptations while I am away.
LORD GORING:	Dear Mabel, while you are away, there are none. It makes me horribly dependent on you. 215
	[Enter LADY CHILTERN.]
LADY CHILTERN:	Good morning, dear! How pretty you are looking!
MABEL CHILTERN:	How pale you are looking, Gertrude! It is most becoming!
LADY CHILTERN:	Good morning, Lord Goring! 220
LORD GORING:	[Bowing.] Good morning, Lady Chiltern!
MABEL CHILTERN:	[Aside to LORD GORING.] I shall be in the conservatory under the second palm tree on the left.
LORD GORING:	Second on the left?
MABEL CHILTERN:	[With a look of mock surprise.] Yes; the usual palm tree. 225 [Blows a kiss to him, unobserved by LADY CHILTERN, and goes out.]
LORD GORING:	Lady Chiltern, I have a certain amount of very good news to tell you. Mrs. Cheveley gave me up Robert's letter last night, and I burned it. Robert is safe. 230
LADY CHILTERN:	[Sinking on the sofa.] Safe! Oh! I am so glad of that. What a good friend you are to him—to us!
LORD GORING:	There is only one person now that could be said to be in any danger.
LADY CHILTERN:	Who is that? 235
LORD GORING:	[Sitting down beside her.] Yourself.
LADY CHILTERN:	I? In danger? What do you mean?
LORD GORING:	Danger is too great a word. It is a word I should not have used. But I admit I have something to tell you that may distress you, that terribly distresses me. Yesterday 240 evening you wrote me a very beautiful, womanly letter, asking me for my help. You wrote to me as one of your oldest friends, one of your husband's oldest friends. Mrs. Cheveley stole that letter from my rooms.
LADY CHILTERN:	Well, what use is it to her? Why should she not have it? 245
LORD GORING:	[Rising.] Lady Chiltern, I will be quite frank with you. Mrs. Cheveley puts a certain construction on that letter and proposes to send it to your husband.
LADY CHILTERN:	But what construction could she put on it? . . . Oh! not that! not that! If I in—in trouble, and wanting your help, 250 trusting you, propose to come to you . . . that you may advise me . . . assist me . . . Oh! are there women so horrible as that . . .? And she proposes to send it to my husband? Tell me what happened. Tell me all that happened.
LORD GORING:	Mrs. Cheveley was concealed in a room adjoining my 255 library, without my knowledge. I thought that the person

who was waiting in that room to see me was yourself.
Robert came in unexpectedly. A chair or something fell in
the room. He forced his way in, and he discovered her. We
had a terrible scene. I still thought it was you. He left me in   260
anger. At the end of everything Mrs. Cheveley got possession of your letter—she stole it, when or how, I don't know.

LADY CHILTERN: At what hour did this happen?

LORD GORING: At half-past ten. And now I propose that we tell Robert the
whole thing at once.   265

LADY CHILTERN: [Looking at him with amazement that is almost terror.] You
want me to tell Robert that the woman you expected was
not Mrs. Cheveley, but myself? That it was I whom you
thought was concealed in a room in your house, at half-
past ten o'clock at night? You want me to tell him that?   270

LORD GORING: I think it is better that he should know the exact truth.

LADY CHILTERN: [Rising.] Oh, I couldn't, I couldn't!

LORD GORING: May I do it?

LADY CHILTERN: No.

LORD GORING: [Gravely.] You are wrong, Lady Chiltern.   275

LADY CHILTERN: No. The letter must be intercepted. That is all. But how can
I do it? Letters arrive for him every moment of the day. His
secretaries open them and hand them to him. I dare not
ask the servants to bring me his letters. It would be impossible. Oh! why don't you tell me what to do?   280

LORD GORING: Pray be calm, Lady Chiltern, and answer the questions I
am going to put to you. You said his secretaries open his
letters.

LADY CHILTERN: Yes.

LORD GORING: Who is with him to-day? Mr. Trafford, isn't it?   285

LADY CHILTERN: No. Mr. Montford, I think.

LORD GORING: You can trust him?

LADY CHILTERN: [With a gesture of despair.] Oh! how do I know?

LORD GORING: He would do what you asked him, wouldn't he?

LADY CHILTERN: I think so.   290

LORD GORING: Your letter was on pink paper. He could recognise it without reading it, couldn't he? By the colour?

LADY CHILTERN: I suppose so.

LORD GORING: Is he in the house now?

LADY CHILTERN: Yes.   295

LORD GORING: Then I will go and see him myself, and tell him that a certain
letter, written on pink paper, is to be forwarded to Robert
to-day, and that at all costs it must not reach him. [Goes to
the door, and opens it.] Oh! Robert is coming upstairs with
the letter in his hand. It has reached him already.   300

LADY CHILTERN:	[With a cry of pain.] Oh! you have saved his life; what have you done with mine?
	[Enter SIR ROBERT CHILTERN. He has the letter in his hand, and is reading it. He comes towards his wife, not noticing LORD GORING'S presence.] 305
SIR ROBERT CHILTERN:	'I want you. I trust you. I am coming to you. Gertrude.' Oh, my love! Is this true? Do you indeed trust me, and want me? If so, it was for me to come to you, not for you to write of coming to me. This letter of yours, Gertrude, makes me feel that nothing that the world may do can 310 hurt me now. You want me, Gertrude?
	[LORD GORING, unseen by SIR ROBERT CHILTERN, makes an imploring sign to LADY CHILTERN to accept the situation and SIR ROBERT'S error.]
LADY CHILTERN:	Yes. 315
SIR ROBERT CHILTERN:	You trust me, Gertrude?
LADY CHILTERN:	Yes.
SIR ROBERT CHILTERN:	Ah! why did you not add you loved me?
LADY CHILTERN:	[Taking his hand.] Because I loved you.
	[LORD GORING passes into the conservatory.] 320
SIR ROBERT CHILTERN:	[Kisses her.] Gertrude, you don't know what I feel. When Montford passed me your letter across the table—he had opened it by mistake, I suppose, without looking at the handwriting on the envelope—and I read it—oh! I did not care what disgrace or punishment was in store for me, I 325 only thought you loved me still.
LADY CHILTERN:	There is no disgrace in store for you, nor any public shame. Mrs. Cheveley has handed over to Lord Goring the document that was in her possession, and he has destroyed it. 330
SIR ROBERT CHILTERN:	Are you sure of this, Gertrude?
LADY CHILTERN:	Yes; Lord Goring has just told me.
SIR ROBERT CHILTERN:	Then I am safe! Oh! what a wonderful thing to be safe! For two days I have been in terror. I am safe now. How did Arthur destroy my letter? Tell me. 335
LADY CHILTERN:	He burned it.
SIR ROBERT CHILTERN:	I wish I had seen that one sin of my youth burning to ashes. How many men there are in modern life who would like to see their past burning to white ashes before them! Is Arthur still here? 340
LADY CHILTERN:	Yes; he is in the conservatory.
SIR ROBERT CHILTERN:	I am so glad now I made that speech last night in the House, so glad. I made it thinking that public disgrace might be the result. But it has not been so.
LADY CHILTERN:	Public honour has been the result. 345

SIR ROBERT CHILTERN:	I think so. I fear so, almost. For although I am safe from detection, although every proof against me is destroyed, I suppose, Gertrude . . . I suppose I should retire from public life? [He looks anxiously at his wife.]
LADY CHILTERN:	[Eagerly.] Oh yes, Robert, you should do that. It is your duty to do that.
SIR ROBERT CHILTERN:	It is much to surrender.
LADY CHILTERN:	No; it will be much to gain. [SIR ROBERT CHILTERN walks up and down the room with a troubled expression. Then comes over to his wife, and puts his hand on her shoulder.]
SIR ROBERT CHILTERN:	And you would be happy living somewhere alone with me, abroad perhaps, or in the country away from London, away from public life? You would have no regrets?
LADY CHILTERN:	Oh! none, Robert.
SIR ROBERT CHILTERN:	[Sadly.] And your ambition for me? You used to be ambitious for me.
LADY CHILTERN:	Oh, my ambition! I have none now, but that we two may love each other. It was your ambition that led you astray. Let us not talk about ambition. [LORD GORING returns from the conservatory, looking very pleased with himself, and with an entirely new buttonhole that some one has made for him.]
SIR ROBERT CHILTERN:	[Going towards him.] Arthur, I have to thank you for what you have done for me. I don't know how I can repay you. [Shakes hands with him.]
LORD GORING:	My dear fellow, I'll tell you at once. At the present moment, under the usual palm tree . . . I mean in the conservatory . . . [Enter MASON.]
MASON:	Lord Caversham.
LORD GORING:	That admirable father of mine really makes a habit of turning up at the wrong moment. It is very heartless of him, very heartless indeed. [Enter LORD CAVERSHAM. MASON goes out.]
LORD CAVERSHAM:	Good morning, Lady Chiltern! Warmest congratulations to you, Chiltern, on your brilliant speech last night. I have just left the Prime Minister, and you are to have the vacant seat in the Cabinet.
SIR ROBERT CHILTERN:	[With a look of joy and triumph.] A seat in the Cabinet?
LORD CAVERSHAM:	Yes; here is the Prime Minister's letter. [Hands letter.]
SIR ROBERT CHILTERN:	[Takes letter and reads it.] A seat in the Cabinet!
LORD CAVERSHAM:	Certainly, and you well deserve it too. You have got what we want so much in political life nowadays—high character, high moral tone, high principles. [To LORD GORING.] Everything that you have not got, sir, and never will have.

350

355

360

365

370

375

380

385

390

LORD GORING:	I don't like principles, father. I prefer prejudices.
	[SIR ROBERT CHILTERN is on the brink of accepting the Prime Minister's offer, when he sees wife looking at him with her clear, candid eyes. He then realises that it is impossible.] 395
SIR ROBERT CHILTERN:	I cannot accept this offer, Lord Caversham. I have made up my mind to decline it.
LORD CAVERSHAM:	Decline it, sir!
SIR ROBERT CHILTERN:	My intention is to retire at once from public life.
LORD CAVERSHAM:	[Angrily.] Decline a seat in the Cabinet, and retire from pub- 400 lic life? Never heard such damned nonsense in the whole course of my existence. I beg your pardon, Lady Chiltern. Chiltern, I beg your pardon. [To LORD GORING.] Don't grin like that, sir.
LORD GORING:	No, father. 405
LORD CAVERSHAM:	Lady Chiltern, you are a sensible woman, the most sensible woman in London, the most sensible woman I know. Will you kindly prevent your husband from making such a . . . from taking such . . . Will you kindly do that, Lady Chiltern? 410
LADY CHILTERN:	I think my husband is right in his determination, Lord Caversham. I approve of it.
LORD CAVERSHAM:	You approve of it? Good heavens!
LADY CHILTERN:	[Taking her husband's hand.] I admire him for it. I admire him immensely for it. I have never admired him so much 415 before. He is finer than even I thought him. [To SIR ROBERT CHILTERN.] You will go and write your letter to the Prime Minister now, won't you? Don't hesitate about it, Robert.
SIR ROBERT CHILTERN:	[With a touch of bitterness.] I suppose I had better write 420 it at once. Such offers are not repeated. I will ask you to excuse me for a moment, Lord Caversham.
LADY CHILTERN:	I may come with you, Robert, may I not?
SIR ROBERT CHILTERN:	Yes, Gertrude.
	[LADY CHILTERN goes out with him.] 425
LORD CAVERSHAM:	What is the matter with this family? Something wrong here, eh? [Tapping his forehead.] Idiocy? Hereditary, I suppose. Both of them, too. Wife as well as husband. Very sad. Very sad indeed! And they are not an old family. Can't understand it. 430
LORD GORING:	It is not idiocy, father, I assure you.
LORD CAVERSHAM:	What is it then, sir?
LORD GORING:	[After some hesitation.] Well, it is what is called nowadays a high moral tone, father. That is all.

LORD CAVERSHAM:	Hate these new-fangled names. Same thing as we used to call idiocy fifty years ago. Shan't stay in this house any longer.	435
LORD GORING:	[Taking his arm.] Oh! just go in here for a moment, father. Third palm tree to the left, the usual palm tree.	
LORD CAVERSHAM:	What, sir?	440
LORD GORING:	I beg your pardon, father, I forgot. The conservatory, father, the conservatory—there is some one there I want you to talk to.	
LORD CAVERSHAM:	What about, sir?	
LORD GORING:	About me, father,	445
LORD CAVERSHAM:	[Grimly.] Not a subject on which much eloquence is possible.	
LORD GORING:	No, father; but the lady is like me. She doesn't care much for eloquence in others. She thinks it a little loud.	
	[LORD CAVERSHAM goes out into the conservatory. LADY CHILTERN enters.]	450
LORD GORING:	Lady Chiltern, why are you playing Mrs. Cheveley's cards?	
LADY CHILTERN:	[Startled.] I don't understand you.	
LORD GORING:	Mrs. Cheveley made an attempt to ruin your husband. Either to drive him from public life, or to make him adopt a dishonourable position. From the latter tragedy you saved him. The former you are now thrusting on him. Why should you do him the wrong Mrs. Cheveley tried to do and failed?	455
LADY CHILTERN:	Lord Goring?	460
LORD GORING:	[Pulling himself together for a great effort, and showing the philosopher that underlies the dandy.] Lady Chiltern, allow me. You wrote me a letter last night in which you said you trusted me and wanted my help. Now is the moment when you really want my help, now is the time when you have got to trust me, to trust in my counsel and judgment. You love Robert. Do you want to kill his love for you? What sort of existence will he have if you rob him of the fruits of his ambition, if you take him from the splendour of a great political career, if you close the doors of public life against him, if you condemn him to sterile failure, he who was made for triumph and success? Women are not meant to judge us, but to forgive us when we need forgiveness. Pardon, not punishment, is their mission. Why should you scourge him with rods for a sin done in his youth, before he knew you, before he knew himself? A man's life is of more value than a woman's. It has larger issues, wider scope, greater ambitions. A woman's life revolves in curves of emotions. It is upon lines of intellect that a man's life progresses. Don't make any terrible mistake,	465 470 475

	Lady Chiltern. A woman who can keep a man's love, and love him in return, has done all the world wants of women, or should want of them.	480
LADY CHILTERN:	[Troubled and hesitating.] But it is my husband himself who wishes to retire from public life. He feels it is his duty. It was he who first said so.	485
LORD GORING:	Rather than lose your love, Robert would do anything, wreck his whole career, as he is on the brink of doing now. He is making for you a terrible sacrifice. Take my advice, Lady Chiltern, and do not accept a sacrifice so great. If you do, you will live to repent it bitterly. We men and women are not made to accept such sacrifices from each other. We are not worthy of them. Besides, Robert has been punished enough.	490
LADY CHILTERN:	We have both been punished. I set him up too high.	
LORD GORING:	[With deep feeling in his voice.] Do not for that reason set him down now too low. If he has fallen from his altar, do not thrust him into the mire. Failure to Robert would be the very mire of shame. Power is his passion. He would lose everything, even his power to feel love. Your husband's life is at this moment in your hands, your husband's love is in your hands. Don't mar both for him.	495
		500
	[Enter SIR ROBERT CHILTERN.]	
SIR ROBERT CHILTERN:	Gertrude, here is the draft of my letter. Shall I read it to you?	
LADY CHILTERN:	Let me see it.	
	[SIR ROBERT hands her the letter. She reads it, and then, with a gesture of passion, tears it up.]	505
SIR ROBERT CHILTERN:	What are you doing?	
LADY CHILTERN:	A man's life is of more value than a woman's. It has larger issues, wider scope, greater ambitions. Our lives revolve in curves of emotions. It is upon lines of intellect that a man's life progresses. I have just learnt this, and much else with it, from Lord Goring. And I will not spoil your life for you, nor see you spoil it as a sacrifice to me, a useless sacrifice!	510
SIR ROBERT CHILTERN:	Gertrude! Gertrude!	
LADY CHILTERN:	You can forget. Men easily forget. And I forgive. That is how women help the world. I see that now.	515
SIR ROBERT CHILTERN:	[Deeply overcome by emotion, embraces her.] My wife! my wife! [To LORD GORING.] Arthur, it seems that I am always to be in your debt.	
LORD GORING:	Oh dear no, Robert. Your debt is to Lady Chiltern, not to me!	520
SIR ROBERT CHILTERN:	I owe you much. And now tell me what you were going to ask me just now as Lord Caversham came in.	

LORD GORING:	Robert, you are your sister's guardian, and I want your consent to my marriage with her. That is all. 525
LADY CHILTERN:	Oh, I am so glad! I am so glad! [Shakes hands with LORD GORING.]
LORD GORING:	Thank you, Lady Chiltern.
SIR ROBERT CHILTERN:	[With a troubled look.] My sister to be your wife?
LORD GORING:	Yes. 530
SIR ROBERT CHILTERN:	[Speaking with great firmness.] Arthur, I am very sorry, but the thing is quite out of the question. I have to think of Mabel's future happiness. And I don't think her happiness would be safe in your hands. And I cannot have her sacrificed! 535
LORD GORING:	Sacrificed!
SIR ROBERT CHILTERN:	Yes, utterly sacrificed. Loveless marriages are horrible. But there is one thing worse than an absolutely loveless marriage. A marriage in which there is love, but on one side only; faith, but on one side only; devotion, but on one 540 side only, and in which of the two hearts one is sure to be broken.
LORD GORING:	But I love Mabel. No other woman has any place in my life.
LADY CHILTERN:	Robert, if they love each other, why should they not be married? 545
SIR ROBERT CHILTERN:	Arthur cannot bring Mabel the love that she deserves.
LORD GORING:	What reason have you for saying that?
SIR ROBERT CHILTERN:	[After a pause.] Do you really require me to tell you?
LORD GORING:	Certainly I do.
SIR ROBERT CHILTERN:	As you choose. When I called on you yesterday evening 550 I found Mrs. Cheveley concealed in your rooms. It was between ten and eleven o'clock at night. I do not wish to say anything more. Your relations with Mrs. Cheveley have, as I said to you last night, nothing whatsoever to do with me. I know you were engaged to be married to her once. 555 The fascination she exercised over you then seems to have returned. You spoke to me last night of her as of a woman pure and stainless, a woman whom you respected and honoured. That may be so. But I cannot give my sister's life into your hands. It would be wrong of me. It would be 560 unjust, infamously unjust to her.
LORD GORING:	I have nothing more to say.
LADY CHILTERN:	Robert, it was not Mrs. Cheveley whom Lord Goring expected last night.
SIR ROBERT CHILTERN:	Not Mrs. Cheveley! Who was it then? 565
LORD GORING:	Lady Chiltern!

LADY CHILTERN:	It was your own wife. Robert, yesterday afternoon Lord Goring told me that if ever I was in trouble I could come to him for help, as he was our oldest and best friend. Later on, after that terrible scene in this room, I wrote to him telling 570 him that I trusted him, that I had need of him, that I was coming to him for help and advice. [SIR ROBERT CHILTERN takes the letter out of his pocket.] Yes, that letter. I didn't go to Lord Goring's, after all. I felt that it is from ourselves alone that help can come. Pride made me think that. 575 Mrs. Cheveley went. She stole my letter and sent it anonymously to you this morning, that you should think . . . Oh! Robert, I cannot tell you what she wished you to think. . . .
SIR ROBERT CHILTERN:	What! Had I fallen so low in your eyes that you thought that even for a moment I could have doubted your goodness? 580 Gertrude, Gertrude, you are to me the white image of all good things, and sin can never touch you. Arthur, you can go to Mabel, and you have my best wishes! Oh! stop a moment. There is no name at the beginning of this letter. The brilliant Mrs. Cheveley does not seem to have noticed 585 that. There should be a name.
LADY CHILTERN:	Let me write yours. It is you I trust and need. You and none else.
LORD GORING:	Well, really, Lady Chiltern, I think I should have back my own letter. 590
LADY CHILTERN:	[Smiling.] No; you shall have Mabel. [Takes the letter and writes her husband's name on it.]
LORD GORING:	Well, I hope she hasn't changed her mind. It's nearly twenty minutes since I saw her last. [Enter MABEL CHILTERN and LORD CAVERSHAM.] 595
MABEL CHILTERN:	Lord Goring, I think your father's conversation much more improving than yours. I am only going to talk to Lord Caversham in the future, and always under the usual palm tree.
LORD GORING:	Darling! [Kisses her.]
LORD CAVERSHAM:	[Considerably taken aback.] What does this mean, sir? You 600 don't mean to say that this charming, clever young lady has been so foolish as to accept you?
LORD GORING:	Certainly, father! And Chiltern's been wise enough to accept the seat in the Cabinet.
LORD CAVERSHAM:	I am very glad to hear that, Chiltern . . . I congratulate you, 605 sir. If the country doesn't go to the dogs or the Radicals, we shall have you Prime Minister, some day. [Enter MASON.]
MASON:	Luncheon is on the table, my Lady! [MASON goes out.] 610
MABEL CHILTERN:	You'll stop to luncheon, Lord Caversham, won't you?

LORD CAVERSHAM:	With pleasure, and I'll drive you down to Downing Street afterwards, Chiltern. You have a great future before you, a great future. Wish I could say the same for you, sir. [To LORD GORING.] But your career will have to be entirely domestic. 615
LORD GORING:	Yes, father, I prefer it domestic.
LORD CAVERSHAM:	And if you don't make this young lady an ideal husband, I'll cut you off with a shilling.
MABEL CHILTERN:	An ideal husband! Oh, I don't think I should like that. It sounds like something in the next world. 620
LORD CAVERSHAM:	What do you want him to be then, dear?
MABEL CHILTERN:	He can be what he chooses. All I want is to be . . . to be . . . oh! a real wife to him.
LORD CAVERSHAM:	Upon my word, there is a good deal of common sense in that, Lady Chiltern. 625
	[They all go out except SIR ROBERT CHILTERN. He sinks in a chair, wrapt in thought. After a little time LADY CHILTERN returns to look for him.]
LADY CHILTERN:	[Leaning over the back of the chair.] Aren't you coming in, Robert? 630
SIR ROBERT CHILTERN:	[Taking her hand.] Gertrude, is it love you feel for me, or is it pity merely?
LADY CHILTERN:	[Kisses him.] It is love, Robert. Love, and only love. For both of us a new life is beginning.
	CURTAIN

Critical Thinking Topics

1. Oscar Wilde is known for his clever phrasing and sharp wit. Choose two witticisms from this play. Explain how each one illustrates a character trait of the speaker and how each illustrates an aspect of Victorian society.

2. Mrs. Cheveley hopes to blackmail Sir Robert Chiltern based on her knowledge that he once committed a criminal fraud, which earned him his political position. Since that time, Sir Robert has been honest and honorable, but the revelation of his crime would ruin his career. How important is it for a politician to be and to always have been completely honest? Explain your response.

3. The title of the play is *An Ideal Husband.* Is there an ideal husband in this play, or even more than one? If so, who? And what qualities make him (or them) "ideal"? If not, explain why none of the husbands is "ideal."

Writing Topic

Lady Chiltern, Mrs. Cheveley, and Mabel Chiltern have wildly different personalities, but they are all strong and empowered women. During the Victorian era, women's rights in Britain were beginning to improve, in large part due to the efforts of privileged women like Lady Chiltern. Research British and American laws and customs regarding courtship and marriage in the late nineteenth century. How has the social and legal position of women improved in the last century in Britain and the United States, and what improvements still need to be made (if any)? Use specific examples to elaborate.

8.24 Nonfiction

The nine nonfiction pieces in this section, spanning the years from 1865 through 2018, explore topics and issues related to the theme of power and responsibility.

8.25 Abraham Lincoln, Second Inaugural Address (March 4, 1865)

At this second appearing to take the oath of the presidential office, there is less occasion for an extended address than there was at the first. Then a statement, somewhat in detail, of a course to be pursued, seemed fitting and proper. Now, at the expiration of four years, during which public declarations have been constantly called forth on every point and phase of the great contest which still absorbs the attention, and engrosses the energies of the nation, little that is new could be presented. The progress of our arms, upon which all else chiefly depends, is as well known to the public as to myself; and it is, I trust, reasonably satisfactory and encouraging to all. With high hope for the future, no prediction in regard to it is ventured.

On the occasion corresponding to this four years ago, all thoughts were anxiously directed to an impending civil war. All dreaded it—all sought to avert it. While the inaugural address was being delivered from this place, devoted altogether to *saving* the Union without war, insurgent agents were in the city seeking to *destroy* it without war—seeking to dissol[v]e the Union, and divide effects, by negotiation. Both parties deprecated war; but one of them would *make* war rather than let the nation survive; and the other would *accept* war rather than let it perish. And the war came.

One eighth of the whole population were colored slaves, not distributed generally over the Union, but localized in the Southern part of it. These slaves constituted a peculiar and powerful interest. All knew that this interest was, somehow, the cause of the war. To strengthen, perpetuate, and extend this interest was the object for which the insurgents would rend the Union, even by war; while the government claimed no right to do more than to restrict the territorial enlargement of it. Neither party expected for the war, the magnitude, or the duration, which it has already attained. Neither anticipated that the *cause* of the conflict might cease with, or even before, the conflict itself should cease. Each looked for an easier triumph, and a result less fundamental and astounding. Both read the same Bible, and pray to the same God; and each invokes His aid against the other. It may seem strange that any men should dare to ask a just God's assistance in wringing their bread from the sweat of other men's faces; but let us judge not that we be not judged. The prayers of both could not be answered; that of neither has been answered fully. The Almighty has his own purposes. "Woe unto the world because of offences! for it must needs be that offences come; but woe to that man by whom the offence cometh!" If we shall suppose that American Slavery is one of those offences which, in the providence of God, must needs come, but which, having continued through His appointed time, He now wills to remove, and that He gives to both North and South, this terrible war, as the woe due to those by whom the offence came, shall we discern therein any departure from those divine attributes which the believers in a Living God always ascribe to Him? Fondly do we hope—fervently do we pray—that this mighty scourge of war may speedily pass away. Yet, if God wills that it continue, until all the wealth piled by the bond-man's two hundred and fifty years of unrequited toil shall be sunk, and until every drop of blood drawn with the lash, shall be paid by another drawn with the sword, as was said three thousand years ago, so still it must be said "the judgments of the Lord, are true and righteous altogether."

With malice toward none; with charity for all; with firmness in the right, as God gives us to see the right, let us strive on to finish the work we are in; to bind up the nation's wounds; to care for him who shall have borne the battle, and for his widow, and his orphan—to do all which may achieve and cherish a just and lasting peace, among ourselves, and with all nations.

Critical Thinking Topics

1. What do you see as Lincoln's primary purpose in this address?
2. Identify passages that illustrate each of the rhetorical appeals—*ethos, logos,* and *pathos.*
3. List several value assumptions about leadership that Lincoln's address illustrates. Then think of at least two individuals—living now or from recent history, people you know or just know about—who represent the leadership values you listed. Describe how each person demonstrates the attributes of a leader.

Writing Topics

1. Select a passage that stands out for you. Write out the passage; read it out loud; and write a three-part response:
   - Creative reading—consider the sound and rhythm, diction and imagery.
   - Critical reading—consider the tone and message.
   - Synthesis of creative and critical readings—consider political speech today and in recent times. Write about one or more leaders whose speeches have motivated and inspired a diverse audience. If you cannot think of any such leaders, discuss the reasons why they do not exist.
2. What is the state of public speech and political rhetoric as a persuasive tool today? Is it constructive or destructive? What is working well, and what seems to have broken down? In the era of social media—including tweets—has public speech become an outdated tool? Use examples to elaborate. (In responding, you might wish to consider Bret Stephens's "The Dying Art of Disagreement," also in this chapter.)

8.26 Chief Joseph, "I will fight no more forever" (October 5, 1877)

I am tired of fighting. Our chiefs are killed. Looking Glass is dead. Toohoolhoolzote is dead. The old men are all dead. It is the young men who say, "Yes" or "No." He who led the young men [Olikut] is dead. It is cold, and we have no blankets. The little children are freezing to death. My people, some of them, have run away to the hills, and have no blankets, no food. No one knows where they are—perhaps freezing to death. I want to have time to look for my children, and see how many of them I can find. Maybe I shall find them among the dead. Hear me, my chiefs! I am tired. My heart is sick and sad. From where the sun now stands I will fight no more forever.

Critical Thinking Topics

1. Read about Chief Joseph online and in the Authors' Biographical Notes in this text. In the 140 years since he spoke these words when formally surrendering to the U.S. Army, to what extent have circumstances changed for Native Americans?

2. Recall a time in your life when you or someone close to you suffered an injustice but decided to accept it rather than keep fighting. What circumstances and considerations led to that decision? What emotions accompanied that decision?

Writing Topics

Chief Joseph's brief speech touched the hearts of a great many Americans, and he became a famous figure in popular culture. He met presidents Hayes and Roosevelt in Washington D.C. His surrender speech creates a strong appeal to *pathos*; cite several examples of this appeal in Chief Joseph's speech. Discuss the strengths as well as the weaknesses of the appeal to *pathos*, using the example of Chief Joseph's speech and words spoken by other public figures who have succeeded in capturing the hearts of the American public.

8.27 Richard Wright, from Black Boy (American Hunger) (1937)

One morning I arrived early at work and went into the bank lobby where the Negro porter was mopping. I stood at a counter and picked up the Memphis *Commercial Appeal* and began my free reading of the press. I came finally to the editorial page and saw an article dealing with one H. L. Mencken. I knew by hearsay that he was the editor of the *American Mercury,* but aside from that I knew nothing about him. The article was a furious denunciation of Mencken, concluding with one, hot, short sentence: Mencken is a fool.

I wondered what on earth this Mencken had done to call down upon him the scorn of the South. The only people I had ever heard denounced in the South were Negroes, and this man was not a Negro. Then what ideas did Mencken hold that made a newspaper like the *Commercial Appeal* castigate him publicly? Undoubtedly he must be advocating ideas that the South did not like. Were there, then, people other than Negroes who criticized the South? I knew that during the Civil War the South had hated northern whites, but I had not encountered such hate during my life. Knowing no more of Mencken than I did at that moment, I felt a vague sympathy for him. Had not the South, which had assigned me the role of a non-man, cast at him its hardest words?

Now, how could I find out about this Mencken? There was a huge library near the riverfront, but I knew that Negroes were not allowed to patronize its shelves any more than they were the parks and playgrounds of the city. I had gone into the library several times to get books for the white men on the job. Which of them would now help me to get books? And how could I read them without causing concern to the white men with whom I worked? I had so far been successful in hiding my thoughts and feelings from them, but I knew that I would create hostility if I went about the business of reading in a clumsy way.

I weighed the personalities of the men on the job. There was Don, a Jew; but I distrusted him. His position was not much better than mine and I knew that he was uneasy and insecure; he had always treated me in an offhand, bantering way that barely concealed his contempt. I was afraid to ask him to help me get books; his frantic desire to demonstrate a racial solidarity with the whites against Negroes might make him betray me.

Then how about the boss? No, he was a Baptist and I had the suspicion that he   5
would not be quite able to comprehend why a black boy would want to read Mencken. There were other white men on the job whose attitudes showed clearly that they were Kluxers or sympathizers, and they were out of the question.

There remained only one man whose attitude did not fit into an anti-Negro category, for I had heard the white men refer to him as a "Pope lover." He was an Irish Catholic and was hated by the white southerners. I knew that he read books, because I had got him volumes from the library several times. Since he, too, was an object of hatred, I felt that he might refuse me but would hardly betray me. I hesitated, weighing and balancing the imponderable realities.

One morning I paused before the Catholic fellow's desk.

"I want to ask you a favor," I whispered to him.

"What is it?"

"I want to read. I can't get books from the library. I wonder if you'd let me use your   10
card?"

He looked at me suspiciously.

"My card is full most of the time," he said.

"I see," I said and waited, posing my question silently.

"You're not trying to get me into trouble, are you, boy?" He asked, staring at me.

"Oh, no sir."   15

"What book do you want?"

"A book by H. L. Mencken."

"Which one?"

"I don't know. Has he written more than one?"

"He has written several."   20

"I didn't know that."

"What makes you want to read Mencken?"

"Oh, I just saw his name in the newspaper," I said.

"It's good of you to want to read," he said. "But you ought to read the right things."

I said nothing. Would he want to supervise my reading?   25

"Let me think," he said. "I'll figure out something."

I turned from him and he called me back. He stared at me quizzically.

"Richard, don't mention this to the other white men," he said.

"I understand," I said. "I won't say a word."

A few days later he called me to him.   30

"I've got a card in my wife's name," he said. "Here's mine."

"Thank you, sir."

"Do you think you can manage it?"

"I'll manage fine," I said.

"If they suspect you, you'll get in trouble," he said.   35

"I'll write the same kind of notes to the library that you wrote when you sent me for books," I told him. "I'll sign your name."

He laughed.

"Go ahead. Let me see what you get," he said.

That afternoon I addressed myself to forging a note. Now, what were the names of books written by H. L. Mencken? I did not know any of them. I finally wrote what I thought would be a foolproof note: *Dear Madam: Will you please let this nigger boy*—I used the word "nigger" to make the librarian feel that I could not possibly be the author of the note—*have some books by H. L. Mencken?* I forged the white man's name.

I entered the library as I had always done when on errands for whites, but I felt that   40
I would somehow slip up and betray myself. I doffed my hat, stood a respectful distance from the desk, looked as unbookish as possible, and waited for the white patrons to be taken care of. When the desk was clear of people, I still waited. The white librarian looked at me.

"What do you want, boy?"

As though I did not possess the power of speech, I stepped forward and simply handed her the forged note, not parting my lips.

"What books by Mencken does he want?" she asked.

"I don't know, ma'am," I said, avoiding her eyes.

"Who gave you this card?"   45

"Mr. Falk," I said.

"Where is he?"

"He's at work, at the M—— Optical Company," I said. "I've been in here for him before."

"I remember," the woman said. "But he never wrote notes like this."

Oh, God, she's suspicious. Perhaps she would not let me have the books? If she   50
had turned her back at that moment, I would have ducked out the door and never gone back. Then I thought of a bold idea.

"You can call him up, ma'am," I said, my heart pounding.

"You're not using these books, are you?" she asked pointedly.

"Oh, no, ma'am. I can't read."

"I don't know what he wants by Mencken," she said under her breath.

I knew now that I had won; she was thinking of other things and the race question   55
had gone out of her mind. She went to the shelves. Once or twice she looked over her

shoulder at me, as though she was still doubtful. Finally she came forward with two books in her hand.

"I'm sending him two books," she said. "But tell Mr. Falk to come in next time, or send me the names of the books he wants. I don't know what he wants to read."

I said nothing. She stamped the card and handed me the books. Not daring to glance at them, I went out of the library, fearing that the woman would call me back for further questioning. A block away from the library I opened one of the books and read a title: *A Book of Prefaces*. I was nearing my nineteenth birthday and I did not know how to pronounce the word "preface." I thumbed the pages and saw strange words and strange names. I shook my head, disappointed. I looked at the other book; it was called *Prejudices*. I knew what that word meant; I had heard it all my life. And right off I was on guard against Mencken's books. Why would a man want to call a book *Prejudices*? The word was so stained with all my memories of racial hate that I could not conceive of anybody using it for a title. Perhaps I had made a mistake about Mencken? A man who had prejudices must be wrong.

When I showed the books to Mr. Falk, he looked at me and frowned.

"That librarian might telephone you," I warned him.

"That's all right," he said. "But when you're through reading those books, I want   60
you to tell me what you get out of them."

That night in my rented room, while letting the hot water run over my can of pork and beans in the sink, I opened *A Book of Prefaces* and began to read. I was jarred and shocked by the style, the clear, clean, sweeping sentences. Why did he write like that? And how did one write like that? I pictured the man as a raging demon, slashing with his pen, consumed with hate, denouncing everything American, extolling everything European or German, laughing at the weaknesses of people, mocking God, authority. What was this? I stood up, trying to realize what reality lay behind the meaning of the words . . . Yes, this man was fighting, fighting with words. He was using words as a weapon, using them as one would use a club. Could words be weapons? Well, yes, for here they were. Then, maybe, perhaps, I could use them as a weapon? No. It frightened me. I read on and what amazed me was not what he said, but how on earth anybody had the courage to say it.

Occasionally I glanced up to reassure myself that I was alone in the room. Who were these men about whom Mencken was talking so passionately? Who was Anatole France? Joseph Conrad? Sinclair Lewis, Sherwood Anderson, Dostoevski, George Moore, Gustave Flaubert, Maupassant, Tolstoy, Frank Harris, Mark Twain, Thomas Hardy, Arnold Bennett, Stephen Crane, Zola, Norris, Gorky, Bergson, Ibsen, Balzac, Bernard Shaw, Dumas, Poe, Thomas Mann, O. Henry, Dreiser, H. G. Wells, Gogol, T. S. Eliot, Gide, Baudelaire, Edgar Lee Masters, Stendhal, Turgenev, Huneker, Nietzsche, and scores of others? Were these men real? Did they exist or had they existed? And how did one pronounce their names?

I ran across many words whose meanings I did not know, and I either looked them up in a dictionary or, before I had a chance to do that, encountered the word in a context that made its meaning clear. But what strange world was this? I concluded the book with the conviction that I had somehow overlooked something terribly important in life. I had once tried to write, had once reveled in feeling, had let my crude imagination roam, but the impulse to dream had been slowly beaten out of me by experience. Now it surged up again and I hungered for books, new ways of looking and seeing. It was not a matter of believing or disbelieving what I read, but of feeling something new, of being affected by something that made the look of the world different.

As dawn broke I ate my pork and beans, feeling dopey, sleepy. I went to work, but the mood of the book would not die; it lingered, coloring everything I saw, heard, did. I now felt that I knew what the white men were feeling. Merely because I had read a book that had spoken of how they lived and thought, I identified myself with that book. I felt vaguely guilty. Would I, filled with bookish notions, act in a manner that would make the whites dislike me?

I forged more notes and my trips to the library became frequent. Reading grew into   65
a passion. My first serious novel was Sinclair Lewis's *Main Street.* It made me see my boss, Mr. Gerald, and identify him as an American type. I would smile when I saw him lugging his golf bags into the office. I had always felt a vast distance separating me from the boss, and now I felt closer to him, though still distant. I felt now that I knew him, that I could feel the very limits of his narrow life. And this had happened because I had read a novel about a mythical man called George F. Babbitt.

The plots and stories in the novels did not interest me so much as the point of view revealed. I gave myself over to each novel without reserve, without trying to criticize it; it was enough for me to see and feel something different. And for me, everything was something different. Reading was like a drug, a dope. The novels created moods in which I lived for days. But I could not conquer my sense of guilt, my feeling that the white men around me knew that I was changing, that I had begun to regard them differently.

Whenever I brought a book to the job, I wrapped it in newspaper—a habit that was to persist for years in other cities and under other circumstances. But some of the white men pried into my packages when I was absent and they questioned me.

"Boy, what are you reading those books for?"

"Oh, I don't know, sir."

"That's deep stuff you're reading, boy."   70

"I'm just killing time, sir."

"You'll addle your brains if you don't watch out."

I read Dreiser's *Jennie Gerhardt* and *Sister Carrie* and they revived in me a vivid sense of my mother's suffering; I was overwhelmed. I grew silent, wondering about the life around me. It would have been impossible for me to have told anyone what I derived from these novels, for it was nothing less than a sense of life itself. All my life had shaped me for the realism, the naturalism of the modern novel, and I could not read enough of them.

Steeped in new moods and ideas, I bought a ream of paper and tried to write; but nothing would come, or what did come was flat beyond telling. I discovered that more than desire and feeling were necessary to write and I dropped the idea. Yet I still wondered how it was possible to know people sufficiently to write about them? Could I ever learn about life and people? To me, with my vast ignorance, my Jim Crow station in life, it seemed a task impossible of achievement. I now knew what being a Negro meant. I could endure the hunger and I had learned to live with hate. But to feel that there were feelings denied me, that the very breath of life itself was beyond my reach, that more than anything else hurt, wounded me. I had a new hunger.

Source: Wright, Richard: Excerpt from pp. 244-50 from BLACK BOY by RICHARD WRIGHT. Copyright 1937, 1942, 1944, 1945 by Richard Wright: renewed © 1973 by Ellen Wright. Reprinted by permission of HarperCollins Publishers.

Critical Thinking Topics

1. After reading the excerpt from Richard Wright's *Black Boy (American Hunger)*, read Langston Hughes's poem "Democracy" and Claude McKay's "America" (both in this chapter). Using examples from all three of these works, explain why Wright chose to use the words *American Hunger* in the title of his work.

2. This excerpt from *Black Boy (American Hunger)* ends with the words "I had a new hunger." What was that hunger, and to what extent was it tied to his being African American?

Writing Topic

Have you ever wanted or needed something that someone in power denied you? If so, did the situation make you angry? Like James Baldwin and other African American writers, musicians, and other artists, Richard Wright spent years as an expatriate living in France. Look up "expatriate" in a dictionary. Describe a situation that might lead you to become an expatriate.

8.28 Frank Schaeffer and John Schaeffer, My Son the Marine? (2002)

When two Marine recruiters showed up at our Salisbury, Mass., home in dress blues, they bedazzled my younger son, John. He had talked to recruiters from the Army, Navy and Air Force too, but his eyes lit up while the Marines spoke. I watched, inwardly alarmed. John seemed to relate to these stern, clean men with their insanely flawless uniforms in some basic way that I could barely comprehend. My wife, Genie, looking concerned and a bit drawn, turned to one of the men and asked, "But when he's done with the Marines, I mean—what will he have?"

The recruiter said, "Have, ma'am? I don't understand."

"I meant, what will he get out of it?"

The man's cheeks flushed. "He'll be a United States Marine, ma'am!"

There were no promises of college funds, "signing bonuses" or great "civilian   5
opportunities" later on in life. Instead, the Marines promised that if John joined the Corps, he would find standards that had not been lowered. A young man wanting to measure himself against the tradition of maximum endurance would not be disappointed. "Boot camp's still tough as hell," one of the recruiters told us.

When the men left, John said to me, "I'm not sure I want to go into the military, Dad. But if I do, it'll be the Marines. Otherwise, what's the point?"

I was born in Switzerland to American missionaries, the youngest of four children. Perhaps because they were overprotective of me after I contracted polio—I wore a leg brace— my parents home-schooled me, and then sent me to private schools in England and Wales.

Genie and I married in 1970 and moved to America ten years later. In September 1980, our son John was born. From the moment he entered our lives to his last high school poetry reading, I doted on him. He made the meaning of life clear to me.

So when he finally decided to join the Marines, I had no picture of how things would go. I felt ignorant. I vaguely imagined my son leaving for boot camp, and then after he graduated, being sent off to the ends of the earth. Why the hell was John going into the Marines?

It had been hard enough sending my two older children off to college. The normal separations were just about unbearable. Our daughter, Jessica, went to New York University, and our other son, Francis, to Georgetown. Couldn't John have gone on to college first? No other parent in our affluent town on the North Shore of Boston had a son or daughter who was going into the military, let alone as an enlisted recruit.

When I told another parent of John's decision to join the Marines, the man was incredulous. "He's so bright and talented and could do anything!" the man said. "What a waste!"

The day John left for boot camp at Parris Island in South Carolina, I woke very early. I had to get him to the local recruiting office by 4:30. At our front door, John and his mother hugged and she cried steady, silent tears. John told his mother he loved her.

At the recruiting office, I looked at my son as he shook the staff sergeant's hand and thought, *What is he trying to prove?* More than once during the last few months, I had asked him, "Why do you want to do this?" Sometimes he'd say, "I want self-discipline." The best answer he gave was, "I just do." We parted with a hug and a handshake. "I'll miss you, boy," I said. "I'll write every day."

"Okay."

"I love you, John."

"I love you, Dad."

Driving home, I lost my way twice on a road I'd driven a thousand times. I'd never experienced pride and fear as one emotion before. *Oh, Lord, please protect my boy and bring him home safe!* was all I could think as I peered forlornly into the gloom while trying to remember my way home.

After a brief call letting us know he'd arrived—plus two form letters sent by the Marines—John was not allowed to contact us. I bought a book by Thomas E. Ricks called *Making the Corps,* which, with its day-by-day account of boot-camp training, quickly became my bible. I followed John's activities: drill marching; classes in subjects like Tactical Weapons of Opportunity (i.e., using things like rocks and sticks to smash the enemy with when a rifle wasn't handy); and physical training—miles of running, thousands of repetitions of exercises, pugil stick fighting, and endless humps (marches in full combat gear and pack).

Writing to John was a poignant experience. There was something so unequal about writing to him from the lap of luxury when he had essentially died and gone to hell.

For the first time in both our lives, my son was beyond my help. Did he have it in him to become a Marine? I knew that John's idea of a good time was to curl up in front of the fireplace and reread his favorite bits of *The Hobbit.* When he caught fish, he let them go. How could my son become a Marine? What sort of a person would he be when the Corps was done with him? Would John be absolutely devastated if he failed? I felt sick.

But he did not fail. Three months after John had left us, Genie and I went down to Parris Island for his graduation. We stood in the stands for the ceremony and watched our son parade in, third man from the front, a tall Marine—my son.

I wiped my eyes and looked around. It occurred to me that this was the first time I'd been in an integrated crowd of this size dedicated to one purpose and of one mind. We were dark-skinned, weather-beaten, Spanish-speaking grandfathers; black kids wearing head rags; Southern-accented mothers with big hair and tight sweat suits; and some people who looked like us.

The platitudes my educated friends mouthed about "racial harmony" and "economic and gender diversity" were nothing compared to the spirit shared among the people gathered in the stands that day to honor our Marines. Our children would room together as they had in boot camp, drink together, work together, united by a high purpose: the defense of our country and loyalty to the Corps.

Nearly two years later, I was packing my bags to fly down to Florida to visit John at his new base, where he was a squad leader and had been nominated by his platoon to represent it as "Marine of the Quarter," the best performer of his unit for that time period. My biggest worry was whether I would have trouble checking the cooler full of food I was bringing to John. It was September 10, 2001.

The next day, all flights were canceled, and civil air traffic over the United States   25 was shut down for the first time in history. The cooler of food was forgotten. I was so scared for John. I longed to hold on to my son for dear life.

I finally spoke to him the next day, on September 12. He sounded calm and confident.

"Hey, Dad, this is worse for you than for me," he said.

"How's that?"

"All you have to do with yourself is worry, but we have a job to do." He paused. "Dad? I love you."

After I hung up the phone, I stared at the television. There were fire-fighters, cops   30 and military personnel struggling to find survivors and thousands of dead. I felt deeply frustrated at being able to do nothing. At least I knew that I could look the men and women in uniform in the eye. My son, after all, was one of them.

Source: From Keeping Faith: A Father-Son Story About Love and the United States Marine Corps by John Schaeffer and Frank Schaeffer, copyright © 2002. Reprinted by permission of Da Capo Press, an imprint of Perseus Books, LLC, a subsidiary of Hachette Book Group, Inc.

Critical Thinking Topics

1. In analyzing an argument, you look at the choices the writer made: Why did the writer choose to begin the piece in this way? Why did he place the evidence in this order? Why did she use this particular metaphor or this descriptive phrase? In "My Son the Marine?" why did the writers choose to mention the son's "last high school poetry reading"? Find at least three examples of details that caught your attention, and discuss how each detail contributes to the persuasive power of the piece.

2. Describe the tone of the writing—the voice you hear as reader. Explain how the tone affects your assessment of the writers' credibility.

3. Which of the three rhetorical appeals (*ethos, logos,* or *pathos*) is most prominent? Point to details as examples. Is this an effective persuasive strategy? Why or why not?

4. There is no explicit claim in "My Son the Marine?" but can you articulate an implied claim? What might the authors want readers to believe after reading this piece? Do you agree or disagree with this claim? Why?

Writing Topic

Think of a personal experience that was meaningful to you, and imagine relating it to other people. Write out a sentence in which you succinctly state what you would like them to conclude (your explicit claim). Now write out a description of the experience that will enable readers to understand your claim without seeing it stated in a specific sentence (your implied claim—for example, a description of an automobile accident might imply that drinking and driving is not a good thing to do).

8.29 Barack Obama, Second Inaugural Address (January 21, 2013)

Vice President Biden, Mr. Chief Justice, Members of the United States Congress, distinguished guests, and fellow citizens:

Each time we gather to inaugurate a president, we bear witness to the enduring strength of our Constitution. We affirm the promise of our democracy. We recall that what binds this nation together is not the colors of our skin or the tenets of our faith or the origins of our names. What makes us exceptional—what makes us American—is our allegiance to an idea articulated in a declaration made more than two centuries ago: "We hold these truths to be self-evident, that all men are created equal, that they are endowed by their Creator with certain unalienable rights, that among these are Life, Liberty, and the pursuit of Happiness."

Today we continue a never-ending journey to bridge the meaning of those words with the realities of our time. For history tells us that while these truths may be self-evident, they have never been self-executing; that while freedom is a gift from God, it must be secured by His people here on Earth. The patriots of 1776 did not fight to replace the tyranny of a king with the privileges of a few or the rule of a mob. They gave to us a Republic, a government of, and by, and for the people: entrusting each generation to keep safe our founding creed.

For more than two hundred years, we have.

Through blood drawn by lash and blood drawn by sword, we learned that no union   5
founded on the principles of liberty and equality could survive half-slave and half-free. We made ourselves anew, and vowed to move forward together.

Together, we determined that a modern economy requires railroads and highways to speed travel and commerce, schools and colleges to train our workers.

Together, we discovered that a free market only thrives when there are rules to ensure competition and fair play.

Together, we resolved that a great nation must care for the vulnerable, and protect its people from life's worst hazards and misfortune.

Through it all, we have never relinquished our skepticism of central authority, nor have we succumbed to the fiction that all society's ills can be cured through government alone. Our celebration of initiative and enterprise—our insistence on hard work and personal responsibility—these are constants in our character.

But we have always understood that when times change, so must we; that fidelity   10
to our founding principles requires new responses to new challenges; that preserving our individual freedoms ultimately requires collective action. For the American people

can no more meet the demands of today's world by acting alone than American soldiers could have met the forces of fascism or communism with muskets and militias. No single person can train all the math and science teachers we'll need to equip our children for the future, or build the roads and networks and research labs that will bring new jobs and businesses to our shores. Now, more than ever, we must do these things together, as one nation, and one people.

This generation of Americans has been tested by crises that steeled our resolve and proved our resilience. A decade of war is now ending. An economic recovery has begun. America's possibilities are limitless, for we possess all the qualities that this world without boundaries demands: youth and drive; diversity and openness; an endless capacity for risk and a gift for reinvention. My fellow Americans, we are made for this moment, and we will seize it—so long as we seize it together.

For we, the people, understand that our country cannot succeed when a shrinking few do very well and a growing many barely make it. We believe that America's prosperity must rest upon the broad shoulders of a rising middle class. We know that America thrives when every person can find independence and pride in their work, when the wages of honest labor liberate families from the brink of hardship. We are true to our creed when a little girl born into the bleakest poverty knows that she has the same chance to succeed as anybody else, because she is an American, she is free, and she is equal, not just in the eyes of God but also in our own.

We understand that outworn programs are inadequate to the needs of our time. We must harness new ideas and technology to remake our government, revamp our tax code, reform our schools, and empower our citizens with the skills they need to work harder, learn more, and reach higher. But while the means will change, our purpose endures: a nation that rewards the effort and determination of every single American. That is what this moment requires. That is what will give real meaning to our creed.

We, the people, still believe that every citizen deserves a basic measure of security and dignity. We must make the hard choices to reduce the cost of health care and the size of our deficit; but we reject the belief that America must choose between caring for the generation that built this country and investing in the generation that will build its future. For we remember the lessons of our past, when twilight years were spent in poverty, and parents of a child with a disability had nowhere to turn. We do not believe that in this country, freedom is reserved for the lucky, or happiness for the few. We recognize that no matter how responsibly we live our lives, any one of us, at any time, may face a job loss, or a sudden illness, or a home swept away in a terrible storm. The commitments we make to each other—through Medicare, and Medicaid, and Social Security—these things do not sap our initiative; they strengthen us. They do not make us a nation of takers; they free us to take the risks that make this country great.

We, the people, still believe that our obligations as Americans are not just to ourselves, but to all posterity. We will respond to the threat of climate change, knowing that the failure to do so would betray our children and future generations. Some may still deny the overwhelming judgment of science, but none can avoid the devastating impact of raging fires, and crippling drought, and more powerful storms. The path towards sustainable energy sources will be long and sometimes difficult. But America cannot resist this transition; we must lead it. We cannot cede to other nations the technology that will power new jobs and new industries—we must claim its promise. That's how we will maintain our economic vitality and our national treasure—our forests and waterways; our croplands and snow-capped peaks. That is how we will preserve our planet, commanded to our care by God. That's what will lend meaning to the creed our fathers once declared.

We, the people, still believe that enduring security and lasting peace do not require perpetual war. Our brave men and women in uniform, tempered by the flames of battle, are unmatched in skill and courage. Our citizens, seared by the memory of those we have lost, know too well the price that is paid for liberty. The knowledge of their sacrifice will keep us forever vigilant against those who would do us harm. But we are also heirs to those who won the peace and not just the war, who turned sworn enemies into the surest of friends, and we must carry those lessons into this time as well.

We will defend our people and uphold our values through strength of arms and rule of law. We will show the courage to try and resolve our differences with other nations peacefully—not because we are naive about the dangers we face, but because engagement can more durably lift suspicion and fear. America will remain the anchor of strong alliances in every corner of the globe; and we will renew those institutions that extend our capacity to manage crisis abroad, for no one has a greater stake in a peaceful world than its most powerful nation. We will support democracy from Asia to Africa, from the Americas to the Middle East, because our interests and our conscience compel us to act on behalf of those who long for freedom. And we must be a source of hope to the poor, the sick, the marginalized, the victims of prejudice—not out of mere charity, but because peace in our time requires the constant advance of those principles that our common creed describes: tolerance and opportunity; human dignity and justice.

We, the people, declare today that the most evident of truths—that all of us are created equal—is the star that guides us still; just as it guided our forebears through Seneca Falls, and Selma, and Stonewall; just as it guided all those men and women, sung and unsung, who left footprints along this great Mall, to hear a preacher say that we cannot walk alone; to hear a King proclaim that our individual freedom is inextricably bound to the freedom of every soul on Earth.

It is now our generation's task to carry on what those pioneers began. For our journey is not complete until our wives, our mothers, and daughters can earn a living equal to their efforts. Our journey is not complete until our gay brothers and sisters are treated like anyone else under the law—for if we are truly created equal, then surely the love we commit to one another must be equal as well. Our journey is not complete until no citizen is forced to wait for hours to exercise the right to vote. Our journey is not complete until we find a better way to welcome the striving, hopeful immigrants who still see America as a land of opportunity; until bright young students and engineers are enlisted in our workforce rather than expelled from our country. Our journey is not complete until all our children—from the streets of Detroit, to the hills of Appalachia, to the quiet lanes of Newtown—know that they are cared for, and cherished, and always safe from harm.

That is our generation's task—to make these words, these rights, these values— of Life, and Liberty, and the Pursuit of Happiness—real for every American. Being   20 true to our founding documents does not require us to agree on every contour of life; it does not mean we all define liberty in exactly the same way, or follow the same precise path to happiness. Progress does not compel us to settle centuries-long debates about the role of government for all time—but it does require us to act in our time.

For now decisions are upon us, and we cannot afford delay. We cannot mistake absolutism for principle, or substitute spectacle for politics, or treat name-calling as reasoned debate. We must act, knowing that our work will be imperfect. We must act, knowing that today's victories will be only partial, and that it will be up to those who stand here in four years, and forty years, and four hundred years hence to advance the timeless spirit once conferred to us in a spare Philadelphia hall.

My fellow Americans, the oath I have sworn before you today, like the one recited by others who serve in this Capitol, was an oath to God and country, not party or faction—and we must faithfully execute that pledge during the duration of our service. But the words I spoke today are not so different from the oath that is taken each time a soldier signs up for duty, or an immigrant realizes her dream. My oath is not so different from the pledge we all make to the flag that waves above and that fills our hearts with pride: they are the words of citizens, and they represent our greatest hope.

You and I, as citizens, have the power to set this country's course.

You and I, as citizens, have the obligation to shape the debates of our time—not only with the votes we cast, but with the voices we lift in defense of our most ancient values and enduring ideals.

Let us each of us now embrace, with solemn duty and awesome joy, what is our 25 lasting birthright. With common effort and common purpose, with passion and dedication, let us answer the call of history, and carry into an uncertain future that precious light of freedom.

Thank you, God bless you, and may He forever bless these United States of America.

Critical Thinking Topics

1. Rhetorical devices can be used to enhance the appeal of both written and spoken prose. There are many such devices, but Obama makes prominent use of one specifically: *syntheton,* linking two words or phrases, most commonly with "and" or "or," to create emphasis and a pleasing sound. Four examples of syntheton early in Obama's speech (par. 5 and 6) are "blood drawn by lash and blood drawn by sword," "railroads and highways," "travel and commerce," and "schools and colleges." List at least six additional examples of syntheton in Obama's speech. Read each example out loud. Does Obama's extensive use of syntheton enhance or detract from his persuasiveness? Explain why.

2. Speakers, especially politicians, typically attempt to appeal to *ethos.* How does Obama create his appeal to *ethos?* With what and with whom does he align himself?

Writing Topic

Traditionally, an inaugural speech outlines the path a president plans to follow during his coming term in office. When you analyze Obama's speech, you will see that he refers to us as being on a journey and then talks about the duty of citizens. Write about your own views on the duty of citizens in a democracy.

8.30 Bret Stephens, The Dying Art of Disagreement (2017)

Let me begin with thanks to the Lowy Institute for bringing me all the way to Sydney and doing me the honor of hosting me here this evening.

I'm aware of the controversy that has gone with my selection as your speaker. I respect the wishes of the Colvin family and join in honoring Mark Colvin's memory as a courageous foreign correspondent and an extraordinary writer and broadcaster. And I'd particularly like to thank Michael Fullilove for not rescinding the invitation.

This has become the depressing trend on American university campuses, where the roster of disinvited speakers and forced cancellations includes former Secretaries of State Henry Kissinger and Condoleezza Rice, former Harvard University President Larry Summers, actor Alec Baldwin, human-rights activist Ayaan Hirsi Ali, DNA co-discoverer James Watson, Indian Prime Minister Narendra Modi, filmmaker Michael Moore, conservative Pulitzer Prize–winning columnist George Will and liberal Pulitzer Prize–winning columnist Anna Quindlen, to name just a few.

So illustrious is the list that, on second thought, I'm beginning to regret that you didn't disinvite me after all.

The title of my talk tonight is "The Dying Art of Disagreement." This is a subject 5 that is dear to me—literally dear—since disagreement is the way in which I have always earned a living. Disagreement is dear to me, too, because it is the most vital ingredient of any decent society.

To say the words, "I agree"—whether it's agreeing to join an organization, or submit to a political authority, or subscribe to a religious faith—may be the basis of every community.

But to say, I disagree; I refuse; you're wrong; *etiam si omnes—ego non*—these are the words that define our individuality, give us our freedom, enjoin our tolerance, enlarge our perspectives, seize our attention, energize our progress, make our democracies real, and give hope and courage to oppressed people everywhere. Galileo and Darwin; Mandela, Havel, and Liu Xiaobo; Rosa Parks and Natan Sharansky—such are the ranks of those who disagree.

And the problem, as I see it, is that we're failing at the task.

This is a puzzle. At least as far as the United States is concerned, Americans have rarely disagreed more in recent decades.

We disagree about racial issues, bathroom policies, health care laws, and, of 10 course, the 45th president. We express our disagreements in radio and cable TV rants in ways that are increasingly virulent; street and campus protests that are increasingly violent; and personal conversations that are increasingly embittering.

This is yet another age in which we judge one another morally depending on where we stand politically.

Nor is this just an impression of the moment. Extensive survey data show that Republicans are much more right-leaning than they were twenty years ago, Democrats much more left-leaning, and both sides much more likely to see the other as a mortal threat to the nation's welfare.

The polarization is geographic, as more people live in states and communities where their neighbors are much likelier to share their politics.

The polarization is personal: Fully 50 percent of Republicans would not want their child to marry a Democrat, and nearly a third of Democrats return the sentiment. Inter-party marriage has taken the place of interracial marriage as a family taboo.

Finally the polarization is electronic and digital, as Americans increasingly inhabit   15 the filter bubbles of news and social media that correspond to their ideological affinities. We no longer just have our own opinions. We also have our separate "facts," often the result of what different media outlets consider newsworthy. In the last election, fully 40 percent of Trump voters named Fox News as their chief source of news.

Thanks a bunch for that one, Australia.

It's usually the case that the more we do something, the better we are at it. Instead, we're like Casanovas in reverse: the more we do it, the worse we're at it. Our disagreements may frequently hoarsen our voices, but they rarely sharpen our thinking, much less change our minds.

It behooves us to wonder why.

Thirty years ago, in 1987, a philosophy professor at the University of Chicago named Allan Bloom—at the time best known for his graceful translations of Plato's "Republic" and Rousseau's "Emile"—published a learned polemic about the state of higher education in the United States. It was called *The Closing of the American Mind*.

The book appeared when I was in high school, and I struggled to make my way   20 through a text thick with references to Plato, Weber, Heidegger and Strauss. But I got the gist—and the gist was that I'd better enroll in the University of Chicago and read the great books. That is what I did.

What was it that one learned through a great books curriculum? Certainly not "conservatism" in any contemporary American sense of the term. We were not taught to become American patriots, or religious pietists, or to worship what Rudyard Kipling called "the Gods of the Market Place." We were not instructed in the evils of Marxism, or the glories of capitalism, or even the superiority of Western civilization.

As I think about it, I'm not sure we were taught anything at all. What we did was read books that raised serious questions about the human condition, and which invited us to attempt to ask serious questions of our own. Education, in this sense, wasn't a "teaching" with any fixed lesson. It was an exercise in interrogation.

To listen and understand; to question and disagree; to treat no proposition as sacred and no objection as impious; to be willing to entertain unpopular ideas and cultivate the habits of an open mind—this is what I was encouraged to do by my teachers at the University of Chicago.

It's what used to be called a liberal education.

The University of Chicago showed us something else: that every great idea is really   25 just a spectacular disagreement with some other great idea.

Socrates quarrels with Homer. Aristotle quarrels with Plato. Locke quarrels with Hobbes and Rousseau quarrels with them both. Nietzsche quarrels with everyone. Wittgenstein quarrels with himself.

These quarrels are never personal. Nor are they particularly political, at least in the ordinary sense of politics. Sometimes they take place over the distance of decades, even centuries.

Most importantly, they are never based on a misunderstanding. On the contrary, the disagreements arise from perfect *comprehension*; from having chewed over the ideas of your intellectual opponent so thoroughly that you can properly spit them out.

In other words, to disagree well you must first *understand* well. You have to read deeply, listen carefully, watch closely. You need to grant your adversary moral respect; give him the intellectual benefit of doubt; have sympathy for his motives and participate empathically with his line of reasoning. And you need to allow for the possibility that you might yet be persuaded of what he has to say.

The Closing of the American Mind took its place in the tradition of these quarrels.   30
Since the 1960s it had been the vogue in American universities to treat the so-called "Dead White European Males" of the Western canon as agents of social and political oppression. Allan Bloom insisted that, to the contrary, they were the best possible instruments of spiritual liberation.

He also insisted that to sustain liberal democracy you needed liberally educated people. This, at least, should not have been controversial. For free societies to function, the idea of open-mindedness can't simply be a catchphrase or a dogma. It needs to be a personal habit, most of all when it comes to preserving an open mind toward those with whom we disagree.

That habit was no longer being exercised much 30 years ago. And if you've followed the news from American campuses in recent years, things have become a lot worse.

According to a new survey from the Brookings Institution, a plurality of college students today—fully 44 percent—do not believe the First Amendment to the U.S. Constitution protects so-called "hate speech," when of course it absolutely does. More shockingly, a narrow majority of students—51 percent—think it is "acceptable" for a student group to shout down a speaker with whom they disagree. An astonishing 20 percent also agree that it's acceptable to use violence to prevent a speaker from speaking.

These attitudes are being made plain nearly every week on one college campus or another.

There are speakers being shouted down by organized claques of hecklers—such   35
was the experience of Israeli ambassador Michael Oren at the University of California, Irvine. Or speakers who require hundreds of thousands of dollars of security measures in order to appear on campus—such was the experience of conservative pundit Ben Shapiro earlier this month at Berkeley. Or speakers who are physically barred from reaching the auditorium—that's what happened to Heather MacDonald at Claremont McKenna College in April. Or teachers who are humiliated by their students and hounded from their positions for allegedly hurting students' feelings—that's what happened to Erika and Nicholas Christakis of Yale.

And there is violence. Listen to a description from Middlebury College professor Allison Stanger of what happened when she moderated a conversation with the libertarian scholar Charles Murray in March:

> The protesters succeeded in shutting down the lecture. We were forced to move to another site and broadcast our discussion via live stream, while activists who had figured out where we were banged on the windows and set off fire alarms. Afterward, as Dr. Murray and I left the building . . . a mob charged us.
>
> Most of the hatred was focused on Dr. Murray, but when I took his right arm to shield him and to make sure we stayed together, the crowd turned on me. Someone pulled my hair, while others were shoving me. I feared for my life. Once we got into the car, protesters climbed on it, hitting the windows and rocking the vehicle whenever we stopped to avoid harming them. I am still wearing a neck brace, and spent a week in a dark room to recover from a concussion caused by the whiplash.

Middlebury is one of the most prestigious liberal-arts colleges in the United States, with an acceptance rate of just 16 percent and tuition fees of nearly $50,000 a year. How does an elite institution become a factory for junior totalitarians, so full of their own certitudes that they could indulge their taste for bullying and violence?

There's no one answer. What's clear is that the mis-education begins early. I was raised on the old-fashioned view that sticks and stones could break my bones but words would never hurt me. But today there's a belief that since words can cause stress, and stress can have physiological effects, stressful words are tantamount to a form of violence. This is the age of protected feelings purchased at the cost of permanent infantilization.

The mis-education continues in grade school. As the Brookings findings indicate, younger Americans seem to have no grasp of what our First Amendment says, much less of the kind of speech it protects. This is a testimony to the collapse of civics education in the United States, creating the conditions that make young people uniquely susceptible to demagogy of the left- or right-wing varieties.

Then we get to college, where the dominant mode of politics is identity politics, 40 and in which the primary test of an argument isn't the quality of the thinking but the cultural, racial, or sexual standing of the person making it. *As a woman of color I think X. As a gay man I think Y. As a person of privilege I apologize for Z.* This is the baroque way Americans often speak these days. It is a way of replacing individual thought—with all the effort that actual thinking requires—with social identification—with all the attitude that attitudinizing requires.

In recent years, identity politics have become the moated castles from which we safeguard our feelings from hurt and our opinions from challenge. It is our "safe space." But it is a safe space of a uniquely pernicious kind—a safe space *from* thought, rather than a safe space *for* thought, to borrow a line I recently heard from Salman Rushdie.

Another consequence of identity politics is that it has made the distance between making an argument and causing offense terrifyingly short. Any argument that can be cast as insensitive or offensive to a given group of people isn't treated as being merely wrong. Instead it is seen as immoral, and therefore unworthy of discussion or rebuttal.

The result is that the disagreements we need to have—and to have vigorously—are banished from the public square before they're settled. People who might otherwise join a conversation to see where it might lead them choose instead to shrink from it, lest they say the "wrong" thing and be accused of some kind of political -ism or -phobia. For fear of causing offense, they forgo the opportunity to be persuaded.

Take the arguments over same-sex marriage, which you are now debating in Australia. My own views in favor of same-sex marriage are well known, and I hope the Yes's win by a convincing margin.

But if I had to guess, I suspect the No's will exceed whatever they are currently   45
polling. That's because the case for same-sex marriage is too often advanced not by reason, but merely by branding every opponent of it as a "bigot"—just because they are sticking to an opinion that was shared across the entire political spectrum only a few years ago. Few people like outing themselves as someone's idea of a bigot, so they keep their opinions to themselves even when speaking to pollsters. That's just what happened last year in the Brexit vote and the U.S. presidential election, and look where we are now.

If you want to make a winning argument for same-sex marriage, particularly against conservative opponents, make it on a conservative foundation: As a matter of individual freedom, and as an avenue toward moral responsibility and social respectability. The No's will have a hard time arguing with that. But if you call them morons and Neanderthals, all you'll get in return is their middle finger or their clenched fist.

One final point about identity politics: It's a game at which two can play. In the United States, the so-called "alt-right" justifies its white-identity politics in terms that are coyly borrowed from the progressive left. One of the more dismaying features of last year's election was the extent to which "white working class" became a catchall identity for people whose travails we were supposed to pity but whose habits or beliefs we were not supposed to criticize. The result was to give the Trump base a moral pass it did little to earn.

So here's where we stand: Intelligent disagreement is the lifeblood of any thriving society. Yet we in the United States are raising a younger generation who have never been taught either the how or the why of disagreement, and who seem to think that free speech is a one-way right: Namely, their right to disinvite, shout down or abuse anyone they dislike, lest they run the risk of listening to that person—or even allowing someone else to listen. The results are evident in the parlous state of our universities, and the frayed edges of our democracies.

Can we do better?

This is supposed to be a lecture on the media, and I'd like to conclude this talk   50
with a word about the role that editors and especially publishers can play in ways that might improve the state of public discussion rather than just reflect and accelerate its decline.

I began this talk by noting that Americans have rarely disagreed so vehemently about so much. On second thought, this isn't the whole truth.

Yes, we disagree constantly. But what makes our disagreements so toxic is that we refuse to make eye contact with our opponents, or try to see things as they might, or find some middle ground.

Instead, we fight each other from the safe distance of our separate islands of ideology and identity and listen intently to echoes of ourselves. We take exaggerated and histrionic offense to whatever is said about us. We banish entire lines of thought and attempt to excommunicate all manner of people—your humble speaker included—without giving them so much as a cursory hearing.

The crucial prerequisite of intelligent disagreement—namely: shut up; listen up; pause and reconsider; and only then speak—is absent.

Perhaps the reason for this is that we have few obvious models for disagreeing 55 well, and those we do have—such as the Intelligence Squared debates in New York and London or Fareed Zakaria's show on CNN—cater to a sliver of elite tastes, like classical music.

Fox News and other partisan networks have demonstrated that the quickest route to huge profitability is to serve up a steady diet of high-carb, low-protein populist pap. Reasoned disagreement of the kind that could serve democracy well fails the market test. Those of us who otherwise believe in the virtues of unfettered capitalism should bear that fact in mind.

I do not believe the answer, at least in the U.S., lies in heavier investment in publicly sponsored television along the lines of the BBC. It too, suffers, from its own form of ideological conformism and journalistic groupthink, immunized from criticism due to its indifference to competition.

Nor do I believe the answer lies in a return to what in America used to be called the "Fairness Doctrine," mandating equal time for different points of view. Free speech must ultimately be free, whether or not it's fair.

But I do think there's such a thing as private ownership in the public interest, and of fiduciary duties not only to shareholders but also to citizens. Journalism is not just any other business, like trucking or food services. Nations can have lousy food and exemplary government, as Great Britain demonstrated for most of the last century. They can also have great food and lousy government, as France has always demonstrated.

But no country can have good government, or a healthy public square, without 60 high-quality journalism—journalism that can distinguish a fact from a belief and again from an opinion; that understands that the purpose of opinion isn't to depart from facts but to use them as a bridge to a larger idea called "truth"; and that appreciates that truth is a large enough destination that, like Manhattan, it can be reached by many bridges of radically different designs. In other words, journalism that is grounded in facts while abounding in disagreements.

I believe it is still possible—and all the more necessary—for journalism to perform these functions, especially as the other institutions that were meant to do so have fallen short. But that requires proprietors and publishers who understand that their role ought not to be to push a party line, or be a slave to Google hits and Facebook ads, or provide a titillating kind of news entertainment, or help out a president or prime minister who they favor or who's in trouble.

Their role is to clarify the terms of debate by championing aggressive and objective news reporting, and improve the quality of debate with commentary that opens minds and challenges assumptions rather than merely confirming them.This is journalism in defense of liberalism, not liberal in the left-wing American or right-wing Australian sense, but liberal in its belief that the individual is more than just an identity, and that free men and women do not need to be protected from discomfiting ideas and unpopular arguments. More than ever, they need to be exposed to them, so that we may revive the arts of disagreement that are the best foundation of intelligent democratic life.

The honor the Lowy Institute does tonight's nominees is an important step in that direction. What they have uncovered, for the rest of you to debate, is the only way by which our democracies can remain rational, reasonable, and free.

Source: From *The New York Times*, 9/24/2017 © 2017. *The New York Times*. All rights reserved. Used by permission and protected by the Copyright Laws of the United States. The printing, copying, redistribution, or retransmission of this Content without express written permission is prohibited.

Critical Thinking Topics

1. Bret Stephens's lecture presents an argument on the state of public discourse in the United States today. Write a summary sentence (in your own words) of each of three key points of his argument. Then discuss your own perspective on each of the three points.

2. Describe and evaluate the variations in Stephens's tone. On several occasions, for example, Stephens interjects a humorous tone, even though his subject matter most certainly is serious. Identify brief passages that illustrate shifts from one tone to another, and discuss how each tonal shift contributes to or detracts from Stephens's argumentative purpose.

3. According to Stephens, who or what forces are responsible for the poor state of public discourse today? In responding, identify several passages on this subject, explain what each says, and discuss your own perspective on each.

4. Stephens is addressing an audience of journalists and, thus, specifically targets journalists in his closing call to action. Even if we are not journalists, what responsibility does each one of us have to "distinguish a fact from a belief and again from an opinion; [to understand] that the purpose of opinion isn't to depart from the facts but to use them as a bridge to a larger idea called 'truth'" (par. 60)? And what responsibility does each of us have "to [preserve] an open mind toward those with whom we disagree" (par. 31)? Use an example (real, observed, or fictional) to explain how engaging in thoughtful disagreement can empower an individual.

Writing Topic

In examining the reasons for the flawed state of discourse, Stephens reflects on his own educational experiences—in particular, at the University of Chicago: "Education, in this sense, wasn't a 'teaching' with any fixed lesson. It was an exercise in interrogation. . . . To listen and understand; to question and disagree . . . . It's what used to be called a liberal education" (par. 21–24). By using the past tense, he implies that, regrettably, liberal education has lost its place to a weak surrogate. Do you agree or disagree with Stephens's viewpoint on the purpose of an education? Can reading "great books" provide preparation for the workplace and practice in career-specific skills? Reflecting on Stephens's viewpoint, your educational experiences, and your personal and career goals, discuss your viewpoint on the purpose of a college education. Use specific details to elaborate on your response.

8.31 Emily Anthes, A Floating House to Resist the Floods of Climate Change
(2018)

Last June, not long after a catastrophic thunderstorm swept through southern Ontario, bringing a month's worth of rain in just a few hours, a group of seventy-five architects, engineers, and policymakers from sixteen countries gathered in the city of Waterloo to discuss how humanity will cope with its waterlogged future. The timing of the conference was a fitting meteorological coincidence; in a world increasingly transformed by climate change, heavy rains and major floods are becoming more common, at least in some areas. In the summer of 2017 alone, Hurricane Harvey dumped more than fifty inches of rain over Texas, a monster monsoon season damaged more than eight hundred thousand homes in India, and flash floods and mudslides claimed at least five hundred lives in Sierra Leone. In the past two decades, the world's ten worst floods have done more than a hundred and sixty-five billion dollars' worth of damage and driven more than a billion people from their homes.

It was statistics like these that animated the experts who had assembled in Ontario for the International Conference on Amphibious Architecture, Design and Engineering, a three-day event organized by Elizabeth English, an associate professor at the University of Waterloo. Unlike traditional buildings, amphibious structures are not static; they respond to floods like ships to a rising tide, floating on the water's surface. As one of English's colleagues put it, "You can think of these buildings as little animals that have their feet wet and can then lift themselves up as needed." Amphibiation may be an unconventional strategy, but it reflects a growing consensus that, at a time of climatic volatility, people can't simply fight against water; they have to learn to live with it. "With amphibious construction, water becomes your friend," English told me. "The water gets to do what the water wants to do. It's not a confrontation with Mother Nature—it's an acceptance of Mother Nature."

English began her career focussed on an altogether different force of nature: wind. After earning degrees in architecture and engineering, she eventually landed at Louisiana State University's Hurricane Center, where she studied the effects of wind loads on buildings and the aerodynamics of windborne debris. In August of 2005, Hurricane Katrina hit New Orleans, about seventy miles southeast of her home in Baton Rouge. The storm's high-speed winds peeled roofs off of buildings and flung debris through windows, but it was the flooding that really shocked English. "Katrina was much more of a water event than a wind event," she said. "I started looking at the implications of all the flood damage and the social disruption that it caused, and I became very, very angry about the cultural insensitivity of the solutions that were being proposed."

In the aftermath of the storm, the federal government recommended that residents permanently elevate their houses, lifting them up onto raised foundations or stilts. But English worried that hoisting the city's low-slung, shotgun-style houses into the air would ruin its sense of community, making it more difficult for residents to chat with neighbors and passersby. "People didn't want to move up," English said. "And it visually thoroughly destroyed the neighborhoods. There had to be a better way."

She discovered that better way in another perpetually sodden locale—the Nether-   5
lands, where developers were building a cluster of amphibious homes in a flood-prone
region along the Maas River. The houses sat on hollow concrete boxes attached to
large steel pillars. During a flood, the boxes would function like the hull of a ship, providing buoyancy. As the waters rose, the buildings would rise, too, sliding up the pillars and floating on the water's surface. When the waters receded, the houses would
descend to their original positions.

It was an elegant solution, English thought, but not quite what she was looking
for. Building a hollow foundation is a major construction project; English wanted to give
New Orleanians an easy and inexpensive way to modify their existing homes. In 2006,
she founded a nonprofit called the Buoyant Foundation Project and began working with
a group of architecture and engineering students to devise a method for retrofitting local
homes with amphibious foundations. A typical New Orleans shotgun house sits slightly
above the ground, resting atop short piers; the researchers could, they thought, fasten
a steel frame to the underside of a house and affix a set of foam buoyancy blocks. Then
they could sink posts into the ground and attach them to the corners of the frame,
allowing the house to rise up off the piers without floating down the street.

English and her students built a full-scale prototype of the system, and in the summer of 2007 they put it to the test. They borrowed some corral panels from the College
of Agriculture and built a temporary flood tank around their model amphibious home,
pumping in water straight from the Mississippi River. The tank filled with two, three, four
feet of water, and the house began to rise. By the time they stopped pumping, it was
hovering about a foot above the piers. "It was a religious experience when it lifted off,"
English recalled.

The system was simple and cheap; it could be installed by two reasonably handy
people without heavy equipment for between ten and forty dollars a square foot. It left a
building's appearance and structure almost unchanged, and it was more resilient than
permanent elevation, which can cost two or three times as much and make a building more susceptible to wind damage. "This is not a one-size-fits-all solution," English
said, noting that the system would not provide adequate protection against high-speed
waves. "But it's an excellent solution for some circumstances."

English became so enamored of the approach that she began to think beyond the
bayou. In the past decade, she and her colleagues at the Buoyant Foundation Project have designed amphibious-housing prototypes for low-income, flood-threatened
regions in Nicaragua and Jamaica. They have also consulted with indigenous communities in Canada and Louisiana. (English kept her house there after she moved from
L.S.U. to Waterloo, in 2007.) Thanks in part to the project's work, the gospel of amphibiation is spreading. Amphibious buildings are popping up everywhere from the U.K.,
where the firm Baca Architects recently built a buoyant, light-drenched three-bedroom
home on an island in the Thames, to Bangladesh, where a master's student designed
a sustainable affordable-housing unit that relies on eight thousand empty plastic water
bottles for buoyancy.

Still, amphibious structures remain more of an innovative curiosity than a bona-fide   10
building trend. It probably doesn't help that the premise is profoundly counterintuitive.
When English first started telling people about her work, they laughed at her. "It seemed
so outlandish," she said. But the biggest hurdles, English told me, are more prosaic.
In the United States, federal law requires most homeowners living in high-risk flood

zones to purchase flood insurance, but buildings with amphibious foundations are not eligible for the subsidized policies offered by the National Flood Insurance Program. In one of English's academic papers, she mentions the story of a developer who built an amphibious house in New Orleans, then found himself unable to acquire an N.F.I.P. policy; the building remained unsold until he replaced the amphibious foundation with a traditional one.

In 2007, after English began promoting her concept on the Buoyant Foundation Project Web site, an official at the Federal Emergency Management Agency, which administers the N.F.I.P., wrote to her. He urged her not to release more information about her design and suggested that communities that permitted the floatable foundations could "jeopardize" their "good standing" with the N.F.I.P. A decade later, FEMA continues to maintain that more research is needed. "Although amphibious-building technology is changing, these systems raise several engineering, floodplain-management, economic, and emergency-management concerns," an agency spokesperson said in a statement. "A technology that relies on mechanical processes to provide flood protection is not equivalent to the same level of safe protection provided by permanent elevation."

English isn't giving up. A few months after the conference, she flew to Vietnam, where she is designing two new amphibious houses that are slated to be built in January. She also has a grant from the National Research Council of Canada to begin developing guidelines for amphibious construction that the government can include in its official building code. English and other experts say that opinions about amphibious architecture are beginning to shift, especially as climate change makes innovative building solutions more urgent. "Usually, after a conference presentation, I'll have people coming up to me and saying, 'I've never heard of this before, this is such a great idea, how can I do this in my community?'" English said. "People don't laugh at me anymore."

Source: Emily Anthes/The New Yorker © Conde Nast.

Critical Thinking Topics

1. The article quotes architect and engineer Elizabeth English as saying, after Hurricane Katrina, "I became very, very angry about the cultural insensitivity of the solutions being proposed." In what sense were the proposed housing solutions to the threat of flooding culturally insensitive?

2. Amphibious construction has run into opposition from the Federal Emergency Management Agency and the National Flood Insurance Program. Explain the objections of these two agencies. What is your assessment of their objections?

3. Discuss the metaphorical significance of the title.

Writing Topic

The power of mother nature is immense and often destructive, yet humanity continues its largely futile attempts to tame her. The innovation advocated by architect Elizabeth English avoids continuing these misguided attempts, and it runs counter to traditional housing designs. However, English's idea seems to have potential as a solution to building in areas prone to flooding, despite the resistance some have to this kind of radical change. In general, people prefer the comfort of continuity, relying on past theories and practices. Select a problem a specific group of people faces, perhaps a situation at work or school or perhaps something on a larger scale. Propose a responsible and innovative solution, and address the opposition your proposal might encounter.

8.32 Lisa L. Lewis, Why We Still Allow Bullying to Flourish in Kids' Sports
(2018)

In the cellphone video, a teenage boy stands at the front of the classroom as his football teammates laugh. The coach walks to the door and closes it. "We don't want no witnesses," he says, to more laughter. After hesitating, the boy complies with the coach's orders to close his eyes and clasp his hands behind his head. Then the coach punches him in the stomach. The boy doubles over and falls to the floor as his teammates laugh some more.

The clip, shot at California's Beaumont High School, made headlines after it was turned over to local police in October. Equally shocking, however, were the expressions of support by many of the players and their parents, who downplayed the incident and lauded the coach, Will Martin, for his mentoring influence. "If it's so bad, why are the kids laughing?" one mom asked, while another parent characterized Martin as a "man of God."

Martin's behavior may be an extreme example, but physical and emotional bullying by youth coaches is often still accepted or even defended as a way to improve performance and build character. Some coaches use exercise as punishment, including one in Des Moines, who was subsequently fired for it in 2012. And verbal abuse by coaches such as name-calling and belittling players is common at all levels of sports. In one study of 800 youth athletes, more than a third of the respondents said their coaches had yelled at a kid angrily for making a mistake, and 4 percent said the coach had hit, kicked or slapped someone on the team. (The authors note that if their sample is seen as representative of the larger population of youth athletes, this equates to close to 2 million kids being on the receiving end of this type of physical bullying each year.)

In any other setting, that behavior would immediately be recognized as physical abuse, noted Jennifer Fraser, the author of "Teaching Bullies: Zero Tolerance on the Court or in the Classroom." "Imagine two women in a staff meeting," she suggested. "Would this be seen as motivating? Would she (the victim) be a better employee as a result?"

In many cases, coaches are simply replicating what was done to them or may be   5
taking out their frustration on their players. "When a coach is yelling like that, they're modeling poor emotional control," said Kristen Dieffenbach, an associate professor of athletic coaching education at West Virginia University and an executive board member of the Association for Applied Sport Psychology. "When I coach soccer and hockey, I yell—sometimes you need to in order to get the kids to pay attention to you. But there's a difference between high energy and 'What the hell is wrong with you?'"

For kids and adolescents, the impact of being yelled at and belittled—or having a coach slap, kick or even punch them—is long-lasting. (Even though the majority of the research looks at peer-to-peer bullying, the dynamic in coach-player bullying is consistent with the imbalance of power that's generally used in definitions of bullying.)

Players may hesitate to speak up for fear of retaliation. And parents who do so risk being seen as helicopter parents, Fraser noted.

And in fact, there's no evidence to suggest that this type of domineering coaching is what wins championships. Instead, coaches who use positive methods have a better track record of keeping kids from dropping out of youth sports, increasing player engagement and developing skills and character, which in turn help teams win. The nonprofit Positive Coaching Alliance, based in Mountain View, Calif., and featuring an all-star advisory board lineup that includes winning coaches, such as Phil Jackson, Bruce Bochy and Steve Mariucci, calls this double-goal coaching, which focuses on winning and even more so on teaching life lessons.

Similarly, experts like Dieffenbach believe the best way to combat old-school coaching is through education. Dieffenbach said coaches often get frustrated and resort to dictatorial techniques because they lack other tools. "Is your job as a coach to dominate, or to lead and develop?" she asked.

Requirements for high school coaches vary by state—in Illinois, for example, pro- 10 spective coaches only need coaching certification if they don't already have an Illinois teaching, school counseling or similar certificate. And in Hawaii, the governing body for high school sports only requires that coaches participating in state championship events take a "Fundamentals of Coaching" course and allows them two years to do so, even though they're coaching players in the interim. The course is offered by the National Federation of State High School Associations, which oversees interscholastic sports federations in each state and the District of Columbia and is one of the main groups offering courses to meet these varying state requirements. Dan Schuster, who oversees educational services for the association, noted that the fundamentals course addresses bullying in the context of providing a safe and respectful environment and refers coaches to additional optional resources on the topic.

In addition to educating coaches, though, we need to look at the broader culture that's made these bullying behaviors seem acceptable. Rationalizing it through a "win at all costs" mind-set or accepting that it's embedded in competitive sports—particularly in aggressive ones like football—only perpetuates it. Joe Ehrmann, a former NFL defensive lineman who spent most of his career with the Baltimore Colts and is now a minister, has said, "The great myth in America today is that sports builds character... (but) sports doesn't build character unless the coach models it, nurtures it and teaches it."

We need to make sure that when we talk about bullying, we're clear about exactly what that means. In a paper published last month in the Sport Journal, Charles Bachand noted that being able to determine whether bullying in sports is increasing or decreasing depends on having a standard definition. Some of the research to date doesn't even include key components such as the imbalance of power inherent in the coach-player dynamic, Bachand pointed out.

Of course, most coaches are hard-working, well-meaning and passionate about sports. Those who do end up bullying may simply be frustrated or misguided about athlete development.

But when they do bully players, we have a responsibility to avoid defending or normalizing it. I have a son who plays high school varsity football, and I was sickened not just by the clip of the Beaumont High School coach, but by the parents who defended his behavior. A teen who's been punched in the stomach by his coach has already been failed once by adults and doesn't need to be failed again.

Source: Used by permission of the author.

Critical Thinking Topics

1. Find and write out the author's claim. Is it a claim of fact, policy, or value?
2. What evidence does the author use to support her claim? How convincing is her argument? Support or refute her claim using examples from your own experience or observation.

Writing Topic

The author mentions that the definition of bullying is unclear. How would you determine if an action constitutes bullying? Craft a definition of bullying that would clarify why bullying is inappropriate behavior. Use specific examples of behaviors that would and would not be classified as bullying.

8.33 Eva Hagberg Fisher, How I Learned to Look Believable (2018)

On the morning of March 31, 2016, I put on a pair of Gap jeans (the ones without holes); a beige silky top I'd bought at the Gap outlet in Sedona, Ariz., where I had briefly lived; and a short-waisted gray zip-up jacket. I parted my hair on the right, as I always do, and put it up in a messy bun. I never wear makeup, so I also didn't wear makeup. Later, of course, I would wear makeup. I was on my way to deliver an 11-page account of sexual harassment by my former graduate school adviser. I wanted to look good. I also wanted to look credible.

Over the course of the last year and a half, since filing that report, I have been asked to participate in a number of legal, semi-legal and legal-adjacent events. Among the processes that can be involved when a person files a sexual harassment complaint in an academic setting are the following: investigation interviews with a Title IX coordinator; appearances at school-sponsored forums where a person may hide in the back while attempting to keep her heart rate manageable as she listens to lots of powerful people proudly talking about what a great job they're doing despite the person making accusations hearing nothing from any of them and quite frankly having no idea what's going on; newspaper photo shoots; television appearances; short impromptu speeches in front of a crowd of fellow students who had just learned their professor was accused of sexual harassment; meetings

For going on TV, make sure to show as little skin as possible by wearing a conservative black turtleneck. These worn-in loafers also demonstrate your lack of camera-readiness, and therefore your reliable honesty.

Jason LeCras/The New York Times/Redux

with a lawyer; meetings with the lawyer's partner lawyer; meetings with a number of lawyers, some of whom may be moderately annoyed with you; meetings with the department chair, who will refuse to speak to you for inexplicable reasons; and, finally and perhaps most important, six hours in front of a group of faculty who will watch, calmly, as you are excoriated. As your emails are read out loud to you, with a special emphasis on your use of exclamation points. As you are asked, triumphantly, about that time in your early 20s that you dated someone older than you.

Over the last year and a half, I have needed a lot of outfits. I have also needed to be consistent. I have needed to be ready, at every moment, to be seen as both a poverty-stricken graduate student and a reliable adult. As an accuser, I need to be a news-team-ready correspondent and someone who certainly wasn't doing this for the limelight. I didn't know any of this when I started. I learned this all on the full-time job that is being an objector to sexual harassment in America.

Some of what I learned to wear I learned on my own, by thinking to myself about what I needed to exhibit. Some of it—you must always put your hair up and never show any skin—came from a politically savvy friend. She is the reason I'm wearing a black turtleneck on four news shows. I refused to be photographed at home, or sitting down. I wanted to project strength, and also a kind of neutrality.

But at the time, I just wanted to be credible. Strong. I didn't want to look like what I imagined a victim looks like. I didn't want to look so downtrodden that I would look obsessed with being a victim, as it was suggested. I didn't want to look so feminine and girlish that I wouldn't be taken seriously; I'd seen the way young-looking women are treated. And yet, I didn't want to look too aggressive, too much like a "rabble-rouser" with an "agenda." Of course I had been cautioned about that.

5

Don't wear this flower-patterned Banana Republic skirt with a top that shows a little midriff; the combination of Georgia O'Keeffe symbolism and skin would be a little too much.

Jason LeCras/The New York Times/Redux

For that photo shoot I wore the same jacket that I wore to report. I did try to expand my wardrobe, going to J. Crew the day before the shoot. Saying, in the shop, "I need something that looks like I'm destroying the patriarchy," didn't lead us in a lot of helpful directions, and, besides, I didn't want to wear a blazer—particularly not a freshly pressed new one. That would make me look like a rich person, not a beleaguered graduate student. It has been important to show that I am but a simple lowly student. It takes a measure of hapless powerlessness.

I have not been as powerless behind the scenes. When I realized the university wasn't doing anything on its own, I hired a lawyer to help exert a little pressure. The first time I met with her, I wore orange suede J. Crew loafers. My friend Jessie Conradi came with me. She's a lawyer, too; she was also wearing loafers. We took a picture of our shoes, posted it to Instagram and tagged it "loafers of justice."

One of the things that's been most challenging is the confidentiality that a legal proceeding requires. When I couldn't outright say what I was doing, I could at least post loafer pics. I also wanted to show my lawyer that, hey, I might be crushed under the weight of the patriarchy but I can also be, you know, fun. I'd seen too much skepticism around victims. Felt the ripple in the air when a woman starts telling her story. Sure, we might believe that she's been harassed. But the later effects of being harassed, the subtler, more insidious and downstream effects—the way in which I started to wonder who was with me and who was against me; the lack of trust I could feel myself developing for almost everyone I encountered in the halls of my former department; the shame I felt at being told that my former cohort had mostly abandoned my cause; my double shame at using words like "shame" and "abandon"—are the forces my clothing is fighting against.

When I filed my complaint, I had already been through a life-threatening, and public, illness. Being a sexual harassment complainant felt, often, like just too much. No wonder I wanted to seem like the coolest cucumber in town.

I learned many things about the law, one of which is that there comes a time where a case may

Definitely do not wear this Banana Republic cocktail dress on TV or anywhere on campus; the neckline, the body-hugging stretch and the length bring it a shade too close to "overtly sexy," and you always want to stay "just plausibly sexy enough to look like you could have been harassed but 100 percent weren't asking for it."

Jason LeCras/The New York Times/Redux

10

move to litigation, or not! Sometimes that decision comes as a collective choice. On a Thursday night in October, after meeting with my lawyer and going over my experiences, I stopped at the Westfield Center in San Francisco. Michael Kors, first I got my purse there, and I believe it makes me look like a real grown-up. I walked in, ignoring the studded fur vests, and was asked if I needed help.

I hadn't really learned from my J. Crew experience and tried a similar opening gambit. "I need something that will help bring the patriarchy down," I said. The helpful salesperson pointed me in the direction of a tight black knee-length dress, dotted with metallic studs. "Maybe for after, when it's all done," I said.

I tried the same line at Club Monaco, where I found better reception. "I need something that'll make me look credible, but not superrich," I said. I hoped I wasn't insulting the place (I grew up in Canada, home of the original store; I'm incapable of insulting it). My vaguely enthusiastic interlocutor—I wish I could have told her more, but the law prevented me—brought me a pair of black dress pants that were short enough to work on my actually kind of short legs and a gray V-neck sweater with black blocks on the sleeves. The gray and black were just exciting enough to say, "Hey, I'm a person with personality!" The black pants were just professional enough to show that I was taking things seriously.

"These'll work," I said to her. At home, I added a white collared shirt—Banana Republic—underneath and then, to show that I hadn't been completely subjugated by the deafening silence in the aftermath of the initial investigation's completion, my Banana Republic polka-dot loafers. After years of being a J. Crew-only girl, I'd both turned 35 and realized that Banana Republic was actually where it's at.

You know where else it's at? The Alexander Wang bootees with rose gold that I bought for myself at the beginning of the semester, when I knew it would be a tough couple of quasi-legal months. They were my Wonder Woman-inspired boots, my "I can do this" boots. They were the most expensive thing I've ever bought for myself, and that includes my wedding dress. Yet I've mostly left them in my closet. I wish that we lived in a world where I could both wear high-heeled gold-detailed boots and be utterly reliable and credible, but the patriarchy is still too strong. Talk about a narrow path to victory.

The right outfit for recounting your experiences in front of assorted lawyer types. The well-fitting Theory blazer, white collar and gray sweater makes you look like someone who takes these proceedings seriously.

Jason LeCras/The New York Times/Redux

The coup de grâce, though, was in November. The protocol for sexual harassment cases at the University of California, Berkeley that are found to have violated the faculty code of conduct is that the defendant is charged with a sanction. This can include dismissal. This happens after the completion of first a Title IX investigation and then an internal investigation. Then comes a letter from the vice provost, followed by multiple opportunities for settling or a variety of face-saving resignations, including that of Geoff Marcy, a Berkeley astronomy professor.

This is all outlined in the very helpful Academic Senate manual, which I have read many times in an effort to find the answers that no one employed by the university will give me. It is my understanding that these hearings are basically like courtrooms— where the plaintiff is the administration and the defendant is the accused. When the University of California professor Blake Wentworth was fired, it was after an Academic Senate committee hearing.

I can't say whether I participated in such a hearing, but I can say that on the morning of Nov. 2 I carefully showered, sprayed my hair with leave-in conditioner, put on my VPL-free underwear I'd bought the year before at Uniqlo, put on those same Club Monaco dress pants, and took the black and gray sweater out of its drawer.

But what shirt? The day before, as seems to be habit, I'd gone to Anthropologie and Madewell in Berkeley. Anthropologie didn't find me any clothes, though I did buy a $7 sea salt bath bar and four face masks. (It's good to have pearly bright skin if you're ever in a position where your credibility may be at stake.) At Madewell, I bought a short-sleeved gray flannel collared shirt and a black button-down printed with gold stars. I obviously wanted to wear the star shirt—if nothing else, this experience has brought me face to face with my own brightness—but it was too bulky for the sweater. And you know what they say about harassment victims with visible shirttails: They're lying.

I played it relatively safe and went with a classic, a purple checked J. Crew shirt I'd bought years before; I discovered, once I posted it on Instagram for something else, that it's known as #thatjcrewshirt. And, again, those polka-dot loafers.

That day I recounted my history as a drug addict, something I'm very open about but seems never to fail to entertain at least some lawyers; I recalled within earshot of a group of assorted faculty that yes, I had brought my husband home with me the night I first met him, and I was glad that I'd chosen the clothes I had. I was glad that I'd put my hair up in a low bun, that I'd carefully parted it to the side. I was glad that I had my perfectly fitting, $169.50-but-on-sale-for-$99 Club Monaco pants, and I was also glad that my shirt collar was a little wrinkly. It showed that I'm not a perfect victim.

I'm not even very good at performing being a perfect victim. We don't always know exactly what to say and how to be, we don't really get a lot of training for how we should act, and we're figuring this out as we go along, and we have done things before and will do things again later that don't fit perfectly into a narrative. Mostly, it shows that we are not a tide of anonymous women making allegations, that we are not interchangeable.

My own legal case was settled in December of last year, but the disciplinary case with the university continues. As I write this, I'm wearing black jeans, a denim shirt, a gray cashmere sweater and a denim jacket. If you could see me now, do you think you would believe me?

Source: "From *The New York Times*, 1/30/2018 © 2018. *The New York Times*. All rights reserved. Used by permission and protected by the Copyright Laws of the United States. The printing, copying, redistribution, or retransmission of this Content without express written permission is prohibited.

20

The wrong outfit. The star shirt is delightful but distracting. The metallic Michael Kors sneakers make you look more like a fun person out for a Mall of America hike than a speaker of truth to power.

Jason LeCras/The New York Times/Redux

This is a great everyday outfit for those campus days when you have no idea whom you might run into. The double denim is relatable and approachable, the shoes just this side of professional, and the high-necked Michael Kors top provides almost as much coverage as a turtleneck.

Jason LeCras/The New York Times/Redux

Critical Thinking Topics

1. The author uses the word "believable" in her title, but she also uses other adjectives throughout her essay to describe how she might want to look. Review her descriptive choices, and, using these adjectives as a guide, summarize how she wants others to see her.

2. The author is discussing something serious in a less-than-serious tone. How would you characterize the tone of this essay? How does the author create this tone, and what is its effect on her overall point?

Writing Topic

In Shakespeare's *Hamlet*, Polonius (whom Hamlet describes as a "tedious old fool") advises his son Laertes that "the apparel oft proclaims the man." A modern version of this idea would be: "Clothes make the man [or woman]." Consider the politics of fashion (as seen, for example, in the elaborate gowns worn at the annual Met Gala at New York's Metropolitan Museum of Art, the black dresses worn to express solidarity with the #MeToo Movement, and the flowers from the British Commonwealth embroidered into Meghan Markle's wedding veil for her marriage to Prince Harry, sixth in line to the British throne). You might also consider the power of a uniform (military dress or sports uniforms, such as the blackout uniforms sometimes used in football). Does formal dressing increase an individual's power, or is the significance of clothing overrated? Give specific examples to support your argument.

8.34 Chapter Activities

The series of activities on the following pages invite you to apply the concepts and ideas embodied in the readings and brought out in the critical thinking topics and writing topics throughout this chapter.

8.34.1 Topics for Writing Arguments

1. The 15-year-old narrator in Mark Spragg's short story in this chapter, "A Boy's Work," reflects, "A lesser horse would have died in the tangled wire. I feel he has made this effort for me" (par. 73). Later, he thinks, "I have just killed a horse so that a man can display the hair of an animal in his den" (par. 83). The narrator clearly feels an intimate bond with the horse and implies that the horse shared that bond; the boy also acknowledges a sense of responsibility for the well-being of animals, both domesticated and wild. Moreover, he implies that men who shoot wild animals for sport are selfishly indulging their egos. Even so, some people would argue that the boy is, like many people, being overly sentimental about animals, if not anthropomorphizing

them, and that animals, domesticated or wild, should serve humankind's needs and desires. Others, however, would contend that animals should have equal rights with humans and, furthermore, that we humans have an ethical and a moral responsibility to support their well-being. In this debate, a contentious issue concerns the reintroduction of wild animal populations in areas where they have disappeared—most recently (at the time of this writing), the reintroduction of wolves and grizzly bears into the lower forty-eight states, notably, western states, where ranching is often a livelihood. In 2018, the Trump administration proposed restarting an Obama-era project to reintroduce grizzly bears on public lands in certain rural areas, thereby re-igniting the simmering debate. Research the topic of the reintroduction of wild animal populations—or a different topic of your choice related to the ethics and morals of our relationship with animals. Based on your analysis of the information, develop an argument centered on a claim of policy.

2. Edith Wharton's "The Choice" and Lucia Berlin's "A Manual for Cleaning Women" (two of the short stories in this chapter) and Oscar Wilde's play *An Ideal Husband* (also in this chapter) are vastly different in setting and situation, yet they all depict one or more assertive female characters jockeying for a position of power in an environment that imposes restrictions. These characters use intelligence and wit to gain control in circumstances that would seem to put them at a disadvantage.

   One situation where women, and girls, often have found themselves disempowered is in sexual relationships. (Such disempowerment, of course, is not limited to one gender.) More recently, we have seen women take charge of their sexual lives, as evidenced by the ever-building momentum of the #MeToo Movement. However, as women's allegations of sexual abuse and assault by men mount, so do responses alleging the absence of abuse or assault, often centered on the issue of consent—that the woman consented to sex. But what is real consent, and what is real refusal—when is yes, in fact, yes; when is no, in fact, no; and how is communication blurred by the nature of the sexual encounter?

   Specifically, college administrations have wrestled with designing policies to address sexual assault on campus. According to statistics from the National Sexual Violence Resource Center, about twenty percent of women are sexually assaulted while in college. Research the college administration's approach to the issue of sexual assault at your campus. Consider seeking out the campus's police and student services personnel who engage directly with incidents of alleged sexual assault. Is the campus community addressing sexual assault effectively? What is working, and what is not? What would you propose to strengthen the effectiveness of campus efforts to mitigate the problem? Develop an argument based on the results of your analyses and evaluation.

3. Early in his second inaugural address, in 2013 (in this chapter), President Barack Obama issued a call to action to "fellow citizens": "Now, more than ever, we must do these things together, as one nation, and one people." Then, towards the closing of his speech, he asserted, "You and I, as citizens, have the power to set this country's course." Over 150 years earlier, in 1865 as the Civil War finally was drawing to a close, President Abraham Lincoln, in his second inaugural address (also in this chapter), issued a different call to action, in this case, action to foster harmony and healing: "With malice toward none; with charity for all; with firmness in the right, as God gives us to see the right, let us strive on to finish the

work we are in; to bind up the nation's wounds; to care for him who shall have borne the battle, and for his widow, and his orphan—to do all which may achieve and cherish a just and lasting peace, among ourselves, and with all nations." Both presidents used their platform and position to motivate and empower citizens, "we the people."

Today, often fueled by social media, citizen actions that may begin with a single individual can quickly expand into formidable grassroots movements, channeling the energies of those who are impatient with the inaction of lawmakers or dissatisfied with policies that seem to serve the few and not the many. In 2018, for example, after watching state education budgets plummet and having their salaries cut or stagnate, public school teachers around the country began staging walkouts and demonstrations at state capitols, thereby making their voices heard. In 2016, a grassroots campaign propelled Bernie Sanders from being a relatively unknown U.S. senator from Vermont to challenging—and coming close to defeating—Hillary Clinton for the Democratic presidential nomination. Think of a problem that concerns you—either a local problem affecting your campus or your community or a state or national problem—and imagine that you are organizing a grassroots campaign to address the problem. Write a call to action that would motivate your fellow citizens to become actively engaged in the campaign. Include a specific plan for proceeding with the campaign.

4. Look back at your responses to the Prewriting and Discussion tasks at the beginning of this chapter; then, keeping in mind your reading, writing, and discussion experiences related to the chapter's reading selections, reflect on these questions about the themes of power and responsibility:
   - How have your ideas and perspectives about those themes been shaped by those experiences?
   - Which three reading selections have most influenced your thinking about those themes? How and why?

8.34.2 Taking a Global Perspective: "Killer Robots" and Warfare: Eliminating Human Error and Human Decision Making—for Better or for Worse?

Tim O'Brien's short story in this chapter, "The Things They Carried," depicts the boots-on-the-ground combat experience of soldiers during the Vietnam War: they toil day after day in a hostile environment; they fear for their lives; they kill and they die. Blaming himself for the death of one of his men, platoon leader Lieutenant Jimmy Cross feels shame, and he grieves: "One thing for sure, he [Kiowa] said. The lieutenant's in some deep hurt. I mean that crying jag . . . it was real heavy-duty hurt. The man cares" (par. 52). Although fictional, the story accurately represents ground warfare at that time—that is, prior to the large-scale use of autonomous weapons. Recent developments have led to the distinct possibility—even probability—that future wars will be waged by self-directed "killer robots" operating without constant human oversight. At the national and international levels, debates over the benefits and dangers of robotized warfare are thriving. Will these robots cut down on the loss of human life, among both combatants and civilians? Or will they magnify the human tragedies of war? Proponents argue that robots can surpass humans in making quick and accurate decisions; however, opponents rebut that argument, pointing out that robots are not capable of feeling compassion and empathy, feelings that, in real combat situations, should influence decisions involving "gray" factors, such as whether to fire on child combatants.

Can robotic weapons be used responsibly, and who should bear the responsibility for their use—military commanders, government leaders, or fighters on the battlefield? With compelling arguments on all sides, advocates and opponents of robotized warfare are calling on the international community to work toward an international resolution. Research the topic of autonomous weapons, or "killer robots," and warfare. Imagine you are representing your nation (the United States or otherwise) at an international convention on the use of autonomous weapons. Based on your research, develop an argument based on a claim of policy that you would make on behalf of your country—whether it be to support the use of autonomous weapons, to ban their use, or to adopt a middle-position set of regulations. If you argue for a middle position, what specific regulations would you propose for adoption?

8.34.3 Collaborating on a Rogerian Argument

For this activity, you will work in small groups to research and write a Rogerian argument on a contemporary issue that has emerged from your exploration of readings in this chapter. The writing topics that follow the readings can help you identify an issue. (See Chapter 4 for a discussion of Rogerian argument and a suggested organizational approach to developing a Rogerian argument essay.) Here are some suggested guidelines for this collaborative activity:

- Identify an issue.
- Divide the research and writing responsibilities as follows:
  - Student one: introduction section
  - Student two: body section, affirmative position
  - Student three: body section, opposing position
  - Student four: conclusion, summation, and middle-ground position

  For an effective collaboration, each team member should take responsibility for
- Collecting information related to the issue.
- Completing assigned work on time.
- Listening to and considering the viewpoints of the other team members.

Sample Topic: Online Activity and Personal Data—Who Is Responsible for Data Breaches?

In May 2018, Facebook founder and CEO Mark Zuckerberg announced that the social network would not compensate its millions of users whose data were breached by Cambridge Analytica. Despite what Zuckerberg conceded was a "breach of trust," users did not suffer financial losses as a result, he pointed out in his announcement. A month earlier, investigators' identification of suspected Golden State killer Joseph James DeAngelo through their use of a public genealogical database raised the specter of violation of the data security and privacy rights of users of these increasingly popular databases, such as 23AndME and Ancestry. If I send a sample of my saliva to an ancestry database for analysis, will law enforcement officers and others have access to highly personal and sensitive information about my very own DNA? These databases do have policies in place to which users must agree, designed to protect users' privacy. Even so, as the Facebook and Cambridge Analytica scandal revealed, such policies typically have loopholes, and the databases typically have technical weaknesses, allowing both lawbreakers and law enforcers to access "private" information. Yet online databases are a rich source of useful information for vast numbers of people, and social networks offer limitless opportunities for constructive interactions among users; thus, most of us are not going to retreat from engaging online with databases or social media.

Certainly, the question of who is responsible for ensuring the privacy of one's data does not have a simple answer. The choice is not as easy as assigning responsibility either to the company that maintains the database or social media platform or to the users themselves. Nevertheless, despite the complexity of the issue, we cannot retreat from grappling with it and attempting to arrive at a reasonable and practical resolution. As a Rogerian argument team, your assignment is just that: to develop a creative solution, one that may not completely solve the problem of assigning responsibility for the breach of personal data but one that will make it easier to determine responsibility in most cases, will provide a procedure for determining responsibility in exceptionally difficult cases, and will provide guidelines for compensating users when responsibility for the breach is not theirs. Keep in mind that responsibility might sometimes have to be shared between the companies and the individual users.

8.34.4 Arguing Themes from Literature

1. In several selections in this chapter, individuals derive their power over others through manipulation and fear. Choose two individuals from the reading selections in this chapter who meet this description, and explain how they wield their power and how their victims react. Use specific passages for support.

2. For some of the individuals in the reading selections in this chapter, power springs from behaving honorably and overcoming obstacles. Choose two of those individuals and explain how they use their power responsibly. Include specific passages for support.

3. Bread often symbolizes a universal need, both in literature and in our culture. This universal need also represents an opportunity for the providers of bread (or what it symbolizes) to demonstrate their responsibility in caring for others. Both Claude McKay in "America" ("bread of bitterness") and Langston Hughes in "Democracy" ("I cannot live on tomorrow's bread") weave the symbol of bread into their poems. Explain the significance of this symbol in each poem and connect the symbol to the concept of responsibility.

8.34.5 Multimodal Activity: The New Frontier: AI and Human Experience

Artificial intelligence (AI) is increasingly prevalent in real life and in pop culture. We have all probably interacted with some form of AI—whether with virtual personal assistants (like Siri or Alexa) or with predictive ads on Facebook or movie suggestions on Netflix. Perhaps you have seen a YouTube video of a young child who gets frustrated with Alexa or, like *New York Times* writer Rachel Botsman, witnessed a child speaking rudely to a virtual personal assistant. The dilemma of how to relate ethically to AI "entities" or systems has frequently been explored in popular media—for example, in the films *2001: A Space Odyssey, War Games,* and *Her;* in the TV series *Westworld* and *Silicon Valley;* and in productions involving the Marvel character Vision. As the human characters interact with AI characters in these narratives, they often reveal their own human strengths and weakness. Choose an example of a fictional encounter between a human and an AI character (either from the list above or from another source). Explain how the human character's responsibility to and power over the AI character reveal the human character's positive or negative traits.

Glossary

Academic argument A written or spoken statement made with the purpose of persuading an audience to accept a conclusion; academic argument is characterized by a logical approach and a respectful tone, to encourage an exchange of viewpoints.

Active reading Reading with the goal of balancing creative, or exploratory, responses with critical, or analytic, responses and then synthesizing these responses to arrive at fresh insights and new conclusions.

Ad hominem (from the Latin for "against the person") A logical fallacy: using personal attack instead of addressing the issue.

Ambiguity A way of inviting diverse interpretations of a work's themes or characters. The successful use of ambiguity does not make the work unclear; rather, it challenges us to debate and discuss its meaning, with the result that our reading experience is enriched and our thinking is expanded.

Annotated bibliography A preliminary or final bibliography with sentences of critical commentary on each source, evaluating the usefulness of the information in the source.

Argument, *see* **Academic argument**

Assertion, *see* **Claim**

Assumptions General principles, generalizations, or commonly accepted beliefs that underlie an argument, typically based on values that the arguer believes the audience shares; assumptions may be stated explicitly but are frequently unstated—that is, implied.

Audience In academic argument, the global academic community, an educated body of the writer's peers.

Authority In argument, a type of evidence—information from people who are widely recognized as experts in the field of the argument and therefore have credibility in that field.

Begging the question A logical fallacy: assuming exactly what the argument is attempting to prove.

Black-and-white fallacy, *see* **Either–or reasoning**

Claim The assertion made in an argument—the main point, thesis, or conclusion of the argument, revealing the writer's purpose in addressing the audience.

Claim of fact A claim that something is either true or false.

Claim of policy A claim stating that a specific action should or should not take place.

Claim of value A claim that makes a judgment, labeling something as good or bad.

Common knowledge Information that may not require documentation because the information is very commonly known—for instance, the information that the U.S. military suffered hundreds of thousands of casualties during World War II.

Concessions In argument, statements that acknowledge the validity of one or more points in a counterargument.

Counterarguments Arguments in opposition to an arguer's own argument.

Creative reading Reading with the goal of exploring a text, considering its relevance to your own life or how it exposes you to a new viewpoint.

Critical inquiry The process of asking questions that advance our thinking about issues, thereby laying the groundwork for developing astute critical thinking skills.

Critical reading Reading with the goal of analyzing a text—scrutinizing it and taking it apart to examine its components or elements.

Critical thinking Thinking that involves analyzing all the elements of a situation and considering all the possible outcomes; critical thinking skills are essential to developing academic arguments.

Direct quotation An exact, word-for-word restatement of a writer's or a speaker's words.

Dramatic context   In imaginative literature, the actions, words, and thoughts of the characters; by examining the characters' claims and arguments, readers gain a clearer perception of their own positions.

Either–or reasoning   A logical fallacy: over-simplifying by implying that there are only two ways of looking at an issue.

Equivocation   A logical fallacy: intentionally using a word that has more than one inter-pretation, in order to confuse an issue.

Ethos   A rhetorical appeal: an arguer makes believable claims to earn the trust of the audience.

Evidence   In argument, the information used to support a claim; information can be drawn from both primary sources and secondary sources.

Explicit claim   A direct statement of the claim in an argument, clearly presented within the text of the argument.

Fallacy, *see* **Logical fallacy**

False analogy   A logical fallacy: making a false or illogical comparison ("comparing apples and oranges").

False cause fallacy, *see* **Post hoc ergo propter hoc**

False dilemma fallacy, *see* **Either–or reasoning**

Hasty generalization   A logical fallacy: jumping to a broad conclusion based on too little evidence (for example, stereotyping).

Implicit claim (also called *implied claim*)   In an argument, a claim that is not stated directly but can be inferred based on evi-dence within the text of the argument.

Issue question   A question on which reason-able people might disagree.

Logical fallacy   An error or flaw in reason-ing; logical fallacies are often used deliber-ately, in order to mislead an audience.

Logos   A rhetorical appeal: an arguer's use of clear and sensible reasoning to draw in the audience.

Paraphrasing   A writer's or speaker's own original rephrasing of material in a source, expressing the ideas accurately in a passage of approximately the same length as the original.

Pathos   A rhetorical appeal: an arguer's use of sincere emotion and shared values to connect with the audience.

Personal experience   In argument, a type of evidence—typically, talking about one's own experiences using descriptive details and a sincere tone to persuade the audience of the validity of the argument by creating a strong, emotional response, particularly among audience members who have had similar experiences.

Plagiarism   A writer's failure to give credit for words or concepts from another source.

Post hoc ergo propter hoc (from the Latin for "after this, therefore because of this")   A logical fallacy: incorrectly attributing a cause-and-effect relationship between events just because one comes after the other.

Preliminary bibliography   A list of poten-tial sources for an argument essay, often including bibliographic information and annotations for each source.

Propaganda   Usually, information spread by a government to promote a political cause.

Purpose   In argument, a writer's motivation for initiating a conversation on a subject.

Red herring   A logical fallacy: distracting readers and leading them astray by bring-ing up a different issue as bait to capture readers' interest.

Refutations   Arguments against one or more points in a counterargument.

Reports   In argument, a type of evidence—objective facts gathered from outside sources to support the argument.

Rhetorical appeals   Fundamentals of persua-sion used by most writers and speakers—for example, *ethos, logos,* and *pathos.*

Rhetorical context   The conversation, both written and oral, surrounding an issue.

Rogerian argument strategy   The strategy of approaching a highly charged issue with the goal of advancing the dialogue constructively and finding common ground on which to build a compromise; arguers demonstrate an understanding of opposing arguments and treat the issue as an oppor-tunity to solve a mutual problem.

Signal phrase   A phrase used to introduce a paraphrase, summary, or quotation—for example, "Smith says . . ." and "Jones asserts that . . . ."

Slippery slope   A logical fallacy: falsely suggesting that a single event will trigger a series of increasingly undesirable effects.

Social context   The conditions and events within society at the time a literary work was written; the social context can provide evidence to support the writer's claim.

Subject   In argument, an issue, a debatable topic.

Summarizing   Concisely rewriting a passage from a source in your own words; unlike paraphrasing, summarizing yields a passage that is much shorter than the original.

Theme   A central or controlling idea in a work.

Two wrongs make a right   A logical fallacy: justifying wrongdoing by pointing to another's wrongdoing.

Value assumption   In argument, an assumption that the audience shares a specific value with the arguer, a belief that something is good or bad (for example, the arguer believes that child labor is bad or that strict gun control laws are good, and assumes that the audience shares the belief).

Authors' Biographical Notes

Abbey, Edward (1927–1989)   Although born and raised on a farm in Pennsylvania, Abbey lived in the Southwest from 1947 until his death. A passionate defender of wilderness, his book *Desert Solitaire* (1968) helped to launch the environmental movement. His novel *The Monkey Wrench Gang* (1975), about a group of environmental guerillas' plot to blow up the Glen Canyon Dam, on the Colorado River, is credited with influencing radical environmental groups such as Earth First!

Anthes, Emily   Anthes is a science journalist and author. She is the author of *Frankenstein's Cat: Cuddling Up to Biotech's Brave New Beasts* (2013) and *Instant Egghead Guide: The Mind* (2009). Anthes has a master's degree in science writing from MIT and a bachelor's degree in the history of science and medicine from Yale, where she also studied creative writing. She lives in Brooklyn, New York.

Bacon, Francis (1561–1626)   Bacon was an English author, a courtier, a philosopher, and an advocate of inductive reasoning in science.

Ballou, Sullivan (1829–1861)   Ballou was a major in the U.S. Army. A lawyer in Rhode Island at the outbreak of the Civil War, he volunteered for military service and was killed at the First Battle of Bull Run.

Bass, Rick (b. 1959)   An environmental activist and a writer, Bass lives in Montana. He is the author of numerous books of fiction and nonfiction, including *The Sky, the Stars, the Wilderness* (1977), *The Watch* (1994), *Colter: The True Story of the Best Dog I Ever Had* (2000), and *Why I Came West* (2008), which was a finalist for a National Book Critics Circle Award.

Berlin, Lucia (1936–2004)   An American short story writer, Berlin was born in Juneau, Alaska. Her collection of stories *A Manual for Cleaning Women* was published posthumously in 2015, making *The New York Times* bestseller list. Berlin also won an American Book Award in 1991 for *Homesick: New and Selected Stories* and was awarded a fellowship from the National Endowment for the Arts.

Bierce, Ambrose (1842–1914?)   Bierce was a master of the short story, but also wrote poetry, news articles, and the satirical *Devil's Dictionary* (1906). He fought for the Union during the American Civil War. He left for Mexico in 1914 to observe, and perhaps fight for, Pancho Villa and his revolution. He was never heard from again, and the date and circumstances of his death have remained a mystery.

Blake, William (1757–1827)   Born in London, Blake became an apprentice to an engraver at the age of fourteen. Both in his poetry and in his etchings and engravings, Blake was an experimentalist as a creative artist and a radical thinker for his time. His most famous books of poetry—*Songs of Innocence* (1789), *The Marriage of Heaven and Hell* (1790), and *Songs of Experience* (1794)—include his illustrations in hand-colored engravings. The poems in *Songs of Experience* center on topics of political corruption and social injustice.

Brooks, David (b. 1961)   Born in Canada, Brooks is an American journalist and political commentator. In 2003, he became a regular contributor to *The New York Times* Op-Ed page. Currently, Brooks is a commentator on *The NewsHour with Jim Lehrer* and a frequent commentator on NPR's *All Things Considered*.

Brooks, Gwendolyn (1917–2000)   Brooks, whose poems reflect the language of black street life, won the Pulitzer Prize for poetry in 1950 for her collection *Annie Allen* (1949), becoming the first African American to win this award. She was named poet laureate of Illinois in 1969. Her other collections include *The Bean-Eaters* (1960), *Beckonings* (1975), and *To Disembark* (1981).

Browning, Robert (1812–1889)   A major poet of the Victorian age in England, Browning is acclaimed for his mastery of the dramatic monologue. Also a playwright and writer of children's verse, he is the author of "The Pied Piper of Hamelin," which along with "Porphyria's Lover" and "My Last Duchess" is collected in *Dramatic Lyrics* (1842). In 1844,

Browning and poet Elizabeth Barrett were married. Among Browning's most well-regarded works are *Men and Women* (1855), which he dedicated to his wife, and *The Ring and the Book* (1868–1869), based on a 1698 murder trial in Rome.

Bussey, Jennifer   Bussey holds a master's degree in interdisciplinary studies and a bachelor's degree in English literature. She is an independent writer specializing in literature and criticism.

Chief Joseph (1840–1904)   When his father, Joseph the Elder, died, Chief Joseph assumed leadership of the Nez Perce tribe of Native Americans in their struggle for a permanent homeland territory in the United States. He and other Nez Perce chiefs renegotiated a peace treaty with the United States with new reservation boundaries, but before the Native Americans could move, new conflicts with the U.S. army broke out, and Chief Joseph retreated with his people toward Canada. Exhausted, the tribe stopped near the Bear Paw Mountains, in the Montana Territory, 40 miles south of Canada; there, in 1877, Chief Joseph delivered his famous surrender speech. In the following years, he petitioned the U.S. government for his people's return to the Oregon Territory. In 1885, the Nez Perce were granted a return to the Northwest, miles, however, from their original homeland area.

Chopin, Kate (1851–1904)   In defiance of contemporary restraints, Chopin often wrote about strong, independent female characters. She also wrote frankly about her characters' sexual feelings and, for that reason, caused a literary scandal. Her novels, notably, *The Awakening* (1899), have recently found a sympathetic audience.

Cleary, Michael (b. 1945)   Cleary grew up in upstate New York and now teaches college English in Fort Lauderdale, Florida, where he writes poetry. His first book of poems, *Hometown*, was published in 1992. He has two more poetry collections: *Halfway Decent Sinners* (2006) and *Bearable Weight* (2011).

Cooper, Sharon E.   Cooper is a New York City–based playwright and screenwriter. Her plays have been produced across the United States and in Germany, England, Hungary, India, Australia, and Singapore. She attended Longwood University, in Virginia, and has a Master's Degree from New York University.

Culp, Meri   Culp teaches and writes in Tallahassee, Florida. She has been published in various journals, including *Limestone Review, Off the Coast, Southeast Review, Apalachee Review, Rose & Thorn, Nomads, Snug,* and *Sweet: A Literary Confection*. Her poems have also appeared online in *True/Slant, Poets for Living Waters,* and *USA Today* and in the anthologies *Howl, 2016; The Gulf Stream: Poems of the Gulf Coast; Love You Madly: Poetry About Jazz; North of Wakulla; Think: Poems for Aretha Franklin's Inauguration Day Hat;* and *All of Us: Poems from Our First Five Years*. She was a finalist in the 2013 Peter Meinke Poetry Competition, the 2014 Crab Orchard Open Series in Poetry Competition, and the 2014 Crab Orchard First Book Award Competition.

Daudet, Alphonse (1840–1897)   Daudet was a French novelist, playwright, short-story writer, and poet who began his career as a schoolteacher in the south of France, the setting of the majority of his works. He worked for a time as a journalist for *Le Figaro* and served as secretary to the French statesman Charles de Morny. He did not support the French Republic but was a monarchist. He had a successful literary career and still maintains his popularity within France. He died in Paris from complications of syphilis.

Dickinson, Emily (1830–1886)   Born in Amherst, Massachusetts, Dickinson rarely left her family home throughout her adult life. From a prominent family, she received more formal education than most of her peers, male or female. Dickinson's poems are noted for their syntactical and rhythmic improvisation, their conciseness, and their profundity. However, her poems were not published until after her death, first in the collection *Poems* (1890). Despite her lack of recognition during her lifetime, Dickinson is now considered to be one of America's most important poets.

Doyle, Arthur Conan (1859–1930)   Born in Edinburgh, Scotland, and educated as a doctor, Doyle is famous for his Sherlock Holmes stories and novels. Doyle also wrote science fiction, historical romances, and nonfiction on subjects such as the Congo and World War I. In 1902, he was knighted for his pamphlet explaining and defending the Boer War.

Engle, Margarita (b. 1951)   Born in California, Engle is a Cuban American poet, journalist, and author of numerous award-winning books for children, young adults, and adults, including *The Surrender Tree: Poems of Cuba's Struggle for Freedom*, which was awarded a Newbery Honor in 2009. Engle served as the 2018–2019 national Young People's Poet Laureate. She is also the author of a novel in verse for young adults, *Jazz Owls: A Novel of the Zoot Suit Riots* (2018).

Erdrich, Louise (b. 1954) Erdrich is the author of numerous novels, including *Love Medicine* (1984), *The Beet Queen* (1986), *The Master Butchers Singing Club* (2003), and *Home of the Living God* (2017). She has also written poetry, children's stories, and nonfiction and is coauthor with her late husband, Michael Dorris, of the novel *The Crown of Columbus* (1991). Her novel *The Round House* won the 2012 National Book Award for Fiction. Born in Minnesota to Chippewa and German parents, Erdrich is a member of the Turtle Mountain Band of Chippewa Indians, a band of the Anishinaabe.

Espada, Martín (b. 1957) Born in Brooklyn, New York, Espada highlights the social inequities of urban America in his poetry. His book *Rebellion Is the Circle of a Lover's Hands* won the Peterson Poetry Prize in 1991. His collection *The Republic of Poetry* (2006) was a finalist for the Pulitzer Prize; his most recent collection is *The Trouble Ball* (2012). Espada is the recipient of the 2018 Ruth Lilly Poetry Prize. A former attorney, Espada is a professor of English at the University of Massachusetts–Amherst.

Fennelly, Beth Ann (b. 1971) Poet laureate of Mississippi, Fennelly teaches poetry and nonfiction at the University of Mississippi. Her first collection of poetry, *Open House*, won the 2001 Kenyon Review Prize. Her other works include the nonfiction *Great with Child: Letters to a Young Mother* (2006) and *The Tilted World* (2013), a novel coauthored with her husband, Tom Franklin.

Franklin, John Hope (1915–2009) A history professor and an author, Franklin was awarded the Presidential Medal of Freedom in 1995 and served as the chair of the President's Initiative on Race. His books include *From Slavery to Freedom: A History of Negro Americans* (1947), *Racial Equality in America* (1976), and *The Color Line: Legacy for the Twenty-first Century* (1993).

Frost, Robert (1874–1963) Frost was born in San Francisco but is best known in relationship to New England, where he lived most of his life. *A Boy's Will*, his first collection of poems, was published by 1913, and Frost continued to write and publish poetry through 1962. He won four Pulitzer Prizes for his work and will always be remembered for reading his poems "Dedication" and "The Gift Outright" at the inauguration of President John F. Kennedy in 1961.

Glaspell, Susan (1876–1948) The work of this Pulitzer Prize–winning writer was heavily influenced by her rural Iowa upbringing. Glaspell embarked upon a career as a journalist at age 18, making an early impact in a male-dominated field. By age 20, she was writing her own column. Through the years, Glaspell wrote novels, short stories, and plays. The play *Trifles* (1916), one of her most famous works, earned her widespread critical acclaim.

Grahn, Judy (b. 1940) After growing up in New Mexico, where she worked at several blue-collar jobs, Grahn moved to California and founded the Diana Press. Her work includes volumes of poetry and the nonfiction work *Another Mother Tongue: Gay Words, Gay Worlds* (1984). Grahn's collection of poems *love belongs to those who do the feeling* (2008) won the 2009 Lambda Literary Award for Lesbian Poetry. Other awards include a grant from the National Endowment for the Arts, an American Book Review award, and an American Library Award. Grahn's 2017 poetry collection, *Hanging On Our Own Bones*, features seven long narratives.

Hagberg Fisher, Eva An architect and writer, Hagberg Fisher is the author of *How to Be Loved: A Memoir of Lifesaving Friendship*. Her writing has appeared in *The New York Times*, *Tin House*, *Wired*, and *Dwell*. She has written two books about architecture, *Nature Framed* (2011) and *Dark Nostalgia* (2009). Hagberg Fisher also has written a bestselling memoir, *It's All in Your Head* (2013), about brain surgery, the specter of a cancer diagnosis, and friendship.

Hardy, Thomas (1840–1928) A major British novelist whose works include *The Mayor of Casterbridge* (1886) and *Tess of the D'Urbervilles* (1891) among many others, Hardy also wrote poems throughout his career. At age sixty, he turned entirely to poetry, publishing *Late Lyrics and Earlier* in 1922. *Winter Words in Various Moods and Metres* was published posthumously in 1928.

Hawthorne, Nathaniel (1804–1864) A Massachusetts author whose fiction draws on romance and psychological realism, Hawthorne found much of his material in New England's Puritan history. Besides his many short stories, he is best known for his novels *The Scarlet Letter* (1850) and *The House of the Seven Gables* (1851).

Hayden, Robert (1913–1980) Hayden was a professor of English at several universities, primarily Fisk University, in Nashville, Tennessee. During his teaching years, he published multiple volumes of poetry, including *The Night-Blooming Cereus* (1972).

Henning, Peter J. (b. 1957) Henning is a law professor at Wayne State University, in Detroit, Michigan, and the author of ten books about criminal justice procedure and white-collar crimes. A contributing writer at *The New York Times*, Henning frequently writes about contemporary issues in business and finance.

Henry, O. (1862–1910) O. Henry was the pen name used by William Sydney Porter. He likely inherited his literary flair from his artistic mother, who died when Porter was three. Porter eventually settled in Austin, Texas, where he married and had a daughter. In 1894, while working as a bank teller, he was accused of embezzlement and lost his job. Facing trial on those charges in 1896, Porter fled to Honduras, but he returned in 1897, stood trial, and was found guilty in 1898. While serving a five-year prison sentence, he began writing short stories under the pen name O. Henry. Details of his legal troubles were not made fully public until after his death. Popular collections of his short stories include *The Four Million* (1906) and *Options* (1909). Several volumes of his short stories were also published posthumously.

Hitler, Adolf (1889–1945) Born in Austria, Hitler served as a corporal in the German army during World War One (1914–1918). In 1923, he was imprisoned for a failed attempt to overthrow the Bavarian government in Munich. While in prison, he began his work on *Mein Kampf*, an autobiography that details his war experience, his political philosophy, and his racist explanation of "the Jewish peril." He became the *Führer* (leader) of the fascist Nazi party, served as chancellor of Germany, and initiated World War II (1939–1945) with his invasion of Poland. Beyond the tens of millions of military and civilian deaths and the widespread devas-

tation associated with the world war, he was responsible for the many programs that persecuted Jews, the Romani people, homosexuals, the sick and disabled, and political dissidents, leading to the deaths of over 11 million people, including 6 million Jews.

Holtry, Mercedez A lifelong resident of Albuquerque, New Mexico, Holtry is a slam poet and Chicana feminist. Passionate about the spoken word and poetry, she is the author of two collections of poetry, *My Blood Is Beautiful* (2015) and *I Bloomed a Resistance from My Mouth* (2018). At the time of this writing, Holtry is on track to graduate from the University of New Mexico in December 2018 with a degree both in journalism and communications and in Chicano studies.

Horick, Randy Horick is a Tennessee-based writer whose editorials have been featured in diverse publications including *Nashville Scene* and *The Tennessean*. His writings explore areas such as sports, politics, and religion. Horick owns Writers Bloc, Inc., and uses his journalism skills to work as a writing consultant.

Housman, Alfred Edward (1859–1936) A. E. Housman was an English poet and scholar. He became a professor at Cambridge in 1911, where he taught for the remainder of his career.

Hughes, Langston (1902–1967) Born in Joplin, Missouri, Hughes became a major force in the Harlem Renaissance of the 1920s. He was among the first successful African American writers in the United States and published poetry (including the book-length poem *Montage of a Dream Deferred* [1951]), novels, and plays (including *Mule Bone* [1931], coauthored with Zora Neale Hurston), as well as children's books and song lyrics. In 1935, Hughes received a Guggenheim Fellowship (one among many honors and awards), and in 1981, his Harlem home at 20 East 127th Street was given New York City Landmark status and renamed the "Langston Hughes Place."

Irving, Washington (1783–1859) Irving grew up a child of privilege, hailing from a wealthy New York family. He found himself fascinated with New York City high society and legends of areas upstate. After he studied law and dabbled in writing, Irving moved to England to run a family business. When that business dissolved, Irving opted to pursue writing full-time. He is most famous for his tales "The Legend of Sleepy Hollow," "Rip Van Winkle," and "The Spectre Bridegroom," which were all included in his collection *The Sketch Book* (1819–1820).

Jackson, Shirley (1916–1965)   Born in San Francisco, Jackson began writing as a teenager. She pursued this interest when she moved to New York with her family and entered the University of Rochester. Though she withdrew from college in 1936, she spent a year practicing her craft by producing 1,000 words per day. By 1940, she had earned her college degree and met her husband, Stanley Edgar Hyman, with whom she founded the literary magazine *Spectre*. In 1948, Jackson rose to fame with *The New Yorker*'s publication of her short story "The Lottery." The piece is said to have generated more mail than any other story ever published in *The New Yorker*'s history. Though most readers reacted negatively to "The Lottery," the story became one of the most famous short stories of the twentieth century.

Johnson, Robert (b. 1948)   Johnson is a professor of justice, law, and society at American University, in Washington D.C. He is a prolific writer, with published articles and books on crime and punishment. Johnson also writes poems focusing on the criminal justice system and incarceration in America, including the 2004 poetry collection *Poetic Justice: Reflections on the Big House, the Death House, and the American Way of Justice*.

Jordan-Young, Rebecca (b. 1963)   An American sociomedical scientist, Jordan-Young is the chair of the Department of Women's, Gender and Sexuality Studies at Barnard College, Columbia University. She is the author of *Brain Storm: The Flaws in the Science of Sex Differences* (2011). In 2016, Jordan-Young and Katrina Karkazis were jointly awarded a Guggenheim Fellowship.

Karkazis, Katrina (b. 1970)   A senior visiting fellow at Yale University and senior research scholar at Stanford University, Karkazis received her PhD in medical and cultural anthropology from Columbia University. She is the author of *Fixing Sex: Intersex, Medical Authority, and Lived Experience* (2008) and, in 2016, was jointly awarded a Guggenheim Fellowship with Rebecca Jordan-Young.

Kelley, Robin D. G. (b. 1962)   Kelley is currently the Distinguished Professor of History and the Gary B. Nash Endowed Chair in United States History at the University of Southern California; he served as William B. Ransford Professor of Cultural and Historical Studies at Columbia University from 2005 to 2007. Kelley is the author of numerous books, including *Hammer and Hoe: Alabama Communists During the Great Depression* (1990), *Yo' Mama's DisFunktional!: Fighting the Culture Wars in Urban America* (1997), *Freedom Dreams: The Black Radical Imagination* (2002), and *Thelonious Monk: The Life and Times of an American Original* (2009).

Kenan, Randall (b. 1963)   Born in Brooklyn, New York, Kenan grew up in North Carolina and received his bachelor's in English from the University of North Carolina in 1985. A former editor at Alfred A. Knopf, he currently teaches creative writing at the University of North Carolina. Kenan's literary awards include a grant from the New York Foundation of the Arts (1989), a MacDowell Colony Fellowship (1990), and the 1993 Lambda Literary Award, Gay Men's Fiction, for *Let the Dead Bury Their Dead*, which includes the short story "The Foundations of the Earth." Kenan's nonfiction works include *Walking on Water: Black American Lives at the Turn of the Twenty-First Century* (1999) and *The Fire This Time* (2007).

Kincaid, Jamaica (b. 1949)   Born as Elaine Potter Richardson on the island of Antigua, she studied photography as a young woman at the New York School for Social Research and also attended Franconia College in New Hampshire for a year. She changed her name to Jamaica Kincaid in 1973. Since then, Kincaid has published a number of novels, including *Annie John* (1986), *At the Bottom of the River* (1992), *The Autobiography of My Mother* (1996), and *See Now Then* (2013).

Knight, Etheridge (1933–1991)   Knight, who grew up in the South, was arrested for armed robbery in 1960 and served eight years in Indiana State Prison. *Poems from Prison* was published in 1968, and he won the American Book Award in 1987 for *The Essential Etheridge Knight* (1986).

Kumin, Maxine (1925–2014)   Winner of the Pulitzer Prize for Poetry and the Ruth Lily Poetry Prize, Kumin was the author of eighteen collections of poetry, numerous novels, and children's and nonfiction books. She served as Poet Laureate Consultant in Poetry to the Library of Congress from 1981 to 1982.

Lawrence, D. H. (1885–1930)   David Herbert Lawrence, born the son of working class parents in England, battled poverty and rose to become a highly respected artist. Lawrence is celebrated not only for his writing, but also for his paintings, which became famous after his death. "Snake" (1921) is one of his best-known poems; *Lady Chatterley's Lover* (1928), perhaps his most popular novel, was banned in both America and the United Kingdom for a number of years due to its erotic content.

Lewis, Lisa L.   Lewis is a California-based freelance writer who often writes about issues affecting education and public health. Her writing has appeared in *The Los Angeles Times, The Washington Post,* and *Slate.*

Lincoln, Abraham (1809–1865)   Born in a cabin in Hardin County, Kentucky, Lincoln became the sixteenth president of the United States. Shortly after his inauguration on March 4, 1861, the Civil War began. In 1863, he issued the Emancipation Proclamation, laying the groundwork for the passage of the Thirteenth Amendment, which outlawed slavery in the United States. On April 14, 1865, he was shot by John Wilkes Booth and died the next day, just a few weeks after delivering his second inaugural address, on March 4.

Mansfield, Katherine (1888–1923)   A native of New Zealand, Mansfield achieved fame as a short-story writer. She published two collections, *Bliss* (1920) and *Garden Party* (1922). She died of tuberculosis at the age of thirty-four.

Marquis, Don (1878–1937)   Donald Robert Perry Marquis was a newspaper columnist, humorist, poet, and playwright. Author of about thirty-five books, Marquis was born in Walnut, Illinois. He is best known for his books of humorous poetry about Archy the cockroach and Mehitabel the cat.

McKay, Claude (1890–1948)   Originally from Jamaica, McKay was an important figure during the Harlem Renaissance, when black writers found their voice in America. He wrote novels and plays but is best remembered for his poems. His novel *Home to Harlem* was published in 1928.

Meier, Barry (b. 1949)   Meier joined *The New York Times* as a staff writer in 1989. His book *Pain Killer: An Empire of Deceit and the Origin of America's Opioid Epidemic* was published in 2003. In 2006, he was a finalist for a Pulitzer Prize in beat reporting for his stories on a defective, life-threatening heart defibrillator.

Meinke, Peter (b. 1932)   Meinke was born in Brooklyn, New York, and attended Hamilton College. He received his doctorate in literature from the University of Minnesota. His poetry has appeared in many magazines and journals since the 1970s. His books include *Liquid Paper: New and Selected Poems* (1991) and *Lucky Bones* (2014). Meinke's short story collection *The Piano Tuner* received the Flannery O'Connor Award for Short Fiction in 1986. He is a professor emeritus of literature at Eckerd College, in St. Petersburg, Florida, and was appointed poet laureate of Florida in 2015.

Miller, Arthur (1915–2005)   Although *Death of a Salesman* (1945) continues to be his most successful play, Miller had a long career as a playwright, winning both the Pulitzer Prize and the New York Drama Critics Circle Award. His play *The Crucible* (1953) grew out of his disdain for the anticommunist persecutions of the McCarthy-era House Un-American Activities Committee.

Milton, John (1608–1674)   Milton worked for Oliver Cromwell during the civil war in England between the king and the parliament and was arrested and briefly imprisoned after the monarchy was restored. Completely blind during the last fourteen years of his life, he retired from public life and, by dictation to aides, wrote his epic poems *Paradise Lost* (1667) and *Paradise Regained* (1671).

Nye, Naomi Shihab (b. 1952)   An American singer and writer with Palestinian roots, Nye has published children's books as well as poetry. Her poetry collections include *Hugging the Jukebox* (1982), *Words Under the Words: Selected Poems* (1995), and *Fuel* (1998).

Obama, Barack (b. 1961)   Obama is a graduate of Harvard Law School; he worked as a civil rights attorney and a law professor before entering politics in 1997. In 2004, he was elected to serve as U.S. Senator for Illinois. Obama served two terms as the 44th President of the United States (2009–2017). In 2018, Obama and his wife, Michelle Obama, entered into a multiyear agreement to produce films and series for Netflix.

O'Brien, Tim (b. 1946) After graduation from college, O'Brien served as an infantryman in Vietnam, where he was awarded a Purple Heart. Upon returning home, he began to write about his war experiences. His Vietnam novel *Going After Cacciato* (1978) won the National Book Award for Fiction in 1979. His novel *July* was published in 2002. O'Brien received the Dayton Literary Peace Prize Foundation's Richard C. Holbrooke Distinguished Achievement Award in 2012.

O'Connor, Flannery (1925–1964) O'Connor was a Southern American writer of essays, novels, and short stories. Her writing contains elements of the Southern Gothic genre, examining religious and ethical issues through grotesque and often violent characters. O'Connor's *Complete Stories* won the 1972 National Book Award for Fiction.

Oliver, Mary (b. 1935) Oliver was born in Cleveland and attended Ohio State University and Vassar College. Her poetry collections include *No Voyage and Other Poems* (1963); *American Primitive*, winner of the 1984 Pulitzer Prize for Poetry; and *New and Selected Poems*, winner of the 1992 National Book Award for Poetry. Other publications include *The Truro Bear and Other Adventures: Poems and Essays* (2008), *Swan: Poems and Prose Poems* (2010), and *Upstream: Selected Essays* (2016).

Orwell, George (1903–1950) A writer and socialist, Orwell lived in poverty and associated with laborers early in his writing career. He later fought in the Spanish Civil War and went on to write *Animal Farm* (1945) and *1984* (1949), both reflecting his distaste for totalitarian governments.

Owen, Wilfred (1893–1918) Owen was an English poet who died in France during World War I at the young age of twenty-five, before his career ever began. Twenty-four of his poems were published after his death.

Penny, Laurie An English author, journalist, and activist, Penny writes frequently about women's issues. Her published books include *Meat Market: Female Flesh Under Capitalism* (2011), *Unspeakable Things: Sex, Lies and Revolution* (2014), and *Bitch Doctrine: Essays for Dissenting Adults* (2017).

Piatote, Beth H. Piatote, an associate professor of Native American studies at the University of California, Berkeley, received her PhD from Stanford University. Piatote's first book, *Domestic Subjects: Gender, Citizen-* *ship, and Law in Native American Literature* (2013), was awarded an MLA book prize; she also has published scholarly essays and short fiction in journals, including *American Quarterly*, *Kenyon Review*, and *SAIL: Studies in American Indian Literature*.

Piercy, Marge (b. 1936) Piercy has written numerous novels and collections of poetry, as well as nonfiction. Her collections of poetry include *The Moon Is Always Female* (1980), *Mars and Her Children* (1992), *What Are Big Girls Made Of?* (1996), *The Hunger Moon: New and Selected Poems, 1980–2010* (2011), and *Made in Detroit* (2015). Piercy's cyberpunk novel, *He, She and It*, won the 1993 Arthur C. Clarke Award. Piercy presently lives in Massachusetts, on Cape Cod.

Poe, Edgar Allan Poe (1809–1849) An American writer whose name is synonymous with horror (though many of his works are not in that genre), Poe composed an amazing trove of tales, poems, and essays during his brief life. Among Poe's best-known works are the short stories "The Fall of the House of Usher," "The Cask of Amontillado," and "The Murders in the Rue Morgue," which is seen as marking the invention of detective fiction. "The Raven," notable for its gripping rhymes and rhythms and for the repeated line "Quoth the Raven, 'Nevermore,'" is regarded as one of the best American poems.

Randall, Dudley (1914–2000) Randall founded Broadside Press in 1965, where he published African American writers. His collected poetry is found in *More to Remember: Poems of Four Decades* (1971) and *A Litany of Friends: New and Selected Poems* (1981).

Rexroth, Kenneth (1905–1982) Born in South Bend, Indiana, Rexroth was a poet, translator, and critical essayist. Expelled from high school in Chicago, he began supporting himself with odd jobs. After hitchhiking around the country and traveling in Europe, he moved to San Francisco in 1927 and began publishing his first poems in small magazines. Rexroth's first collection of poems, *In What Hour*, was published in 1940. He is considered instrumental in launching the late 1940s San Francisco Renaissance, and in 1955, he organized and emceed the Six Gallery reading at which Allen Ginsberg unleashed "Howl." In 1975, Rexroth received the Copernicus Award from the Academy of American Poets in recognition of his lifetime work.

Rich, Adrienne (1929–2012) Rich was a Phi Beta Kappa graduate of Radcliffe College in 1951, the year she published her first collection of poetry, *A Change of World*. Since then, she has won many awards, including the National Book Award for poetry in 1974. Rich published numerous collections of poetry, including *An Atlas of the Difficult World* (1992); *The School Among the Ruins: Poems, 2000–2004*; and *Tonight No Poetry Will Serve: Poems, 2007–2010*. In 2006, Rich was awarded the National Book Foundation Medal for Distinguished Contribution to American Letters.

Rilke, Rainer Maria (1875–1926) Rilke is one of the most well known and widely read German poets. Living in Paris from 1902 until 1910, Rilke served for a time as secretary to the French sculptor Rodin, who also became his mentor. His works include *New Poems* (1907) and, while living in Switzerland, *Sonnets to Orpheus* and *The Duino Elegies*, both published in 1923.

Robinson, Edwin Arlington (1869–1935) In his poems, Robinson created psychological portraits of small-town citizens. He received three Pulitzer Prizes for his work.

Rodriguez, Richard (b. 1944) Rodriguez's book *Hunger of Memory: The Education of Richard Rodriguez* (1982) focuses on the issues of education and ethnic identity. *Days of Obligation* (1992) was nominated for a Pulitzer Prize. His most recent work is *Darling: A Spiritual Autobiography* (2013). Rodriguez's essays have been published in *Harper's Magazine*, *Time*, and *Mother Jones*, and he has made regular appearances on PBS's *NewsHour*.

Roethke, Theodore (1908–1963) Roethke grew up in Michigan and attended the University of Michigan and Harvard University. He won the Pulitzer Prize for poetry in 1954 for *The Waking: Poems 1933–1953*. He also won two National Book Awards for poetry.

Sanders, Scott Russell (b. 1945) Born in Memphis, Sanders has published many essay collections, novels, and children's books. His collections of essays include *Hunting for Hope* (1998), *The Country of Language* (1999), *A Conservationist Manifesto* (2009), and *Earth Works* (2012). Sanders is a distinguished professor emeritus of English at Indiana University.

Schaeffer, Frank (b. 1952) Schaeffer is an author, film director, screenwriter, and public speaker. He has written nonfiction books relating to the U.S. Marine Corps, including *Keeping Faith: A Father-Son Story About Love and the United States Marine Corps* (2002), which he coauthored with his son John Schaeffer.

Schaeffer, John (b. 1980) Schaeffer joined the Marines right out of high school, serving from 1999 to 2004. He has coauthored a book with his father, the writer Frank Schaeffer, *Keeping Faith: A Father-Son Story About Love and the United States Marine Corps* (2002). Schaeffer graduated from the University of Chicago and works in the financial technology industry.

Shakespeare, William (1554–1616) Born in Stratford-upon-Avon, in England, Shakespeare married Anne Hathaway in 1582. In the 1590s, Shakespeare began to establish himself as an actor and a playwright and became an owner of one of London's acting companies, as well as an investor in the Globe Theater in 1599. Shakespeare created a number of his classic plays between 1598 and 1609, including *As You Like It, Henry V, Julius Caesar, Twelfth Night, Hamlet, Othello, King Lear*, and *Macbeth*. Culminating this period of creative productivity was the publication in 1609 of his 154 sonnets, dedicated to the still-unidentified "Mr. W. H." From 1603 until 1616, Shakespeare divided his time between London and Stratford, where he died on his fifty-second birthday.

Snyder, Gary (b. 1930) Born in San Francisco, Snyder studied Asian languages at the University of California, Berkeley; worked as a logger; studied Buddhism in Japan; and shipped as a crew member on oil tankers. His poems draw on images from nature, Native American culture, and Buddhism. His many books of poetry include *Regarding Wave* (1970) and his latest collection, *This Present Moment: New Poems* (2015). Snyder's awards include a Pulitzer Prize for Poetry (1975), an American Book Award (1984), the John Hay Award for Nature Writing (1997), and the Ruth Lilly Poetry Prize (2008).

Song, Cathy (b. 1955) Born in Hawaii, Song received a master's degree in creative writing from Boston University in 1981. In 1982, she was the recipient of the Yale Series of Younger Poets Award for her collection *Picture Bride* (2003). Song's collections of poetry include

School Figures (1994), *The Land of Bliss* (2001), and *Cloud Moving Hands* (2007).

Spragg, Mark (b. 1952) Spragg grew up in Wyoming. After graduating from the University of Wyoming, he worked various jobs, including on an oil rig and leading pack trips, as he began his writing career. His first book, the memoir *Where Rivers Change Direction* (1999), focuses on the rugged outdoor life he experienced in childhood. Spragg later published three novels, including *An Unfinished Life* (2004), which was made into a film starring Morgan Freeman.

Stephens, Bret (b. 1973) Stephens, a journalist and political commentator, became an Op-Ed columnist for *The New York Times* in 2017; prior to that, he was a foreign affairs columnist and then deputy editorial-page editor for *The Wall Street Journal*. In 2003, Stephens won a Pulitzer Prize for commentary; he is the author of the 2014 book *America in Retreat: The New Isolationism and the Coming Global Disorder*.

Suárez, Virgil (b. 1962) Born in Cuba, Suárez moved to the United States in 1974, after four years in Spain. He is a poet, novelist, essayist, and short story writer. Suárez teaches creative writing and Latino/a literature at Florida State University.

Udall, Brady (b. 1971) Udall, who grew up in the Southwest, is a graduate of the Iowa Writers Workshop. He found critical recognition with his collection of short stories *Letting Loose the Hounds* (1997). His novels include *The Secret Life of Edgar Mint* (2001) and *The Lonely Polygamist* (2011), which became a *New York Times* bestseller. Udall teaches at Boise State University.

Vega, Ed (1936–2008) Vega, a Puerto Rican fiction writer, made his home in New York. His novels include *The Comeback* (1985), which satirizes ethnic autobiography and identity crisis, and *Casualty Report* (1991).

Vest, George Graham (1830–1904) Vest was an American politician and lawyer, serving as a U.S. senator and a Confederate congressman. He was known for his skills in public speaking. He also worked to protect Yellowstone National Park.

Vickers, Lu Vickers is the author of one novel and several books on Florida history, including *Weeki Wachee Mermaids: Thirty Years of Underwater Photography* (2012) and

Cypress Gardens, America's Tropical Wonderland: How Dick Pope Invented Florida (2010). She has also received three Individual Artists grants for fiction, from Florida's Division of Cultural Affairs. In 2014, as she was in the final stages of writing *Remembering Paradise Park: Tourism and Segregation at Silver Springs* (2015), Vickers was awarded a National Endowment for the Arts Fellowship for excerpts from a novel in progress.

Villanueva, Alma Luz (b. 1944) Villanueva is a poet, novelist, and short story writer. Her novel *The Ultraviolet Sky* won the 1989 National Book Award. Her other books include *Weeping Woman: La Llorona and Other Stories* (1994), the novel *Song of the Golden Scorpion* (2013), and the collection of poetry *Gracias* (2015).

Walker, Margaret (Abigail) (1915–1998) Born in Birmingham, Alabama, the daughter of college professors, Walker published *Jubilee* in 1966, a novel that imagines the Civil War and emancipation from a slave's point of view. Her collection of poetry *For My People* was published in 1942.

Wharton, Edith (1862–1937) Wharton pushed back against the established gender roles of her time to pursue her passion for writing. She was born into a wealthy family, and the privilege of travel gave her an intense thirst for education. Wharton's parents, particularly her mother, discouraged her pursuit of a writing career, preferring her to concentrate on the role of rich debutante. Even so, her nonstop pursuit of authorship led to some of the most famous American novels and short stories, including *The House of Mirth, Ethan Frome, The Age of Innocence*, "Roman Fever," "The Choice," and a collection of ghost stories that includes "Mr. Jones."

Wilde, Oscar (1854–1900) Born in Dublin, Ireland, Wilde became a popular playwright and lecturer in Victorian England. He graduated from Oxford University with honors and had highly successful lecture tours in America and then in England and Ireland. He was a leading proponent of the aesthetic movement. He wrote poetry, children's stories, and essays, but he was best known for the novel *The Picture of Dorian Gray* (1890) and for his 1894 plays, *The Importance of Being Earnest* and *An Ideal Husband*. In 1895, he was arrested, tried, and convicted of "gross indecency" (that is, homosexuality) and was imprisoned until 1897. Impoverished and with his health impaired by his imprisonment, he went into exile in France, where he died.

Williams, William Carlos (1883–1963) A poet, novelist, playwright, essayist, and pediatrician, Williams is best known as an imagist poet. In 1963 he won a Pulitzer Prize for his last book, *Pictures from Brueghel* (1962).

Wright, Richard (1908–1960) Born in Roxie, Mississippi, and often close to starvation during his youth, Wright graduated as valedictorian of his high school class in 1925. Fifteen years later, he published his novel *Native Son*, and in 1945, his autobiography, *Black Boy*, which brought him much critical acclaim.

Author/Title Index

Subject Index

U.S. Census Bureau, 200
U.S. Department of Veteran Affairs, 122
U.S. Supreme Court, 488

V
Valid assumptions, 390
Value assumptions, 52, 190, 194, 479
Values of community, 180
Veterans, 162
  posttraumatic stress disorder (PTSD), 101–105
Victim-persecutor relationships, 270
Victorian society, 36, 563–564
Videos, 100
Vietnam veterans, 161, 162
Vietnam War, 597–598
Visual argument, 62–63, 71
Voice, 485
Voluntary manslaughter, 306

W
War
  bonding and friendship, 450
  boots-on-the-ground combat experience, 597–598
  killer robots, 597–598
  personal conflict of, 266
  waging, 368
War Games (movie), 600
Watergate scandal, 127–128
Wayne, John, 484–486
Wells Fargo Bank, 393
White-collar criminals, 393
White-collar workers, 39

Wild animal populations, 596
Wilderness, 51–52
Witch hunt, 30–31
Witticisms, 563
Women
  art brought to life, 44
  gender assumptions, 270
  growing up in hard circumstances, 185
  independence, 185
  life for, 192
  meaning of, 40–42
  men's assumptions about, 382
  mother's advice and admonitions, 62
  sexual abuse, 596
  strong, 194
  Victorian society, 333, 563–564
Words
  obsolete, 259
  unfamiliar, 283
Working class, sympathy, compassion, or respect from upper classes, 139
Works Cited page, 112, 113, 116–119
World War II veterans, 162
Writing tone, 573
Wrongful imprisonment, 345

Y
YouTube, 600

Z
Zero draft, 78
Zoos, 479
Zuckerberg, Mark, 49, 598